Critique of
Dialectical Reason

VOLUME I

Critique of Dialectical Reason

VOLUME 1

Theory of Practical Ensembles

JEAN-PAUL SARTRE

Translated by Alan Sheridan-Smith

Edited by Jonathan Rée

VERSO

London · New York

First published as *Critique de la Raison Dialectique*
by Editions Gallimard, Paris 1960
This translation first published 1976
This corrected edition, published by Verso in 1991,
is based on the revised French edition of 1985
© Editions Gallimard 1960, 1985
Translation © New Left Books 1976

Verso
UK: 6 Meard Street, London W1V 3HR
USA: 29 West 35th Street, New York, NY 10001-2291

Verso is the imprint of New Left Books

British Library Cataloguing in Publication Data
Sartre, Jean-Paul *1905-1980*
  Critique of dialectical reason.
  1.: Theory of practical ensembles
  1. Marxism. Dialectical materialism — Philosophical perspectives
  I. Title II. Rée, Jonathan *1948-* III. [Critique de la raison dialectique précédé de
  questions de méthode].
  English
  335.4

  ISBN 0-86091-757-6

US Library of Congress Cataloging-in-Publication Data available
Library of Congress No. 90-25658

Typeset in Monotype Fournier
Printed in Great Britain by Biddles Ltd, Guildford and Kings Lynn

Contents

Introduction

1
The Dogmatic Dialectic and the Critical Dialectic

2
Critique of Critical Investigation

BOOK I   From Individual Praxis to the Practico-Inert

1

Individual Praxis as Totalisation

2

Human Relations as a Mediation between Different Sectors of Materiality

3
Matter as Totalised Totality:
a First Encounter with Necessity

4
Collectives

BOOK II   From Groups to History

1
The Fused Group

2
The Statutory Group

3
The Organisation

4
The Constituted Dialectic

Editor's Note

The text translated here was originally published in 1960 in a volume entitled *Critique de la Raison Dialectique, précédé de Questions de Méthode, Tome I, Théorie des Ensembles Pratiques*. The projected second volume, of which two chapters were completed shortly after the first, has not been published. *Questions de Méthode* was originally published as a separate essay, and is available in English (entitled either *The Problem of Method* or *Search for a Method*). It is therefore not translated here. None of the material translated here has appeared in English before except in small fragments.

Sartre's text was written hastily, and is not easy to translate. The glossary explains how various neologisms and technical terms have normally been translated; but it must be admitted that in many cases, including such crucial terms as *'expérience'* and *'dépassement'* (which we have translated by 'investigation' and 'transcendence' respectively), no completely satisfactory English equivalent has been found.

Many of Sartre's longer sentences and paragraphs have been divided, as have his chapters. Most of the divisions into chapters, sections and subsections, along with their titles, are our own. So too are most of the footnotes. In these and other matters, the German translation by Traugott König (Rowohlt 1967) has been very useful to us.

Jonathan Rée

Introduction

The Dogmatic Dialectic and the Critical Dialectic

1 Dialectical Monism

Everything we established in *The Problem of Method*[1] follows from our fundamental agreement with historical materialism. But as long as we present this agreement merely as one option among others we shall have achieved nothing, and our conclusions will remain conjectural. I have proposed certain methodological rules; but they cannot be valid, in fact they cannot even be discussed, unless the materialist dialectic can be assumed to be true. It must be proved that a negation of a negation can be an affirmation, that conflicts – within a person or a group – are the motive force of History, that each moment of a series is *comprehensible* on the basis of the initial moment, though *irreducible* to it, that History continually effects totalisations of totalisations, and so on, before the details of an analytico-synthetic and regressive-progressive method can be grasped.

But these principles cannot be taken for granted; indeed most anthropologists (*anthropologistes*) would reject them. Of course, the determinism of the positivists is necessarily a form of materialism: whatever its subject matter, it endows it with the characteristics of mechanical materiality, namely inertia and exterior causation. But it normally rejects the reinteriorisation of the different moments in a synthetic progression. Where we see the developmental unity of a single process, the positivists will attempt to show several independent, exterior factors of which the event under consideration is the resultant. What the positivists reject is a *monism* of interpretation. Take,

1. Though a separate essay, this is printed at the beginning of the French edition of *Critique*. It is available in English as *The Problem of Method*, trans. Hazel E. Barnes (London, Methuen, 1964). The American edition is published under the title *Search for a Method*. [Ed.]

for example, the excellent historian Georges Lefebvre. He criticises Jaurès[2] for claiming to see the *unity* of a process in the events of 1789. 'As presented by Jaurès, 1789 was one simple event. The cause of the Revolution was the ripening of the power of the bourgeoisie, and its result was the legalisation of that power. But it is now well known that the Revolution of 1789 as a specific event required a truly abnormal and unpredictable set of immediate causes: a financial crisis aggravated by the war in America; unemployment, caused by the commercial treaty of 1786 and by the war in the Far East; and, finally, high prices and shortages brought about by the poor harvest of 1788 and by the edict of 1787 which had emptied the granaries.'[3]

As for underlying causes, Lefebvre stresses the fact that without the abortive aristocratic revolution, which began in 1787, the bourgeois revolution would have been impossible. He concludes: 'The rise of a revolutionary class is not necessarily the only cause of its victory; nor is its victory inevitable; nor need it lead to violence. In this instance, the Revolution was begun by those whom it was to annihilate rather than by those who profited from it, and . . . there is no reason to suppose that great kings could not have checked the progress of the aristocracy in the eighteenth century.'[4]

I do not wish to analyse this text, at least at present. Certainly, Lefebvre may be right to say that Jaurès' interpretation is simplistic, that the unity of a historical process is more ambiguous, more 'polyvalent' than he says – at least in its origins. One might try to find the unity of the disparate causes in a broader synthesis, to show that the incompetence of the eighteenth century kings was effect as much as cause, etc., to rediscover circularities, and to show how chance is *integrated* into those 'feed-back' devices which are the events of History; and that it is instantly incorporated by the whole so that it appears to everyone as a manifestation of providence, etc. But this misses the point. It is not a matter even of showing that such syntheses are possible, but of proving that they are *necessary*: not any particular one, but in general that the scientist must adopt, in every case and at every level, a totalising attitude towards his subject matter.

Let us not forget that anthropologists never reject the dialectical method *absolutely*. Even Lefebvre does not formulate a general criti-

2. Jean Jaurès, *Histoire socialiste de la révolution française*, Paris 1901–4 and 1922–4. [Ed.]
3. *Études sur la Révolution française*, Paris 1954, p. 247.   4. *Ibid.*

cism of *every* attempt at totalisation. On the contrary, in his celebrated lectures on the French Revolution he approached the relations between the Assembly, the Commune and various groups of citizens, from 10 August to the September Massacres, *as a dialectician*; he gave the 'First Terror' the unity of a developing totalisation. But Lefebvre refused to adopt the totalising attitude *consistently*. In response to our questions, he would no doubt say that History is not a *unity*, that it obeys diverse laws, that an event may be produced by the pure accidental coincidence of independent factors, and that it may, in turn, develop according to totalising schemata which are peculiar to it. In short, Lefebvre would simply say that he rejects monism, not because it is monism, but because it seems to him *a priori*.

The same attitude has been formulated in other branches of knowledge. The sociologist Georges Gurvitch has described it very accurately as dialectical hyper-empiricism.[5] This is a neo-positivism which rejects every *a priori*; neither the exclusive appeal to analytical Reason, nor the unconditional choice of dialectical Reason can be justified rationally. We must accept the object as it is and let it develop freely before our eyes, without prejudging what types of rationality we will encounter in our investigations. The object itself dictates the method, the manner of approach. Gurvitch calls his hyper-empiricism 'dialectical', but this hardly matters since all he means is that his object (social facts) presents itself to investigation as dialectical. His dialecticism is thus itself an empirical conclusion. This means that the attempt to establish totalising movements, reciprocities of conditioning – or, as Gurvitch quite correctly puts it, reciprocities of 'perspectives' – etc., is based on past investigations and is *confirmed* by present ones. Generalising this attitude, one might, I think, speak of a neo-positivism which discovers in a given region of anthropology now a dialectical field, now a field of analytical determinism, and now, if occasion demands, other types of rationality.[6]

5. Georges Gurvitch, 'Hyper-Empirisme dialectique', *Cahiers Internationaux de Sociologie* XV, 1953. [Ed.]
6. Theoretical psychoanalysis simultaneously employs determinism, the dialectic, and 'paradox' in the Kierkegaardian sense of the term. Ambivalence, for example, cannot now be regarded as a contradiction or exactly as a Kierkegaardian *ambiguity*. Given the way the concept is used, one is tempted to think of a real contradiction with interpenetrating terms, or in other words, of a contradiction without opposition. In my opinion, what psychoanalysts lack is *opposition*, at least in certain respects (for there is dialectical conflict between the id, the super-

Within the limits of an empirical anthropology this distrust of the *a priori* is perfectly justified. I have shown in *The Problem of Method* that this is necessary if a living Marxism is to incorporate into itself the disciplines which have hitherto remained external to it. However, whatever else one may say about it, this incorporation must consist in revealing beneath the classical determinism of particular 'fields', their dialectical connection with the whole or, where we are dealing with processes whose dialectical character is already recognised, in revealing this regional dialectic as the expression of a deeper totalising movement. In the end, this means that we are confronted once again with the need to establish the dialectic as the universal method and universal law of anthropology. And this amounts to requiring Marxists to establish their method *a priori*: whatever relations are investigated, there will never be enough of them to establish a dialectical materialism. Such an extrapolation – that is, an infinitely infinite extrapolation – is radically different from scientific induction.

2   Scientific and Dialectical Reason

The attempt to ground the Marxist dialectic on anything other than its content, that is to say, the knowledge which it provides, might be de-

---

ego and the ego). They have nonetheless constructed a rationality and what might be called a logic of ambiguity – which would scandalise poor Kierkegaard. This logic is non-Aristotelian (because it expresses the connection between facts and attitudes which transcend one another, meet again, and struggle against each other and because, in the last analysis, it is applicable to neuroses, that is to say, to *circular beings*); but this logic is not entirely Hegelian either, since it is concerned with reciprocity of conditioning rather than with totalisation. However, to the extent that, for such a logic, a particular action is an expression of the circularity of the conditions and of the individual history, the analysed subject appears as a true whole. The truth is, however, that his being is passivity, at least in 'classical' psychoanalysis. The fact that Freudian analysts have been led to attribute greater and greater importance to the functions of the ego scarcely affects this. The simple fact that Anna Freud (following so many others) can refer to these functions as 'defence mechanisms' imprints upon the *work* of the ego an *a priori* inertia. In the same way physics speaks of 'forces' and of 'work' without ever abandoning the terrain of exteriority.

nounced as idealism. In the first place, it might be said that Diogenes demonstrated motion by walking; but what if he had been momentarily paralysed? There is a crisis in Marxist culture; there are many signs today that this crisis is temporary, but its very existence prohibits us from justifying the principles by their results.

The supreme paradox of historical materialism is that it is, at one and the same time, the only truth of History and a total *indetermination* of the Truth. The totalising thought of historical materialism has established everything except its own existence. Or, to put it another way, contaminated by the historical relativism which it has always opposed, it has not exhibited the truth of History as it defines itself, or shown how this determines its nature and validity in the historical process, in the dialectical development of *praxis* and of human experience. In other words, we do not know what it means for a Marxist historian to *speak the truth*. Not that his statements are false – far from it; but he does not have the concept of *Truth* at his disposal. In this way, Marxism presents itself to us, as ideologists,[7] as an unveiling of being, and at the same time as an unanswered question as to the validity of this unveiling.

In response to this, it may be claimed that physicists are not concerned with the ground of their inductions. This is true. But there is a general, formal principle; that there are strict relations between facts. This means: the real is rational. But is this really a principle, in the ordinary sense of the term? Let us say, rather, that it is the condition and fundamental structure of scientific *praxis*. Through experimentation, as through any other form of activity, human action posits and imposes its own possibility. *Praxis* does not, even dogmatically, affirm the *absolute* rationality of the real, if this means that reality obeys a definite system of *a priori* principles and laws, or, in other words, that it complies with a kind of *constituted* reason. Whatever the object of his research, whatever its orientation, the scientist, in his activity, assumes that reality will always manifest itself in such a way that a provisional and fluid rationality can be constituted in and through it. This amounts to saying that the human mind will accept *everything* presented to it by investigation and will subordinate its conception of

7. '*Idéologues*'. Sartre defines this word in *The Problem of Method*: 'Those intellectuals who come after the great flowering and who undertake to set the systems in order . . . should not be called philosophers. . . . These *relative* men I propose to call "ideologists" '. *The Problem of Method*, trans. Hazel E. Barnes, p. 8. [Ed.]

logic and of intelligibility to the actual data revealed by its investigations. Bachelard has shown clearly how modern physics *is* in itself a
new rationalism: the only presupposition of the *praxis* of the natural
sciences is an assertion of *unity* conceived as the perpetual unification
of an increasingly real diversity. But this unity depends on human
activity rather than on the diversity of phenomena. Moreover, it is
neither a knowledge, nor a postulate, nor a Kantian *a priori*. It is action
asserting itself within the undertaking, in the explanation of the field
and the unification of the means by the end (or of the sum of experimental results by the aim of the experiment).

This is why any comparison between the scientific principle of
rationality and the dialectic is absolutely unacceptable.

Scientific research can in fact be unaware of its own principal
features. Dialectical knowledge, in contrast, is knowledge of the dialectic. For science, there is not any formal structure, nor any implicit
assertion about the rationality of the universe: Reason *is developing*, and
the mind prejudges nothing. In complete contrast, the dialectic is both
a method *and* a movement in the object. For the dialectician, it is
grounded on a fundamental claim both about the structure of the real
and about that of our *praxis*. We assert simultaneously that the process
of knowledge is dialectical, that the movement of the object (whatever
it may be) is *itself* dialectical, and that these two dialectics are one and
the same. Taken together, these propositions have a *material content*;
they themselves are a form of organised knowledge, or, to put it
differently, they define a rationality of the world.

The modern scientist sees Reason as independent of any particular
rational system. For him, Reason is the mind as an empty unifier. The
dialectician, on the other hand, locates himself within a system: he
defines *a* Reason, and he rejects *a priori* the purely analytical Reason of
the seventeenth century, or rather, he treats it as the first moment of a
synthetic, progressive Reason. It is impossible to see this as a kind of
practical assertion of our detachment; and equally impossible to make
of it a postulate, or a working hypothesis. Dialectical Reason transcends
the level of methodology; it *states* what a sector of the universe, or,
perhaps, the whole universe is. It does not merely direct research, or
even pre-judge the mode of appearance of objects. Dialectical Reason
legislates, it defines what the world (human or total) must be like
for dialectical knowledge to be possible; it simultaneously elucidates
the movement of the real and that of our thoughts, and it elucidates
the one by the other. This particular rational system, however, is

supposed to transcend and to integrate all models of rationality. Dialectical Reason is neither constituent nor constituted reason; it is Reason constituting itself in and through the world, dissolving in itself all constituted Reasons in order to constitute new ones which it transcends and dissolves in turn. It is, therefore, both a type of rationality and the transcendence of all types of rationality. The certainty of always being able to transcend replaces the empty detachment of formal rationality: the ever present possibility of *unifying* becomes the permanent necessity for man of totalising and being totalised, and for the world of being an ever broader, developing totalisation. But knowledge of such scope would be a mere philosophical dream if it did not have all the marks of apodictic certainty. This means that practical successes are not enough; even if the assertions of the dialectician were infinitely confirmed by research, this permanent confirmation would not get us beyond empirical contingency.

So we must take up the whole problem once again, and explore the limits, the validity and the extent of dialectical Reason. We cannot deny that a *Critique* (in the Kantian sense of the term) of dialectical Reason can be made only by dialectical Reason itself; and indeed it must be allowed to ground itself and to develop itself as a free critique of itself, at the same time as being the movement of History and of knowledge. This is precisely what has not been done until now: dialectical Reason has been walled up in dogmatism.

3 Hegelian Dogmatism

The source of this dogmatism lies in the basic problem of 'dialectical materialism'. In setting the dialectic back on its feet Marx revealed the true contradictions of realism. These contradictions were to be the very substance of knowledge, but they have been concealed. We must therefore take them as our starting-point.

The superiority of Hegelian dogmatism, for those who believe in it, lies precisely in that part of it which we now reject – its idealism. For Hegel, the dialectic had no need to prove itself. In the first place Hegel took himself to be at the beginning of the end of History, that is to say, at that moment of Truth which is death. The time had come to judge, because *in future* the philosopher and his judgement would never be required again. Historical evolution required this Last Judgement; it culminated in its philosopher. Thus the totalisation was complete: all that remained was to bring down the curtain. Besides, and most important, the movement of Being and the process of Knowledge are inseparable. This implies, as Hyppolite rightly says, that Knowledge of the Other (object, world, nature) is self-Knowledge, and conversely. Thus Hegel could write: 'Scientific knowledge, however, demands precisely that we surrender to the life of the object, or, which means the same thing, that one hold present and express the internal necessity of this object.'[8] Absolute empiricism becomes identical with absolute necessity: the object is taken as given, at its moment in the history of the World and of Spirit. But this means that consciousness returns to the beginning of its Knowledge and allows this Knowledge *freely* to reconstitute itself within consciousness – it reconstitutes knowledge for itself; it means, in other words, that consciousness can see the strict necessity of the sequence and of the moments which gradually constitute the world as a concrete totality, because it is consciousness itself which constitutes itself for itself as absolute Knowledge, in the absolute freedom of its strict necessity. The reason why Kant could preserve the dualism of noumena and phenomena is that, for him, the unification of sense experience was effected by formal and non-temporal principles: the content of Knowledge could not change the mode of knowing. But if form and knowledge were modified together, and by each other, if necessity no longer belonged to a pure conceptual activity, but to a perpetual, and perpetually total, transformation, then it would have to be suffered *in the realm of Being* in order to be recognised in the development of Knowledge; and it would have to be lived in the movement of knowledge in order to be attributed to the development of the object. *In Hegel's time*, this seemed to imply the identity of Knowledge and its object. Consciousness was consciousness of the Other, and the Other was the being-other of consciousness.

8. G. W. F. Hegel, *Phenomenology of Spirit*, (Preface) trans. Kaufman in Walter Kaufman, *Hegel*, London, Weidenfeld and Nicholson, 1966, p. 434. [Ed.]

4 The Dialectic in Marx

Marx's originality lies in the fact that, in opposition to Hegel, he demonstrated that History *is in development*, that *Being is irreducible to Knowledge*, and, also, that he preserved the dialectical movement *both in* Being *and in* Knowledge. He was correct, *practically*. But having failed *to re-think the dialectic*, Marxists have played the Positivist game. Positivists often ask Marxists how they can claim, given that Marx had the good sense to realise that 'pre-history' had not yet come to an end, to detect the 'ruses' of History, the 'secret' of the proletariat, and the direction of historical development. For Positivists, prediction is possible only to the extent that the current order of succession re-enacts a previous order of succession; and so the future repeats the past. Hegel could have answered them by saying that he had only *predicted the past*, in that his history was finished and complete and that, as a matter of fact, the moment which posits itself for itself in the process of living History can only guess the future, as the truth of its own incompleteness, unknowable *for it*. The Marxist future, however, is a genuine future: it is *completely* new, and irreducible to the present. Nevertheless, Marx does make predictions, and long term rather than short term ones. But in fact, according to Positivist Rationalism, Marx had disqualified himself from doing this, and given that he himself was pre-historical and within pre-history, his judgements can have only a relative and historical significance – *even* when they concern the past. Thus Marxism *as dialectic* must reject the relativism of the positivists. And it must be understood that relativism rejects not only vast historical syntheses, but also the most modest assertions of dialectical Reason: whatever we may say or know, however close we may be to the present or past event which we attempt to reconstitute in its total-ising movement, Positivism will always deny us the right. It does not regard the synthesis of all knowledge as completely impossible (though it envisages it as an inventory rather than as an organisation of Knowledge): but it considers such a synthesis impossible *now*. It is therefore necessary to demonstrate, in opposition to Positivism, how, *at this very moment*, dialectical Reason can assert certain totalising truths – if not the whole Truth.

5 *Thought, Being and Truth in Marxism*

But that is not all. For Hegel, as we have seen, the apodicticity of dialectical knowledge implied the identity of *being, action* and *knowledge*. Marx, however, began by positing that material existence was irreducible to knowledge, that *praxis* outstrips Knowledge in its real efficacy. Needless to say, this is my own position. However, this position gives rise to new difficulties: how can we establish that one and the same movement animates these different processes? In particular, thought is both Being and knowledge of Being. It is the *praxis* of an individual or a group, in particular conditions, at a definite moment of History. As such, thought is subject to the dialectic as its law, just like the historical process, considered either as a whole or in its particular details. But it is also knowledge of the dialectic as Reason, that is, as the law of Being. But this presupposes an explanatory separation from dialectical objects, allowing us to unveil their movement. Is there not an inevitable contradiction between the knowledge of Being and the being of knowledge? The demonstration that thought, *as Being*, is carried along in the same movement as the whole of History, does not dissolve all contradictions. In fact it is precisely to this extent that thought is incapable of grasping itself in the necessity of its own dialectical development.

In the *Phenomenology of Spirit*, consciousness apprehends its own necessity in the Other and, at the same time, it apprehends in itself the necessity of the Other. But, once again, the totalising operation is carried out in the past – according to Hegel, Christianity and scepticism provide the means for understanding the previous moment, Stoicism – and, in general, Being is Knowledge, and thought itself is *simultaneously* both constituent and constituted. In one and the same movement it *is subject to its law* in so far as it is constituted, and it *knows this law* in so far as it is constituent. But if thought were no longer the whole, it would see its own development as if it were an empirical succession of moments, and this lived experience (*le vécu*) would appear as contingency and not as necessity. If thought were to understand itself as a dialectical process, it could not formulate its discovery except as a simple fact. Still less could thought pretend to settle the question whether the movement of its object is modelled on the movement of thought, or whether the movement of thought is modelled on that of its object. If material being, *praxis* and knowledge are indeed irreducible realities, do we not have to appeal to a pre-established harmony in order to relate their developments? In other words, if the search for Truth is to be dialectical in its methods, how can it be shown *without idealism* that it corresponds to the movement of Being? And on the other hand, if Knowledge is to allow Being to develop itself according to its own laws, how can we prevent whatever processes are involved from appearing as *empirical?* Moreover, in the latter case, the question arises how passive, and *therefore* non-dialectical, thought can evaluate the dialectic; or in ontological terms, how it can be that the only reality which lies beyond the laws of synthetic Reason is that which decrees them. Let no one think that he can get out of these dilemmas by means of some pseudo-dialectical answer such as: Thought is dialectical *by virtue of its object*, it is simply the dialectic as the movement of the real. For, even if it is true that History becomes intelligible when considered dialectically, the example of the Positivists shows that this can be regarded as mere determinism. For this reason, one must already be *situated* within constituent dialectical Reason in order to see History as constituted dialectical Reason. But if dialectical Reason *creates itself* (rather than suffering itself), how can one prove that it corresponds to the dialectic of Being, without relapsing into idealism? This old problem recurs whenever traditional dogmatic dualism is revived. No doubt it will seem surprising that I refer to Marxist monism as a dualism; it is, in fact, both monist and dualist.

It is dualist because it is monist. Marx's ontological monism consisted in affirming the irreducibility of Being to thought, and, at the same time, in reintegrating *thoughts* with the real as a particular form of human activity. This monistic claim, however, appears as a dogmatic Truth. But we must distinguish it from conservative ideologies which are mere *products* of the universal dialectic: in this way thought as the vehicle of truth can recover what it has lost ontologically since the collapse of idealism, and become a Norm of Knowledge.

Of course dialectical materialism has a practical advantage over contemporary ideologies in that it is the ideology of the rising class. But if it were merely the inert expression of this rise, or even of revolutionary *praxis*, if it did not direct its attention back upon this rise so as to explain it, to reveal it to itself, how could we speak of a progress of *consciousness?* How could the dialectic be regarded as the real movement of History unfolding itself? Like philosophical liberalism today, it would be no more than a mythical reflection. Besides, for the dialectician, *even* ideologies, however mystifying, contain an element of truth, as Marx often emphasised. But how is this partial truth to be established? Materialist monism, in short, has successfully eliminated the dualism of thought and Being in favour of total Being, which is thereby grasped in its materiality. But the effect of this has only been to re-establish, as an antinomy – at least an apparent one – the dualism of Being and Truth.

6 The External Dialectic in Modern Marxism

This difficulty has appeared insurmountable to modern Marxists. They have seen only one solution: to refuse to acknowledge thought itself as a dialectical activity, to dissolve it into the universal dialectic, and to eliminate man by dispersing him into the universe. This enables them to substitute Being for Truth. There is no longer *knowledge* in the strict sense of the term; Being *no longer manifests itself* in any way whatsoever: it merely evolves according to its own laws. The dialectic of Nature is Nature without men. There is therefore no more need for certainty, for criteria; even the attempt to criticise and establish knowledge becomes useless. Knowledge of whatever form is a relation between man and the world around him, and if man no longer exists this relation disappears.

The source of this unfortunate approach is well known: as Whitehead said, a law begins by being a hypothesis and ends by becoming *a fact*. When we say that the earth revolves, we no longer feel that we are stating a theory, or that we are relying on a system of knowledge; we feel that we are in the presence of the fact itself, which immediately eliminates us as knowing subjects in order to restore to us our 'nature' as objects of gravitation. For anyone with a realist view of the world, knowledge therefore destroys itself in order to *become the world*, and this is true not only of philosophy but also of all scientific Knowledge. When dialectical materialism claims to establish a dialectic of Nature it does not present itself as an attempt at an extremely general synthesis of human knowledge, but rather as a mere ordering of the facts. And its claim to be concerned with facts is not unjustified: when Engels speaks of the expansion of bodies or of electric current, he is indeed referring to the facts themselves – although these facts may undergo essential changes with the progress of science. This gigantic – and, as we shall see, abortive – attempt to allow the world to unfold itself by itself and to *no one*, we shall call *external*, or transcendental, dialectical materialism (*le matérialisme dialectique du dehors ou transcendental*).

7 The Dialectic of Nature

It is clear that this kind of materialism is not Marxist, but still it is defined by Marx: 'The materialist outlook on nature means nothing more than the conception of nature just as it is, without alien addition.'[9] On this conception, man returns to the very heart of Nature as one of its objects and develops before our eyes in accordance with the laws of Nature, that is, as pure materiality governed by the universal laws of the dialectic. The object of thought is Nature as it is, and the study of History is only a particular form of it: we must trace the movement that produces life out of matter, man out of primitive forms of life, and social history out of the first human communities. The advantage of this conception is that it avoids the problem: it presents the dialectic, *a priori* and without justification, as the fundamental law of Nature. This external materialism lays down the dialectic as exteriority: the Nature of man lies outside him in an *a priori* law, in an extra-human nature, in a history that begins with the nebulae. For this universal dialectic, partial totalisations do not have even provisional value; they do not exist. Everything must always be referred to the totality of *natural history* of which human history is only a particular form. Thus all real thought, as it *actually* forms itself in the concrete movement of History, is held to be a complete distortion of its object. It becomes a truth again only if it is reduced to a dead object, to a result; and thus a position outside man, and on the side of things, is adopted so that the idea can be seen as a thing signified by things rather than as a signifying

9. This sentence appears to be by Engels and not by Marx. It is part of an unused section of a draft of Engels, *Ludwig Feuerbach and the Outcome of Classical German Philosophy*. The text of this unused section appears as a section of *Dialectics of Nature*, trans. C. P. Dutt, Moscow, Progress Publishers, 1934, pp. 195–9. Sartre refers to the same remark in *The Problem of Method*, p. 32, n. 9, and also below, p. 181 [Ed.]

act. In this way, that 'alien addition' which is man – concrete, living man with his human relations, his true or false thoughts, his actions, his real purposes – is removed from the world. An *absolute object* is put in his place: 'What we call a *subject* is only an object considered as the centre of particular reactions.'[10] The notion of *truth* is replaced by those of success or normality as applied to performances in tests: 'As the centre of more or less delayed reactions, the body performs movements which organise themselves as behaviour. This produces actions. (Thinking is an action. Suffering is an action.) These actions can be regarded as "tests" . . ., as trials.'[11] Thus we get back to the disguised scepticism of 'reflection'. But when everything has apparently culminated in sceptical objectivism, we suddenly realise that it has been imposed on us dogmatically, that it is the Truth of Being as it appears to universal consciousness. Spirit *sees* dialectic as the law of the world. Consequently we fall back into complete dogmatic idealism.

Scientific laws are experimental hypotheses verified by facts; but at present, the absolute principle that 'Nature is dialectical' is not open to verification at all. You may claim that some set of laws established by scientists *represents* a certain dialectical movement *in the objects of these laws*, but you cannot prove it.[12] Neither the laws nor the 'great theories' will change, however you view them. Your problem is not whether light transmits energy particles to the bodies it illuminates, but whether quantum theory can be integrated into a dialectical totalisation of the universe. You need not question the kinetic theory of gases; you need only see whether it weakens the totalisation. You are reflecting on Knowledge. And since the law discovered by the scientist, taken in isolation, is neither dialectical nor anti-dialectical (it is only a quantitative determination of a functional relation), the consideration of scientific facts (that is to say, of established laws) cannot furnish, or even suggest, a proof of the dialectic. Dialectical Reason can only be captured *elsewhere*, so that it can be forcibly imposed on

10. Pierre Naville, *Introduction générale à 'La Dialectique de la Nature' de Frédéric Engels*, Paris, Librairie Marcel Rivière, 1950, p. 59.

11. *Ibid.*

12. These remarks apply, of course, only to the dialectic conceived as an abstract and universal law of Nature. However, when the dialectic is applied to human history, it loses none of its *heuristic* value. Concealed, it directs the collection of facts; then it reveals itself by making them comprehensible, by totalising them. This comprehension reveals a new dimension of History, and finally, its truth, its intelligibility.

the data of physics and chemistry. *It is well known*, in fact, that the notion of dialectic emerged in History along quite different paths, and that both Hegel and Marx explained and defined it in terms of the relations of man to matter, and of men to each other. The attempt to find the movement of human history within natural history was made *only later*, out of a wish for unification. Thus the claim that there is a dialectic of Nature refers to the totality of material facts – past, present, future – or, to put it another way, it involves a totalisation of temporality.[13] It has a curious similarity to those *Ideas* of Reason which, according to Kant, were regulative and incapable of being corroborated by any particular experience.

8 Critique of the External Dialectic

Thus a system of ideas is contemplated by a pure consciousness *which has pre-constituted their law for them*,[14] though utterly incapable of justifying this ukase. But in order to grasp materiality as such, it is not sufficient to discuss the word 'matter'. Language is ambiguous in that words sometimes designate objects and sometimes concepts; and this is why materialism as such is not opposed to idealism. In fact, there is a materialist idealism which, in the last analysis, is merely a discourse on the idea of matter; the real opposite of this is realist materialism – the thought of an individual who is *situated* in the world, penetrated by every cosmic force, and treating the material universe as something which gradually reveals itself through a 'situated' *praxis*. In the present case, we are evidently confronted with an idealism which has appropriated the vocabulary of science in order to express ideas of such poverty that one can see straight through them. But the important point is this: if you are hunting for the Truth (as a *human* undertaking) of the Universe, you will find it, in the very words you use, as the object of an absolute and constituting consciousness. This means that it is impossible to get away from the problem of Truth. Naville deprives his

13. There is such a thing as a *totalisation from within* of temporalisation as the meaning of History. But this is something completely different.
14. In *The Dialectics of Nature*, Engels goes so far as to defend the theory of the Eternal Return.

'centres of delayed reactions' of the ability to distinguish between True and False; he imposes the dialectic on them without allowing them knowledge of it; but *what he says* thereby becomes an absolute truth without foundation.

How can we accept this doubling of personality? How can a man who is lost in the world, permeated by an absolute movement coming from everything, *also* be this consciousness sure both of itself and of the Truth? It is true that Naville observes that 'these centres of reaction elaborate their behaviour according to possibilities which, at the level both of the individual and of the species, are subject to an unalterable and strictly determined development . . .', and that 'experimentally established reflex determinations and integrations enable one to appreciate the narrowing margin within which organic behaviour can be said to be autonomous'. We obviously agree with this; but the important thing is Naville's application of these observations, which inevitably leads to the theory of reflection, to endowing man with constituted reason; that is, to making thought into a form of behaviour strictly conditioned by the world (*which of course it is*), while neglecting to say that *it is also* knowledge of the world. How could 'empirical' man think? Confronted with his own history, he is as uncertain as when he is confronted by Nature, for the law does not automatically produce knowledge of itself – indeed, if it is passively suffered, it transforms its object into passivity, and thus deprives it of any possibility of collecting its atomised experiences into a synthetic unity. Meanwhile, at the level of generality where he is situated, transcendental man, contemplating laws, cannot grasp individuals. Thus, in spite of ourselves, we are offered two thoughts, neither of which is able to think *us*, or, for that matter, *itself*: the thought which is passive, given, and discontinuous, claims to be knowledge but is really only the delayed effect of external causes, while the thought which is active, synthetic and desituated, knows nothing of itself and, completely immobile, contemplates a world without thought. Our doctrinaires have mistaken for a real recognition of Necessity what is actually only a particular form of alienation, which makes *their own lived thinking* appear as an object for a universal Consciousness, and which reflects on it *as though it were the Thought of the Other*.

We must stress this crucial fact: Reason is neither a bone[15] nor an

15. Cf. Hegel, *Phenomenology of Mind*, 'Phrenology', trans. J. B. Baillie, London, Unwin, 1910, pp. 351–72. [Ed.]

accident. In other words, if dialectical Reason is to be *rationality*, it must provide Reason with its own reasons. From this point of view, analytical rationalism demonstrates itself, because, as we have seen, it is the pure affirmation – at a quite superficial level – of the bond of exteriority as permanent possibility. But let us see what Engels says about 'the most general laws' of 'the history of nature and human society'. It is this:

'. . . they can be reduced in the main to three:
The law of the transformation of quantity into quality, and vice versa;
The law of the interpenetration of opposites;
The law of the negation of the negation.
All three are developed by Hegel in his idealist fashion as mere laws of *thought*. . . . The mistake lies in the fact that these laws are foisted on nature and history as laws of thought, and not deduced from them.'[15a]

Engels' uncertainty is revealed by his words, for abstraction is not the same as deduction. And how can universal laws be deduced from a set of particular laws? If you want a name, it can only be called *induction*. And as we have seen, the only dialectic one will find in Nature is a dialectic that one has put there oneself. But let us suppose for a moment that universal laws can actually be *induced*, that is to say, that they provide both a means of ordering scientific Knowledge and a heuristic procedure. For all that, they will remain only probabilities. Let us suppose, also, that their probability is very high and that, consequently, we are obliged to accept them as true. Where will this get us? To a discovery of the laws of Reason in the universe, like Newton's discovery of the principle of gravitation. When Newton said '*Hypotheses non fingo*', he meant that while calculation and investigation permitted him to prove *the de facto existence* of gravitation, he would not try to establish it *de jure*, to explain it, to reduce it to some more general principle. Thus, to his contemporaries, rationality seemed to come to a halt with demonstrations and proofs; the fact in tself remained inexplicable and contingent. Science does not have to *account for* the facts that it discovers; it firmly establishes their existence and their relations with other facts. Later, the movement of scientific thought itself was to lift this mortgage, for in contemporary physics gravitation is treated quite differently; without ceasing to be a

15a. Engels, *Dialectics of Nature*, trans. Dutt, Moscow, 1934, p. 62. [Ed.]

fact, it is no longer the *untranscendable final fact*; it is part of a new conception of the universe and we know now that every contingent fact, however untranscendable it may appear, will be transcended in its turn, by other facts.

But what are we to make of a doctrine which presents the laws of Reason in the same way as Newton presented those of gravitation? If someone had asked Engels: Why are there three laws rather than ten, or just one?; Why are the laws of thought *these* and not others?; Where do they come from?; Is there some more general principle from which they might be deduced, instead of appearing as having the contingency of a fact?; Is there some way of uniting them in an organised synthesis, and putting them in some order?; etc., he would probably have shrugged his shoulders and replied, like Newton, '*Hypotheses non fingo*'. The upshot of this is paradoxical: Engels criticises Hegel for imposing the laws of thought on matter, but he does precisely the same himself, in that he expects the sciences to verify a dialectical reason which he discovered in the social world. But, in the historical and social world, as we shall see, there *really* is a dialectical reason; by transferring it into the 'natural' world, and forcibly inscribing it there, Engels stripped it of its rationality: there was no longer a dialectic which man produced by producing himself, and which, in turn, produced man; there was only a contingent law, of which nothing could be said except *it is so* and not otherwise. In short, Reason once more becomes a bone, since it is merely a fact and has no knowable necessity. It so happens that opposites interpenetrate. Rationality is merely a final and universal law; and *therefore* it is irrationality pure and simple. However one looks at it, transcendental materialism leads to the irrational, *either* by ignoring the thought of empirical man, *or* by creating a noumenal consciousness which imposes its law as a whim, *or again*, by discovering in Nature '*without* alien addition' the laws of dialectical Reason in the form of contingent facts.

9   The Domain of Dialectical Reason

Must we then *deny* the existence of dialectical connections in inanimate Nature? By no means. Indeed, in the present state of our knowledge,

I do not see that we are in a position to affirm or deny it. Every one is free either to *believe* that physico-chemical laws express a dialectical reason, or *not to believe it*. In any case, in the domain of the facts of inorganic Nature, the claim must be extra-scientific. We merely ask for the restoration of the order of certainties and discoveries: for if there is such a thing as a dialectical reason, it is revealed and established in and through human *praxis*, to men in a given society at a particular moment of its development. On the basis of this discovery, the limits and scope of dialectical certainty have to be established. The dialectic will be an effective method as long as it remains *necessary* as the law of intelligibility and as the rational structure of Being. A materialist dialectic will be meaningless if it cannot establish, within human history, the primacy of material conditions as they are discovered by the *praxis* of particular men and as they impose themselves on it. In short, if there is to be any such thing as dialectical materialism, it must be a *historical* materialism, that is to say, a materialism from within; it must be one and the same thing to produce it and to have it imposed on one, to live it and to know it. Consequently, this materialism, if it exists, can be *true* only within the limits of our social universe. It is at the heart of a society which is organised and stratified – and which is also rent by strife – that the appearance of a new machine will bring profound changes which will reverberate from the infrastructures to the superstructures; it is *within* a society which possesses tools and institutions that the material facts – the poverty or richness of the subsoil, the climate, etc. – which condition it and in relation to which it is itself defined, will be discovered.

As for the dialectic of Nature, it cannot be anything more than the object of a metaphysical hypothesis. The procedure of *discovering* dialectical rationality in *praxis*, and then projecting it, as an unconditional law, on to the inorganic world, and then *returning* to the study of societies and claiming that this opaquely irrational law of nature conditions them, seems to us to be a complete aberration. A human relation, which can be recognised only because we are ourselves human, is encountered, hypostasised, stripped of every human characteristic and, finally, this irrational fabrication is substituted for the genuine relation which was encountered in the first place. Thus in the name of monism the practical rationality of man making History is replaced by the ancient notion of a blind Necessity, the clear by the obscure, the evident by the conjectural, Truth by Science Fiction. If there is a dialectic now, and if we are to establish it, we shall have to seek it

B

where it is. We shall accept the idea that man is a material being among other material beings and, as such, does not have a privileged statute; we shall even refuse to reject *a priori* the possibility that a concrete dialectic of Nature will one day be discovered, which would mean that the dialectical method would become a heuristic in the natural sciences and would be used by scientists themselves and under experimental control. All I say is that dialectical Reason must be turned over once again, that it must be recognised *where it is there to be seen*, instead of being dreamed of in areas where we cannot yet grasp it. There is such a thing as historical materialism, and the law of this materialism is the dialectic. But if, as some writers imply, dialectical materialism is to be understood as a monism which is supposed to control human history from outside, then we are compelled to say that there is no such thing as *dialectical materialism*, at least for the time being.[16]

This long discussion has not been useless: it has enabled us to formulate our problem; it has revealed *the conditions under which* a dialectic can be established. No doubt these conditions are *contradictory*, but it is their moving contradictions which will throw us into the dialectical movement. Engels' mistake, in the text we quoted above, was to think that he could extract his dialectical laws from Nature by non-dialectical procedures – comparison, analogy, abstraction and induction. In fact, dialectical Reason is a whole and must ground itself by itself, or dialectically.

(1) The failure of dialectical dogmatism has shown us that the

16. It may be said that the metaphysical hypothesis of a dialectic of Nature becomes more interesting when it is used to explain the passage from inorganic matter to organic bodies, and the evolution of life on earth. This is true. But it should be noted that this *formal* interpretation of life and evolution will never be more than a pious dream as long as scientists have no way of using the notions of 'totality' and 'totalisation' as a guiding hypothesis. Nothing is gained by proclaiming that the evolution of the species or the appearance of life are moments of the 'dialectic of Nature' as long as we are ignorant of *how* life appeared and *how* species are transformed. For the present, biology, in its actual research, remains positivistic and analytical. It is possible that a deeper knowledge of its object, through its contradictions, will force biology to consider the organism in its totality, that is to say, dialectically, and to consider all biological facts in their relation of interiority. This is *possible*, but it is *not certain*. In any event, it is curious that Marxists, as dialecticians of nature, denounce as idealists those who, like Goldstein, attempt (rightly or wrongly) to consider organic beings as totalities although this only involves showing (or trying to show) the dialectical irreducibility of the 'state of matter' which is life, to another state – inorganic matter – which nevertheless generated it.

dialectic as rationality must be open to direct, everyday investigation, both as the objective connection between facts and as the method for knowing and fixing this connection. But at the same time, the provisional character of *dialectical hyper-empiricism* forces us to the conclusion that dialectical universality must be imposed *a priori* as a necessity. The '*a priori*', here, has nothing to do with any sort of constitutive principles which are prior to experience. It relates to a universality and necessity which are contained in every experience but which transcend any particular experience. But since, as Kant showed, experience provides facts but not necessity, and since we reject all idealist solutions, there is obviously a contradiction here. Husserl could speak of apodictic certainty without much difficulty, but this was because he remained on the level of pure, formal consciousness apprehending itself in its formality; but, for us, it is necessary to find our apodictic experience in the concrete world of History.

(2) We have noticed the aporias of being and knowledge in Marx. It is clear that the former is irreducible to the latter. On the other hand, the 'dialectic of Nature' has shown us that *knowledge* vanishes when reduced to one modality of being among others. Nevertheless, this dualism, which threatens to lead us into some form of disguised spiritualism, must be rejected. The possibility that a dialectic exists is itself dialectical; or, to put it another way, the only possible unity of the dialectic as law of historical development and the dialectic as knowledge-in-movement of this development is the unity of a dialectical movement. Being is the negation of knowledge, and knowledge draws its being from the negation of being.

(3) 'Men make their own History . . . but under circumstances . . . given and transmitted from the past.'[17] If this statement is true, then both determinism and analytical reason must be categorically rejected as the method and law of human history. Dialectical rationality, the whole of which is contained in this sentence, must be seen as the permanent and dialectical unity of freedom and necessity. In other words, as we have seen, the universe becomes a dream if the dialectic controls man from outside, as his unconditioned law. But if we imagine that every one simply follows his inclinations and that these molecular collisions produce large scale effects, we will discover *average* or statistical results, but not *a historical development*. So, in a sense, man

17. Karl Marx, *The Eighteenth Brumaire of Louis Bonaparte*, in Marx and Engels, *Selected Works*, (1962) Vol. 1, p. 247. [Ed.]

submits to the dialectic as to an enemy power; in another sense, he *creates it*; and if dialectical Reason is the Reason of History, this contradiction must itself be lived dialectically, which means that man must be controlled by the dialectic in so far as he *creates* it, and *create* it in so far as he is controlled by it. Furthermore, it must be understood that there is no such thing as man; there are people, wholly defined by their society and by the historical movement which carries them along; if we do not wish the dialectic to become a divine law again, a metaphysical fate, it must proceed *from individuals* and not from some kind of supra-individual ensemble. Thus we encounter a new contradiction: the dialectic is the law of totalisation which creates *several* collectivities, *several* societies, and *one* history – realities, that is, which impose themselves on individuals; but at the same time it must be woven out of millions of individual actions. We must show how it is possible for it to be both a *resultant*, though not a passive average, and a *totalising force*, though not a transcendent fate, and how it can continually bring about the unity of dispersive profusion and integration.

(4) We are dealing with a *materialist dialectic*; and by this I mean – from a strictly epistemological point of view – that thought must discover its own necessity in its material object, at the same time as discovering in itself, *in so far as it is itself a material being*, the necessity of its object. This could be done within Hegelian idealism, and either the dialectic is a dream or it can be done in the real material world of Marxism. This inevitably refers us from thought to action. Indeed, the former is only a moment of the latter. We must therefore inquire whether, in the unity of an apodictic experience, every *praxis* is constituted, in and through the material universe, as the transcendence of its object-being (*être-objet*) by the Other, while revealing the *praxis* of the Other as an object. But, at the same time, a relation must be established, by and through the Other, between each *praxis* and the universe of things, in such a way that, in the course of a perpetual totalisation, the thing becomes human and man realises himself as a thing. It must be shown, in concrete reality, that the dialectical method is indistinguishable from the dialectical movement; indistinguishable, that is to say, both from the relations which each person has with everyone through inorganic materiality, and from those which he has with his materiality and with his own organic material existence, through his relations with others. We must show, therefore, that the dialectic is based on this, everyone's permanent experience: in the universe of exteriority, one's relation *of exteriority* to the material

universe and to the Other is always accidental, though always present; but one's relation of interiority with men and with things is fundamental, though often concealed.

(5) The dialectic, however, if it is to be a reason rather than a blind law, must appear as untranscendable intelligibility. The content, the development, the order of appearance of negations, of negations of negations, of conflicts, etc., the phases of the struggle between opposed terms, and its outcome – in short, *the reality* of the dialectical movement, is governed in its entirety by the basic conditions, the structures of materiality, the initial situation, the continuous action of external and internal factors, and the balance of the forces involved. Thus there is no *one* dialectic which imposes itself upon the facts, as the Kantian categories impose themselves on phenomena; but the dialectic, if it exists, is the individual career of its object. There can be no pre-established schema imposed on individual developments, neither in someone's head, nor in an intelligible heaven; if the dialectic exists, it is because certain regions of materiality are *structured* in such a way that it cannot not exist. In other words, the dialectical movement is not some powerful unitary force revealing itself behind History like the will of God. It is first and foremost a *resultant*; it is not the dialectic which forces historical men to live their history in terrible contradictions; it is men, as they are, dominated by scarcity and necessity, and confronting one another in circumstances which History or economics can inventory, but which only dialectical reason can explain. Before it can be a *motive force*, contradiction is a result; and, on the level of ontology, the dialectic appears as the only type of relation which individuals, situated and constituted in a certain way, and on account of their very constitution, can establish amongst themselves. The dialectic, if it exists, can only be the totalisation of concrete totalisations effected by a multiplicity of totalising individualities. I shall refer to this as dialectical *nominalism*. Nevertheless, the dialectic cannot be valid for all the particular cases which recreate it, unless it always appears *as necessity* in the investigation which reveals it, nor is it valid unless it provides us with the key to the process which expresses it, that is, unless we apprehend it as *the intelligibility* of the process in question.[18]

The combination of the necessity and intelligibility of dialectical Reason, with the need to discover it empirically *in each instance*,

18. And, from this point of view, nominalism is also a dialectical *realism*.

leads to several reflections. In the first place, no one can *discover* the dialectic while keeping the point of view of analytical Reason; which means, among other things, that no one can discover the dialectic while remaining *external* to the object under consideration. Indeed, for anyone considering a given system in exteriority, no specific investigation can show whether the movement of the system is a continuous unfolding or a succession of discrete instants. The stance of the de-situated experimenter, however, tends to perpetuate analytical Reason as the model of intelligibility; the scientist's passivity in relation to the system will tend to reveal to him a passivity of the system in relation to himself. The dialectic reveals itself only to an observer situated in interiority, that is to say, to an investigator who lives his investigation both as a possible contribution to the ideology of the entire epoch and as the particular *praxis* of an individual defined by his historical and personal career within the wider history which conditions it. In short, in order to preserve the Hegelian idea (that Consciousness knows itself in the Other and knows the Other in itself), while completely discarding its idealism, I must be able to say that the *praxis* of everyone, as a dialectical movement, must reveal itself to the individual as the necessity of his own *praxis* and, conversely, that the freedom, for everyone, of his individual *praxis* must re-emerge in everyone so as to reveal to the individual a dialectic which produces itself and produces him in so far as it is produced. The dialectic as the living logic of action is invisible to a contemplative reason: it appears in the course of *praxis* as a necessary moment of it; in other words, it is created anew in each action (though actions arise only on the basis of a world entirely constituted by the dialectical *praxis* of the past) and becomes a theoretical and practical method when action in the course of development begins to give an explanation of itself. In the course of this action, the dialectic appears to the individual as rational transparency in so far as he produces it, and as absolute necessity in so far as it escapes him, that is to say, quite simply, in so far as it is produced by others. Finally, to the extent that the individual becomes acquainted with himself in the transcendence (*dépassement*) of his needs, he becomes acquainted with the law which others impose on him in transcending their own (he becomes acquainted with it: this does not mean that he submits to it), and becomes acquainted with his own autonomy (in so far as it can be, and constantly is, exploited by the other – shamming, manoeuvring, etc.) as an alien power and the autonomy of the others as the inexorable law which enables him to coerce them. But, through the very reciprocity of coercions and autonomies, the law ends up by escaping everyone, and in the revolving movement of totalisation it appears as dialectical Reason, that is to say, external to all because internal to each; and a developing totalisation, though without a totaliser, of all the totalised totalisations and of all the de-totalised totalities.

If dialectical Reason is to be possible as the career of all and the freedom of each, as experience and as necessity, if we are to display *both* its total translucidity (it is no more than ourself) and its untranscendable severity (it is the unity of everything that conditions us), if we are to ground it as the rationality of *praxis*, of totalisation, and of society's future, if we are then to *criticise* it as analytical Reason has been criticised, that is to say, if we are to determine its significance, then we must realise the situated experience of its apodicticity *through ourselves*. But let it not be imagined that this experience is comparable to the 'intuitions' of the empiricists, or even to the kind of scientific experiments whose planning is long and laborious, but whose result can be observed instantaneously. The experience of the dialectic is itself dialectical: this means that it develops and organises itself on all levels. At the same time, it is the very experience of living, since to live is to act and be acted on, and since the dialectic is the rationality of *praxis*. It must be *regressive* because it will set out from lived experience (*le vécu*) in order gradually to discover all the structures of *praxis*. However, we must give notice that the investigation we are undertaking, though in itself historical, like any other undertaking, does not attempt to discover the movement of History, the evolution of labour or of the relations of production, or class conflicts. Its goal is simply to reveal and establish dialectical rationality, that is to say, the complex play of *praxis* and totalisation.

When we have arrived at the most general conditionings, that is to say, at materiality, it will then be time to reconstruct, on the basis of the investigation, the schema of intelligibility proper to the totalisation. This second part, which will be published later,[19] will be what one might call a synthetic and progressive definition of 'the rationality of action'. In this connection, we shall see how dialectical Reason extends beyond analytical Reason and includes *within itself* its own critique and its own transcendence. However, the limited character of the project cannot be emphasised sufficiently. I have said – and I repeat – that the only valid interpretation of human History is historical

19. The second volume of the *Critique* has in fact never appeared. [Ed.]

materialism. So I shall not be restating here what others have already done a thousand times; besides, it is not my subject.

If a summary of this introduction is required, however, one could say that in the field of dialectical rationality historical materialism is its own proof, but that it does not provide a foundation for this rationality even, and above all, if it provides the History of its development as constituted Reason. Marxism is History itself becoming conscious of itself, and if it is valid it is by its material content, which is not, and cannot be, at issue here. But precisely because its reality resides in its content, the internal connections which it brings to light, in so far as they are part of its real content, are indeterminate in form. In particular, when a Marxist makes use of the notion of 'necessity' in order to characterise the relation of two events within one and the same process, we remain hesitant, even if the attempted synthesis convinces us completely. This does not mean that we reject necessity in human affairs – quite the opposite; but simply that dialectical necessity is by definition *different* from the necessity of analytical Reason and that Marxism is not concerned – why should it be? – with determining and establishing this new structure of being and of experience. Thus our task cannot *in any way* be to reconstruct real History in its development, any more than it can consist in a concrete study of forms of production or of the groups studied by the sociologist and the ethnographer. Our problem is *critical*. Doubtless this problem is itself raised by History. But it is precisely a matter of testing, criticising and establishing, *within History* and at this particular moment in the development of human societies, the instruments of thought by means of which History thinks itself in so far as they are also the practical instruments by means of which it is made. Of course, we shall be driven from *doing* to *knowing* and from *knowing* to *doing* in the unity of a process which will itself be dialectical. But our real aim is theoretical. It can be formulated in the following terms: on what conditions is the knowledge *of a History* possible? To what extent can the connections brought to light be *necessary*? What is dialectical rationality, and what are its limits and foundation? Our extremely slight dissociation of ourselves from the letter of Marxist doctrine (which I indicated in *The Problem of Method*) enables us to see the meaning of this question as the disquiet of the genuine experience which refuses to collapse into non-truth. It is to this disquiet that we are attempting to respond. But I am far from believing that the isolated effort of an individual can provide a satisfactory answer – even a partial one – to so vast a question, a question which engages with the totality of History. If these initial investigations have done no more than enable me to define the problem, by means of provisional remarks which are there to be challenged and modified, and if they give rise to a discussion and if, as would be best, this discussion is carried on collectively in working groups, then I shall be satisfied.

2

Critique of
Critical Investigation

1   The Basis of Critical Investigation

We know the abstract conditions which this investigation must
satisfy if it is to be possible. But these conditions leave its individual
reality undetermined. In the same way, in the sciences of Nature we
can have a general idea of the aim of an experiment (*expérience*) and
the conditions for it to be valid, without knowing what physical fact is
to be investigated, what instruments it will employ, or what experimental system it will identify and construct. In other words, a scientific
hypothesis includes its own experimental requirements; it indicates, in
broad outline, the conditions that the *proof* must satisfy; but this
initial schema can be distinguished only formally from the conjecture
which is to be tested. This is why the hypothesis has sometimes been
called an experimental idea. It is historical circumstances (the history of
the instruments, the contemporary state of knowledge) which give the
projected experiment its peculiar physiognomy: thus Faraday, Fou-
cault and Maxwell, for example, constructed such and such a system
in order to get such and such a result. But our concern is with the
problem of a totalising investigation, and this clearly means that it
bears only an extremely distant resemblance to the experiments of the
exact sciences. Nevertheless, it too must present itself in its technical
particularity, detail the instruments of thought it employs, outline the
concrete system it will constitute (that is to say, the structural reality
which will be exteriorised in its experimental *practice*). This is what we
shall now specify.[20] By what particular *experimentation* can we expect

20. These moments are in fact for the most part inseparable. But it is appropriate that methodological reflection should at least register an example of the
stubbornness of reason.

to expose and demonstrate the reality of the dialectical process? What instruments do we need? What is their point of application? What experimental system must we construct? On the basis of what facts? What type of extrapolation will it justify? What will be the validity of its proofs?

2   *Dialectical Reason as Intelligibility*

In order to answer these questions we must have some guide-line; and this is provided purely by what the object demands. We must turn, therefore, to this basic demand. But if this demand is reduced to the simple question, 'Are there ontological regions where the law of being and, correlatively, that of knowledge can be said to be dialectical?', there is a serious risk of making it unintelligible and of relapsing either into some form of hyper-empiricism or into the opacity and contingency of the laws formulated by Engels. If we were to discover these regions in the same way as *natural* regions (for example, an area of the earth, together with its climate, hydrography, orography, flora and fauna, etc.) are discovered, then the discovery would share the opacity of something merely *found*. If, on the other hand, we were to ground our dialectical categories on the impossibility of experience without them, as Kant did for positivist Reason, then we would indeed attain necessity, but we would have contaminated it with the opacity of facts. Indeed, to say, 'If there is to be any such thing as experience, the human mind must be able to unify sensuous diversity through synthetic judgements', is, ultimately, to base the whole critical edifice on the unintelligible judgement (a judgement of fact), 'But experience does occur.' And we shall see later that dialectical Reason is itself the intelligibility of positivist Reason; and this is precisely why positivist Reason presents itself at first as the unintelligible law of empirical intelligibility.[21]

21. I am thinking here of the *Critique of Pure Reason* rather than of Kant's later works. It has been clearly demonstrated that, in the very last part of Kant's life, the requirement of intelligibility led him right up to the threshold of dialectical Reason.

If, however, dialectical Reason has to be grasped initially through human relations, then its fundamental characteristics imply that it appears as apodictic experience in its very intelligibility. It is not a matter of simply asserting its existence, but rather of directly experiencing its existence through its intelligibility, independent of any *empirical discovery*. In other words, if the dialectic is the reason of being and of knowledge, at least in certain regions, it must manifest itself as double intelligibility. Firstly, the dialectic as the law of the world and of knowledge must itself be intelligible; so that, unlike positivist Reason, it must include its own intelligibility within itself. Secondly, if some real fact – a historical process, for example – develops dialectically, the law of its appearing and its becoming must be – from the stand-point of knowledge – the pure ground of its intelligibility. For the present, we are concerned only with original intelligibility. This intelligibility – the translucidity of the dialectic – cannot arise if one merely proclaims dialectical laws, like Engels and Naville, unless each of these laws is presented as a mere sketch, revealing the dialectic as a totality. The rules of positivist Reason appear as separate instructions (unless this Reason is envisaged as a limiting case of dialectical Reason and from its point of view). Each of the so-called 'laws' of dialectical Reason is the *whole* of the dialectic: otherwise the dialectic would cease to be a dialectical process, and thought, as the *praxis* of the theoretician, would necessarily be discontinuous. Thus the basic intelligibility of dialectical Reason, if it exists, is that of a totalisation. In other words, in terms of our distinction between being and knowledge, a dialectic exists if, in at least one ontological region, a totalisation is in progress which is immediately accessible to a thought which unceasingly totalises itself in its very comprehension of the totalisation from which it emanates and which makes itself its object.

It has often been observed that the laws stated by Hegel and his disciples do not at first seem intelligible; taken in isolation, they may even seem false or gratuitous. Hyppolite has shown convincingly that the negation of the negation – if this schema is envisaged in itself – is not necessarily an affirmation. Similarly, at first glance, the opposition between contradictories does not seem to be necessarily the motive force of the dialectical process. Hamelin, for example, based his whole system on the opposition between contraries. Or, to give another example, it is difficult to see how a new reality, transcending contradictions while preserving them within itself, can be both irreducible to them and intelligible in terms of them. But, these difficulties arise only because the dialectical 'principles' are conceived either as mere data or as induced laws; in short, because they are seen from the point of view of positivist Reason in the same way as positivist Reason conceives its own 'categories'. Each of these so called dialectical laws becomes perfectly intelligible when seen from the point of view of totalisation. It is therefore necessary for the critical investigation to ask the fundamental question: is there a region of being where totalisation is the very form of existence?

3   Totality and Totalisation

From this point of view, and before taking the discussion any further, we must make a clear distinction between the notions of totality and totalisation. A totality is defined as a being which, while radically distinct from the sum of its parts, is present in its entirety, in one form or another, in each of these parts, and which relates to itself either through its relation to one or more of its parts or through its relation to the relations between all or some of them. If this reality is *created* (a painting or a symphony are examples, if one takes integration to an extreme), it can exist only in the imaginary (*l'imaginaire*), that is to say, as the correlative of an act of imagination. The ontological status to which it lays claim by its very definition is that of the in-itself, the inert. The synthetic unity which produced its appearance of totality is not an activity, but only the vestige of a past action (just as the unity of a medallion is the passive remnant of its being struck). Through its being-in-exteriority, the inertia of the in-itself gnaws away at this appearance of unity; the passive totality is, in fact, eroded by infinite divisibility. Thus, as the active power of holding together its parts, the totality is only the correlative of an act of imagination: *the* symphony or *the* painting, as I have shown elsewhere, are imaginaries projected through the set of dried paints or the linking of sounds which function as their *analogon*. In the case of practical objects – machines, tools, consumer goods, etc. – our present action makes them seem like totalities by resuscitating, in some way, the *praxis* which attempted to totalise their inertia. We shall see below that these inert totalities are of crucial importance and that they create the kind of relation between men which we will refer to, later, as the practico-inert. These *human* objects are worthy of attention in the human world, for it is there that they attain their practico-inert statute; that is to say, they lie heavy on our destiny because of the contradiction which opposes *praxis* (the labour which made them and the labour which utilises them) and inertia, within them. But, as these remarks show, they are products; and the *totality*, despite what one might think, is only a regulative principle of the totalisation (and all at once disintegrates into the inert ensemble of its provisional creations).

If, indeed, anything is to appear as the synthetic unity of the diverse, it must be a developing unification, that is to say, an activity. The synthetic unification of a habitat is not merely the labour which has produced it, but also the activity of inhabiting it; reduced to itself, it reverts to the multiplicity of inertia. Thus totalisation has the same statute as the totality, for, through the multiplicities, it continues that synthetic labour which makes each part an expression of the whole and which relates the whole to itself through the mediation of its parts. But it is a *developing* activity, which cannot cease without the multiplicity reverting to its original statute. This act delineates a practical field which, as the undifferentiated correlative of *praxis*, is the formal unity of the ensembles which are to be integrated; within this practical field, the activity attempts the most rigorous synthesis of the most differentiated multiplicity. Thus, by a double movement, multiplicity is multiplied to infinity, each part is set against all the others and against the whole which is in the process of being formed, while the totalising activity tightens all the bonds, making each differentiated element both its immediate expression and its mediation in relation to the other elements. On this basis, it is easy to establish the intelligibility of dialectical Reason; it is the very movement of totalisation. Thus, to take only one example, it is within the framework of totalisation that the negation of the negation becomes an affirmation. Within the practical field, the correlative of *praxis*, every determination is a negation, for *praxis*, in differentiating certain ensembles, excludes them from the group formed by all the others; and the developing unification appears *simultaneously* in the most differentiated products (indicating the direction of the movement), in those which are less differentiated (indicating continuities, resistances, traditions, a tighter, but more superficial, unity), and in the conflict between the two (which expresses the present state of the developing totalisation). The new negation, which, in determining the less differentiated ensembles, will raise them to the level of the others, is bound to eliminate the negation which set the ensembles in antagonism to each other. Thus it is only within a developing unification (which has already defined the limits of its field) that a determination can be said to be a negation and that the negation of a negation is necessarily an affirmation. If dialectical Reason exists, then, from the ontological point of view, it can only be a developing totalisation, occurring where the totalisation occurs, and, from the epistemological point of view, it can only be the accessibility of that totalisation to a knowledge which is itself, in principle, totalising in its procedures. But since totalising knowledge cannot be thought of as attaining ontological totalisation as a new totalisation of it, dialectical knowledge must itself be a moment of the totalisation, or, in other words, totalisation must include within itself its own reflexive re-totalisation as an essential structure and as a totalising process within the process as a whole.

4 Critical Investigation and Totalisation

Thus the dialectic is a totalising activity. Its only laws are the rules produced by the developing totalisation, and these are obviously concerned with the relation between unification and the unified,[22] that is

---

22. A few examples: the whole is entirely present in the part as its present meaning and as its destiny. In this case, it is opposed to itself as the part is opposed to the whole in its *determination* (negation of the whole) and, since the parts are opposed to one another (each part is both the negation of the others and the whole, determining itself in its totalising activity and conferring upon the partial structures the determinations required by the total movement), each part is, as such, mediated by the whole in its relations with the other parts: within a totalisation, the multiplicities (as bonds of absolute exteriority – i.e., quantities) do not eliminate, but rather interiorise, one another. For example, the fact *of being a hundred* (as we shall see when we discuss groups) becomes for each of the hundred a synthetic relation of interiority with the other ninety-nine; his individual reality is affected by the numerical characteristics of *being-the-hundredth*. Thus quantity can become quality (as Engels said, following Hegel) only within a whole which reinteriorises even relations of exteriority. In this way, the whole (as a totalising act) becomes the relation among the parts. In other words, totalisation is a mediation between the parts (considered in their determinations)

to say, the modes of *effective* presence of the totalising process in the totalised parts. And knowledge, itself totalising, is the totalisation itself in so far as it is present in particular partial structures of a definite kind. In other words, totalisation cannot be consciously present to itself if it remains a formal, faceless activity of synthetic unification, but can be so only through the mediation of differentiated realities which it unifies and which effectively embody it to the extent that they totalise *themselves* by the very movement of the activity of totalising. These remarks enable us to define the first feature of the *critical investigation*: it takes place *inside* the totalisation and can be neither a contemplative recognition of the totalising movement, nor a particular, autonomous totalisation of the known totalisation. Rather, it is a real moment of the developing totalisation in so far as this is embodied in all its parts and is realised as synthetic knowledge of itself through the mediation of certain of these parts. In practice, this means that the critical investigation can and must be anyone's reflexive experience.

---

as a relation of interiority: within and through a totalisation, each part is mediated by all in its relation to each, and each is a mediation between all; negation (as determination) becomes a synthetic bond linking each part to every other, to all, and to the whole. But, at the same time, the linked system of mutually conditioning parts is opposed to the whole as an act of absolute unification, *to precisely the extent* that this system in movement does not and cannot exist except as the actual embodiment and present reality (here and now) of the whole as a developing synthesis. Similarly, the synthetic relations that two (or $n + 1$) parts maintain between themselves, precisely because they are the effective embodiment of the whole, oppose them to every other part, to all the other parts as a linked system and, consequently, to the whole in its triple reality as a developing synthesis, as an effective presence in every part, and as a surface organisation. Here we are only giving a few abstract examples; but they are sufficient to illustrate the meaning of the bonds of interiority within a developing totalisation. Obviously these oppositions are not static (as they might be if, as might happen, the totalisation were to result in totality); rather they perpetually transform the interior field to the extent that they translate the developing act into its practical efficacity. It is no less clear that what I call a '*whole*' is not a totality, but the unity of the totalising act in so far as it diversifies itself and embodies itself in totalised diversities.

5 Critical Investigation and Action

But we must both deepen and delimit our terms. For when I say that the investigation must be *reflexive*, I mean that, in the particularity of its moments, it cannot be separated from the developing totalisation any more than reflection can be distinguished from human *praxis*. I have shown elsewhere that reflection must not be conceived as a parasitical, distinct consciousness, but as the distinctive structure of certain 'consciousnesses'. If a totalisation is developing in a given region of reality, it must be a unique process occurring in unique conditions and, from the epistemological point of view, it will produce the universals which explain it and individualise them by interiorising them. (Indeed, all the concepts forged by history, including that of man, are similarly individualised universals and have no meaning apart from *this* individual process.) The critical investigation can only be a moment of this process, or, in other words, the totalising process produces itself as the critical investigation of itself at a particular moment of its development. And this critical investigation apprehends the individual movement through reflection, which means that it is the particular moment in which the act gives itself a reflexive structure. Thus the universals of the dialectic – principles and laws of intelligibility – are individualised universals; attempts at abstraction and universalisation can only result in schemata which are continually valid *for that process*. Later, we shall see how far formal extrapolations are conceivable (on the abstract hypothesis that other, as yet unknown, ontological regions are *also* totalisations); but, at any rate, such extrapolations cannot claim to be knowledge and their only utility, if they are possible, is to throw more light on the particularity of the totalising process where the investigation takes place.

6 The Problem of Stalinism

This makes clear how we are to understand the word 'anyone'. If the totalisation produces a moment of critical consciousness as the necessary incarnation of its totalising *praxis*, then obviously this moment can only appear at particular times and places. In its deep reality as well as in its modes of appearance, it is conditioned by the synthetic rule characteristic of *this* particular totalisation as well as by prior circumstances which it must transcend and retain within itself according to this rule. To make myself clearer, let me say that – if, as we assume, the region of totalisation is, for us, human history – the critique of dialectical Reason could not appear *before* historical totalisation had produced that individualised universal which we call the dialectic, that is to say, before it was posited for itself in the philosophies of Hegel and Marx. Nor could it occur *before* the *abuses* which have obscured the very notion of dialectical rationality and produced a new divorce between *praxis* and the knowledge which elucidates it. Indeed, *Critique* derives its etymological meaning and its origin from the real need to separate the true from the false, to define the limits of totalising activities so as to restore to them their validity. In other words, critical investigation could not occur *in our history*, before Stalinist idealism had sclerosed both epistemological methods and practices. It could take place only as the intellectual expression of that re-ordering which characterises, in this 'one World' of ours, the post-Stalinist period. Thus, when we claim that *anyone* can carry out the critical investigation, this does not mean it could happen at any period. It means anyone *today*. What, then, does 'anyone' mean? We use this term to indicate that, if the historical totalisation is to be able to exist, then any human life is the direct and indirect expression of the whole (the totalising movement) and of all lives to precisely the extent that it is opposed to everything and to everyone. Consequently, in any life (though more or less explicitly, depending on the circumstances) totalisation effects the divorce of blind unprincipled *praxis* and sclerosed thought, or, in other words, the obscuring of the dialectic which is a moment of the totalising activity of the world. Through this contradiction, lived in discontent and, at times, in agony, the totalisation compels everyone, as part of his individual destiny, to re-examine his intellectual tools; and this represents in fact a new, more detailed, more integrated and richer moment of human development. In fact, we are witnessing *today* the emergence of numerous attempts – all of them interesting and all of them debatable (including, of course, this one) – to interrogate the dialectic about itself. This means not only that the origin of critical investigation is itself dialectical, but also that the appearance of a reflexive and critical consciousness in everyone takes the form of individual attempts to grasp the moment of historical totalisation through one's own life, conceived as an expression of the whole. Thus, in its most immediate and most superficial character, the critical investigation of totalisation is the very life of the investigator in so far as it reflexively criticises itself. In abstract terms, this means that only a man who lives within a region of totalisation can apprehend the bonds of interiority which unite him to the totalising movement.

7 The Problem of the Individual

These remarks coincide with those I made in *The Problem of Method* about the need to approach social problems by *situating* oneself in relation to the ensembles under consideration. They also remind us that the epistemological starting point must always be *consciousness* as apodictic certainty (of) itself and as consciousness *of* such and such an object. But we are not concerned, at this point, with interrogating consciousness about itself: the object it must give itself is precisely the *life*, the objective being, of the investigator, in the world of Others, in so far as this being totalises itself from birth and will continue to totalise itself until death. On this basis, the individual disappears from historical categories: alienation, the practico-inert, series, groups, classes, the components of History, labour, individual and communal *praxis* – the individual has lived, and he still lives, all of these in interiority. But if there is a movement of dialectical Reason, it is this movement which produces this life, this membership of a particular class, of certain milieux and of certain groups; it is the totalisation itself which brought about his successes and his failures, through the vicissitudes of his community, and his personal joys and sorrows. Through his love or family relations, through his friendships and through the 'relations of production' that have marked his life, the dialectical bonds reveal themselves. For this reason, his understanding of his own life must go so far as to deny its distinctiveness so as to seek its dialectical intelligibility within human development as a whole. What I have in mind is not an act of consciousness which would make him grasp the *content* of his life in terms of concrete history, of the class to which he belongs, its characteristic contradictions and its struggles against other classes: we are not trying to reconstruct the real history of the human race; we are trying to establish the *Truth of History*.

The point is, therefore, that the critical investigation should bear on the nature of bonds of interiority (if they exist), on the basis of the human relations which define the investigator. If he is to be totalised by history, the important thing is that he should re-live his membership of human ensembles with different structures and determine the reality of these ensembles through the bonds which constitute them and the practices which define them. And to precisely the extent that the investigator is in himself (like any other individual) a living mediation between these different kinds of ensembles, his critical investigation must reveal whether this mediating bond is itself an expression of totalisation. In short, if there is such a thing as the unity of History, the experimenter must see his own life as the Whole and the Part, as the bond between the Parts and the Whole, and as the relation between the Parts, in the dialectical movement of Unification; he must be able to leap from his individual life to History simply by the practical negation of the negation which defines his life. From this point of view, the order of the investigation becomes clear: it must be regressive. The critical investigation will move in the opposite direction to the synthetic movement of the dialectic *as a method* (that is to say, in the opposite direction to Marxist thought, which proceeds from production and the relations of production to the structures of groups, and then to their internal contradictions, to various milieux and, where appropriate, to the individual); it will set out from the immediate, that is to say from the individual fulfilling himself in his abstract[23] *praxis*, so as to rediscover, through deeper and deeper conditionings, the totality of his practical bonds with others and, thereby, the structures of the various practical multiplicities and, through their contradictions and struggles, the absolute concrete: historical man. This is tantamount to saying that the individual, the investigator under investigation, is both *myself* and no one. The *bond* between collectives and groups remains: through the lived interconnection between affiliations, we shall, through this disappearing *self*, grasp the dynamic relations between the different social structures in so far as they transform

23. I am using the term 'abstract' here in the sense of *incomplete*. The individual is not abstract from the point of view of his individual reality (one could say that he is the concrete itself); but only *on condition* that the ever deeper determinations which constitute him in his very existence as a historical agent and, at the same time, as a product of History, have been revealed.

themselves in History. For instance, we must grasp the group in the moment it constitutes itself from the dissolution of the collective, or, similarly, the return of certain groups to sociality through the very movement of common *praxis* and its decomposition.

8   *Totalisation and History*

But we have neglected a crucial dimension of the critical investigation: the past. It is clear how *I* dissolve myself practically in the process of human development, but this still leaves us on the synchronic plane. It remains the case that the totalisation differs from the totality in that the latter *is* totalised while the former totalises itself. In this sense, it is obvious that to totalise *itself* means to temporalise *itself*. Indeed, as I have shown elsewhere, the only conceivable temporality is that of a totalisation as an individual process. If the totalisation is to be revealed as a developing totalisation, this means not only that it becomes and that it will become, but also that it *has become*. In this instance, *my* life, in its individual movement, is too short for us to hope to grasp the diachronic process of totalisation within it, except in so far as the totalising bond with the past which constitutes the individual *may* serve as a symbol of a totalisation of individuals.

All this is true; or rather it *would be true* if we were to ignore the *cultural* structure of every diachronic experience. Now, if culture is more than an accumulation of heteroclite knowledge and dates (in short – and this is the question – if a totalisation is developing), then what I *know* exists both within me and outside me as a field of particular tensions; *bodies of knowledge*, however disparate their content or the dates of their appearance (both in the world and in my cultural apprenticeship), are linked by *relations of interiority*. Besides, *within* modern culture as a whole, my knowledge must be dialectically conditioned by my ignorance. Once again, at the present time, this does not appear self-evident: there seems to be no reason why culture should not be a collection, or, at the very most, a superimposition of strata whose only bond (the superimposition itself) is external. One might even, like our eclectics, imagine some cultural regions which condition one another in interiority, others which remain mere aggregates, and still others which (depending on the state of knowledge) possess both characteristics. Equally, cultural regions might be defined on the basis of their internal, dialectical conditioning while their inter-relations were supposed to be ones of pure contiguity (or certain *exterior* bonds).

But if History is a totalisation which temporalises itself, culture is itself a temporalising and temporalised totalisation, despite the 'dis-parateness' of *my* knowledge and perhaps of knowledge *in general* within *the objective Culture* of this century. This problem must be resolved according to whether dialectical investigation is, or is not, possible. Supposing, for a moment, that it is possible, it is immediately clear that *my* culture cannot be treated as a subjective accumulation of knowledge and methods 'in *my* mind'; instead, this culture which I call mine must be conceived as a specific participation in interiority in the objective culture. And instead of me being a particular social atom which itself defines the cultural possibilities, this participation defines me (in a specific way). As soon as I reflexively grasp this bond of in-teriority which links me to the cultural totalisation, I disappear as a cultivated individual and emerge as the synthetic bond between every-one and what might be called the *cultural field*. And this connection will itself appear in all its complexity (relation of the Whole to the Whole for my mediation, opposition of the Whole to the part and to the Whole, opposition between *some* parts and *the* part and the Whole, etc.). Moreover – still on the assumption that dialectical investigation is possible – this very bond gives us access to *the Culture* itself as totalisation and temporalisation. In this way, I find myself dialectically conditioned by the totalised and totalising past of the process of human development: as a 'cultured' man (an expression which applies to *every* man, whatever his culture, and even if he is an illiterate) I totalise myself on the basis of centuries of history and, in accordance with my culture, I totalise this experience. This means that my life itself is centuries old, since the schemata which permit me to under-stand, to modify and to totalise my practical undertakings (and the set of determinations which go with them) have *entered the present* (present in their effects and past in their completed history). In this sense, diachronic evolution is present (as past – and, as we shall see later, as future) in synchronic totalisation; their relations are bonds of interiority and, to the extent that critical investigation is possible, the temporal depth of the totalising process becomes evident as soon as I reflexively interpret the operations of my individual life.

Of course, the individual is here only the methodological point of departure, and his short life soon becomes diluted in the pluridimensional human ensemble which temporalises its totalisation and totalises its temporality. To the extent that its individual universals are perpetually aroused, in my immediate as well as my reflective life, and, from the depths of the past in which they were born, provide the keys and the rules of my actions, we must be able, in our regressive investigation, to make use of *the whole of contemporary knowledge* (at least in principle) to elucidate a given undertaking or social ensemble, a particular avatar of *praxis*. In other words, the first use of culture must be in the unreflected content of critical reflexion, to the extent that its first grasp of synchronisms is through the present individual. Far from assuming, as certain philosophers have done, that we know nothing, we ought as far as possible (though it is impossible) to assume that we know everything. At any rate, we use the whole of knowledge in order to decipher the human ensembles which constitute the individual and which the individual totalises by the very style in which he lives them. We use this knowledge because the dream of an absolute ignorance which reveals pre-conceptual reality is a philosophical folly, as dangerous as the dream of the 'noble savage' in the eighteenth century. It is possible to be nostalgic about illiteracy, but this nostalgia is itself a cultural phenomenon, since absolute illiteracy is not aware of itself – and, if it is, it sets about eliminating itself. Thus the starting point of 'supposing we know nothing', as a negation of culture, is only culture, at a certain moment of totalising temporalisation, choosing to ignore itself *for its own sake*. It is, one might say, a sort of *pre-critical* attempt to criticise knowledge, at a time when the dialectic has not reached the stage of criticising itself.

Our critical investigation, on the other hand, will make use of everything that comes to hand because, in an individual life, each *praxis* uses *the whole* of culture and becomes both synchronic (in the ensemble of the present) and diachronic (in its human depth); and because our investigation is itself a cultural fact. In the methodical reconstruction of History it is practically forbidden to follow analogies of content, and to interpret, for example, a revolution such as Cromwell's in terms of the French Revolution. On the other hand, if we are trying to grasp formal bonds, (for example, any kind of bonds of interiority) between individuals or groups, to study the different forms of practical multiplicities and the kinds of interrelations which exist within them, the best example is the clearest provided by culture regardless of date. In other words, the dialectic is not the culmination of history; it can only exist as the original movement of totalisation. Of course, the dialectic must in the first instance be the immediate, simple lived *praxis*, and, in so far as it acts upon itself in the course of time so as to totalise itself, it *discloses* itself and progressively mediates itself through critical reflection. But for this reflection, by definition, the immediate no longer exists in relation to either present or past *praxis*. The former, contemporary with the critical investigation, acquires a reflexive structure at the moment of its constitution; the latter, precisely because it has been preserved (at least vestigially) or reconstituted, is *already mediated* when it is brought to light: in this case reflexive scissiparity becomes a kind of *distantiation*. But a reflexive critique forms part of what we shall call reconstituting *praxis* (that of the historian or the ethnographer); and reconstituting *praxis* – in so far as it effects reconstitution – is indissolubly linked to reconstituted *praxis*. (It constructs past, that is to say transcended, reality, by rediscovering it in the present transcendence which preserved it; and it is itself constructed by this resuscitated past which transforms it in so far as it restores it.) Furthermore, as a transcended past, the reconstituted *praxis* necessarily forms part of our present *praxis* as its diachronic depth. Thus, the reflexive critique becomes critical and quasi-reflexive knowledge when it seeks its examples and its explanations in the objective Culture. And let us not forget that the choice of social memories defines both the present *praxis* (in so far as it motivates this choice) and social memory in so far as it has produced our *praxis* along with its characteristic choice.

This being so, reflexive investigation and quasi-reflexive knowledge are completely homogeneous in bringing to light the synthetic bonds of History. The content of these bonds, in its materiality, can be used only to distinguish and to differentiate: it must be recognised that a friendship in Socrates' time has neither the same meaning nor the same functions as a friendship today. But this differentiation, which completely rules out any belief in 'human nature', only throws more light on the synthetic bond of *reciprocity* (which will in any case be described below) – an individualised universal, and the very foundation of all human relations. Bearing in mind these difficulties, we may select the best examples of this fundamental reciprocity from the past which we did not live, but which is nevertheless, through the *medium* of culture, completely ours. We are proposing not the rewriting of human history, but the critical investigation of bonds of interiority, or, in other words, the discovery, in connection with real, though quite ordinary, undertakings, structures and events, of the answer to this all-important question: in the process of human history, what is the respective role of relations of interiority and exteriority? And if this total investigation – which can be summed up as that of my whole life in so far as it is dissolved in the whole of history, and of the whole of history in so far as it is concentrated in an entire life – establishes that the *bond of exteriority* (analytical and positivist reason) is itself *interiorised* by practical multiplicities, and that it acts within them (as a historical force) only to the extent that it becomes an interior negation of interiority,[24] we will find ourselves situated, through the investigation itself, at the heart of a developing totalisation.

9 Primary and Secondary Intelligibility

But our task involves more than establishing the existence of an ontological region of totalisation within which we are situated. For if dialectical reason exists, the totalising movement must, at least in principle, be *intelligible* to us everywhere and at all times. (Sometimes our information may not be sufficient to make an event accessible to us; but even if this were usually so, intelligibility *in principle* would still have to be guaranteed by our investigation.) This is a matter of secondary intelligibility. Primary intelligibility, if it is to be possible, that is to say, if there is such a thing as a totalising temporalisation – must, as we have seen, consist in reducing the laws of the dialectic to moments of the totalisation. Instead of grasping certain principles *within ourselves*, *a priori* (that is to say, certain opaque limits of thought), we must grasp the dialectic *in the object* and understand it – to the extent that each of us, simultaneously individual and *the whole* of human history, *produces* it from this double point of view and is subject to it in producing it – as the totalising movement. Secondary intelligibility, however, is not the translucidity of dialectical Reason: it is the intelligibility of partial moments of the totalisation, resulting from the totalisation itself in its

---

24. We shall see later, for example, how a numerical multiplicity, in order to become a group, must interiorise its *number* (its quality as exteriority).

temporalisation, that is to say, through the critical application of dialectical schemata. We have seen that dialectical Reason, when applied to the sciences of Nature, cannot be 'constitutive': in other words, it is no more than the empty idea of totalisation projected beyond the strict and quantitative laws established by positivist Reason. Within the totalisation *where* we are and *which* we are, however, dialectical Reason must prove its *constant* superiority for the understanding of historical facts: it must dissolve the positivist, analytical interpretation from within its own totalising activity; it must reveal certain structures, relations and meanings which necessarily elude all positivism. Moreover, in the limiting case of perfect information, the event itself must become transparent, that is to say, it must reveal itself as accessible only to dialectical Reason. This means that the movement by which totalising agents, in transcending their contradictions, produce new and irreducible moments of the totalisation must present itself to us both as reality and as elucidation. In other words, if there is any such thing as dialectical Reason, it must be defined as the absolute intelligibility of the irreducibly new, in so far as it is irreducibly new. It is the opposite of the positivist analytical enterprise of explaining new facts by reducing them to old ones. And, in a sense, the positivist tradition is so firmly anchored in us, even today, that the requirement of intelligibility may seem paradoxical. The new, *in so far as it is new*, seems to elude the intellect: the new *quality* is regarded as a brute fact or, at best, its irreducibility is taken to be temporary, and analysis is expected to reveal old elements in it. But in fact it is man who brings novelty into the world: it is his *praxis* (at the level of perception: colours, odours) which, through the partial or total reorganisation of the practical field, produces a new instrument in the new unity of its appearance and function; it is the *praxis* of users which, coordinated with that of producers, will maintain the tool in the human world and, through use, link together its so-called 'elements' in such a way as to preserve its irreducibility, in relation to men.

'Human reality' is a synthesis at the level of techniques, and at the level of that universal technique which is thought. This much is clear. It is also clear – and it will become clearer – that analytical Reason is a synthetic transformation to which thought intentionally subjects itself: this thought must become a thing and control itself in exteriority in order to become the *natural* milieu in which the object under investigation defines itself *in itself*, as conditioned in exteriority. In this respect, as we shall see in detail later, thought, when it *makes itself* into directed inertia in order to act on inertia, conforms to the rule of the practical organism at every level. But, while making itself the object of this transformation, thought also controls it and realises it in connection with the inert system it is trying to study. It becomes the law of bodies in motion (at first as an indeterminate schema and *in order to become* this specific law), or the rule of chemical combination (as the simple, *a priori* certainty that such combinations cannot be totalisations). Thus analytical Reason, as the pure, universal schema of natural laws, is really only the result of a synthetic transformation or, so to speak, a particular practical moment of dialectical Reason: this latter, like animal-tools, uses its organic powers to make certain regions of itself into a *quasi-inorganic residue deciphering the inert by means of its own inertia*; scientific thought is synthetic in its internal movement (*creation* of experiments and hypotheses), and (in the case of the sciences of Nature in their present state) analytical in its noemic projection of itself. Its hypotheses are synthetic in virtue of their unifying function ($y = f(x)$) and analytical in virtue of the dispersive inertia of their material content. If our experiment is a success, we shall see later that dialectical Reason sustains, controls and constantly re-creates positivist Reason as its relation of exteriority with natural exteriority. But this positivist Reason, produced like the chitinous carapaces of certain insects, has its foundation and intelligibility only in dialectical Reason. If it is sometimes true and intelligible that an object gets its unity from exterior forces, and if these forces are themselves systematically conditioned by the indefinite exteriority of the universe, this is because man is part of this universe and is strictly conditioned by it; because all *praxis*, and consequently all knowledge, must unify molecular dispersal (either by constructing a tool, or by unifying social multiplicity within a group by interiorising it). Thus the sciences of Nature are analytical with respect to their content, whereas scientific thought is both analytical in its particular procedures and synthetic by virtue of its ultimate aims.

But if there is such a thing as totalisation, it would be wrong to suppose that the existence of organising and creative thought is *the unintelligible fact* about the human race, or some kind of *unconscious* activity revealed only through the use of the methods and the knowledge of the natural sciences. To understand a mathematical or experimental proof is to understand the method and orientation of thought. In other words, it is to grasp both the analytical necessity of the calculations (as a system of equivalences, and so as the reduction of change to zero) and the synthetic orientation of these equivalences towards the creation of new knowledge. Indeed, even if a reduction of the new to the old were to be rigorously proved, the emergence of *proved* knowledge where before there was only a vague hypothesis which at any rate lacked *Truth*, must be seen as an irreducible novelty in the order of knowledge and its practical applications. And if there could be no complete intelligibility of this irreducibility, there could be neither any consciousness of its *aim* nor any understanding of the gradual progress of the proof (on the part either of the scientist who invented the experiment or of the student listening to an account of it). Thus natural science has the same structure as a *machine*: it is controlled by a totalising thought which enriches it and finds applications for it and, at the same time, the unity of its movement (accumulation) totalises ensembles and systems of a *mechanical* order *for man*. Interiority exteriorises itself in order to interiorise exteriority.

The transparence of *praxis* (let us say, for the moment, of *individual praxis*) has its source in the indissoluble connection between negation (which totalises *in situation* what it negates) and a project which defines itself in terms of an abstract and still formal *whole* which the practical agent projects into the future and which appears as the reorganised unity of the negated situation. In this sense, the very temporalisation of an undertaking is accessible since it can be understood on the basis of the future which conditions it (that is to say of the *Whole* which *praxis* conceives as having to be realised). Thus in the very act of negating, negation creates a temporary totality; it totalises *before* becoming partial. Furthermore, when it resolves to negate a particular structure of the rejected situation, it does so on the basis of a provisional totalisation; the particularisation of the negation is not *pure analysis*, but, on the contrary, a dialectical moment: the secondary structure appears within the provisional whole as expressing the totality and as incapable of changing without the totality itself being modified (or even, as incapable of changing except as a result of the prior modification of the totality). This unification, in fact (and the discovery which is effected in the totalised field) *is* intelligibility in the first instance, in so far as human *praxis*, transparent to itself as the unity in act either of a rejection or of a project, defines its own practical understanding as the totalising grasp of a unified diversity (to understand, for a technician, is to see the whole – the entire functioning of a machine to be repaired, for example – and to search for the particular structures which obstruct its functioning *on the basis* of this overall function). It is a case, in fact, of what we were talking about a moment ago: totalisation diversifies itself and integration grows proportionately stronger. But it is also a movement from the future (for example, the machine in working order) towards the past: *repairing* something means grasping its integrity both as a temporal abstract and as the future state which is to be reconstituted. On this basis, all the activities of a practical agent are to be understood *through the future* as a perpetual re-totalisation of the provisional totality. And the ensemble of these moments, themselves re-totalised by the temporalisation, is in fact original intelligibility, for the practical agent is transparent to himself as the unifying unity of himself and his environment. In this sense, the *new* is immediately intelligible to him in his activity itself (in so far as this activity *produces* it, not in so far as it comes from outside), since, for the practical agent, it is nothing but his own *practical* unity in so far as he constantly produces it outside himself as the mark of an ever deeper diversity. Thus dialectical intelligibility rests on the intelligibility of every new determination of a practical totality, in so far as this determination is nothing other than the preservation and the totalising transcendence of all previous determinations and in so far as this transcendence and preservation are explicable by a totality which has to be realised.[25]

These remarks do not prejudge the outcome of the critical investigation which we are about to undertake. They merely indicate its intention. It is possible that, on some plane, individual *praxis* is transparent to itself and that, in this transparence, it provides the model and the rules of full intelligibility; but this still has to be proved. It is also conceivable, at least hypothetically, that human thought (in so far as it is itself *praxis* and a moment of *praxis*) is fundamentally the understanding of novelty (as a perpetual re-organisation of the given in accordance with acts explicable by their end).[26] But it is clear that this

25. This totality is only a moment of practical totalisation. If the agent regards it as definitive, this can only be for reasons external to the pure diversifying unification, such as its utility. Besides, we shall see that the created totality will elude him to the extent that its very realisation causes it to relapse into original inertia and into pure exteriority.

26. From the point of view of the future totality, each new state of the organised system is in reality a *pre-novelty*, and it shows its intelligibility only in so far as it is *already transcended* by the future unity, in so far as it is not *new enough*. Take the simple example of intuitive (and dialectical) certainty as compared with a geometrical proof. It is quite *certain* – first and foremost for a child – that a

straight line which intersects a circle at any given point must also intersect it at another point. The child or the untutored person will grasp this truth on the basis of the circle itself; he will say of the line drawn on the blackboard: since it enters the circle it must come out. A mathematician will not be satisfied with this naive certainty: he requires a proof. This is partly for all the well known reasons which make geometry rigorously systematic, and which imply that a proposition can be integrated into the system only if it is demonstrated, that is, proved according to the proper rules of geometry. But it is also, and above all, because proof is analytic whereas the intuitive certainty which I have described is dialectical. The circle-as-sensible-object is eliminated, relegated to the background, and replaced by one of its properties: there is a point inside the circle equidistant from every point on the circle; all points on the circle are equidistant from a point called 'the centre'. Let us take a point and baptise it 'centre'; it is connected to a given line by a line segment baptised 'radius'. Then one can prove that there is another point on the line which can be connected to the centre by a segment equal to the first. The actual proof does not concern us here, though we shall come back to it when we discuss necessity. What is important for us now is that the proof destroys the sensible and qualitative unity of the *circle-gestalt* in favour of the inert divisibility of 'geometrical loci'. The *gestalt* now exists only to the extent that it is compressed into implicit knowledge. All that remains is exteriority, that is to say, the residue of the generative movement. The *circle-gestalt*, in contrast, is much more than a sensible form: it is an organising movement which has been going on since the very conception of the figure, and which the eye constantly recreates. This enables us to see that this human determination of spatial indifference is *practical*, or rather that it is abstract *praxis* including within itself all the practices of enclosure. Similarly, the line in question is no longer a set of particular points; it is a *movement*: the shortest path between two points, and thus both a charting of the route and a strict law of a given movement. These considerations enable us to understand the *dialectical* intelligibility of the theorem under consideration. The circle, as the abstract idealisation of enclosure, *confines*. The straight line, as the idealisation of a disciplined journey, *shatters obstacles* in its path. Or, if it could not shatter them, it would 'mark time' before a rampart or a hill, and it would have to demolish the wall or bore a tunnel. But since we are concerned with an infinite journey, and so one without any real obstacles, we immediately see, in the geometrical diagram, that the line has *arrived* outside the circular enclosure and, in short, we grasp its movement only on the basis of points not represented on the blackboard or the sketch, and which are implicit in what we see as the destiny, the direction, the future of the line. But, to the extent that this infinitely distant future is already present in the perception of the straight line, what we see of it is *already left behind* what we cannot see of it. In a sense the present is *already past* since the movement has already reached infinity: the line becomes a vestige, a trail on the point of disappearing. Thus we see it, in the upper right-hand corner of the blackboard, for example, taking off into the sky. And thus the two points where it crossed the circle which was drawn in the middle of the blackboard appear within the diagram itself as a *transcended past*. However limited and abstract it may be, a schematic temporalisation (which the transformation of the straight line into a vector only serves to explicate) totalises the *career* (*aventure*) of the line. The line, like the circle, is individualised, however vaguely, by the process of human development (*aventure*). And when we *encounter* this movement crossing a closed curve, we are really *re-encountering* it: the straight line has already reached infinity when we see it cut the circle. And indeed the encounter with this double organisation is a new piece of knowledge. But here intelligibility originates in the intuitive apprehension of two contradictory practices (for example, an enclosure and a rail) one of which dominates the other by submitting to its law. The absolute hardness of the movement and the inflexible rigidity of its path come to terms with the circular resistance of the enclosure. The meaning of the latter is to form an *interior* (and there, too, the completed movement will make us grasp the circle, whether drawn by the mathematician or constructed by men in danger, as a totalised temporalisation). All we need to understand here is the generating act, the synthesis which collects the palissades or which holds together the abstract elements of space. The *new* is the trace left by a totalising temporalisation on the absolute, inert dispersal which represents space. It is intelligible *in so far* as the dispersive inertia which it collects *itself adds nothing to it* and is only the congealed reproduction of the generating act. At every point on the curve, the circle is both in the process of being formed and already finished. At every point on the curve, the movement to be made (the rule of construction) is understood on the basis of the movement already accomplished (the temporalised totality of the synthesis), and conversely (the *new* opacity of sensible determination is dissolved in the rule which produces it; it becomes, at each point, the sketch of the movement's past and future).

As for the relationship between the straight line and the closed curve, it appears here as a temporal and quasi-particularised process: it is the synthesis of two contradictory and already executed sets of instructions. The closed curve resists exteriority, and doubly so: it presents a barrier to every exterior force; and within this barrier it encloses an interiority. But the straight line which crosses it, when it breaks down the barrier, finds itself subjected to the law of interiority: it must return to the exterior out of which it came, following the rule which defines its movement. Thus the 'entry' of the movement demands its 'exit' because the entry has transformed it into a determination of the interiority of the circle. But conversely, the straight line realises the exteriority of the interior content by crossing the curve. Thus it is this new organisation which provides the practical intelligibility of the geometrical process by realising, *through us* and through the movement which we recreate, the exteriorisation of the interior (the action of the line on the circle) and the interiorisation of the exterior (the line makes itself interior in order to traverse the obstacle, it conforms to the structures of the circle). But this synthesis of contradictories in its transcended novelty, is decoded on the basis of future totalisations, that is to say, on the basis of operations which are performed through the mere indication that they must be.

If we examine this extremely simple case closely, it is clear that sensible intuition is simply the generative act which produces the two spatial determinations, in so far as the agent understands his partial operation in terms of a double total *praxis* (draw the line, close the circle). In short, dialectical certainty elucidates the developing act by means of the totalised act, and the nature of the material intervenes only in order to qualify the informing *praxis* (of course, this is no longer so if the material in question becomes concrete, and we shall have occasion to discuss this point at length; but at any rate the principle of dialectical certainty must be

is not the important point; it is not just a matter of studying an individual at work. A critique of dialectical Reason must concern itself with the field of application and the limits of this reason. If there is to be any such thing as the Truth of History (rather than *several* truths, even if they are organised into a system), our investigation must show that the kind of dialectical intelligibility which we have described above applies to the process of human history as a whole, or, in other words, that there is a totalising temporalisation of our practical multiplicity and that it is intelligible, even though this totalisation does not involve a grand totaliser. It is one thing to claim that individuals (possibly 'social atoms') totalise dispersals through their very existence (but individually and each within the private region of his work), and it is quite another to show that they totalise *themselves, intelligibly,* without for the most part showing any concern about it.

10 *The Plan of this Work*

If History is totalisation and if individual practices are the sole ground of totalising temporalisation, it is not enough to reveal the totalisation developing in everyone, and consequently in our critical investigations, through the contradictions which both express and mask it. Our critical investigation must also show us *how* the practical multiplicity (which may be called 'men' or 'Humanity' according to taste) realises, in its very dispersal, its interiorisation. In addition, we must exhibit

---

the perception of a developing *praxis* in the light of its final term). If this immediate understanding of practical novelty seems, in the example we have just considered, useless and almost childish this is because geometry is concerned not with acts but with their vestiges. It matters little for geometry whether its geometrical figures are abstractions, limiting schemata of real work; geometry is concerned only to reveal relations of radical exteriority beneath the seal of interiority which is stamped on these figures when they are generated. But this means that intelligibility disappears. In effect, practical syntheses are studied in so far as the synthesising action becomes a pure passive designation making way for the establishment of relations of exteriority between the elements which it has brought together. We shall see later how the practico-inert rediscovers this passive exteriorisation of practical interiorisation and how, in tracing this process, it is possible to define *alienation* in its original form.

the dialectical necessity of this totalising process. Indeed, the multi-plicity of dialectical agents (that is, of individuals producing a *praxis*) seems at first sight to involve a second-order atomism, through the multiplicity of totalisations. If this were so, we should return on a new level, to the atomism of analytical Reason. But since our starting point is individual *praxis*, we must carefully follow up every one of those threads of Ariadne which lead from this *praxis*, to the various forms of human ensembles; and in each case we shall have to determine the structures of these ensembles, their real mode of formation out of their elements, and finally their totalising action upon the elements which formed them. But it will never be sufficient to show the production of ensembles by individuals or by one another, nor, conversely, to show how individuals are produced by the ensembles which they compose. It will be necessary to show the dialectical intelligibility of these trans-formations in every case.

Of course, this is a matter of *formal* intelligibility. By this I mean that we must understand the bonds between *praxis*, as self-conscious, and all the complex multiplicities which are organised through it and in which it loses itself as *praxis* in order to become *praxis-process*. However – and I shall have occasion to repeat this still more emphati-cally – it is no part of my intention to determine the concrete history of these incarnations of *praxis*. In particular, as we shall see later, the practical individual enters into ensembles of very different kinds, for example, into what are called *groups* and what I shall call *series*. It is no part of our project to determine whether series precede groups or vice versa, either originally or in a particular moment of History. On the contrary: as we shall see, groups are born of series and often end up by serialising themselves in their turn. So the *only* thing which matters to us is to display the transition from series to groups and from groups to series as constant incarnations of our practical multiplicity, and to test the dialectical intelligibility of these reversible processes. In the same way, when we study class and class-being (*l'être de classe*) we shall find ourselves drawing examples from the history of the working class. But the purpose will not be to define the particular class which is known as the proletariat: our sole aim will be to seek the constitution of a class in these examples, its totalising (and detotalising) function and its dialectical intelligibility (bonds of interiority and of exteri-ority, interior structures, relations to other classes, etc.). In short, we are dealing with neither human history, nor sociology, nor ethno-graphy. To parody a title of Kant's, we would claim, rather, to be laying the foundations for 'Prolegomena to any future anthropology'.

If our critical investigation actually yields positive results, we shall have established *a priori* – and not, as the Marxists *think* they have done, *a posteriori* – the heuristic value of the dialectical method when applied to the human sciences, and the necessity, with any fact, provided it is *human*, of reinserting it within the developing totalisation and understanding it on this basis. Thus the critical investigation will always present itself as a double investigation: *if* totalisation exists, the investigation will supply us with, *on the one hand* (and in the regressive order), all the *means* brought into play by the totalisation, that is to say the partial totalisations, detotalisations and retotalisations in their functions and abstract structures and, *on the other hand*, it must enable us to see how these forms dialectically generate one another in the full intelligibility of *praxis*. Moreover, in so far as our investigation proceeds from the simple to the complex, from the abstract to the concrete, from the constituting to the constituted, we must be able to settle, without reference to concrete history, the incarnations of individual *praxis*, the formal structural conditions of its alienation[27] and the abstract circumstances which encourage the constitution of a common *praxis*. This leads to the principal divisions of this first volume: *the constituent dialectic* (as it grasps itself in its abstract translucidity in individual *praxis*) finds its limit within its own work and is transformed into an *anti-dialectic*. This anti-dialectic, or dialectic against the dialectic (dialectic *of passivity*),[28] must reveal *series* to us as

27. This means: the dialectical investigation of alienation as an *a priori possibility* of human *praxis* on the basis of the *real* alienations to be found in concrete History. It would indeed be inconceivable that human activity should be *alienated* or that human relations should be capable of being *reified* if there were no such thing as alienation and reification in the *practical* relation of the agent to the object of his act and to other agents. Neither the un-situated freedom of certain idealists, nor the Hegelian relation of consciousness to itself, nor the mechanistic determinism of certain pseudo-Marxists can account for it. It is in the concrete and synthetic relation of the agent to the other through the mediation of the thing, and to the thing through the mediation of the other, that we shall be able to discover the foundations of all possible alienation.

28. The dialectic of passivity is in no way reducible to analytical reason, which is the *a priori* construction of the inert (spatio-temporal) framework of exteriority as such, or which, as it were, is the dialectic giving itself exteriority in order to grasp the exterior and manifesting itself implicitly only in the unitary direction of the passive behaviour of exteriorised exteriority. What we call the dialectic of passivity, or anti-dialectic, is the moment of intelligibility corresponding to a *praxis* turned against itself in so far as it is reinstated as the per-

a type of human gathering and alienation as a mediated relation to the other and to the objects of labour in the element of seriality and as a serial mode of co-existence.[29] At this level we will discover an equivalence between alienated *praxis* and worked inertia, and we shall call the domain of this equivalence the *practico-inert*. And we shall see the group emerge as a second type of dialectical gathering, in opposition both to the *practico-inert* and to impotence. But I shall distinguish, as will be seen, between the constituted dialectic and the constituent dialectic to the extent that the group has to constitute its common *praxis* through the individual *praxis* of the agents of whom it is composed. Therefore, if there is to be any such thing as totalisation, the intelligibility of constituted dialectical Reason (the intelligibility of common actions and of *praxis*-process) must be based on constituent dialectical reason (the abstract and individual *praxis* of man at work). Within the context of our critical investigation, we shall be able at this point to define the limits of dialectical intelligibility and, by the same token, the specific meaning of totalisation. It may then appear that realities such as class, for example, do not have a unique and homogeneous kind of being, but rather that they exist and they create themselves on all levels at once, through a more complex totalisation than we expected (since the anti-dialectic must be integrated and totalised, but not destroyed, by the constituted dialectic which, in turn, can totalise only on the basis of a constituent dialectic).

At this level, it will become evident that the regressive investigation has reached bedrock. In other words, we shall have grasped our individual depth in so far as, through the movement of groups and series, our roots reach down to fundamental materiality. Every moment of the regress will seem more complex and general than the

---

manent seal of the inert. At this level we shall have to turn our attention to the way inertia itself becomes dialectical through having this seal placed upon it: not *in so far* as it is pure inertia, but in so far as we must station ourselves at the point of view of inert exteriority in order to discover passivised *praxis* (for example, the circulation of currency). On the surface, this pseudo-dialectic or inverted dialectic has the appearance of magic, but in fact it has its own type of rationality which we shall have to reveal.

29. Obviously alienation is a much more complex phenomenon and its conditions, as we shall see, are present at all levels of experience. Nevertheless we must here indicate its ground. For example, alienation exists as a constant danger within the practical group. But this is intelligible only in so far as the most lively and united group is always in danger of relapsing into the series from which it came.

isolated, superficial moment of our individual *praxis*, yet from another point of view, it remains completely abstract, that is, it is still no more than a *possibility*. Indeed, whether we consider the relations between group and series formally, in so far as each of these ensembles may produce the other, or whether we grasp the individual, within our investigation, as the practical ground of an ensemble and the ensemble as producing the individual in his reality as historical agent, this formal procedure will lead us to a dialectical circularity. This circularity exists; it is even (for Engels as much as for Hegel) characteristic of the dialectical order and of its intelligibility. But the fact remains that reversible circularity is in contradiction with the irreversibility of History, as it appears to investigation. Though it is true in the abstract that groups and series can indifferently produce each other, it is also true that historically a particular group, through its serialisation, produces a given serial ensemble (or conversely) and that, if a new group originated in the serial ensemble, then, whatever it might be, it would be irreducible to the serial ensemble. Moreover, such a regressive investigation, though it brings certain conflicts into play, only reveals our underlying structures and their intelligibility, without revealing the dialectical relations between groups and series, between different series or between different groups.

Thus, dialectical investigation in its regressive moment will reveal to us no more than the static conditions of the possibility of a totalisation, that is to say, of a history. We must therefore proceed to the opposite and complementary investigation: by progressively recomposing the historical process on the basis of the shifting and contradictory relations of the formations in question, we shall experience History; and this dialectical investigation should be able to show us whether the contradictions and social struggles, the communal and individual *praxis*, labour as producing tools, and tools as producing men and as regulator of human labour and human relations, etc., make up the unity of an intelligible (and thus directed) totalising movement. But above all, though these discoveries have to be made and consolidated in relation to these particular examples, our critical investigation aims to recompose the intelligibility of the historical movement within which the different ensembles are defined by their conflicts. On the basis of synchronic structures and their contradictions, it seeks the diachronic intelligibility of historical transformations, the order of their conditionings and the intelligible reason for the irreversibility of History, that is to say, for its direction. This synthetic progression, though merely formal, must fulfil several functions: by recomposing instances in terms of process, it must lead us, if not to the absolute concrete, which can only be individual (*this* event at *this* date of *this* history), at least to the absolute system of conditions for applying the determination '*concrete* fact' to the fact of *one* history.

In this sense it could be said that the aim of the critical investigation is to establish a structural and historical anthropology, that the regressive moment of the investigation is the basis of the intelligibility of sociological Knowledge (without prejudging any of the individual components of this Knowledge), and that the progressive moment must be the basis of the intelligibility of historical Knowledge (without prejudging the real individual unfolding of the totalised facts). Naturally, the progression will deal with the same structures as those brought to light by regressive investigation. Its sole concern will be to rediscover the moments of their inter-relations, the ever vaster and more complex movement which totalises them and, finally, the very direction of the totalisation, that is to say, the 'meaning of History' and its Truth. The multiple, fundamental bonds between the constituent dialectic and the constituted dialectic and vice versa through the constant mediation of the anti-dialectic, will become clear to us in the course of these new investigations. If the results of the investigation are positive, we shall finally be in a position to define dialectical Reason as the constituent and constituted reason of practical multiplicities. We shall then understand the meaning of totalisation without a totaliser, or a de-totalised totalisation, and we shall finally be able to prove the strict equivalence between *praxis* with its particular articulations and the dialectic as the logic of creative action, that is to say, in the final analysis, as the logic of freedom.

Volume I of the *Critique of Dialectical Reason* stops as soon as we reach the 'locus of history'; it is solely concerned with finding the intelligible foundations for a structural anthropology – to the extent, of course, that these synthetic structures are the condition of a directed, developing totalisation. Volume II, which will follow shortly,[30] will retrace the stages of the critical progression: it will attempt to establish that there is *one* human history, with *one* truth and *one* intelligibility – not by considering the material content of this history, but by demonstrating that a practical multiplicity, whatever it may be, must unceasingly totalise itself through interiorising its multiplicity at all levels.

11   The Individual and History

The link of our critical investigation is none other than the fundamental identity between an individual life and human history (or,
from the methodological point of view, the 'reciprocity of their perspectives'). Strictly speaking, the identity of these two totalising
processes must itself be proved. But in fact critical investigation proceeds from exactly this hypothesis and each moment of the regression
(and, later, of the progression) directly calls it into question. The
continuity of the regression would be interrupted at every level if
ontological identity and methodological reciprocity did not in fact
always appear both as fact and as necessary and intelligible Truth. In
reality, the hypothesis which makes the critical investigation feasible is
precisely the one which the investigation aims to prove. If there is a
dialectic we must submit to it as the unavoidable discipline of the
totalisation which totalises *us* and grasp it, in its free practical spontaneity, as the totalising *praxis* which we are; at each stage in our investigation we must rediscover, within the intelligible unity of the
synthetic movement, the contradiction and indissoluble connection
between necessity and freedom, though, at each moment, this connection appears in different forms. In any case, if my life, as it deepens,
becomes History, it must reveal itself, at a deep level of its free development, as the strict necessity of the historical process so as to
rediscover itself at an even deeper level, as the freedom of this necessity
and, finally, as the necessity of freedom.[31]
    The critical investigation will reveal this interplay of aspects in so
far as the totaliser is always also the totalised, even if, as we shall see,
he is the Prince in person. And, if the investigation is successful, and
we reveal the rocky sub-soil of necessity beneath the translucidity of

31. Though I present the final relation between these realities in this form, I am
not halting the enumeration of these contradictory unities on account of the two
terms of the comparison: nothing would prevent us from *circularly* conceiving
other dialectical moments in which the succession of the unities mentioned would
turn out to take place in the opposite order. If I halt the enumeration here, this
is because the very movement of structural and historical totalisation requires, as
we shall see, that these unities, *and these alone*, should mark the moments of our
investigation.

free individual *praxis*, we will be able to hope that we have taken the right track. Then we shall be able to glimpse what these two volumes together will try to prove: that *necessity*, as the apodictic structure of dialectical investigation, resides neither in the free development of interiority nor in the inert dispersal of exteriority; it asserts itself, as an inevitable and irreducible moment, in the interiorisation of the exterior and in the exteriorisation of the interior. This double movement will be that of our entire regressive investigation: a thorough examination of individual *praxis* will show us that it interiorises the exterior (in delimiting, through action itself, a practical field); but conversely, we shall grasp in the tool and in objectification through labour an intentional exteriorisation of interiority (of which a *seal* is both the symbol and the example); similarly, the movement by which the practical life of the individual must, in the course of the investigation, dissolve itself into sociological or historical totalisations, does not preserve the translucid interiority of the totalising agent in the new form, which appears as the objective reality of life (series, group, system, process). To put it more vividly if less precisely, it is *initially within itself* that free subjectivity discovers its objectivity as the intelligible necessity of being a perspective within totalisations which totalise it (which integrate it in synthetic developing forms). Subjectivity then appears, in all its abstraction, as the verdict which compels us to carry out, freely and through ourselves, the sentence that a 'developing' society has pronounced upon us and which defines us *a priori* in our being. This is the level at which we shall encounter the *practico-inert*.

However, it must be understood that *praxis* presupposes a material agent (the organic individual) and the material organisation of an operation on and by matter. Thus we shall never find men who are not mediated by matter at the same time as they mediate different material regions. A practical multiplicity is a certain relation of matter to itself through the mediation of the *praxis* which transforms the inert into worked matter, just as the collection of objects which surrounds us imposes its mediation on the practical multiplicity which totalises us. Thus, the history of man is an adventure of nature, not only because man is a material organism with material needs, but also because worked matter, as an exteriorisation of interiority, produces man, who produces or uses this worked matter in so far as he is forced to re-interiorise the exteriority of his product, in the totalising movement of the multiplicity which totalises it. The *external* unification of the inert, whether by the seal or by law, and the introduction of inertia at the heart of *praxis* both result, as we have seen, in producing necessity as a strict determination at the heart of human relations. And the totalisation which controls me, in so far as I discover it within my free lived totalisation, only takes the form of necessity for two fundamental reasons: first, the totalisation which totalises me has to make use of the mediation of inert products of labour; second, a practical multiplicity must *always* confront its own external inertia, that is to say, its character as a discrete quantity. We shall see that the interiorisation of number is not always possible and that, when it does take place, quantity produces in each member of a group a thick layer of inertia (exteriority within interiority), though it is lived dialectically in interiority. Consequently, the problem of necessity, which is immediately given as a structure of our critical investigation, necessarily leads us to the fundamental problem of anthropology, that is, to the relations of practical organisms to inorganic matter. We must never lose sight of the fact that exteriority, (that is to say, quantity, or, in other words, Nature), is, for every multiplicity of agents, a threat both from without and from within (we shall see its role in the anti-dialectic), and that it is both the permanent means and the profound occasion for totalisation. We shall also see that it is the *essence* of man in the sense that essence, as transcended past, is inert and becomes the transcended objectification of the practical agent (thus producing within everyone and within every multiplicity the continually resolved and constantly renewed contradiction between man-as-producer and man-as-product).[32] In the second volume we will also learn that exteriority is the inert motive force of History in that it is the only possible basis for the *novelty* which places its seal on it and which it preserves both as an irreducible moment and as a memory of Humanity. Whether as inert motive force or as creative memory, inorganic matter (always organised by us) is never absent from the history of our organic materialities; it is the condition of exteriority, interiorised so as to make history possible, and this fundamental condition is the absolute requirement *that there must be* a necessity in History at the very heart of intelligibility – and perpetually dissolved in the movement of

---

32. The objectification of man places a seal on the inert. Thus, a transcended objectification, in so far as it is the space of the practical man, is, in the last analysis, a robot. In the strange world which we are describing the robot is the essence of man: he freely transcends himself towards the future, but he thinks of himself as a robot as soon as he looks back on his past. He *comes to know himself in the inert* and is therefore a victim of his reified image, even prior to all alienation.

practical understanding.[33] Thus, our critical investigation must present us with apodicticity as the indissoluble unity – at every totalising and totalised level – of the organic and the inorganic through all the forms that this connection can assume (from the presence of the inorganic within the organism itself and all around it, up to and including the

---

33. There is, in fact, a contradiction between intelligibility and necessity. Intelligibility makes the new perfectly clear on the basis of the old; it enables us to witness the transparent practical production of the new on the basis of previously defined factors and in the light of totalisation. However, *precisely* because this light is shed everywhere, it dissolves that external control which, as we shall see, necessity is and remains, even within processes of thought. For necessity merely eliminates all possibility by simply positing *from the exterior* the impossibility, given y and z, that x should not occur (and of course this impossibility also applies to processes of thought). Dialectical understanding, in so far as it offers a full, temporalised intuition of the organising movement whereby y and z are unified in x simply through their connection of interiority (within the developing totalisation), tends to get absorbed into the very temporalisation of this certainty. Transparency is its own guarantee, and the basic problem is not that of ruling out possibilities, but that of grasping, the full realisation of *one* possibility, in every one of its moments, and on the basis of a future totality. Certainty tends to avoid apodicticity to the extent that necessity tends to repel certainty. But in so far as historical certainty must always display the bonds of interiority, to the extent that these unite and partially transform an *exterior* diversity (every element of which is external to the others, external to itself and controlled from the exterior), to the extent, also, that these interior bonds are affected through their very activity with a quasi-exteriority, necessity appears within certainty as the formal inertia of intelligibility; every adjustment tends to dissolve it in the very movement which circumscribes the inert diversity and seems, for a moment, to endow it with an internal and autonomous strength. But necessity reappears at the very end of the partial totalisation as the bony structure, the skeleton of certainty: thus the intelligibility of *praxis* comes to depend on the *result* of the *praxis*, both as it was projected and yet *always different*, and this result, *in so far as it differs* (that is to say, in so far as it *too* is connected to the whole by exteriority) will appear as *incapable* of being different than it is (and by the same token all totalising processes of thought will appear as having been incapable of being other than they are). It is worth recalling – as an illustration rather than an example – that the reading of novels and plays is a totalisation (as is the life of the reader). On the basis of the double totalisation effected by History, and as his own individual life, the reader approaches the work as a totality to be re-totalised in its own individuality. The understanding of actions or of dialogues must, if the work is to satisfy the mind, be both the translucidity of the unforseen, (one witnesses the intelligible birth of a response, for example, as the partial re-totalisation of the situation and of the conflicts) and, in so far as each moment falls within a past of inertia, the impossibility, to which immediate memory is subjected, that this moment should have been different.

organisation of the inorganic and the presence of number as pure exteriority within number interiorised by organised practical multiplicity). It is in this way that we rediscover the schema of the critical investigation. In the regressive moment, we shall find the constituent dialectic, the anti-dialectic and the constituted dialectic. And in the moment of synthetic progression, we shall trace the totalising movement which integrates these three partial movements within a total totalisation. On this basis we shall be able to put the question of *possibility* in history (and, in general, in *praxis*), and of historical *necessity* in its true light. It is thus in this progressive moment that we shall finally understand our original problem: what is Truth as the *praxis* of synthetic unification, and what is History? Why is there such a thing as human history (ethnography having acquainted us with societies with no history)? And what is the *practical* meaning of historical totalisation in so far as it can reveal itself today to a (totalising and totalised) agent situated within History in development?

1 2 Intellection and Comprehension

The close connection between *comprehension* (*la compréhension*), as I defined it in *The Problem of Method*,[34] and *intellection* (*l'intellection*), as we must be able to define it if there is such a thing as dialectic, will no doubt have been noticed. *Comprehension* is simply the translucidity of *praxis* to itself, whether it produces its own elucidation in constituting itself, or recognises itself in the *praxis* of the other. In either case, the comprehension of the act is effected by the (produced or reproduced) act; and the teleological structure of the activity can only be grasped within a project which defines itself by its goal, that is to say, by its future, and which returns from this future in order to elucidate the present as the negation of the transcended past. From this point of view, every *praxis* is a partial re-totalisation of the practical field (in so far as this is defined by its negation — the first *internal* totalisation

34. '*Comprehension* is nothing other than my real life; it is the totalizing movement which gathers together my neighbour, myself, and the environment in the synthetic unity of an objectification in process'. *The Problem of Method*, trans. H. E. Barnes, p. 155. [Ed.]

effected by the agent or the practical multiplicity), and it is because my life is a perpetual (horizontal and vertical) re-totalisation that I have access to the other's present on the basis of his future. Now, dialectical intelligibility is, as we have seen, defined by the degree of transparency of the developing totalisation and the practical agent can temporalise an intelligible certainty only in so far as, situated within this totalisation, he is himself both totalising and totalised. It might seem, therefore, that 'intellection' is only another word for comprehension – in which case it would seem to be useless. However, it is usual to oppose intellection (restricted to the processes of analytical Reason) to comprehension (which occurs only in the human sciences).

This distinction, however commonplace, is quite meaningless. There is no such thing as *intelligibility* in the sciences of Nature: when *praxis* puts its seal on a region of the exteriority of inertia, it produces and reveals necessity in the form of the impossibility that the facts in question should be other than they are; and as we have seen, Reason then *makes itself* into a system of inertia in order to rediscover sequences in exteriority and in order both to produce and to discover necessity as their sole *exterior* unity. Necessity as succession in exteriority (the moments are *exterior* to each other and they cannot occur in a different order) is only the mind producing and discovering its own limit, that is to say, producing and discovering *the impossibility of thinking in exteriority.*[35] The discovery of thought as impossibility is the complete opposite of understanding, for understanding can only be the recognition of the accessibility of the real to a rational *praxis.* *Comprehension*, on the other hand, which recognises this accessibility within the human sciences, is insufficiently grounded and, unless it is reduced to *praxis* producing itself along with its elucidation, it is in danger of becoming irrational or mystical intuition (sympathy, etc.). If we are to see *comprehension* as a moment of *praxis*, then it goes without saying that it is totalising and that it grasps the temporalising and temporalised certainty of practices, wherever they occur, in so far as they are totalisations.

The opposition between the intelligible and the comprehensible ought really to be rejected. It is not as though there are two fundamentally different kinds of certainty. If we retain the two terms in

35. When I say 'producing', it is obvious that I am not thinking of Kantian 'categories'. The *seal* impressed upon exteriority is only a *practical* operation (such as the construction of a mechanical model or an experimental system).

spite of this, it is because comprehension is a kind of species of which intellection is the genus. We shall in fact retain the term 'comprehensible' to designate any *intentional praxis* (whether of an individual or of a group). And of course affectivity itself is *practical*. Thus we do not mean to confine comprehension to pure straightforward action and labour. Whenever a *praxis* can be traced to the intention of a practical organism or of a group, even if this intention is implicit or obscure to the agent himself, there is comprehension. However, critical investigation will reveal actions without an agent, productions without a producer, totalisations without a totaliser, counter-finalities and infernal circularities. We shall also discover multiplicities producing totalised thoughts and acts without reference to the individuals composing them, indeed without their even being aware of it. In such cases, and in many others which will turn up in due course, either the Truth of History *is not unified,* or totalising intellection *must be possible.* Vagabond and authorless, these free actions, which can overturn a society or its dead institutions, and which have always lost their meaning (and, perhaps, taken on a new meaning), must be totalisable, cannot remain foreign bodies within developing History; consequently, they must be intelligible. Intellection, being more complex, must be able to grasp, on the basis of the developing totalisation, the source of such things, the reasons (*within History*) for their inhumanity and for their accessibility, as such, to a totalising anthropology: it must see them arise and dissolve themselves in the unity of a dialectical process, that is, in direct connection with *praxis* itself and as the transitory exteriority of an interiority. For this reason, I shall call any temporalising dialectical certainty, in so far as it is capable of totalising *all* practical realities *intellection,* and reserve the term *comprehension* for the totalising group or any *praxis* in so far as it is intentionally produced by its author or authors.

Book I

From Individual Praxis
to the Practico-Inert

Individual Praxis
as Totalisation

1 Need

If the dialectic is possible, we must be able to find answers to the following four questions:

(1) How can *praxis* in itself be an experience both of necessity and of freedom since neither of these, according to classical logic, can be grasped in an empirical process?

(2) If dialectical rationality really is a logic of totalisation, how can History – that swarm of individual destinies – appear as a totalising movement, and how can one avoid the paradox that in order to totalise there must already be a unified principle, that is, that only actual totalities can totalise themselves?

(3) If the dialectic is comprehension of the present through the past and through the future, how can there be a historical future?

(4) If the dialectic is to be materialist, how are we to comprehend the materiality of *praxis* and its relation to other forms of materiality?

It should be recalled that the crucial discovery of dialectical investigation is that man is 'mediated' by things to the same extent as things are 'mediated' by man. This truth must be born in mind in its entirety if we are to develop all its consequences. This is what is called dialectical *circularity* and, as we shall see, it must be established by dialectical investigation. But if we were not already dialectical beings we would not even be able to comprehend this circularity. I present it at the outset not as a truth, nor even a conjecture, but as the type of thought which is necessary, *prospectively*, in order to elucidate a self-developing investigation.

On the most superficial and familiar level, the investigation *first* reveals, in the unity of dialectical connections, unification as the movement of individual *praxis*, plurality, the organisation of plurality, and the plurality of organisations. One need only open one's eyes to see this. Our problem concerns these connections. If there are individuals, *who*, or *what*, totalises?

A simple but inadequate answer is that there would not even be the beginnings of partial totalisation if the individual were not totalising *through himself*. *The entire historical dialectic rests on individual* praxis *in so far as it is already dialectical*, that is to say, to the extent that action is itself the negating transcendence of contradiction, the determination of a present totalisation in the name of a future totality, and the real effective working of matter. This much is clear, and is an old lesson of both subjective and objective investigation. Our problem is this: what becomes of *the* dialectic if there are only particular men each of whom is dialectical? As I have said, the investigation provides its own intelligibility. We must therefore see what is the real rationality of action, at the level of individual *praxis* (ignoring for the moment the collective constraints which give rise to it, limit it or make it ineffective).

Everything is to be explained through *need (le besoin)*; need is the first totalising relation between the material being, man, and the material ensemble of which he is part. This relation is *univocal*, and *of interiority*. Indeed, it is through need that the first negation of the negation and the first totalisation appear in matter. Need is a negation of the negation in so far as it expresses itself as a *lack* within the organism; and need is a positivity in so far as the organic totality tends to preserve itself *as such* through it. The original negation, in fact, is an initial contradiction between the organic and the inorganic, in the double sense that lack is defined in relation to *a totality*, but that a *lacuna*, a *negativity*, has as such a *mechanical* kind of existence, and that, in the last analysis, *what is lacking* can be reduced to inorganic or less organised elements or, quite simply, to dead flesh, etc. From this point of view, the negation of this negation is achieved through the transcendence of the organic towards the inorganic: need is a link of *univocal immanence* with surrounding materiality in so far as the organism *tries to sustain itself* with it; it is already totalising, and doubly so, for it is nothing other than the living totality, manifesting itself as a totality and revealing the material environment, to infinity, as the total field of possibilities of satisfaction.

On the level which concerns us here, there is nothing mysterious in this transcendence through need since the basic behaviour associated with need for food reproduces the elementary processes of nutrition: chewing, salivation, stomach contractions, etc. Transcendence here takes the form of a simple unity of a totalising function working in a vacuum. Without a unity of basic behaviour within the whole, there would be no such thing as hunger; there would only be a scattering of disconnected, frantic actions. Need is a function which posits itself for itself and totalises itself as a function because it is reduced to an empty gesture, functioning for itself and not within the integration of organic life. And this isolation threatens the organism as a whole with disintegration – the danger of death. This initial totalisation is *transcendent* to the extent that the being of the organism lies outside it, immediately or mediately, in inanimate being; need sets up the *initial contradiction* because the organism, in its being, depends directly (oxygen) or indirectly (food), on unorganised being and because, conversely, the control of its reactions imposes a biological statute on the inorganic. In fact, this is really a matter of two statutes of the same materiality, since everything points to the fact that living bodies and inanimate objects are made of the the same molecules.[1] Yet these statutes contradict one another, since one of them presupposes a bond of interiority between the whole as a unity and molecular relations, whereas the other is purely external. Nevertheless, negativity and contradiction come to the inert through organic totalisation. As soon as need appears, surrounding matter is endowed with a passive unity, in that a developing totalisation is reflected in it as a totality: matter revealed as passive totality by an organic being seeking its being in it – this is Nature in its initial form. Already, it is in terms of the total field that need seeks possibilities of satisfaction in nature, and it is thus totalisation which will reveal in the passive totality its own material being as abundance or scarcity.

But while Nature appears, through the mediation of need, as a false organism, the organism exteriorises itself in Nature as pure materiality. In effect, a biological statute is superimposed, in the organism, on a physico-chemical statute. And while it is true that, in the interiority of nutritive assimilation, molecules are controlled and filtered in close coordination with the permanent totalisation, yet when it is seen from the point of view of exteriority the living body obeys all the exterior laws. In this sense, one could say that the matter outside it subjects the living body to an inorganic statute precisely to the extent that it is itself transformed into a totality. The living body is therefore *in danger* in the universe, and the universe harbours the possibility of the

1. Though this has not been proved by any *definite* investigation.

non-being of the organism. Conversely, if it is to find its being within Nature or to protect itself against destruction, the organic totality must transform itself into inert matter, for it is only as a mechanical system that it can modify the material environment. The man of need is an organic totality perpetually making itself into its own tool in the milieu of exteriority. The organic totality acts on inert bodies through the medium of the inert body *which it is* and which it *makes itself*. It *is inert* in as much as it is already subjected to all the physical forces which reveal it to itself as pure passivity; it *makes itself* inert in its being in so far as it is only externally and through inertia itself that a body can act on another body in the milieu of exteriority.

The action of a living body on the inert can be exercised either directly or through the mediation of another inert body, in which case we call the intermediary a tool. But once the organised body takes its own inertia as mediation between inert matter and its own need, instrumentality, purpose and labour are given together: the totality to be preserved is, in effect, projected as the totalisation of the movement by which the living body uses its inertia to overcome the inertia of things. At this level, the transcendence of exteriority towards interiorisation is characterised both as existence and as *praxis*. Organic functioning, need and *praxis* are strictly linked in a dialectical manner; dialectical time came into being, in fact, with the organism; for the living being can survive only by renewing itself. This *temporal* relation between the future and the past, through the present, is none other than the functional relation of the totality to itself; the totality is its own future lying beyond a present of reintegrated disintegration. In short, a living unity is characterised by the decompression of the temporality of the instant; but the new temporality is an elementary synthesis of change and identity, since the future governs the present in so far as this future strictly identifies itself with the past. The cyclical process – which characterises both biological time and that of primitive societies[2] – is interrupted *externally*, by the environment, simply because the contingent and inescapable fact of scarcity disrupts exchanges. This disruption is lived *as negation* in the simple sense that the cyclical move-

---

2. This is not because these societies are *organic*, for, as we shall see, organicism has to be absolutely rejected, but because their individual members remain very close to the organic temporality of cyclical repetition, and because the mode of production helps to maintain the process of repetition – at first through itself, and then through the type of mediation and integration which it introduces into the institutional relations between men.

ment or function continues in a vacuum, thus denying the identity of the future and the past and relapsing to the level of a *present* circular organisation conditioned by the past. This dislocation is necessary if the organism is to become, not the milieu and destiny of the function, but its end.

The only real difference between primitive synthetic temporality and the time of elementary *praxis* lies in the material environment which, by not containing what the organism seeks, transforms the totality as future reality into *possibility*. Need, as a negation of the negation, is the organism itself, living itself in the future, through present disorders, as its own possibility and, consequently, as the possibility of its own impossibility; and *praxis*, in the first instance, is nothing but the relation of the organism, as exterior and future end, to the present organism as a totality under threat; it is function exteriorised. The real difference is not between function as internal assimilation and the construction of tools with an end in view. Many species of animals, in fact, make tools of themselves: that is to say, organised matter produces the inorganic or the pseudo-inert out of itself. I have said that organisms cannot act on the environment without temporarily returning to the level of inertia; but animal-tools make themselves permanently inert in order to protect their lives or, to put it another way, instead of using their own inertia they hide it behind a created inertia. It is at this ambiguous level that the dialectical transition from function to action can be seen. The *project*, as transcendence, is merely the exteriorisation of immanence; transcendence itself is already present in the functional fact of nutrition and excretion, since what we find here is a relation of univocal interiority between two states of materiality. And, conversely, transcendence contains immanence within itself in that its link with its purpose and with the environment remains one of exteriorised interiority.

2   *The Negation of the Negation*

Thus although *in the first instance* the material universe may make man's existence impossible, it is through man that negation comes to man and to matter. It is on this basis that we can understand in its original intelligibility the celebrated law of 'the negation of the nega-tion' which Engels erroneously presents as, basically, an irrational 'abstraction' from natural laws. In reality, the dialectic of Nature – whether one seeks it in 'changes of state' in general or makes it the *external dialectic* in human history – is incapable of providing an an-swer to two essential questions: why should there be any such thing as negation either in the natural world or in human history? And why and in what specific circumstances does the negation of a negation yield to affirmation? Indeed, it is not clear why transformations of energy – even if they are 'vectoral' as M. Naville would have it, *even if certain among them are reversible and others irreversible, even if, as in chemical experiments, certain partial reactions occur within an overall reaction and alter it[3] – should be regarded as negations, except *by men* and as a convention for indicating the direction of the process. There is no denying that matter passes from one state to another, and this means that change takes place. But a material change is neither an affirmation nor a negation; it cannot *destroy* anything, since nothing was *constructed*; it cannot *overcome resistances*, since the forces involved simply produced the result they had to. To declare that two opposed forces applied to a membrane *negate each other* is as absurd as saying that they *collaborate* to determine a certain tension. The only possible use for the *order of negation* is to distinguish one direction from an other.

3. I am thinking, for example, of what has been known, since Sainte-Claire Deville, as *chemical equilibrium*: when the chemist attempts, by putting two sub-stances, *a* and *b*, together in certain experimental conditions to produce two other substances, *c* and *d*, the direct reaction, $a + b = c + d$, is normally accompanied by the inverse reaction, *c* and *d* reacting with one another to form *a* and *b*. Thus a chemical equilibrium is reached; the transformation stops half-way. Here, we have indeed *two forms of reaction* and there is nothing to stop the scientist calling one of them positive and the other negative, *provided* that this is in relation to his human undertaking, whether experimental or industrial. If 'inverse' reactions are regarded as *negative*, this means that their existence prevents the achievement of a certain result; they are impediments *in relation* to the directed ensemble. If one is dealing with strictly *natural* reactions, reactions occurring outside the laboratory and having no connection with any preconceived hypothesis, it is still possible to regard one of them as a positive and the other as a negative quantity, but only as an indication of the order in which they occur. *In any case* this is a molecular re-distribution which, though directed, is not in itself either positive or negative. Moreover, even if the inverse reaction is regarded as the negation of the direct reaction, the definitive result is not a synthetic form but an inert equilibrium, a mere coexistence of results – all of them 'positive' too, whether their origins are 'positive' or 'negative'.

Resistance and. consequently, negative forces can exist only within a movement which is determined *in accordance with the future*, that is to say, in accordance with a certain form of integration. If the end to be attained were not fixed from the beginning, how could one even conceive of a restraint? In other words, there is no negation unless the future totalisation is continually present as the de-totalised totality of the ensemble in question. When Spinoza says 'All determination is negation,' he is right, *from his point of view*, because substance, for him, is an infinite totality. This formula is thus an intellectual tool for describing and comprehending the *internal relations of the whole*. But if Nature is an immense dispersive decompression, if the relations between natural facts can only be conceived in the mode of exteriority, then the individual couplings of certain particles and the little solar system which temporarily results from them are not *particularisations*, except in a purely formal, logical and idealist sense. To say that *through* entering into a given combination, a molecule thereby *does not* enter another, is merely to reiterate the proposition one wishes to affirm in a negative form – like a logician replacing 'All men are mortal' by 'All non-mortals are non-men'.

Determination will be real negation only if it identifies the determined within a totalisation or a totality. Now, *praxis*, born of need, is a totalisation whose movement towards its own end *practically* makes the environment into a totality. It is to this double point of view that the movement of the negative owes its intelligibility. On the one hand, the organism engenders the negative as that which destroys its unity: discharge and excretion, as a directed movement of rejection, are just opaque and biological forms of negation. Similarly, *lack* appears through function, not only as a mere inert lacuna, but also as an opposition of function to itself. Finally, need posits negation by its very existence in that it is itself an initial negation of lack. In short, the intelligibility of the negative as a structure of Being can be made manifest only in connection with a developing process of totalisation; negation is defined on the basis of a primary force, as an *opposing force* of integration, and in relation to a future totality as the destiny or end of the totalising movement. At a still deeper level, and more obscurely, the organism itself as a transcendence of the multiplicity of exteriority is a univocal primary negation in that it preserves multiplicity within itself and unites itself against this multiplicity, without being able to eliminate it. Multiplicity is its danger, the constant threat to it; and, at the same time, it is its mediation with the material universe which surrounds it and which can negate it. Thus negation is determined by unity; indeed it is *through unity* and *in unity* that it can manifest itself. In the first instance, negation manifests itself not as a contrary force, but, what amounts to the same thing, as partial determination of the whole in so far as this partial determination is posited for itself.

On this basis, a dialectical logic of negation conceived as the relation of internal structures both to each other and to the whole within a complete totality or within a developing totalisation, could be constructed. It would then become clear that, within the field of existence and tension determined by the whole, every particular exists in the unity of a fundamental contradiction: it *is* a determination of the whole and, consequently, it is the whole which gives rise to it; in a certain sense, in so far as the being of the whole demands that it be present in all its parts, *every particular is the whole itself.* But at the same time, as arrest, as turning-back upon themselves, as delimitation, particulars are not the whole, and in fact it is in opposition to the totality (rather than to beings which transcend it) that they particularise themselves. But in the context of this fundamental contradiction, particularisation is precisely the negation of interiority – as particularisation *of the whole* it is the whole opposing itself through a particular which it governs and which depends on it; and as determination – that is, as limitation – it becomes the nothing which stands in the way of the retotalisation of the whole and which would destroy itself in such a retotalisation. It is the existence of this non-being as a *developing relation* between the constituted whole and the constituent totalisation, that is to say, between the whole as the future, abstract, *but already present* result and the dialectic as a process tending to constitute in its concreteness the totality which defines it as its future and its end; it is the existence of this nothingness, which is both active (totalisation positing its moments) and passive (*the whole as the presence of the future*), which constitutes the first intelligible dialectical negation. And it is within the totality, as the abstract unity of a field of forces and tension, that the negation of a negation becomes an affirmation.

Thus, however, it manifests itself – whether as the liquidation of a partial moment or as the appearance of other moments in conflict with the first (in short, the differentiation or even fragmentation of the partial totality into smaller parts) – the new structure is the negation of the first (either directly or by attracting, through its very presence, the relation of the first to the whole). In this way, the whole manifests itself in the second structure, which it also produces and preserves, as a totality resuming within itself the particular determinations, and erasing them, either by simply destroying their particularity or by differentiating itself around and in relation to them, in such a way as to insert them into a new order which in its turn becomes the whole itself as a differentiated structure.

Such a logic of totalisations would be an abstract system of propositions concerning the multiplicity of possible relations of a whole to its parts and of different parts amongst themselves, either direct or mediated by their relation to the whole. It would be completely useless to devise this system here; it is something which everyone can work out for himself. Let me just remark that the content of these propositions, though abstract, would not be *empty*, like the analytical judgements of Aristotelean logic, and that, though these propositions are synthetic, they possess in themselves a *genuine intelligibility*. In other words, they need only be established on the basis of a totality (*any* totality) in order to be *comprehended* as certain. We shall return to this later.

Let us return to need. When the project passes through the surrounding world towards its end – in this case, the restoration of a negated organism – it unifies the field of instrumentality around itself, so as to make it into a totality which will provide a foundation for the individual objects which must come to its aid in its task. The surrounding world is thus constituted practically as the unity of materials and means. However, since the unity of the means is precisely the end, and since the end itself represents the organic totality in danger, a new, inverted relation between the two 'states of matter' emerges here *for the first time*: inert plurality becomes totality through unification by the end into an instrumental field; it is in itself the end fallen into the domain of passivity. Its character as a completed totality, however, far from being damaged by its inertia, is actually preserved by it. In the organism, bonds of interiority overlay those of exteriority; in the instrumental field, it is the other way round: a bond of internal unification underlies the multiplicity of exteriority, and it is *praxis* which, in the light of the end, constantly reshapes the order of exteriority on the basis of a deeper unity. On this basis, a new type of negation arises, for this is a new type of totality which is both passive and unified, but which is constantly reshaping itself, either through the direct action of man or in accordance with its own laws of exteriority. In either case the changes occur on the basis of a pre-existing unity and become the destiny of this totality even if their sources lie elsewhere, at the furthest corner of the world. Everything which takes place within a totality, even disintegration, is a total event of the totality as such and is intelligible only in terms of the totality. But as soon as the ferment of the totalised plurality produces a few passive syntheses, it shatters the relation of immediate integration between the elements and the whole, within the constituted whole.

The relative autonomy of the part thus formed necessarily acts as a brake on the overall movement; the whirlpool of partial totalisation thus constitutes itself as a negation of the total movement. By the same token, even in the case of a transformation necessary for *praxis*, its determination *becomes* its negation: the relation of the integrated elements to the partial whole is more precise, less 'indeterminate' than its relation to the overall totalisation, but poorer and less comprehensive. As a result of its new bond of exteriorised interiority, the element loses the set of objective possibilities which each element possessed within the general movement; it becomes impoverished. Thus the relation of this partial totality to the total totality takes the form of conflict; absolute integration requires that every particular determination should be eliminated to the extent that it threatens to constitute a new plurality. Conversely, inertia and the necessities of partial integration require each part of the relative totality to resist the pressures of the whole. Finally, the determination of a partial totality, within the detotalised totality, must also determine the ensemble which remains outside this integration, *as a partial totality*, albeit negatively. The unity in exteriority of those regions which lie outside the zone of partial integration (in the first instance, those which *have not* been integrated) is transformed into a unity of interiority, that is, into an integrating determination, simply because, within a totality, even exteriority is expressed by relations of interiority. At the same time, the relation of the new totalisation to the whole varies: it may start to posit itself for itself, in which case the developing totalisation is completely shattered; it may identify itself with the whole itself and strive to reabsorb the new enclave; finally, it may be torn apart by contradiction, positing itself *both* as the whole, or at any rate, as the very process of totalisation, *and* as a partial moment which derives its determinations from its opposition to the Other.

3 *Labour*

Man, who produces his life in the unity of the material field, is led by *praxis* itself to define zones, systems and privileged objects within this inert totality. He cannot construct his tools – and this applies to the agricultural tools of primitive peoples as much as to the practical use of atomic energy – without introducing partial determinations into the unified environment, whether this environment is the whole world or a narrow strip of land between the sea and the virgin forest. Thus he sets himself in opposition to himself through the mediation of the inert; and, conversely, the constructive power of the labourer opposes the part to the whole in the inert within the 'natural' unity. We shall come across many examples of this later. It follows, in the first place, that negation becomes internal in the very milieu of exteriority, and secondly, that it is a real opposition of forces. But this opposition comes to Nature through man in two ways, since his action constitutes both the whole and its disruption. *Labour* of any kind always exists only as a totalisation and a transcended contradiction. Once it has constituted the environment as the milieu in which the labourer produces himself, every subsequent development will be a negation precisely to the extent that it is positive. And such negations can be grasped only as moments which posit themselves for themselves, since the force of inertia increases their separation within the whole. Hence the subsequent task of labour must be to put the created object back in contact with the other sectors within the whole and to unite them from a new point of view; it negates separation.

But this new process, the negation of the negation, derives its intelligibility, once again, from the original totality. In a realist and materialist system there can be no justification for asserting, *a priori*, that the negation of a negation must give rise to a new affirmation, as long as the type of reality in which these negations occur remains undefined. Even in the human universe, the universe of totalities, there are quite definitive and classifiable situations in which the negation of the negation is a new negation, because in these special cases there is interference between totality and recurrence. But this is not our present concern. At all events, it is clear that the negation of a negation produces an indeterminate ensemble *unless* it is regarded as arising within a totality. But even within a totality the negation of the negation would be a return to the starting point if it did not involve a totality being transcended towards a totalising end. The elimination of the partial organisations of the instrumental field would simply bring us back to the original non-differentiation of the unified environment (as when one destroys the traces of an event, an experience or a construction), unless the movement to eliminate them is accompanied by an effort to preserve them – that is, unless they are regarded as a step towards a unity of *differentiation* in which a new type of subordination of the parts to the whole and a new co-ordination of the parts with one another is to be achieved. And this is what has to happen given that the aim is not to preserve the unity of the field of action in and for itself, but to find in it material elements capable of preserving or restoring the organic totality it contains. Thus, in so far as body is function, function need and need *praxis*, one can say that *human labour*, the original *praxis* by which man produces and reproduces his life, is *entirely* dialectical: its possibility and its permanent necessity rest upon the relation of interiority which unites the organism with the environment and upon the deep contradiction between the inorganic and organic orders, both of which are present in everyone. Its primary movement and its essential character are defined by a twofold contradictory transformation: the unity of the project endows the practical field with a quasi-synthetic unity, and the crucial moment of labour is that in which the organism makes itself inert (the man applies his weight to the lever, etc.) in order to transform the surrounding inertia.

The oscillation which opposes the human thing to the thing-man will be found at every level of dialectical investigation. But the meaning of labour is provided *by an end*, and need, far from being a *vis a tergo* pushing the labourer, is in fact the lived revelation of a goal to aim at, and this goal is, in the first instance, simply the restoration of the organism. Eventually, action really converts the material surroundings into a real whole on the basis of which an organisation of means to an end is possible. In the simplest forms of activity, this organisation is given by the end itself: that is to say, it is merely an exteriorisation of function. The totality defines its means through its lacks: the hunter or fisherman *lies in wait*; the food-gatherer *searches*: the field has been unified so as to provide a basis on which the object sought may be more readily *apprehended*. Thus labour organises itself by *synthetic determinations* of the ensemble, by discovering or constructing tighter and tighter relations within the practical field so as to convert what was originally only a vague relation of the parts to the whole and to one another into a complete circle of conditioning.

Determination of the present by the future, oscillation between the inert and the organic, negation, transcended contradictions, negation of the negation – in short, developing totalisation: these are the moments of *any* form of labour, until – at a dialectical level that we have yet to consider – society develops the division of labour to the point of the specialisation of machines. The process is then inverted: the semi-automatic machine defines its environment and constructs its man, so that the inorganic comes to be characterised by a false but effective interiority, and the organic by exteriority. Man becomes the machine's machine; and to himself he is his own exteriority. But in all other cases, the dialectic appears as the logic of labour. To consider *an individual* at work is a complete abstraction, since in reality labour is as much a relation between men as a relation between man and the material world. I do not claim to have revealed the historically primary moment of the dialectic: I have merely tried to show that our most everyday experience, which is surely labour, considered at the most abstract level, that is as the action of an isolated individual, immediately reveals the dialectical character of action. Or, to put it another way, even if we accept the molecular theories of analytical rationalism, the dialectic is already present, even at the highest level of abstraction, in the elementary but complete form of a law of development and a schema of intelligibility. It goes without saying that, although the real existence of organic totalities and totalising processes reveals a dialectical movement, the existence of organic bodies can in no way be derived from the dialectic. However biology may develop in future, organic bodies can never be regarded as any more than *de facto* realities; we have no means of establishing their existence by reason alone. The theory that they originate from unorganised matter is a reasonable and economical hypothesis, on which even Christians can agree. But this hypothesis is no more than a belief. Thus neither analytical Reason, which applies to relations in exteriority, nor dialectical Reason, which derives its intelligibility from totalities, and which governs the relations of wholes to their parts and of totalities to one another in a process of increasing integration, can establish a statute of intelligibility for organised bodies. If they emerged from inorganic matter, there was a passage not only from the inanimate to life, but also from one rationality to the other.

It might be thought that this merely brings us back to the irrationalities of Engels. But it is not so. For Engels, it is the laws which are irrational – opaque formal principles of thought and nature. For us, however, what is contingent is the existence of certain objects. But just as analytical Reason is not qualified to ask why matter exists instead of nothing, so dialectical Reason is not bound to inquire why there are organised wholes rather than merely inorganic matter. These questions *may* become scientific (for one cannot set *a priori* limits to science), but at present they are not. The essential point is, however, that if there are organised wholes, then their type of intelligibility is the dialectic. Since the individual worker is just such a totalisation, he can only understand himself in his acts, and in his relation to Nature (and indeed, as we shall see, in his relations with others) if he interprets every partial totality in terms of the overall totalisation, and all their internal relations in terms of their relations to the developing unification, the means in terms of the end and the present in terms of the relation which links the future to the past. On the other hand, his *praxis* is dialectical and contains its own intelligibility. To take but one example, the law of the interpenetration of opposites, baldly proclaimed by Engels, becomes perfectly intelligible when related to a *praxis* seen in the light of its future totalisation and of the completed totalities which surround it. Within a totality (whether completed or developing), each partial totality, as a determination of the whole, contains the whole as its fundamental meaning and, consequently, also contains the other partial totalities; the secret of each part therefore lies in the others. In practical terms, this means that each part determines all the others in their relations to the whole, that is to say, in their individual existence. At this level, the truly dialectical type of intelligibility appears, combining the *direct* conflict between the parts (to the extent that dialectical Reason includes and transcends analytical Reason) with the constantly shifting hidden conflict which modifies each part *from within* in response to internal changes in any of the others, and establishing alterity in each part both as what it *is* and as what it is *not*, as that which it possesses and as that by which it is possessed.

With these remarks I have merely described the form of connection proper to these objects, namely the bond of interiority. At this level, dialectical investigation may be difficult to *describe*, but it is universal and constant. It *is true* that most people speak according to the rules of analytical rationality, but this does not mean that their *praxis* is not conscious of itself. In the first place,[4] dialectical Reason includes analytical Reason, just as totality includes plurality. In the process of labour, the practical field must already be unified before the worker can undertake an analysis of its problems. An 'analysis of the situation' is carried out in accordance with the methods and mode of intelligibility of analytical Reason; and though indispensable it presupposes totalisation. Ultimately it leads to the underlying plurality, that is, to the elements *as united* by the bonds of exteriority. But the practical movement, which transcends this molecular dispersal of conditions, will recover a unity through itself, in creating both the problem and the solution. Moreover, this unity was never lost, since it was *within it* that the dispersal was sought. But the analysis is *initially* carried out by discourse and thought, even if it requires a material expression later; the *production* of the object, on the other hand, is entirely *practical*. And although *praxis* is self-explanatory and transparent to itself, it is not necessarily expressible in words. In fact, *knowledge* appears as the explanation of the practical field of perception by the end, that is to say, by future non-being. It would be a simple task, though too lengthy to undertake here, to show that only the dialectic can establish the intelligibility of knowledge and truth because neither knowledge nor truth can be a positive relation of being to being; they are, on the contrary, negative relations mediated by a nothingness. The transcended and its transcendence can be explained only in terms of a future which does not yet exist, and within the practical unity of a developing totalisation. But such a discovery can only be practical; in a society which, as a whole, confuses knowledge and contemplation, it cannot be frozen in discourse. Thus we all try to express our dialectical investigation of everything in the terms of analytical, mechanical rationality. Nevertheless, as long as we are aware of this situation, all of us can characterise our fundamental experience at any given moment. Man as a totalising project is himself the active intelligibility of the totalisations; and since alienation has not yet come into the picture (simply because we cannot deal with everything at once), doing and understanding are indissolubly linked.

---

4. We shall see later that the dialectical investigation is not only permanent, in that men always have worked and always will, but also the result of becoming, in that it is the discovery at a particular point in time of the dialectic as the intelligibility of History.

The investigation, however, in its elucidation of the logic of wholes and of the intelligibility of the relations of man to the universe, still cannot be regarded as apodictic. The full comprehension of act and object remains the temporal development of a practical intuition, rather than apprehension of a necessity. For necessity can never be given in intuition, except as a horizon, an intelligible limit of intelligibility.

Human Relations as a Mediation Between Different Sectors of Materiality

1 Isolated Individuals

Immediate experience reveals being at its *most concrete*, but it takes it at its most superficial level and remains in the realm of abstractions. We have described the man of need and seen his labour as dialectical development. But we must not assume that there are no such things as isolated labourers. Isolated labourers, in fact, exist wherever the social and technical conditions of their work require that they work alone. But their very isolation is a historical and social characteristic: in a given society, and given a certain level of technical development, etc., peasants work in complete isolation at certain times of year and this is a social mode of the division of labour. And the labourer's work, his manner of *producing himself*, conditions not only the satisfaction of his need, but also the need itself.

In southern Italy, the agricultural day labourers, the semi-employed *bracciante*, eat only once a day or even, sometimes, once every two days. In this situation, hunger ceases to exist *as need* (or rather, it appears only if it suddenly becomes impossible for the labourers to get their single meal every one or two days). It is not that hunger has ceased to exist, but that it has become interiorised, or structured, as a chronic disease. Need is no longer the violent negation which leads to *praxis*: it has passed into physical generality as *exis*, as an inert, generalised lacuna to which the whole organism tries to adapt by degrading itself, by idling so as to curtail its exigencies (*exigences*). In spite of this, given that the labourer is alone, and given that he chooses *this* or *that* piece of work and decides on his order of means, (at the present time, in present society, and given his particular objectives and the tools at his disposal), he can be made the object of a regressive investigation, and *his praxis* can be grasped and located as temporalising *itself* through all the conditionings. But it must be noticed that this moment of the regression, though true as a first approximation within a dialectical investigation, would be false and idealist if it were taken no further. *Conversely,* when our whole investigation is complete, we shall see that individual *praxis*, always inseparable from the milieu which it constitutes, and which conditions and alienates it, is at the same time constituent Reason (*la Raison constituante*) itself, operating within History seen as constituted Reason.

For precisely this reason, the second moment of the regression cannot be *directly* the relation of the individual to social bodies (inert or active) and to institutions. Marx clearly indicated that he distinguished *human relations* from their reification or, in general, from their alienation within a particular social system. He says, in effect, that in feudal society, based on different institutions and tools, a society which presented different questions, its *own* questions, to its members, the exploitation of man by man did exist, together with the fiercest oppression, but that everything happened *differently* and, in particular, human relations were neither reified nor destroyed. It is obvious, however, that he was not trying to evaluate or compare two systems, both built on exploitation and institutionalised violence. He merely stated that the connection between the serf or the black slave and the proprietor is often *personal* (which, in a sense, makes it even more intolerable and humiliating) and that the relations between labourers and employer (or of labourers among themselves in so far as they are subject to forces of massification) is a simple relation of exteriority. But this relation of exteriority is itself inconceivable except as a reification of an objective relation of interiority. History determines the content of human relations in its totality, and all these relations, even the briefest and most private, refer to the whole. But History itself does not cause there to be human relations in general. The relations which have established themselves between those *initially separate* objects, men, were not products of problems of the organisation and division of labour. On the contrary, the very possibility of a group or society being constituted – around a set of technical problems and a given collection of instruments – depends on the permanent actuality of the human relation (whatever its content) at every moment of History, even between two separate individuals belonging to societies with different systems and entirely ignorant of one another.

This is why the habit of skipping the abstract discussion of the human relation and immediately locating ourselves in the world of productive forces, of the mode and relations of production, so dear to Marxism, is in danger of giving unwitting support to the atomism of liberalism and of analytical rationality. This error has been made by several Marxists: individuals, according to them, are *a priori* neither isolated particles nor directly related activities; it is always up to society to determine which they are through the totality of the movement and the particularity of the conjuncture. But this reply, which is supposed to avoid our 'formalism', involves complete formal acceptance of the *liberal* position; the individualistic bourgeoisie requires just one concession: that individuals passively submit to their relations and that these are conditioned in exteriority by all kinds of other forces; and this leaves them free to apply the principle of inertia and positivistic laws of exteriority to human relations. From this point of view it hardly matters whether the individual really lives in isolation, like a cultivator at certain periods, or whether he lives in highly integrated groups: *absolute separation* consists in the fact that individuals are subject to the historical statute of their relations to others in radical exteriority. In other words – and this amounts to the same thing, though it misleads certain undemanding Marxists – absolute separation is when individuals as products of their own product (and therefore as passive and alienated) *institute* relations among themselves (on the basis of relations established by earlier generations, of their own constitution and of the forces and requirements of the time).

This brings us back to our problem in the first part of this book:[5] what does it mean to *make* History on the basis of earlier conditions? I then said: if we do not distinguish the project, as transcendence, from circumstances, as conditions, we are left with nothing but inert objects, and History vanishes. Similarly, if human relations are a mere product, they are in essence reified and it becomes impossible to understand what their reification really consists in. My formalism, which is inspired by that of Marx, consists simply in recognising that men make History to precisely the extent that it makes them. This means that relations between men are always the dialectical consequence of *their activity* to precisely the extent that they arise as a transcendence of dominating and institutionalised human relations. Man exists for man only in given circumstances and social conditions, so every human

5. i.e. *The Problem of Method*. [Ed.]

relation is historical. But historical relations are human in so far as they are *always* given as the immediate dialectical consequence of *praxis*, that is to say, of the plurality of *activities* within a single practical field. A good example is *language*.

Words are matter. *In appearance* (an appearance which has its truth as such), words make a material impression on me, as disturbances of the air producing certain reactions in my organism, in particular certain conditioned reflexes which materially reproduce the words in me (I *understand* them in *forming* them at the back of my throat). Accordingly, one can say, more briefly, and with a measure of both truth and falsity, that words *enter* the interlocutors as vehicles of their meaning. They carry the projects of the Other into me and they carry my own projects into the Other. Language might well be studied on the same lines as money: as a circulating, inert materiality, which unifies dispersal; in fact this is partly what philology does. Words live off the death of men, they come together through men; whenever I form a sentence its meaning escapes from me, is stolen from me; meanings are changed *for everyone* by each speaker and each day; the meanings of the very words in my mouth are changed by others.

There can be no doubt that language is *in one sense* an inert totality. But this materiality is *also* a constantly developing organic totalisation. Nor can there be any doubt that speech separates as much as it unifies; or that it reflects the cleavages, the stratifications and the inertias of the group; or that dialogues are partly dialogues of the deaf. Bourgeois pessimism decided long ago to rest content with this observation; the original relation of men to one another would be reduced to the pure and simple exterior coincidence of immutable substances. This being so, it is obvious that a person's every word must depend, in its present meaning, on its references to the total system of interiority and that it must be the object of an incommunicable comprehension. But this incommunicability – in so far as it exists – can have meaning only in terms of a more fundamental communication, that is to say, when based on mutual recognition and on a permanent project to communicate; or rather, on the permanent, collective, institutional communication of, for example, all French people, through the constant mediation of verbal materiality, even in silence; and on people's actual projects of particularising this general communication.

Every word is in fact *unique*, external to everyone; it lives *outside*, as a public institution; and speaking does not consist in inserting a vocable into a brain through an ear, but in using sounds to direct the interlocutor's attention to this vocable as public exterior property. From this point of view, the totality of language as a set of *internal* relations between objective senses is given, for and to everyone; words are simply specifications expressed against the background of language;[6] the sentence is an actual totalisation where every word defines itself in relation to the others, to the context and to the entire language, as an integral part of a whole. To speak is to modify each vocable by all the others against the common background of the word (*verbe*); language contains every word and every word is to be understood in terms of language as a whole; it contains the whole of language and reaffirms it. But this fundamental totality can only be *praxis* itself in so far as it is directly expressed to others; language as the practical relation of one man to another is *praxis*, and *praxis* is always language (whether truthful or deceptive) because it cannot take place without signifying itself. Languages are the product of History; as such, they all have the exteriority and unity of separation. But language *cannot have come to man*, since it presupposes itself: for an individual to discover his isolation, his alienation, for him to suffer from silence or, for that matter, to become integrated into some collective undertaking, his relation to others, as manifested in and by the materiality of language, must constitute him in his own reality.

This implies that, if the *praxis* of the individual is dialectical, his relation to the other must be dialectical too and that it is contemporary with his original relation to materiality both inside and outside him. And this relation should not be seen as a potentiality present in everyone as a kind of 'opening to the other' which is actualised in a few particular cases. This would be to shut up these relations in 'natures' like boxes and to reduce them to mere subjective dispositions: and then we would relapse into analytical reason and molecular solipsism. 'Human relations' are in fact inter-individual structures whose common bond is language and which *actually* exist at every moment of History. Isolation is merely a particular aspect of these relations.

The reversal of our investigation shows us *the same men*: but whereas we started by considering them in so far as each of them was ignorant of most (in fact, almost all) the others, we are now considering them in so far as each is bound by work, interest, family ties, etc., to

6. It is in this sense that every vocable is *the whole* of actualised Language. Specification is totalisation.

several others, each of these to others, etc. This is not really a totalisation, or even a totality; it is rather a changing indefinite dispersal of reciprocities. And our investigation is not yet in a position to comprehend the structures of this group; it still seeks the elementary bond which conditions all structurations. It is necessary to know at the simplest level, the level of duality and trinity, whether the relation between men is unique and, if so, *in what respect* it is so. This, like everything else, will have to be revealed in simple everyday *praxis*.

Since we began with the dispersal of human organisms, we shall consider individuals who are completely isolated by institutions, by their social condition, or by accidents of fortune. We shall try to reveal in this very separation, and therefore in a relation which tends towards absolute exteriority, their concrete historical bond of interiority.

2 *Duality and the Third Party*

From my window, I can see a road-mender on the road and a gardener working in a garden. Between them there is a wall with bits of broken glass on top protecting the bourgeois property where the gardener is working. Thus they have no knowledge at all of each other's presence; absorbed as they are in their work, neither of them even bothers to wonder whether there is anybody on the other side. Meanwhile, I can see them without being seen, and my position and this passive view of them at work situates me in relation to them: I am 'taking a holiday', in a hotel; and in my inertia as witness I realise myself as a petty bourgeois intellectual; my perception is only a moment of an undertaking (such as trying to get some rest after a bout of 'over-working', or some 'solitude' in order to write a book, etc.), and this undertaking refers to possibilities and needs appropriate to my profession and milieu. From this point of view, my presence at the window is a passive activity (I want 'a breath of fresh air' or I find the landscape 'restful', etc.) and my present perception functions as a means in a complex process which expresses the whole of my life. Hence my initial relation to the two workers is negative: I do not belong to their class, I do not know their trades, I would not know how to do what they are doing, and I do not share their worries.

But these negations have a double character. In the first place, they can be perceived only against an undifferentiated background consisting of the synthetic relations which support me together with them in an *actual* immanence: I could not contrast their ends with mine without recognising them as ends. The basis of comprehension is complicity in principle with any undertaking, even if one then goes on to combat or condemn it. Any new end, once determined, is set against the organic unity of all human ends. In certain pathological states (e.g. 'de-personalisation') man appears as the representative of an alien species because he is no longer seen in his teleological reality, that is, because the link between the patient and his own ends is temporarily broken. To anyone who believes himself to be an angel, the activities of other people will seem absurd, because he tries to transcend the human undertaking by having nothing to do with it.

But it would be a mistake to suppose that my perception reveals me to myself as *a man* confronted by two other *men*: the concept of man is an abstraction which never occurs in concrete intuition. It is in fact as a 'holiday-maker', confronting a gardener and road-mender, that I come to conceive myself; and in making myself what I am I discover them as they make themselves, that is, as their work produces them; but to the extent that I cannot see them as ants (as the aesthete does) or as robots (as the neurotic does), and to the extent that I have to project myself through them before their ends, in order to differentiate their ends from mine, I realise myself as a member of a particular society which determines everyone's opportunities and aims; and beyond their present activity, I rediscover their life itself, the relation between needs and wages, and, further still, social divisions and class struggles. In this way, the affective quality of my perception depends both on my social and political attitude and on contemporary events (strikes, threats of civil or foreign war, occupation of the country by enemy troops or a more or less illusory 'social truce').

Secondly, every negation is a relation of interiority. By this I mean that the reality of *the Other* affects me in the depths of my being to the extent that it *is not* my reality. My perception provides me first with a multiplicity of tools and apparatuses, produced by the labour of Others (the wall, the road, the garden, the fields, etc.) and it unifies them according both to their objective meaning and to my own project. Every *thing* maintains with all its inertia the particular unity which a long forgotten action imposed upon it; things in general are indifferent to the living, but ideal act of unification which I perform in perception.

But I see the *two people* both as objects situated among other objects in the *visual field* and as prospects of escape, as outflow-points of reality. In so far as I understand them on the basis of their work, I perceive their gestures in terms of the aims they set themselves, and so on the basis of the future which they project. The movement of intra-perceptual comprehension, then, is achieved by reversing the simple perception of the inanimate: the present is explained by the future, particular movements by the overall operation, in short, the detail in terms of the totality.

In the same way, their material environment eludes me in so far as it is made the object or the means of their activity. Their practical relation to the things I see implies a concrete exposure of these things within *praxis itself*; and this exposure is implied in my perception of their activity. But to the extent that this activity defines them as *other than me*, to the extent that it constitutes me as an intellectual confronting manual workers, the exposure which is a necessary moment of it appears to me to reveal, within objectivity, an *objectivity-for-the-other* which escapes me.[7] Each of the two men is re-conceived and located in the perceptual field by my act of comprehension; but with each of them, through the weeding, pruning or digging hands, or through the measuring, calculating eyes, through the entire body as a lived instrument, I am robbed of an aspect of the real. Their work reveals this to them[8] and in observing their work, I feel it as a lack of being. Thus their negative relation to my own existence constitutes me, at the deepest levels of myself, as definite ignorance, as inadequacy. I *sense* myself as an intellectual through the limits which they prescribe to my perception.

Each of these men therefore represents a point of haemorrhage of the object and qualifies me objectively in my very subjectivity; and that is how they are linked at first in my perception, that is to say, as two centrifugal and divergent 'slips' (*glissements*) within the same world. But, since it is the same world, they are united, by my personal perception, within the universe as a whole, and in so far as each deprives the Other of it. The mere fact, for each of them, of seeing what

7. But, as we shall see in the next chapter, it *eludes me as objectivity*, which, in specific circumstances, I may define or even divine, and is part of the obiectivity of the totalised practical field.

8. The act in effect defines the areas of competence and ignorance both in real extension and in relation to the past.

the Other does not see, of exposing the object through a special kind of work, establishes a relation of reciprocity in my perceptual field which transcends my perception: each of them constitutes the ignorance of the Other. Of course these mutual ignorances would not come into objective existence without me: the very notion of ignorance presupposes a questioning or knowing third party; otherwise it could be neither experienced nor described; the only real relation would be contiguity, or co-existence in exteriority. But my perception makes me a real and objective mediation between these two molecules: if I can, in effect, constitute them in a reciprocity of ignorance, it is because their activities jointly affect me and because my perception defines my limits by revealing the duality of my internal negations. Even my subjectivity is objectively designated by them as Other (another class, another profession, etc.), and in interiorising this designation, I become the objective milieu in which these two people realise their mutual dependence *outside* me.

It is important not to reduce this mediation to a subjective impression: we should not say that *for me* the two labourers are ignorant of one another. They are ignorant of one another *through me* to the extent that I become what I am *through them*. In the same way, each enters into the environment of the Other as an implicit reality; each sees and touches what the other would see and touch in his place, but each reveals the world through a *particular practice* which regulates this process. Thus, by limiting me, each constitutes the limit of the Other, and deprives him, as he deprives me, of an objective aspect of the world. But this mutual theft is nothing like the haemorrhage they make in my own perception: they are both manual workers, and they are both from the country; they differ from each other less than they differ from me and, in the last analysis, their reciprocal negation is, for me, a kind of deep complicity. A complicity against me.

In fact, in the moment of discovering either of them, the project of each displays the world, as the objective envelope of his work and his ends: and this spherical unveiling returns to him so as to situate him in relation to what lies behind him as much as to what lies in front of him, in relation both to what he sees and to what he does not see. The objective and the subjective are indistinguishable; the worker produces himself through his work as a certain exposure of the world which objectively makes him the product of his own product. Thus each of them, as the *objectification of self in the world*, reaffirms the unity of the world by inscribing himself in it through his work and through the particular unifications which this work brings about; thus each of them can discover the Other, as an object actually present in the universe, *within his own situation*. And – as these possibilities can be objectively seen from my window, as my mediation suffices to uncover the real routes which might bring them closer – separation, ignorance, and simple juxtaposition in exteriority appear as mere accidents concealing the fundamental, immediate and permanent possibility of mutual discovery, and, therefore, the existence of a human relation.

At this fundamental level, I myself am picked out and put in question. Three objective possibilities are given in my perception: the first is to establish a human relation with one or the other; the second is to become a *practical* mediation enabling them to communicate with one another, or, in other words, to be revealed by them as the objective milieu which I already am; the third is to play a passive part in their meeting and to observe them constituting a closed totality from which I am excluded. In the third case, I am directly *involved* in the exclusion and it forces a practical choice on me: either I submit to it or I adopt it and co-operate with it (for example, I close the window and go back to my work) or I myself enter into collaboration with them. But in this way I change them in changing myself.[9] However, whichever choice I make each of the two men, in his ignorance of the Other – an ignorance which becomes real through me[10] – will interiorise in his behaviour what was an exteriority of indifference, even if they never meet. The *hidden* existence of a human relation relegates physical and social objects, or the world of inertia, to the level of inessential reality. This permanent inessentiality exists as a passive possibility: either simple recognition abolishes distance, or work projects onto matter the inanimate movement of convergence.

In short, the organisation of the practical field in the world determines a real relation for everyone, but one which can only be defined by the experience of all the individuals who figure in this field. This comes down to unification through *praxis*; and everyone, unifying to the extent that his acts determine a dialectical field, is unified within this field by the unification of the Other, that is to say, in accordance with the *plurality of unifications*. The reciprocity of relations – which we will

9. See below, section 3.
10. When I count on it, it becomes a reality. If a military leader uses the enemy's ignorance to destroy two units which do not know their relative positions, this ignorance becomes *lack of co-ordination*, *incompetence*, etc.

examine in detail later – is a new moment of the contradiction between the unifying unity of *praxis* and the exteriorising plurality of human organisms. This relation becomes inverted in that the exteriority of multiplicity is a condition of the synthetic unification of the field. But multiplicity also remains a factor of exteriority since, within this multiplicity of totalising centralisations, each eluding the Other, the only true bond is *negation* (at least as the moment we have now reached). Each centre stands in relation to the Other as a point of flight, as an *other* unification. This is a negation of *interiority*, but not a totalising negation. Everyone *is not* the Other in an active, synthetic manner, since *not to be* someone is in this case to make him serve, in a more or less differentiated way, as an object – an instrument or a conflicting purpose – in the very activity which grasps the unity of the practical field, since it is both to constitute this unity against him (in so far as he is himself constituent) and to deprive him of an aspect of things. The plurality of doubly negated centres at the level of practical unification becomes a plurality of dialectical movements, but this plurality of exteriority is interiorised in that it characterises every dialectical process in interiority, simply because a dialectical development can be recognised from the inside only by characteristics which are dialectical (that is, synthetically organised within the whole).

Thus, this new stage of the investigation reveals the human relation within pure exteriority in so far as objective exteriority turns out to be lived and transcended in the interiority of my *praxis*, and to indicate an *elsewhere* which escapes me and escapes all totalisation because it is itself a developing totalisation. Conversely, one might say that I find that this negative rudiment of the human relation is an objective and constituent interiority for everyone in so far as I find myself in the subjective moment of *praxis* to be objectively characterised by this interiority. In this elementary sense, the individual's movement from the subjective to the objective no longer involves knowing his *being* from the point of view of matter as it used to do; it now involves realising *his human objectivity* as the unity of all the negations which connect it internally to the interior of others, and of his project as the positive unification of these negations. It is impossible *to exist amongst men* without their becoming objects both for me and for them through me, without my being an object for them, and without my subjectivity getting its objective reality through them as the interiorisation of my human objectivity.

The foundation of the human relation as the immediate and

perpetual determination of everyone by the Other and by all is neither an *a priori* communication engineered by a kind of Great Telephone Operator, nor the indefinite reiteration of essentially separate patterns of behaviour. This synthetic connection, arising always for particular individuals at a definite moment of History and on the basis of determinate relations of production, but which also turns out to be *a priori*, is simply *praxis*, that is, the dialectic as the development of living action in everyone in so far as it is pluralised by the multiplicity of men within a single material *zone*. Every *existent* integrates the other into the developing totalisation and thereby, even if he never sees him, and in spite of barriers, obstacles and distances, defines himself in relation to the actual totalisation which the Other is performing.

But it should be noted that the relation revealed itself through the mediation of a third party. It is through me that ignorance became *reciprocal*. And yet this reciprocity no sooner came into being than it repulsed me; as we saw, it closed in upon itself. If the triad is necessary in the extreme case of a relation stranded in the universe, and *actually* linking two individuals who are ignorant of each other, it is broken up by the exclusion of the third party as soon as people or groups either help one another or fight one another *deliberately and self-consciously*. The human mediator cannot help transforming the elementary relation whose essence is to be lived with no other mediation than matter into *something else*. (The meaning of this metamorphosis will become clear later.) But this is not all. Even when men are face to face, the reciprocity of their relation is actualised through the mediation of this third party and at once closes itself off from it.

Following Mauss, Lévi-Strauss has shown that potlatch is 'supra-economic' in character: 'The best proof . . . is that . . . greater prestige results from the destruction of wealth than from its distribution, because however liberal it may be, distribution always requires a similar return.'[11] And it cannot be denied that in this case the gift has

---

11. *The Elementary Structures of Kinship*, (1949), London and Boston, 1969, p. 55. Lévi-Strauss emphasises, of course, the fact that its economic aspect persists, 'although it is always limited and qualified by the other aspects of the institution of exchange'. By way of objection, one might refer to some interesting observations made by Georges Bataille (*La Part maudite*) to the effect that, in certain societies and in certain conditions, extravagance (which is tightly bound up with other institutions of a political-religious character) is an economic function. Economics as the science of the production, distribution and consump-

a basic quality of reciprocity. But it should be noted that in its destructive form the gift is not so much an elementary form of exchange as a mortgage of *the one* for *the other*: the period of time which separates the two ceremonies, even if reduced to a minimum, masks their reversibility; in effect, the first donor issues a challenge to the second. Mauss has emphasised the ambiguous character of potlatch being an act both of friendship and of aggression. In effect, in its simplest form, the act of giving is a material sacrifice whose object is to put the absolute Other under an obligation. When, in the course of a migration, members of a tribal group come across a strange tribe, they suddenly discover man as an alien species, that is, as a fierce carnivorous beast who can lay ambushes and make tools.[12] This terrified discovery of alterity necessarily implies *recognition*: human *praxis* confronts them as a hostile force. But this recognition is crushed by the quality of strangeness which it itself produces and supports. And the gift, as a propitiatory sacrifice, is offered both to a god whose anger is being appeased, and to a beast which is tamed by being fed. It is *the material object* which, by its mediation, *sets reciprocity free*. But it is not experienced as such: whoever receives a gift, provided he agrees to receive it, conceives the gift both as proof of non-hostility and as an obligation *on himself* to treat the newcomers as guests; the threshold is crossed, that is all.

The importance of *temporality* cannot be overemphasised: the gift *is and is not* an exchange; or, to put it another way, it is exchange experienced as irreversibility. So that its temporal character can be dissolved in absolute reciprocity, it must be *institutionalised*, that is to say, apprehended and located through an objective totalisation of lived time. Duration then appears as a material object, as a mediation between two acts which determine one another in their interiority; it may be defined

---

tion of goods in a context of scarcity ought to pay attention to *gratuitous expenditure* in consumption societies.

12. Cf. Lévi-Strauss's excellent descriptions of the relation between strangers who are forced to share the same restaurant table or the same railway compartment *in our society* (p. 59). 'A conflict exists . . . between the norm of privacy and the fact of community.' See also his description of the former markets of the Chukchee. 'Everyone came armed, and the products were offered on spear points. Sometimes a bundle of skins was held in one hand and a bared knife in the other so that one was ready for battle at the slightest provocation. The market was also formerly designated by the one word, *Elpu'rIrkIn* "to exchange", which was also applied to the vendetta' (p. 60).

by reference to tradition or law, so that the homogeneity of instants conceals the heterogeneity of succession. But institutions, such as marriage between cross-cousins, are themselves manifested against the background of the 'dualistic organisation' of which Lévi-Strauss has given such a striking description, and whose origin lies in a reaction against the pluralisation of primitive groups. Migratory movements 'have introduced allogenic elements', the absence of central power has encouraged 'fissions', etc. Thus a dualistic ordering is 'superimposed' on a plurality of clans and 'sections' and functions as a 'regulating principle'. The Mekeo of New Guinea themselves say that the 'apparent confusion of their groups' actually conceals a dualistic order based on reciprocal tributes. This is because reciprocity as a *relation within the totality* can be conceived only from the point of view of totality, that is, by each group in so far as it can claim to be integrated with all the others. The whole precedes the parts, in this case, not as a static substance but as a turning totalisation. We shall come back to this point later. But what has emerged clearly here is that duality, both as a general rule and in each particular case, is released by a sort of commutative trinity which presupposes plurality: it is only the third party in fact who can, through his mediation, show *the equivalence* of the goods exchanged and consequently of the successive acts. For this *exterior* third party, the use-value of the goods exchanged is clearly transformed into exchange-value. Thus to precisely the extent that he is not an *agent* in the operation, he negatively determines the potlatch, and, for those who do it, he illuminates their reciprocal recognition. And here, whatever the society, the third party is everyone and everybody; thus reciprocity is lived by everyone as *diffuse objective possibility*. But as soon as it is actualised, or rather unmasked, it closes in upon itself. The dualistic ordering is based on the ever turning totalisation and negates this totalisation as soon as it is established.[13]

Similarly, reciprocity becomes isolated as a human relation between individuals; it presents itself as the fundamental, concrete lived bond. If I try to locate myself in the social world, I discover around me various ternary or binary formations, the first of which are constantly disintegrating and the second of which arise from a turning totalisation and may at any moment integrate themselves into a trinity. Thus it is inconceivable that a temporal process should begin with a dyad

---

13. As we shall see, it will lay claim to it again at a later moment of its development.

and culminate in a triad. A binary formation, as the immediate relation of man to man, is the necessary ground of any ternary relation; but conversely, a ternary relation, as the mediation of man amongst men, is the basis on which reciprocity becomes aware of itself as a reciprocal connection. If the idealist dialectic misused the triad, this is primarily because the *real* relation between men is necessarily ternary. But this trinity is not a designation or ideal mark of the human relation: it is inscribed *in being*, that is to say, in the materiality of individuals. In this sense, reciprocity is not the thesis, nor trinity the synthesis (or conversely): it is lived relations whose content is determined in a given society, and which are conditioned by materiality and capable of being modified only by action.

3 Reciprocity, Exploitation and Repression

But let us go back to the binary formation. We take it first because it is the simplest, but we must not lose sight of the synthetic ensemble in relation to which it defines itself. As we have seen, it is not something which can come to men from outside, or which they can establish between themselves by common consent. Regardless of the action of the third party, and however spontaneous the mutual recognition of the two strangers who have just met may seem, it is really only the actualisation of a relation which is given as *having always existed*, as the concrete and historical reality of *the couple which has just been formed*. It is important to see in this how each of them exists, or *produces his being*, in the presence of the Other and in the human world. In this sense, reciprocity is a permanent structure of every object: defined as things *in advance*, by collective *praxis*, we transcend our being by producing ourselves as men among men and we allow ourselves to be integrated by everyone else to the extent that they are to be integrated into our own project. And since the historical content of my project is conditioned by the fact of my already being amongst men, and being recognised by them in advance as a man of a certain kind and milieu, with my place in society already fixed by meanings engraved in matter, reciprocity is always concrete. It cannot be based on a universal abstract bond, like Christian 'charity'; nor on an *a priori* willingness to treat the human person, in myself and in the Other, as an absolute end; nor on a purely contemplative intuition revealing 'Humanity' to everyone as the essence of his fellows. It is the individual's *praxis*, as the realisation of his project, which determines his bonds of reciprocity with everyone.

And the quality of being a *man* does not exist as such: *this* particular gardener recognises in *this* particular road-mender a concrete project, which is expressed in his behaviour and which others have *already recognised* by the very task which they have set him. Thus everyone recognises the Other on the basis of a social recognition to which his clothes, his tools, etc., passively bear witness. From this point of view, the mere act of speaking, the simplest gesture, and the elementary structure of perception (which, moving from future to present, from totality to particular moments, discloses the behaviour of the Other) imply mutual recognition. And capitalist exploitation and oppression are no counterexample to this. The swindle of capitalist exploitation is based on a contract. And though this contract necessarily transforms labour, or *praxis*, into an inert commodity, it is, formally, a reciprocal relation; it is a free exchange between two men who *recognise each other* in their freedom; it is just that one of them pretends not to notice that the Other is forced by the constraint of needs to sell himself as a material object. The clear conscience of the employer is based entirely on that moment of exchange in which the wage-labourer appears to offer his labour-power *in complete freedom*. And if he is not free in relation to his poverty, he is juridically free in relation to his employer, since, at least in theory, the employer does not put any pressure on the workers when he hires them, and merely fixes a top rate and turns away those who ask for more. Here, once again, competition and antagonism between workers moderate their demands; the employer himself has nothing to do with it. This example shows clearly enough that man becomes a *thing* for the Other and for himself only to the extent that he is initially posited as human freedom by *praxis* itself. Absolute respect for the freedom of the propertyless is the best way of leaving him at the mercy of material constraints, at the moment of the contract.

As for oppression, it consists, rather, in treating the Other as an *animal*. The Southerners, in the name of their respect for animality, condemned the northern industrialists who treated the workers as material; but in fact it is animals, not 'material', which are forced to work by breaking-in, blows and threats. However, the slave acquires his animality, through the master, only *after* his humanity has been recognised. Thus American plantation owners in the seventeenth century refused to raise black children in the Christian faith, so as to keep the right to treat them as sub-human, which was an implicit recognition that they were *already* men: they evidently differed from their masters only in lacking a religious faith, and the care their masters took to keep it from them was a recognition of their capacity to acquire it. In fact, the most insulting command must be addressed by one man to another; the master must have faith in man in the person of his slaves. This is the contradiction of racism, colonialism and all forms of tyranny: in order to *treat a man like a dog*, one must first recognise him as a man. The concealed discomfort of the master is that he always has to consider the *human reality* of his slaves (whether through his reliance on their skill and their synthetic understanding of situations, or through his precautions against the permanent possibility of revolt or escape), while at the same time refusing them the economic and political status which, *in this period*, defines human beings.

Thus reciprocity, though completely opposed to alienation and reification, does not save men from them. As we shall see later, a dialectical process produces these *inhuman* relations out of their opposite. Reciprocal ternary relations are the basis of *all* relations between men, whatever form they may subsequently take. Though reciprocity is often concealed by the relations which are established and supported by it (and which may, for example, be oppressive, reified, etc.), it becomes evident whenever it manifests itself that each of the two terms is modified in its very existence by the existence of the Other. In other words, men are bound together by *relations of interiority*. It might be objected that this reciprocal relation is *unintelligible*: for we have tried to show that the intelligibility of the synthetic bond either manifests itself in the process of a totalising *praxis*, or remains congealed in an inert totality. But in this case there is neither totality nor totalisation, and these relations manifest themselves as plurality within exteriority. The primary answer to this objection is that, while we are at this stage of the investigation, we are not dealing with *one* dialectic, but with the external relation between several, a relation which must be *both* dialectical and external. In other words, the relation of reciprocity and the ternary relation are neither of them totalising: they are multiple adhesions between men which keep a 'society' in a colloid state. Besides, in order to gain comprehension, we must – in this as in every other case – make use of the totality of the moments of the investigation which have already been established. It is true that the dialectical materiality of everyone is not sufficient to account for a reciprocity; the least that is necessary is a quasi-totality. And this quasi-totality, as we know, exists in the form of worked matter in so far as it mediates between men; it is on the basis of this negative inert unity that reciprocity arises. This means that it always arises on an inert foundation of institutions and instruments by which everyone is already defined and alienated.

We must not suppose that we have entered the kingdom of ends and that, in reciprocity, everyone recognises and treats the Other as an absolute end. This would be formally possible only in so far as every-one treated himself, or treated the human person in himself, as an un-conditioned end. Indeed this hypothesis would throw us back into absolute idealism: only an idea amongst other ideas can posit itself as its own end. But man is a material being set in a material world; he wants to change the world which crushes him, that is, to act on the world of materiality through the mediation of matter and hence to change himself. His constant search is for a different *arrangement* of the universe, and a different statute for man; and in terms of this new order he is able to define himself as *the Other whom he will become*. Thus he constantly makes himself the instrument, the means, of this future statute which will realise him as other; and it is impossible for him to treat his own present as an end. In other words, man as the future of man is the regulative schema of every undertaking, but the end is always a remoulding of the material order which *by itself* will make man possible.

Or, to approach the question from a different angle, Hegel's mistake was his belief that within everyone there is something to objectify and that work reflects the individuality of its author. In fact, however, objectification as such is not the goal, but the consequence attached to the goal. The aim is the production of a commodity, an object of con-sumption, or a tool, or the creation of a work of art. And it is through this production, this creation, that man creates himself, or in other words detaches himself gradually from things as he inscribes his work in them. Consequently, in so far as my project is a transcendence of the present towards the future, and of myself towards the world, I always treat myself as a means and cannot treat the Other as an end. Reci-procity implies, first, that the Other is a means to the extent that I myself am a means, that is to say, that the Other is the means of a transcendent end and not *my* means; second, that I recognise the Other as *praxis*, that is to say, as a developing totalisation, at the same time as integrating him as an object into my totalising project; third, that I recognise his movement towards his own ends in the same movement by which I project myself towards mine; and fourth, that I discover myself as an object and instrument of his ends through the same act which constitutes him an objective instrument of my ends.

In this way, reciprocity can be either positive or negative. In the first case, everyone may make himself a means within the project of the other so that he becomes a means within his own project; and in this case the two transcendent aims remain separate. This is what happens with *exchange* or the provision of services. Alternatively, the end may be shared (a collective undertaking or work), everyone making himself the Other's means in order that their collective effort shall realise their single transcendent aim. In the case of negative reciprocity, the four necessary conditions are fulfilled but on the basis of a reciprocal refusal: each refuses to serve the Other's end and, while recognising his own objective being as a means within the adversary's project, he uses his own instrumentality *in others* to make them an instrument of his own ends in spite of themselves. This is *struggle*; in it, everyone reduces himself to his materiality so as to act on that of the Other; through pretences, stratagems, frauds and manoeuvres everyone allows himself to be constituted by the Other as *a false object, a deceptive means*. But here again it would be quite wrong to think that the aim is the annihilation of the adversary or, to use Hegel's idealist language, that each consciousness seeks the death of the Other. The origin of struggle always lies, in fact, in some concrete antagonism whose material condition is *scarcity (la rareté)*,[14] in a particular form, and the real aim is objective conquest or even creation, in relation to which the destruction of the adversary is only the means. Hatred – a form of *recognition* – even if it is posited for itself, is really only a mobilisation of all one's strength and passions in the service of an aim which requires such total commitment. Hegel, in other words, ignored matter as a mediation between individuals. Even if one uses his terminology, one has to say that while each consciousness is the counterpart of the Other, this reciprocity can take an infinity of different forms, positive or negative, and that it is the mediation of matter which determines these forms in every concrete case.

But this relation, *which comes to all from each in so far as he makes himself a man amongst them*, contains a contradiction: it is a totalisation

14. This theme will be developed in the next chapter.

which has to be totalised by what it totalises. It presupposes the complete equivalence of two systems of reference and of two actions; in short, it does not posit its own unity. The limit of unification lies in the mutual recognition which occurs in the process of two synthetic totalisations: however far the two integrations are carried, they *respect one another, there will always be two* of them, each integrating the entire universe.

Two men are performing a certain task together. Each adapts his behaviour to that of the Other, each approaches or withdraws according to the requirements of the moment, each makes his body into the Other's instrument to the extent that he makes the Other into his, each anticipates the Other's movement in his body, and integrates it into his own movement as a transcended means; and in this way each of them acts in such a way as to become integrated as a means into the Other's movement. But this intimate relation in its reality is the negation of *unity*. Of course, there is always the objective possibility of unification; it is foreseen, even required, by the material environment, that is, by the nature of the tools, the structure of the workshop, the job to be done, the materials to be used, etc.

But it is always a *third party* which picks them out, through the mediation of objects; or, in other words, the unity of the work team is inscribed in matter as an inanimate imperative. Each of them is defined in reality as a class individual by the objects which he uses or modifies, to the extent that he uses them, that is, to the extent that he arouses and sustains materialised meanings by his *praxis*;[15] he *makes* himself into the manual worker, the proletarian, which *this* particular machine requires. But their unity lies in matter, or rather, it goes from tool to material: their double *praxis* is objectified as a *common praxis* in the finished product; but in this way it loses its quality as the unity of a duality and becomes merely the *unity of the object*, that is to say, the crystallisation of anonymous labour, with no characteristics which enable one to judge *a priori* how many workers produced it.

Of course, while doing the work, each of them will see this objective unity coming into existence, and will see his own movement reflected in the object both as his own and as other. Of course, when each of them approaches the Other, each will see this approach as coming to him from outside. And of course, *every* moment of this *continuum* must be ambivalent since the *praxis* of each resides in that of the Other, as its

---

15. See below, 'class being'.

secret exteriority and its deep interiority. Nevertheless, this reciprocity is lived in separation; and since mutual integration implies the being-an-object of each for the Other, it could not be otherwise. Each reflects his own project to the Other as coming to him within the objective; but these experiences, ordered and connected *in interiority*, are not integrated into a synthetic unity.

The fact is that in their mutual *recognition* each of them discloses and respects the project of the Other, as also existing outside his own project; that is, they define it as a transcendence which cannot be reduced to its simple objectivity as transcended transcendence, but which produces itself in the direction of its own ends, through its own motivations. But precisely because it is experienced *over there*, or *outside*, every transcendence, in its subjective reality, recedes from the Other and can be referred to, in the objectivity of behaviour, only as a *signification* with no graspable content. It is therefore impossible to unite a work team in a totalising movement since such a developing totalisation actually contains an element of disintegration: the Other appears as a totalised object referring beyond its project to a different, transcendent, lived totalisation, and one in which the first, in its turn, features as a similarly destructive object. Another reason why unification is impossible is that each totalisation *here and now* posits itself as essential to the extent that it affirms the co-essentiality of the Other.

Thus each lives within the absolute interiority of a relation which lacks unity; his concrete certainty is mutual adaptation within separateness; it is the existence of a two-centred relation which he can never grasp in its totality. This disunity within solidarity (whether positive or negative) is caused by an excess rather than a deficiency: it is the product, in effect, of two synthetic and strictly equivalent unifications. Here we encounter ambiguity in a real material object, for the terms of the relation are incapable *both* of being reckoned as distinct quantities *and* of effectively realising their unity. In effect, the only possible unity of these epicentres is a transcendent hyper-centre. In other words, the unity of a dyad can be *realised* only within a totalisation performed from outside by a third party. Each member of the team comes upon this unity as a negation, as a lack, in a kind of disquiet; it is at once an obscure deficiency arising from the very requirements of each totalisation, and an imprecise reference to an absent witness, and the lived but unarticulated certainty that the total reality of the collective undertaking can only exist *elsewhere*, through the mediation of an Other and as *a non-reciprocal object*.

Thus the mutual relation is haunted by its unity as if it were an inadequacy of being transforming its original structure. This *disquiet* of reciprocity, in its turn, is intelligible as the moment in which the dialectic of each experiences the dialectic of the Other as a limitation on the project of totalisation, imposed in and by the very attempt at synthesis. For this reason, it is always possible for reciprocity to collapse into its terms as a false, crushing totality. And this can be positive as well as negative. A collective undertaking can become a kind of infernal impulsion when each insists on continuing it out of consideration for the Other. Apprentice boxers are often dominated *by their fight*, as if they were drowning in this ever disintegrating unity; hitting at the air, suddenly leaning against each other in a common fatigue which hints at the shadow of a positive reciprocity, or pursuing each other to the four corners of the ring, they are possessed: they become inessential while the match becomes essential.

Of course, in actual fact, each of them has at his disposal an array of abstract designations with which to express this fleeting unity to the Other and with which to refer to it in the void. But it must be observed, in the first place, that these designations, and the possibility of employing them, that is of conceiving the double totalisation as an objective totality, depend on the presence of a third party. For, as we have seen, the third party makes reciprocity visible to itself, while reciprocity closes in upon itself by denying the third party, and yet referring to him through its own inadequacy. In this sense, the relation between third parties, in so far as each is preoccupied with mediating a reciprocal relation, is one of separation postulating reciprocity as the fundamental bond between men. *However*, lived reciprocity always refers back to the third party and in its turn shows that a ternary relation is both its foundation and its culmination. It is this new relation which we must now investigate: what is the significance for a binary relation of being integrated into a ternary one?

Let us return to our example of two labourers performing a joint task. Let us suppose that a norm is being established. The presence of a timekeeper and his specific task reanimate inert meanings. His aim is to regulate a particular event: he sees each movement in its objectivity in terms of a certain objective purpose, namely, increasing productivity. The irreducible heterogeneity of the dyad is concealed because from the point of view of the task to be done, the workers and tools appear as a homogeneous ensemble; the two reciprocal actions together constitute *the object* of his inquiry. And, since his task is to determine this rhythm as precisely as possible, the common rhythm, in the light of the objective end, appears as the living unity which animates the two workers. Thus the movement of objectivity is inverted: what the time-keeper initially sees as the meaning and unity of his own project, is the aim which he pursues. He has to *measure speeds*; and through this relation which is definitive of his *praxis*, he grasps the end which is imposed upon the workers in its full objectivity; for it is not the same as his own end though it is intimately linked with it. As the end of Others it is the essential means for him to do his job. The objective and subjective connection between his own end and that of others makes him see the rhythm as his object and the workers as the means of maintaining or increasing its speed. Reciprocity as the real bond of a double heterogeneity is relegated to another level; this interiority without a centre, this intimacy lived in separation, is abruptly dislo-cated and torn apart so as to become a single *praxis* whose end lies outside itself. This end which belongs to Others, reveals itself as *their* end and as *his* means and is presented to the witness in its objective totality. And as it discloses its content, which refers back to the activity of the whole factory and to the entire social system, it reveals itself as a structure of control set up from outside by technicians in accordance with the requirements of production. It is this disclosure which defines the relation of the timekeeper to the two workers and to his superiors, or in other words, which designates his objective being in his very subjectivity: he is the one *through whom* the end is posited as a structure of transcendence in relation to the workers. Thus he reveals it as an autonomous object. But this structure of control refers, in its very objectivity, to the subjectivity of those whom it controls: this *goal has to be achieved*, it imposes itself on them as a common imperative. This imperious goal, though entirely present in the objective field, cannot be grasped by the witness; it closes in on the two subjectivities which it equalises and shows them its inner surface – which the timekeeper has to see as pure meaning, as a dimension of flight at the heart of plenitude.

Objectively, the totality includes the two simultaneous actions; it defines and limits them at the same time as enveloping them, and so masking them from direct perception. It is a structure of the world, which exists through itself; it is expressed and sustained by a double *praxis*, but only in so far as this is subjected to the pre-established im-perative which conditions it. Objectively, and *through* the third party, the independence of the end turns reciprocity into a binding together of movement, and mutual adaptation into the internal self-determination of *praxis*; it transforms a double action into a single event which controls the two workers as secondary structures whose particular relations depend on overall relations and who communicate through the mediation of the whole. This living totality, comprising men, their objects and the material on which they work, is both an event as a temporalisation of the objective imperative and – though this amounts to the same thing – the regressive disclosure of the end (from the future to the present) as the concrete unity of the event.

Subjectivities are enveloped within this moving totality as necessary but elusive significations; but they define themselves as a common relation to a transcendent end rather than as each apprehending its own ends in a reciprocity of separations. Thus these significations, in their objective meaning, become homogeneous, and come together and merge into one another in their recognition of the transcendent imperative. Thus this imperative is expressed, through the mediation of the Other, as essential, and subjectivity becomes its inessential means of making itself felt as imperative. In this way, subjectivity is merely the internal milieu which mediates the imperative as the interiorisation of control; in this milieu the individual appears as an *a posteriori* and arbitrary determination of the subjective substance. As in wave mechanics, the principle of individuality is not really applicable. Whatever their external differences, individuals are defined on the basis of the end as a complete interiorisation of the entire imperative, and therefore by the presence in them of the *whole* of subjectivity.

Here the social group appears reduced to its simplest expression. It is the objective totality in so far as it defines its subjectivity simply by interiorisation of values and objective ends and, within a given undertaking, controls real individuals as simple interchangeable modes of subjective *praxis*. Through the intervention of third parties, the subjectivity of the group is shown to be indivisible, and circulates freely within the object as milieu, substance and *pneuma*; it expresses itself in self-temporalising objectivity as intersubjective reality. And intersubjectivity expresses itself in the most fortuitous and temporary groupings; for a taxi-driver looking at some people staring into a river, they are united by one and the same curiosity. And their *active* curiosity (they push one another, lean over, and stand on tiptoe) shows the existence of a transcendent, but invisible end: there is *something* that *has* to be looked at. The mediation of the third party reanimates the objective significations, already inscribed in things, which constitute the group as a totality. These crystallised significations already represent the anonymous *praxis* of the Other and produce, in matter, a solidified revelation. In awakening them the third party makes himself a mediator between objective thought as Other and concrete individuals; through him a rigid universality *constitutes* them by its own activity.

Thus duality is unified *from outside* through the *praxis* of the third party; and we shall see in a moment how the members of a group interiorise it. At present it is still a transformation which transcends him. True, the relation of the third party to the dyad is one of interiority in that he modifies himself in modifying it. But this relation is not reciprocal: in transcending the dyad towards his own ends, the third party shows it to be an *object-unity*, that is a *material unity*. Of course, the relation of the integrated terms is neither external nor molecular, but, in so far as each of them excludes the Other through their *actual recognition*, or in so far as this relation can only *link* but not unify, unity is imprinted from outside and, in the *first moment*, passively received. The dyad becomes a team not by producing its totality, but, initially, by being subjected to it *as a determination of being*.

It will no doubt have been noticed that this Trinity seems like an embryonic hierarchy: the third party as mediator is a synthetic power and the bond between him and the dyad is unreciprocal. It will therefore be asked what this spontaneous hierarchy is based on, given that we are considering it in the abstract, as a synthetic bond, without examining the historical circumstances in which it arises. The answer to this question is provided by two points, and these will enable us to make further progress in our regressive investigation. First, if there is no reciprocity between the dyad and the third party, this is because of the very structure of *the third party relation*; but this does not generate any *a priori* hierarchy since any member of the Trinity might become the third party in relation to the Other two. Only the conjuncture (and therefore History in its entirety) can determine whether this changing relation shall be commutative (each member becoming the third party in turn, like in children's games where everyone takes turns at being the general or the bandit chief) or whether it is to be fixed in the form of a primitive hierarchy. It is already fairly obvious, in fact, that the problem will become infinitely complex since social reality comprises an indefinite multiplicity of third parties (because the relation changes even if the number of individuals is finite) and an indefinite multiplicity of reciprocities; and also because individuals can constitute themselves as group third parties, and there can be reciprocities of reciprocities, and reciprocities of groups; finally, individuals or groups can be engaged in reciprocal actions even while defining themselves as third parties.

At present we are not equipped to *think* these moving, indefinite relations in their intelligibility, for we have not yet mastered all our instruments. But it is worth recalling, to conclude, that the human relation really exists between all men and that it is no more than the relation of *praxis* to itself. The only origin of the complication which gives birth to these new relations is *plurality*, that is, the multiplicity of *active* organisms. So, quite apart from any question of antagonism, every *praxis* both affirms and negates the other, in so far as it transcends it as its object, and also causes itself to be transcended by it. And every *praxis*, as a radical unification of the practical field, adumbrates, in its relation to all others, the project of unifying them all by eliminating the negation of plurality. This plurality is none other than the inorganic dispersal of organisms; and given that this plurality always arises within an existing society, it is in fact never wholly *natural* and, as we have seen, is always expressed in techniques and social institutions – which transform it to the extent that it occurs within them. But, although natural dispersal cannot be any more than the abstract sense of real, social dispersal, it is always the case that, within a given society, the negative element of mechanical exteriority always conditions that peculiar relation of reciprocity which negates not only plurality, through the adhesion of activities, but also unity, by a plurality of recognitions, and also the relation of a third party to a dyad, which defines itself as exteriority within pure interiority. Moreover, the designation of a third party as the actualisation in a given individual of this universal relation always occurs, as we have seen, in a given practical situation and under the pressure of material circumstances.

Thus our investigation is reversed: starting from the isolated worker, we showed individual *praxis* to be the complete intelligibility of dialectical movement; but, moving on from this abstract moment, we have found that the first relation between men is the indefinite adherence of each to each; and these formal conditions for all History are immediately seen to be conditioned by inorganic materiality, both as the fundamental condition determining the content of human relations, and as an external plurality within the commutative reciprocity and within the Trinity. It can also be seen that this commutativity, though by degrees it unites each to all, is in itself incapable of realising totalisation as the movement of History, since the jelly-like substance which constitutes human relations involves the infinite interiorisation of bonds of dispersive exteriority, rather than their elimination or totalising transcendence. No doubt it does transcend them, but only because the discrete multiplicity of organisms happens to be engaged in a kind of dance with an unlimited, circulating multiplicity of epicentres.

This ambiguity accounts well enough for our private relations with friends, companions, casual customers or chance acquaintances, and even with colleagues (in an office, or a factory) *in so far as* they are *both* the living milieu which unites us to everyone *and* the mechanical indifference which separates them from us when work is over. But this ambiguity cannot explain the structured relations which at all levels produce active groups, classes, and nations, any more than it can explain institutions or the complex ensembles known as *societies*. The reversal of the investigation takes place through historical materialism: if *totalisation* is a historical process, it comes to men through *matter*. In other words, *praxis* as the free development of the organism has now totalised the material environment in the form of a practical field; and in a moment we shall see the material milieu as the first totalisation of human relations.

3

Matter as Totalised Totality – A First Encounter with Necessity

1   *Scarcity and Mode of Production*

Pure, non-human inorganic matter – that is, not matter *in itself* but matter from the point of view of the *praxis* in which it is the object of scientific experiment – is governed by laws of exteriority. If it is true that matter effects an initial union between men, this can only be so *to the extent that* man has already made a practical attempt to unify it, and that it has passively received the seal of that unity. In other words, a passive synthesis whose unity conceals a molecular dispersal conditions the totalisation of organisms whose deep bonds of interiority cannot be masked by their dispersal. This synthesis, therefore, represents the material condition of historicity. At the same time, it is what might be called the passive motor of History. Human history – an orientation towards the future and a totalising preservation of the past – is in fact also defined in the present by the fact that *something is happening to men.*

As we shall see later, the inert totality of worked matter, which, functioning as an inert universal memory, records and conserves the forms impressed on it by earlier labour, is the *only* factor in any given social field which allows every particular historical situation to be transcended by the total process of History. In addition, as a kind of material synthetic judgement, it makes possible the continuous *enrichment* of historical events. But since inorganic materiality which has received the imprint of *praxis* appears as a *passive unity (unité subie)*, and since the unity of interiority which belongs to the dialectical moments of action returns into itself and can only be preserved *through exteriority* (that is to say, to the extent that there is no external force to destroy it), it is *necessary*, as we shall soon see, that human history should be lived, at this level of the investigation, as non-human history. This does not mean that historical events are going to appear to us as an arbitrary succession of irrational facts; *on the contrary*, it means that they are going to assume the totalising unity of a negation of man. History, at this level, has a fearful and depressing meaning: it appears as though what unites men is an inert demonic negation, taking away their substance, that is to say, their labour, and turning it against all men in the form of *active inertia* and totalisation by extermination. We shall see that this peculiar relation, together with the initial alienation which results from it, will produce its own dialectical intelligibility, as soon as the relation of a multiplicity of individuals to the practical field which surrounds them is investigated, in so far as this relation is for everyone a univocal relation of interiority, and as soon as it is linked dialectically to the reciprocal relations which unite them.

At the same time, it is worth pointing out that this univocal relation of surrounding materiality to individuals is expressed *in our History* in a particular and contingent form since the whole of human development, at least up to now, has been a bitter struggle against *scarcity*. Thus at every level the basis of the passive actions of worked and socialised materiality will turn out to be the original structure of scarcity as a primary unity transmitted to matter through men and returning to men through matter. But we should not be disturbed by the fact that the relation of scarcity is contingent. It is indeed logically possible to conceive of other organisms on other planets having a relation to their environment other than scarcity. (However we are completely incapable of *simply imagining* such a relation, and supposing that there is life on other planets, it is most likely that it too would suffer from scarcity.) Above all, although scarcity is *universal*, at a given historical moment it may vary from one region to another. (And while some of the causes of these variations, such as over-population or under-development, are historical, and are therefore fully intelligible within History itself, others, such as climate, or the richness of the sub-soil, given a certain level of technical development, condition History through social structures without being conditioned by it.)

The fact is that after thousands of years of History, three quarters of the world's population are undernourished. Thus, in spite of its contingency, scarcity is a very basic human relation, both to Nature and to men. In this sense, scarcity must be seen as that which makes us into *these* particular individuals producing *this* particular History and defining *ourselves* as men. It is perfectly possible to conceive of a dialectical *praxis*, or even of labour, without scarcity. In fact, there is no reason why the products required by the organism should not be practically inexhaustible, while a practical operation was still necessary in order to extract them from the earth. In that case, the inversion of the unity of human multiplicities through the counter-finalities of matter would still necessarily subsist. For this unity is linked to labour as to the original dialectic. But what would disappear is our quality as *men*, and since this quality is historical, the actual specificity of our History would disappear too. So today everyone must recognise this basic contingency as the necessity which, working both through thousands of years and also, quite directly, through the present, forces him to be exactly what he is.

In the progressive moment of our investigation, we shall study the problem of the contingency of History; and we shall see that the problem is particularly important from the point of view of a future for man. In the case which we are considering, scarcity appears to grow less and less contingent in that we ourselves produce new forms of it as the milieu of our life, on the basis of an original contingency – which shows, one might say, both the necessity of our contingency and the contingency of our necessity. Nevertheless, an attempted critique must distinguish between this determinate relation and the general relation, independent of historical determination, between dialectical, multiple *praxis* and materiality. However, since scarcity is a determination of this general relation and the latter is manifested to us only through the former, it will be safest to discuss scarcity first and then to let the universal relations between the dialectic and the inert emerge later.

Our description of the relation of scarcity will be brief, because there is nothing new to say about it. In particular, historical materialism, as the interpretation of *our* History, has provided the necessary explanations here. But what has never been attempted is a study of the type of passive action which materiality as such exerts on man and his History in returning a stolen *praxis* to man in the form of a counter-finality. The point must be emphasised: History is more complex than some kinds of simplistic Marxism suppose; man has to struggle not only against nature, and against the social environment which has produced him, and against other men, but also against his own action as it becomes other. This primitive type of alienation occurs within other forms of alienation, but it is independent of them, and, in fact, is their foundation. In other words, we shall reveal, through it, that a permanent anti-*praxis* is a new and necessary moment of *praxis*. If we do not try to define this moment, historical intelligibility – that is, certainty within the complexity of temporal development – loses one of its essential moments and is transformed into unintelligibility.

(*i*) *Scarcity and History*

Scarcity is a fundamental relation of *our* History and a contingent determination of our univocal relation to materiality.

Scarcity, as the lived relation of a practical multiplicity to surrounding materiality within that multiplicity itself, is the basis of the possibility of human history. But this calls for two explicit qualifications. First, for a historian situated in 1957, scarcity is not the basis of the possibility of *all* History. We have no way of telling whether, for different organisms on other planets – or for our descendants, if technical and social changes shatter the framework of scarcity – a different History, constituted on another basis, and with different motive forces and different internal projects, might be logically conceivable. (By this I do not simply mean that we cannot tell whether the relation of organic beings to inorganic (*inorganisés*) ones might somewhere be something other than scarcity; first and foremost, I mean that it is impossible to know *a priori* whether the temporalisation of such beings would take the form of a history.) But to say that our History is a history of men is equivalent to saying that it is born and developed within the permanent framework of a field of tension produced by scarcity.

The second qualification is this. Scarcity is the basis of the possibility of human history, but not of its reality. In other words, it makes History possible, but other factors (yet to be determined) are necessary if History is to be produced. The reason for this restriction is that there are some backward societies which, in a sense, are more prone than others to famine or to seasonal depressions of food resources, but which are, nevertheless, correctly classified by ethnographers as societies with no history, societies based on repetition.[16] This means

16. In fact, as we shall see, they have begun to interiorise *our* History, because they have been subjected to colonialism as a historical event. What historialises them, however, is not a reaction to their *own* scarcity.

that scarcity can exist on a very large scale. If a state of equilibrium is established within a given mode of production, and preserved from one generation to the next, it is preserved as *exis* – that is to say, both as a physiological and social determination of human organisms and as a practical project of keeping institutions and physical corporate development at the same level. This corresponds ideologically to a decision about human 'nature'. *Man* is a stunted misshapen being, hardened to suffering, and he lives in order to work from dawn till dusk with *these* (primitive) technical means, on a thankless threatening earth. We shall see later that certain scarcities can condition a moment of History, if, in the context of changes of technique (which will themselves have to be explained), they take the form of abrupt changes in the standard of living. History is born from a sudden imbalance which disrupts all levels of society. Scarcity is the basis of the possibility of human history – and of no more than its possibility – because, through the internal adaptation of organisms, it can, within certain limits, be lived as an equilibrium. From this point of view, there is no logical (dialectical) absurdity in the idea of a country with no History, where human groups would vegetate and never break out of a cycle of repetition, producing their lives with primitive techniques and instruments and knowing absolutely nothing of one another.

Some people, of course, have said that these societies with no History are in fact societies whose History has come to a halt. That is quite plausible, since they do indeed have their techniques, and, however primitive their tools may be, there must have been a temporal process to bring them to *this* degree of efficiency, by means of social forms which themselves, in connection with this process, are in spite of everything differentiated, so that they, too, refer back to this temporalisation. But this way of presenting matters disguises the *a priori* desire of some ideologists,[17] idealists as well as Marxists, of basing History on some essential necessity. From this point of view, non-historical societies would in fact be very special moments in which historical development had slowed itself down and stopped, by turning its power against itself.

For the *critical* position, however, this conception, though pleasing in that it reinstates necessity and unity everywhere, is unacceptable simply because it offers itself as a conception of the world which the facts could neither confirm nor refute. (It is true that many groups

---

17. See above, p. 19, n. 7 [Ed.]

which here settled into repetition have a legendary history; but this is irrelevant, for legend is a negation of History, its function being to re-introduce the *archetype* into sacred moments of repetition.) The only conclusion we can draw from the examination of the validity of a dia-lectic is that scarcity could never be sufficient by itself either to initiate a historical development or, in the course of a development, to burst some log jam which has transformed History into repetition. On the contrary, it is *always* scarcity, as a real and constant tension both between man and his environment and between man and man, which explains fundamental structures (techniques and institutions) – not in the sense that it is a real force and that it has produced them, but because they were produced in the *milieu of scarcity*[18] by men whose *praxis* interiorises this scarcity even when they try to transcend it.

Scarcity can be seen, in the abstract, as a relation of the individual to the environment. Practically and historically, that is, in so far as we exist in particular situations, the environment is a ready-constituted practical field, which relates everyone to collective structures (we shall explain what this means later). The most fundamental of these struc-tures is scarcity as the negative unity of the multiplicity of men (of *this* concrete multiplicity). This unity is negative in relation to men because it is transmitted to man by matter *in so far as* matter is non-human (that is to say, in so far as its being human is possible *only* through struggle on this earth). This means, therefore, that the first totalisation effected by materiality manifests itself (in a given society and between independent social groups) *both* as the possibility of universal destruction *and* as the permanent possibility that this des-truction through matter might come to any individual through the *praxis* of other men. This first aspect of scarcity *can* condition the unity of the group, in that the group, taken collectively, may organise itself to react collectively. But this dialectical and properly human aspect of *praxis* cannot possibly be contained within the relation of scarcity itself, precisely because the positive dialectical unity of a common action is the negation of negative unity as surrounding materiality turning on the individuals who have totalised it. In fact, scarcity as tension and as force-field is the expression of a quantitative fact (more or less strictly defined). There will be an insufficient quantity of a

18. As we shall see, *scarcity* is a milieu in that it is a unitary relation of a plu-rality of individuals. In other words, it is an individual relation and a social milieu.

particular natural substance or manufactured product in a particular social field, *given* the number of members of the groups or inhabitants of the region. *There is not enough for everybody.*

Thus the world (the ensemble) exists for anyone in so far as the consumption of such and such a product elsewhere, by others, deprives him *here* of the opportunity of getting and consuming something of the same kind. In examining the indefinite and universal relation of indeterminate reciprocity we have noticed that men can be united with each other indirectly through a series of adhesions, without having the slightest idea of the existence of this or that other person. In the milieu of scarcity, however, even if individuals are unaware of each other, even if social stratifications and class structures completely sever reciprocity, everyone within the particular social field still exists and acts in the presence of everyone else. Perhaps *this* member of *this* society does not even know how many individuals it contains. He may not know the exact relation of man to natural substances, to instruments and to human products – the relation which strictly defines scarcity. And he may account for present poverty in ways which are completely untrue and absurd. All the same, the other members of the group do exist for him *collectively*, in that each one of them is a threat to his life – in other words, in that the existence of every one of them is the interiorisation and absorption by a human life of the environment as a negation of mankind. But this individual member, if he realises himself, through his need and *praxis*, as being *amongst men*, will see everyone *in terms of* the object of consumption or the manufactured product, and, on this basic level, he will recognise them as the mere possibility of the consumption of something he himself needs. In short, he will find each of them to be the material possibility of his being annihilated through the material annihilation of an object of primary necessity.

Of course, these remarks describe a still very abstract moment of our regressive investigation: in reality, all the social antagonisms in a given society are qualified and structured, and the society itself defines the bounds of scarcity, at least within certain limits, both for each of its constituent groups, and in the fundamental matter of collective scarcity – that is, in terms of an original relation between forces and relations of production. But the important thing for us now is simply to record, *in order*, the structures of dialectical intelligibility. Now, from this point of view, it is easy to see that the totalisation effected by scarcity is circular. Scarcity is not the absolute impossibility of the human organism surviving (although, as I have shown, one might wonder whether this statement would remain true in this form: the radical impossibility of the human organism surviving *without labour*). But in a given situation, whether it be the raft of the *Medusa*,[19] an Italian city under siege, or a modern society (which, of course, discreetly selects its dead simply by distributing items of expenditure in a particular way, and which, at its deepest foundations, is already in itself a choice of who is well provided for and who is to go hungry), scarcity makes the passive totality of individuals within a collectivity into an impossibility of co-existence. The group or the nation is defined *by its surplus population* (*ses excedentaires*); it has to reduce its number in order to survive.

This *numerical reduction*, of course, though always present as a practical necessity, need not take the form of murder. People can simply be allowed to die, as was the case with surplus children under the *Ancien Régime*. Or birth control can be used, in which case the potential child, as a future consumer, is designated as undesirable. This may be conceived either, as in bourgeois democracies, in terms of the impossibility of continuing to feed its brothers in an individual family, or, in a socialist nation such as China, in terms of the impossibility of maintaining a certain rate of population growth until a certain rate of production growth can be reached. But when there is no question of controlling the birth rate, the negative requirements of materiality take a purely *quantitative* form: the size of the surplus population can be determined, but not their individual characters.[20]

Here we see the full force of *commutativity*, whose importance will become clearer later, and which marks each member of the group *both* as a possible survivor and as a dispensable surplus member. And each member is constituted in this way in his objectivity both by himself and by everyone. The direct movement of need affirms him unconditionally as having to survive; this is the practical message of hunger and labour; and a direct challenge to it is inconceivable since it itself expresses man's transcendence of a radical threat by matter. But at the same time the individual's *being* is put in doubt by everyone, and by the very

19. Reference to the sinking of the *Medusa* in 1816. [Ed.]

20. As I have said before, social institutions will be seen later as a society's stratified inert selection of its dead – though, of course, this is only *one* aspect of them. But even when this choice is made, even when an oppressed and exploited class has to submit to it, there is still indeterminacy both within the class and at the level of individuals.

movement which transcends all threats. Thus *his own activity* is turned against him and returns to him *as Other* through the social milieu. Through socialised matter and through material negation as an inert unity, man is constituted as Other than man. Man exists for everyone as *non-human man*, as an alien species. And this does not necessarily mean that conflict is *already* interiorised and lived as a fight for survival. It simply means that the *mere existence* of everyone is defined by scarcity as the constant danger of non-existence *both for another and for everyone*. Better still: this constant danger of the annihilation of myself and of everyone is not something I see only in *Others*. *I am myself* that danger in so far as I am Other, and designated by the material reality of the environment as potentially surplus *with Others*. This concerns an objective structure of my being because I *really* am a danger to Others and, through the negative totality, to myself, in so far as I am a part of that totality. We shall see below why both sellers and buyers in a free market can fix prices only to the extent that they are *Others* in and for themselves. But at present we must confine ourselves to drawing certain consequences from these observations.

When I say that man exists as Other in the guise of non-human man, this must obviously be understood as applying to all the human occupants of the social field under consideration, for others and for themselves. In other words, everyone *is* a non-human man for all Others, and considers all Others as non-human men, and actually treats the Other without humanity (the meaning of this will become clear later). These remarks of course must be understood in a proper sense, that is to say, in the light of there being no such thing as human *nature*. However, at least up to this moment of our pre-history, scarcity, in some form or other, has dominated all *praxis*. It must therefore be understood both that man's non-humanity does not come from his nature, and that far from excluding his humanity, it can only be understood through it. But it must also be understood that, as long as the reign of scarcity continues, *each and every man* will contain an inert structure of non-humanity which is in fact no more than material negation which has been interiorised. So let us understand that non-humanity is a relation between men and could not be anything *else*. No doubt it is possible to be wantonly cruel to some animal. But any punishment or blame for this cruelty can only be in the name of human relations. For who could believe that this carnivorous species – which rears animals in their hundreds of thousands in order to kill them or to make them labour, and which systematically destroys others, for the sake of hygiene, or for self-protection, or gratuitously, for fun – who could believe that this predatory species has put its values and its real definition of itself into its relations with animals, except for ones which are castrated and domesticated, and then only by means of a simplistic symbolic mechanism?

Now, *human* relations (positive or negative) are reciprocal. This means that each individual's *praxis*, in its practical structure and for the sake of the completion of its project, *recognises* the *praxis* of the other, which means, basically, that it sees the duality of activities as inessential and the unity of *praxes* as such as essential to them. In reciprocity, my partner's *praxis* is, as it were, at root *my praxis*, which has broken in two by accident, and whose two pieces, each of which is now a complete *praxis* on its own, both retain from their original unity a profound affinity and an immediate understanding. I do not claim that the relation of reciprocity ever existed in man *before* the relation of scarcity, man being, after all, the historical product of scarcity. But without this human relation of reciprocity the non-human relation of scarcity would not exist. Indeed, scarcity as a univocal relation of each and of all to matter, finally becomes an objective social structure of the material environment, and in that way its inert finger points to every individual as both a cause and a victim of scarcity. And everyone interiorises this structure in that by his behaviour he makes himself *a man of scarcity*. His relation to the Other *in so far as* it comes from matter is a relation of exteriority: in the first place, because the Other is the pure (living but abstract) possibility of the destruction of the necessary product, so that he defines himself in exteriority as a threatening but contingent possibility inherent in the product itself, as an external object; in the second place, because scarcity, as a rigid schema of negation, organises, through everyone's *praxis*, every group of potentially surplus people as a totality *which has to be negated*, as a totality which negates everything except itself. Thus the negative unity which comes from matter totalises men falsely, or inertly, as molecules of wax are inertly united *externally* by a seal. But since relations of reciprocity survive, exteriority penetrates *into them*. This means that everyone's understanding of the *praxis* of the Other continues to exist, but that this other *praxis* is understood from within only to the extent that the interiorised materiality of the agent constitutes the Other as an inert molecule separated from every other molecule by an external negation.

In pure reciprocity, that which is Other than me *is also the same*. But in reciprocity as *modified by scarcity*, the same appears to us as anti-human in so far as *this same man* appears as radically Other – that is to say, as threatening us with death. Or, to put it another way, we have a rough understanding of his ends (for they are the same as ours), and his means (we have the same ones) as well as of the dialectical structures of his acts; but we understand them as if they belonged to *another species*, our demonic double. Nothing – not even wild beasts or microbes – could be more terrifying for man than a species which is intelligent, carnivorous and cruel, and which can understand and outwit human intelligence, and whose aim is precisely the destruction of man. This, however, is obviously our own species as perceived in others by each of its members in the context of scarcity.

This, at any rate, is the basic abstract matrix of every reification of human relations in any society. At the same time, it is the first stage of *ethics*, in so far as this is *praxis* explaining itself in terms of given circumstances. The first movement of ethics, in this case, is the constitution of radical evil and of Manichaeism; it values and evaluates the breaking of the reciprocity of immanence by interiorised scarcity (though we cannot go into the production of values here), but only by conceiving it as a product of the *praxis* of the Other. The anti-human (*le contre-homme*) in fact tries to destroy men by sharing their ends and adopting their means. The break occurs the moment this deceptive reciprocity reveals the deadly danger which it contains, or, in other words, when it reveals that it is impossible for *all* those bound by reciprocal links to stay on the soil which supports and feeds them. And let us not make the mistake of thinking that this interiorised impossibility characterises individuals *subjectively*; on the contrary, it makes everyone *objectively dangerous* for the Other and makes the concrete existence of each individual endanger that of the Other. Thus man is *objectively* constituted as non-human, and this non-humanity is expressed in *praxis* by the perception of evil as the structure of the Other. The somewhat confused clashes, whose origin is highly ambiguous, which take place between nomadic tribes when they happen to encounter one another, have for this reason been interpreted by historians and ethnographers as a challenge to some of the elementary truths of historical materialism. It is certainly true that the economic motive is not always essential, and is even sometimes not to be found at all. These wandering groups have the whole savannah to themselves; they do not *trouble* one another. But this is not the point. It is not always necessary for scarcity to be explicitly involved; but, in each of these tribes, the man of scarcity encounters, in the other tribe, the man of scarcity in the form of the anti-human. All of them are so constituted by their struggle against the physical world and against people (often within their own group) that the appearance of strangers, which presents them both with the bond of interiority and with the bond of absolute exteriority, makes them see man as an alien species. The strength of their aggressiveness and hatred *resides in need*, and it makes very little difference if this need has just been satisfied: its constant renewal and everyone's anxiety mean that whenever a tribe appears, its members are constituted as famine being brought to the other group in the form of a human *praxis*. And, when there is a clash, what the adversaries try to destroy in each other is not the simple threat of scarcity, but *praxis* itself in so far as it is a betrayal of man in favour of the anti-human.

For this reason, I believe that, at the level of need and through it, scarcity is experienced in practice through Manichaean action, and that the ethical takes the form of the destructive imperative: evil *must* be destroyed. And at this level, too, *violence* must be defined as a structure of human action under the sway of Manichaeism and in a context of scarcity. Violence always presents itself as *counter-violence*, that is to say, as a retaliation against the violence of the Other. But this *violence of the Other* is not an objective reality except in the sense that it exists in all men as the universal motivation of counter-violence; it is nothing but the unbearable fact of broken reciprocity and of the systematic exploitation of man's humanity for the destruction of the human. Counter-violence is exactly the same thing, but as a process of restoration, as a response to a provocation: if I destroy the non-humanity of the anti-human in my adversary, I cannot help destroying the humanity of man in him, and realising his non-humanity in myself. I may try to kill, to torture, to enslave, or simply to mystify, but in any case my aim will be to eliminate alien freedom as a hostile force, a force which can expel me from the practical field and make me into 'a surplus man' condemned to death. In other words, it is undeniable that what I attack is man as man, that is, as the free *praxis* of an organic being. It is man, and nothing else, that I hate in the enemy, that is, in myself as Other; and it is myself that I try to destroy in him, so as to prevent him destroying me in my own body.

These relations of exteriority in reciprocity, however, are complicated by the development of *praxis* itself, which re-establishes reciprocity in the negative form of antagonism, as soon as a real struggle develops. In terms of the concrete necessities of strategy and tactics, one is bound to lose if one does not *recognise* the enemy as another human group, capable of inventing traps, and of getting out of them, and of allowing itself to be caught by some of them. Conflicts of scarcity, from nomad wars to strikes, are always oscillating between two poles, one of which turns the conflict into the Manichaean struggle of men against their terrifying counterparts, while the other reduces it to human proportions as a dispute which is being resolved by violence because the possibilities of reconciliation have been exhausted or because mediation has broken down. The important point here is that, as soon as it is constituted as the action of an army, a class, or even of a lesser group, *praxis in principle* transcends the reifying inertia of the relations of scarcity.

This shows, I think, that the inert morality of Manichaeism and radical evil presupposes a suffered distance, a lived impotence, and, in a way, the discovery of scarcity as destiny – in short, a veritable domination of man by the interiorised material environment. So it is not a permanent structure, in the sense that it must always remain rigid and inert at a given level of human density, but rather a certain moment of human relations, which is constantly being transcended and partially destroyed, but which is always being reborn. In fact, this moment is located midway between the destruction of positive reciprocities by scarcity (to whatever degree of social *praxis* this destruction goes) and the reappearance, under the sway of scarcity, of negative and antagonistic reciprocities. And this intermediate moment is identical with the first moment and the productive schema of the complex process of reification. In this moment, the individuals belonging to a given social field live in a false relation of reciprocity with the environment (that is to say, they allow themselves and others to be defined by matter as pure quantity), and they carry this relation into the social milieu by living their reciprocity as human beings as a negated interiority or, in other words, by living it falsely in exteriority.

It may be said that we have not explained how matter as scarcity can unite men in a common practical field when free human relations, abstracted from economic constraint, reduce themselves to constellations of reciprocity. In other words, given that the possibility of totalising comes from *praxis*, how can matter control *totalising actions* through scarcity so as to make them totalise every individual totalisation? The question contains its own answer. It must be recognised that neighbouring groups, though differing in structure – like, for example,

Chinese peasants and nomads on the frontiers of China during the T'ang dynasty – can in fact be materially united in one and the same place, defined by a particular material configuration, and by a particular state of techniques, especially communications. The nomads have a limited freedom of movement and always remain on the edge of the desert; while the pioneering army of Chinese peasants advances step by step seizing a little more arable land from the unproductive desert every day. The two groups are aware of each other: they are both divided and united by an extreme tension. For the Chinese, the nomads are robbers capable only of stealing the fruit of the labour of others; and for the nomads, the Chinese are pure colonialists, gradually driving them into an uninhabitable desert. For each group, as *praxis*, the Other is an object in the unity of its practical field (we shall return to groups later); and everyone is aware of being an object for the Other's group. This utilitarian knowledge will be expressed in such things as the peasants' precautions against surprise attack, and the nomads' care in preparing their next raid. And it is *precisely this* that prevents the two movements of practical unification from constituting two *different fields of action* in the same environment. For each of them, the existence of the Other as the object for which it is itself the object, simply constitutes the material field as undermined, or as having a double foundation. In this co-existence, the only duality is a duality of meanings for every material object. The field is practically constituted as a means which can be used by the Other; it is a mediation between the two groups in that each makes it a means against the means of the Other. Everything is both a trap and a display; the secret reality of the object is what the Other makes of it. And while the pure surrounding materiality becomes the contradictory unity of two opposed totalisations, each group, as an object among objects, that is to say, as a means chosen by the Other to achieve his own ends, is objectively totalised as material fragility along with all the other material structures of the field. As a *praxis* which has been transcended and outwitted, as a freedom which has been misled and used against its will (I sketched these relations in *The Problem of Method*), every individual and every village will realise itself as objectively characterised by the inertia of the surroundings; and these objective characteristics will become more and more clear as the peasants who dread the raids take stricter measures to avoid them by transcending their environment. In a solitary *praxis*, as we have seen, the farmer makes himself into an inert object in order to act on the soil; but at this point, his inertia reappears, transmitted to him through other people. But, if the balance of forces in some clash is favourable to him, he will find a new form of labour (for war is a labour of man upon man) in the shape of *power*. And this means something entirely new, namely the power of one human *praxis*, through matter, against the *praxis* of the other, and the possibility of transforming an objectifying object into an absolute one. But what is particularly interesting from our point of view is that every square metre of the practical field totalises the two groups and their two activities for all their members, in so far as the terrain presents itself as a permanent possibility of alienation for everyone. The negative unity of scarcity, which is interiorised in the reification of reciprocity, is re-exteriorised for us all in the unity of the world as the common locus of our antagonisms; and we will re-interiorise this unity in turn, in a new negative unity. We are united by the fact that we all live in a world which is determined by scarcity.

It goes without saying that scarcity, as indeed we have already seen, can be the occasion for the formation of new groups whose project is to combat it. Man, in fact, produces his life in the midst of other men who are also producing theirs, or at least causing others to produce it; he produces his life in the social field of scarcity. I do not intend to study the types of groups, collectives and institutions which arise *within this social field*; I am not trying to reconstitute the moments of History or the descriptions of sociology. Besides, this is not the place for a description of those human fields which are unified under the pressure of an active organisation of multiplicity, with differentiated functions. We must pursue our investigation in the regressive order and return to materiality as the inert synthesis of human plurality. However, we must not move on from this stage of our inquiry without making some observations about those groups which are united and differentiated in a unique way by struggling against scarcity and by being conditioned in their structures by scarcity. They constitute and institutionalise themselves not because scarcity appears to everyone in need through the need of Others, but because it is negated, in the unified field, by *praxis, by labour*. This obviously means that labour, as we have seen, is *primarily the organism* which reduces itself to a controlled inertia so as to act upon inertia and satisfy itself as need. Clearly this does not in itself mean *either* that labour exists in the field of scarcity, *or* that it must be defined as a struggle against scarcity. But given a social field which is defined by scarcity, that is, given the historical human field, labour for man has to be defined as *praxis* aimed at satisfying need *in the context of scarcity* by a particular negation of it. In hunting, for example, which is a matter not of systematically producing some tool, but of *finding* animals already in the field, it must not be forgotten that the speed of the 'game', its *average* distance (a flock of migrant birds in the sky, etc.), and all kinds of dangers, constitute *causes of scarcity*. And so a hunting weapon appears as creative, both negatively, in that it partially destroys distance, and sets its own speed against that of the hunted animal, and positively, in that for the hunter it multiplies the amount of possible prey or, in other words, his chances of catching one of them. And from our point of view, it is important that in the *present* context there is no difference between saying, on the one hand, that the chances of an individual or family being fed are multiplied by the tool in a given practical field (since the practical field, at this level, is not *really changed* by the tool), and saying, on the other hand, that the tool transforms the practical field for people who live by fishing and hunting, if not in its extent, then at least in its differentiation and fertility.

Thus the human labour of the individual, and, consequently, of the group, is conditioned in its aim, and therefore in its movement, by man's fundamental project, for himself or for the group, of transcending scarcity, not only as the threat of death, but also as immediate suffering, and as the primitive relation which *both* constitutes Nature through man *and* constitutes man through Nature. But *for precisely this reason* scarcity will, without ceasing to be the fundamental relation, come to qualify the group or the individual who struggle against it by *making themselves scarce so as to destroy it*. In certain historical conditions, provided that techniques enable a certain level of scarcity to be transcended – provided, in other words, that the milieu worked by previous generations and the quantity and quality of the tools available enable a definite number of workers to expand production by a certain amount – it is men who become scarce or risk becoming so – men as units of labour which destroy scarcity by means of organised production. Again we must be clear what we mean: it is the scarcity of products which defines men as scarce in certain social fields (though not in all) *even if* it still defines them commutatively as surplus in so far as they are men of need. And, of course, the scarcity of men can refer to various structures of organisation (shortage of manual labour, of skilled workers, of technicians, or of managers). In any case, what matters is that within a given group the individual is constituted in his humanity by other individuals *both* as expendable and as scarce. His expendability is immediate; and his *scarcity* appears in the most primitive forms of practical association and creates a constant tension in any given society. But in particular societies, with particular modes of production, the scarcity of men in relation to tools can be transformed, as a result of its own effects, into a scarcity of tools in relation to men. But the basic issue is the same. For a given society the quantity of tools in itself defines the producers, and thus the combination of producers and means of production defines the limits of production and the margin of non-producers (that is to say, of rejected producers) which the society can permit itself. The remaining non-producers represent a surplus which can either vegetate in malnutrition or disappear.

It goes without saying that this new form of scarcity presupposes a society based on *particular* kinds of work performed in common by an organised group. But this is not sufficient to define any particular historical society. Chinese society in imperial times (in so far as it was conditioned primarily by its rivers), and Roman society (in so far as it secured domination of the Mediterranean world by constructing an enormous system of communications), both satisfy the necessary conditions just as well as capitalism, although this type of scarcity has essentially developed as part of the process of modern industrialisation. But, in the same way, in certain structured historical situations, the institutionalised inequality of classes and conditions can cause a complete reversal of the situation – *a scarcity of consumers in relation to products*. Of course such relative scarcity is caused *both* by some material rigidity of production (which must not fall below certain levels) *and* by the institutionalised social choice of consumers (or rather of the hierarchy of consumers, which itself reflects the social structures which crystallise around the mode of production – what Marxists call 'relations of production'). It is all too clear that this reversal is particularly marked in our capitalist society and that it is an expression of its fundamental contradiction – over-production. And it is the absence of home markets capable of absorbing the entire product which has forced maritime societies since antiquity to trade by sea in order to search for new products or raw materials; it is this which has forced the continental powers into military imperialism.

But this scarcity of man in relation to the product, the final twist of the dialectic of scarcity, presupposes as its essential condition the scarcity of the product in relation to man. And this scarcity is a fundamental determination of man: as is well known, the socialisation of production does not put an end to it except possibly through a long dialectical process of which we cannot yet know the outcome. The scarcity of consumers in relation to a particular product is conditioned by the scarcity of all products in relation to all consumers. Indeed, it is because of this fundamental scarcity that certain relations of production have arisen, defined on the basis of the mode of production, which institutionally exclude certain social groups from full consumption, reserving it for other groups, insufficient in number to consume everything.

There would be no point in expounding the dialectic of 'overproduction' and its crises here. But it is important to notice that, taking the process as a whole, the capitalist is ruined, because of lack of outlets under competition, precisely to the extent that the proletariat is impoverished, that is to say, to the extent that the process produces a scarcity of objects of primary necessity. It is perfectly logical, at this level of the contradiction, for a given society to destroy some of its members as surplus to requirements at the same time as destroying part of its product because production exceeds consumption. And of course even if these products were distributed free to those whom society would otherwise allow to die, this would scarcely improve their lot. There would have to be a change at the level of the mode of production and of the basic relations to which it gives rise if the scarcity of consumers were to be made absolutely impossible and the reality of basic scarcity eliminated in the long term. The important thing, from the point of view of the logical structures of History, is that the historical process is constituted in the field of scarcity; and if it actualises all its dialectical possibilities, this is because of its actual contingent materiality, the outcome of an original contingency. But although, if we consider each case in isolation, it would have been possible for some of these dialectical moments not to have developed (we have only to consider peoples with no history, or those Asiatic nations which were forced to *interiorise* the fundamental relation of man to machine in the form in which the capitalist West initially imposed it on them in colonialism), once these moments appear as structures of intelligibility in a developing history, they alone enable it to be seen as a total rationality.

(*ii*) *Scarcity and Marxism*

It should be noted that Marx[21] – so clear and intelligible in his dialectical reconstruction of the capitalist process and in demonstrating its
necessity – always refused, and rightly so, to present Marxism as 'a
general historico-philosophical theory the supreme virtue of which
consists in being supra-historical'.[22] But at the same time, he believed –
correctly, though without historical proof – that historical materialism
was applicable to every moment of the historical process. In a remarkable passage, he criticised our contemporary Marxists and their dogmatism.

'(The plebeians) of ancient Rome were originally free peasants, each
cultivating his own piece of land on his own account. In the course of
Roman history they were expropriated. The same movement which
divorced them from their means of production and subsistence involved the formation not only of big landed property but also of big
money capital. Thus one fine morning there were to be found, on the
one hand, free men stripped of everything except their labour power
and on the other, the owners of all the acquired wealth ready to exploit
this labour. What happened? The Roman proletarians became not
wage labourers but a *mob* of do-nothings . . . and alongside them there
developed a mode of production which was not capitalist but based on
slavery. Thus events strikingly analogous but taking place in different
historical surroundings led to totally different results. By studying
each of these forms of evolution separately, and then comparing them
one can easily find the clue to this phenomenon. . . .'[23]

This passage clearly shows that, for Marx, the history of the non-

21. Since Marx constituted the materialist dialectic out of and in opposition to
the bourgeois economists of scarcity, the discussion which follows is necessary,
though it may appear to be a digression. Its aim is to re-integrate scarcity into
human history as a *human fact*, rather than as the malignity of a cruel Nature.

22. Karl Marx, Letter to the editorial board of the *Otechestvenniye Zapiski*,
Nov. 1877, in Marx and Engels, *Selected Correspondence*, Moscow, 1975, p. 294.
[Ed.]

23. *Ibid.* The object is to show that the proletarianisation of the Roman
plebs, despite its similarity to the proletarianisation of a section of the contemporary peasant class, does not produce the same results and that, consequently,
the march of Russia towards socialism will be different from that of the advanced
capitalist countries.

capitalist and pre-capitalist societies of the past *is not over and done with*. It is important to study the development of these societies, and to compare them amongst themselves and with modern societies, at least when there are compelling analogies; and intelligibility will be produced by these separate studies and by their comparison. Of course, the comparison will make them intelligible *in so far as they differ* through occurring in entirely different surroundings. But it is not based purely on the external similarity of the processes: the similarity is founded, although it in turn provides a foundation for difference. It is based *essentially* on the dialectical development of certain relations of man to his *praxis*, that is, to his labour (*free* peasants, that is, peasants freely working their fields; concentration of landed property and monetary capital reducing the expropriated to the condition of *possible labourers* for whom, nevertheless, labour, as the condition of the production of life, has become the primary scarcity). But all this is only roughly sketched, and consequently the evolution of the transformations of Roman society has the form of a story which lacks genuine intelligibility.

I hope it will not be suggested that the reason for the differentiation between the two processes resides in the radical difference between the two modes of production. It is *true*, in a sense, that the constitution of the Roman plebs presupposed that there was no industry in the modern sense at the time. But this is merely to say that the proletarianisation of the peasants driven from the countryside directly depended, in our own case, on industrialisation and industrial concentration. In other words, the movement towards industrialisation is a source of positive intelligibility for the contemporary phenomenon; but its absence, for Rome and the Romans, has meaning only for us, and only as a strict negation of total exteriority. It is a negative source of intelligibility, for instance, to show that a nation lost a war through the inadequacy of its armaments compared to the enemy's. It would be completely senseless to say that Napoleon was beaten at Waterloo because he did not have an air force. In short, the Roman process must provide its positive sources of intelligibility from within itself.

It is worth observing that the schemata of pre-history, antiquity, the Middle Ages and the pre-capitalist period are very seldom presented by Marx in an *intelligible* form. Firstly, he did not hesitate to reshape them in response to the work of non-Marxist historians – and this is to his credit. For instance, he presented his theory of class struggle as a very general truth, based on experience: 'The history of all hitherto existing society is the history of class struggles.'[24] Later Engels added the following note: 'That is, all *written* history. In 1847, the pre-history of society, the social organization existing previous to recorded history, was all but unknown. Since then . . . (it has been discovered that) common ownership of land . . . and . . . village communities . . . have been the primitive form of society. . . . With the dissolution of these primeval communities society begins to be differentiated into separate and finally antagonistic classes.'

'It has been discovered'. . . . By whom? Haxthausen, Maurer and Morgan. They studied the data of pre-history, made conjectures and judged that they were confirmed by events. On the basis of this *probability*, Engels (and Marx before him) did not hesitate to change his conception of History, and thus to substitute an empirical conditioning for an intelligible development. On the basis of recent work in pre-history and ethnography, he would no doubt change again and recognise that the truth, though not proving him entirely wrong, is more complex than the simplistic historians of the nineteenth century ever imagined.

Buy *why* did this dissolution occur? First, Engels himself believed that it did not take place everywhere; he liked the Iroquois and wished to believe that original purity had lasted longer in them. Secondly, he cited many societies in which it occurred at very different periods, and often *from outside*, through contact with more 'evolved' societies. For instance, he wrote in the *Anti-Dühring*: 'For thousands of years, Oriental despotism and the changing rule of conquering nomad peoples were unable to injure these old communities; the gradual destruction of their primitive home industry by the competition of products of large-scale industry brought these communities nearer and nearer to dissolution'.[25] And Marx, referring to the Russian commune, described Russia as 'the only European country where the "village community" has been maintained on a national scale down to our own day.'[26] These considerations inevitably bring us back to the difficult problem of peoples with no history. But they amplify and exaggerate the problem, since they make the temporal order of different histories seem completely contingent. I certainly would not claim that Marx and

24. Marx and Engels, *The Communist Manifesto*, (1848). See Marx and Engels, *Selected Works*, (1962), Vol. I, p. 34. [Ed.]

25. Engels, *Anti-Dühring*, Moscow, 1947, p. 194. [Ed.]

26. Letter to Vera Zassulitsch, first draft, Marx and Engels *Werke*, Vol. 19, p. 389. [Ed.]

Engels regarded this *particular* contingency as irreducible – irreducible, for example, to the more general contingency *of there being* a history, which we will discuss more fully later. What is certain is that in the cases under consideration we are confronting vast hypotheses about the succession of events which have no dialectical intelligibility. But let us see how Engels himself described the dissolution of village communities. Here are two passages from the same work. In the first we read:

'Private property . . . already existed, though limited to certain objects, in the ancient primitive communes of all civilized peoples. It developed into the form of commodities within these communes, at first through barter with foreigners. The more the products of the commune assumed the commodity form, that is, the less they were produced for their producers' own use and the more for the purpose of exchange, and the more the original natural division of labour was extruded by exchange also within the commune, the more did inequality develop in the property owned by the individual members of the commune, the more deeply was the ancient common ownership of the land undermined, and the more rapidly did the commune develop towards its dissolution and transformation into a village of small-holding peasants'.[27]

Exactly. This is an example of a law in the positivist sense, that is to say, of *a function* and the determination of its variable. $Y = f(X)$. The rate at which a commune changes into a village of property-owning peasants is directly proportional to the rate at which increasing numbers of 'natural' products are transformed into commodities. But then, because this law, like every law of Nature, merely describes a universal relation between possibilities, its content is non-historical; on the contrary, it is for History to explain how and why in a given society the rate suddenly accelerates while in another there is practically no change. And *this History* must provide its own intelligibility as a temporal process; no analytical law can explain it. And it is striking that Engels tried in the sentence that follows to provide just such an example of this dissolution as historical intelligibility, and that he took the example from the Asiatic communes. The sentence, in fact, has already been quoted. It says that these communes managed to *resist everything* except the entirely modern competition of large-scale industry. Of course this sentence must be taken in context; Engels was rightly

27. *Anti-Dühring*, p. 194. [Ed.]

trying to prove to Dühring that private property is not based on violence. Nevertheless he gave the effect of an industrialised society on a peasant commune as an example. The other example he chose is even more conclusive. It explains the *contemporary* dissolution of arable lands into agricultural properties on the banks of the Moselle or in the Hochwald as follows: 'The peasants simply find it to their advantage that the private ownership of land should take the place of common ownership.'[28] In their interests, of course – today, in an industrialised Germany. But earlier generations certainly did not see their interests in this way. So it is curious that the explanation of History relies on examples showing societies with no history being engulfed and dissolved by the history of Others. But this is precisely what needs to be explained. And it is pointless to conclude that 'Wherever private property evolved it was the result of altered relations of production and exchange, in the interest of increased production and in furtherance of intercourse – hence as a result of economic causes.'[29] This tries to say everything but means nothing, and is still no more than a universal function.

It will have been noticed that, in this passage, Engels makes commodity production the source of inequalities of wealth. But it could not possibly be maintained that these inequalities in themselves produce *classes*; and Engels himself did not believe it: in part three he gave a completely different interpretation of the division into classes:

'The separation of society into an exploiting and an exploited class, a ruling and an oppressed class, was the necessary consequence of the deficient and restricted development of production in former times. So long as the total social labour only yields a produce which but slightly exceeds that barely necessary for the existence of all; so long, therefore, as labour engages all or almost all the time of the majority of the members of society – so long, of necessity, this society is divided into classes. Side by side with the great majority, exclusively bond slaves to labour, arises a class freed from directly productive labour, which looks after the general affairs of society: the direction of labour, state business, law, science, art, etc. It is, therefore, the law of division of labour that lies at the basis of the division into classes.'[30]

---

28. *Ibid.* [Ed.]   29. *Ibid.* [Ed.]

30. *Anti-Dühring*, pp. 333–4. Apart from the contradictions which will be noted below, it is curious that Engels can treat government and justice as factors engendering classes when he maintains elsewhere, and with more justification,

Here the explanation is *historical*, and this is what makes it possible to see what is wrong with it. To begin with, it is clear that past societies – those which belong to 'written' History and are therefore characterised by classes – are divided into a *plurality of classes*, whose number tends to be gradually reduced by their struggles, rather than into the schematic duality which does not apply even *today* in industrialised countries. Besides, how can we accept the idea that the upper class is *initially* constituted as a *ruling* class and frees itself from directly productive labour by means of its new function when Engels himself says that the institution of slavery frees the majority of 'free men' from a part of the constraints of labour? Or when the moment of the expropriation and concentration of landed property, according to Marx, follows that of the individual ownership of land by peasants; and when this moment in fact creates a defenceless proletariat confronting a class of big proprietors (together with other intermediary classes)? Similarly, in the Middle Ages, as Marc Bloch has said, a noble was originally a person who owned a horse; and if the peasants gathered around the castle, accepted the constraints of serfdom, forced labour and the communal kitchen, this was indeed due to a certain division of labour, but not the one Engels mentions. The peasant asks the noble to undertake the labour of war, that is to say, to defend him with violence against violence *in the milieu of scarcity*.

What is striking in Engels' interpretations, and often in Marx's too, is that the references to scarcity are almost incomprehensible and, what is more, ambiguous. We find traces of it in this explanation of class duality; but the imagined society is assumed to produce *a little more* than necessary. And the scarcity is not a scarcity of goods, or of tools or of men, but of *time*. Of course, this scarcity reflects the others: if time is scarce for the worker (because he does not have enough of it to exercise his own sovereignty), we must obviously conclude that scarcity of goods and producers has been transposed and converted into scarcity of time. But this quintessentialised form does not take account of the reality of malnutrition which is universal today *even under socialist régimes*. The historical interpretations of Marx and

---

that the dominant class produces the State as one of its organs. No doubt this is not a contradiction, but the 'circularity' is very suspicious. A class which developed on the basis of its political and judicial sovereignty would not have the characteristics of the owners of landed property or of the bourgeoisie of the Ancien Régime.

Engels, taken literally, would have us believe that societies always have enough of what is necessary, given the instruments at their disposal and the needs which have become stratified in their organisms; and that it is the mode of production which, through the institutions that it conditions, produces the social scarcity of its product, that is to say, class inequality.

In *Wage Labour and Capital* Marx wrote: 'In production, men not only act on nature but also on one another. They produce only by co-operating in a certain way and mutually exchanging their activities. In order to produce, they enter into definite connections and relations with one another and only within these social connections and relations does their action on nature, does production, take place.'[31] And a little further on: '*The relations of production in their totality constitute what are called the social relations, society.*'[32] I entirely agree with Marxism on this point. *Given the existence of classes*, that is to say, once 'co-operation' has revealed the deep antagonism which underlies it, it provides us with the bases for a true intelligibility. The entire problem – and we can now see that there is only one problem here, the problem of the historical disintegration of agricultural communes being merely an aspect of it – is how, within Marxism, to conceive the transition from positive to negative. In Engels, we see workers creating their administrators; and in Marx, we see the direct co-operation of individuals around a mode of production which determines its conditions. But why *must* these direct transformations, which even look something like a Rousseauan contract, inevitably become antagonisms? Why should the social division of labour, which is a positive differentiation, be transformed into class struggle, that is, into a *negative* differentiation? After all, *today*, militant trade unionists are the organisers and administrators of the working class; and in certain countries they have taken on too much importance, or the leadership is becoming bureaucratic; the workers, however, have not claimed that they form a class or are going to become one. Is this because the differentiation occurs within the exploited class and against other classes? Undoubtedly. But when a group which is absorbed in labour which takes up all its time, produces apparatuses for supervision, management and control, these apparatuses, according to Engels, are maintained *within* this rudimentary society and their purpose is to counter internal

31. Marx, 'Wage Labour and Capital', *Selected Works*, Vol. I, p. 89. [Ed.]
32. *Ibid.*, p. 90. [Ed.]

divisions, natural dangers and enemies. Why should they break the unity of the society and produce classes? The only possible answer – not as the historical Reason for any particular process, but as the foundation of the intelligibility of History – is that negation must be given *in the first instance* in the original indifferentiation, whether this is an agricultural commune or a nomadic horde. And this negation, of course, is the interiorised negation of a number of men by scarcity, that is to say, the necessity for society to choose its dead and its underfed. In other words, it is the existence of a practical dimension of non-humanity in the man of scarcity.

Marx says very little about scarcity. The reason for this, I believe, is that it was a commonplace of classical economics, made fashionable by Adam Smith and developed by Malthus and his successors. Marx took it for granted and, rightly, since this is what Marxism consists in, preferred to treat labour as producing tools and consumption goods, and, at the same time, as producing definite relations between men. But in addition, when Marx did mention scarcity, in connection with the surplus part of the population, and resulting emigration, the only *negative* Reason for this seemed to him to be ignorance. 'In Antiquity, in fact, forced emigration . . . was a constant element of the social structure. . . . Because the Ancients were ignorant of the application of the sciences of Nature to material production, they had to stay few in number in order to remain civilised.'[33] But, as we saw above, this negative Reason is really a nothingness of Reason. It is as though Marx tried to transform an internal negation of the Greek or Roman groups into an external negation which had fallen out of the sky – that is to say, out of the year 1853. Besides, he only gave this example in order to contrast it with that of emigration in the capitalist period which is explained by *surplus*: 'It is not the poverty of the productive forces which creates the surplus population; it is the increase in productive forces which demands a decrease in population and gets rid of the surplus by famine or emigration.'[34] Of course, this is only a passing allusion to technological unemployment and the growing impoverishment of the working class through industrialisation. But the juxtaposition is typical. In the first case Marx evokes a negative Reason (the inadequacy of knowledge and, therefore, of the productive forces) only to make it vanish; and, in the second, he gives an *entirely positive cause* (the increase of the productive

33. *New York Tribune*, 9 February 1853; Marx and Engels *Werke*, Vol. VIII, p. 493. [Ed.]   34. *Ibid.*

forces) for an *entirely negative event* (the liquidation of surplus population by famine or emigration). This is just the conclusion he wanted to reach: in the capitalist period the mode of production itself produces scarcity (surplus population in a given society, decrease of purchasing power for each of them), because it comes into contradiction with the relations of production.

This means that, according to Marx, the Revolution – which he believed to be imminent – would not simply be the heir of bankruptcy, and that, by transforming the relations of production, the proletariat would soon be in a position to reabsorb this *social* scarcity into a new society. The truth will appear later on when new contradictions will arise in a socialist society owing to the gigantic struggle against scarcity. It is this positive certainty which prevented Marx and Engels from emphasising scarcity as a negative unity through matter in labour and man's struggles. And it was this same certainty which gave such uncertainty to Engels's reflections on violence. For, in a sense, he saw violence everywhere and, like Marx, made it the midwife of change; and if words have any meaning, struggle involves violence. But in another sense, Engels refused, quite rightly, to follow Dühring when he tried to base property and exploitation on violence. Now Dühring was a fool, and his robinsonades are absurd; but Engels did not see that his idealist and romantic ideas and all their follies required the presence of the *negative* in History. And this is what Dühring meant by 'violence': the historical process cannot be understood without a permanent element of negativity, both exterior and interior to man. This is the perpetual possibility *in man's very existence* of being the one who sends Others to their deaths or whom Others send to his – in other words, of scarcity.

The errors of the classical economists and of Dühring are exact opposites. The former, like everyone else at the time, believed in human nature. They placed man in situations of scarcity – this is what defined the economy – and tried to study his behaviour and the resulting relations between the objects of the economy. But it is assumed that man *is what he is* at the outset and that scarcity conditions him externally. Dühring, on the other hand, immediately attributed to man a capacity for violence and a will to use it which could only come from his enslaved will. This wicked creature's behaviour when there is no bread is not difficult to imagine. But violence is not necessarily an action; and Engels succeeded in showing that *as an action* it is absent from a great many processes. Nor is it a feature of Nature or a hidden potentiality. It is the constant non-humanity of human conduct as interiorised scarcity; it is, in short, what makes people see each other as the Other and as the principle of Evil. Thus the idea that the economy of scarcity is violence does not mean that there must be massacres, imprisonment or any visible use of force, or even any present project of using it. It merely means that the relations of production are established and pursued in a climate of fear and mutual mistrust by individuals who are always ready to believe that the Other is an anti-human member of an alien species; in other words, that the Other, whoever he may be, can always be seen by Others as 'the one who started it'.

This means that scarcity, as the negation of man in man by matter, is a principle of dialectical intelligibility. But I am not trying *either* to give an interpretation of pre-history *or* to fall back on the notion of classes and show, as so many others have done, how they originated. Such a project exceeds the powers of one individual; and in any case it is not what I intend. I simply wish to show that the dissolution of agricultural communes (where they existed), like the appearance of classes (*even* if we admit, with Engels, that they originate in a differentiation of functions), is intelligible only in terms of an original negation, whatever the real conditions of such events may be. From a material point of view, if workers produce *a little more* than society really needs, and if they are administered by a group which is freed from productive labour and whose members, necessarily few in number, can share out the surplus, there seems no reason at all why the situation should ever change. However, if we assume that differentiation occurs in a society whose members always produce *a little less* than everyone needs (which is always so, whatever the level of technique and so of demand), so that the constitution of an unproductive group depends on general malnutrition, and so that one of its essential functions is the selection of surplus population to be eliminated – if we assume all this, then, it seems to me, we will have grasped the very framework of the transformations, and their intelligibility.

No one has the right to regard the fear of famine which is so striking in underdeveloped societies, or the Great Fears of peasants under feudalism confronting the spectre of starvation, as mere subjective feelings. On the contrary, they represent the interiorisation of objective conditions and are in themselves an origin of *praxis*. History has developed, through the differentiation of functions and sub-groups, within a humanity in which even today millions of men *literally* die of hunger. So it is immediately obvious that administrative, managing and ruling groups are both *the same* as those they administer (in so far as the latter accept them) and *other than them*. For not only are they responsible for determining *the Others* in the group, that is, for choosing the victims of the new system of distribution; but also, they are themselves *the Others* in the sense that they are completely dispensable, consuming without producing and constituting a pure threat for everybody. In the context of scarcity, the differentiation of functions (however this takes place, for Engels saw it in a very simplistic way) *necessarily* implies the constitution of a dispensable (but accepted) group and the formation, by this group, with the complicity of many Others, of a group of under-nourished producers. Conversely, the unproductive groups, which are perpetually in danger of liquidation because they are the absolute Other (living off the labour of Others), interiorise this ambivalent alterity and behave towards individuals either as if they were Other than man (positively, as gods) or as if they alone were men in the midst of a different, sub-human species. As for the sacrificial group, its relation with Others can truly be described as struggle. For even if violence is not used, such a group will be negated by everyone, that is, by scarcity in everyone and it will reply by negating this negation – not, however, at the level of *praxis*, but simply through that negation of negation which is need.

We shall see later how in reality these acts and attitudes become beings, or collectives. We shall also see the true structure of groups. But it has been important to explore the primary conditioning of men by interiorised matter, this first, constant reassertion of control by the inertia of exteriority which contradicts *praxis* within *praxis* itself. This provides a foundation for the intelligibility of that cursed aspect of human history, both in its origins and today, in which man constantly sees his action being stolen from him and totally distorted by the milieu in which he inscribes it. It is *primarily* this tension which, by inflicting profound dangers on everyone in society, by creating diffused violence in everyone, and by producing the possibility for everyone of seeing his best friend approaching him as an alien wild beast, imposes a perpetual statute of extreme urgency on every *praxis*, at the simplest level, and, whatever its real aim, makes the *praxis* into an act of aggression against other individuals or groups. If one grants Marx and Engels the idea of class struggles, that is, of the negation of classes by one another; in other words, if one grants them negation, then they are able to comprehend History. But then we still have to explain negation *in the first place*. And we have just seen that, under the rule of scarcity, the negation of man by man, adopted and interiorised by *praxis*, was the negation of man by matter in so far as the organism has his being outside him in Nature. But we cannot stop here, for two reasons. In the first place, scarcity is a fundamental but contingent expression of the reaction of matter to the organism, which means that we must attempt a general theory of the relations of matter and *praxis* in the inevitable framework of scarcity which ceaselessly produces us, but without dealing with scarcity in isolation. Secondly, goods, products, etc., have a double character in relation to man. On the one hand, they are scarce; on the other hand, *this particular product*, for example, is a real and present being, which I produce, possess, consume, etc. And no doubt scarcity dwells in it as a negative being through the very precautions I take in using it. But to the extent that I produce it and make use of it I *also* have relations with it by which I transcend it towards my own ends, by which my *praxis* is its negation; relations by which the result inscribed in it is, within man's univocal bond of interiority with Nature, a *positive* acquisition. The creation of a tool or an object of consumption diminishes scarcity – by a negation of the negation. It *ought* therefore, as such, to relax the tensions of alterity in the group, especially in so far as individual productive labour is also *social labour*, that is, in so far as, whether individual or collective, it increases the wealth of the community.

Now, *at this level of positivity*, that is to say, precisely at the level of *objectification*, worked matter can be seen in all its docility both as a new totalisation of society and as its radical negation. At this level the real foundations of alienation appear: matter alienates in itself the action which works it, not because it is itself a force nor even because it is inertia, but because its inertia allows it to absorb the labour power of Others and turn it back against everyone. In the moment of passive negation, its interiorised scarcity makes everyone appear to Others as Other. In the moment of labour – the *human* moment in which man objectifies himself in producing his life – the inertia and material exteriority of objectification mean that, whatever else human relations may be, *it is the product* which defines men as Others and constitutes them as another species, as anti-human; and that it is in the product that people produce their own objectivity, which returns to them as an enemy and constitutes them as Other. Historical society could not produce itself through class struggles if the *praxis* which has been detached from it did not return to men as an independent and hostile reality – not only in the context of the capitalist process, but also at every other moment of the historical process. Marx explained the material conditions for the appearance of *capital*, a social force which ultimately imposes itself on individuals as anti-social. But our concern is to carry out a concrete investigation of the general, dialectical conditions which produce a determinate inversion in the relations of man and matter as a moment of the overall process; and which produce, within that determinate moment, through the *praxis* of Others, and through his own *praxis* as Other, the domination of man by matter (by *this* particular already-worked matter) and the domination of matter by man. It is within this complex of dialectical relations that the possibility of the capitalist process constitutes itself as one of the possible historical moments of alienation.

In other words: we have seen how production establishes itself and how it makes alterity a characteristic of the relations of production in the context of scarcity, or the negation of man by materiality as an inert absence of matter, and we shall now investigate how alienation becomes the rule of objectification in a historical society to the extent that materiality, as the positive presence of worked matter (of the tool), conditions human relations. We shall then understand, through the connection of these two dialectical moments, *how classes are possible*. But in the moment in which our *praxis* experiences its alienation, an internal and external structure of objectification appears, and this is precisely *Necessity*. So the rest of the regressive investigation need not be confined to displaying the *intelligibility* of class formation (on the basis of the mode of production and in the context of scarcity, as complex structures of stratified alterities, of interiorised and subsequently re-exteriorised contradictions and of antagonisms); it also introduces us to its first structure of apodicticity.[35]

35. It must be clearly understood here that the rediscovery of scarcity in this investigation makes absolutely no claim either to oppose Marxist theory, or to complete it. It is of a different order. The essential discovery of Marxism is that labour, as a historical reality and as the utilisation of particular tools in an already determined social and material situation, is the real foundation of the organisation of social relations. This discovery *can no longer* be questioned. What we are arguing, however, is this: the possibility of these social relations becoming contradictory is itself due to an inert and material negation re-interiorised by man. We are also arguing that *violence* as a negative relation between one *praxis* and another characterises the immediate relation of all men, not as a real action but as an inorganic structure re-interiorised by organisms and that the possibility of reification is present in all human relations, even in the pre-capitalist period, and

2 *Worked Matter as the Alienated Objectification of Individual and Collective Praxis*

It is important to be clear about what is meant by saying that a society designates its undernourished producers and selects its dead. It sometimes happens than an organised power consciously and deliberately decides to overpower and exploit certain groups for the advantage of others. This is the case, for instance, when one nation conquers another, and plunders and enslaves the defeated. But this is certainly not the most usual kind of case; on the contrary. Engels was right to say that very often, when two groups engage in a series of contractual exchanges, one of them will end up expropriated, proletarianised and, often, exploited, while the other concentrates the wealth in its own hands. This takes place *in violence*, but not *by* violence: and experiencing exchange as a duel in this way is characteristic of the man of scarcity.

---

even in family relations or relations between friends. As for scarcity itself, it has a formal dialectic which we have already sketched: scarcity of products, scarcity of tools, scarcity of workers, and scarcity of consumers; it also has a historical, concrete dialectic about which we will be silent since it is for historians to retrace its moments. Indeed, it would be necessary to show the double transition, under the influence of production itself, from scarcity as the dispensability of each individual in relation to all, to scarcity as the designation by society of groups of under-consuming producers. At this point the relation between groups becomes *violence* – not necessarily because it was established by violence – Engels is right about this – but because it *is* in itself a relation of violence between violent men. The second aspect of the transition is from absolute scarcity, as a determinate impossibility of all the members of the group existing together in certain definite material conditions, to relative scarcity, as the impossibility that the group, in certain circumstances, should grow beyond a certain limit without any change in the mode or the relations of production (that is to say, scarcity in the form of the discreet liquidation of non-producers in a given society according to certain rules, and *also* as the selection of undernourished producers). This relative scarcity, which itself has a historical dialectic (an intelligible history), acquires, in class societies, the status of *an institution*. The analytical study of institutions of scarcity is political economy. This implies that in giving due weight to scarcity we are not reverting to a pre-Marxist theory of the pre-eminence of 'consumption', but merely throwing into relief negativity as the implicit motive force of the historical dialectic and making it intelligible. *In the context of scarcity* all the structures of any given society depend on the mode of production.

Though the result is appropriated *in* violence by the dominant class, it is not foreseen by the individuals who compose it.

The striking thing about Marxist descriptions, however, is not so much exchange as the constraints of tools. Late eighteenth and nineteenth century society was completely dependent on the iron and coal complex. In other words, coal as a source of energy itself conditioned the means of harnessing that energy (for instance, the steam engine) and, through these new tools, it conditioned new methods of working iron. (The meaning and intelligibility of this observation will become clear later.) In this way, mankind came into possession of a source of accumulated energy derived from vanished vegetable matter; one might describe it as capital bequeathed to mankind by other living beings. But at the same time every proprietor was eating away his own capital; for mines are not inexhaustible. This peculiar feature of mining, as well as favouring industrialisation in its initial stages, made this first moment of industrial capitalism violent and feverish in character. All exploitative activities come to be based on the mode of exploitation of the mines; they are constituted in the perspective of rapid, brutal gains before the raw material is exhausted. And this gave rise to steam transport, railways (which are very directly linked to mining since their original function was to serve it), gas-lighting, etc. And within this complex of materials and instruments, there had to be a division of labour: mines and factories created their capitalists, their technicians and their workers.

Marx and many later thinkers have shown the meaning of these constraints *of matter* – how the iron and coal complex presents itself at the basis of a society as the condition for class mobility, for new functions and institutions, for more extreme differentiations and for changes in the system of property, etc. But the undeniable result of what has sometimes been called the 'palaeotechnical' period was the partial destruction of the structures of the old society, the proletarianisation of certain groups and their subjugation to the two inhuman forces of physical fatigue and scarcity. And as a result of all this, a new kind of men came into being, 'iron and coal men', produced by mining and by new smelting techniques, the industrial proletarians (and, of course, industrialists and technicians, etc.). All this is well known. But still, it seems paradoxical that the ruthless proletarianisation of the peasants, which continued throughout the century, arose and developed from an incredible growth in the wealth of mankind and from absolute progress in its techniques. The historical reasons for this are well known.

To take just two well understood examples, it has been shown hundreds of times how industry under the Second Empire itself produced a concentration of landed wealth, once industrialists had decided to construct the agricultural implements which enabled rich peasants to get richer while forcing poor, ruined peasants to sell their land and migrate to the towns. It has also been shown how steam ships caused the demographic transformation of England at the end of the last century by causing an unprecedented agricultural crisis simply by bringing Argentinian corn within *a few days* of England.

From the point of view of intelligibility, the important thing is to comprehend how a positive fact, such as the large scale use of coal, could become the source of deeper and more violent divisions between people within a *working society*, a society which was also seeking to increase its social wealth by all available means; and to understand, too, how the constraints of the material complex which men inherit can negatively define the new expropriated, exploited and undernourished groups. Of course, this new mode of production could not have abolished scarcity, so it was not even conceivable that the means of production should be socialised. But this negative explanation is no more valuable than the attempt to explain the emigration of ancient Greeks by reference to their ignorance of the sciences of Nature. It would be both more reasonable and more intelligible to exhibit industrialisation as a process which developed out of *previous* scarcity, which is a real factor in History (in so far as it is crystallised in institutions and practices), and therefore on the basis of the negation of men by matter through other men. It is obvious, for instance, that the first people to work in factories and mines in England were *paupers*, that is to say, peasants who had been designated, sometimes from father to son, as dispensable, surplus population as a result of the complex movement of agricultural economies and the hard policies of bourgeois land-owners. It was left to machines to shatter the last positive bond: the parish had formerly fed its poor; this was an ethico-religious practice, and the only vestige of feudal relationships built around the Church. (And as is well known, Marx said that *in these* relationships, oppression and exploitation did not altogether hide a non-reified human relation.) Industry, and the political representatives of industrialists, in so far as they made themselves political servants of industrialisation, however, condemned the poor. They were torn from their villages, and immense movements of population took place, and individuals were reduced to interchangeable units of an abstract labour power, the same in everyone. This labour power itself became a commodity, and finally massification constituted workers in this first aspect: *mere inert things* who relate to other workers through competitive antagonism, and to *themselves* through the 'free' possibility of selling that other *thing*, their labour power, which also means the possibility of working as a man rather than an animal, of *organising one's praxis* so as to contribute more to production, and of being a man in general, since *praxis* is the real humanity of man. In *all these specific negations*, scarcity and pre-capitalist social structures are no longer to be found, although of course the new negations were based on the old ones; they actually owe their negative character to the mode of production in so far as it rests on this incredible wealth. In an altogether different context, and with a very different intention, Engels noted this paradoxical character very clearly: negation as the result of positivity.

'The natural division of labour within the family cultivating the soil made possible, at a certain level of well-being, the introduction of one or more strangers as additional labour forces. This was especially the case in countries where the old common ownership of the land had already disintegrated. . . . Production had developed so far that the labour-power of a man could now produce more than was necessary for its mere maintenance; the means of maintaining additional labour forces existed; likewise the means of employing them; labour power acquired a *value*. But the community . . . yielded no available, superfluous labour forces. On the other hand, such forces were provided by war, and war was as old as the simultaneous existence alongside each other of several groups of communities. Up to that time, . . . prisoners of war . . . had . . . simply been killed. . . . But . . . now . . . the prisoners acquired a value; one therefore let them live and made use of their labour. . . . Thus force, instead of controlling the economic situation was on the contrary pressed into the service of the economic situation. *Slavery* had been invented.'[36]

Considered in the context of economic evolution, slavery represents progress, and therefore in itself it expresses a positive response to the positive conditions which gave rise to it: after all, it is *true* that it was the basis of Ancient Greece and of the Roman Empire. Again, considered in itself, it can also be seen as a humanisation of war and a positive element in that prisoners of war acquired value on account of their potential labour (on the highly dubious assumption that slavery

<hr />

36. *Anti-Dühring*, pp. 215–16.

can be explained in such simplistic terms). But from the first point of view, we could also say that, as far as the technical and even ethical progress of humanity are concerned, the industrial proletariat is a positive gain, because industrialisation involves proletarianisation and because the worker thus produced is destined to carry out the sentence which capitalism passes on itself.

Marxism in no way conflicts with this; however, today, from the point of view of *making* History, it presents the positive character of the proletariat as the negation (human negation = *praxis*) *of a negation.* Similarly, from the point of view of the entire ancient world, the emancipation of the few through the enslavement of the many presents itself as the negation of the enslavement of all, and as an enslavement imposed only on some. Slavery prevents a possible enslavement. But when Engels shows us the origins of slavery, (or what he takes to be its origins), slavery appears as the negative result of a positive development of production. Free men, working for themselves and their community, are reduced to their labour power, are forced to use it entirely for the advantage of some foreigner. That this negative side was perfectly evident to groups in which slavery existed is sufficiently proved by the frequent wartime oaths to die rather than become a slave. So it would be absolutely wrong to say that the massacre of prisoners, when it occurred, expressed the victor's indifference about the defeated. What it expressed was, rather, a certain statute of violence, in which death was a bond of antagonistic reciprocity; slavery was seen *as positive in that* positive extra labour power was actually present in exploitation, and it was seen *as a negation of war, under the threat of war,* perpetually, as the danger of a new statute being imposed on everyone. Besides, even if the transformation in the fate of prisoners of war due to economic development is, in this simplistic form, romanticised history, it is nevertheless clear that, when the practice became institutionalised, a complex system was constituted in response to the scarcity of slavery, involving a multiplication of wars and raids *for the sake of* conquering slaves, and also for the organisation of the slave-trade.

It would be pointless for us to take up a moral position – which would be entirely meaningless – and to condemn the ancient system of slavery. Our concern has simply been to show that Engels wrote his paragraph on slavery using exclusively *positive* words and expressions, as against Dühring, who saw enslavement as simple violence and therefore as nothing but a fundamental *negation* of man by man. But Engels's collection of *positive* propositions does not conceal the fact that slavery originally appeared as a choice of a category of under-nourished sub-humans, by men who were conscious of their own humanity and that, as such, in spite of the false, specious argument based on war, it appeared as negativity. But should this negativity be attributed to a displacement of scarcity? Scarcity of labourers, replacing a scarcity of tools and raw materials? Yes indeed; but this only takes us back to the heart of the problem, since this displacement of scarcity, as a negation which had to be negated, emerged out of a positive process. And this production of negativity did not result directly from scarcity *felt* as need, since it occurred in groups (in particular, families) which were quite 'well off'. They could conceive it only as *a lack which had to be acquired*, that is, in so far as it was expressed – in tools, in cultivation, and in the technical organisation of familial exploitation – as a positive possibility creating its own negation in its very positivity. In this case, the materiality revealed by action is really entirely positive: in the practical field, the soil is revealed as soil to be cultivated. This means that materiality also indicates the means of cultivation – it reveals itself as such through the tools and organisation which have actually cultivated some other part of the same soil. But this positive ensemble is lived as a negative turning back, and conditions all negativity (the *raid* in which men are captured like animals, and the statute which assigns them to a place in the new society as both necessary producers and dispensable consumers reduced to underconsumption and which, in constituting the Other as sub-human, makes of the slave-owner a man *other than man*).[37]

---

37. This is not a return to Hegelianism, which makes the Slave the *Truth* of the Master. Apart from the idealism of the celebrated passage on 'Master and Slave', Hegel can be criticised for describing *the* Master and *the* Slave, that is to say, ultimately, for describing the relations of *a* master with *his* slave through universals, without reference to their relations to other slaves or other masters. In reality, the plurality of masters and the serial character of every society cause the Master as such, even in idealist terms, to find *a different truth* within the ensemble of his class. Slaves are the truth of masters, but masters are also the truth of masters, and these two truths oppose one another as do these two categories of individuals. Besides, except at the time of great concentrations of landed wealth, in Rome and later, the *Master also worked*. So the problem was no longer to compare an idle whim with slave labour (which thereby became identified with labour in general), but rather, (to take for example a Greek artisan), to compare free (manual) labour with the slave labour which is its condition (but which is no longer identified with labour in general, since the slave is only given unpleasant tasks requiring no skill). If the slave possesses the secret of the master this is

Within *praxis*, therefore, there is a dialectical movement and a dialectical relation between action as the negation of matter (in its present organisation and on the basis of a future re-organisation), and matter, as the real, *docile* support of the developing re-organisation, as the negation of action. And this negation of action – which has nothing in common with obstruction – can be expressed in action only in terms of action itself; that is to say, its positive results, in so far as they are inscribed in the object, are turned against and into it in the form of objective, negative exigencies. This should surprise no-one; everyone understands the necessity of social transformations in terms of material and technical complexes. Today, everyone finds a true intelligibility in the objective process (which is much more complex than Engels's Marxism portrayed it) which adumbrates the slave as the sub-human future of still undetermined individuals *on the basis of* a technical progress and an increase in wealth which will rescue certain groups (including, in many cases, ones which will be reduced to slavery) from what Engels called the constraint of animality. Today everyone understands, or can understand, how machines, by their structure and functions, determine the nature of their servants as the rigid and imperious future of undetermined individuals and, thereby, *create men*.

It is true that the intelligibility and objective necessity contained in the whole process sustain and illuminate our knowledge of it; but, on the other hand, they remain hidden in so far as they are absorbed by a material content which then reveals them to knowledge *through* its own temporalisation and as the special rule of its historical development. We are unable to give a dialectical account of our social and historical language. In his excellent book, Mumford says: 'Since the steam engine *requires* constant care on the part of the stoker and engineer, steam power was more efficient in large units than in small ones. . . . Thus steam power *fostered* the *tendency* toward large industrial plants. . . .'[38] I do not wish to question the soundness of these observations, but simply to note the strange language – language which has been ours since Marx and which we have no difficulty in understanding – in which a single proposition links finality to necessity so indissolubly that it is impossible to tell any longer whether it is man or machine which is a

because his labour is destined to approach a moment where it will cost more than it produces, thereby bringing about the ruin of the ancient world.

38. Lewis Mumford, *Technics and Civilization*, 1934, p. 162. The italics are Sartre's. [Ed.]

practical project. We all *feel* that this language is correct, but also realise that we cannot explain or justify this feeling. Similarly, when we learn that gas-lighting, which was a consequence of the use of coal as a source of energy, *enabled* employers to make their workers work fifteen or sixteen hours a day, we do not quite know whether it was the industrial ensemble dominated by coal which, through the medium of the men it produced, required a working day of sixteen hours, or whether it was the industrialist, in the coal-based economy, who used gas-lighting to increase production or, again, whether the two formulations do not refer to two aspects of a single dialectical circularity. It is precisely at this level that a dialectical investigation must supply its own intelligibility, as the general condition of the relation of *praxis* to tools and, generally speaking, to materiality. This means that the translucidity of the individual *praxis* as the free, re-organising transcendence of particular conditionings, is really an abstract moment of the dialectical investigation – even though this moment can develop as a concrete reality in any particular undertaking, even in the wage earner's manual labour (for instance, when a skilled worker, though conscious of having sold his labour power, remains the organiser of his professional *praxis*). The deepening of the investigation must also be a deepening of *praxis*. It is in *praxis* itself, in so far as it objectivises itself, that we will find the new moment of dialectical intelligibility, which constitutes the result of a negation of the undertaking. This new structure of rationality can be called dialectical intelligibility because in its immediate purity it is simply a new dialectical determination produced on the basis of existing structures, and without any new factors apart from those it itself produces on the basis of these structures as the totalisation of their transcendence and as the strict necessity of this transcendence.[39]

39. *After* the transcendence the totalisation itself becomes particular, both as an alienated objectification and in relation to the transcended structures which still exist, *also* in freedom (that is to say, in the strict conditioning of their reciprocal determinations and beyond all transcendence). So the particularised totalisation becomes, with others, the object of a new totalising transcendence which we shall have to discuss later. By way of an example, I would refer the reader to the observations I made in *The Problem of Method* (p. 72) on some studies by Kardiner, in particular the inquiry into the natives of the Marquesas islands.

(i) *Matter as inverted praxis*

Every *praxis* is primarily an instrumentalisation of material reality. It envelops the inanimate thing in a totalising project which gives it a pseudo-organic unity. By this I mean that this unity is indeed that of a whole, but that it remains social and human; *in itself* it does not achieve the structures of exteriority which constitute the molecular world. However, if the unity persists, it does so through material *inertia*. But this unity is nothing other than the passive reflection of *praxis*, that is to say, of a human enterprise undertaken in particular circumstances, with well defined tools and in a historical society at a certain point in its development, and therefore the object produced reflects the whole collectivity. But it reflects it in the dimension of passivity. Take, for example, the act of *sealing* something. It is performed on certain ceremonial occasions (treaties, contracts, etc.) with a special tool. The wax *returns* (*retourne*) the act; its inertia reflects the *doing* as pure *being-there*. At this level, practice absorbed by its 'material' becomes a material caricature of the human. The manufactured object proposes itself to men and imposes itself on them; it defines them and indicates to them how it is to be used. In order to incorporate this set of indications into a general theory of signs, one would have to say that the tool is a *signifier* and that man *here* is a *signified*. In fact, the tool can have meaning only through man's labour, and man can only signify what he knows. In a sense, therefore, it appears that tools reflect to individuals nothing but their own knowledge. One can see this in the routine of a craftsman, in which the worker apprehends, through the tool he has himself made, the eternal return of the same movements, defining a permanent statute within the corporation or the town, in relation to an unchanging clientèle.

But precisely because signification takes on the character of materiality, it enters into relation with the entire Universe. This means that infinitely many unforeseeable relations are established, through the mediation of social practice, between the matter which absorbs *praxis* and other materialised significations.

Inert *praxis* which imbibes matter transforms natural, meaningless forces into quasi-human practices, that is to say, into passivised actions. Chinese peasants, as Grousset rightly says, are colonialists. For four thousand years, they have been appropriating arable land on the frontiers of their territory, from Nature and from the nomads. One aspect of their activity is the deforestation which has been going on for centuries. This *praxis* is living and real, and retains a traditional aspect: even recently the peasant was still tearing up scrub to clear a place for millet. But, at the same time, it inscribes itself on nature, both positively and negatively. Its positive aspect is that of the soil and the division of cultivation. Its negative aspect is a signification of which the peasants themselves are not aware, precisely because it is an absence – *the absence of trees*. A European flying over China *today* is immediately struck by this feature; China's present leaders have perceived it and are aware of the seriousness of the danger. But traditionalist Chinese in previous centuries could not perceive it since their goal was conquest of the soil. They saw only the plenty represented by their harvests and had no eyes for *the lack*, which was for them, at most, a simple process of liberation, the elimination of an obstacle. On this basis, deforestation, as a passivised practice which had become *characteristic* of the mountains, particularly those that dominate Szechwan, transformed that physico-chemical sphere which can be called 'wild' in the sense that it begins where human practice leaves off. To begin with, this wild sector is human in that it expresses the historical limit of society at a particular moment. But above all deforestation as the elimination of obstacles becomes negatively a lack of protection: since the loess of the mountains and peneplains is no longer retained by trees, it congests the rivers, raising them higher than the plains and bottling them up in their lower reaches, and forcing them to overflow their banks. Thus, the whole history of the terrible Chinese floods appears as an intentionally constructed mechanism.[40]

If some enemy of mankind had wanted to persecute the peasants of the Great Plain, he would have ordered mercenary troops to deforest the mountains systematically. The positive system of agriculture was transformed into an infernal machine. But the enemy who introduced the loess, the river, the gravity, the whole of hydrodynamics, into this destructive apparatus was the peasant himself. Yet, taken in the moment of its living development, his action does not include this rebound, either intentionally or in reality. In *this* particular place, and for *this* particular man cultivating his land, all that existed was an organic connection between the negative (removal of the obstacle) and the positive (enlargement of the arable sector). The first thing that is necessary for counter-finality to exist is that it should be adumbrated

40. Cf. my remarks about counter-finality, above.

by a kind of *disposition* of matter (in this case the geological and hydro-graphic structure of China). It seems that in order to remove the danger of flooding completely it would not have been sufficient *not to* deforest. From ancient times, *reforestation* would have been necessary. Second, human *praxis* has to become a fatality and to be absorbed by inertia, taking on *both* the strictness of physical causation *and* the obstinate precision of human labour. Destruction by Nature is imprecise: it leaves little islands, even whole archipelagos. Human destruction is systematic: a particular farmer proceeds on the basis of an approach to a limit which conditions his *praxis* – quite simply, the idea that every tree growing in his field should be destroyed. Thus the absence of trees, which is an inert and thus a material negation, also has the systematic character of a *praxis* at the heart of materiality. Last, and most important, the activity must be carried on *elsewhere*: peasants *everywhere* must burn or uproot the scrub. These actions, which are legion and, as actions, both *identical* and *irreducible*, are united by the matter they unify. Through molecular homogeneity, the multiplicity of actions is diffused in the 'community' of being. Imprinted on the red soil, which offers itself as an infinite deployment of materiality, particular actions lose both their individuality and their relation of identity (in space and time): they spread themselves out without frontiers, carried along by this material deployment, and lose themselves in it; there is just *one* seal impressed on just one land.

But the passive movement of this deployment is itself the result of an initial *praxis*; the changing links between groups, by river, canal and road created *closeness* and *distance* within an initial unity, which was the life lived in common under the same geographical conditions by a society already structured by its tools and its labour. Thus deforestation as the material unity of human actions is inscribed as a universal absence on an initial inert synthesis, which itself is already the materialisation of the human. And passive unity, as the synthetic appearance of pure dispersal and as the exteriorisation of the bond of interiority, is for *praxis* its unity *as Other* and in the domain of the Other.[41] On this basis, deforestation as the action of Others becomes everyone's action as Other *in matter*; objectification is alienation, and at first this primitive alienation does not express exploitation, though it is inseparable from it, but rather the materialisation of recurrence. There is no joint

41. Obviously my example can be understood only in the context of scarcity and as a displacement of it.

undertaking, but still the infinite flight of particular undertakings inscribes itself in being as a joint result. By the same token, Others are fused, as Others, in the passive synthesis of a false unity; and, conversely, the Oneness stamped on matter reveals itself as Other than Oneness. The peasant becomes his own material fatality; he produces the floods which destroy him.[42]

Thus human labour, though only just 'crystallised', is enriched with new meanings precisely to the extent that it eludes the labourer through its materiality. At this elementary stage, by inscribing itself in the natural milieu, it extends to the whole of Nature and incorporates the whole of Nature within itself: *in* and *through* labour Nature becomes both a new source of tools and a new threat. In being realised, human ends define a field of counter-finality around themselves. Through the unity of this counter-finality, deforestation negatively unites the enormous masses who people the great plain of China: it creates universal solidarity in the face of a single danger. But at the same time it aggravates antagonisms, because it represents a *social future* both for the peasants and for the land-owners. This future is both absurd, in that it comes to man from the non-human, and rational, in that it merely accentuates the essential features of the society. Future floods *are lived* as a traditional feature of Chinese societies. They bring about a perpetual shift of fortunes, and equalisation through catastrophe followed by renewed inequality; – hence the immemorial feudalism in which repetition replaces transformation, and in which, apart from the great landowners, the rich man is almost always a *nouveau riche*. Later, when it is recognised as the foremost danger, deforestation remains a *threat to be eliminated*, in the form of a common task whose success will give benefits to all.

This first relation of man to the non-human – where Nature becomes the negation of man precisely to the extent that man is made *anti-*

---

42. The extraordinary separation of rural workers in China, which the commune system has only recently caused to disappear, is obviously linked with the primitiveness and stagnation of techniques. These facts condition and express a definite system of social relations and a definite form of property. But although exploitation as alienation is inscribed in materiality with its own characteristics and mingles there indissolubly with alienation through recurrence, the latter cannot be reduced to the former. The former defines the relation of forms of production to productive forces in a concrete historical society; the latter, although it appears in the relevant aspect only at a certain technical level, is a permanent type of separation *against which* men unite, but which attacks them even when united.

physis and that the actions in exteriority of the atomised masses are united by the communal character of their results – does not as yet integrate materiality with the social, but makes mere Nature, as a brutal, exterior limitation of society, into the unity of men. What has happened is that, through the mediation of matter, men have realised and perfected a joint undertaking because of their radical separation. Nature, as an exterior constraint on society, *at least in this particular form*, constrains society as an interiority based on the objectification in exteriority of that society. This limit, however, is re-interiorised and institutionalised precisely to the extent that deforestation as a practical result appears as the means chosen by the Other for bringing about floods and to the extent that, throughout historical society, these floods appear as scourges which have to be combated, which necessarily implies a 'river civilisation', involving large-scale public works, movements of population, and the absolute authority of the rulers, etc. Thus we can begin to see an actual state of labour as a univocal relation of interiority between man and surrounding matter, a state in which there is a constant transformation of man's exigencies in relation to matter into exigencies of matter in relation to man. In this state, man's needs for material products, in so far as they express his being in their finality and rigidity as interiorised exteriority, are homogeneous in relation to the exigencies of matter in so far as these express a crystallised, inverted human *praxis*.

These rational connections will become clearer at a more complex level of integration. *Praxis* uses tools which are not only the means by which the organism realises its own inertia in order to act on the inert milieu, but also the support of this inertia which has been exteriorised by an inorganic inertia, and the passive unity of the practical relation between an undertaking and its result. Thus Nature, though transcended, reappears *within society*, as the totalising relation of all materiality to itself and of all workers to one another. It is at this level that matter can be studied as an *inverted praxis*. As an example, we shall consider the role of *precious metals* in a given historical situation – Spanish hegemony, the decline of the Mediterranean, merchant capitalism struggling against feudal forms, and the exploitation of gold mines in Peru by new techniques. The precious metals will be considered as simultaneously products, commodities, signs, powers and instruments, and as themselves becoming exigencies, constraints, undertakings and non-human activities (in the sense that the non-human is a different species), while in a different way remaining for everyone the passive indication of a definite if temporary purchasing power. Obviously we do not intend to make an economic or historical study. But, given the work of historians and economists on the circulation of precious metals in the Mediterranean world during the Renaissance, we will try to grasp the intelligible bond of exteriority and of interiority in real life within that circulation, observing how, in the case of gold and silver as materiality, and in the case of man as the product of his product, it transforms human *praxis* into *antipraxis*, that is to say, into a *praxis without an author*, transcending the given towards rigid ends, whose hidden meaning is counter-finality. I shall apply myself, therefore, to an example, drawn from Spanish history, which has the advantage of showing the process of the inversion of *praxis* in all its clarity. It goes without saying that this process develops in class societies with class divisions. But it is not classes which we will be trying to understand in it, but rather, other things being equal, the dialectic of *antipraxis* as an objective relation between matter and man. On the basis of this inquiry, we shall, perhaps, be able to determine the conditions for the dialectical intelligibility of the constitution of classes as schism and conflict within a given grouping.

In the example we have chosen, as in those quoted above, a social heritage turns into a disaster; and plenty itself becomes negativity (as also happened later, in the age of mining). The discovery of the Peruvian mines seemed at the time to be an increase of wealth and, in the middle of the sixteenth century, it caused a new technique of metallic amalgamation to be perfected. The continual increase in stocks of precious metals *in Spain*, however, eventually resulted in an increased cost of living on the whole of the Mediterranean seaboard, worsening poverty for the exploited classes, the paralysis of business and the ruin of many merchants and industrialists. The Spanish terror, caused by the *outflow of gold*, must be seen, finally, as containing not only the prophetic announcement of the decline of Spain and the Mediterranean, but also its result and one of its conditions. How can the affirmation of an affirmation produce a negation?

As soon as the first Spanish gold coins had been struck, a living bond between them, other Spanish coins, and the coins of all other countries, and also between all these and all the gold mines established itself, through the apparatus and structures of mercantile capitalism and the historical *praxis* of Charles V and Philip II. The bond was initially a human one: mining, transport, melting down, minting – so many modalities of labour – defined techniques and social structures. Circu-

lation and hoarding are forms of *praxis*. It was the labour in the Peruvian mines, the long and difficult journey along the routes crossing the
isthmus of Panama, and the comings and goings of the Spanish fleet
which, under the *Ancien Régime*, placed Spanish currency as a whole in
a permanent relation with mining as the source of constant, limited
expansion. But it was the instruments of mining, the means of transport, the techniques of minting, etc. which, at least in part, accounted
for the reserves of money at any particular moment in the reign of
Philip II.

At the beginning of the sixteenth century, the Mediterranean suffered
a 'gold famine': African sources were exhausted. America was replacing them, and up to 1550, Spain was importing both gold and
silver. But in the second half of the century, silver predominated, and
this was because Bartolomeo de Medina had introduced a new amalgamation process into the American mines. Between 1580 and 1630
imports of precious metals increased tenfold. This is a case of matter
acting on matter: the treatment of silver ore with mercury conditioned
the whole evolution of money up to the middle of the following
century. But this instrumental materiality was materialised practice.
Later, as prices rose, the effects of the increase were felt particularly in
Florence and in Castille. Braudel explains why: 'Continental prices
reflected the constant tension in economies affected by the hostile
distances separating them from the sea.'[43] But these *hostile distances*
also express materialised *praxis*: distance as materiality is a function of
the state of the roads, of the means of communication, and of conflicts
between towns: Florence was *now* close to the sea. In short, at this
level, matter as a limit to signification becomes a mediation between
significations. It is in and through matter that significations (crystallised *praxis*) combine into new but still inert syntheses.

American gold and silver took on their true character within these
passive totalisations. Coins *became human quantities* under the influence of the inert actions surrounding them. In a sense, indeed, quantity
was already in them, since it cannot be separated from materiality, nor,

43. F. Braudel, *The Mediterranean and the Mediterranean World in the Age of
Philip II* (1949). [English translation of second edition by Sian Reynolds, Collins,
1972 – Ed.] The whole of the exposition which follows is no more than a commentary on this admirable work. See, in particular, Part Two. 'Collective
Destinies and General Trends', chapter two, 'Economies: Precious Metals, Money
and Prices'. [The sentence quoted by Sartre is on p. 413 of the first, French
edition, and does not occur in the second – Ed.]

above all, from *being in exteriority*. But it was not a differentiated quantum; and, above all, it did not concern coins *as such*. I am not referring to the *value* of coins, which is something we shall come to later. If it were only a question of their weight, even that would have its concrete reality only in relation to the galleons which transported them and the carts which brought them to the capital from the coast. And how could their number be determined except in relation to a definite vessel in which they accumulated without being able to escape? Such a vessel existed: it was Spain itself, 'a country traditionally protectionist, fenced around with customs barriers. . . . So, in principle, the huge American treasure was being drawn into a sealed vessel.'[44] It was the unity of the vessel, the customs barriers and the authoritarianism of the absolute monarchy which allowed the amount of coins or precious metal to be checked and counted. It was in relation to this unit that this quantity would be reckoned as abundance or as scarcity. It was at the bottom of this crucible that the heavy burden of ingots and coins began to *weigh*; it was in and through it that real relations came to be established between this mineral and other material objects – manufactured products, food-stuffs, etc. Should this crucible, this unbreakable vessel (unbreakable in theory at least) be called *material*, on the grounds that the very nature of the Spanish frontiers (the sea, the Pyrenees) constitutes in itself a natural barrier, and that institutions, social structures and the system of government are crystallised practices? Or should it be called *praxis*, on the grounds that governments pursuing a precise policy and supported by the ruling classes appointed quite definite people – administrators, policemen, customs officials, etc. – to keep watch over the outflow of gold and silver?

In reality, it is completely impossible to separate the first interpretation from the second: at this point we reach concrete and fundamental reality. Matter as the receptacle of passivised practices is indissolubly linked to lived *praxis*, which simultaneously adapts to material conditions and inert significations, and renews their meaning, *re-constituting* them by transcending them, if only to transform them. At this level, the process of revelation is constitutive in the sense that it *realises* a unity which, without man, would be instantly destroyed. Spain was the living unity of an undertaking, and restored their value and meaning to the signs inscribed in a sector of matter: and, *at the same time*, it was a material entity, a set of geographical, geological and

44. Braudel, trans. Reynolds, p. 476.

climatological conditions which sustained and modified the institutional meanings which it created and, in this way, conditioned the *praxis* of the men who were subject to that *de facto* unity, even in the movement which enabled them to transcend it. At this level of the double, regressive and progressive, approach we find a new structure of the real dialectic: every *praxis* is a unifying and revelatory transcendence of matter, and crystallises in materiality as a signifying transcendence of former, already materialised, actions. And all matter conditions human *praxis* through the passive unity of prefabricated meanings. There are no material objects which do not communicate among themselves through the mediation of men; and there is no man who is not born into a world of humanised materialities and materialised institutions, and who does not see a general future prescribed for him at the heart of the movement of History.

In this way, society in its most concrete movement is shot through with passivity, and unceasingly totalises its inert multiplicities and inscribes its totalisation in inertia, while the material object, whose unity is thereby recreated, re-discovered and imposed, becomes a strange and living being with its own customs and its own movement. It is this point of view which enabled Braudel to write: 'The Mediterranean as a unit, with its creative space, the amazing freedom of its sea-routes (its automatic free trade as Ernest Labrousse called it), with its many regions, so different yet so alike, its cities born of movement . . .'[45] This is not a metaphor. To preserve its reality as a *dwelling* a house must be *inhabited*, that is to say, looked after, heated, swept, repainted, etc.; otherwise it deteriorates. This vampire object constantly absorbs human action, lives on blood taken from man and finally lives in symbiosis with him. It derives all its physical properties, including temperature, from human action. For its inhabitants there is no difference between the passive activity which might be called 'residence' and the pure *re-constituting praxis* which protects the house against the Universe, that is, which mediates between the exterior and the interior. At this level one can speak of 'the Mediterranean' as a real symbiosis of man and things, and as tending to petrify man in order to *animate* matter. Within a historical society, a definite economy based on particular types of exchange and, in the last analysis, on a particular kind of production, the Mediterranean, as a conditioned condition, emerges as a 'creative space'. *For* and *through* ships it expresses the

45. *Ibid.*, p. 1239.

freedom of its sea-routes, etc. In transcending his material condition man objectifies himself in matter through labour. This means that he loses himself for the sake of *the human thing*,[46] and that he can rediscover himself in the objective as the meaning for man of his product.

Two types of human mediation must, however, be distinguished. The first is communal, premeditated, synthetic *praxis* uniting men (whether exploited or not) in a single enterprise aimed at a single object. Such – to return to our example – was the *policy* of Philip II's government, in particular, in relation to precious metals. This concerted undertaking[47] led to the accumulation of ingots and coins in the depths of the crucible of Spain. Through this mediation matter directly produced its own idea. But this has nothing to do with philosophical or religious conceptions, constituted at the level of 'superstructures' as dead possibilities far removed from reality. The idea of the thing is in the thing, that is to say, it is the thing itself revealing its reality through the practice which constitutes it, and through the instruments and institutions which define it. In the sixteenth century, the use of colonial mines necessarily meant importing unprocessed products from the colonies into the metropolitan country, and therefore accumulating precious metals in Spain. But this very practice revealed gold and silver as commodities, and this, moreover, corresponded to the mercantilism of the age. Money revealed itself as a commodity because it was treated as a commodity: since the necessities of colonisation implied the accumulation of gold in the colonising country, it is obvious that the labour expended on transport defined gold *as real wealth*. But it is even more obvious that the density and material opacity of the object, its weight and brilliance also turned it into an autonomous substance which was apparently sufficient to itself; the physical reality of the coin proved its *bonitas intrinseca*.[48] Price became an intrinsic relation between the values of two commodities: that of the object you wished to buy and that of the monetary unit.

46. Hence the profundity of Zola's title for one of his most famous novels, *La Bête Humaine* – the humanised machine, man with his animal needs, man as prey to the machine and the machine acquiring a parasitic life from man.

47. In due course we will come back to these *collective undertakings* in so far as they *make* history. But we do not yet have the means to think them.

48. On the other hand it would not have occurred to anyone in 1792 to regard *assignats* (promissory notes) as commodities. However, the metalist theory being then at its height, they were regarded as fiduciary signs *backed by money-commodities* which themselves served to mediate between the note and the national wealth.

This *idea* of matter is naturalistic and materialistic in that it is matter itself producing its own idea. It is materialistic because it is simply the instrument itself conceived in its visible and tangible materiality; it is naturalistic because natural properties of the physical object are given as the source of its utility.[49] But, above all, it is *praxis* reverberating through a thing. Each *praxis* contains its own ideological justification: the movement of accumulation necessarily involves the idea that the accumulation of goods leads to prosperity; and since gold and silver are accumulated, it must be the case that the more ingots or coins you have, the richer you are. Thus the value of a unit must be constant, since wealth consists in the simple addition of monetary units. But is this *idea* of gold coins true? . . . or false? In fact, it is neither. In the importation process, the idea is gold revealing itself as a *precious metal*; but, at the same time, it is inert; it is not an invention of the mind, but a petrification of action. The idea is true *of* and *in* the coin, for the individual, for the moment, and as a direct connection between man and his product. But it becomes false, or incomplete, as soon as the play of recurrence totally falsifies the group's unitary, concerted undertaking. *Here*, and for this *particular* merchant, whatever the circumstances and however prices may fluctuate, it is still true that he will be *richer this evening* if he gets an extra thousand ducats. But *in the process as a whole* it is not the case that collectivities are enriched by the accumulation of monetary signs. Here, matter as passive activity and counter-finality contradicts its own idea through its movement.

These remarks bring us to the second type of human mediation, which is serial. In this case, the same or different men constitute themselves at the margins of the undertaking *as Others* in relation to the common *praxis*. In other words, the synthetic interiority of the group at work is penetrated by the reciprocal exteriority of individuals, in so

49. Marx wrote in *Capital*: 'To Hegel, the life-process of the human brain, *i.e.*, the process of thinking, which, under the name of "the Idea", he even transforms into an independent subject, is the demiurgos of the real world, and the real world is only the external, phenomenal form of "the Idea". With me, on the contrary, the ideal is nothing else than the material world reflected by the human mind, and translated into forms of thought'. ('Afterword to the Second German Edition', in *Capital*, Vol. I, trans. Moore and Aveling, London, Lawrence and Wishart, 1970, p. 19.) This is entirely correct, provided we add: and this material world has already transformed and translated human *praxis* into its own language, that is to say, into terms of inertia. The money-commodity is opaque matter in the head of a Spanish minister precisely to the extent that, *in the gold coin*, it is an idea.

far as this constitutes their material separation. In spite of customs barriers, prohibitions and police investigations, precious metals entered Spain only to leave it again: gold escaped across every frontier. First, there were illegal dealings: in this period, the Mediterranean world needed gold; trade was active and Sudanese gold was exhausted; and foreign merchants who had settled in Spain sent cash back to their own countries. Then there were legal outlets: imports of cereals and of certain manufactured products necessitated payment in cash. Finally, Spain's imperialist policy cost her dear, for the Netherlands swallowed up a large part of the Peruvian gold. So Braudel concludes that 'the Peninsula . . . acted as a reservoir for precious metals'.[50a] Indeed, in so far as frauds were perpetrated by *Others* (by and for foreigners), and in so far as Spanish imperialism was constituted as the policy of the Other in relation to money, in other words, in so far as the king was other than himself when he contradicted his own decisions, it becomes impossible to discern any *communal* action; there were only innumerable separate actions, without any concerted link. Whether they cheated individually or in small organised groups, the illegal operators did not usually know one another, since they were forced to act in secrecy; the king *did not know* his own contradiction; the purchase of corn and of essential products was immediately seen *from another* point of view in connection with the vital needs of Spain.

But these isolated actions had an exterior bond in the inert unity of the stock of gold and in the inert idea which was inscribed on every ingot. Precious metal presented itself as *the* wealth of Spain, that is to say, it appeared, through the legal activities of merchants and of the government, as a material synthetic power liable both to increase and to decrease. Thus the losses of gold were regarded by the Cortes *as a systematic impoverishment* of the country. The unity of the concerted process of accumulation gave matter its passive unity as wealth; and this material unity in its turn unified the amorphous growth in fraud and in imports. In this way, matter itself became the essential thing, and individuals disappeared unrecognised into inessentiality. What had to be stopped was the *outflow of gold*. This outflow *through the Other* became a spontaneous movement of matter as *Other*, in so far as it was, in its very humanisation, *Other than man*. But since it was Other through its inertia, through its molecular structure, and through the reciprocal exteriority of its parts, that is to say, *as matter*, it absorbed

50a. Braudel, *op. cit.*, p. 479

recurrence and made of it a sort of spontaneous resistance on the part of matter to the wishes and practices of men. In this case, inertia itself *merged with alterity*, and became a synthetic principle producing new forces. But these forces were negative: gold took on a 'life of its own' mediating between real *praxis*, whose unifying power and negativity it absorbed, and the mere succession of physical phenomena, whose dispersal in exteriority it re-affirmed. The characteristics of this magical *life*, which turns *praxis* back on itself and transforms ends into counter-ends, cannot be analysed here; but I will examine one example, which I shall call *bewitched quantity*.

The Spanish government accumulated gold, *yet* the gold flowed out. On this plane, we have first a positive, logical action of quantity: it seems, in short, that gold flowed out faster and more abundantly as the monetary potential of the country rose. Hence Braudel's metaphor: 'Spain was a reservoir'. If this action was negative, it was so only in relation to human undertakings. But this only means that the action's powers of destroying accumulation have to be seen *in the same light* as, for instance, the limits on the size of a galleon's cargo. If the galleon foundered, the shipwreck was due to the *positive* action of overloading; the *more* ingots it carried, the *more* it weighed. In reality this is not so clear, since any given current contains negativity. But, after all, a historian or an economist may use a physical symbol to describe the phenomenon as a whole.

However, it is the other aspect of the complex fact of 'accumulation-outflow' that we shall refer to as a 'bewitchment of quantity'. American wealth stayed for a while in Spain, and was then discharged into other Mediterranean countries; for nearly a century the Spanish reserves were reconstituted and increased by new imports. Here a contradiction arises between the material idea of the money-commodity and economic reality. The quantitative notion enters into the *idea*; if the value of the monetary unit is fixed, then the *greater* the sum, the *greater* its value. And as I have shown, this is always true *for the individual*. But, while *for him* every new quantity increases his wealth, in the national community it *devalues* the unit; and thus individual wealth constantly deteriorates in the hands of the merchant or the industrialist, and his own increasing prosperity is partially responsible. Without any doubt, there are physical laws stating functional relations between *two* quantities, one of which increases as the other diminishes. This is what allowed the metalists of the liberal period to present the phenomenon of devaluation in terms of a relation between two variables, the money-commodity and non-money commodities: if the quantity of money in circulation increases, then prices rise. But when the use-value of commodities – as well as their labour-value – remains fixed, then *ex hypothesi* the price rises solely because the value of the monetary unit has slumped. So we come back to this basic fact: the *value* of coins diminishes as they increase in number. Yesterday I had 5,000 ducats; today I have 10,000. Consequently *this* particular ducat, which has never left my pocket, has, without changing in nature, undergone a sort of deterioration or loss of power (always assuming, of course, that increase in wealth is related to the growth of reserves).

Apparently the rise of prices in Spain 'seemed mad at the time'. A ship of 500 tons was worth 4,000 ducats in the time of Charles V and 15,000 in 1612. Earl J. Hamilton[50b] has shown that 'the correlation between the rate of imports of precious metals from America and prices is so obvious that they seem to be connected by a physical, mechanical link. Everything was governed by the increase in the stock of precious metals.' This stock tripled in the course of the sixteenth century and the monetary unit lost two thirds of its value. In short, it was *partly* a matter of a mechanical bond; but there was *also* the dialectical action of the whole on its parts. For mechanical bonds, strictly speaking, are bonds of exteriority: the forces acting on an object are independent of each other, and the elements of a system are invariable. It is for precisely this reason that they can be treated as quantities: the whole does not act on the parts for the simple reason that there is no whole. There are ensembles or sums: relations change, but the terms they relate are not modified by these changes.

In the case of the price-rises, however, we find what might be called a phantom totality; in other words, the sum acts negatively on its parts *as if it were a whole*. As we have seen, the increase in reserves governed the devaluation of each unit. So the elements are constantly conditioned by their relations. But still, such a relation appears quantitative; in fact, it is a relation between quantities. But this relation of exteriority is eroded by a relation of interiority. This will be even clearer if we put the phenomenon back into the temporality of *praxis* instead of confining it to the timeless present of mechanism. A future then appears: inside the concerted action, which defines itself, as we have seen, in terms of its future totality, and which therefore takes the form of a

50b. Cf. Earl J. Hamilton, *American Treasure and the Price Revolution in Spain, 1501–1650*, Harvard, 1934. [Ed.]

totalisation, the process of devaluation itself becomes a movement, whose future (the prospect of an even larger increase of reserves) determines the present itself and the *praxis* of groups or individuals (this is why it later became possible to speculate 'bearishly'). Ultimately, devaluation came to the Spaniards from the future, and they could foresee it. Admittedly, the metalist theory caused confusion in the sixteenth century, and merchants did not realise that the increase in reserves governed the economy as a whole. On the other hand, they did realise that prices would continue to rise. They realised this because they extrapolated from the rise itself: and *as a continuing process* it projected its own future through them.

Various acts and decisions followed from this: they would have to protect themselves against the present danger, but without losing sight of the continually worsening situation; in particular, industrialists would try to keep wages down. Wages in Spain (taking 1571–1580 = 100 as base) stood at 127.84 in 1510, and after several ups and downs reached 91.31 in 1600. Thus price rises, through the mediation of *praxis in alterity* (for the limitation of wages was not achieved by the government, but was the result of innumerable private initiatives[51]) produced far-reaching changes in other sectors of society. There was as yet no concerted *praxis* which could oppose these changes. Lacking the means to defend themselves, workers were controlled by an iron law, which *also* reveals to us the action of quantity *as totalisation*. When wages rocketed again in 1611 (130.56), this was because poverty and epidemics had 'considerably reduced the population of the Peninsula'.

This shows us three things. First, the action of the employers, like that of the Chinese peasants, produced the opposite of what they hoped for. By lowering the standard of living they placed the population at the mercy of famine and epidemics, and thereby brought about a man-power crisis. Secondly, the masses, 'atomised' as they were by their lack of political unity, were *materialised* by the forces of massification. Here we can see them in their mechanical reality, for the organic and human aspect of each of them did not stop their relation to others being purely molecular *from the point of view of the defence of wages*. The isolation of everyone resulted in the ensemble of wage-earners being constituted as a vast, externally conditioned inert system. At this level,

---

51. Of course, it expresses a class attitude; but we are not yet equipped to think the action and interests of a class. See below.

this shows that inanimate matter is not defined by the actual substance of the particles composing it (which may be inert or living, inanimate or human), but by their relations among themselves and to the universe. We can also observe here, in this elementary form, the Nature of reification. It is not a metamorphosis of the individual into a thing, as is often supposed, but the necessity imposed by the structures of society on members of a social group, that they should live the fact that they belong to the group and, thereby, to society as a whole, as a molecular statute. What they experience or do *as individuals* is still, immediately, real *praxis* or human labour. But a sort of mechanical rigidity haunts them in the concrete undertaking of living and subjects the results of their actions to the alien laws of totalising addition. Their objectification is modified externally by the inert power of the objectification of others. Thirdly, it is materiality which opposes materiality: depopulation increases the value of the individual. This relation is the reverse of that which we found to apply to money: in this case *less* creates *more*. Here again it would be pointless to try and establish a functional relationship between the number of human commodities and their wages. For, from this point of view, the reality of the man-thing, that is to say, his instrumentality, is already his labour, decomposed, detotalised and divided into the *external* atoms of hours of labour; and the only reality of the hour of labour is social: the price it fetches.[52] Thus abundance produces devaluation, and consequently human material becomes scarce; therefore scarcity revalues social molecules. In this example, increasing scarcity plays the same role as a growth of monetary reserves: through the mediation of supply and demand, numerical decrease acts on its units as a totalisation by increasing the quantity of each of them. The possibility of being added up as discrete amounts, that is to say, the fact of *not being together*, becomes *a kind of bond of interiority* for the workers. A double transformation has taken place: the atomised group has become a mechanical system, but the pure exteriority of the summation has become a human or pseudo-human totality, and acts against employers *in the manner* of a general strike.[53]

52. One of the mystifications of surplus value is that the dead time of working hours is substituted for the concrete, human time of real labour, that is, of a totalising, human undertaking. Marx says this, though without stressing it. We shall return to it elsewhere.

53. This transformation of matter and materialisation of the human in the individual himself is also to be found in marginalism. From this point of view,

The process as a whole retained a human meaning in Spain because, in a way, everything from the outflow of gold to the outbreak of epidemics, including the price rises, can be regarded as the result of the deliberate and persistent practice of monetary accumulation. In the other Mediterranean countries, however, precious metal appeared, through various individual frauds, *as an invasion*. Governments had no legal means of encouraging the influx of money; the most they could do was to close their eyes to this automatic accumulation. In this case, money appeared in its material dispersal, in small separate sums[54] or on the occasion of legal transactions, but with no other relation than temporal co-existence. Once again, the unity is human: the 'hunger for gold'. But this means a diffuse need on the part of Mediterranean industry and trade, felt *through* individuals unknown to one another. The unity was not a *lived reality* for anyone; it was a material reality expressed by a cloud of particular demands. In a sense, every merchant

---

personal desires and needs are objectified and alienated in the use-values of the thing in which they become quantities. But, at the same time, the 'units' (*doses*) are no longer forced to co-exist like coins in a stocking; or rather, their co-existence becomes an internal relation. The 'marginal unit' – that with the lowest use-value – determines the value of all the others. And this is not a real synthesis, but a phantom interiorisation. In a real synthesis, the relation would establish itself between real, concrete and individuated parts. In marginalism, *the final unit could be any one of them*. Any of my ten gold coins can be regarded as the one which I shall use last; each of the employer's ten workers can be regarded as *the last one*, and his labour can always be seen in terms of its *marginal productivity*. But what makes this link of interiority commutative is the materialisation of need. It is this which, through the decomposition due to Gossen's law, impregnates the sum of marginal *units* with its unitary project. The truth of marginalism does not lie *outside*, in pure quantity; nor does it lie *inside*, in the 'psychological': it lies in the dialectical uncovering of a constant exchange between interiority and exteriority which bases a pseudo-mathematics on a pseudo-psychology and crystallises the lived time of satisfied need in a hidden ordinalism of cardinals. This pseudo-mathematics is in fact more like a logistic. There is nothing to prevent the construction of a symbolism once some universal relations of pseudo-interiority have been defined. It is sufficient that exteriority should be present somewhere. It is the true interiority of relations – that is to say, the individuated part's concrete membership of the whole – which is always absolutely unamenable to symbolisation. In other words, certain moments of the dialectic can be expressed algebraically; but the dialectic itself in its real movement lies beyond any mathematics.

54. 'In 1554 . . . Don Juan de Mendoza searched the passengers travelling on his galleys from Catalonia to Italy. The result was the confiscation of 70,000 ducats, most of it on Genoese merchants,' (Braudel, *op. cit.*, p. 478.)

who demanded money realised the totalisation of the economy outside himself in institutions and social structures. Thus the influx of
money was both *summoned* and *suffered*: an attraction was surrendered
to like an invasion. The attraction was concrete and active when it
affected individuals or particular companies; but in the case of a whole
city or State it was passively suffered. Thus, if it is true that the State
can be viewed as the destiny of every citizen, then, conversely, in the
milieu of recurrence and alterity the atomised ensemble of citizens (at
least, of members of the merchant bourgeoisie) appears as the destiny
of the State. On the Mediterranean markets, Spanish ducats and silver
réals were at a premium, and they were even worth more than money
minted in the country in question. A form of Spanish presence and
hegemony were imposed through them and through the price rises
they brought about. We need not labour the point, but it should also
be noted how, through Spanish money, the social reality of the bourgeois class imposed itself as an intolerable constraint on the world of
the workers. But the bourgeoisie was its own victim: as a class it
suffered from the dealings of its members. Bankers and manufacturers
were hit hard by inflation. It is indisputable that through this monetary
revolution the Mediterranean world, violently *impeded* in its economic
development, learned the fatality of its own decadence.

What can we learn from this rapid survey? *First*, that significations
are *composed* of matter alone. Matter retains them as inscriptions and
gives them their true efficacity. In losing their human properties,
human projects are engraved in Being, their translucidity becomes
opacity, their tenuousness thickness, their volatile lightness permanence. They *become Being* by losing their quality as lived events; and in
so far as they are Being they cannot be dissolved into knowledge even
if they are deciphered and known. Only matter itself, beating on
matter, can break them up. The meaning of human labour is that man
is reduced to inorganic materiality in order to act materially on matter
and to change his material life. Through trans-substantiation, the
project inscribed by our bodies in a thing takes on the substantial
characteristics of the thing without altogether losing its original
qualities. It thus possesses an inert future within which we have to
determine our own future. The future comes to man through things in
so far as it previously came to things through man. Significations as
passive impenetrability come to replace man in the human universe:
he delegates his powers to them. They affect the entire material universe both by contact and by passive action *at a distance*. This means

not only that they have been inscribed in Being, but also that Being has been poured into the mould of significations. It also means, however, that these heavy, inert objects lie at the basis of a community whose bonds are, *in part*, bonds of interiority. It is through this interiority that one material element can act on another from a distance; for example, the fall in the output of American mines put an end to inflation in the Mediterranean towards the middle of the seventeenth century. Through such modifications, however, an element may help to break the bond of interiority which unites men to one another.

From this point of view, it is possible to accept both Durkheim's maxim and 'treat social facts as things', and the response of Weber and many contemporaries, that 'social facts are not things'. That is to say, social facts are things in so far as *all things* are, directly or indirectly, social facts. The foundation of the synthetic growth of wealth must be sought not, as it was by Kant, in a synthetic *a priori* judgement, but rather in an inert collection of significations *in so far as they are forces*. To the extent, however, that these forces are forces of inertia, that is to say, to the extent that they are communicated by and to matter *from the outside*, they introduce exteriority in the form of passive unity as *a material bond of interiority*. Thus materialised *praxis* (the minted coin, etc.) has the effect of uniting men precisely to the extent that it separates them by imposing on every one a meaningful reality infinitely richer and more contradictory than they anticipated individually. Materialised practices, poured into the exteriority of things, impose a common destiny on men who know nothing of one another, and, at the same time, by their very being, they reflect and reinforce the separation of individuals. In short, alterity comes to things through men and comes back to men from things in the form of atomisation: it was the Other that produced the outflows of gold. But gold, as an inert dispersal of monetary units, imbibed this alterity and became Other than man; through it, alterity was reinforced in everyone. However, as this alterity became the unity of an object or process (Gold, the Outflow of Gold), and as the unity arose within a human dispersal *both* as a community of destiny *and* as a conflict of interests, as a project of union and as lived separation, it became, for everyone, a synthetic determination of each in relation to all and, *consequently*, a more or less antagonistic connection between men. Thus worked matter reflects our activity back to us as inertia, and our inertia as activity, our interiority with the group as exteriority and our exteriority as a determination of interiority. In worked matter, the living is transformed into the mechanical, and the mechanical is raised to a kind of parasitic life; it is our inverted reflection, and in it, to make use of a celebrated phrase of Hegel's, 'Nature appears as the Idea in the form of Otherness'. There is, simply, no Idea here at all, but only material actions performed by individuals. Matter is this changing reflection of exteriority and interiority only within a social world which it surrounds completely and penetrates, in so far as it is *worked*.

If materiality is everywhere and if it is indissolubly linked to the meanings engraved in it by *praxis*, if a group of men can act as a quasi-mechanical system and a thing can produce its own idea, what becomes of *matter*, that is to say, Being totally without meaning? The answer is simple: it does not appear *anywhere* in human experience. At any moment of History things are human precisely to the extent that men are things. A volcanic eruption destroys Herculaneum; in a way, this is man destroying himself by the volcano. It is the social and material unity of the town and its inhabitants which, within the human world, confers the unity of an event on something which without men would perhaps dissolve into an indefinite process without meaning.

Matter could not be matter except for God and for pure matter, which is absurd. But does this lead us back to dualism? Not at all. We situate man in the world, and we simply note that for and through man this world cannot be anything but human. But the dialectic is precisely a form of monism, in that oppositions appear to it as moments which are posited for themselves for an instant before bursting. If we were not wholly matter, how could we act on matter, and how could it act on us? If man were not a specific entity which lives its condition in totalising transcendence, how could there *be* a material world? How could we conceive of the general possibility of any activity whatever? We always experience material reality as a threat to our lives, as resistance to our labour, as a limit to our knowledge and also as actual or possible instrumentality. But we experience it *in society*, where inertia, automatism and impenetrability act as a brake on our action, as well as in inert objects which resist our efforts. In both cases we experience this passive force within a process of signifying unification. Matter eludes us precisely to the extent that it is given *to us* and *in us*. The universe of science is a strict chain of *significations*. These are produced by practice and return to it in order to illuminate it. But each of them appears as *temporary*; even if it is still in the system tomorrow, the permanent possibility of the overthrow of the ensemble will modify it. The monism which *starts from the human world* and *situates* man in

Nature is the monism of materiality. This is the only monism which is realist, and which removes the *purely theological* temptation to contemplate Nature 'without alien addition'.[55] It is the only monism which makes man neither a molecular dispersal nor a being apart, the only one which *starts* by defining him by his *praxis* in the general milieu of animal life, and which can transcend the following two true but contradictory propositions: all existence in the universe is material; everything in the world of man is human.

But how can we ground *praxis*, if we treat it as nothing more than the inessential moment of a radically non-human process? How can it be presented as a real material totalisation if the whole of Being is totalised through it? Surely man would become what Walter Biemel, in his commentary on Heidegger, calls 'the bearer of the Opening of Being'.[56] This is not a far fetched comparison. The reason why Heidegger payed tribute to Marxism is that he saw Marxist philosophy as a way of showing, as Waelhens says (speaking of Heideggerian existentialism), 'that Being is Other in me . . . (and that) man . . . is himself only through Being, which is not him.'[57] But any philosophy which subordinates the human to what is Other than man, whether it be an existentialist or Marxist idealism, has hatred of man as both its basis and its consequence: History has proved this in both cases. There is a choice: either man is primarily himself, or he is primarily Other than himself. Choosing the second doctrine simply makes one a victim and accomplice of real alienation. But alienation presupposes that man *is primarily action*. Servitude is based on freedom; the human relation of exteriority is based on the direct bond of interiority as the basic type of human relation. Man lives in a universe where the future is a thing, where the idea is an object and where the violence of matter is the 'midwife of History'. But it is man who invests things with his own *praxis*, his own future and his own knowledge. If he could encounter

55. Friedrich Engels, *Dialectics of Nature*, p. 198. See above, p. 27, n. 9.

56. Walter Biemel, *Le Concept du Monde chez Heidegger*, Paris, 1950, pp. 85–6. Biemel adds that, in his writings after *Sein und Zeit*, 'Heidegger begins with Being and ends up with an interpretation of man' (*Ibid.*). This method brings him close to what we have called the external materialist dialectic. It, too, begins with Being (Nature without alien addition) and ends up with man; it too regards knowledge-reflection as 'an opening to Being (*l'Étant*) maintained in man by the Been (*l'Été*).'

57. Alphonse de Waelhens, *Phénoménologie et Vérité, essai sur l'évolution de l'idée de vérité chez Husserl et Heidegger*, Paris, Collection Épiméthée, 1953, p. 16.

pure matter in experience, he would have to be either a god or a stone; and in either case, it *would not affect him*: either he would produce it out of the incomprehensible fulguration of his intuitions, or else *action* would disappear and be replaced by mere energy equations. The only temporal movement would be decay, that is to say, an inverted dialectic moving from the complex to the simple, from the concrete wealth of the earth to the indifferentiation of a perfect equilibrium: in short there would be involution and dissolution instead of evolution.

In our example we saw how things can absorb the whole of human activity, and then materialise and return it: it could not be otherwise. Nothing happens to men or to objects except in their material being and through the materiality of Being. But man is precisely the material reality from which matter gets its human functions. Every effect of Spanish money was a transformation and reflection of human activity: wherever we find that an *action of gold* disrupts human relations without being willed by anyone, we discover an underlying profusion of human undertakings, directed towards individual or collective ends and metamorphosed through the mediation of things. In the indissoluble couple of 'matter' and 'human undertakings', each term modifies the other: the passive unity of the object determines material circumstances which the individual or group transcend by their *projects*, that is, *by a real and active totalisation* aimed at changing the world. This totalisation, however, would be pure negation if it were not inscribed in Being, if Being did not take hold of it as soon as it occurred, so as to transform it again into the pseudo-totality of the tool, and relate it as a finite determination to the whole universe. The totalising extraction from inert meanings involves a more or less profound and explicit decoding and understanding of the signifying ensemble. A project *awakens* significations; it momentarily restores their vigour and true unity in the transcendence which finally engraves this totality in some completely inert but already signifying material, which might be iron, marble or language, and which others animate with their movement from beneath, like stage-hands creating waves by crawling around under a piece of canvas. Everything changes and becomes confused; different meanings come together and merge in a passive recomposition which, by substituting the fixity of Being for the indefinite progress of the actual totalisation, encloses the totality-object within its limits and produces the ensemble of contradictions which will set it in opposition to the Universe. For it is not comprehension which solidifies meanings; it is Being.

In this sense, the materiality of things or institutions is the radical negation of invention or creation; but this negation comes to Being through the project's negation of previous negations. Within the 'matter-undertaking' couple, man causes himself to be negated by matter. By putting his meanings (that is to say, the pure totalising transcendence of previous Being) into matter, man allows himself to lend it his negative power, which impregnates materiality and transforms itself into a destructive power.[58] Thus negation, as a pure extraction from Being and an unveiling of the real in the light of a rearrangement of previous givens, becomes an inert power to crush, demolish and degrade. In the most adequate and satisfactory tool, there is a hidden violence which is the reverse of its docility. Its inertia always allows it to 'serve some other purpose', or rather, it *already* serves some other purpose; and that is how it creates a new system. Those who, in their turn, transcend this system must therefore have a project with a double aim: to resolve the existing contradictions by a wider totalisation, and to diminish the hold of materiality by substituting tenuousness for opacity, and lightness for weight; in other words it must create immaterial matter.

Through the contradictions which it carries within it, worked matter therefore becomes, *by* and *for* men, the fundamental motive force of History. In it the actions of all unite and take on a meaning, that is to say, they constitute for all the unity of a common future. But *at the same time* it eludes everyone and breaks the cycle of repetition because this future, always projected in a framework of scarcity, is non-human; its finality in the inert milieu of dispersal either changes into a counter-finality or, while remaining itself, produces a counter-finality for some or all. It therefore produces a necessity for change *of itself*, and as a synthetic summary of all actions, that is, of all inventions, creations,

58. This is what primitive man immediately realises when he dreads and reveres his own power, become maleficent and turned against him in the arrow or the axe. In this sense, there is nothing surprising about religious ceremonies in which a supernatural power is conferred on weapons whose effectiveness is shown every day by technique and experience. For this effectiveness is *both* a crystallisation of some human labour (the labour *of an other*) *and* a solidified indication of future behaviour. This fusion of the Other and himself in a kind of eternity, this possession of the hunter by the technical capacities of the blacksmith and, in the end, the petrification of both – primitive man sees in these both a beneficent power and a threat. He guesses at the hidden hostility of worked matter beneath its instrumentality. As has been known for a long time, this contradiction is characteristic of the relation to the sacred.

etc. It is not only the social memory of a collectivity, but also its transcendent but interior unity, the totality made up of all its dispersed activities, the solidified threat of the future and the synthetic relation of alterity by which men are connected. It is both its own Idea and the negation of the Idea, and in any case the perpetual enrichment of all. Without it, thoughts and actions would disappear, for they are inscribed in it as a hostile power, and it is through it that they act materially or mechanically on men and on things, and in it that they are subjected to the mechanical action of things and of reified ideas. A coin as a human object in circulation is subject to the laws of Nature through other human objects, such as caravels, waggons, etc. These laws of Nature are *unified in it* in so far as its circulation is a parasitic inertia which vampirises human actions. Through this changing unity of natural laws, as through the strange human laws which result from circulation, it produces an inverted unity of men. This can be summarised in one word: *praxis* as the unification of inorganic plurality becomes the *practical* unity of matter. Material forces gathered together in the passive unity of tools or machines *perform actions*: they *unify* other inorganic dispersals and thereby impose a material unification on the plurality of men. The movement of materiality, in fact, derives from men. But the *praxis* inscribed in the instrument by past labour defines behaviour *a priori* by sketching in its passive rigidity the outline of a sort of mechanical alterity which culminates in a division of labour. Precisely because matter mediates between men, men mediate between materialised *praxes*, and dispersal orders itself into a sort of quasi-synthetic hierarchy reproducing the particular ordering imposed on materiality by past labour in the form of a human order.

At the level which we have now come to, our investigation has already reached richer meanings, but is still abstract. Obviously the human world contains more than this non-humanity; and it will be necessary to pass through further layers of intelligibility before completing our dialectical investigation. Nonetheless, whatever its relations with other moments of the investigation, it is correct to present this moment as the determination of a specific structure of real History, namely the domination of man by worked matter. But, in so far as we have been able to follow the movement of this domination in our example, we have seen the expression of that terrible aspect of man in which he is the product of his product. (We have also seen that, at this stage of the inquiry, he is nothing more than this.) We must now study this within the unity of this moment of the investigation and in close connection with the non-human humanisation of materiality. In effect we have been inquiring into what type of intelligibility can be attributed to those curious synthetic everyday locutions, which we think we understand, in which finality and necessity, *praxis* and inertia, etc., are united in an indissoluble totalisation. We also claimed that these locutions apply *equally* to human action and to the 'behaviour' of worked matter, as if man in so far as he is produced by his product and matter in so far as it is worked by man approached total equivalence through the gradual elimination of all their original differentiations; and even as if that equivalence, once realised, allowed us, by using these notions, to designate and to think objects which appear different but are of the same nature, one of them being a man or a group of men, and the other, for instance, a railway system or a group of machines. But this is not how it always is. Normally, at the present level of our investigation, the human object and the inanimate tool do not *become identical*; rather, an indissoluble symbiosis is set up between the humanised matter of the material ensembles and the dehumanised men of the corresponding human ensemble. Thus we use phrases like 'the factory' or 'the business' to refer either to a particular complex of instrumentality, surrounded by walls which materially determine its unity, or to the personnel within them, or to both at once in deliberate indifferentiation. But this totalisation, in the sense in which we understand it here, can occur only to the extent that the material and the personal factors are adapted to one another, without being strictly equivalent. Indeed, if individuals, as products of their labour, were simply free *praxis* organising matter – which, amongst other things, they really are at a more superficial level – the bond of interiority would remain univocal and it would be impossible to speak of the very distinctive unity which expresses itself in the social field as passive activity, as active passivity, and as *praxis* and destiny. In order that the social object thus constituted should have a being, it is necessary for man and his product to exchange their qualities and statutes in the process of production itself. Soon we shall examine the being of primitive social objects; but we must now turn to man in so far as he is dominated by worked matter.

In this respect, man is still the man of need, of *praxis* and scarcity. But, in so far as he is dominated by matter, his activity is no longer directly derived from need, although this remains its fundamental basis: it is occasioned in him, from the outside, by worked matter as the practical exigency of the inanimate object. In other words, the object designates its man as one who is expected to behave in a certain way. In the case of a circumscribed social and practical field, the worker's need and the necessity of producing his life (or of selling his labour power so as to purchase his subsistence) are sufficient to create the unifying and totalising tension of the field for everyone. But this need is not necessarily present 'in person'; it is simply that to which the *praxis* as a whole refers. On the other hand, in so far as this social field (the factory or workshop, for example) is unified by all the others by means of an already constructed hierarchy, the individual worker is subjected to this unification in things themselves, as an alien power and, at the same time, as his own power. (This is quite apart from the structure of alienation, strictly so called, in so far as this is linked to capitalist exploitation.) And this unification, which relates him both to Others and to himself as Other, is quite simply the collective unity of labour (of the workshop, the factory, etc.), to the extent that he can grasp it concretely only from the point of view of his own labour. Indeed, if he were to *observe* other men working, his knowledge of the unification of their movements would be abstract. But he lives in his own labour as the labour of Others, of all the Others of whom he is one, to the extent that the general movement of the collective *praxis* awakens the practical meanings which were *given to* the tools by labour which was completed in other times and places.

A tool is in fact a *praxis* which has been crystallised and inverted by the inertia which sustains it, and this *praxis* addresses itself in the tool to anyone: a brace and bit and a monkey-wrench designate me as much as my neighbour. But when these designations are addressed to me, they generally remain abstract and purely logical, because I am a petty-bourgeois intellectual, or rather, because I am designated as a petty-bourgeois intellectual by the very fact that these relations remain pure, dead possibilities. However, in the practical field of actual common labour, the skilled worker is really and directly designated by the tool or the machine to which he is assigned. The *method of using* the machine, as established in the past by its producer, does not in fact designate him any more than it does me; it is only a particular way of being useful, and this constitutes the object itself, whoever uses it. But through this dead designation of inertia, the group of workers designates him, to the extent that the labour of all depends on the labour of each.

But, as Marx has shown, the passive materiality of the machine realises itself as the *negation* of this human interdependence, and interposes itself between labourers to precisely the extent that it is indispensable for their work; the living solidarity of the group is destroyed even before it can take shape. What one man expects of another, if their relation is human, is defined in reciprocity, for expectation is a human act. There can only be such a thing as *passive exigency* between them *if*, within a complex group, divisions, separations and the rigidity of the organs of transmission replace living bonds by a mechanical statute of materiality (we shall come back to this point later). For it is possible for *praxis* as such to unite itself to *praxis* in reciprocal action, and for everyone to propose his own end in so far as he recognises that of the Other; but no *praxis* as such can even formulate an imperative, simply because exigency does not enter into the structure of reciprocity.[59]

As for *sovereignty*, which, as we shall see, is possessed by the third party, it is, as I shall try to show, nothing but freedom positing itself for itself. On the other hand, the expectation of others, affecting the individual labourer through the machine, is qualified by the machine itself. Simply by virtue of its structure, the machine says what task is to be performed. But even while human expectation – at least provided it achieves self-consciousness, and the group is not too large – relates to the worker *in person*, with his name and character, etc., the machine absorbs and depersonalises it, translating it into anyone's expectation; that is, into the expectation of the worker himself, in so far as he is not *himself*, but is defined by a universal pattern of behaviour, and is therefore other. In this way, it also makes his comrades Other than themselves, since they are merely the men who happen to be serving other machines, and by means of its demand it refers to the demand made on Others by other machines; so that it ends up as a group of machines imposing a demand on *any* men, regardless of who they are. But this demand on the part of a tool designed to be used in a particular way, with particular rhythms, etc., is also transformed by its very materiality: it becomes *exigency* through receiving the double quality of alterity and passivity.

Exigency, in fact, whether in the form of an order or a categorical imperative, constitutes itself in everyone as other than him. (He cannot modify it, but simply has to conform to it; it is beyond his control, and he may change entirely without it changing; in short, it does not

---

59. We shall see below how the individual can affect himself with inertia by means of a pledge; exigency then becomes possible.

enter into the dialectical movement of behaviour.) In this way, exigency constitutes him as other than himself. In so far as he is characterised by *praxis*, his *praxis* does not originate in need or in desire; it is not the process of realising his project, but, in so far as it is constituted so as to achieve an alien object, it is, in the agent himself, the *praxis* of another; and it is another who objectifies himself in the result. But in order to escape this dialectical movement from the objective to the objective which, as it progresses, totalises everything, *praxis* itself must occupy the domain of inertia and exteriority. What characterises the imperative is perseverance through inertia; in short, materiality. An order is only an order in so far as it can no longer be changed. (Whoever issued it has gone away; one can only carry it out.) Precisely for this reason the basic form of exigency lies in the inert expectation on the part of the instrument or material, designating the worker as *the Other who is expected to do certain things*. If we put this exigency in a concrete context, that is, if we realise that the broken solidarity of the workers is really their common subservience to production, and remember that the tension of the practical field originates fundamentally and more or less directly in need, then we can conclude, without even going into the specifically capitalist structure of exigency[60] (labour/commodity), that all forms of imperative come to man through worked matter, to the extent that it *signifies* him in his generality within the social field. In other words, at the level under consideration, the univocal relation of interiority changes into an interior relation of false reciprocity: man as Other affirms his pre-eminence over man through matter. Thus the machine *demands* (*exige*) to be kept in working order and the practical relation of man to materiality becomes *his response* to the exigencies of the machine.

Of course, it is easy to object that the inert matter of which the machine consists cannot demand anything at all. However, to the extent that, as I have said, we *never* make contact with anything but worked and socialised matter, this argument ceases to have any value. A given machine in a society which already has a capitalist structure, is not only the real product of real labour (by unknown workers); it is also, as capital, the private property of an individual or group which is structured as a function of property; and it is the possibility for these men of producing a certain quantity of goods in a given time, through other

60. In socialist societies this description would at least apply to particular factories in particular circumstances.

men animating it with their labour power; and, for the manual labourers, it is the very object of which they are the objects and in which their actions are inscribed in advance. But this machine arises in the milieu of industrial competition: it is the product of this competition and serves to intensify it. Competition as recurrent antagonism determines even the employer as *Other than himself* in so far as it determines his action as a function of the Other and of the Other's action on Others. It was imported into France *as Other*, and was to inaugurate new destinies and antagonisms *for all* and *between all*. (Consider, for example, the first cautious importation of English machinery around 1830 by *a few* producers in the textile industry.) These defined classes and milieux within this perspective by necessarily constituting them *as Others*. (We shall see that about 1830 labourers and artisans, disqualified and proletarianised by these machines, lived their destinies like a conjuring trick which reduced them to ruins and completely transformed them without touching them.) There can be no doubt that a particular machine of a particular type, which by its form expresses the techniques and social structures of the age, is, *in itself*, and as a means of realising, maintaining and expanding a certain sector of production, exactly *what I said*, namely, *the Other* in the milieu of the Other. Nor can it be doubted that, in this milieu, it has already absorbed into itself both the tensions of competition, so as to reflect them to the employer *as exigency*, and those of need and social constraint so as to turn them into exigencies in relation to the workers.

In this way, every object, in so far as it exists within a given economic, technical and social complex, will in its turn become exigency through the mode and relations of production, and give rise to other exigencies in other objects. The basic intelligibility of this transformation *at a distance* of one material object by others naturally lies in the serial action of men; but this intelligibility requires precisely that the action of man should be constituted as inessential, that is, that it should take note of its own impotence and make itself a *means* to the accomplishment of some non-human end – that of worked matter in so far as it presents itself as *passive activity, and sole producer of goods* – in the name of which it appears as a social force, as a social power and as unconditioned exigency.

Admittedly it is logically and abstractly possible to consider material exigencies as hypothetical imperatives, such as 'If you want your wages . . .' or 'If productivity is to be increased and the number of workers reduced . . .' But this abstract view belongs in the milieu of analytical Reason. It is true that the possibility of taking one's own life is not given with life itself, the only reality of which is the perpetuation of its being. However, it appears in definite historical and social conditions. For example, for the Indian population it was the result of the establishment of Europeans in Central and South America, which brought about a transformation of the mode of labour and of life of the conquered, enslaved peoples and, through their very organism and its perpetual maladaptation, led to a threat to their survival.[61]

Thus the hypothetical 'If you want your wages . . .' cannot appear concretely in anyone's *praxis* unless society itself has already threatened the lives of its members through the changes which it requires of them. In the milieu of organic life as the absolute positing of itself the sole aim of *praxis* is the indefinite reproduction of life. In so far as the means of subsistence are determined by society itself, together with the types of activity which will allow them to be procured either directly or indirectly, on the other hand, the vital tension of the practical field effectively results in exigency being presented as a categorical imperative. And to the extent that the employer, as we shall see, subordinates his *praxis* to his Being-outside-himself in the world under the common name of *interest* (such as a factory, property in the soil or what lies beneath it, or a group of machines), the imperative comes to him too from need itself, even if this need is not felt at the time or even directly brought into question. (For even if the employer is ruined, he is not necessarily unable to satisfy his needs or those of his family.)

However, we must also approach the object from the opposite direction. In so far as it is a categorical imperative for Others and in the milieu of the Other, of which every one is a part, it comes back to everyone as an imperative power which condenses in itself the whole of social dispersal reunited by the negation of materiality. Thus the categorical imperative, lived in the direct milieu of vital urgency, turns round and addresses everyone categorically as Other, that is to say, as a mediation between the material object and the imperative of Others. It might be said here that the imperative has a double – and doubly categorical – structure, because for everyone the tension of life sustains serial alterity, which reacts on it and conditions it. In this way, individuals in an organisation interiorise the exigency of matter and

---

61. It seems, in fact, that they suffered even more as a result of the abrupt change, *without transition*, from nomadic life to the settled labour of the peasant than as a result of defeat and servitude.

re-exteriorise it as the exigency of man. Through supervisors and inspectors, machines demand a particular rhythm of the worker: and it makes no difference whether the producers are supervised by particular *men* or whether, when the equipment allows it, the supervisors are replaced by a more or less automatic system of checks. In either case, material exigency, whether it is expressed through a machine-man or a human machine, comes to the machine through man to precisely the extent that it comes to man through the machine. Whether *in the machine*, as imperative expectation and as power, or *in man*, as mimicry (imitating the inert in giving orders), as action and coercive power, exigency is *always* both man as a practical agent and matter as a worked product in an indivisible symbiosis.

More precisely, *a new being* appears as the result of a dialectical process, in which the total materialisation of *praxis is* the negative humanisation of matter, and whose true reality transcends the individual as an isolated agent and inorganic matter as an inert and sealed reality, that is to say, *the labourer*. On this basis, we can comprehend how 'steam *initiated* the tendency towards larger factories', how 'the poor performance of locomotives on inclines of more than 2 per cent at first *compelled* new lines to follow water-courses and valleys' and how, among other factors, some of which were much more important, this characteristic of railways '*tended* to drain away the populations of the hinterland'. Of course, these material factors in no way depend either on God the Father or on the Devil: it is by and through men that these exigencies arise, and they would disappear if men did. But still, the example of the locomotive shows that the exigency of matter ends up by being extended to matter itself through men. Thus the very *praxis* of individuals or groups is altered in so far as it ceases to be the free organisation of the practical field and becomes the re-organisation of one sector of inert materiality in accordance with the exigencies of another sector of materiality. Even before it is made, an invention may, in certain circumstances, be an exigency of the *practico-inert Being* which we have defined. In so far as a mine is 'capital' which is progressively destroyed, and in so far as its owner is forced by the exigency of the object to open up new galleries, the net cost of the mineral extracted must increase.[62]

62. These exigencies were already *objective* in the social world of the sixteenth century, since Hero, Porta, Caus and Cardan all grasped them *practically*, in suggesting the use of steam.

But, in so far as coal had become the main exigency of an industrial world in the process of equipping itself, the necessity of 'devouring oneself' affected both the mine and its owner, in so far as they were *Others*, fused by demand into a common alterity. Common exigency, then, arose out of the mine, as if matter itself could interiorise the exigency of other material sectors as a new imperative. To reduce costs, water *had* to be removed from the deep galleries; and the labour of men and beasts was not sufficient for this. In the eighteenth century, the first steam pump, which was made in England, inscribed itself within a tradition of effort and research which was itself crystallised in material objects, in experiments to be *repeated* and meanings deposited in books. In other words, the exigency of matter working through its men ended by nominating the material object it required. Papin and Newcomen had defined that particular exigency, and had thereby established the schemata and general principles of the invention *before it was made*: in this way, sustained by the growing consumption of coal and the gradual exhaustion of certain galleries, it was the object itself, as defined but not yet made, which became an exigency of being. And, through competition, the exigency which put every engineer under an obligation to make one, became, *through Others*, a matter of urgency for all potential inventors: a pump had to be made *as quickly as possible*. So, when Watt constructed his steam-engine, it already existed and his invention was no more than an improvement involving the separate condensation chamber.

But this improvement was also a realisation, in that it was a means of increasing output – this being the justification for the industrial production of such machines. The same years (roughly the last decade of the eighteenth century) saw the appearance of other essential objects, in particular steamboats. The fundamental exigency determined similar exigencies in other sectors: it was negatively totalising, as inert matter must be. At the same time it produced *exigency-man*; that is, new generations, or certain groups within them, interiorised, as their own exigencies, the diffuse exigencies of materiality which previous generations had lived as *their limits*. The inventor is a technician who makes himself into an *exigency-man*, an inessential mediation between present materiality and the future it demands (*exige*). A man who invents a steam-engine must *himself be a steam-engine*, as an inert ensemble of known principles relating to it; he must himself be *the lack* of a sufficiently powerful pump, as the *old*, but still real, exigency of the mine, and the future objectification of past *praxis* in a realisation which demands realisation through the future. Thus we rediscover the dimensions of *praxis*, which was only to be expected, since everything is sustained by individual *praxis*. But through it coal produces its own means of extraction, by becoming the fuel and energy source for the machine which will make it possible to excavate new galleries.

The moment of *exigency* as inert, imposed finality makes it possible to conceive of the kind of negativity known as *objective contradiction*. We shall see that the deep structure of every contradiction lies in the opposition between human groups within a given social field. But at the level of technical ensembles of the *activity/inertia* type, contradiction is the counter-finality which develops within an ensemble, in so far as it opposes the process which produces it and in so far as it is experienced as negated exigency and as the negation of an exigency by the totalised ensemble of practico-inert Beings in the field. What must in fact be comprehended is that, at the level of practico-inert Being, counter-finalities are highly structured and become, through the mediation of certain groups which stand to benefit, *finalities against* (des *finalités contre*) others. And, at the same time, since each inert finality is both the exigency of the Other and Other reality, each of them is equally a *counter-finality*. The over-industrialisation of a country is a counter-finality for the rural classes who become proletarianised to precisely the extent that is is a finality for the richest landowners because it enables them to increase their own productivity. But within the ensemble of a nation it may, once a particular threshold has been passed, become a counter-finality in so far as the country is now further away from its new rural bases.[63] The transcendence of this contradiction *between things* will be found only in over-industrialisation itself – for example, in the development of a merchant fleet with bigger and faster ships and of a navy one of whose functions is to defend the trading ships. Here again, the transcendence is adumbrated by the contradiction itself; and, to this extent, we can rediscover this contradiction in a different form on the basis of the transcendence. Alternatively, the finality of a *praxis* can be presented as changing, for a group or class, into counter-finality *of its own accord* – within the context of the class struggle, no doubt, but still as a relatively autonomous development of the material fact itself.

There can be no doubt that the first industrial revolution (coal, iron,

---

63. Colonies, under-developed countries selling their corn in order to buy manufactured products, etc.

steam-engines, concentration of workers around towns, etc.) involved *air pollution* for the constantly growing urban populations. It goes without saying that the biological effects were essentially harmful to the workers, in the first place because their habitat and mode of work brought them closer to the sources of the pollution; and secondly, because their starvation wages forced them to work all the time so that they had to stay in the smoke of the factories year in year out; and lastly, because the poison would have more effect on exhausted and undernourished bodies. In this sense, this counter-finality simply reproduces the class struggle (whose existence we are assuming, though we have not yet established its intelligibility): it is *one aspect* of that struggle. All the same we must notice that air pollution presupposes the iron-coal complex and, although it is obvious that this complex conditions one particular aspect of the class struggle and no other, air pollution is *another* consequence of the complex, contemporaneous with the structuring of the class but of a different order.

And, in fact, pollution is also a counter-finality for the employer, or so, at least, one might think. Admittedly, he has sufficient means to spend his evenings and his Sundays out of town, in his country cottage. But still he does not breathe in less coal dust during the days. In a way, there was appreciably less inequality from the point of view of air pollution during working hours between the employer and the wage-earners, and between the office clerks and the labourers. Bourgeois children themselves suffered in their development from this pollution, which sometimes reached truly cataclysmic proportions. (For example, in 1930 in the Upper Meuse region an excessive concentration of noxious gas produced a suffocating cloud which spread throughout the whole region killing sixty-five people.)

Moreover, to stay with our example, coal fumes contain another definite counter-finality from the point of view of the employers. They are costly, as the following figures prove. In order to maintain the *normal* standard of cleanliness of any industrial city, Pittsburgh is committed to *extra* expenditure (over and above the average cleaning expenses for a city of its kind and with its population) amounting to 1,500,000 dollars for household washing, 7,500,000 dollars for general cleaning and 360,000 dollars for curtains. And in order to estimate the total cost we should have to add losses due to the corrosion of buildings, additional electricity consumption for those periods when concentrations of gas over the city make it necessary to switch on the lights in offices and workshops, etc.

So what is the difference between the bourgeoisie and the working class in this case? In the first place, from the beginnings of urban concentration the workers have been aware of the danger which threatens their lives. (The contrast is obvious for proletarianised peasants.) But before union organisations had been formed the demand for a hygiene policy was a luxury which the first resistance and combat groups could not afford: it was quite hard enough to prevent wages from falling. Besides, their impotence at that time made them prefer the factory, with all its *counter-finalities*, which allowed them to sell their labour power, to the disappearance of the factory, which would necessarily lead to the total destruction of dispensable groups. In the end, therefore, as a result of their situation at the time, counter-finality threw them back on the employers *as a universal exigency which constituted the employers as a special group to precisely the extent that they failed to satisfy it.* In other words, the nineteenth century industrialists, indifferent to the mortal dangers which threatened the working population, and to the real danger and even to the real costs that public squalor represented for them, were *truly* characterised as a special group by their refusal to constitute this effect of industrialisation as a universal counter-finality, though it could have been constituted as such through a well defined *praxis*. (Of course, *this* is not what made them a special group; but it was *in this*, amongst other things, that their distinctiveness was expressed.)

From the outset means were in fact available of lessening the pollution if not of ending it entirely. Franklin had already suggested that coal smoke could be reused, since it was really just incompletely consumed carbon. Ultimately, smoke expressed the limitations of the machine at this time. Ninety per cent of the heat generated was lost as the fuel escaped up the chimney. But the failure to see this human and technical exigency, or to see it and take it seriously, is *precisely* what characterises the *praxis* of the bourgeoisie at this time. (Today the ensemble of safety and health measures is due to union pressures; and in the most advanced countries, the initiative sometimes reverts to the employers, in so far as they want to increase the productivity of labour; but the problems in this case are different.) Mines, as capital subject to a gradual process of exhaustion, created the first employing class (*patronat*), a curious mixture of traditionalist prudence and of wastage (wastage of human lives, of raw materials and of energy). They were constituted as a class (in this particular respect) by a refusal to see the effects of air pollution *on the other class* as a counter-finality. But they

were constituted as an *archaic* type of industrialist (for us and in relation to us) by their indifference to the effects which this pollution
might have on themselves and by their refusal – which, as we have
seen, was not due to ignorance – to develop industrial techniques to
alleviate the situation.

Here we have the complexity of a practico-inert process: finality,
counter-finality discovered and suffered by particular powerless
groups, counter-finality denounced in theory but, in a particular period, never *recognised in practice* by the other groups which had the power
to alter the situation. Counter-finality can become an end for certain
ensembles: the first steam-engines were noisy, and engineers, Watt in
particular, tried to reduce the noise. But in a practico-inert ensemble
(for instance, the iron and coal 'complex', the first employers' class, or
the first appearances of mechanisation), noise, like the black smoke
which rose from the factory chimneys, demanded to be maintained as a
material affirmation of new-found human power, that is, of the power
of a new class produced in the context of a changing mode of production, and therefore *in opposition* both to landowners and to workers.
The counter-finality which *has to be removed* (though it is really a
counter-finality only for the exploited class, since it is the workers who
live amid the noise, whereas the employers merely *pass through it*),
becomes *a finality which had to be maintained*, and in this way it appears,
in the ensemble under consideration, as *negative exigency*, and itself
develops the ensemble of its 'advantages' and 'disadvantages' within
practical inertia as a series of contradictions (this reveals their original
active structure) which are *passive* (they are structured in exteriority).
'There are pros and cons.' At this negative level transcendence is
inconceivable. In the inert struggle of pros and cons, which takes
place outside everyone, in the milieu of alterity, there is either a
balance, or a victory for the pros (like a superior *weight* and not as a
totality which returns to its contradictory and enfolds it in itself), or
victory for the cons. Here we encounter another, slightly different
aspect of the indissoluble unity of the inert and of finality. To sum up,
the intelligibility of material contradictions within a developing process is due to the fact that, through negation as a material unity within
the social field, every finality is a counter-finality; and to the fact that,
on the other hand, to the extent that all movements of matter are
sustained and directed by men, every counter-finality is objectively,
at its own level, and from the point of view of particular practico-
inert ensembles, a finality.

(*ii*) *Interest*

A new characteristic of the symbiosis we are uncovering is what economists and some psychologists have called *interest*. In a way, this is merely a specific form of *exigency*, in particular conditions and amongst particular individuals or groups. Interest is being-wholly-outside-oneself-in-a-thing in so far as it conditions *praxis* as a categorical imperative. Considered in himself, in his simple, free activity, an individual has needs and desires, he is a project, he realises ends through his work; but in this fictitious abstract state, he has no *interest*; or rather, ends reveal themselves spontaneously in his *praxis* as objectives *which have to be* reached or tasks *which have to be* carried out, without any return into himself to link these tasks and objectives with subjective aims. And if, at the level of scarcity, he sees a man coming towards him as a threat to his life, it is *his life* which is at stake and which affirms itself by becoming objectified as violence (that is to say, which constitutes the Other as a being who is capable of doing harm as well as *being harmed*); but interest has no real existence either as motivation or as *stratification of the past*. Interest is a certain relation between man and thing in a social field. It may be that it reveals itself fully, in human history, only with what is called real property. But it exists in a more or less developed form wherever men live in the midst of a material set of tools which impose their techniques on them. In fact, the dialectical possibility of its existence is already given with the biological organism, since this already has its being-outside-itself-in-the-world, in so far as its possibilities of survival are given outside itself in its milieu.

The origin of interest, as an abstract foundation, is therefore the univocal relation of interiority which connects the human organism to its environment. But interest does reveal itself in the practico-inert moment of the investigation in so far as man constitutes himself in the exterior milieu as *this* particular practico-inert set of worked materials, while establishing its practical inertia within his real person. To take the clearest example, real bourgeois property, the first moment of the process is the identification of the being of the owner with the ensemble of his property. This ensemble – if for example it is a house with a garden – confers *human interiority* on the ensemble, by raising walls to hide his wealth from the world; through his very life, as we have seen, he communicates a certain unity to the ensemble; he lays out his memory in drawers or on tables, until in the end it is everywhere, as is the ensemble of his practices and habits; when everything is outside him, sheltered behind the walls, in rooms where each piece of furniture is the materialisation of a memory, one can say that his interior life (*la vie intérieure*) is literally none other than his home life (*la vie d'intérieur*) and that his thoughts are defined by the inert and changing relations between his various pieces of furniture. But at the same time the exteriority of the thing becomes his own human exteriority. The inert separation which encloses his intimate life as a signifying materiality between four walls constitutes him as a material molecule among molecules: the relation he has, on this level, with other human beings, taken as a social, institutionalised practice, is in effect the absolute negation of any relation of interiority in the positive guise of mutual respect for possessions (and consequently for private life). It then becomes possible for the proprietor to assert that 'human beings are impenetrable', because he has given them in his person the impenetrability of matter (that is to say, the impossibility of distinct bodies occupying the same place at the same time). What we have here is an everyday phenomenon of reification; but the proprietor will find his truth and reality more completely in the thing possessed, which already addresses him as his own visible and tangible essence, the more he experiences, in his direct relation with this metamorphosis into an inanimate power, his mechanical isolation in the midst of a molecular dust.

However, this dual, complementary aspect of private property is as yet no more than an abstraction: this property exists in a particular society, at a particular moment of History, and is dependent on the institutions of this society, which are themselves based on the development of the mode of production. Beneath the molecular relation between owners, we discover their serial conditioning within a structured social field and within a certain general movement of History. For example, in the case of rural properties, it may happen that the movement of investments which have been diverted, for other historical reasons, from agricultural enterprises results in disposable capital being concentrated for a time in rapidly developing industries. At this stage, agriculture, deprived of capital, will stick at the same technical level, the yield of the land will not increase, nor, consequently, its value. But by gradually improving the means of communication the development of industry may have the effect of raising land values. And if a sector of industry starts producing new agricultural tools, yields will increase and there will be a concentration of land, accompanied by expropriation. Throughout all these transformations, our proprietor's income and the value of his possessions will change (or at least they may change) from one year to another and they will change, as it were, *in his hands*, even if, like Gustave Flaubert, he is a bachelor and an artist and remains entirely passive. In other words, this interior-being as possessed materiality turns out to be conditioned by the whole of exteriority. His real person as an isolated molecule is separated from all others by an absolute vacuum and his personality-matter, as the object that he *is*, is subjected to the shifting laws of exteriority, as a perverse and demoniac interiority. Lastly, throughout the ups and downs, the crises and the good years, everything drives him back into need, through the fear of privation (in negative moments), or into expansion of his property as a real intensification of his powers. In other words, the negative moment sends him back to the immediate and absolute exigency of the organism as such; the positive moment becomes his own possible expansion as inert materiality, or as exigency. As soon as an objective ensemble is posited in a given society as the definition of an individual in his *personal* particularity and when *as such* it requires this individual to act on the entire practical and social field, and to *preserve it* (as an organism preserves itself) and *develop it at the expense of the rest* (as an organism feeds itself by drawing on its exterior milieu), the individual *possesses an interest.*

But the material ensemble, being practico-inert, is already of itself a passive action on the practico-inert world around it; it reflects the exigencies of this world in the negative unity of passivity, and as its own exigencies, while at the same time it is already a teleological process acting on the whole of the field and reflected as an exigency by all sectors of materiality. In this way, to the small extent that the individual can escape or act, he becomes, in fact, the mediation between the exigencies of the material totality (mediated by everyone) and those of the limited totality *which is himself.* His being-outside-himself has become essential and, in so far as its truth lies in the practico-inert totality, it dissolves within him the characteristics of pseudo-interiority which appropriation gave him. Thus the individual finds his reality in a material object, conceived initially as an interiorising totality which functions, in effect, as an integrating part of an exteriorised totality; the more he tries to conserve and increase the object which is himself the more the object becomes the Other as dependent on all Others and the more the individual as a practical reality determines himself as inessential in his molecular isolation, in short as a mechanical element. In the extreme case, in the structure of interests, men consider themselves as a sum of atoms or as a mechanical system and their *praxis* is used to preserve their material being in an inorganic ensemble seen as a totality.

At the level of individual interest, the relation of *interest* therefore involves the massification of individuals as such and: heir practical communication through the antagonisms and affinities of the matter which represents them. A French industrialist who, in 1830, in the good old days of the family business, was wise enough to introduce English machines 'because it was in his interest to do so' related to these machines only through the medium of his factory. Although the basis of his *praxis* was, as I have suggested, the fear of privation or the desire for expansion, it should be remembered that this fear was merely a horizon; he certainly never had to face the following dilemma: increase the number of machines or go begging. Similarly, the desire for expansion (like all the acts of violence covered by such terms as will-to-power, *conatus*, etc.) is simply the real expansion of his factory in so far as he controls it through his *praxis*, and in so far as his *praxis* transcends it towards a teleological future (that is to say, in so far as this *praxis*, as an activity necessarily orientated towards an objective, uncovers in its very movement and as its own end what amounts to the objective expansion of the factory in a favourable conjuncture). He is *already* his factory, in the sense, for example, that he inherited it from his father and that he finds in it the unity and slow rise of his family.

If he introduces English machines, it is because the factory requires it in a particular competitive field, and therefore, already, because it is Other and conditioned by Others. It might be a question, for example, of benefiting from a few prosperous years in order to make a new investment and to reduce costs by increasing productivity and reducing labour. This decision is imposed on him as an exigency by the milieu of competition (beating competitors by undercutting them), but in a negative manner, because competition (and the possibility that other factories may also resort to English machines) imperil him in so far as he has constituted himself as a *factory*. But the machine has only to be installed for the interest to shift. His own interest, that is to say, his subjection to his being-outside-himself, was the factory; but the interest of the factory becomes the machine itself; from the moment it is put into operation, it is the machine which determines production, and which forces him to disrupt the old equilibrium between supply and demand and to seek new markets, that is to say, to condition demand by supply. The interest of the factory has changed, the prudence and stability which characterised this interest are transformed into calculated risk and expansion; the manufacturer has established an irreversible mechanism in the workshops of his factory. This irreversibility (the machine cannot stop) characterises him in his being as well as his *praxis*; or rather, it realises in him as a social object the identity of Being (as a structure of inertia) and *praxis* (as developing realisation).

But in the milieu of antagonisms of alterity (in this case, the competitive milieu) the interest of each manufacturer is *the same* precisely to the extent that he constitutes himself *as Other*; or, to put it another way, the need continually to reduce costs by installing new and improved machines appears to each manufacturer as *his* interest (as the real exigency of the factory) *in so far as it is the interest of Others* and in so far as *for Others* he himself constitutes this interest as the interest of the Other. In a given sector of industry, each manufacturer determines the interest of the Other to the extent that he is an *Other for this Other*, and each determines himself by his own interest to the extent that this interest is experienced by the Other as the interest of an Other. This is to a large extent the case today with the forward planning by American factories in certain sectors which have still remained at least partly competitive: there is an initial calculation, on the basis of known data, of the production of the factory in future years (as possibilities of this abstract system, other things being equal); then there is an attempt to situate this estimate, and the alterations that it involves, in the overall national output for the sector. The management of a particular factory commits itself to a set of wagers, strictly based on an estimate of probabilities, resting on factual data concerning competitors' production in the same period, suppliers of raw material, etc. These wagers bear *above all* on the present decisions of these other groups in so far as they make, or will make, their decisions on the basis, first, of their own possibilities and, second, of a set of wagers bearing on the production which is expected and decided by Others and, in particular, by the factory in question. This factory makes its decision therefore as a result of a system of wagers concerning the unknown decisions that it itself conditions as an unknown decision. It thus becomes a condition of itself *as Other* and

once the rhythm of production has been established it will always contain within itself its structure of alterity.[64]

Being-outside-oneself as worked materiality therefore unites under
the name of interest, individuals and groups by the negation, always
other and always identical, of each by all and of all by each. In other
words, the interest-object acts (through the mediation of the individual)
under the negative pressure of similar exigencies developed in other
interest-objects. At this level, to take an example from the 'liberal' era
of the nineteenth century, it is impossible to say whether *profit* is an
end or a means for the industrialist. In the movement of interest as
negative exigency – that is, in the perpetual and necessary transformation of the means of production – most of the profit is reinvested in the
enterprise itself. In one sense, the end of such transformations is to
maintain or increase the rate of profit but, in another sense, profit is the
only possible means for the capitalist to realise these transformations –
that is to say, in a way, to adapt the enterprise to exterior changes and
to see that it benefits from them, and at the same time to prevent the
transformations of others from putting his enterprise out of business –
so that in the unity of the total process, the factory as the *possession-
power* of an individual or group of individuals constitutes itself in its
maintenance and development as its own end, changing either in order
to remain the same or in order to develop itself by means of the profit
it produces. From the impossibility of stopping the movement of production without destroying the object, to the need to find new markets
for increased production and to increase this production in order to
maintain market positions, there is the movement of growth and
maturation of a *quasi-organism*, that is to say, of the inverted simulacrum of an organism – a false totalised totality in which man loses
himself in order that it can exist, a false totalising totality which groups
together all men in the practical field in the negative unity of alterity.
The interest of the manufacturer is simply the factory and its machines
in so far as their development requires his participation in the form of
exigency, and in so far as, through his bond of interiority with their
exteriorised pseudo-interiority, he is in constant danger in the world of
practical and social materiality. But, in this and in every other case, at

64. In reality, other factors intervene, and the calculation is much more complicated, since the entire national economy and its orientation have to be taken
into account through customers. But still, the predictions and wagers in a particular sector have a partial autonomy and, furthermore, at the level of the conjuncture, the factory under consideration reappears as an other.

every other moment of History in which interest appears, the essential point is that *my* (or *our*) interest first appears to us to the extent that it is that of the Other and that I have to negate it in the Other (in the Other's being-outside-himself) in order to realise it in my own being-outside-myself; *or* in so far as it is revealed as the negation of the Other's being-outside-himself by my own. There are just two reasons why a Rouen manufacturer should buy English machinery: either *urgency* (his competitors are going to import machines or at least they may do so), or *counter-attack* (machinery has been imported by *an Other* and the manufacturer can no longer struggle against this competition; his costs must be lowered because of the lowering of the Other's). Interest is the negative life of the human thing in the world of things in so far as man reifies himself in order to serve it. It goes without saying that in the hierarchy of social structures, the human thing can use its *tangibility* without necessarily ceasing to be: it is enough that it is the rigid law of man and that in the practico-inert world it opposes man to himself as Other in so far as it pursues the destruction of another object, which is really itself in the milieu of antagonism.

It goes without saying that these attenuated forms of materiality, which we will encounter again in the superstructures, have their basis and their rationality in solid, elementary forms; and we shall come back to this. Nevertheless, one can speak of ideological interests, for example. This does not mean considering an author's work as providing him with income (interest does exist at this level but it is not ideological); but rather considering it as a set of inert meanings, supported by verbal material, to the extent that the author has constituted his being-outside-himself in it. On this basis, indeed, we can state, *first*, that it is not always possible for this work to be *reactualised* in its totality by its author and that, therefore, the detailed set of meanings which compose it remains purely material (not because they are black marks on a sheet of paper, but because, as significations, they remain inert and the ensembles they form are an unbalanced synthesis of mechanical summations and totalising integrations). But *secondly* this perpetual reactualisation (as long as we are dealing with a sufficiently well known published work, of course) perpetually operates *elsewhere* and everywhere *through Others*, that is to say, through beings who are similar to the author, but who negate him (because of their age – a new generation – or their milieu, or the perspectives which constitute their practical opening to the same world) and who, above all, through reading as a *praxis* of transcendence, reactualise significations towards themselves and towards the material and social world and transform these meanings by elucidating them in terms of a new context (a book written ten years ago and read today, in this historical moment, by a young man of twenty). Whether or not the author continues to write books, however, and whether or not he rereads them from time to time, his ideological interest consists in the fact that he has his being-outside-himself in material meanings (which he might still be said to know and understand though without producing them and living them), whose pseudo-organic ensemble has constituted itself as the inorganic reality of his practical organism and through which he is perpetually *threatened* in the world by the Other, unless he constantly comes back to them, explains them, and shows (or tries to show) that they are compatible with new findings and practices, and that they cannot die through Others as they died through him (in so far as they were a movement of living objectification transforming itself into objectivity). If he tries to defend himself or to complement himself to the extent that he is this work, to show that he was not wrong to write this or that, etc., he finds himself thrown back into dependence on the whole of History in the making, by the object in which he had taken refuge against History. His ideological interest will be to combat new theories and new works – anything that threatens to declass him (and also to try to absorb and digest everything in order to constitute other works, to complement and justify his previous work).

It will be noted that the relation of reciprocal pseudo-interiority between man and his object is not, at this level, that of the owner to the possession: in fact, on one plane, whatever the society's institutions for controlling the relation between an author and a book in so far as the book is the author's livelihood (pension, salaries, royalties, etc.), the relation between creator and creation – in so far as the latter is merely the former as a consumable product – is not one of possession. It is not necessary for us to investigate this dependence in itself: I simply wish to point out that, although it is strikingly exemplified in the case of private property, it would be quite improper to limit *interest* to the real property of our bourgeois societies. Interest is a negative practical relation between man and the practical field, mediated by the thing which he is outside; or, conversely, a relation between *the thing* and other things in the social field, mediated by its human object.

It is this, and not the optimistic harmonies of liberal economics, which explains how individual interest can, in particular conditions, be transformed into group (or class) interest. To conceive of group or class interest in terms of the subjective characteristic of one individual coinciding with the subjective characteristics of all the Others, one would in fact have to begin by forgetting the dialectic of alterity which renders this agreement as such impossible. But, even if this could be done, it would still be necessary to understand the agreement of these molecular subjectivities: if one begins by positing them as different, it is not clear why a common exterior situation should not aggravate these differences; indeed, in the true milieu of alterity, in particular conditions, a common danger may, by its very urgency, accentuate antagonisms and conflicts. On the other hand, it is easy enough to point out that special interest as a material object in the world already has a structure of generality because it offers itself as the same for everyone in that it is this sameness that creates antagonisms in the milieu of alterity. But of course this is not altogether true: interest does not begin the same, and then divide into an infinity of oppositions; rather, in so far as the unity of the same equipment, the same techniques, and the same skills, constitutes the fundamental practical basis of all antagonism, it is the oppositions in a given social field which, through one another and in their confrontation, define the unity of all of them, in so far as they negate each of them as the universal characteristic of particular interests.

Thus, classical economics tried to define identical interests as if they existed equally in every individual member of a group, and it did not take account of the fact that this very identity was the result of a serial process. In other words, when they stated some obvious truth, for example, that in a capitalist system the interest of the producer is, at least within limits, to intensify production and lower costs, they took themselves to be stating *logically* an analytical, Aristotelian truth, of the same kind as 'all men are mortal'. But, in fact, it is something quite different, partly because this interest involves a structure of serial alterity of the individual being-outside-himself, and partly because it cannot be acquired by an individual except in certain totalising conditions, *and through others*. (For instance, in a France where a sort of tacit understanding and very real, if secret, agreements stifled any competition which small enterprises would have been unable to resist, in the name of Malthusianism, the interest of the employer, which seldom situated itself in a European or world context, was to increase productivity without increasing production; and thus this interest came to him from Others.) Thus the universality of particular interests can appear only to a form of thought (a rationality) which I will define below when I deal with serial transfinites. And from this point of view, the universality of particular interests ('everyone pursues his own interest', etc.) finally becomes the material and transcendent unity of all interests as reciprocal conditionings by a single, fundamental, inert negation which basically offers itself as the self-destructive result of all antagonisms.

'Everyone follows his own interest' means: the general characteristic of particular interests is never to be able to transform themselves into general interests or to realise themselves in stability as particular interests. But it should also be observed that we have presupposed in this investigation that the practical field was occupied by a multiplicity of individuals who began with more or less equal opportunities, and that this field remained *free*, that is to say, it was assumed that there was no action by any other grouping, dominating or exploiting the individuals under consideration from the outside. This therefore involved an abstract moment of the investigation, so that, for example, a free practical field amongst the high capitalist bourgeoisie was investigated without other classes being taken into account. But, to go back to the example of nineteenth century French industrialisation, we must realise that the machine is also a determination of the practical field of the working population and – this is the third characteristic of practico-inert Being – that it is *destiny* for the workers to precisely the extent that it is *interest* for the employer.

The worker who serves the machine *has his being in it* just as the employer does; and just as the employer reinvests his profits in it, so the worker finds himself objectively forced to devote his wages to the upkeep (at minimum cost) of a servant for the machine who *is none Other than himself.* Indeed, we saw above how tools, in the field of the need and labour of Others (and of himself, as Other) expressed their exigencies as *imperatives*; and how his very organism was attacked by the counter-finalities of a machinery of which he was the true animator. But we must not be misled by this apparent symmetry: the machine is not, and cannot be, the worker's *interest.* The reason for this is simple: far from the worker objectifying himself in it, the machine objectifies itself in him. In so far as industrialisation and concentration determine the proletarianisation of a section of the rural classes, they constitute not only the opportunity for the new proletarians of selling their labour power, but also, in the field of practico-inert Being, a force of attraction which tears the peasant away from agriculture and puts him in a workshop before a loom.

Now, the individual thus signified by material practice is, in a different sense, reduced to a nonentity: he need only satisfy a few universal conditions (being an expropriated peasant, or a peasant in danger of being expropriated, or the son of a large, penurious peasant family, etc.); as a worker he is no more than a particular labour power used for various tasks, and renewed each day by his daily wage. Thus not only does his being exist before and outside him, in the movement of the economy, and ultimately in *this* particular machine (or *these* tools) which lay claim to him; but also, this Being represents the pure abstraction of himself. His object-being awaits him and patiently produces him from a distance: for example, the industrialisation of certain agricultural processes, by gradually preparing the ruin and expropriation of his father, patiently shapes the son until penury turns him into a *free* worker – an exploited man whose exploitation resides entirely in freedom of contract. The machine shapes its man to precisely the extent that man shapes machines (I shall deal with this process of shaping more extensively below). This means that it constitutes its servant, by a temporal, teleological process, as a machine for operating machines. It inverts the relations *within* the practical agent; it is a categorical imperative, which makes him an absolute but conscious means (in that he *knows* the imperative); a distributor of wages, which transforms his *praxis* (or labour power) into a commodity, that is, an inert product, while preserving for him the power of unifying a practical field. Indeed, to the extent that he makes himself a force of inert exteriority (or uses his substance in energy transformations which are inorganic in nature), it itself becomes a living thing and a pseudo-organism.

Thus the machine defines and produces the reality of its servant, that is to say, it makes of him a practico-inert Being who will be a machine in so far as the machine is human and a man in so far as it remains, in spite of everything, a tool to be used: in short, it becomes his exact complement as an inverted man. At the same time, it determines his future as a living organism, just as it defines that of the employer. The difference is that it defines him negatively as an impossibility of living in the more or less long term. The machine does this not only through the counter-finalities which we have described (air pollution, destruction of the environment, occupational diseases, etc.), but also through representing, *for him*, in so far as it develops his being in the practical field of industrialisation, a permanent threat of reduced wages, of technological unemployment and of becoming disqualified.

This has its rationality in the true meaning of industry: that the machine is made to replace man. It is obvious that in certain conditions, and for certain societies, this may signify that it will relieve man of labour. But *apart from its historical appearance* in the social context of the period, its function is to replace *certain men* – manual workers in fact – because it costs less to maintain. Thus, while the employer sees in the factory the being-outside-itself of his own individuality, his own possibility of expansion according to certain rules, and an object to serve and, of course, develop – but only because it is his own positive materiality and his power over the world – the worker finds in it his being as indifferent generality, his *praxis* as already materialised in predetermined tasks as inert exigencies to be satisfied, and his future as impotence; and in the end he finds his prefabricated destiny in the inert design of the machine whose purpose is to eliminate its servants.

This means that the machine could *never* be the particular interest of the worker; on the contrary, it is the *a priori* negation both of his particularity and of any possibility of his having an interest. In so far as his objective being is in the machine and in the wages it gives him, he is effectively prevented from engaging it elsewhere: there is no other object which can be described as the particular being-outside-himself of the worker in the world. Of course, his labour power is treated as an inert commodity; but, although it does in fact become a commodity in social terms, it represents in the worker the perpetual need to turn himself into an inorganic means to an end which has nothing to do with him, rather than an exterior materiality in which he might objectify himself. On the other hand, he is objectified in his product, but only to the extent that this product does not belong to him. No doubt the mere fact of treating labour power as a commodity creates a labour market in which workers oppose one another in antagonistic competition; this means that they become sellers in a market structured by capitalism itself. But this antagonism has a dual origin, of need directly felt or immediately anticipated, and of the relative scarcity of demand (a scarcity which machines themselves enable employers to maintain). *It is not the interest of the worker to work*: the situation is quite different, since, under the constraint of need, his work exhausts him and its ultimate results (the construction of machines) contribute to his elimination. As for the antagonism between workers on the market, it necessarily culminates in results which are entirely opposed to the 'interests' of individuals or of the class (if it can have interests), since it enables the employers to get starvation wages freely accepted and to intimidate strikers by threatening to replace them immediately.

But to precisely the extent that the machine signifies the worker as a practico-inert being, deprived of any particular interest (and of all possibility of having one), it also designates him as a general individual, that is, as a class individual (using the word 'class' at this stage only in the very abstract sense of 'collectivity'). And in this case to produce and to signify are clearly the same thing. Of course, this does not mean that machines produce abstract beings which lack individuality; even within reification, the human agent is a constituent, dialectical totality: in fact, everyone puts the particularity of his *praxis* into the way he constitutes himself, and allows himself to be constituted, as generality; and the generality of everyone characterises everyone's relations; everyone discovers his generality in the Other, and *personal* relations are constructed on this basis. In the early stages of industrialisation, inert generality, as the milieu of the working class, cannot be regarded as the real, totalising unity of the workers in a factory, a city or a country; and we shall return to this. It presents itself to them on the basis of worked matter, like the false negative unities discussed above, and it is constitutive of each and every individual as the negative unity of a destiny which condemns him. But, by the same token, in the negative milieu of generality, everyone sees the general destiny (which, at this stage, is the general destiny not of a totality of workers but of an indeterminate number of similar instances connected by their identical condition) of everyone in the very generality of his own destiny; in other words, he sees the destiny of the worker, as the negation of the possibility of his own existence, in the generality of machines as possessions of the generality of Others.

It is too early to describe the way in which the class or a section of it can unify itself into an organised group, that is, transform generality and identity into a unifying totalisation. But, at this stage of the investigation, all I have wanted to show is that there is no difference between realising the active totality of the group (whether in trade union or political terms), and constituting the totality of industrial machinery, in a capitalist society, in relation to this group (in so far as it represents the developing unification of the class) and in opposition to it, as the total being-outside-itself of the working class (and the totality of production as the totality of objectified and inverted *praxis*). In this way, in so far as it organises itself so as to reappropriate its total class destiny through the socialisation of the means of production, and, indeed, in so far as, at the level, for example, of trade union struggle, it struggles against particular effects of the private ownership of machines in the development of a specific moment of the historical process, as a fundamental relation of production, the *praxis* of the group, through the practical negation of its being-outside-itself *as destiny*, constitutes its destiny as *future interest* (through the material object), and as exigency contained in the destiny-materiality of changing itself into interest-materiality.

The contradiction of the machine in the capitalist period is that it both creates and negates the worker; this contradiction is materialised into a general destiny and becomes a fundamental condition of the assumption of consciousness, that is to say, of the negation of the negation. But the only negation which is possible as *the unity of all*, is not the negation of the machine in itself (which was attempted, about 1830, by craftsmen thrown out of work and by disqualified workers whose wages were steadily falling) and, consequently, of the worker in so far as he is its product and in so far as it is his being; it is the negation of the machine *in so far as* it is destiny in exteriority for the man it produces because, *within a given social system*, it controls him and he cannot control it in return. Thus all the worker can wish for is that the means of production and products as a whole should represent *the material expansion of his class* (there is no need to show here how this *praxis* moves towards the exigency of a classless society), that is to say, that *this ensemble*, simply through the movement which negates its character as destiny (organisation and struggle), should become his interest.

This does not mean that a real socialisation of the means of production must, in a particular historical development, lead to the total elimination of interest itself as linking men *in alterity* through matter. On the contrary, interest *arises*, as always, out of *alterity* as the primary human practical relation, but as deformed by the matter which mediates it; and it maintains itself in the milieu of alterity. There are *several* workers' interests, but only *one* working class interest. This is because the employers, by introducing new machines within the framework of capitalism and appropriating them *as their interest*, constitute the destiny of the workers as the *interest of the Other, controlling them in the form of counter-interest* (destiny), and because *in* the moment of social struggle, that is to say, of the *negation of the negation*, the real material objective can only be the negation of the capitalist's interest in so far as it has become the worker's destiny, that is to say, the negation of the *interest of the other as negation*. And so, at a particular historical moment of unification, the negation of the Other's interest realises itself as an affirmation of the true interest of the working class.

The whole of my description here applies, really, to the first stages of capitalism (the existence of activist groups and of workers' institutions, as well as the achievement of socialism in certain countries, completely transforms the problem). But there can be no doubt that about 1830 the workers who broke up machines and even the Lyon silk-weavers (who were protesting against *a reduction of wages*) had only one demand: the stabilisation of their destiny. Nothing contributed more to workers' organisation, under Louis-Philippe, than the inexorable lowering of real wages which was linked to a certain phase of industrialisation (above a certain threshold, wages were to rise during the second phase of industrialisation, between 1870 and 1914). This showed workers that the stabilisation of their destiny was impossible in that their destiny was simply the impossibility of any stabilisation. This was due not to the physical, technological materiality of the machine, but to its social materiality (to its practico-inert being); in other words, to the impossibility of controlling this materiality and orienting it towards the real reduction of human labour *for all* rather than towards the negation of the workers, or at least of their humanity. The interest of the working class, therefore, inscribes itself in the practico-inert ensemble which, in the contradiction of struggles, and about the middle of the nineteenth century, represents both its future interest and its present destiny: its destiny, when a hardening of employers' attitudes, or a failure of attempts to form unions, or unsuccessful strikes, or strikes which end in bloody defeat, relegate the realisation of socialisation as a total process to an indeterminate future; and its interest, on the other hand, when, as a result of industrial expansion, the value of labour, and therefore the power of the workers, increases, so that activities of unification and the production of *apparatuses* and *organs* within the class itself, increase too. But, of course, in all capitalist countries from the middle of the nineteenth century to the present day, these two structures have always occurred together: in defeat, socialisation *remains to be achieved* and defeat itself teaches new methods of struggle; the bitterest disappointment of the *present* generation (these machines are *my* destiny) is necessarily negated by the existence of generations to come; conversely, the greatest working-class victories in the capitalist countries have not, by definition, eliminated appropriation by individuals or groups, even if profit margins are fixed by the social ensemble, and even if the employers are effectively supervised by trade unions in matters of hygiene, security and even of management. But the workers' interest never appears to the worker as an inert object of contemplation, but rather as the variable, practical meaning of his daily struggle against the necessary consequences of the capitalist process, and therefore both as *present* (to the extent that any successful action, however local, presents itself as the human negation of a destiny and, concretely, as the practical, negative use of machines against the employer in the milieu of liberal competition itself);[65] and as *future* in a perspective whose opening and depth are conditioned by *praxis* itself as it assumes its total historical meaning. Thus, though we are not yet able to answer our questions: – how can a *class* be dialectically intelligible, and how can a *practical group* be formed; and what type of dialectical reality can it represent? – our investigation already gives us the rational certainty that workers do not have particular interests (as individuals subjected to forces of massification) and that their unification, if it occurs, is indissolubly bound up with the constitution of general interest (as such still undetermined) as *class interest.*

It is on this basis that class interest arises amongst employers: the moment which is, in effect, passed over in silence in the constitution of their material property as their private interest, is that neither land nor machines *on their own* can be productive; or, in other words, they need *human means* in order to be made to work. When I say 'passed over in silence', this does not imply any particular reflection on the attitude of employers to workers: in false innocence they may believe in the absolute value of the free wage contract; or, while having no illusions as to the nature of profit, they may believe that the workers are massified and too impotent to initiate anything. This abstract position, while making it possible to merge the worker and the machine in the real symbiosis of their common social activity, legitimates for them the constitution of a single social field: that of *the employers*, whose *properties*, as materials and means of production, oppose one another in their practico-inert being and thus oppose them. In a way, the multiplicity of these antagonisms has always been integrated into the ab-

---

65. Strikes, as the collective refusal to use machines, turn machines – in so far as they require a certain level of production in particular circumstances – into the workers' weapon against the employers and, if the strike continues and shows signs of succeeding, the employer in turn will discover his destiny as a distant future possibility (for succeeding generations if not for him) through the medium of his present interest.

stract forms of unity and universality. Although divided to the extent that each of them produces *the same commodity* as the other, two industrialists will, in one way or another, affirm their positive unity as producers of wealth for mankind as a whole. This is the true meaning of Calvinism since the sixteenth century and of Puritanism up to the twentieth: the bourgeois is the man of God because God has put him on earth to continue the work of creation; and the pride of the Victorian industrialist watching his factory chimneys poisoning his native town involves a collective structure: even if he is the most powerful, he is not alone and, indeed, he needs other powerful men in order to be more powerful than them.

What these abstract integrations really express is simply *the other side of particular interest*: based on the diversification of production and causing an increasingly extreme division of functions and of labour (at least in the nineteenth century), the private ownership of a factory implies solidarity *in matter* between the industrialist, his suppliers and his customers. We are in fact still in the domain of the practico-inert: it is *the machine* which requires certain materials (and which is thereby affected, for example, by improvements in communication), and again, it is the machine which demands certain markets (that is to say, at a certain level of production, customers who are themselves producers). This is expressed in the practical field, and under the aberrant appearance of 'private life', in *social* relations between employer-suppliers and employer-customers. (This is an extreme simplification because these social relations in fact concern the entire social field of production in so far as it is the private interest of the capitalists, and because such 'private' social relations *also* connect financiers and senior civil servants.) But these social relations – simple activities aimed at establishing the human relations between employers that their machines demand – are in fact eroded by exteriority (in so far as it is reconstituted in competition). Nothing *really* connects a particular supplier to a particular customer, other than a material situation which is itself given as variable (it only requires a lowering of transportation costs for it to become the particular interest of *this* particular customer to obtain his supplies elsewhere). In this sense, the negative unity of 'everyone follows his own interest' erodes and neutralises the positive unity of their supposed solidarity in differentiation. In the drawing-rooms of the rich bourgeois, machines pay visits on one another and manifest their temporary concord.

The concrete unity of the bourgeois class can be realised only through a common opposition to the common *praxis* of the workers.

The exploited classes manifest themselves *as exploited* simply through the unity which, in the class milieu, makes the worker appear a man: for the employer, isolated in his private interest, the absolute refusal of the exploited to regard the machine as their destiny manifests itself as the possibility that his own interest will be transformed into a destiny for him – not only through the still distant socialisation of the means of production, but also simply through the workers' resistance (to wage cuts, raising of norms, etc.), which *in principle* implies a reduction of profits, and therefore possible ruin (through competitors). But the *unity* of the workers' *praxis*, through the geographical dispersal of factories in the social field, gives each employer the possibility of a destiny, *in so far as* this possibility applies to him *both* as a general individual *and* as a particular moment of the capitalist process in its totality. In this sense, it is *through the unity of the workers* that the capitalists realise capital as the totality of the process instead of as a mere dispersal of interests which sometimes support and sometimes contradict one another.

This change occurred towards the end of the eighteenth century and it can be observed in a number of writings of that period. Nasmyth wrote at the time that 'strikes do more good than harm because they serve to encourage inventions'. And Ure said: 'If capital takes science into its service, the recalcitrant labourer will be forced to be docile.' In reality, there is a circle here: the machine causes strikes precisely in so far as it aims to eliminate workers. The crucial fact is that capital becomes self-conscious *in so far as it is unified in the milieu of the Other*, and therefore in so far as it is an *other totality*; its general (and total) interest comes to it therefore *as other*, and negatively, as the need to destroy any possibility of the other class transforming its destiny into interest. This emerges very clearly in a remark by another classical economist: 'As far as most of our tools and powerful, automatic machines are concerned, industrialists could be led to adopt them only when forced to do so by strikes.' This, too, is only partially true: it is equally true, in fact, that in a period of competition the machine produces the machine, since it is the machine which determines the flow of investments. But this admission is historically interesting, in the sense that it shows the historical development of capital as producing itself for the bourgeois themselves under pressure *from the Other class*. And, in so far as the machine becomes an exigency for the capitalist himself, to the extent that it is his private interest, and in so far as the expansion of production directly or indirectly defines all the social and political activities of a human grouping, and in so far as the discovery of new sources of energy in certain countries becomes an external destiny for less favoured countries, the totality of 'capital', as the common interest of the capitalist class, also controls everyone as his destiny. At this level the State, as a class organ, represents an apparatus of struggle against *capital as the destiny of the capitalists*; and it is at this level, too, that the organs of the workers' struggle will create, *in the other class, as an Other for itself*, agreements and employers' organisations whose structure is determined by that of the workers' organisations. However, as long as the competitive system is not directly challenged by employers' organisations struggling against the counter-finalities of capital it-self,[66] the fractured unity of the social field of the capitalists is due to the fact that they can unite only to impose the changing multiplicity of their contradictions. In short, the capitalists' class interest, up to the end of the nineteenth century, was to maintain a system ruled by the conflict of private interests. Or, to take them in their being-outside-themselves, their interest was the material totality of production goods – in so far as this totality, in its social materiality, negated the

66. In this sense, monopolies, cartels, agreements, and even State intervention, in so far as they define the semi-competitive system in which we live, derive *both* from the transformation of the means of production (electric power, etc.) *and* from the working class itself in so far as, by the same process, it becomes one of the essential markets for mass-production. However, it should be remarked that this is an attempt on the part of industry to mitigate a structural contradiction of the capitalist process in itself. Producers find that, in themselves and as con-sumers, they are the destiny of capital, to precisely the extent that the capitalists' need to reinvest most of their profits has the contradictory double result of expanding production and diminishing the overall buying power of the working masses. Thus the destiny of the workers, as the negation of their standard of living by machines, becomes the destiny of the machine (in the social field of capitalism) as the negation of the possibility of selling its products; and this destiny exercises its control through *crises*. The policy of paying high wages in the context of controlled mass-production (which implies at least a partial nega-tion of the competitive system), in the 'second industrial revolution', was un-doubtedly an attempt at conscious organisation by the employers, in certain sectors of industry and in the most advanced countries, to transcend the deep contradictoriness of the capitalist process by making the producers themselves the consumers of their own products. At this level of the investigation, a new theoretical conflict will set Marxists (who think that the contradiction is simply veiled) in opposition to technocrats (who claim that it has been overcome). We cannot go into this here; but it was worth explaining the reversal which, for the capitalists, transforms the destiny of the proletariat (even in grinding poverty) into the destiny of capitalism, in the field of consumption itself.

practical totalisation which the class without property wanted (namely, socialisation) and in so far as it affirmed the negative dispersal of the owners of capital with the whole of its practico-inert being. Thus everything becomes *Other*: for the possessors the threat of Others constitutes their general interest as Other, and this material interest is the exigency that relations between capitalists should be relations of Other to Other or, in other words, the exigency that in so far as it determines the relations of production, the capitalist mode of production cannot unite the members of the dominant class except through their radical alterity. Thus we see, in effect, how particular interests ultimately express material being-outside-itself in the medium of the Other and one's own coming to oneself as Other than self.

These formal remarks cannot, of course, claim to add *anything at all* to the certainty of the synthetic reconstruction which Marx carried out in *Capital*; they are not even intended to be marginal comments on it. By its very certainty, the reconstruction in effect defies commentary. But my remarks, though they are possible only on the basis of this reconstruction, which simultaneously recreates its method and its object, belong, logically, *before* this historical reconstruction, at a higher level of greater indeterminacy and generality: in so far as they have fixed certain relations of the practico-inert field in its generality, their purpose is simply to define the type of intelligibility which is involved in the Marxist reconstruction. I have simply tried to establish without prejudice (the inquiry is not yet complete) the basic relations between *praxis* and the material environment (in so far as it organises a practical field and defines the relations between men through their objects, and the relations between objects through men) in which a rational foundation for the certainty of dialectical investigations (*l'évidence de l'expérience dialectique*), which any reader of Marx can experience, can be found. And, as for conflicts of interest, in particular, my own investigations, as conducted in this book, have provided a means to pay off the hedonistic, utilitarian mortgage which makes of interest an irrational mixture of subjective *conatus* and objective conditions.

There is a choice: either 'everyone follows his interest', which implies that divisions between men are *natural* – or it is divisions between men, resulting from the mode of production, which make interest (particular or general, individual or class) appear as a real moment of the relations between men. In the first case, interest as a fact of nature is an entirely unintelligible *datum*; indeed, the induction which posits it as an *a priori* reality of human nature could never be justified. The whole of History, in so far as its motive force is provided by conflicts of interest, sinks entirely into the absurd; in particular, Marxism becomes no more than an irrational hypothesis: if conflicts of interest are *a priori* then relations of production are determined by them rather than by the mode of production; in other words, the mode of production is not *praxis* objectifying itself and finding the basis of its contradictions in its objectification, that is to say, in its becoming-matter; instead, it is a mere mediation through which individual interests determine the type and intensity of their conflicts. In effect, the immediate consequence of the law of interest (or the Darwinian 'struggle for life') is that human relations are *a priori* antagonistic.

This being so, it is hardly surprising that one conservative ideology condemns all attempts at socialisation in the name of human nature (that is, in the name of the obscure law of interest): human beings are not going to change, etc. But it is more surprising that several Marxist writers seem to hesitate between the law of interest and the Marxist conception of History, that is to say, between a sort of biological materialism and historical materialism. They make the concept of need completely opaque. Having made it completely *unintelligible*, they are satisfied with calling this unintelligibility 'objective reality' and then consider this inert dark force, this exteriority within interiority, as *interest*. As a result, it is no longer possible to comprehend anything about human conflicts, since most of them, especially those which oppose an oppressed or exploited group to a group of oppressors or exploiters, seem to involve 'interests' of completely different level, complexity and structure. And, to take the example of a factory on strike, if we were told – as might be perfectly true – that the strikers were fighting desperately and had their backs to the wall because, in this particular case, they could no longer bear the slightest reduction in their income, whereas the employers, who could afford a readjustment of wages, have an interest in refusing it in the context of the economic situation and in view of their forecasts and production plans (or alternatively they might give in because the country was becoming industrialised and the value of labour was increasing), then we are dealing with heterogeneous realities which are being grouped together under the same name in spite of being constituted on different levels. In this case, the interest of the worker would simply be fundamental needs, while the interest of the employer would be a necessity (or possibility) imposed on him by production itself, that is, through all the structures of capitalist society, and which, as we have seen, relates only very indirectly to need itself, although need is always present *as tension*. The same would apply to a kind of quasi-socialist idealism which represented the employers as *necessarily rapacious*, that is to say, if the pursuit of profit, power, etc. (which exists only in and through a particular society and whose character and even intensity depend on the historical situation as a whole and on particular institutions) was treated as the natural force which moves individuals. We would then find, as we often do, the same unintelligible heterogeneity when confronted with workers grouped into unions and acting in accordance with *the interests of their class* against vampire-employers giving in to their rapacious instincts.

In both these cases, the transition from false individual objectivity (*conatus* conceived as an external force) to the objective, abstract generality of the process simply becomes incomprehensible. And if the workers were fundamentally these interests posited in divergence and antagonism as natural realities, if their class interest were not negatively inscribed for everyone in the destiny prefabricated by machines, no propaganda, no political or union education, no emancipation would be possible. For every individual or class, interests are constituted in and through matter itself in so far as it defines and produces, as instruments, the men and relations suited to serving it (to serving production). For the men or groups under consideration their interests do not differentiate themselves from their being-outside-themselves in matter at work in so far as this being-outside-themselves controls the Other as destiny (through other men or groups). The structure of the material equipment alone determines what kind of interests are operative. (It is this structure which creates a practical field of individual interests for one class and a field of general interest as its only possibility for another.) From this point of view, conflicts of interest are defined at the level of relations of production, or rather, they *are* these relations themselves: they appear as directly caused by the movement of worked matter, or rather as this matter itself in its exigencies and movement, in so far as each group (or person) struggles to regain control of it (in order to control production in and through their being-outside-themselves-in-it, that is to say, through the inert but powerful objectification of themselves in it) and to wrest this control from the Other.

In this sense, it is not diversity of interests which gives rise to conflicts, but conflicts which produce interests, to the extent that worked matter imposes itself on struggling groups as an independent reality through the temporary impotence which emerges from their balance of forces. And, in this sense, interest is always a negation not only of the Other but also of the practico-inert being both of matter and of men in so far as this being is constituted by everyone as the destiny of the Other. But, in the same moment, it is precisely this interchangeability of man and his product in the medium of the practico-inert. The contradiction of interest is that it reveals itself in the individual or collective attempt to rediscover the original univocal bond between man and matter, that is to say, free constituent *praxis*, but that it is already in itself the perversion and petrification of this attempt by matter as the false counterpart of human action. In the practico-inert field, in other words, active man, inert in his product, becomes the only way of preventing his interest from becoming destiny, or of transforming his destiny into interest. But, as destiny and interest are two contradictory statutes of being-outside-oneself, and as these two statutes always exist together (although the one may enclose the other and veil it), they mark the limits of the practico-inert field, in so far as worked matter produces, as means to its ends, its men with their conflicts and their work relations, that is to say at that moment of the dialectical investigation in which man, defined by his being-outside-himself (whether this is the seal he impresses on matter or the prefabrication of his functions by the coming together and passive organisation of material exigencies), is defined as *bewitched matter* (that is, precisely as an inorganic, worked materiality which develops a non-human activity because its passivity synthesises the serial infinity of human acts which sustain it).

Thus *for this being* who reveals himself in the perpetual appropriation of his *praxis* by the technical and social environment, destiny threatens as a mechanical fatality; and his struggle against destiny as such cannot itself be conceived as free human affirmation: it must appear as a means of safeguarding, or at least serving, *his interest*. Interest therefore appears as the inorganic materiality of the individual or group seen as an absolute and irreducible being which subordinates itself to *praxis* as a way of preserving itself in its practico-inert exteriority. In other words, it is the passive, inverted image of freedom, and the only way in which freedom can produce itself (and become conscious of itself) in the shifting hell of the field of practical passivity.

3   *Necessity as a New Structure of Dialectical Investigation*

At its most immediate level, dialectical investigation (*l'expérience dialectique*) has emerged as *praxis* elucidating itself in order to control its own development. The certainty of this primary experience, in which *doing* grounded its consciousness of itself, provides us with one certainty: it is reality itself which is revealed as presence to itself. The only concrete basis for the historical dialectic is the dialectical structure of individual action. And, in so far as we have been able provisionally to abstract this action from the social milieu in which it is in fact embedded, we have discovered a complete development of dialectical intelligibility as the logic of practical totalisation and of real temporalisation. But this investigation, just because it is its own object, provides us with complete transparency *but not necessity*. Since man becomes dialectical by acting on matter, and since knowledge is action in so far as action is knowledge, this constitutes an *indubitable fact*. Indubitability, however, is not necessity.

And as soon as we tried to reach the more complex, more concrete reality of everyday life, we discovered a multiplicity of discrete quantities, which is capable of being studied by analytical Reason. The fact that this multiplicity reveals itself on the level of totalising synthesis rather than on that of simple living organisms is irrelevant; and so is the fact that the origin of dispersal is itself dialectical: the plurality of human actions is still a negation of the dialectical unity of each *praxis*. But since these actions as a whole – of which some are done by groups, and others by individuals – act *on a single material field* (an isolated Indian village in the virgin forest of Brazil, or the soil and sub-soil of a country or of the whole world), and since this field, which was originally united by its bond of univocal practical interiority to everyone is, in its passivity, the basis and support of the multiplicity of determinations, we have discovered, by deepening our investigation, that men unwittingly realise their own unity in the form of antagonistic alterity through the material field in which they are dispersed and through the multiplicity of unifying actions which they perform upon this field. Thus while the plurality of bodies and actions, if it is conceived directly, produces isolation, it is transformed into a unifying factor if it is reflected to men through worked matter.

This is apparent in the most everyday objectivity: from my window I can see men who do not know each other walking across a square to jobs which, at least at the present level of the investigation, isolate them from one another; I can also see a group of people waiting for a bus, while none of them pays the slightest attention to the others – all eyes are turned towards the rue de Rennes, looking out for the bus which is about to arrive. In this state of semi-isolation, it is obvious that they are united by the street, the square, the paving-stones and the asphalt, the pedestrian crossings, and the bus, that is to say, by the material underside of a passivised *praxis*. But this unity is itself that of a material system, and in this sense it is highly ambiguous. It can be called dialectical in so far as the ensemble under consideration has been totalised by actions; and also in so far as scarcity, in any form, transforms separation into antagonism. But from another point of view, if dialectic is totalisation, materiality cannot be said to totalise: the avatars of Spanish gold did not totalise the practices of the nations and cities of the Mediterranean; they absorbed them and gave them the passive unity of interpenetration. Moreover, the inversion of activity into passivity, combined with the transformation of the diverse into a totalised inertia, has the effect of inverting *both* relations of exteriority *and* relations of interiority: quantity controls reified men in so far as these same men magically haunt quantity. Everything changes its sign when we enter the domain of the negative; from the point of view of this new logic, the unity of men through matter can only be their separation. In other words, separation ceases to be a pure relation of exteriority and becomes a bond of lived interiority. People are separated by *alterity*, by antagonisms, by their place in the system; but these separations, such as hatred, flight, etc., are also modes of connection. However, since matter unites men in so far as it binds them together and forces them to enter a material system, it unifies them in so far as they are inertia.

We have already seen how, through its quality as inorganic inertia, the organism can come into contact with the non-organised world; what we find here is passive materiality, as an elementary structure of the human organism, in thrall to an inorganic matter which has taken away its power of transcendence towards organised action. To stop at this level would lead to a very elementary and very false picture of the materialist dialectic – which is, unfortunately, most widespread:

scarcity, the antagonisms of need, tools, and organisation around tools. These are all acceptable in themselves, but they are explained in a way which gives priority to the inert, to inverted *praxis*, in short, to inorganic matter over the historical agent. However, we ought not to leave this moment of the investigation yet. What has to be established is that the introduction of new elements does not destroy dialectical *intelligibility* and that, for the first time, the agent has objective experience of necessity.

Complex as they may be, the facts which we have taken as examples are in fact accessible only to dialectical Reason. There can never be any hope of analytical Reason explaining the metamorphoses of Spanish gold, just because, as we have seen, the quantitative bonds of exteriority, though they do not disappear, are turned back or diverted by bonds of interiority; in other words, each piece of gold is *both* a unit in a sum and, through its relations to all the other pieces, a part in a whole. Dialectical intelligibility, however, is entirely preserved, since it enables one to grasp, in terms of the proliferation of acts, the type of negative unity represented by materiality. The transparency of *praxis* is certainly not to be found at this level. But it must be understood that there is a dialectic within the dialectic. That is to say, from the point of view of a realist materialism, the dialectic as totalisation produces its own negation as absolute dispersal. It does this *both* because the confrontation of activities is a union in separation, *and* because it is only through it and in it that plurality as dispersal can have a meaning. It is not that the dialectic as Idea produces exteriority as the reverse side of the Idea; it is the real *analytical* dispersal of specifically dialectical agents, which they have to live as the interiorisation of exteriority. Thus it is not a process which is transparent to itself in so far as it is produced in the unity of a project, but an action which escapes from itself and diverts itself according to laws which we know and clearly understand in so far as they effect an unbalanced synthesis between interior and exterior. In so far as, having achieved our own goal, we understand that we have actually done *something else* and why our action has been altered outside us, we get our first dialectical experience of necessity.[67]

But necessity must not be confused with constraint. We are sub-

---

67. As every means is a provisional end, it is obvious that the experience of necessity occurs not just when the action is complete, but during the entire development of the *praxis*.

jected to constraint as to an exterior force, with all the contingent opacity of a fact; it appears as violence in so far as it opposes itself to free *praxis*. Nor is the discovery of necessity to be found in that gradual confinement of action which finally reduces the number of possibilities to *one*, in relation to a given end, and on the basis of certain already constructed means. When only one course is possible (for moving a material ensemble from one state to another, for going from one place to another, or from one person to another, or from one idea to another), and when this course exists and opens or offers itself, then *praxis* will conceive of itself as creating it – and rightly so, since, without it, neither the possibilities nor the means would exist as such. Thus the synthetic, royal road to comprehension, in the domain of thought, is a synthetic advance which is given negatively, as incapable of being otherwise, through the positive consciousness of becoming everything it can become. The unfolding of action and the conformity between the result achieved and the result intended cannot in fact give rise to any apodicticity except of the Other and by means of the Other, and on another level of the investigation.

This shows that the first practical experience of necessity occurs in the unconstrained activity of the individual to the extent that the final result, though conforming to the one anticipated, also appears as radically Other, in that it has never been the object of an intention on the part of the agent. This elementary type of necessity is already to be found in mathematics; at the end of a proof, the last proposition is transformed into *an other* which is just a statement of the theorem to be demonstrated. The difference is that the mathematician uses the dialectical fact of the transformed result *as a method*. The moment of necessity in practical experience is the simultaneous recognition of the same as Other and of the Other as the same. Let there be no misunderstanding: a solitary activity involving a tool undergoes transformations due to the nature of the chosen instrument or of the object on which it is used. But these transformations, transcended, corrected and controlled, do not alter *praxis*, even if they force it to modify itself, to make deviations, etc.: the metamorphoses of *praxis* are dialectical and form part of *praxis* as inevitable, living moments linked by relations of interiority; failure itself is integrated into the movement, as a final term and destruction of the dialectic in the same way as our death may be said to be part of our life. Moreover, in the case of solitary activity, failure returns to throw light upon the whole of the *praxis* and reveals within it the real reasons for our defeat:

we were wrong to undertake it, or we chose the wrong means. In general, failure, illuminating past movement, shows us that we were already certain to fail, or, in other words, that an objectively inappropriate action produces in interiority in one form or another (stubbornness, haste, etc.) the knowledge of its inappropriateness. But when this knowledge is absent, failure still exists within *praxis* itself as a dialectical possibility of negation.

Necessity appears in experience when we are robbed of our action by worked matter, *not* in so far as it is pure materiality but in so far as it is materialised *praxis*. In this moment, the tool made by an Other represents *an element of exteriority* in the dialectical field of interaction; but this exteriority does not derive from the external connections which are characteristic of inorganic materiality. All these connections are effectively taken up in the practical field of action. *Exteriority* exists to the extent that the tool *as materiality* is part of other fields of interiority. Finally, it is primarily a matter not of fields determined by the deliberate *praxis* of individuals or groups, but of the quasi-dialectical field whose fugitive unity does not come from anyone, but proceeds *from matter* to men who mediate between different sectors of materiality. In this way, a magical field of quasi-dialectical counter-finality comes to be constituted: everything acts on everything else from a distance, and the slightest novelty produces complete devastation, just *as if* the material ensemble were a true totality. And the instrument used by a given individual or community is transformed externally within the very hands which use it.

During the period of Spanish hegemony, for example, gold could be real power for a person or collectivity. And, in so far as a historical agent is defined by his objective reality, and therefore by his objectification, this precious metal became, for a given society, this objectification itself; and objectifying *praxis* came to be defined, in turn, by its use of gold, that is to say, by the distribution of wealth (capitalisation, the financing of enterprises, items of expenditure, etc.). But in addition to being the mode of exteriorising interiority for particular individual or collective agents, what gold represented for the agent was existence in total exteriority, since its value at any particular time was determined by the whole of History; and in this way, to the extent that a prince or merchant realised his objective reality, it eluded him. But this exteriority refers back to material totalities in which every element acts *at a distance* as in an organic whole (the discovery of a mine, a massive influx of precious metals, the discovery of a new technical process, etc.). In this way, the haemorrhage of objective reality, which is emptied of its meaning in the hands of the agent, takes on a *definite meaning* when interpreted in terms of the developing totality. The ruin of a particular Genoese merchant can be interpreted from within his *praxis*, but in order for it to be intelligible it must also be seen as coming *from outside* as a result of the accumulation of stocks of precious metals, etc., to the extent that the Mediterranean is, as Braudel says, a material unity.

There is no *a priori* reason why the transformation of the result should be understood by the agent: everything depends upon the instruments of thought provided for him by his period, class and historical circumstances. On the other hand, at the present level of development of our knowledge, it is possible to claim that this transformation is always intelligible, provided one has the necessary instruments at one's disposal; in other words, it defines its own type of rationality. The point is to conceive the *praxis* and its result from two inseparable points of view: that of objectification (or of man acting on matter) and that of objectivity (or of totalised matter acting on man). It is necessary to grasp how the concerted result of a practice, as a new fact, can produce a universal modification in the material quasi-totality, and how it can receive from this moving, inorganic totality a sort of passive modification which makes it Other than it is. The example of deforestation is very clear: uprooting a tree in a field of sorghum becomes *deforestation* from the point of view of a large plain and of terraces of loess, united by the work of separate men; and *deforestation* as the real meaning of the individual action of uprooting is simply the negative union of all those who are isolated by the material totality which they have produced. Thus the transformation of the act is completely intelligible from the point of view of a process of comprehension which, having evaluated its end in isolation, strives to comprehend it *in terms* not only of the massification of the peasants (identity of work, repetition), but also of the constitution of a material totality which abolishes separations in the common unity of a destiny (floods) and, lastly, of new material totalities created on this basis and separately. Although this doubly referring work can be done by an isolated agent only with difficulty, there is no reason in principle why he should not do it; in other words, it is possible for anyone to comprehend *himself* in *his* action both from the outside and from within: this is proved by the fact that the Chinese government's propaganda against deforestation explained the totalised meaning of his familial *praxis* to everyone. The experience of necessity is all the more obvious, all the more blinding, to the extent that every moment of the *praxis* has been clear and conscious, and that the choice of means has been deliberate. And it should be remembered that, as it becomes richer, *praxis* gradually reduces the number of possibilities to one and, in the end, eliminates itself, as dialectical unfolding and as work, in favour of a result inscribed in things.

We have seen that the agent's real aim, and (this comes to the same thing) the agent himself, can only be assessed in the light of the result. It is Madame Bovary who illuminates Flaubert, not the reverse. But if an *other*, broader result, bound up with the present totality, always superimposes itself on the result which has been intended and achieved, then what is assessed from the point of view of totalised objectivity is not only the aim, but also the agent himself in so far as he is nothing Other than his objectification through *praxis*. It is therefore necessary to recognise oneself as *Other* in one's own individual objectification on the basis of an *other result*. And this recognition is an experience of necessity because it shows us an *unconstrained* irreducibility inside the framework of intelligibility. This individual experience can occur only through the freedom of *praxis* (as I defined it in *The Problem of Method*); it is the free fullness of successful action providing me with the objective result as irreducibility: if I have made mistakes or been subject to constraints, it is always possible that they have falsified the result. But if I take full responsibility for the operation, I shall discover necessity as ineluctable. In other words, the basic experience of necessity is that of a retroactive power eroding my freedom, from the final objectivity to the original decision, but nevertheless emerging from it; it is the negation of freedom in the domain of complete freedom, sustained by freedom itself, and proportional to the very completeness of this freedom (degree of consciousness, instruments of thought, practical success, etc.). In this sense, it is the experience of the Other, not in so far as he is my adversary, but in so far as his dispersed *praxis*, totalised by matter, turns back on me in order to transform me; it is the historical experience of matter as *praxis* without an author, or of *praxis* as the signifying inertia which signifies me. We shall find that this experience becomes more complex as our investigation progresses, but for the present we may say: the man who looks at his work, who recognises himself in it completely, and who also does not recognise himself in it at all; the man who can say both: 'This is not what I wanted' and 'I understand that this is what I have done and that I could not do anything else', and whose free *praxis* refers him to his prefabricated being and who recognises himself equally in both – this man grasps, in an immediate dialectical movement, necessity as the *destiny in exteriority of freedom*.

Should we describe this as alienation? Obviously we should, in that *he returns to himself as Other*. However, a distinction must be made: alienation in the Marxist sense begins with exploitation. Should we go back to Hegel who sees alienation as a constant characteristic of all kinds of objectification? Yes and no. We must recognise that the original relation between *praxis* as totalisation and materiality as passivity obliges man to objectify himself in a milieu which is not his own, and to treat an inorganic totality as his own objective reality. It is this relation between interiority and exteriority which originally constituted *praxis* as a relation of the organism to its material environment; and there can be no doubt that as soon as man begins to designate himself not as the mere reproduction of his life, but as the ensemble of products which reproduce his life, he discovers himself as *Other* in the world of objectivity; totalised matter, as inert objectification perpetuated by inertia, is in effect *non-human* or even *anti-human*. All of us spend our lives engraving our maleficent image on things, and it fascinates and bewilders us if we try to understand ourselves *through it*, although we are ourselves the totalising movement which results in *this* particular objectification.[68]

---

68. It is the necessity for the practical agent to discover himself in the organised inorganic as a material being, and this necessary objectification as grasping himself in the world and outside himself in the world, which makes man into what Heidegger calls a 'being of distances'. But it is very important to notice that he first discovers himself as the real object of his *praxis* in a milieu which is not that of his practical life, so that his knowledge of himself is knowledge of himself as inertia stamped with a seal (whereas, in fact, he is the movement by which he transcends material conditioning through the act of placing his seal on the inorganic). Thus the practical agent is an organism transcending himself by an action, and his objective perception of himself presents him as an inanimate object, the result of an operation, whether it is a statue, a machine or his particular interest. For those who have read *Being and Nothingness*, I can describe the foundation of necessity as practice: it is the For-Itself, as agent, revealing itself initially as inert or, at best, as practico-inert, in the milieu of the In-Itself. This, one might say, is because the very structure of action as the organisation of the unorganised primarily relates the For-Itself to its alienated being as Being in itself. This inert materiality of man as the foundation of all knowledge of himself by himself is, therefore, an alienation of knowledge as well as a knowledge of alienation. Necessity, for man, is conceiving oneself originally as Other than one is

4   Social Being as Materiality – Class Being

In the moment where we reach the apodictic structure of dialectical experience, still in its most abstract form, the discovery by the agent of the alienation of his *praxis* is accompanied by the discovery of his objectification as alienated. This means in fact that through a *praxis* which effaces itself before an inert, alienated objectivity, he discovers his being-outside-in-the-thing as his fundamental truth and *his reality*. And this being-outside constitutes itself (or is constituted) for him as practico-inert matter; either he himself, as a particularity, is roughly conditioned in exteriority by the whole universe, or, alternatively, his being awaits him from outside, prefabricated by a conjuncture *of exigencies*. In either case, human *praxis* and its immediate aims can appear at this level only in *subordination*: human *praxis* is subordinated to the direct and lifeless exigency of a material ensemble, and is the means of fulfilling this exigency, the immediate aims appearing as the means of initiating *praxis*. 'It is *useful* that workers should strike since this encourages inventions.' Inventions are required by production itself (which sets itself the absolute aim: accumulation of wealth on God's earth); production demands from it the means of intensifying itself; the employers finance and encourage research through the militancy of the workers.

According to this optimistic way of thinking, which is perfectly adapted (as capitalist thinking) to the practico-inert hell which produced it, strikes, conceived as a means of determining employers to break out of absolute inertia, are characterised by two things, which we will recognise immediately. *First*, they lose their quality of collective *praxis* (the motives, objectives, and unity which, in the early stages,

---

and in the dimension of alterity. Certainly, *praxis* is self-explanatory (*se donne ses lumières*); it is always conscious of itself. But this non-thetic consciousness counts for nothing against the practical affirmation that *I* am what I have done (which eludes me while constituting me as other). It is the necessity of this fundamental relation which explains why, as I have said, man *projects himself* in the milieu of the In-Itself-For-Itself. Fundamental alienation does not derive, as *Being and Nothingness* might mislead one into supposing, from some prenatal choice: it derives from the univocal relation of interiority which unites man as a practical organism with his environment.

had been so difficult to create, the calculation of chances, courage, adoption of a plan, the relation between elected representatives and their comrades, etc., in short everything which is or can be the moment of constitution of the group as human activity) and become a universal *exis*. They become – as a special quality of the mechanical ensemble known as the working population – the turbulence which is manifested in its anonymous generality in odd anecdotes which, in themselves, are without interest; thus the Birmingham or Sheffield strike becomes not a particular human undertaking within the development of human history, but the exemplification of a concept. Having said this, we must not treat this abject way of thinking as a mistake; for it is true at the level where employers take account of the likelihood of strikes (calculated on the basis of previous years) in their production forecasts. *Secondly*, they control an inert milieu from outside: disturbances amongst the workers, as a general reality and negative force (like 'physical force', as it was conceived at about the same time) impinges on the employers' milieu as an inert ensemble, communicates to it a certain energy which produces internal reactions and, in particular, invention.

Inertia, exteriority: classical economics aspires to be like *physics*. But, at the same time, this inertia and exteriority are, for this way of thinking, human characteristics (that is to say, they both refer back *to praxis* as their sole intelligibility). Employers are blamed for this inertia: it is said that *they do not know their own interest*; that militant employers would not need external incentives; moreover, the authors quoted above also express annoyance at working class disturbances, which, when not resolved in definite, historical events, appear to them as an *evil failing*. (The working class can never be cured of it; but, by constantly maintaining the fear of being sacked or replaced, and by constant maintenance of a threat of replacement by the victims of technological unemployment, it is secured, *externally*, that disturbances are opposed by terror as a physical force.) But just as disturbances, which they see simply as chaotic expressions, are not just a force, but an *exis*, so *terror* – as one can read in every line of these frightful books – is a *moral* as well as a physical reaction: it is justified punishment – or the revenge of terrorised employers (which amounts to the same thing). Here we have a mixture of inertia (the stability of equal and constant forces in equilibrium) and practice (*values* imposed on the *exis* of disturbances, and on their punishment.)

The fact that such thinking is incomplete or false, and that it belongs to the employers, is unimportant; and we can say with assurance that this is how capitalism saw itself at the beginning of the first industrial revolution: an inert milieu in which transmutations of energy could take place provided they were produced by an exterior energy source. However, this need not correspond to any particular manufacturer's judgement of himself when he tries to know himself as an individual: on the contrary, he will regard himself as a bold innovator (if he has just bought a new machine, if his factory is expanding) or as a wise man (if he is refusing to take an interest in some invention). Employers as Other, (the ensemble of his competitors, suppliers and clients) however, he will judge in this way; but this *Other* body of employers exists in him as his own (relative or total) powerlessness to change anything ('Personally, I would be only too happy to . . .'). Thus he will rediscover in himself, as his negative social being and as caused impotence, the inertia which he considers to be a constituent characteristic of the being of Others.

He is not entirely mistaken. It must be recognised that his impotence is created for him out of the inertia of Others, and is lived by Others as an other inertia reducing them to impotence. It should also be understood that, for him and for Others, impotence is simply the level of his production in so far as it is conditioned by total production in terms of the system and the conjuncture. It is on the basis of this being-outside in a field of unifying materiality on the part of everyone that Marx can describe the process of capital as an 'anti-social force' developed within a definite social field and positing itself for itself. But this inertia of impotence, in so far as it can also be conscious of itself as impotence through inertia (circumstances, or a competitor's innovation can define a manufacturer's pseudo-impotence as inertia for him: 'I should have suspected something, I should have accepted so and so's proposal,' etc.). And in so far as it constitutes itself as the reality of the individual (or group), and as the negative medium in which external transmutations of energy produce *praxis* in the form of a transformation of energy conditioned from the outside but producing itself as *human value*, we can regard it as the *social Being* of man at the fundamental level, that is to say, in so far as there are *several people* within a practical field totalised by the mode of production. At an elementary level of the social (and we shall see that there are others), everyone must become conscious *of his being* as the inorganic materiality of the outside interiorising itself in the form of a bond linking him to everyone else. We shall try to see *social Being* from the point of view of the practico-inert in so far as it really determines a structure of inertia from the inside, first in individual *praxis*, then in common *praxis*; and finally we shall see it as the inorganic substance of the first *collective beings*: we shall then be in a position to see the primary structure of class *as social and collective Being*.

If the reader is surprised to see the *external being* which is *my being* determining a structure of inertia in my *praxis* (whereas *praxis* is precisely the transcendence of all the inertia of the 'material conditions' towards an objective), I have not entirely succeeded in explaining my approach: the beings, objects and people we are talking about, though still abstract, *are real*. In a given practical field, we really are practico-inert beings. I am not providing *symbolic headings* to indicate the results of human activities which have been dispersed and reunited by materiality: the flight of gold and the crisis of the Ancien Régime are realities. But these realities are produced at a certain level of concrete experience; they exist neither by nor for the block of stone in the mountain, nor for God, nor for isolated individuals, for illiterates, for example, though they may well be subjected to its effects. It is social men who produce and reveal these realities, as these realities reveal and create them, through other social realities which serve as a mediation and which have already constituted themselves.

Thus we have managed to refine our definition of the contradiction between being and doing. This contradiction does not exist in the individual considered in isolation, apart from his social relations; but on the contrary, it breaks out in the region of the practico-inert, since the first basis of the social field is this very contradiction. In this connection we have recognised that human existence is constituted through a practical project which transcends and negates given characteristics towards a totalising rearrangement of the field. Do we also have to admit that one is a worker or petit-bourgeois *passively*? Existentialism denied the *a priori* existence of essences; must we not now admit that they do exist and that they are the *a priori* characteristics of our passive being? And if they exist, how is *praxis* possible? I used to say that one never *is* a coward or a thief. Accordingly, should I not now say that one *makes oneself* a bourgeois or a proletarian? This is the question which we must now turn to.

There can be no doubt that one *makes oneself* a bourgeois. In this case, every moment of activity is embourgeoisement. But in order to make oneself bourgeois, one must be bourgeois. There is no comparison between cowardice, courage and other such useful summaries of complex activity, and membership of a class. At the origin of this membership, there are passive syntheses of materiality. And these syntheses represent both the general conditions of social activity and our most immediate, crudest objective reality. They already exist; they are simply the *crystallised practice* of previous generations: individuals find an existence already sketched out for them at birth; they 'have their position in life and their personal development assigned to them by their class'.[69] What is 'assigned' to them is a type of work, and a material condition and a standard of living tied to this activity; it is a fundamental *attitude*, as well as a determinate provision of material and intellectual tools; it is a strictly limited field of possibilities. Thus Claude Lanzmann is right when he says: 'A working woman who earns 25,000 francs a month and contracts chronic eczema by handling Dop shampoo eight hours a day is wholly reduced to her work, her fatigue, her wages and the material impossibilities that these wages assign to her: the impossibility of eating properly, of buying shoes, of sending her child to the country, and of satisfying her most modest wishes. Oppression does not reach the oppressed in a particular sector of their life; it constitutes this life in its totality. They are not people plus needs: they are completely reducible to their needs. There is no distance between self and self, no essence is hidden within the bounds of interiority: the person exists outside, in his relation to the world, and visible to all; he coincides exactly with his objective reality.'[70]

But this objective reality involves an obvious contradiction: it is both the individual and his predetermination through generality: the working woman is expected in bourgeois society, her place is marked in advance by the capitalist 'process', by national production requirements and by the particular needs of the Dop shampoo factory. Her life and destiny can be determined *before she gets her job*, and this prefabricated reality must be conceived in the mode of *being*, in the pure materiality of the in-itself. The role and attitude imposed on her by her work and consumption have never even been the object of an *intention*; they have been created as the negative aspect of an ensemble of directed activities; and as these activities are teleological, the unity of this prefabrication remains human, as a sort of negative reflection of ends pursued outside it, or, in other words, as a result of *counter-*

69. *The German Ideology*, Moscow, 1964, pp. 69–70.
70. *Les Temps Modernes*, special issue on the Left, Nos 112–13, (1955), p. 1647.

finality. At the same time, this material apparatus in which everything is meticulously controlled as if by a sadistic will *is* the working woman herself. This is what Marx elucidated in *The German Ideology*: 'The conditions under which individuals have intercourse with each other, so long as the above-mentioned contradiction is absent, are conditions appertaining to their individuality, in no way external to them; conditions under which these definite individuals, living under definite relationships, can alone produce their material life and what is connected with it, are thus the conditions of their self-activity and are produced by this self-activity.'[71]

Marx here refers to the contradiction which opposes the productive forces to the relations of production. But this is really the same contradiction as that mentioned above, which forces the working woman to live a prefabricated destiny as *her reality*. She would try in vain to take refuge in intimate 'privacy'; such a remedy would betray her directly, and become simply a mode of subjective realisation of objectivity. When semi-automatic machines were first introduced, investigations showed that specialised women workers indulged in sexual fantasies as they worked: they recalled their bedrooms, their beds, the previous night – everything that specially concerns a person in the isolation of the self-enclosed couple. But it was the machine in them which was dreaming of love: the kind of attention demanded by their work allowed them neither distraction (thinking of something else) nor total mental application (thinking would slow down their movements). The machine demands and creates in the worker an inverted semi-automatism which complements it: an explosive mixture of unconsciousness and vigilance. The mind is absorbed but not used; it is concentrated in *lateral* supervision; and the body functions 'mechanically' while yet remaining *under surveillance*. Conscious life overflows the job; the minutes of false distraction have to be lived one by one; they must be lived without concentration, and there can be no attention to detail, or to systematic ideas; otherwise the lateral function of supervision would be impeded, and movements would be slowed down. It is therefore appropriate to sink into passivity.

In similar situations, men have less tendency to indulge in erotic fantasies; this is because they are the 'first sex', the active sex; if they were to think of '*taking*' a woman, their work would suffer; conversely, work, by absorbing their total activity, cuts them off from sexuality.

71. *The German Ideology*, p. 89.

The woman worker thinks about *sexual abandonment*, because the machine requires her to live her conscious life in passivity in order to preserve a flexible, preventive vigilance without ever mobilising herself into active thought. Naturally, rumination can have various aspects, and may attach itself to different objects: the woman may recall the pleasure of the night before, or dream of the night to come, or constantly relive her troubled feelings while reading a book or magazine; or she may avoid sexuality and ruminate on the bitterness of her social condition instead. Nevertheless, it is essential that the *object* of her daydreams should also be the subject, that there should always be *adherences*: if the object posits itself for itself (if the woman emerges from her daydream, and *thinks* about her husband or her lover), the work will stop or slow down. That is why mothers are practically unable to think about their children – objects of their attention and worries – and why, very often, a woman's sexual ruminations do not correspond to her *sexual attitude* in married life. The truth is that when the woman worker thinks she is *escaping* from herself, she is really finding an indirect way of making herself what she is; the vague uneasiness which she maintains – and which, indeed, is limited by the constant movement of the machine and of her body – is a means of preventing thought from reforming, of confining consciousness and absorbing it in flesh, even while making use of it. Is she conscious of this? Yes and no: no doubt she tries to people the desert of boredom produced by the specialised machine. But *at the same time*, she tries to fix her mind within the limits allowed by the operation, by the objective task: she is the unwilling accomplice of employers who have determined norms and minimum output in advance. Thus the deepest interiority becomes a means of realising oneself as total exteriority.

In this sense, the conditioning of the person is itself a future contradiction, which will eventually break out, but it is this contradiction in its present ambiguity or, as Marx says, in its 'incompleteness'; it will not be evident until after it has broken out and 'thus exists (only) for the later individuals'.[72] In fact, wherever one places oneself in history, one will find some oppositions which are entrenched and others which are uncertain, since we are always both those who come before and those who come after. *It is true* that 'for the proletarians . . . the condition of their existence, labour, and with it all the conditions of

72. *Ibid.*, p. 89.

existence governing modern society have become something acci-dental'.[73] This implies that the individual enters into conflict with the situation in which he finds himself. But *it is also true* that all the actions he carries out *as an individual* merely reinforce and emphasise the objective being imposed on him: when the woman in the Dop shampoo factory has an abortion in order to avoid having a child she would be unable to feed, she makes a free decision in order to escape a destiny that is made for her; but this decision is itself completely manipulated by the objective situation: she *realises* through herself what she *is already*; she carries out the sentence, which has already been passed on her, which deprives her of free motherhood.

On this first point dialectical intelligibility is unimpaired and exis-tential principles are unaffected. In *Being and Nothingness* I said, following Hegel, that essence is past, transcended being. And, indeed, this is precisely what the being of the worker *primarily* is, in that in a capitalist society, it is prefabricated by already performed, already crystallised labour. And his personal *praxis*, as a free productive dia-lectic, in turn transcends this prefabricated being by the very movement which it impresses on the lathe or machine-tool. Inertia comes to him from the fact that previous work has constituted in the machine *a future which cannot be transcended* in the form of exigency (that is to say, specifically, the way the machine is to be used and its ability, in definite conditions, to increase production by a definite proportion), and from the fact that this untranscendable future is actualised in all its urgency by present circumstances (the capitalist process as a whole and the conjuncture in the unity of historical totalisation). Thus the *inertia of praxis*, as a new characteristic of it, removes none of its previous characteristics: *praxis* remains a transcendence of material being to-wards a future reorganisation of the field. But passivising *annulment* modifies it from the future towards the past within the petrified frame-work of exigency: this is because the future to be realised is already fabricated as mechanical inertia *in the way in which past being is trans-cended*. And indeed it can always be said that any material circumstance which has to be transcended, even the configuration of the land in the course of a walk, imposes a certain content on the future towards which it is transcended. It restricts certain possibilities and provides a certain instrumentality which will characterise the final result. However, it does not *produce* that future; the future comes to material circumstances

73. *Ibid.*, p. 96.

through men, and if material circumstances are preserved in it as significations, it is not because it is homogeneous with them (and passive like them), but on the contrary because human *praxis* has given it a human future by projecting it (as transcended and preserved) into this future. On the contrary, *precisely* because they have been worked and assembled by men, who have made them anti-human, the machine and the combination of exigencies contain the movement of transcendence in themselves and, in connection with this inert movement, the future of the ensemble is the mechanico-practical meaning of this totality in so far as it *functions* (that is to say, in so far as an *exterior* force enables it to realise itself as a pseudo-organic function). Thus the reason why past being cannot be transcended is that it is itself the inscription in being of a *praxis* which produces, beyond any particular human *praxis*, its own meaning as transcendent being. So the human *praxis* which lives in symbiosis with this inert practice and which is controlled by it as exigency constitutes itself as a mechanical means (in exteriority) of introducing mechanics amongst its characteristics as a human undertaking. It remains entirely what it is (if one takes it abstractly as a pure, isolated *praxis*) but its own future as transcendence of its past being is transcended by this very past-being in so far as it is already signified by the future.

As I have said already, if the stratagems of the enemy lead a regiment to retreat towards an emplacement which seems protected but which has in fact been heavily mined, the practical freedom of the commanders who execute this retreat remains unimpaired in each of its dialectical moments, but their ignorance of the trap the enemy has prepared for them means that their free *praxis* is the necessary means selected by the enemy of bringing this military unit to inevitable destruction. Thus some other freedom, supported by powerful material means, may force a *praxis* into the role of a blind process leading men toward a passive future which cannot be transcended: that of their own destruction. And, if we assume that – as is usually the case – the commanders *could not* know that the field was mined, their *praxis* should not even be described as *playing this role*, but rather as objectively being this necessity itself. In any case, it should be noted that a *praxis* can constitute itself in this way only in the milieu of a *praxis* which transcends it and knows it better than it knows itself. Of course, it often happens that, in trying to avoid some annoyance, we fall into worse trouble; but if nobody has deliberately arranged the first danger in order to lead us into the second through the complicity of our personal activity, this involves nothing more than the inherent uncertainty of *praxis*; for every *praxis*, to some degree, takes account of its areas of ignorance, reckons on *probabilities* (in the strict sense of the term), makes wagers, and takes risks.

The freedom of an action which ends in failure is simply freedom which fails, since the fundamental relation of the organism to its environment is univocal. Matter does not make a constitutive return to *praxis* in order to transform it into a controlling fatality. In the case of a trap, however, it is clear that the freedom of the enemy, through the complex of material means involved, from the initial shot to the mine field, *has given our own freedom a negative aspect* (*envers*), and has made it objectively a practico-inert process of counter-finality: so much so that the soldier who falls into the trap will, if he escapes, discover an extraordinary (but easily understood) paradox, conveyed by the colloquial expression: 'We've really been *had*.' To have: that is, to possess an enemy *in so far as* he is an inalienable *praxis* (and not, for example, because one is stronger or better armed). This petrification of freedom as such is obvious in military stratagems because once the material machine which forces us to destroy ourselves is set in motion, it is sustained and controlled by the living, practical freedom of the enemy. In the case of class-being as inertia which infiltrates freedom, the thing seems less obvious: for one thing, the workers who created the machines through their work are absent, perhaps dead; and in any case, it is not they but others − their exploiters − who desired our enslavement; indeed they did not desire it directly, but were essentially trying to increase their profit; besides, the empty position which each worker is expected to fill derives thereby from the diverse variety of exigencies which have come together without any particular action having presided over the process. Thus there is not really a freedom on the part of the employers to constitute *the negative aspect in itself* of the workers' *praxes*. But the univocal relation of interiority has transformed itself through the medium of the real meanings and real exigencies whose material object has been provided by human practices, whether multiple or unified, in false reciprocal interiority. And this false interiority, along with the prefabricated ends which cannot be transcended but which *praxis* must freely realise, is sufficient to transform this transcendence of Being into transcendence transcended by the Being to be transcended. Thus in the complex movement of alienated labour we have the inert Being of machinery as a material circumstance to be transcended, transcendence by *praxis* (setting in motion, use, and supervision) and transcendence of *praxis* (in so far as some exterior norm transfuses it as inert exigency) by that same Being, but to come as an *other* meaning realising itself.

This will apply on every plane and not just that of production. The worker is socially constituted as a practico-inert object to the extent that he receives a wage: he becomes a machine that has to be maintained and fed. Now, in deciding his budget in accordance with the needs created in him by his work (by satisfying above all his hunger, to the detriment of clothes and lodging), the nineteenth-century worker *made himself what he was*, that is to say, he practically and rationally determined the order of priority of his expenditure; he therefore decided in his free *praxis*, and through this very freedom he made himself what he was, what he is, and what he must be: a machine whose wages simply represent maintenance costs.[74] At this level we will encounter the questions raised in *The Problem of Method*. We can now see why *transcending one's class condition* effectively means realising it. And since *praxis*, as the transparent movement of action, cannot alienate itself, we find different actions in everyone: one worker reads, another agitates, another finds time to do both, another has just bought a scooter, another plays the violin, and another does gardening. All these activities are constituted on the basis of particular circumstances, and they constitute the objective individuality of each person. But still, in so far as they are located, in spite of themselves, inside a framework of exigencies that cannot be transcended, they simply realise everyone's class being. Everyone makes himself signify by interiorising, by a free choice, the signification with which material exigencies have produced him as a *signified being*. Class-being, as practico-inert being mediated by the passive syntheses of worked matter, comes to men through men; for each of us it is our being-

74. I say 'the nineteenth-century worker' because contemporary economists increasingly tend to regard wages as the portion of the national income socially assigned to each individual. We may well wonder whether this ethical conception of wages – based on old 'solidarist' theories – has any advantage other than 'drowning the fish' – that is to say, passing over class struggle in silence; whether, in effect, family allowances, social security, etc., do not represent what one might call a *social portion* of wages. It should be observed however that *even so* it is far from being the case that society as a whole provides this national contribution. In any case, the contemporary worker has entirely different characteristics, in many fields, than previous generations. But the problem of class-being, as a logical and dialectical problem of rationality, remains the same for all that.

outside-ourselves in matter, in so far as this produces us and awaits us from birth, and in so far as it constitutes itself through us as a future-fatality, that is to say as a future which will necessarily realise itself through us, through the otherwise arbitrary actions which we choose. It is obvious that this class-being does not prevent us from realising an individual destiny (each life is individual), but this realisation of our experience until death is only one of several possible ways (determined by the structured field of possibilities) of producing our class-being.

However, it should not be thought that class-being realises itself as a simple relation of everyone to instrumentality and thereby to the other class; it is produced, in simultaneous connection with everything, as the structure of a class, that is to say, as a prefabricated relation between people of the same class on the basis of instrumentality. From this point, in a circular movement, it becomes the inert statute of their collective *praxis* in the context of class struggle. Admittedly, we have not yet established the nature of groups as organised activity. But even without examining this (we shall come to it in the next chapter) it will be appropriate to show that they can be organised only on the basis of inert structures representing both a qualification of their action and its objective limit, including its secret inertia. A well-known example will make this clearer.

Corresponding to the iron and coal complex there is the so called 'universal' machine. This means a machine – like the *lathe* in the second half of the nineteenth century – whose function remains indeterminate (in contrast to the specialised machines of automation and semi-automation), and which can do very different jobs provided it is guided, prepared and supervised by a skilful, expert worker. The universality of the machine produces specialisation in its servants: it is accessible only to those who know how to use it, and who have therefore had to undergo an often very long apprenticeship. (Conversely, the specialisation of the machine, fifty years later, in the period of semi-automation, has brought with it the universalisation of its servants: they are interchangeable.) Thus the producer of the machines, through his product and the improvements he makes to it, identifies a certain type of men, namely the skilled workers who are capable of carrying out a complete operation from beginning to end, unaided, that is to say, a dialectical *praxis*.

This practical effect is built into machines themselves in the form of exigency. They reduce specifically physical effort, but require skill. They require that men freed of all secondary labours should devote themselves entirely to them: and in this way, they fix, *first*, the mode of recruitment; then, through the employers, they create employment opportunities and relatively high wages on the labour market; and so a structured future opens up for certain sons of workers, who turn out to have the abilities and means required to become apprentices. (This means sons whose fathers, themselves workers, are in a position to let their sons work for a number of years without being able to support themselves. Generally, the father himself will have to be a skilled worker.) But, in the same process, machines create a lower proletariat which is *not only* the direct result of the rise of an élite of better paid workers, who are selected by apprenticeship, but is *also* directly required by the universal machine, in the form of the ensemble of unskilled workers who, in every workshop, have to be attached to the skilled workers, obey them, and relieve them of all the lowly chores which *Others* can do for them.

Thus, the nineteenth-century machine constitutes *a priori* a passive structure of the proletariat. I shall call this a solar-system structure: the unskilled workers – indistinguishable and defined only as non-specialised (and therefore completely indeterminate) individuals – circle around an equally interchangeable skilled worker in groups of five to ten; but he is defined, in universal terms, by his specialisation. This proletariat, structured by its functions – that is to say, by the role of its members in production – is required not only by the employers (who need to organise and encourage apprenticeship, and fear a crisis of skilled labour), but also by the workers themselves (who have to carry out the selection themselves, under the pressure of needs and in the context of everyone's opportunities). The machine organises men. But this human organisation has nothing in common with a synthetic union, with a community based on a conscious decision; the hierarchy will establish itself in the mechanical dispersal of massified pluralities and *as if by accident*. One child will happen to fulfil the physical, mental and social conditions required to become an apprentice; another – with no apparent relation to the first – will become an unskilled worker because these conditions are not fulfilled. Everyone's relation to machines being, strictly speaking, an individual and relatively autonomous destiny, the statistical relation of the machine to everyone appears as a real redistribution of social molecules in a given society, at a given moment, *by materiality itself*. And it is precisely material inertia which makes this mysterious and rigid, hierarchical unity *in dispersal* possible, just as it is the solidified *praxis* of matter, as the mechanical future of a group, class or society which establishes this hierarchical order *a priori* as the ensemble of those abstract relations which are to unite arbitrary individuals and which will impose themselves on these individuals *whoever they are* in the temporal context of production: the factory, with all its machines, has already decided on the ratio of unskilled to skilled workers, and consequently it has already established, *for everyone*, their chances of joining the élite or remaining in a state of sub-humanity.

Thus the universal machine imposes differentiation on workers as a law of things; but at the same time, by the process described above in connection with Spanish gold, *it becomes its own idea*. As the property of an employer, it relegates its servant to the ranks of the exploited, and maintains and aggravates the contradiction which opposes the propertied class to the working class; but through the skill it demands, it creates a humanism of labour in the hands and body of the person who operates it. To the extent that, through the machine, the skilled worker sees his labour power, his skill and his abilities transformed into a product, that is to say, into social wealth, he will not regard himself as a 'sub-human conscious of his sub-humanity'. Admittedly, his product is taken away from him: but his indignation at being exploited has its deepest source in his pride as a producer. The 'damned of the earth' are precisely the only people capable of changing life, and who do change it every day, who feed, clothe and house humanity as a whole. And since the machine is selective, since, through the competence it exacts and creates, it constitutes work, for the skilled worker, as the honour of the exploited, it produces, in one process, both for the skilled workers and for the working masses, the unskilled worker as an inferior who gets lower wages, and possesses less technical value and less being. In relation to the employer, of course, the unskilled worker is posited as *exploited*; but what is he in relation to the skilled worker? Perhaps someone less fortunate (his father was poor, he started work at the age of twelve), or perhaps someone who lacked courage or ability; perhaps both. There is a tension here. It is not a true antagonism, at least at first: the unskilled worker harbours ambiguous feelings about the skilled worker. He admires him and listens to him: the skilled worker, acquiring political and sometimes scientific knowledge, and regarding himself as the active wing of the proletariat, merely develops the machine's own idea of itself and of its servant; but his positive education and his combativeness deceive the unskilled worker: he follows. But sometimes he will get the impression that the élite workers, incorporating him in their struggles, are not always defending *his* own interests.

Everything I have just described is *inscribed in Being*. The inert idea of labour-dignity, technical operations, differentiation between men, the hierarchy and the tension it produces, are all a product of machines; in other words, in a given factory, they are the practico-inert Being of the workers themselves in so far as the relations between them are *the machine itself* through its servants. But what has to be demonstrated is that these passive structures will induce a quite specific inertia in militant workers' groups in that *praxis* will always be incapable of transcending certain untranscendable structures. I have indicated elsewhere how anarcho-syndicalist organisations, a product of the free efforts of skilled workers, were destined, even before unification was achieved, to reproduce in the form of a 'voluntary' association the structures which had been established through the mediation of the universal machine in different enterprises. But it would be a grave mistake to believe that the machine created the syndicalism of 1900 in the way that a 'cause' produces its 'effect'. If this were the case, both the dialectic and mankind would disappear.

The humanism of labour is in fact the material being of the skilled worker; he realises it in his work, in his hands and his eyes; he receives it in his wages, which express both exploitation and the hierarchy of the exploited; and he creates it by his very influence on the unskilled workers, and through an obscure conflict between them which remains hard to grasp. He still has to find out what he is. This means that his attempt to unite with his equals and to oppose exploitation by a practical negation must be made through the projection of *what he is* into his very *praxis*. How should he transcend exploitation, if not with what it has made of him: the fundamental movement by which skilled workers unite and transcend their antagonisms is also the affirmation of the humanism of labour. The anarcho-syndicalist decries exploitation in the name of the absolute superiority of skilled manual labour over all other activities. And practice fully confirms that this was the situation: in the period of the universal machine, it mattered very little if there was a strike of unskilled workers, whereas the absence of a few skilled workers, who would be very hard to replace, was enough to disrupt a whole workshop. So the *élite* of specialists deprived themselves, *unwittingly*, of the means of protesting against the exploitation of the unskilled workers: admittedly, their poverty angered them, but they could not support the claims of these 'sub-humans' on the grounds of the skill of their work. As soon as machine labour required that the worker should have a sort of suzerainty over his assistants, the fundamental affirmation of the humanism of labour and the related circumstances of the class struggle gave rise to a new device, which might be called the paternalism of the labour élite: unskilled workers must be educated, trained, inspired by example, etc. Thus the organisation against exploitation recreated, rigorously but freely, all the conditions which materiality imposes on alienated man.

The interesting point here is the subtle nothingness at the heart of a positive fullness: the impossibility of *transcending* this humanism. It was in fact transcended when the skills of the skilled workers were rendered useless by specialised machines: this recreated workers' unity (in the advanced capitalist countries) on the basis of the interchangeability of skilled workers. Work took on once again all its negative characteristics: an exhausting burden, a hostile force. Admittedly, manual workers were still proud of their work: but this was because they sustained the whole of society, rather than because of the distinctiveness of the particular quality of their work. A humanism of need, as the direct hold of every man on all men, was being born. But it is crucial that anarcho-syndicalist humanism was unable to transcend itself. The reason, indeed, is simple enough: this practice and theory represented the very life of the group, and the militant group (whether a trade union or the employees of a factory) was simply the unification and reorganisation of the social struggle on existing structural bases. It was *really impossible* that the skilled workers, with their superior education, and their greater militancy and effectiveness, who could bring work to a halt by their mere absence, should merge themselves *in practice* with mass organisations in which the less educated and less militant would have been in a majority. If mass unions are possible and necessary today, it is because the technique of struggle has changed with the class structure, and because the interchangeability of skilled workers forces them to adopt a policy of mass action.

The equality of workers has come both from changes in the means of production and from the practical tasks which these changes impose: hence it is *real*, that is to say, it is constantly being proved by its efficacity. But in 1900 this would have been an idealist position, since the slightest strike could have demonstrated its ineffectiveness. How could one affirm equality as long as a strike could succeed *without the support of unskilled workers* and when *the unskilled workers on their own* could not win a strike at all? And how could one give the same weight to every opinion given that the unskilled workers of that time, with their poor education, their timidity, and their lack of the deeply respectable pride of the skilled workers, *really* were an inert mass which needed to be roused and galvanised into action?

Positively, the humanism of labour appeared as an absorbing, endless task: innumerable monographs prove how seriously these men took it. They had to improve their skills in their trade, to educate themselves, and to educate the unskilled – they regarded themselves as responsible for their assistants; and they had to fight, to forge working-class unity and bring forward the day when they would seize power. In short, it was a free, full world and they developed it tirelessly and passionately. And this living fullness was, at the same time, doomed: confronted by contemptible employers, incapable of exercising a truly productive trade, and surrounded by the unskilled workers whom they were obliged to emancipate, they identified the real, fulfilled human being with the skilled worker. And this false identification (false not in relation to the employers but in relation to the masses) represented a limit which could not be transcended, since it was *themselves*, or in other words, the theoretical and practical expression of their practico-inert relations with other workers. This should not be misunderstood: if, today, someone manages to glimpse absolute equality in his practical efficacity as the only valid form of human relation, his theory is false in so far as it paralyses, and becomes destiny. But when the problem of the structure of unions (whether they should be based on crafts or industries) arose, theory and practice became false in that they were an inert resistance to effective reorganisation; the humanism of labour became false when it led certain syndicalist dreamers to propose a workers' order of chivalry; and the link with the vassals became false when the docility of the unskilled workers gave way to increasing discontent. And above all the ideological and practical ensemble which expressed the struggle of a class which was structured by the universal machine became false when it prevented the unions from encompassing and organising the new masses, produced since before 1914 by the first specialised machines.

But how could this exploited class fight for a proletariat other than itself? And was it not precisely a proletariat which was structured in its being by universal machines, and passively affected by the material idea of 'dignity of labour', which its élite interiorised in *praxis*. By determining what the members of the exploited class were, machines determined what they could be: they even deprived them of the ability to imagine different forms of struggle, at the same time as giving their self-affirmation (that is to say, their ethico-practical reinteriorisation of the machine's exigencies and the temporalising development in action of structures prefabricated by it) the form of the only effective struggle that was possible in *these* circumstances and against *these* employers. In this situation, Being became the prefabricated Future as a negative determination of temporalisation. In other words, it appeared *in action* (at least to some people, in some circumstances, such as, for example, certain antagonistic relations with unskilled workers) as its solidified but incomprehensible contradiction, as an impossibility of going further, of desiring or comprehending any more, like an iron wall in translucidity. In a way, indeed, the limit is given and even *interiorised* by *praxis* itself (in our example, it appears *inside* individual relations themselves: work relations, politico-social relations, personal relations) of both skilled and unskilled workers; it even affects a simple greeting between a skilled and an unskilled worker, just as the relation between classes in the same period is visible in the greeting between an industrialist and one of his workers.

For us, who belong to another society (still capitalist, but one whose structures are governed by new energy sources, new machines and mass production), these interiorised limits appear as the objective meaning of structural relations in the period of anarcho-syndicalism. Of course, we can neither see nor hear these men, and the meaning of their everyday individual *praxis* eludes us. But it is expressed everywhere in the collective actions of which society retains some memory, in the institutions which they produced, in the sectarian conflicts within the unions, in the speeches which express them and even in the dreams of certain anarchist journalists. Elsewhere I have quoted some statements by syndicalist leaders which affirm quite blandly that the exploitation of man by man is more deplorable the more skilled the work (there are thousands of such statements). This can be taken to mean that the exploitation of an illiterate labourer – who has no skill, but who exhausts himself in carrying enormous loads from one end of the workshop to the other – is not completely unjustified. Above all, this proves that such syndicalists (whatever they may have said or written) did not really understand that this illiterate, possibly stupid labourer had been marked by society, even before he was born, as incapable of becoming a skilled worker. So *for us* the meaning of this is blindingly obvious; and this is a measure of our distance from them; and we *too* comprehend it in terms of *our* invisible walls: we can understand every petrified limit of human relations in terms of the invisible limit which reifies our own. I am not saying that *for them* this objective meaning was *a priori* incapable of being achieved: for example, the contacts between two societies with different structures, though *always degrading* for the underdeveloped society, lead certain groups in the underdeveloped society to see certain relations which were formerly simply *produced* in their objectivity. Supposing, for example – though it is historically absurd – that in the name of another trade union movement, established on the basis of mass production in advanced capitalist countries, foreign workers were able, in the course of an international dialogue, to point out to the anarcho-syndicalists certain ossified structures of social *praxis*, there is no *a priori* reason for denying that certain groups or individuals might have become conscious of them (at least it is not logically impossible). However, this does not in any way imply that they would have wanted to alter these structures; it is more likely that they would have engaged in the kind of secondary activity which might be called practices of justification. But, in any case, contacts – between differently structured proletariats – could not have had such a simple meaning at the beginning of the twentieth century, when, unknown to itself, the second industrial revolution was taking place. Today, such contacts exist, but they have a different meaning (France: for a long time backward in its development, with a more homogeneous working class in certain key-industries, and still a hierarchised one in other sectors; the United States: advanced capitalism, a destiny which was for a long time rejected in France, both by Malthusian employers and by the working class).

The fact remains that it is always abstractly possible for any practico-inert limit to a human relation to reveal itself to the men it unites as *the objective Being* of their relation. But at this very moment, their experience of this meaning *as real Being* shows them that it has always existed, interiorised but petrified, in living *praxis*, even at the moment of subjectivity. It is simply that it then appeared both as an incomprehensible nothingness in the full development of some reciprocal activity and as a positive qualification of this practical fullness (suzerainty lived in the relation between the skilled and unskilled worker as the basis of the responsibilities of the suzerain and even of his love for the vassal). And precisely for that reason, the discovery of our Being is frightening (since it generally occurs in the midst of failure and conflict) – because it reveals that what one did not know was something one knew all along, in other words, because it retrospectively constitutes our ignorances of our Being as determined and prefabricated by the Being which we are but of which we were unaware. In this way – and this applies to the group as much as to the individual – inert Being can also be defined in terms of the type of practical choice which prevents one from knowing what one is.

But *above all* it must be emphasised that this prefabricated objectivity does not prevent *praxis* from being free temporalisation and *effective* reorganisation of the practical field in relation to aims discovered and posited in the course of *praxis* itself. Anarcho-syndicalism was *in fact* a vital and effective struggle, which gradually forged its weapons and created trade union unity out of dispersal; today, it even seems that its historical role was precisely to create the first organs of unification in the working class. In other words, it was simply the working class itself, at a particular moment in its development, producing in a rudimentary form its first collective apparatuses. But it must be understood, quite simply, that its form of hierarchical unity was already inscribed in human plurality by universal machines, to the extent that their exigencies had structured hierarchical groups of workers and that the transcendence of real multiplicity, of individual antagonisms, of local peculiarities, of mistrusts, of inertia, etc., in so far as it was a totally human *praxis* (that is to say, one which necessitated theoretical understanding of the situation, organisation of the practical field, constant efforts, courage, patience, and the practical development of an experience which itself brought new technical means of transcending the situation, etc.), simply carried out in a human way – that is to say, practically, dialectically – the sentence which universal machines had passed on the proletariat. The sentence still *had* to be carried out: without human *praxis*, the class remained the inert collective which will be described in the next paragraph; but human *praxis*, occasioned by the very structures of the collective (our discussion of the group will explain the meaning of the word 'occasion'), could only temporalise the same structures which had made it possible, in the unity of an action which was both organisational and tactical, through relations established by men.[75]

75. Although it lies beyond our subject, it is worth remarking that value (in the *ethical* rather than the economic sense of the term, though the former is based on the latter) is precisely the contradictory unity of *praxis* (as free transcendence positing itself as an indeterminate possibility of transcending everything in the translucence of creative action) and of exigency (as the future which cannot be transcended). From pure *praxis*, value derives the translucidity of self-

positing freedom; but *in so far as* the end projected is *in fact* an inert, untranscendable meaning of the prefabricated future, value acquires an independent passive being. Instead of being pure *praxis*, laying down its own laws (which would deprive it of its characteristics of interior exteriority, that is, of transcendence in immanence, and which would reduce it to a mere act of awareness (*prise de conscience*)), it isolates itself. But, since its inertia necessarily makes it *transcendable*, and since its practico-inert characteristic is that it *cannot be transcended*, it posits itself as the transcendent unity of all possible transcendences, (*dépassements*), that is to say, as the term which is untranscendable (because it is situated at infinity) and towards which every action transcends the material conditions which occasion it. In the case of anarcho-syndicalist humanism, for example, skilled labour became *human value* as soon as the conditions which had made it necessary began to make it impossible even to conceive of a different mode of being, constituted on the basis of unskilled labour. If he became conscious of himself, without this *a priori* limit and as a mere historical agent, the skilled worker would certainly have come to see his work as the dialectical, translucent development of human *praxis* within an exploitative system, in short, as the historical, dated actualisation of his reality as a man. But labour became impossible to transcend in him, because it also appeared as other; that is, when the actual *praxis* of the worker constituted itself as having to realise itself as *other than itself*, as a particular embodiment of an inert meaning which, even when embodied, would remain alien to it, or in other words, would remain the sign of all transcendences. However, value is different from exigency. They are two different structures within a single process. The imperative character of exigency is due to the fact that materiality is animated by the *praxis* of the other and to the fact that this *praxis* is revealed to me as both human and alien: it signifies me and awaits me, but it is not *mine*: it is myself as nothing. Value, on the other hand, is in a double movement: both the revealing of *my praxis* in its free development in so far as it posits itself as other within immanence, and the revealing of a future signification as an inertia which necessarily refers back to my freedom. In either case, the original structure is worked materiality as a bond between men, and *praxis* as absorbed and inverted by this matter. But in the first case, the inversion directly *signifies me* in so far as I am the *means of realising* a material aim; whereas in the second case, which arises at a different level of the investigation, I apprehend *primarily* my *praxis*, but only *in so far as* it transcends itself in its very freedom towards the Other-Being of all *praxis*; and, consequently, in so far as a *controlling and created* limit affects it with materiality. This new structure implies that the experience of *praxis* as the creator (or realiser) of value is new (*originale*): there is not any constraint in this case, but rather an (alienated) awareness of an identity between *praxis* itself, at its highest level of conscious translucidity, and a particular inert meaning which absorbs it and gives it its practico-inert statute as materiality. In short, value is not the alienation either of the aim or of realised objectivity; it is the alienation of *praxis* itself. In other words, it is *praxis* unwittingly revealing the inertia with which the practico-inert being of the practical agent affects it. From the point of view of ethics, this means that values are bound up with the existence of the practico-inert field, in other words with hell as the negation of its negation (which shows that their pseudo-positivity is entirely negative) and that if a liquidation of these structures is to be possible – a question which we shall examine in the progressive moment of the investigation-values will disappear with them, allowing *praxis* in its free development to be revealed as the sole ethical relation between people in so far as together they dominate matter. The source of the ambiguity of all morality, past and present, is that freedom as a human relation reveals itself, in the world of exploitation and oppression, in opposition to this world and as a negation of the inhuman *through values*, and that it reveals itself there as alienated and loses itself in it and that, *by means of values*, it realises nevertheless the untranscendable exigency imposed on it by practico-inert being, while still contributing to an organisation which carries within it the possibilities of reorganising the practico-inert field (at least on the basis of new circumstances). Every system of values rests on exploitation and oppression; every system of values effectively negates exploitation and oppression (even aristocratic systems, if not explicitly at least in their internal logic); every system of values confirms exploitation and oppression (even systems constructed by oppressed classes, if not in intention, at least in so far as they are systems); every system of values, in so far as it is based on a social practice, contributes directly or indirectly to establishing devices and apparatuses which, when the time comes (for example, on the basis of a revolution in techniques and tools) will allow *this* particular oppression and exploitation to be negated; every system of values, at the moment of its revolutionary efficacity, ceases to be a system, and values cease to be values: their character was due to the fact that they could not be transcended; and circumstances, overthrowing structures, institutions and exigencies, transform them into transcended significations: systems are reabsorbed into the organisations which they have created and the organisations, transformed by the overthrow of the social field, integrate themselves into new collective actions, carried out in the context of the new exigencies; and they disclose new values. But Marxists can be criticised for confusing systems of values with their expression in language and with the moralities invented by intellectuals on the basis of these systems. This makes it easy to see them as mere dead reflections of practice. By confusing them with the philosophical vocabulary which is used to refer to them, Marxism has avoided a difficult problem: that of accounting for their structure. And in this way, it has had no defence against moralism, because it cannot give an account of them. Nothing is more striking, for example, than the profound moralism of Russian society (which there is no reason for confusing with the collective *praxis* which is constructing, through new contradictions, a socialist society). In the USSR, certain notions, common to all (in particular, that of *life* both as a value to be preserved and as the ethical source of all experience) are expressly presented *as values*, at every level of the society. In order to give an account of them, Marxism must understand that value is produced at the level of elementary *praxis* (individual and collective), as this *praxis* itself in so far as it conceives its own limits in the false guise of a positive fullness which cannot be transcended. What I am trying to show here is that every supposed superstructure is really already contained in the base, as a structure of the fundamental relation of men to worked matter and to other men. If we then see them appear and posit themselves for themselves as abstract moments and as superstructures, this is because a complex process refracts them through other fields and, particularly, in the field of language. But *no idea, no value*, and *no system* would be conceivable if they were not already contained, at every level of the

Thus we have seen *class-being* as the practico-inert statute of individual or common *praxis*, as the future sentence, petrified in past being, which this *praxis* itself has to carry out and in which it must finally recognise itself in a new experience of necessity. But this practico-inert being appeared to us as a real moment of the individual or as the passive statute of an active group or, conversely, as the active pseudo-unity of an inert material ensemble. In order to understand it better, we must investigate a new structure, conditioned by the preceding ones and conditioning them in turn: for, as we have seen, *class-being* is not a mere characteristic of untranscendable materiality existing as a separate quality in discrete entities isolated from one another (like, for example, height or colour of hair). In fact *class-being*, far from manifesting itself as an *identity* of being between independent realities, appears in this investigation (*expérience*) as the material unity of individuals or, in other words, as the collective basis of their individuality. Our examples were designed to show that individuals realise their class statute *through one another*: from elementary *praxis*, from working in a workshop, everyone's *class-being*, in so far as it is a practico-inert exigency of machines, comes to him not only from the class which exploits him, but also from all his comrades; or rather, it comes to him from the class which exploits him and the machines which require him through the medium of his comrades and their universal character as exploited.

At the same time, *class-being* defines itself for everyone as an inert (untranscendable) relation with his class comrades on the basis of certain structures. Destiny, general (and even particular) Interest, Exigency, Class Structures, Values as common limits, all necessarily direct our attention not only to a type of individual being which we have already described, but also, through it, to *a type of collective being* as the basis of all individual reality. I am not referring here to those active collectivities which organise themselves for a definite purpose and which we will study later under the name of groups. Nor am I referring to those ensembles which are *both* hot and cold, like an army, because they possess both the practical and historical activity of an organisation and the inert materiality of an institution. Rather, at a deeper level, as the basis of all individuation as well as all unity, I am

---

experience and in various forms, in all the moments of activity and of alienation, not only as signs, as exigencies in the tool, but also as a revelation of the world through this tool by labour, etc.

referring to *inert collective being*, as the *inorganic common materiality* of all the members of a given ensemble. This indeed is basically what it means to speak of a class. For the term does not primarily mean either the active unification of all the individuals within the organisations which they themselves have produced, or an identity of nature between several separate products. In the first meaning, indeed, the term is not always, or even very frequently, applicable in our investigation; numerous contradictions, born of historical circumstances, often cause deep divisions within a class.

There can be no doubt that the proletariat would be able to approach the unity of a collective *praxis* if the organisations it has produced – in France for example – succeeded in bringing about trade union unity. But, when it is represented by warring parties and unions, must we stop calling it the proletariat? Everyone's experience testifies to the contrary; for it is normal to speak of the *divisions in the working class*, which presupposes a deeper unity, on the basis of which, in certain conditions, it will produce either its active unity as an increasingly developed integration (and totalisation), or its divisions as the destruction of an already existing totality. Or rather: no one would dream of arguing that, because these divisions exist, the working class is being replaced by *several* groups of exploited individuals, more opposed in their aims and their tactics than they are united by common exploitation. These divisions would be described as *threatening to reduce the working class to impotence*. The divisions appear therefore as accidents, which, though undoubtedly very serious *for practice*, cannot affect the fundamental substance, which is *one*.

And it cannot be argued that this substance does not really exist, that there are only individuals threatened by a single destiny, victims of the same exigencies, possessing the same general interest, etc., for it is precisely the ensemble of structures of the practico-inert field that necessarily conditions the substantial unity of the being-outside-oneself of individuals, and conversely, this being-outside-oneself as a substantial and negative unity on the terrain of the Other conditions the structures of this field in its turn. But at the same time, we should avoid thinking in terms of those gelatinous realities, somewhat vaguely haunted by a supra-individual consciousness which, in defiance of all appearances, a discredited organicism still tries to find in the rough, complex field, furrowed with passive activity, which contains *several* individual organisms and inorganic material realities. And in fact, if everyone merges together in a particular common being, this must occur in the practico-inert field *and precisely to the extent* that they *are not* individual organisms, or in other words, in so far as worked materiality itself makes itself into a synthesis (or false synthesis) of their *being-outside-themselves-in-it*. This is clearly reflected in our language, when an individual is said to be born *into* the working class or to have *sprung from* the proletariat (if he has emerged from it) or to *belong* to it, as if the class as a whole was a matrix, a milieu and a sort of passive weight (the idea of class *viscosity* is used to explain a worker's son's chances of emerging from the working class). In a word, class as collective being is in everyone to the extent that everyone is in it, and before 'getting organised' and 'producing apparatuses', it appears in the contradictory aspect of a sort of common inertia as a synthesis of multiplicity. These considerations, which normally satisfy sociologists, obviously cannot establish the intelligibility of fundamental *socialities*. We must abandon such vague descriptions and try to extend our dialectical investigation to include them. But, although *class*, as a fundamental structure, represents at a certain level the very substance of which groups and passive socialities are determinations, and although every collection of human beings, at the present time, expresses this substance in one way or another, or manifests the class divisions of society – both within themselves and in their inertia or *praxis* – we will not immediately attempt a definition of the practico-inert sociality of class. We shall examine the most obvious, immediate and superficial gatherings of the practical field, as they appear in everyday experience. And, since many of them arise as simple internal determinations of a substance with which they are homogeneous, they can be treated formally not in their particularity, but in so far as through themselves they are social beings in the practico-inert field: through themselves they will manifest to us what might be called their ontological intelligibility, and in a later moment we will be able, through them, to understand and fix this more fundamental reality, class. In *The Problem of Method* I called these inorganic social beings *collectives*.

4

Collectives

Social objects (by which I mean any objects which have a collective structure and which, as such, must be the subject matter of sociology) are, at least in their fundamental structure, beings of the practico-inert field. Their being therefore resides in inorganic materiality in so far as, in this field, it is itself practico-inert. I am not referring to the material beings (*produced by human labour*) which are sometimes called rallying points, or symbols of unity: what I have in mind are practical realities, with their exigencies, to the extent that they realise in and through themselves the interpenetration of a multiplicity of unorganised individuals *within them* and that they produce every individual in them in the *indistinction* of a totality. The structure of this 'totality' has yet to be determined; but it ought not to be understood in the same sense as that in which a group of machines becomes the unity of its servants by determining tasks: this unity, as the reverse side of a well-defined division of labour, is simply the inorganic inversion of a differentiated unity of *functions*, and in so far as it turns back on men to produce them, it produces them through distinct exigencies and to the extent that everyone, as a general individual, is the means of a given differentiated function (as Other, as we have seen).

A collective structure, that is to say, a structure of totalising or pseudo-totalising *interpenetration*, could exist within a mechanical ensemble only to the extent that the mechanical ensemble itself existed as an *undifferentiated* practico-inert reality – for example, as a factory which, when it closes its gates, throws two thousand workers out of work, or as an ensemble which is a threat *to everyone* because the employer refuses to take the necessary security measures (though it is hard to draw this distinction in general terms, and the examination of a particular case would take too long). On the other hand, we must emphasise that groups (both as practical organisations, directly established by human *praxis*, and as present, concrete undertakings) can arise only on the foundation of a collective which, however, they do not eliminate (at least not entirely) and, conversely, that in so far as, whatever its aim, it necessarily acts through the medium of the practico-inert field, it must itself, as a free organisation of individuals with a common aim, produce *its collective structure*, that is to say, *exploit its inertia for practice* (this, as we have seen, characterises action at every level). In the end, for reasons whose very intelligibility will be criticised when we come to discuss them, subject to certain circumstances and in certain conditions, groups die and then disintegrate. This means that they ossify, become stratified and return into more general socialities, though without dissolving into them, while retaining their own sociality, as true collectives. Any social field is constituted, very largely, by structured ensembles of groupings which are always both *praxis* and practico-inert, although either of these characteristics may constantly tend to cancel itself out; only experience can indicate the internal relation of the structures in a definite group and as a definite moment of its interior dialectic.

The collective, therefore, will often appear in my examples through living or moribund groups of which it is a fundamental structure. But, in so far as the group constitutes itself as a negation of the collective which engenders and sustains it, and in so far as the collective reappears when a complex of historical circumstances negates the group as an undertaking but does not liquidate it as a determination, we can identify, at the extremes, groups in which passivity tends to disappear entirely (for example, a very small 'combat unit', all of whose members live and struggle together, and never leave each other), and collectives which have almost entirely reabsorbed their group: thus in Budapest, before the insurrection, the Social Democratic Party, which had practically no members left[76], officially retained its emblems and its

---

76. The majority had merged with the Communists to form a new party. Some elements of the right-wing minority had been put on trial, and others had emigrated. The social-democratic tendency, which was very strong among the workers, became *a tendency*, an *exis*, but outside any party. On the other hand, *the headquarters* as worked materiality became the Party itself, not only for the government (which was concerned to show that the grouping had not been eliminated in an authoritarian way, but that it had simply lost its members), but also for the emigré socialists (who found in it the material, transcendent and distant unity of their dispersal, as well as a petrified affirmation of their hope), and for the socialists who had merged with the Communists (as their transcended and, at least for some of them, untranscendable past being) and, lastly, for the non-party sympathisers as the solidified exigency (their own exigency turned

name and its headquarters in a certain building. These extreme – though frequent and *normal* – cases enable us to make a clear separation between the two social realities: the group is defined by its undertaking and by the constant movement of integration which tends to turn it into pure *praxis* by trying to eliminate all forms of inertia from it; the collective is defined *by its being*, that is to say, in so far as all *praxis* is constituted by its being as mere *exis*; it is a material, inorganic object in the practico-inert field in so far as a discrete multiplicity of active individuals is produced *in it* under the sign of the Other, as a *real unity within Being*, that is to say, as a passive synthesis, and to the extent that the constituted object is posited as essential and that its inertia penetrates *every individual praxis* as its fundamental determination by passive unity, that is to say, by the *pre-established* and *given* interpenetration of everyone as Others.

In this new moment of the spiral, we find the same terms enriched by their partial totalisations and reciprocal conditionings: reciprocity as a fundamental human relation, the separation of individual organisms, the practical field with its dimensions of alterity in depth, inorganic materiality as man's being-outside-himself in the inert object and as the inert's being-outside-itself as exigency in man, in the unity of a falsely reciprocal relation of interiority. But specifically, outside the human relation of reciprocity and the relation to the third party, which in themselves *are not social* (although in a sense they condition all sociality and are conditioned by sociality in their historical content), the structural relation of the individual to other individuals remains in itself completely indeterminate until the ensemble of material circumstances on the basis of which the relation is established has been defined, from the point of view of the historical process of totalisation. In this sense, the contrast between 'reciprocity as a relation of interiority' and 'the isolation of organisms as a relation of exteriority', which, in the abstract, conditions an unspecified tension within multiplicities, is in fact transcended, and merged in a new type of 'external-internal' relation by the action of the practico-inert field which transforms contradiction in the milieu of the Other into *seriality*. In order to understand the collective one must understand that this material object realises the unity of interpenetration of individuals as beings-in-the-

---

back on itself) of a temporarily or absolutely impossible integration. And none of these people was unaware of what this collective object produced in the others.

world-outside-themselves to the extent that it structures their relations as practical organisms in accordance with the new rule of *series*.

1   Series: the queue

Let us illustrate these notions by a superficial everyday example. Take a grouping of people in the Place Saint-Germain. They are waiting for a bus at a bus stop in front of the church. I use the word 'grouping' here in a neutral sense: we do not yet know whether this gathering is, as such, the inert effect of separate activities, or whether it is a common reality, regulating everyone's actions, or whether it is a conventional or contractual organisation. These people – who may differ greatly in age, sex, class, and social milieu – realise, within the ordinariness of everyday life, the relation of isolation, of reciprocity and of unification (and massification) from outside which is characteristic of, for example, the residents of a big city in so far as they are united though not integrated through work, through struggle or through any other activity in an organised group common to them all. To begin with, it should be noted that we are concerned here with a plurality of isolations: these people do not care about or speak to each other and, in general, they do not look at one another; they exist side by side alongside a bus stop. At this level, it is worth noting that their isolation is not an inert statute (or the simple reciprocal exteriority of organisms); rather, it is *actually* lived in everyone's project as its negative structure. In other words, the isolation of the organism, as the impossibility of uniting with Others in an organic totality, is revealed through the isolation which everyone lives as the provisional negation of their reciprocal relations with Others. This man is isolated not only by his body as such, but also by the fact that he turns his back on his neighbour – who, moreover, has not even noticed him (or has encountered him in his practical field as a general individual defined by waiting for the bus). The practical conditions of this attitude of semi-unawareness are, first, his real membership of other groups (it is morning, he has just got up and left his home; he is still thinking of his children, who are ill, etc.; furthermore, he is going to his office; he has an oral report to make to his superior; he is worrying about its phrasing, rehearsing it under his breath, etc.); and secondly, his being-in-the-inert (that is to say, his interest). This plurality of separations can, therefore, in a way, be expressed as the negative side of individual integration into separate groups (or into groups that are separate *at this time* and *at this level*); and, through this, as the negative side of everyone's projects in so far as they determine the social field on the basis of given conditions. On the other hand, if the question is examined from the point of view of groups, interests, etc. – in short, of social structures in so far as they express the fundamental social order (mode of production, relations of production, etc.) – then one can define each isolation in terms of the forces of disintegration which the social group exerts on individuals. (These forces, of course, are correlatives of forces of integration, which we shall discuss soon.)

In other words, the intensity of isolation, as a relation of exteriority between the members of a temporary and contingent gathering, expresses *the degree of massification* of the social ensemble, in so far as it is produced on the basis of given conditions.[77]

At this level, reciprocal isolations, as the negation of reciprocity, signify the integration of individuals into one society and, *in this sense*, can be defined as a particular way of living (conditioned by the developing totalisation), in interiority and as reciprocity within the social, the exteriorised negation of all interiority ('No one helps anyone, it's everyone for himself') or, on the other hand, in sympathy (as in Proust's 'Every person is very much alone'). Finally, in our example, isolation becomes, for and through everyone, for him and for others, the real, social product of cities. For each member of the group waiting for the bus, the city is in fact present (as I have shown in *The Problem of Method*) as the practico-inert ensemble within which there is a movement towards the interchangeability of men and of the instrumental ensemble; it has been there since morning, as exigency, as instrumentality, as milieu, etc. And, through the medium of the city, there are given the millions of people who are the city, and whose completely invisible presence makes of everyone *both* a polyvalent isolation (with millions of facets), *and* an *integrated* member of the city (the '*vieux Parisien*', the '*Parisien de Paris*', etc.). Let me add that the mode of life occasions *isolated behaviour* in everyone – buying the paper as you leave the house, reading it on the bus, etc. These are often

77. When I say that the intensity of isolation *expresses* the degree of massification, I mean that it does this in a purely *indicative* way.

operations for making the transition from one group to another (from the intimacy of the family to the public life of the office). Thus isolation is a project. And as such it is relative to particular individuals and moments: to isolate oneself by reading the paper is to make use of the national collectivity and, ultimately, the totality of living human beings, in so far as one is one of them and dependent on all of them, in order to separate oneself from the hundred people who are waiting for or using the same vehicle. Organic isolation, suffered isolation, lived isolation, isolation as a mode of behaviour, isolation as a social statute of the individual, isolation as the exteriority of groups conditioning the exteriority of individuals, isolation as the reciprocity of isolations in a society which creates *masses*: all these forms, all these oppositions co-exist in the little group we are considering, in so far as isolation is a historical and social form of human behaviour in human gatherings.

But, at the same time, the relation of reciprocity remains in the gathering itself, and among its members; the negation of isolation by *praxis* preserves it as negated: it is, in fact, quite simply, the practical existence of men among men. Not only is there a lived reality – for everyone, even if he turns his back on the Others, and is unaware of their number and their appearance, knows that they exist as a finite and indeterminate plurality *of which he is a part* – but also, even outside everyone's real relation to the Others, the ensemble of *isolated* behaviour, in so far as it is conditioned by historical totalisation, presupposes a structure of reciprocity at every level. This reciprocity must be the most constant possibility and the most immediate reality, for otherwise the social models in currency (clothes, hair style, bearing, etc.) would not be adopted by everyone (although of course this is *not sufficient*), and neither would everyone hasten to repair anything wrong with their dress as soon as they notice it, and if possible in secret. This shows that isolation does not remove one from the visual and practical field of the Other, and that it realises itself objectively in this field.

At this level, we recognise the same society (which we just saw as an agent of massification), in so far as its practico-inert being serves as a medium conducive to inter-individual reciprocities: for these separate people form a group, *in so far as* they are all standing on the same pavement, which protects them from the traffic crossing the square, *in so far as* they are grouped around the same bus stop, etc. Above all, these individuals form a group to the extent that they have a *common interest*, so that, though separated as organic individuals, they share a structure of their practico-inert being, and it unites them from outside. They are all, or nearly all, workers, and regular users of the bus service; they know the time-table and frequency of the buses; and consequently they all wait for the *same* bus: say, the 7.49. This object, in so far as they are dependent upon it (breakdowns, failures, accidents), *is their present interest.* But this present interest – since they all live in the district – refers back to fuller and deeper structures of their general interest: improvement of public transport, freezing of fares, etc. The bus they wait for unites them, being their interest as individuals who *this morning* have business on the *rive droite*; but, as the 7.49, it is *their interest as commuters*; everything is temporalised: the traveller recognises himself as a *resident* (that is to say, he is referred to the five or ten previous years), and then the bus becomes characterised by its daily eternal return (it is actually *the very same* bus, with the same driver and conductor). The object takes on a structure which overflows its pure inert existence; as such it is provided with a passive future and past, and these make it appear to the passengers as a fragment (an insignificant one) of their destiny.

However, to the extent that the bus designates the present commuters, it constitutes them in their *interchangeability*: each of them is effectively produced by the social ensemble as united with his neighbours, in so far as he is strictly identical with them. In other words, their being-outside (that is to say, their interest as regular users of the bus service) is unified, in that it is a pure and indivisible abstraction, rather than a rich, differentiated synthesis; it is a simple identity, designating the commuter as an abstract generality by means of a particular *praxis* (signalling the bus, getting on it, finding a seat, paying the fare), in the development of a broad, synthetic *praxis* (the undertaking which unites the driver and conductor every morning, in the temporalisation which is *one* particular route through Paris at a particular time). At this moment of the investigation, the unit-being (*être-unique*) of the group lies outside itself, in a future object, and everyone, in so far as he is determined by the common interest, differentiates himself from everyone else only by the simple materiality of the organism. And already, if they are characterised in their temporalisation as awaiting their being as the being of all, the abstract unity of their common future being manifests itself as *other-being* in relation to the organism which *it is in person* (or, to put it another way, which it *exists*). This moment cannot be one of conflict, but it is no longer one of reciprocity; it must simply be seen as the abstract stage of identity.

In so far as *they have the same objective reality* in the future (a minute later, the same for everyone, and the bus will come round the corner of the boulevard), the *unjustified* separation of these organisms (in so far as it arises from other conditions and another region of being) determines itself as *identity*. There is *identity* when the *common* interest (as the determination of generality by the unity of an object in the context of particular practices) is made manifest, and when the plurality is defined just *in relation to this interest*. In that moment, in fact, it matters little if the commuters are biologically or socially differentiated; in so far as they are united by an abstract generality, they are identical as separate individuals. Their identity is their future practico-inert unity, in so far as it determines itself at the present time as *meaningless separation*. And, since all the lived characteristics which might allow some interior differentiation lie outside this determination, everyone's identity with every Other is their unity elsewhere, as other-being; here and now, it is their common alterity. Everyone is the same as the Others in so far as he is Other than himself. And identity as alterity is *exterior separation*; in other words, it is the impossibility of realising, through the body, the transcendent unity to come, in so far as this unity is experienced as an irrational necessity.[78]

It is at precisely this level that material objects will be found to determine the serial order as the social reason for the separation of individuals. The practico-inert exigency, here, derives from scarcity: *there are not enough places for everyone*. But, apart from scarcity as the contingent but fundamental relation of man to Nature, which remains the context of the whole investigation, *this* particular scarcity is an aspect of material inertia. Whatever the demands, the object remains passively what it is: there is no reason to believe that material exigency must be a special, directly experienced scarcity: we shall find different practico-inert structures of the object as an *individuated being of generality* conditioning different serial relations. I take this example for its simplicity. Thus the specific scarcity – the number of people in relation to the number of places – in the absence of any particular practice, would designate every individual as dispensable; the Other would be the rival of the Other because of their identity; separation would turn into contradiction. But, except in cases of panic – where, in

---

78. It becomes perfectly rational when the stages of the entire process are reconstructed. All the same, the conflict between interchangeability and existence (as unique, lived *praxis*) must be lived at some level as a *scandalous absurdity*.

effect, everyone fights *himself in the Other*, in the whirling madness of an abstract unity and a concrete but unthinkable individuality – the relation of reciprocity, emerging or re-emerging in the exteriority of identity, establishes interchangeability as the impossibility of deciding, *a priori*, which individuals are dispensable; and it occasions some practice whose sole purpose is to avoid conflicts and arbitrariness by creating an order.

The travellers waiting for the bus take tickets indicating the order of their arrival. This means that they accept *the impossibility of deciding which individuals are dispensable in terms of the intrinsic qualities of the individual*; in other words, that they remain on the terrain of common interest, and of the identity of separation as meaningless negation; positively, this means that they try to differentiate every Other from Others without adding anything to his characteristic *as Other* as the sole social determination of his existence. *Serial unity*, as common interest, therefore imposes itself as exigency and destroys all opposition. The ticket no doubt refers to a temporal determination. But this is precisely why it is *arbitrary*: the time in question is not a practical temporalisation, but a homogeneous medium of repetition. Taking his ticket as he arrives, everyone does the same as the Other. He realises a practico-inert *exigency* of the ensemble; and, since they are going to different jobs and have different objectives, the fact of having arrived first does not give *any distinctive characteristic*, but simply the right to get on the bus first. The material justifications for the order have meaning, in fact, only after the event: being the first to arrive is no virtue; having waited longest confers no right. (Indeed, one can imagine fairer classifications – waiting means nothing to a young man, but it is very tiring for an old woman. Besides, war wounded have priority in any case, etc.) The really important transformation is that alterity as such, pure alterity, is no longer *either* the simple relation to common unity, *or* the shifting identity of organisms. As an ordering, it becomes a negative principle of unity and of determining everyone's fate as Other *by every Other as Other*. It matters a lot to me, in effect, that I have the tenth number rather than the twentieth. But I am tenth *through Others* in so far as they are Other than themselves, that is to say, in so far as the Reason for their number does not lie in themselves. If I am after my neighbour, this may be because he did not buy his newspaper this morning, or because I was late leaving the house. And if we have numbers 9 and 10, this depends on both of us and also on all the Others, both before and after.

On this basis, it is possible to grasp our relations to the object in their complexity. On the one hand, we have effectively remained general individuals (in so far as we form part of this gathering, of course). Therefore the unity of the collection of commuters lies in the bus they are waiting for; in fact it *is* the bus, as a simple possibility of transport (not for transporting *all* of us, for we do not act together, but for transporting each of us). Thus, as an appearance and a first abstraction, a structure of universality really exists in the grouping; indeed, everyone is identical with the Other in so far as they are waiting for the bus. However, their acts of waiting are not a communal fact, but are lived separately as identical instances of the same act. From this point of view, the group is not structured; it is a gathering and the number of individuals in it is contingent. This means that any other number was *possible* (to the extent that the individuals are considered as arbitrary particles and that they have not collected together as a result of any common dialectical process). This is the level where *conceptualisation* has its place; that is to say, concepts are based on the molecular appearance of organisms and on the transcendent unity of the group (common interest).

But this generality, as the fluid homogeneity of the gathering (in so far as its unity lies outside it), is just an abstract appearance, for it is actually constituted in its very multiplicity by its transcendent unity as a structured multiplicity. With a concept, in effect, everyone is the same as the Others in so far as he is himself. In the series, however, everyone becomes himself (*as Other than self*) in so far as he is other than the Others, and so, in so far as the Others are other than him. There can be no *concept* of a series, for every member is serial by virtue of his place in the order, and therefore by virtue of his alterity in so far as it is posited as irreducible. In arithmetic, this can be demonstrated by reference to numbers, both as concepts and as serial entities. All whole numbers, or integers, can be the object of the same concept, in so far as they all share the same characteristics; in particular, any whole number can be represented by the symbol $n + 1$ (if we take $n = o$ for the number one). But *for just this reason*, the arithmetical series of integers, in so far as all of them are constituted by adding one to the preceding number, is a practical and material reality, constituted by an infinite series of unique entities; and the uniqueness of each number is due to the fact that it stands in the same relation to the one that precedes it as this one does to the one preceding it. In the case of ordinals, alterity also changes its meaning: it manifests itself in the concept as common to all, and it designates everyone as a molecule identical with all the others; but, in the series, it becomes a rule of differentiation. And whatever ordering procedure is used, seriality derives from practico-inert matter, that is to say, from the future as an ensemble of inert, equivalent possibilities (equivalent, in this case, because no means of forecasting them is given): there is the possibility that there will be one place, that there will be two, or three, etc. These rigid possibilities are inorganic matter itself in so far as it is non-adaptability. They retain their rigidity by passing into the serial order of separate organisms: for everyone, as a holder of a numbered ticket, they become a complex of possibilities peculiar to him (he will get a place if there is room for ten or more people on the bus; he will not do so if there is only room for nine, but then he will be the first for the next bus). And it is these possibilities and these alone which, within the group, constitute *the real content* of his alterity.

But it should be noticed that this constituent alterity must depend both on all the Others, and on the particular possibility which is actualised, and therefore that the Other has his essence in all the Others, in so far as he differs from them.[79] Moreover, this alterity, as a principle of ordering, naturally produces itself as a *link*. Now this link between men is of an entirely different kind from those already examined. On the one hand, it cannot be explained in terms of reciprocity, since the serial movement in our example excludes the relation of reciprocity: everyone is the Reason for the Other-Being of the Other in so far as an Other is the reason for his being. In a sense, we are back with material exteriority, which should come as no surprise since the series is determined by inorganic matter. On the other hand, to the extent that the ordering was performed *by some practice*, and that this practice included reciprocity within it, it contains a *real interiority*: for it is *in his real being*, and as an integral part of a totality which has totalised itself outside, that each is dependent on the Other in his reality. To put it another way: reciprocity in the milieu of identity becomes a false reciprocity of relations: what *a* is to *b* (the reason for his being other), *b* is to *c*, *b* and the entire series are to *a*. Through this opposition between the Other and the same in the milieu of the Other, alterity becomes this paradoxical structure: the identity of everyone as everyone's action of serial interiority on the Other. In the same way, *identity* (as the sheer absurdity of meaningless dispersal) becomes

79. In so far as he is *the same*, he is simply and formally *an other*.

synthetic: everyone is identical with the Other in so far as the others make him an Other acting on the Others; the formal, universal structure of alterity produces the *formula of the series* (*la Raison de la série*).

In the formal, strictly *practical*, and limited case that we have been examining, the adoption of the serial mode remains a mere convenience, with no special influence on the individuals. But this simple example has the advantage of showing the emergence of new pratico-inert characteristics: it reveals two characteristics *of the inactive human gathering*. The visible unity, in this case, in the time of the gathering (the totalised reality which they comprise *for* someone who sees them from a window or from the pavement opposite), is only an *appearance*; its origin for every observer to whom this totality is revealed, is integral *praxis* in so far as it is a perpetual organisation of *its* own dialectical field and, in practico-inert objectivity, the general, inert link between all the people in a field which is limited by its instrumentality, in so far as it is social – that is to say, in so far as its inert, instrumental materiality ultimately refers back to the order of historical movement – combined with their true being-outside-themselves in a particular practical object which, far from being a symbol, is a material being which produces their unity within itself and imposes it on them through the inert practices of the practico-inert field.

In short, the visible unity of a gathering is produced *partly* by accidental factors (accidental at this level of the investigation – their unity will be restored in a broader movement of totalisation), and *partly* by the *real* but *transcendent* unity of a practico-inert object, in so far as this unity, in the development of a directed process, *produces itself* as the real material unity of the individuals in a given multiplicity, which it itself defines and limits. I have already said that this unity is *not* symbolic; it is now possible to see why. It is because it has nothing to symbolise; *it* is what unites everything. And if, in special circumstances, it is possible to see a symbolic relation between the gathering, as a visible assembly of discrete particles (where it presents itself in a visible form), and its objective unity, this is to be found in the small visible crowd which, by its presence as a gathering, *becomes a symbol* of the practical unity of its *interest* or of some other object which is produced as its inert synthesis. This unity itself, in so far as it is practico-inert, may present itself to individuals through a larger *praxis* of which they are either the inert means, the ends or the objects, or a combination of these, and which constitutes the true synthetic field of their gathering and which produces them in the object with their new laws of unified multiplicity. This *praxis* unifies them by producing the object in which they are already inscribed, in which their forms are negatively determined, and, in so far as it is already other (affected by the entire inertia of matter), it is this *praxis* which produces them in common in other unity.

The second point to be made is that the apparent absence of structure in the gathering (or its apparent structures) does not correspond to objective reality: if they were all unaware of each other and if they carried their social isolation behaviour to the limit, the passive unity of the gathering *in the object* would both require and produce an *ordinal* structure from the multiplicity of the organisms. In other words, what presents itself to perception either as a sort of organised totality (men huddled together, waiting) or as a dispersal, possesses, as a collecting together of men by the object, a completely different basic structure which, by means of serial ordering, transcends the conflict between exterior and interior, between unity and identity. From the point of view of the activity-institution (the exact meaning of these terms will be clarified later), which is represented in Paris by the RATP (the public transport authority), the small gathering which slowly forms around the bus stop, apparently by a process of mere aggregation, *already has* a serial structure. It was produced *in advance* as the structure of some unknown group by the ticket machine attached to the bus stop. Everyone realises it for himself and confirms it for Others through his own individual *praxis* and his own ends. This does *not* mean that he helps to create an active group by freely determining, with other individuals, the end, the means, and the division of tasks; it means that he *actualises* his being-outside-himself as a reality shared by several people and *which already exists, and awaits him*, by means of an inert practice, endowed by instrumentality, whose meaning is that it integrates him into an ordered multiplicity by assigning him a place in a prefabricated seriality.

In this sense, the indifferentiation of beings-outside-themselves in the passive unity of an object exists between them as a serial order, as separation-unity in the practico-inert milieu of the Other. In other words, there is an objective, fundamental connection between collective unity as a transcendence which is *given to the gathering* by the future (and the past), and seriality as everyone's practico-inert actualisation of a relation with Others in so far as this relation determines him in his being *and already awaits him*. The thing as *common being* produces seriality as its own practico-inert being-outside-itself in the plurality of practical organisms; everyone realises himself outside himself in the objective unity of interpenetration in so far as he constitutes himself in the gathering as an objective element of a series. Or again, as we shall see more clearly later, whatever it may be, and whatever the circumstances, the series constitutes itself on the basis of the unity-object and, conversely, it is in the serial milieu and through serial behaviour that the individual achieves practical and theoretical participation in common being.

There are serial behaviour, serial feelings and serial thoughts; in other words a *series is a mode of being for individuals both in relation to one another and in relation to their common being* and this mode of being transforms all their structures. In this way, it is useful to distinguish serial *praxis* (as the *praxis* of the individual in so far as he is a member of the series and as the *praxis* of the whole series, or of the series totalised through individuals) both from common *praxis* (group action) and from individual, constituent *praxis*. Conversely, in every non-serial *praxis*, a serial *praxis* will be found, as the practico-inert structure of the *praxis* in so far as it is social. And, just as there is a *logic* of the practico-inert layer, there are *also* structures proper to the thought which is produced at this social level of activity; in other words, there is a *rationality* of the theoretical and practical behaviour of an agent as a member of a series. Lastly, to the extent that *the series* represents the use of alterity as a bond between men under the passive action of an object, and as this passive action defines the general type of alterity which serves as a bond, alterity is, ultimately, the practico-inert object itself in so far as it produces itself in the milieu of multiplicity with its own particular exigencies. Indeed, every Other is both Other than himself and Other than Others, in so far as their relations constitute both him and Others in accordance with an objective, practical, inert rule of alterity (or a formal particularisation of this alterity).

Thus this rule – the *formula of the series* – is common to all precisely to the extent that they differentiate themselves. I say common, but not identical: for identity is separation, whereas the *formula of the series* is a dynamic scheme which determines each through all and all through each. *The Other*, as formula of the series and as a factor in every particular case of alterity, therefore becomes, beyond its structure of identity and its structure of alterity, a being common to all (as negated and preserved interchangeability). At this level, beyond the concept and the rule, the Other is me in every Other and every Other in me and everyone as Other in all the Others; finally, it is the passive Unity of the multiplicity in so far as it exists in itself; it is the reinteriorisation of exteriority by the human ensemble, it is the being-one of the organisms in so far as it corresponds to the unity of their being-in-themselves in the object. But, in so far as everyone's unity with the Other and with all Others is never given in him and the Other in a true relation based on reciprocity, and in so far as this *interior* unity of all is always and for everyone in all the Others, in so far as they are others and never *in him* except *for Others*, and in so far as he is other than them, this unity, which is *ever present but always elsewhere*, again becomes interiority lived in the milieu of exteriority. It no longer has any connection with molecularity: *it is genuinely a unity*, but the unity of a flight.

This can best be understood in the light of the fact that in an active, contractual and differentiated group, everyone can regard himself both as subordinate to the whole and as essential, as the practical local presence of the whole, in his own particular action. In the case of the bond of alterity, however, the whole is a totalisation of flight; Being as material reality is the totalised series of *not-beings*; it is what everyone causes the other to become, as his double, out of reach, incapable of acting on him directly, and, simply in its transformation, subject to the action of an Other. Alterity, as the unity of identities, must always be elsewhere. *Elsewhere* there is only an Other, always other than self and which seems, from the point of view of idealist thought concerning other real beings, to engender them by logical scissiparity, that is to say, to produce the Others as indefinite moments of its alterity (whereas, in reality, exactly the opposite occurs). Ought we to say that this hypostasised serial reason simply refers us back to the *practico-inert object* as the unity outside themselves of individuals? On the contrary, for it engenders it as a particular practical interiorisation of being-outside through multiplicity. In this case, must we treat it as an Idea, that is to say, *an ideal label*? Surely not.

The Jew (as the internal, serial unity of Jewish multiplicities), or *the* colonialist, or *the* professional soldier, etc., are not ideas, any more than *the* militant or, as we shall see, *the* petty bourgeois, or *the* manual worker. The theoretical error (it is not a practical one, because *praxis* really does constitute them in alterity) was to conceive of these beings as concepts, whereas – as the fundamental basis of extremely complex relations – they are *primarily* serial unities. In fact, the being-Jewish of every Jew in a hostile society which persecutes and insults them, and opens itself to them only to reject them again, cannot be the only relation between the individual Jew and the anti-semitic, racist society which surrounds him; it is this relation in so far as it is lived by every Jew in his direct or indirect relations with all the other Jews, and in so far as it constitutes him, through them all, as Other and threatens him in and through the Others. To the extent that, for the conscious, lucid Jew, being-Jewish (which is his statute *for non-Jews*) is interiorised as his responsibility in relation to all other Jews and his being-in-danger, out there, owing to some possible carelessness caused by Others who mean nothing to him, over whom he has no power and every one of whom is himself like Others (in so far as he makes them exist as such in spite of himself), *the* Jew, far from being *the type* common to each separate instance, represents *on the contrary* the perpetual *being-outside-themselves-in-the-other* of the members of this practico-inert grouping. (I call it this *because* it exists within societies which have a non-Jewish majority and because every child – even if he subsequently adopts it with pride and by a deliberate practice – must begin by *submitting to* his statute.)

Thus, for example, if there is an outbreak of anti-semitism, and Jewish members of society are beginning to be accused of 'getting all the best jobs', then for every Jewish doctor or teacher or banker, every other banker, doctor or teacher will constitute him as dispensable (and conversely). Indeed it is easy to see why this should be so: alterity as everyone's interiorisation of his common-being-outside-himself in the unifying object can be conceived as the unity of all only in the form of common-being-outside-oneself-in-the-other. This is because totalisation as an *organised form of social relations* actually pre-supposes (in the abstract and in extreme cases, of course) an original synthetic *praxis* whose aim is the human production of unity as its objectification in and through men. This totalisation – which will be described below – comes to men through themselves. But the totality of the gathering is only the passive action of a practico-inert object on a dispersal. The limitation of the gathering to *these* particular individuals is only an accidental negation (since, in principle, as *identities*, their number is not determined). Transformation into a totality is never the aim of a *praxis*; it reveals itself in so far as men's relations are governed by object-relations, that is to say, in so far as it comes to them as a practico-inert structure whose sealed exteriority is revealed as the interiority of real relations. On this basis, and in the context of *exigency* as an objectivity to be realised, plurality becomes unity, alterity becomes my own spontaneity in the Other and that of everyone in me, and the reciprocity of flights (as a pseudo-reciprocity) becomes a human relation of reciprocity. I have taken the simple and unimportant example of the passengers on the bus only in order to show serial structure as the being of the most ordinary, everyday gatherings: as a fundamental constitution of sociality, this structure does in fact tend to be neglected by sociologists. Marxists are aware of it, but they seldom mention it and generally prefer to trace the difficulties in the *praxis* of emancipation and agitation to organised forces rather than to seriality as the material resistance of gatherings and masses to the action of groups (and even to the action of practico-inert factors).

If we are to encompass the world of seriality, if only in one glance, or to note the importance of its structures and practices – in so far as they ultimately constitute the foundation of all seriality, even that which aims to bring man back to the Other through the organisation of *praxis* – we must abandon the example we have been using and consider what occurs in a domain where this basic reality discloses to our investigation its true nature and efficacity. I call the two-way relation between a material, inorganic, worked object and a multiplicity which finds its unity of exteriority in it *collective*. It defines *a social object*; it is a two-way relation (false reciprocity) because it is possible not only to conceive the inorganic object as materiality eroded by serial flight, but also to conceive the totalised plurality as materialised outside itself as common exigency in the object. Conversely, one can start either from material unity as exteriority, moving towards serial flight as a determinant of the behaviour which marks the social and material milieu with the original seal of seriality, or from serial unity, defining its reactions (as the practico-inert unity of a multiplicity) to the common object (that is to say, the transformations they bring about in the object). Indeed, from this point of view the false reciprocity between the common object and the totalised multiplicity can be seen as an interchangeability of two material statutes in the practico-inert field; but at the same time it must be regarded as a developing transformation of every one of the practico-inert materialities by the Other. In any case, we can now elucidate the meaning of serial structure and the possibility of applying this knowledge to the study of the dialectical intelligibility of the social.

2 Indirect gatherings: the radio broadcast

In order to understand the rationality of alterity as a rule of the social practico-inert field, we must, in effect, understand that this alterity is more complex and concrete than in the superficial and limited example in which we have observed it. Following up our investigation, we may find that some new characteristics emerge as seriality comes to be constituted in a larger field, and as the structure of more complex collectives. *First*, it should be noted that, in accordance with their own structure and passive action, practico-inert objects produce the gathering as a direct or indirect relation between the members of the multiplicity. The relation based on *presence* will be referred to as *direct*. And *presence* will be defined as the maximum distance permitting the immediate establishment of relations of reciprocity between two individuals, given the society's techniques and tools. (This distance obviously varies. In particular, there is the *real presence* of two people speaking on the telephone, each in relation to the other; similarly, an aeroplane can remain in a permanent relation of *presence*, by radio, with all the technical services which ensure its security.)

There are, of course, different kinds of presence, and they depend on *praxis* (some undertakings require that everyone should be present in the perceptual field of the Other – without the mediation of instruments) but, in any case, I define gatherings by the co-presence of their members, not in the sense that there must be relations of reciprocity between them, or a common, organised practice, but in the sense that the possibility of this common *praxis*, and of the relations of reciprocity on which it is based, is immediately given. Housewives queueing in front of a baker's shop, in a period of shortage, are characterised as a gathering with a serial structure; and this gathering is *direct*: the possibility of a sudden unitary *praxis* (a riot) is immediately given. On the other hand, there can be practico-inert objects whose structure is completely determinate but which, within the indeterminate multiplicity of men (of a city, a nation, or the world), themselves constitute a given plurality as an *indirect* gathering. And I define such gatherings by *absence*; by which I mean not so much absolute distance (in a given society, at a given moment in its development) which is, in reality, only an abstraction, as the impossibility of individuals establishing relations of reciprocity between themselves or a common *praxis*, *in so far as* they are defined by this object as members of the gathering.

But the important point is not whether a particular radio listener possesses his own transmitter and can make contact, as an individual, *later*, with some other listener, in another city or country: the mere fact of *listening to the radio*, that is to say, of listening to a particular broadcast at a particular time, establishes a serial relation of *absence* between the different listeners. In this way, the practico-inert object not only produces a unity of individuals outside themselves in inorganic matter, but also determines them in separation and, in so far as they are separate, ensures *their communication through alterity* (and the same applies to all 'mass media'). When I listen to a broadcast, the relation between the broadcaster and myself is not a human one: in effect, I am passive in relation to what is being said, to the political commentary on the news, etc. This passivity, in an activity which develops on every level and over many years, can *to some extent* be resisted: I can write, protest, approve, congratulate, threaten, etc. But it must be noted at once that these activities will carry weight only if a majority (or a considerable minority) of listeners who do not know me do likewise. So that, in this case, reciprocity is a gathering with one voice. Moreover, radio stations represent the point of view of the government or the special interests of a group of capitalists; so the listeners' activities (about programmes or about the opinions that are expressed) are unlikely to have any effect.

It often happens that political and social events which occur at all levels and throughout the country suffice to bring about changes in programmes or in controversial comment. From this point of view, the listener who disagrees with the policy of the government, even if, elsewhere, as a member of organised groups, he plays an effective part in opposing this policy, will see his passive activity – his 'receptivity' – as impotence. And, in so far as this voice gives it exactly the limits of its powers (there was an *excessively* bad drama or music programme), the public can act. Not entirely, however, as many examples have shown: the listener's indignation may simply be the lived discovery of his impotence as a man *confronting a man*. (The same applies if he is enthusiastic; I am taking the negative case because it is simpler, but the same impotence exists if I am delighted by some speaker or singer and demand that he be given a regular programme or that he broadcast more frequently.) For, in a sense, the voice, with its particular inflections and intonations, is the individual voice of a particular person, who has prepared his audience by a series of precise, individual actions. At the same time, there can be no doubt that the voice is addressed to me. To me and to Others, the voice says: 'Dear listeners.' But, although the speaker at a meeting addresses everyone present, each of them is in a position to contradict or even insult him (on condition, of course, that he takes certain risks in certain cases, with the more or less clearly defined intention, according to the circumstances, of 'changing public opinion'). Thus the public speaker really does address *us*, in that both individual reciprocity (*I* shout out my approval or my criticism) and collective reciprocity (we applaud him or shout our disapproval at him) are perfectly conceivable.

The broadcaster's voice, in contrast, in its reality as a human voice, is, in principle, mystifying: it is based on the reciprocity of discourse, and therefore on a human relation, but it is really a reifying relation in which the voice is given as *praxis* and constitutes the listener as the object of *praxis*; in short, it is a univocal relation of interiority, similar to that of the organism acting on the material environment, but one in which I, as an inert object, am subjected as inorganic matter to the human work of the voice. Yet I can, if I wish, turn the knob, and switch off the set or change stations. But here the gathering at a distance emerges. For this purely individual activity changes absolutely nothing in the real work of this voice. It will continue to echo through millions of rooms and to be heard by millions of listeners; I will merely have rushed into the ineffective, abstract isolation of private life, objectively changing nothing. I will not have negated the voice; I will have negated myself as an individual member of the gathering. And, especially in the case of ideological broadcasts, it is really as *Other* that I will have wanted this voice to be silent, that is to say, in so far as it can, for example, harm Others who are listening to it. I may be perfectly sure of myself, I may even belong to some active political group, sharing all its views and adopting all its positions. Nevertheless, the voice is unbearable for me *in so far as* it is listened to by Others – Others who, to be precise, are *the same* in so far as they listen to the radio and Others in so far as they belong to different milieux. I tell myself that it may *convince them*. In fact, I feel as though I could challenge the arguments put forward by this voice in front of these Others, even if they do not share my views; but what I actually experience is *absence* as my mode of connection with the Others. In this case, my impotence does not lie only in the impossibility of silencing the voice: it also lies in the impossibility of convincing, *one by one*, the listeners all of whom it exhorts in the common isolation which it creates for all of them as their inert bond. Indeed, as soon as I imagine some practical action against what the broadcaster says, I can conceive of it only as serial: I would have to take the listeners one by one. . . . Obviously, this seriality is a measure of my impotence and, perhaps, of that of my Party. In any case, if the Party planned to do some counter-propaganda, it would be obliged to adapt itself to the serial structure imposed by the mass media. (And if the listener is a journalist, if he expresses his indignation in his newspaper the next day, then he is opposing one serial action to another: he addresses the four hundred thousand separate listeners in the city in so far as he can reach them as separate readers.)

Thus the impotent listener is constituted by the very voice as an *other-member* (*membre-autre*) of the indirect gathering: with the first words, a lateral relation of indefinite seriality is established between him and *the Others*. Of course, this relation originated in knowledge produced by language itself in so far as it is a means for the mass media. Everyone gets their information about French radio programmes from newspapers and the radio itself. But this knowledge (which is itself of a serial order by virtue of its origin, content and practical objective) has for a long time been transformed into a fact. Every listener is objectively defined by this real fact, that is to say, by the structure of exteriority which has been interiorised in knowledge. Now, when, in a given historical situation and in the context of the conflicts it gives rise to, one listens to the voice in impotent anger, one no longer listens to it *for oneself* (assuming that one can be sure of withstanding the arguments), but from the *point of view* of Others. Which others? This is determined by circumstances and by the individual himself, with his experience and his past. Perhaps he will imagine himself in the situation of his friends the Xs, who are rather impressionable or who seemed more wavering than usual last night. Or perhaps he will try to listen as an abstractly defined kind of listener known only in his generality (as lukewarm, or passive, or, more specifically, as a listener with a particular interest which is being skilfully played up to, etc.).

But in any case, the abstract individual whom he evokes in his alterity has also long been a ready-made notion (a schema forged both in experience and through the schematisations of the mass media) and, conversely, the wavering family which he takes as a reference can really disturb him only in so far as it represents the first term of a series, that is to say, in so far as it is itself schematised as Other. It would be useless to describe the curious attitude of the indignant listener here (everyone can find it in his own experience) and the three moment dialectic: the moment of triumph in which he refutes the argument, or perhaps just thinks he does (this is already *for the Other*, but only in so far as a relation of reciprocity might be possible). Then there is the moment of impotent indignation, in which he realises himself as a member of a series whose members are united solely by the bond of alterity; and finally, the moment of anguish and temptation, in which, placing himself *at the point of view of the Other*, he allows himself to be convinced as Other, up to a certain point, in order to feel the force of the argument. This third moment is that of discomfort and fascination; it involves a violent contradiction: I become, in effect, both someone who knows how to refute such nonsense, and someone who is liable to be convinced by it. And I do not mean that I become both myself and the Other: perhaps the triumphant attitude of the individual who knows is only another form of alterity (I have confidence in Others who are in a position to refute such arguments and I identify myself with them because I share their opinion). The main point is that my inability to act on the series of *Others* (who may allow themselves to be convinced) reverts to me and makes *these Others* my destiny. Of course, this is not because of the broadcast on its own, but because it occurs in a wider context of mystificatory propaganda which lulls them into unawareness.

In this way, the voice becomes *vertiginous* for everyone: it is no longer anyone's voice (even if the broadcaster is named), since reciprocity has been destroyed. But it is *doubly* a collective: on the one hand, as we have just seen, it produces me as an inert member of a series and as Other in the midst of Others; and on the other hand, it appears in itself as the social result of a political *praxis* (of the government, in the case of a state radio station) and as *sustained* in itself by a different serial cross-section of listeners – those who are already convinced, and whose opinions and interests it expresses. Thus, in it and through it, Others (supporters of the policy) influence Others (the waverers, the undecided); but this influence is itself serial (what is not serial, of course, is the political *action* of the government and its propaganda *activities*), since everyone listens from the position of the Other, and as Other and because the voice itself is Other. It is Other for those who reject the policy which inspires it, both as expressing certain Others and as action on Others; it is Other for the waverers, who listen to it *already* as the opinion of Others (of those all-powerful

Others who control the mass media) and who are influenced by the mere fact that this policy has the power to propagate itself publicly; and finally, it is Other for those who support government policy, in that *for everyone* in isolation it is backed up by the approval of Others (those who share his opinion) and by its effect on waverers. For them, the voice expresses their own thinking, but as Other, in that it is *uttered* by an Other, *expressed in other terms* (better than they could have done and differently) and in so far as it exists simultaneously *for all Others* as an Other-Thought. The reactive behaviour occasioned in the listeners by the Other-Thought as the meaning of the Other-Voice is always the *behaviour of alterity*. By this I mean that it has neither the immediate structure of an individual *praxis*, nor the concerted structures of a common, organised *praxis*. It is occasioned *immediately* – as the individual's free reaction – but he cannot produce it under the influence of the collective except in so far as it is itself a lateral totalisation of seriality (indignation, ironical laughter, impotent anger, fascination, enthusiasm, the need to communicate with Others, shock, collective fear,[80] etc.). In other words, the individual, as a member of a series, exhibits behaviour which is *altered* (*alterées*), and every part of which is the action of the Other in him, which means that of itself it is recurrence taken to its limit (that is to say, to infinity).

In developing this example our investigation (*expérience*) of seriality has grown richer. From the very fact that some objects can establish indirect bonds of alterity between individuals who are unaware of each other as such, we can see how the possibility emerges of a series being either finite, indefinite or infinite. When a multiplicity, though numerically determined in itself, remains practically indeterminate as a factor of the gathering, it is indefinite. (This applies, for example, to the radio: there is a definite number of individuals listening to a particular programme at a given moment, but it is as an indeterminate quantity that the broadcast constitutes the seriality of its listeners as a relation of each of them to the Others.) When the multiplicity is

80. In so far as collective fear is manifested as serial behaviour in an isolated listener, it occurs if the broadcast seems audacious or shocking; then it is the fear of anger or of others, it is sacred fear, for it is the fear that these words should have been spoken in the indefinite milieu of seriality, and also the fear in the milieu of the Other of having *heard* these words. These others, in me, condemn this moment of receptivity in which, by my individuality as a practical organism, these words have existed *here* in this room; alterity condemns in me my personal reality, and the Other passes sentence on the Same.

gathered together by a movement of circular recurrence, we have a practically infinite series (at least provided the circular movement continues). Each term, in effect, in so far as it produces the alterity of Others, itself becomes Other to the extent that Others produce it as Other, and that it helps modify them in their alterity in turn.

But we have also noticed that pure, formal alterity (as our first examples showed) is only an abstract moment of the serial process. It is true that it occurs in any group which, for example, is *ordered* in some way or other (a group of shoppers, for example, when there is a scarcity of goods or staff). But the formal purity is maintained here by a deliberate action – the refusal to discriminate between individuals on any basis other than alterity, itself constituted as a rule of succession. Otherwise, that is to say when alterity is not itself a means of selection, individuals in the serial milieu have a few special characteristics which vary among them or from one ensemble to another. Of course, the fundamental structure remains the same: the radio listeners at this moment constitute *a series* in that they are listening to the common voice which constitutes each of them in his identity as an Other. But it is precisely for this reason that an alterity of content arises between them. This alterity is still extremely formal, for it constitutes them on the basis of the object (the voice) and in accordance with their possible reactions to it. It goes without saying that in order to ground these reactions, one would have to enter more deeply into the differences, find other collectives and interests and groups, and, finally, one would have to totalise the historical moment together with its past. But in so far as the gathering *is created by the radio*, it remains at the level of the practical alterity of *listening behaviour*. It is on this basis that alterity as the formula of the series becomes a constituent force of each and for all; for in everyone, the Other is no longer mere formal difference in identity; in everyone, the Other is a different reaction, other behaviour, and everyone is conditioned in the fleeting unity of alterity by these different kinds of behaviour of the Other *in so far as* he cannot modify them in the Other. Thus everyone is as effective in his action on the Other as if he had established human relations with him (either direct and reciprocal, or organised), but his passive, indirect action derives from *his very impotence*, in so far as the Other lives it in himself as his own impotence as Other.

3 Impotence as a bond: the free market

This material, but still abstract, determination of the variable content
of alterity (in other words, of a synthetic alterity which by itself
creates a practico-inert world of alterity) leads us logically to the
investigation (*expérience*) of impotence as a real bond between members of a series. A series reveals itself to everyone when they perceive
in themselves and Others their common inability to eliminate their
material differences. We shall see how, in certain special conditions, a
group constitutes itself as the negation of this impotence, that is to say,
of seriality: I feel my impotence in the Other because it is the Other as
Other who will decide whether my action will remain an individual,
mad initiative and throw me back into abstract isolation or whether it
is to become the common action of the group; in this way, everyone
awaits the Other's action and makes himself the Other's impotence in
so far as the Other is his impotence. But this impotence, as a constituent presence in everyone in the series, does not necessarily correspond
to the pure, passive immobility of the ensemble. On the contrary, it may
become unorganised violence: precisely to the extent that I am impotent through the Other, it is the Other himself who becomes an active
power in me. Incapable of changing the Other's indignation (when I
witness a scene which some people find shocking), this indignation,
lived in impotence, becomes for me an *other-indignation*, in which the
Other in me is angered and guides my action. Provocateurs apart,
there is no difference between Scandal and the Fear of Scandal. In other
words, Scandal is the aggressive Fear of the Other's Scandal. In other
words, Scandal is the Other himself as the transcendent reason of the
serial propagation of acts of violence caused by the fear of Scandal.

But in order to simplify the structure of collectives, we have so far
assumed that series are constituted by isolated terms, whose only, and
fleeting, unity was alterity as impotence. Series of this kind actually
exist; generally speaking, readers of *Le Figaro* or radio listeners
would be an example. But other cases are more complex: for human
relations of reciprocity define the co-existence of men as well as the
statute of massified dispersal. And as these relations constitute complex chains and polyvalent systems, every individual relation, through
the medium of the surrounding material reality, is conditioned by

Others, either negatively or positively. Thus the multiplicity has merely changed position: and in so far as an object in the practico-inert field is the unity-outside-themselves of these inter-individual relations, seriality determines the multiplicities of reciprocal relations, as it determines the multiplicities of individuals. Thus the dispersal of human relations (in so far as each of them is linked to an other, or to several others, and these to others, etc.), in so far as it becomes alterity as the formula of the series, transforms each of them into an *other-relation*, by means of all the other relations. In other words, the Other produces itself as the fleeting unity of all in so far as it appears in each as a *necessary alteration* of direct reciprocity; or, again, in so far as everyone, if he wishes to communicate with an Other, constitutes his relation in practico-inert being on the basis of all the other totalised relations.

This plurality is of a special type: it is better to call it a quasi-plurality. In reality, it is difficult truly to separate links from one another (as one separates terms) and to quantify them – in so far as a human relation of reciprocity can be established between several persons at once. However, serial-being as a rigid alterity within every living relation draws its strength from *practical distancing*, that is to say, from the inconceivable proliferation of other relations, in so far as every gathering of relations (the discontent in a particular workshop about a particular measure taken by the management, in so far as it manifests itself, before exploding into action, in the quasi-plurality of human relations between the workers) refers to other gatherings (other workshops in so far as they have constituted themselves individually *as Others*, in their material difference, through their past conduct in earlier conflicts or in the development of this one), and these gatherings to yet others (outside the factory, but in the same industry) and to others (through individual responsibilities – connected, for example, by the date – they are referred back to the family, and to residential groups as to a branch of lateral seriality, of a secondary, but in fact very important kind) to this extent, distant relations arise for close relations, not as homogeneous relations far away, but, in their inert gathering, *as an inert conducting medium*, that of alteration (*altération*).

Every concrete inter-individual relation therefore arises, in this moment, linked with all the others. The link is serial, as the determination of a more or less definite milieu, which is characterised by a real cohesion, a compact solidity, and which as a whole exerts a *force* of inertia and exhibits the synthetic structure *of the relation*. But the practical reality of this milieu (a simple practico-inert totality of all these relations as alterity *in* each relation) resides simply in its serial structure. In other words, there are human milieux, and *they are men*, in so far as common objects produce them as the milieu of men. But it is wrong for sociologists and historians to study the *milieu*, as a collective – that is to say, as the other-unity of a quasi-plurality of human relations – in the form which it displays to *its individuals*. As it is manifested *to everyone* through relations of reciprocity as their synthetic cohesion, individuals do not perceive it *directly as other*, *as a serial rule of distancing*: what is clear to them when they are themselves the terms of the series is beyond their grasp – in immediate practice – when they are only an interior structure of the terms and when each term is, *in fact*, the relation which unites them. The milieu appears immediately to its members *as a homogeneous container* and as a permanent (practico-inert) *linking* force which unites everyone to everyone without distance; from this point of view, every human relation which establishes itself concretely between two or more individuals arises in the milieu as an inessential *actualisation* of a practico-inert structure already inscribed in Being. At the contingent level of individual histories, such an encounter naturally appears as a more or less intentional, more or less accidental realisation of individual and inter-individual *possibilities*. But, *as a relation belonging to a milieu*, the actualisation of a reciprocal determination in inertia is nothing like the realisation of a possibility. It was possible that *this* particular individual should have met that one, but, to take for example a competitive market (we shall return to this example later), this need not prevent a particular merchant from *being already linked*, as a practico-inert element of multiple (or quasi-plural) relations, with his competitors and customers (that is to say, not only with his real, active customers, but also with all the customers in the market *minus* his own customers, and, in the last analysis, with *all* the customers in the market, including his usual customers). Naturally, these multiple links manifest and transform themselves in the course of practico-inert processes which traverse the milieu.

This *apparent* structure of the milieu makes sociologists like Lewin tend to take it for a *Gestalt* which performs a synthetic action on its structures as a *real totality* and determines the behaviour and processes of every part in so far as it communicates directly with all the others through the real presence of the whole in every one of them. But this apparent structure is only a superficial moment of a preliminary investigation. The next moment reveals the collective as the relation between a totality of worked objects, a unity of inert exteriority (the sixteenth *arrondissement* of Paris, etc.), and the quasi-plurality which is signified by it and which produces unity in it *as an absence*. My relation with my customer arises in the bourgeois milieu of retailing (and more specifically of a particular retail trade, in a particular town, etc.) and contributes to determining it while actualising a predetermined structure; but *the milieu* which unites us is revealed as an active, synthetic force (in the course of business) only in so far as *precise relations* link one term to another, and link the relation itself to other terms and relations (deals between big companies which are trying to lower prices and ruin small businesses or simply approaches to one of my customers by a competitor), on which practical influence is *inconceivable*.

Thus the *true structures* of the milieu, those which produce its real force in the practico-inert field, are in fact structures of alterity. It is true that every relation is linked to every other, but only in particular ways: every element is linked to all elements, but *from its place in the series* and *through its fleeting link with all the intermediate elements*, just as any number is linked to every other number through precise relations which presuppose that every one of them is related to the others *through* the series of numbers which separate them – that is, on the basis that one of them is $(n + 1)$ and the other $(n + 1) + 1$, etc. Similarly, there is the unity of the milieu, which can, in certain cases, be a terrifying collective force. (It can be measured objectively, at least in some cases, by the chances of an individual in the milieu emerging from it, and inversely by the chances of an individual from a particular social category entering it, apart from any constraint exerted by his own milieu.) But the unity of the milieu exists *precisely* in so far as it does not reside in its terms as the whole in the part, in so far as it realises itself for each relation as *those* relations which *elsewhere* condition its concrete existence and its content. It is true that in the serial behaviour of terms which are present, the totality of the others arises as a milieu and as a general conditioning of behaviour. But this totality must not be confused with a positive, concrete totality, with a real *presence*: it is not the result of the unification of a practical field. On the contrary, it is a *real* extrapolation of an infinite series of relations which are both *identical and other* in so far as everyone conditions the Other by his absence. The totality here is the practico-inert totalisation of the series of concrete negations of every totality. The totality manifests itself in every reciprocity as its other-being, in so far as every reciprocity is characterised by the impossibility of any totalisation. The intelligibility of serial action (that is to say, of serial unity as a negative totality) derives from the relation of concrete reciprocity which unites two practical organisms *in so far as* it produces itself as conditioned by its inability to act on all the others and in so far as each of the others has the same inability within a serial field whose structure is determined by an identical relation of everyone to the common object and to its demands. And the distinctive property of the *milieu*, as the indefinite alterity of human relations, is that it offers itself to experience as a unitary synthetic form, totalising but not structured (in the sense in which each part would be a relation with every other and with the whole) and then reveals itself in *praxis* as a serial structure of determination by the other.

However, we must make a closer examination of these structures before we can understand the real (but practico-inert) action of seriality as a force which is suffered in impotence and which acts both on every reciprocal relation and on the series (as totalised in each of them by being taken to its limit). I will take a very simple, schematic example from everyday economics: the determination of current prices in a competitive market. It goes without saying that this determination presupposes a plurality of contractual relations (between buyers and sellers) and of competitive antagonisms, and therefore of negative reciprocities (between sellers on the one hand and buyers on the other). Obviously, we are not going to consider either the origins or the structures of this common object (the price of *this* particular commodity) and we will take the Marxist theory of value and prices for granted. The reader may wish to dispute this theory, but this has no bearing on the rest of our investigation, since we are concerned only with the final readjustment, which, other things being equal, is made at the market stage. Moreover, we will consider neither the components of the price (production cost, etc.), nor the effects of the conjuncture; we will assume the atomicity and fluidity of the sellers and buyers. This pure competitive market is neither a sort of 'state of nature' of the market as eighteenth-century economists believed, nor, as is too often said nowadays, a mere convenient abstraction: it simply represents a constituted reality, dependent on the system as a whole, which appears and disappears in accordance with the overall evolution of the economy, at a particular level of exchange. Up to 1939, for example, the Stock Exchanges (in Paris, London and New York) had all the characteristics of a competitive market, as, indeed, did the other nineteenth-century commercial markets in major international products (wheat, cotton, etc.). If we examined all the conditions affecting markets in general, our conception of 'collectives' as recurrences would be confirmed, but the problem would go beyond the limits of this study. The market has an undeniable reality; it is imposed on everyone in so far as the price and volume of transactions are necessarily determined (in terms of constant elements and within determinate limits) by the quantities on offer, the prices asked, the quantities needed and the prices people want to pay. Now, it is easy to see that the necessity which imposes itself on a merchant in his relation with an *individual* consumer arises from the concrete relations between *other* tradesmen and their customers, and from the relations between other buyers and this seller (who, for them, becomes *Other* than he was for the customer in question) and, finally, from the very fact that the consumer *as such* appears on the market as Other than himself and acts *as Other* on the direct human relation which he tries to form with the seller. The price corresponds to the intersection of the supply and demand curves, as everyone knows: this means that the quantities supplied and demanded *at this price* are equal. If the seller set his price at a lower level, demand would exceed supply; if he set it higher, supply would exceed demand. But there is no direct agreement between two men or two groups, understanding one another directly. A dealer never actually fixes his prices himself. And the mathematical rigour of the object demonstrates precisely that it is the objective representation of a line of flight.

The table opposite is of quantities supplied and demanded.

According to what we have just said, 11,000 units will be sold at the price of 6 francs.

First, it goes without saying that the justification for this quantitative law lies neither in purely mathematical principles, nor in the essential characteristics of quantity. The heart of the proof (that if the price were lower, demand would be higher than supply, and inversely) must refer us back to the seller and to his real action, to the buyer and his real demand. Demands cannot be higher than supply *precisely* because buyers who are in a position to pay more will make new offers and this will have the effect of raising prices. Supply cannot be higher than demand, because the better placed merchants (with lower production costs) will drop their prices immediately. Thus men are considered as *forces* of buying and selling. To simplify matters, let us assume that one buyer corresponds to each unit of demand, and that one seller corresponds to each unit of supply. Now, of the 27,500 supposed sellers, we can see that only 11,000 are prepared to drop the price to 6 francs per unit. And, of these, only 8,500 would go to 5 francs. Of 27,500 sellers, therefore, there are just 2,500 who can go down to 6 francs but no lower, and these 2,500 determine the price for everyone

Price	Quantity demanded	Quantity supplied
1	18,500	0
2	16,500	0
3	15,000	3,000
4	13,500	6,000
5	12,250	8,500
6	11,000	11,000
7	10,000	13,500
8	9,000	15,500
9	8,250	17,250
10	7,500	19,000
11	6,750	20,500
12	6,000	22,000
13	5,250	23,250
14	4,750	24,250
15	4,250	25,250
16	3,750	26,000
17	3,250	26,750
18	2,750	27,500

else. On the one hand, by lowering the price, they effectively exclude from the market 16,500 sellers, who, for one reason or another, cannot match this price reduction. On the other hand, by setting the price at 6 francs, they enable 8,500 sellers to avoid going down to 4 francs a unit, and 3,000 to avoid going to 3 francs. Thus, to confine our attention to them, these 3,000 receive a *seller's profit*, that is to say, they realise 3 francs a unit above their minimum expectations. How, then, do we explain the fate of the 25,000 people, of whom some have sold nothing at all while others have made an unexpected profit? It is due, firstly, to the fact that they are *active*, that is to say, real sellers standing in real relations[81] with their possible customers. Secondly, it is due to the fact that *in the transaction* they are affected by the action of *Other* sellers and that they are treated (by the customer himself) *as Others*: the *real* impossibility of 2,500 sellers going below 6 francs becomes for 8,500 of their competitors a *prohibition* against lowering the price. (I do not mean to give the word 'prohibition' an ethical or psychological sense. But the fact is that they *might*, hypothetically, lower their price and that the action of others creates a new type of impossibility for them, which no longer has anything to do with the cost price or with transport costs: it is no longer a material condition, a real, direct component of the price, but a law laid down from the outside governing their activity as sellers.) And obviously the same might be said about the sellers: 11,000 of them deprive 7,500 people of the possibility of buying the product in question; of these 11,000, 1,000 customers constitute *buyers' profits* for the 10,000 others. Thus, of the 46,000 people who constitute the group of buyers and sellers, 42,500 immediately appear as controlled by the law of the others; for them, the law of the market is a *heteronomy*. But if we consider the 3,500 who appear to have fixed the market, it is obvious that their supposed activity is only an appearance. In effect, if some of them bought *as dear as possible* (for them), and others sold *as cheap as possible*, it is because they were pushed to their utmost limits. The interest of both has been to benefit from the buyer's or seller's 'profit': but it is precisely the people who can go lower or higher than they can who *really* force them to give up additional profit. The sellers, for example, are in a situation of total alterity: 8,500 of them *live* the prohibition against going lower because 2,500 of them are *materially* incapable of doing so. And these 2,500 go down to their limit because the 8,500 others might go even lower.

Thus all their operations are determined by *the action of the Other*. But it is also the action of everyone *in so far as he is Other* (for other sellers and for other customers). Let us suppose that only 10,000 sellers are materially able to lower their price to 7 francs and 10,000 buyers to pay for the unit at this price. The point of intersection of the two curves would then be different, the quantities exchanged would be 10,000

---

81. We shall see that once the 'collective' is established, it has the effect of de-realising these relations and of reifying them.

units, and the price 7 francs. Thus the possibility of lowering prices acts *against them*. Why? Because it reaches the upper limit which characterises a definite number of buyers and which makes possible the equalisation of supply and demand. It should also be noted that there is no correspondence between the number of buyers who could go as far as 6 francs and the number of sellers who could lower their prices to that figure (1,000 and 2,500): it is not a true relation, but, on the contrary, an absence of relation (because we have assumed that every buyer and seller corresponds to *one* unit of supply or demand). What counts, of course, is that this figure of 11,000, arbitrarily fixed by us, determines prices and the equality of the exchanges. There are 11,000 people willing to sell at 6 francs, and 11,000 willing to buy. But this figure is precisely that of alterity since every individual sells or buys as an eleven thousandth, rather than as an individual person. On the other hand, such a number cannot be regarded simply as a sum: for example, if one said that it is the number of products sold at 6 francs, or of dealers who sell at this price, one would be forgetting the vital fact that all these dealers, with their own opportunities and projects, have gone down to this price simply and solely because they number 11,000 relating to 11,000 buyers. But it would be impossible to find any true unity in this collection: 11,000 here represents 11,000 individuals and not the concrete unity of these 11,000 people. The relations between the sellers are competitive and therefore antagonistic. But this antagonism which opposes them to one another finds expression in the fact that each receives his law from the Other (and not, as in direct struggle, that each tries to impose his law on the Other). The link between sellers (within a particular number) is *neither* a simple juxtaposition *nor* a unitary synthesis. They are juxtaposed precisely to the extent that, in its real movement, every direct relation to the buyer is independent of the relation of the Other. They are united by the fact that the *juxtaposition* of men is not that of sardines in a tin: sellers who carry out the same operation determine a social field, simply because the operation is *human* and necessarily concerns Others; in other words because every operation, in addressing itself to the indistinct mass of buyers, *projects a human future*.

I have taken the example of the pure competitive market because it illustrates what Hegel called 'the atomised crowd': but in fact the quantitative relations between physical molecules are radically different from the relations between social atoms. The former act and react in the milieu of exteriority; the latter in that of interiority. Everyone determines both himself and the Other in so far as he is Other than the Other and Other than himself. And everyone observes his direct action deprived of its real meaning in so far as the Other governs it, and in his turn hastens to influence the Other, over there, without any real relation to his intention. There must be a false unity. And it exists: it is the market as a gathering (whether it is a physical place or a system of telecommunications informing everyone of supplies, demands and prices).[82] At the outset, everyone *yields* to the gathering; he already determines it (in alterity) by his expectations, and it already eludes him and determines him. Consequently, the market exists *through him* (in itself and for him) as an object of expectation and as the fleeting determination of his action; but he himself sees it as an ensemble of juxtaposed persons. The totality of the market is thus detotalised.

To take the simplest examples (flower markets, cattle markets, etc.), the unity of place shows that all the individuals are *united* in that they devote themselves to the same direct operation, which allows itself to be determined in exteriority and alterity by all the other similar operations, so that this determination in alterity finally turns them into the object itself and reality: everyone's expectations, in a market that is supposed to be competitive, depend on the hypothesis that atomisation will remain the typical social link at least for the duration of the exchange. Thus, the unity cannot be conceived as a unifying synthesis, but as a form of dispersal as such, when this dispersal is seen as a rule and means for action. Two essential facts must be noted. First, the real difference between the physical molecule and the social molecule is that the first is purely and simply an element of numerical dispersal, while the second is a factor of dispersal only in so far as it begins as a factor of unity. The human molecule does not remain in multiplicity: through its action it organises the multiplicity into a synthetic unity (it is *the* market as the aim and condition of its activity). Dispersal intervenes *in the second degree*: there is a multiplicity, not of simple isolated molecules, but of *unifications* of purely physical multiplicity which have *already* been practically (and sometimes even consciously) *realised*. Everyone unifies, and perceives, and manipulates the market as a total reality (he perceives it through local traditions, habit, periodicity, his own material existence, his project as a producer-seller, etc.).

But these unifications are separated from one another by a *real*

---

82. The market as a gathering (practico-inert place) *itself becomes the price* in so far as it grounds the practico-inert activity of the series.

vacuum, that is to say, by *the fact* that, physically and practically, everyone *is not* the other, that walls really do separate them, as well as practical antagonisms or their real ignorance of their reciprocal existence. And the market is not the synthetic unity of a multiplicity, but the dispersive, real multiplication of its own unity. The unity of the market is not only the foundation of the operation which everyone tries to carry out, but also something which eludes him because the very action of this atomicity is *alienating*; and, finally, it is the fact that the *centre* of a market is *always elsewhere* as well as always present (as the place of the gathering or as all the information about prices); and it is this very contradiction which creates the social object. It is precisely this contradiction that enables the unity of the gathering to be not simply *transcended* by common action (as happens when there is a direct agreement between producers or consumers), or even by indidual action, but on the contrary to present itself both as the common object of an action and as the rigid, external law of every particular action, that is to say, to exist in the manner of an instrumental object, 'to hand', 'before one's eyes' and as an objective but alien necessity in every one of us. It is this second point which has to be emphasised. If prices are agreed between unions (or co-operatives) and monopolies, the price tends to lose its reality as a constraint. Obviously production costs and real wages indicate objective limits of variation; but these conditions are material and visible and can be confronted head-on; the profit margin, in contrast, can be reduced or increased by the direct relation between the forces present. At this level, selling price becomes a 'reciprocal object', that is to say, its opacity for one is based on the direct resistance of the other, and it affords us a glimpse, in its depths, of the action and needs of trusts or co-operatives.

Under Roosevelt's presidency, Americans refused to buy meat in order to struggle against the claims of the trust of slaughter-house owners. In such a situation – as long as the boycott lasts – price remains an ideal sign, since nobody either sells or buys and its meaning refers directly to the trust's will to struggle; it is a mere statement of the trust's determination, of their will to 'hold out' and of the material conditions which occasion or necessitate their attitude. But this is because the unification of the two groups makes a direct relation between them possible. (And as I have said, this unification only displaces recurrence.) When unification does not occur, for example in a competitive market, the price derives its objective and practical reality from the physical and mental separation of the agents; it is *real* because it gathers within it all the real factors of separation – the inadequacy of the available means of communication, the stone walls which separate the retail stores, or the actual time needed to reach one's neighbours and persuade them to transcend antagonism towards co-operation; but *above all*, it is based on a certain type of human relations, which might be called indirect, or lateral. Its strength derives from the impotence (whether temporary or absolute) of every buyer (or seller) in relation to the *series* of other buyers (or sellers); it corresponds to the necessity that if the seller (or buyer) wanted to try to defend himself, he would have to undertake a *serial* action, passing, that is, *from one individual to the next*. This serial action must be both indeterminate (for the number of persons to be directly reached is not given), and circular (for the individual with whom I make direct contact becomes other for me again, as soon as I move away from him in order to reach another; and it will be necessary to return to him). So it is a case of infinite recurrence.

The type of arithmetical reasoning which demonstrates that all the elements of a series possess the same property is well known. It can be divided into three operations. First, we establish a simple universal proposition: if the property exists for any number *a*, it necessarily exists for the number *b* (which comes immediately after *a* in the series); secondly, we verify that some number of the series does, in fact, possess the property in question; and lastly, we proceed to a sort of artificial totalisation, in other words, a sort of passage to the limit which dispenses with an infinite series of operations. (It is true of *a*, and therefore it is true of *b*; if it is true of *b*, then it is true of *c*, therefore *c* possesses the property; but if it is true of *c*, it is true of *d*, etc.) Thus *collective objects* originate in social recurrence: they represent totalisations of impracticable operations. But they do not appear at first as an object of knowledge: above all, they are realities which we are subjected to and which we live, and we learn them, in their objectivity, through acts which we *have to do*. The price imposes itself on me, as a buyer, because it imposes itself on my neighbour; it imposes itself on him because it imposes itself on his neighbour, and so on. But, conversely, I am not unaware that I help to establish it and that it imposes itself on my neighbours because it imposes itself on me; in general, it imposes itself on everyone as a stable collective reality only in so far as it is the totalisation of a series.

The *collective object* is an *index of separation*. This would emerge more clearly if we took as our example a more complex market (in connection with the conjuncture, with State intervention, with the existence of semi-monopolies, and taking into account advertising, the weather – and consequently, fluctuations of production and tooling – etc.), but this would require a treatment beyond the scope of this study. Let us simply take a particular case: that of a market in a period of rapid inflation.[83] The depreciation of money accelerates as everyone tries to get rid of it in order to acquire real values; but this behaviour determines the depreciation *above all* by reflecting it; in other words, it is future depreciation, in so far as it imposes itself on the individual to the extent that he *foresees* it as the unity of a process which conditions him, and it is this future depreciation which determines present depreciation. Now, the individual submits to this future depreciation as the action *of Others* on money. He adapts to it by imitating it: that is to say, he *makes himself Other*. In this way, he acts against his own wages *in so far as he is Other*, because it is he who contributes as much as anyone else to the destruction of the monetary unit; and his own position in relation to money (with its psychological characteristics of pessimism, etc.) has no other basis than the attitude of Others. The phenomenon occurs *as flight*: because I cannot prevent some unknown person from changing his money as quickly as possible into goods which he will stockpile, I hasten to exchange mine for other goods. But it is my own action, in so far as it is already inscribed in economic behaviour as a whole, and my future action, which determine the action of this unknown person. I return to myself as Other and my subjective fear of the Other (whom I cannot reach) appears to me as an alien force, the accelerated depreciation of money. Thus the collapse of the assignat[84] in 1792 was a collective process which could not be stopped: its objectivity was complete, and everyone *suffered* it as a destiny. Indeed, its objective factors were numerous and powerful: monetary circulation had doubled without any increase in production; the

83. Here again, I am ignoring the material conditions of inflation, namely the considerable increase in the quantity of money (which relates to the financial deficit of the government and, therefore, to history as totalisation) and some poverty of the factors of production (no stocks, etc.). These conditions are absolutely necessary for inflation, and their combination makes inflation inevitable. But they cause it *through men* who live the situation and react to it in their behaviour. These men are under-determined by the fact that the Other constantly eludes them and that they can struggle against him only by imitating him.

84. The promissory note issued by the revolutionary government in 1790. [Ed.]

persistence of coinage alongside paper money introduced a bi-monetary system (2,000 million in coin, 2,000 million in paper) and, as is well known, in such situations bad money chases good, that is to say supply exceeds demand, and it devalues rapidly; lastly, we must take account of speculation, forged notes from abroad, etc.[85]

But, apart from the fact that many of them can be effective only in so far as they are lived (for example Gresham's law necessarily refers to *confidence* – good money disappears because *people* hoard it, and they do so because they have no confidence in each other), historians recognise the importance of *political* factors in the decline of the assignat: confidence in it was all the weaker because it was issued by a revolutionary power, which might be overthrown. The failure of the assignat therefore reflects the flight of Louis XVI, the retractions of the Constituent Assembly, the defeat of the revolutionaries at the end of 1791 and, after the first defeats of 1792, the fear of the restoration of absolute monarchy. For the men who came together to struggle against these different events, in so far as they are historical, were directly subjected to them; it was an organised response to the king's treason which expelled him from the Tuileries on 10 August. The collapse of the assignat, however, gives expression to these events in so far as they had lateral effects on everyone, lived as the dispersed reaction of Others, in recurrence and impotence. The same person might belong to a Jacobin club, approve enthusiastically of 10 August, and keep his gold without noticing that the same facts are appearing to him at two distinct levels and that he reacts in contradictory ways depending on the level at which he considers them. As far as the assignat is concerned, the Revolution crumbles in his hands, and he helps it to do so; but as far as the motion which he helped to get carried at his club is concerned, he sees himself as carried along by revolutionary fervour. And supposing someone was aware of the contradiction, would he *receive* payment in assignats but *pay* for things in coin? Recurrence intervenes here; such an act could serve neither as propaganda, nor as an example; hardly anyone would notice it, and the only result would be that if the patriot was a merchant he would be ruined, while if he was a producer, though he would no doubt be saved, he

85. All these factors relate, of course, to the *praxis* of the bourgeoisie, to its economic liberalism (its refusal to give the assignat a power equal to that of coin, a refusal to decree compulsory circulation (this was to come later) and a refusal to shoulder the expenses of war).

would be helping (though to a negligible degree) to maintain the bi-monetarism which was undermining the Revolution.

So must this revolutionary be worried, and suspicious? Yes, profoundly; defiance of the Other, and a vague awareness of recurrence are necessary concomitants of the first steps of a revolution. The suspicion calls for unity *against recurrence* (and not, as some people think, against mere multiplicity), and for totalisation *against indefinite flight* (and not, as Hegel says, universality against specific difference): it is suspicion which engenders and sustains Terror as an attempt at *subjective* unification. But this suspicion, governed by the suspicion of Others, is also counter-revolutionary and presents it.elf in the collapse of the assignat as an alien object. At this level, we come back to money as materiality. But this time, we can consider it in the context of practical relations of reciprocity. Its meaning sums up the totality of the historical process up to the present moment, but it does so by mechanising it; and the agents do not conceive of it as a positive characteristic of the material object (like the Genoese merchants when they carried off the Spanish gold), but as an infinite and regressive absence. Today, the rapid succession of inflations and devaluations has shown everyone the double character of all money, as material presence and as indefinite flight. The real value of a given banknote can be determined only in a specific, dated historical conjuncture; it must refer to the capitalist system, to the relations of production, to the relative strengths of classes, to the contradictions of imperialism and to the relation between France and other bourgeois democracies. But this complex is a flight *for me*; I see it in the 5-franc piece *in so far as* it is lived by the Other, either the buyer who stockpiles in the expectation of war, or the seller who raises his prices, or the producer who reduces his own production. But this absence, this movement of perpetual regression, can be manifested only in a material object of which it constitutes the *human reality*. The diabolical appearance of the *coin* (or note) is that it is apprehended (at successive moments) in its material identity and that I can take it, hold it, and hide it; but that in its very immobility it is affected by an absent change, which always occurs elsewhere and which reflects to me the image of my impotence through atomisation.

I shall develop the example of money in a later work. Here, I simply wish to draw attention to the fact that money, in each of its concrete units, has the double infinity of the universal and of recurrence. *This* particular banknote is constituted in my hands as a universalised abstraction by the fact that it is valid everywhere: it is *the* hundred-franc note. (Hence the familiar phrases: 'How much does that cost?' '*The* hundred-franc note'.) And at the same time, its real purchasing power is the result of an infinite recurrence in which I myself feature as *an other*. We shall therefore treat it as a 'collective'. In so far as their inertia preserves them, all social objects are collectives *in their fundamental materiality*; as long as they last, all of them derive their reality from the perpetual detotalisation of the totality of men; *basically*, they all presuppose a haemorrhage from which material presence drains away. Of course, they have very diverse structures. The competitive market can be conceived of as, at most, the radical atomisation (or massification) of human groups; the ponderous reality *of price*, fixed by common disagreement, is *the collective* (valid for everyone) *expression of the impossibility of a real unity*, of an organisation of buyers (or of sellers). It does not *connect*: rather, it is the consequence of separation, and a factor of new separation; in short, it is *realised separation*. But for men, separation, like union, is *a constructed situation*, resulting from certain actions performed by certain forces. *Price* derives its false unity from the fact that separation is a produced reality, a type of relation between men.

It is this separation which Le Chapelier attempted to effect on the labour market,[86] after some strikes which had worried the bourgeoisie, and which, for the workers, was expressed in the absolute inflexibility of wages. The unity of the collective object therefore becomes stricter, and its rigidity more inflexible as the atomisation of groups develops. And as price originally represents everyone's activity in so far as it is governed laterally, and at a distance, by the activity of *the Other*, its collective character expresses the simplest form of alienation. Wage limits, taxes, and modern State intervention do not *initially* come up against ill will: but such attempts at positive unification, which presuppose (and also try to constitute) a centralisation and organisation of inter-human relations, are in constant danger of dissolving back into the milieu from which they arise, that is to say, into the milieu of recurrence: before they can be lived as a direct relation between a centralising organ and every individual, they will be lived *as other* and *through the other* regardless of the express wish of the rulers. This is why the Convention eludes the Convention member

---

86. The Le Chapelier law of June 1791 deprived the workers of the right of combination.

and takes on an impenetrable depth in so far as it also exists for a non-member, for the *sans-culottes*, for the provincial towns, for the country-side, and for Europe itself (how often revolutionary orators declared: 'The eyes of the world are upon us!'). Originally, this relation is a direct one: the Convention, with its powers, its authority, its tasks, its deputies, exists as a direct object for the elector, for the Jacobin, and for the *représentant en mission*; it is both the organ of government and the elected assembly which is accountable to the nation; it is suffered and resisted, venerated and detested. But what makes us relapse into recurrence is the fact that, in spite of the political clubs, the citizens were not organised in any way, and that, in a way, the Assembly was in the position of a monopoly facing dispersed buyers. This dispersal creates both the power and impotence of the rulers: it reduces the possibility of organised resistance (strikes against maximum wages, etc.) to a minimum, but, at the same time, it erodes its unifying de-crees and dissolves them in itself (the crisis in foodstuffs, the collapse of the assignat, etc.). Representations and beliefs, *always coming from elsewhere*, bear in themselves the mark of recurrence, they are 'over-flowing' ideas (*idées 'débordantes'*): no doubt they express everyone's real situation, but they express it in flight, and mythically; their incon-sistency makes them impenetrable and invincible. When the member of the Convention tries to understand the Convention, as a changing undertaking, *for* his electors or *for* the country, it will elude him com-pletely: *the object* is there, enlarged to the frontiers of France, real, constricting, but, strictly speaking, unthinkable.

4 Series and Opinion: the Great Fear

These last remarks enable us to see a few characteristics of another collective – a most important one from the point of view of rulers. This is *public opinion*. In the context of the process of temporalisation and totalisation, there is undoubtedly such a thing as *opinion*, and it is expressed in words and deeds which refer to certain meanings. It is an everyday matter for some of these words and deeds to form the sub-ject of police reports to the head of government. It is for the leaders themselves to interpret their meanings as *objective realities* and as an effective ideological materiality. Then there will be talk of the *discontent* of a particular social category, of the *tension* developing amongst individuals and groups (in so far as it is expressed in speech and action – brawls, lynchings, etc.). At this level it will be determined whether public opinion does or does not make a direct connection between two facts or objective meanings (for example, between the refusal of the bourgeoisie to finance the war of 1792 from taxation and the fall of the assignat) or whether, in contrast, it creates – rightly or wrongly – a single meaning with two different meanings. So public opinion tends to be seen as a collective consciousness arising from the synthetic unification of the citizens into a nation, and imposing its representations on everyone as an integral part of the whole, just as the totality is present in each of its parts.

The *discontent* of retailers (as revealed both in common actions *and* in wholly distinct ones), the *distrust* of the government amongst industrialists and bankers (as expressed in the refusal of loans), *the revival of anti-semitism* (after a defeat or a national humiliation): all these objective realities should be regarded as totalising schemata. But we should realise that every one of them, in itself and for everyone, is *the Other*, that its signifying structure is infinite seriality, and that it has the practico-inert unity of an index of separation. For example, in so far as retailers have produced their own organs of defence and can affect the government, it is inappropriate to speak of discontent: they fight ministerial power and try to change it. Everything is *praxis*: if it succeeds, everything will be settled amicably. On the other hand, when the isolated small shopkeeper sees taxes and wholesale prices rising when he is unable to raise his retail prices, he feels, in his very person, the fear of ruin and hunger. But his reaction would be pure terror, rather than discontent, unless, in his very fear, he discovered the same discontent among other shopkeepers as a serial totality of impotence, that is to say, unless he discovered himself as dispersed in the seriality of the Other, as affected by the impotence of Others, and as affecting the Others (that is to say, himself as Other to infinity) with his impotence. For this reason, *the common material object* (for example, tax or the index of wholesale prices) in its practico-inert development, creates *the unity of the discontent*. But it creates it outside, in him. In the multiplicity of individuals, this discontent realises itself in the theoretical and practical protests of isolated, discontented individuals (who do not know one another as individuals), as the index of their separation. In this sense, *it is a social reality*; it is a force (as impotence lived individually, it may lead a person to sell his business, to commit suicide, etc.; and in circumstances which will be defined below, it can serve as a basis for regroupment) and this force is simply the practico-inert power of hundreds of thousands of people as potential energy. But this force does not reside *in anyone*, and it is not *the product of everyone*; it is alterity itself to precisely the extent that, for everyone, it is *elsewhere*.

In specific cases where discontent (or some other affective state) has spread through the country, then, rather than being felt and expressed by everyone in *his own right*, people take part in serial propagations which clearly illuminate its character as alterity. One need only recall the Great Fear of 1789, of which Lefebvre has provided such a re-markable study.[87] First he shows that the fear did not break out everywhere at the same time and that it did not cover the whole of France, contrary to what some historians have claimed in the name of a spontaneous organicism. He shows that five different waves of fear ought to be distinguished, and that certain regions were never affected. Finally, he shows that these waves, the origins of each of which can be localised and dated, were propagated *serially*, from town to village and from village to town, and that their routes were determined by quite precise conditions. But the most striking thing in his book is that one constantly feels driven to discovering the intelligibility of a movement in the rationality of the Other. I will simply recall a few observations: the *fear* arose in very specific conditions, but what it expressed, in the provinces and the countryside, was above all a structure of alterity in relation to Paris. News was scarce, slow to arrive, and impatiently awaited: it eventually reached the towns, but it spread unevenly and confusedly in the countryside (it was already stale and distorted when the peasants heard it on market days). Thus the contrast between the rapidity of events in the capital and Versailles and the scarcity of in-formation showed everyone his passivity in relation to those Others (aristocrats, deputies of the Third Estate, the Parisian people) who made History in Paris. Later, Jacobin societies tried to organise the provinces and even the countryside. But at this time, these men – disturbed, anxious and impatient – all felt themselves as *Others* (who suffered History) in so far as they could have no effect on the *subjects* who were making History in Paris.

87. Georges Lefebvre, *The Great Fear of 1789* (1956), trans. Joan White, NLB, 1973. [Ed.]

The conditions which gave rise to the Great Fear must therefore be seen in the context of everyone's discovery of himself as Other (as an object of a History made by others). But it is striking that the fear was essentially born out of 'fear of bandits'. Begging, in fact, was the chronic sore of the countryside: there were beggars and tramps everywhere. Basically, these were just ruined peasants or the children of over-large families. Nevertheless, the farmers did not regard them favourably. The smallholders and even the day-labourers saw them as an agricultural 'lumpen-proletariat' at the same time as recognising themselves in the vagabonds, in that a permanent possibility threatened them too with ruin, with vagabondage, and with being Others. But, for the peasant, the true *other*, *the other class*, was, of course, the landed aristocracy with its feudal rights. Now it is remarkable that, on the news that an aristocratic *plot* was feared in the towns, the synthetic link between aristocrats and vagabonds suddenly became apparent. Of course, one *might* offer a reasonable explanation: the aristocrats had had the vagabonds *in their pay* in order to crush the country people. But this interpretation rationalises *retrospectively* a movement whose intelligibility lies in the process of alterity itself and which makes the vagabond appear as *absolute Other*, that is to say, as doubly Other (Other as a pauper, and Other as a hireling of the oppressing class), combining in himself, in the dimension of alterity, both crime as the anti-human activity of the Other than man, and oppressive domination as a *praxis* aiming to reduce the peasant to a sub-human state. The proof that it was essentially a synthetic union of all alterities in the absolute Other (a cruel man reducing his fellow-men to sub-humanity, a cruel beast exactly like men except that his sole aim is to eliminate them) is that, in regions where memories of the ravages caused by the Hundred Years War still lingered on, bandits were known as 'Englishmen' and that, almost everywhere, with no concern for coherence, the vagabond-hirelings were known as *foreigners*. The 'aristocrat's plot', supported by a professional army, initially had meaning, in fact, only in *Paris and Versailles*: it was conceivable that the aristocracy would use the troops massed around Paris to break the resistance of the Third Estate and of the people (and certain aristocrats actually attempted to impose this policy). But, in the new form that this policy assumed in the eyes of the peasant, it became perfectly absurd. Nevertheless *it was the same*, but seen in the milieu of the Other by individuals whose impotence had dragged them into the world of objects, of Others. *Bandits* were the aristocratic plot as Other, seen in the original milieu of the Other and as a characteristic of absolute alterity; they were History as an enemy force, coming to everyone as alien.

What makes the Great Fear even more complex is that, as Lefebvre has shown, it did not *cause* riots or the looting of châteaux but, on the contrary, was preceded by a series of local insurrections (though naturally there was *far more* looting during and after the Great Fear): peasants besieged châteaux, occupied them, and sometimes damaged them and they also attacked some of the nobles. Now these local actions also helped *to produce the fear* – and not only the fear of the Other's reaction (or of reprisals), for they also appeared, to those who had not taken part in them (and perhaps also, after some time, to the participants themselves) as terrifying, evil actions – rather like a violation of some sacred prohibition or a fearful unleashing of violence. Now, these non-participating peasants were *the same* as those who took part in the riot: by seeing the action (directed against *the same* oppressor they hated) as directed in fact against them, they saw their own violence as that of an Other and their fellows as aliens. Thus setting a château on fire assumed an ambivalent character in popular memory (in the form of alterity as a structure of memory) like the sacred itself: both black and white. It was *both* a legitimate revolt of the people *and* Other violence, violence as Other: which is why it was attributed to *bandits*. Faced with this alien violence, everyone, in effect, as though confronting History, felt himself to be an *other object*. Similarly, the storming of the Bastille, as a piece of news which spread everywhere, assumed both a more or less vague, but true and positive aspect (that the people had stormed the Bastille), and a polymorphous, negative aspect, depending whether it was rationalised (the storming of the Bastille would unleash the vengeance of the aristocracy on the people); and a consequence of the storming of the Bastille was that numerous bandits escaped from Paris and disappeared into the countryside (in this version, Paris becomes, in spite of everything, the negative cause, the source of evil); and lastly, more or less obscurely (elements hostile to the Revolution must have helped), the Bastille was stormed by bandits.

Having said this, neither the economic, political and social causes known to us, nor the fear of bandits or the constitution *of the milieu of the Other* as a refracting medium (*milieu*) of History are enough to explain the Great Fear. The factors referred to, including fear of bandits, are in fact universal. The Great Fear as a real process was broad, but localised. In each case, it had to be triggered off by some local incident which was perceived as Other by those who witnessed it, and seriality had to propagate itself by becoming *actualised.* At first, indeed, what appears is always *taken for something else.* This does not in any way mean that one object is mistaken for another, as in the case of a sensory error: the object correctly conceived actually *returns* as an other meaning in the very movement of propagation. A gang of day-labourers in the Oise valley protest because the farmer refuses to pay what they demand. 'The news,' said a local newspaper, *'spread and grew.* Bells were rung in all the parishes.' In the same region another newspaper offered a different interpretation: 'from a distance,' a group of surveyors had apparently been mistaken for bandits. Elsewhere, town militias or soldiers were mistaken, *from a distance,* for bands of assassins. *From a distance* means: when the information was so poor that it was impossible to know who was coming. In such a case, that is to say, *whenever* witnesses could choose between a positive and a negative interpretation, between reciprocity and alterity, between man and anti-man, they chose the Other, the no, the anti-human. Anyone seen from a distance was other than man because the observer felt himself to be other in this developing History.

We must now show how alterity creates its own laws: the truth becomes obvious for everyone not only in so far as it is negative and relates to the Other, but also in so far as it is transmitted by an Other in so far as he is Other. These are the rules of belief: what everyone believes of the Other is what the Other conveys in so far as he is Other (or in so far as the news comes to him already from an Other). In other words, it is negative information in that neither the person who receives it, nor the one who gives it, could or can verify it. Their *impotence* is simply seriality itself as a negative totality, and it should not be supposed that everyone believed his informer *in spite of it.* On the contrary, this impotence in each of them as Other supports and sustains the belief in the Other as a means of propagating truth as Other. If I believe my informer, it is not *because* I cannot check what he says, or because I trust him (which would re-establish a direct relation of reciprocity), or because, while I may check it sometime it is more prudent to be prepared for the worst. I believe him because, as Other, the truth of a report is its seriality, that is to say, the infinite series of impotences which will be, or are being, or have been actualised, and which constitute me *through Others* as a *practico-inert conveyor* of the truth. I believe it *because it is Other* (that is to say, in accordance with the principle that History is really the history of the Other-than-man and that the worst is always certain), because it shows the

man it describes as an alien species, and because the mode of its communication is other, and has no reciprocity. The informer *propagates*
a material wave; he *does not truly inform*; his report is *a panic*; in a word,
the truth, as Other, is transmitted as a state *by contagion*; it is quite
simply the Other-state of the Other in the face of Others, and it is this
contagion which grounds it for everyone, in so far as it is ultimately
the Other-Being of the series which realises itself through it in him;
if I believe a madman whom I see approaching, running and shouting,
when I am already aware of my own impotence, I become *the same
for another* and run like a madman towards my neighbour. Belief, *in a
process* like the Great Fear, is alterity itself in so far as it temporalises
itself in the actualisation of an already constituted series. Thus the
contagious fact is unintelligible *apart from* the collective and recurrence. Whatever the fundamental historical conditions which gave
rise to it, it would never have produced itself as a chain-disintegration
unless it had taken place in the structured temporality of the practico-
inert field and unless the infinite complex of serialities had *already been
produced* as the very grain and web of this field. Indeed, it was in terms
of seriality and alterity that contemporaries explained it when they
tried to slow it down. One simply changes level: newspapers and local
authorities explain that *foreigners* are spreading rumours to the effect
that there are bandits (or else are passing themselves off as bandits) in
order to spread panic. This amounts to saying: if you plunge into the
milieu of the Other, you are playing the game of *the absolute Other*.

I have used this example in order to exhibit a new temporal object:
a series in the process of actualisation. It is not an historical *event* in the
ordinary sense of the term, that is to say, a developing totalisation of
antagonistic and concerted actions, but rather a *process*. However, in
so far as the practico-inert field is the field of material exigencies, of
counter-finalities and of inert meanings, its unity necessarily remains
teleological and signifying. Thus, the Great Fear appeared to contemporaries *either* as the practical result of a revolutionary agitation which
aimed to set the peasants against the feudal lords (and, in fact, looting
and rioting, as the first *group* reaction against the impotence of the
collective, did increase; and, a little later, the project of federation
also appeared as a reaction against the impotence of the masses), *or* as
the result of an attempt by representatives of the aristocracy (and a
section of the lower clergy) to demoralise the peasant masses and to
set them against the bourgeoisie of the Third Estate. In actual fact, it
involved this double counter-finality only because the series lived

History as Other and on the basis of human impotence. The *opinions* of public opinion arise like the Great Fear, in that everyone makes himself Other by his opinion, that is to say, by taking it *from the Other* because the Other believes it as Other, and makes himself the informer of the Others. At this level, the Idea is a process; it derives its invincible strength from the fact that nobody thinks it. That is to say, it does not define itself as the conscious moment of *praxis* – that is to say, as the unifying unveiling of objects in the dialectical temporalisation of action. Instead, it defines itself as a practico-inert object whose self-evidence, for me, is the same as my double inability to verify it and to transform it in Others.[88]

88. There are also other forms of ideas in the collective: for example, the *Idea-exis*. As we have seen, the practico-inert object (the gold coin, for example) produced its own Idea in the general movement of practice, that is to say, the passive unity of its materiality was constituted by practice as meaning. In so far as this object becomes the common-being-outside-itself of a series, the Idea, as such, becomes the unity of the series as its reason or its index of separation. This is how colonialism, as a material system in the practico-inert field of colonisation, in other words as the *common interest* of the colonists, produced its own Idea in its very development: it became a means of practical choice between those who are the exploited *by essence*, and those who have become exploiters *through merit*. And if it does designate the exploited by their essence (that is to say, as exploitable *sub specie aeternitatis*), it is because it cannot allow any change in their condition, however minimal, without destroying itself. Colonialism defines the exploited as eternal because it constitutes itself as an eternity of exploitation. In so far as the inert sentence passed on the colonised peoples becomes the serial unity of the colonialists (in its ideological form), or their link of alterity, it is the Idea as Other or the Other as Idea; it therefore remains an Idea of stone, but its strength derives from its ubiquity of absence. In this form of alterity, it becomes racism. The essence of racism, in effect, is that it is not a system of thoughts which might be false or pernicious – and the same applies to thousands of other 'theses'; I simply took the first example to come to mind. *It is not a thought at all.* It cannot even be formulated. And the attraction of racism for intelligent, well-meaning people (for example, in the form of an innocent pride: 'One has to admit that the Mediterranean races . . ., etc.') is normally experienced by them (and in an objectively observable way) as the attraction of stupidity, that is to say, as the secret hope that thought is a stone. In reality, racism is the colonial interest lived as a link of all the colonialists of the colony through the serial flight of alterity. As such, like the living Idea, it presents itself as infinite depth. But this depth is both petrified and strictly formal, because it is limited to producing itself as a negation of everyone by serial infinity: in other words, it gives itself *in the abstract* as *other* than each of its particular formulations. At the same time it realises itself constantly in every relation between the colonists and the colonised through the colonial system and, as the basic activity of the colonists amongst themselves, it

is reduced to a few phrases, which have almost no content, but are uniquely guaranteed by alterity in that the Other-Idea guarantees them in a negative way by negating its reduction, as a totalised seriality, to these particular expressions. These determinations of discourse are very familiar: 'The native is lazy, dishonest, and dirty; he doesn't work unless he is forced to; he's an eternal child quite incapable of controlling himself; in any case, he lives on nothing, he never thinks of the next day; the native is properly understood only by the colonialist, etc.' These phrases were never the translation of a real, concrete thought; they were not even *the object* of thought. Furthermore, they have not by themselves any meaning, at least in so far as they claim to express knowledge about the colonised. They arose with the establishment of the colonial system and have never been anything more than this system itself producing itself as a determination of the language of the colonists in the milieu of alterity. And, from this point of view, they must be seen as material exigencies of language (the *verbal milieu* of all practico-inert apparatuses) addressed to colonialists as members of a series and *signifying* them as colonialists both in their own eyes and in those of others, in the unity of a gathering. It is pointless to say that they circulate, that people repeat them to one another in some form; the truth is that they *cannot* circulate because they cannot be objects of exchange. They have *a priori* the structure of a collective and when two colonialists, in conversation, appear to be *exchanging* these ideas, they actually merely reactualise them one after the other in so far as they represent a particular aspect of serial reason. In other words, the sentence which is uttered, as a reference to the common interest, is not presented as the determination of language by the individual himself, but as his *other* opinion, that is to say, he claims to get it from and give it to others, in so far as their unity is based purely on alterity. (Of course, it is possible to imagine colonialist groups associating for the organised defence of their colonial interests; indeed, there have been plenty of cases of it. Naturally, these groups multiply as tension between colonists and colonised increases. But we are here considering only the colonial *milieu*. It is enough to indicate – and we shall come back to this in the next chapter – that the presence of groups constituted *from* the gathering itself must complicate any real description.)

In fact, the affirmative force of this opinion derives from the fact that, in and through everyone, it is the invincible stubbornness of others; and the certainty of the person who affirms it rests on his (cheerfully accepted) inability to occasion any doubt about this subject in any other members of the series. The Idea as a product of the common object has the materiality of a fact because no one thinks it. Therefore, it has the opaque indubitability of a thing. But in the moment where a particular colonialist is pleased to relate to it as to a thing, that is to say, as an unthinkable thought, he presents it as a spontaneous rediscovery, a fresh, new re-creation *elsewhere* (anywhere in the colony): for example, there is this colonial administrator, a nice chap, but terribly young and so foolishly idealistic, and he is just learning the job . . .; in him and through him, the idea becomes a hypothesis, a key to decipher an experience, etc. *Elsewhere*, and therefore in the Other, the inert formula which everyone repeats recovers its pristine force as a discovery; in other words *this* particular colonialist, *as Other*, here repeats a stereotyped formula in the certainty that he *himself, in an Other and as an Other*, is rediscovering it. But, in fact, he has neither the means nor the intention of renewing his experience *for himself,* of testing the Idea, in order to guarantee it anew: the Idea as a living *praxis* emerges in action and as a moment of action as an *ever contestable* key to the world. But there is no need to contest it since the common object is based on the practical avoidance of all testing. The strength of *this* particular colonialist lies in the fact that the Idea (as a common bond) comes to him as the thought of the Other, of totalised alterity, and that he is *entirely the Other* as infinite flight, frozen at the moment he repeats it, while this absolute certainty becomes work, unification and translucidity in Others – in the young, etc. He affirms himself as the Other who *really thinks it elsewhere* by making himself *the Other who repeats it here without thinking.*

In connection with this opacity conceived as *obviousness* and the inability to change the Other conceived as *indubitability,* it should be remembered that each of these Ideas is imposed on everyone as a practico-inert *exigency,* that is to say, as a categorical imperative. In this sense, it is common interest constituting itself as the solidarity of the colonialists against the colonised; but this solidarity, at the level of seriality, can only have a negative form: it is determined in alterity. On this basis, it arises as the (negative) fact that, amongst the small number of colonialists who maintain themselves by force and against the colonised, *everyone is in danger in* the Other; that is to say, everyone is *impotently* in danger of suffering the consequences of some pernicious act occurring somewhere in the series. In fact, in this particular example, the serial unity of the colonists comes to them from the Absolute Other which is the colonised people; and it reflects them as an active grouping (a synthetic, positive unity of plurality). The impotence of the series constitutes itself as a magical power of the colonised people. They are oppressed and, in a way, still impotent – otherwise the colonialists would no longer be there; but, at the same time, 'they know everything, they see everything, they spy on us, they communicate among themselves instantly, etc.'. In this *magical milieu of the colonised Other and of the participation of every native in the whole,* seriality is revealed in its impotence as the threat to each by all, and consequently as an obligation for everyone to maintain the *Other-Action,* which means: not that which has been established by universal agreement, but that which he would like any other to maintain. This act, of course, is *the Other itself* as the formula of the series of colonialists; in other words, it is *the* colonialist in so far as he is always the model who inspires me in an Other. The colonialist produces himself in the Other *without weakness;* he imposes himself within me *as a prohibition:* show no weakness to the native staff; and this brings us to the exigency of the system: no change for the colonised without the destruction of the colonial apparatus. *The colonialist is a particular being who needs to be realised through me* in so far as no one can realise him and in so far as he must remain outside as the negative formula of the series. In a way, every colonialist spontaneously and constantly realises him by his free activities in so far as they express his particular interests as an exploiter in the milieu of the exploited; but at this level, *he is not a being.* He becomes one when the threat of insurrection becomes more concrete. But in this case, his practico-inert relation to everyone is imperative precisely because it produces itself as everyone's responsibility towards the Other in so far as every Other is responsible for everyone. Hence that strange magical bond through the virgin forest of seriality: I try to realise the Other – that is to say, to make myself more deaf, ruthless, and negative to the claims of the native, than my plantation as my own

I have described *serial being* as the determination of the bond of alterity as a unity of plurality by the exigencies and structures of the common object which in itself defines this plurality as such. We have seen that this being is *practical* because it is sustained in reality by the relations which are established in the practico-inert field between the *individual* activities of men. But at the same time as it produces itself as collective in and through the real behaviour of every practical organism, this serial being is constituted as a *negative unity* and a threatening (or paralysing) inter-dependence *by the impotence* of each real action in so far as it derives from the actions of the others through the practical field. Its reality, then, is in itself practico-inert and its transformations are born of a simple dialectic. (Activity is sometimes constituted as collective passivity by failures due

interest actually requires – so that my attempt becomes, for some other who might be tempted to make a concession to the natives, the real presence of the Other, as a magical force of constraint. In fact, of course, there is nothing irrational in this: the Other as the presence-constraint of a negative unity is given to all the members of the series; it is the same imperative for all. In actualising it in my action I actualise it *for all those present* and, by degrees, (by a *real* series of propagation, which, however, like all movements, exhausts itself) for the serial totality. *In fact, the example* is in no way the direct unification of the multiplicity of a gathering by the real activity of a single individual (although the existence of the group will complicate its structures). Originally, the example was quite simply the actualisation in one term of the relation of seriality. In this Other, who behaved *correctly* in public (that is to say, as the Other that he is and that I am) towards the native, I discover *myself as Other* (an identity determined in seriality). Conversely, this particular Other, who has shown himself so perfectly as the Other in all his opacity, becomes for me the common interest as my particular imperative: the Other that I have to be. This makes it clear that *racist ideas*, as structures of the collective opinion of the colonialists, are petrified actions (petrified *from the beginning*) which are manifested as imperatives in the context of the Other to be realised by me. As perpetual exigencies of reaffirmation by individual verbal acts, they indicate the impossibility of a real totalisation of these affirmations, that is to say, the intensity of the imperative is directly proportional to the index of separation. In short, by the very act of repeating them, one shows that it is impossible for everyone to unite simultaneously against the natives, that it is merely shifting recurrence, and that in any case such a unification could occur as an active grouping only so as to massacre the colonised people, which is the perpetual, absurd temptation of the colonialists, and which, if it were possible, would amount to the immediate destruction of colonisation. In this way, *the racist idea*, both as an unthinkable idea and as a categorical imperative, can serve us as a typical example of *the serial idea* as an act of alterity which *realises in urgency* (and for lack of anything better) the practico-inert unity of the gathering, and, in contradiction with the original exigency, manifests this unity as a fundamental negation, that is to say, as impotence grounded on separation.

to *impotence*, that is to say, to a qualification and a transformation which come to the agent from others; serial being becomes immobility *through* innumerable impotent activities, or activities of impotence. And sometimes, as in the case of the colonialists, impotence presents itself as a unitary exigency of action; but, in this case, action is not really *praxis*; it is practico-inert because it realises the Other as a fleeting and prefabricated passivity.) In this way, serial being, as a practico-inert reality, can be defined as a *process*, that is to say, as a development which, though orientated, is caused by a force of exteriority which has the result of actualising the series as the temporalisation of a multiplicity in the fleeting unity of a violence of impotence. These observations have shown us that *the collective* is not simply the form of being of certain social realities,[89] but that it is also the being of sociality itself at the level of the practico-inert field. And I have been able to describe this being as social being in its elementary, fundamental structure because it is at the practico-inert level that sociality is produced in men by things as a bond of materiality which transcends and alters simple human relations. Besides, a collective is in itself a sort of scale model of the practico-social field and of any passive activity carried out in it. It is constructed, moreover, on the false reciprocity of the practical agent and of worked matter; in reality, worked materiality, in bearing the seal *of an other activity* (and entering into human action under the impulse of a series of dispersed *praxes*), becomes in the collective the practico-inert unity of the multiplicity of which it is the common object. Thus the unity of the gathering, far from being organic or practical, manifests itself with all the characteristics of sealed materiality; in other words, inorganic materiality comes to the gathering as such from its inert (or practico-inert) unification by the interiorisation of the seal of its common object. But this materiality, as an inorganic materiality which produces itself in and through practical relations, takes on the determination *of alterity*. Thus, in the dialectical movement which characterises this structure of false reciprocity within the collective, seriality as the seal of the common object projected onto the human multiplicity turns back on the common object and determines it by the action of everyone as an *other-object* (*objet autre*) (that is to say, a common object *as the objectification of the Other* or as *Other objectivity*). It is in this dialectical moment that the object produces its men (as workers, owners, etc.), as the others whose alterity it is and who act on it or suffer its action in so far as it becomes for each of them his Other Destiny or his Other Interest, that is to say, in so far as the activity of everyone – in so

---

89. Though certain of these realities have *no being other than collective being.*

far as it responds to the exigencies of the common object – also reveals the impotence *of everyone* in the objective form of the inflexibility of the object. The celebrated *inexorable laws* of bourgeois economics in the nineteenth century have never been anything but the effect of scarcity appearing in a practico-inert field of serial impotence. Indeed, from this point on, the same practico-inert notions (solidified finality, simultaneous inversion of the dialectical laws of human *praxis* and of the analytical quantitative laws of inorganic materiality) apply within the collective, to matter as the sealed unity of men, to the gathering as the material negation of molecular dispersal and of the human relation, and to the acting individual in so far as his free *praxis* constitutes itself as inessential in relation to the practico-inert activity of the Other and to the practico-inert exigencies of the worked thing. In fact, we rediscover here a real and universal mode of discourse, in so far as discourse itself is a practico-inert designation of the practico-inert field. These verbal structures are genuine tools of thought for thinking the world of passive activity and active passivity; all that is necessary is that a direct, organised practice (on the part of an individual or a group) should take them *in their practico-inert being* and use them, as is only proper, as replacements for things. And in so far as they have been invented by nobody, and in so far as they are language organising itself as passive activity in the milieu of alterity, these verbal structures are, in a collective, the collective itself, that is to say, the common object in so far as it is produced (under everyone's real actions) as a material Idea of the being of man or of the acting individual in so far as he acts and speaks as Other in the milieu of serial impotence. These verbal structurations (practical schemata for constructing an indeterminate series of sentences) are characterised by an absolute refusal to make a distinction at any level between the agent (or agents) as member of a series and the object as producing men as its products. In fact, in the collective, exigency *really is* in the object, because some men have put it there and others maintain it there on the basis of the entire historical process; and it really is inhuman, because inorganic matter, as the conducting medium, necessarily inverts the structures of *praxis*. Conversely, it is *really human* in everyone (in so far as it is grounded on need, etc., and in so far as it manifests itself through a project which transcends past and present conditions towards the future), but it is *dehumanising* in so far as it produces itself as the unification of the gathering by the thing: its reality therefore produces itself in everyone as inflexible in so far as it produces impotence as the negative and totalising link of the series as materiality; furthermore, the structure of alterity which is manifested on the basis of this impotence forces man to *demand,* as Other and as conditioned by Others, (and as conditioning them as an Other) so that, ultimately, everyone's need, though directly present in the organism as a real negation of it, is itself felt through impotence as the need of the Other or Need as Other. At this level, there is no difference between saying that the children of poor districts need sun, that the car needs petrol, that the room needs a good clean, or that France needs children, etc.[90] It would be completely mistaken to reduce these structures and their mode of expression to capitalist societies alone and to regard them as a historical product of capital: others can be found, different in content but similar in essence, in socialist societies too. A Polish journalist indignantly quoted the following sentence which had appeared all over the walls of Warsaw, two years before Poznan: 'Tuberculosis impedes (*freine*) production.' He was both right and wrong to be indignant. He was right because it makes the tubercular worker, as a manual worker, into a mere negative (and inert) relation between a microbe and a machine. Indeeed, there can be few slogans which show more vividly the absolute equivalence between serial multiplicity and the common material object within a collective.[91] But, on the other hand, the slogan is neither stupid nor false: it is the expression of *bureaucracy* as the decomposition (by the exigencies of a practico-inert field) of an active ruling group into a serial gathering. Bureaucracy, in effect, is the Other erected into a principle and a means of government: it means that the decomposition of the group has totally enclosed men in the internal field of the practico-inert. It is not that man has ceased to be the future of man, but that the man of the future comes to man *as a human thing*.

From this point of view, dialectical investigation provides the answer to the question we just posed: it shows us class *at the level of the practico-inert field* as a collective, and *class being* as a statute of seriality

90. On the social and political plane, the point is not to negate these structures of being and language, but to act together in order to liquidate the practico-inert field.

91. *Production,* indeed, as an unconditional imperative, is the quantity of goods produced in so far as they have absorbed as their inessential means the strength and activity of the producers. In so far as the slogan affirms the practical homogeneity of the concepts which it unites, tuberculosis is a disease in so far as it is experienced by nobody, in so far as it is a statistic, that is to say, measured, for example, by the number of working hours which it causes to be lost. Finally, the relation between them is expressed by a word which qualifies the object on the basis of human labour; *impeding* can, in fact, *today*, refer to a natural modification within some mechanical system, but this is *only because,* for millennia, men have been constructing a certain internal relation within worked objects known as the *brake.* This expression therefore results in inserting a Manichean type of counter-finality as a practico-inert relation between a material exigency and its negation by material circumstances.

imposed on the multiplicity which composes it. But a few points still remain to be cleared up. We shall return for a moment to the example of the French proletariat as produced by industrialisation in the first half of the nineteenth century.

5 Series and Class: The French Proletariat

As collectives are both a result of particular undertakings and a radical inversion of finality, they have peculiar powers which may have made it possible to believe in their subjective existence, but which need to be studied in objectivity. Because the economic system of a society is *a collective*, it can be conceived as a system which functions of itself, tending to persevere in its being. In particular, what Marx calls the process of capital must necessarily be understood through the materialist dialectic and in accordance with his rigorous interpretation of it. But if it is true that this process is partially responsible for 'the atomisation of crowds' and also for recurrence,[92] it is also true that it can

---

92. There is no trace of atomisation in medieval communities. They have their own structures, grounded on the relation of man to man (personal dependence). In this period, writes Marx: 'The social relations between individuals in the performance of their labour, appear at all events as their own mutual personal relations, and are not disguised under the shape of social relations between the products of labour....' (*Capital*, I, p. 77). Yet this feudal constitution did nothing to prevent alterity or circular recurrence or even in certain cases the perspective of flight: this is what creates, for example, the reality of *the Church*, which is certainly something more than the set of the personal relations amongst the clergy and between the clergy and the laity. If the enormous, real substratum of religious alienation existed, and weighed on the whole of Europe with the weight of its properties and its privileges, this is not because it was tending to realise its unity as a subjective community of believers, but rather because it remained a detotalised totality and because any attempted action on it, whether from outside or inside, lost itself in a perspective of indefinite flight. The real problem – which we cannot go into here – relates not so much to the past, where recurrence and alienation have always existed, as to the future: to what extent will a socialist society do away with atomism *in all its forms*? To what extent will collective objects, the signs of our alienation, be dissolved into a true inter-subjective community in which the only real relations will be those between men, and to what extent will the necessity of every human society remaining a detotalised totality maintain recurrence, flights and therefore unity-objects as limits to true unifica-

exist as 'a relation determined by production' only in and through this milieu of recurrence which it helps to maintain. 'Capital is a collective product, and only by the united action of many members, nay, in the last resort, only by the united action of all members of society, can it be set in motion. Capital is, therefore, not a personal, it is a social power,' we read in the *Communist Manifesto*.[93] But this social power will impose itself as 'a thing existing outside individuals' through what Marx called an 'interversion and a prosaically real and in no way imaginary mystification'. And a passage in *Capital* explains the origin of this interversion itself: 'In the form of society now under consideration, the behaviour of men in the *social* process of production is purely atomic. Hence their relations to each other in production assume a *material* character independent of their control and conscious individual action. These facts manifest themselves at first by products as a general rule taking the form of commodities. . . . Hence the riddle presented by the money-fetish is but the riddle presented by the commodity-fetish.'[94] Thus it is not so much, as Marx says somewhat unfortunately in the *Manifesto*, 'the united action of many members', but above all their separation and atomisation which endows their real relations of production with the inhuman character of a thing.

Yet this 'uniting of action' does occur; the proof is that bourgeois economists speak quite readily of the solidarity of the interests of workers and employers. Thus, the finished product is presented as if it were the result of a concerted undertaking, that is to say, of an action and work group comprising management, technicians, office staff and workers. But the bourgeois economist does not wish to see that this solidarity is expressed *in inert matter* as an inversion of the real relations; this false unity, as the inert seal which supposedly signifies *men*, can, in fact, refer only to relations of antagonism and seriality. It is the object and the object alone which *combines* human efforts in its inhuman unity: and if it can make people believe in the existence of an original agreement where there is, in fact, only an anti-social (practico-

tion? Must the disappearance of capitalist forms of alienation mean the elimination of *all* forms of alienation? This brings us to the question posed by Jean Hyppolite in his *Études sur Marx et Hegel* (Paris, 1955; translated by John O'Neill as *Studies on Marx and Hegel*, Basic Books, 1969. [Ed.])

93. Marx and Engels, *Selected Works*, Moscow, 1962, Vol. I, p. 47. [Ed.]

94. *Capital*, Vol. I, pp. 92–3. The emphases are Sartre's and the translation is slightly amended. [Ed.] The passage is missing from the French translation. See Maximilien Rubel, *Karl Marx. Essai de biographie intellectuelle*, p. 350.

inert) force, this is because its passive unity, in its radical heterogeneity, cannot refer to any kind of human unification. In other words, it leaves the social origin of a machine as such totally indeterminate (*at a particular moment of History* there is no way of telling, for example, whether a particular machine was produced in a country with a capitalist system or in one where the means of production are socialised).[95] How can one fail to see that 'reification' comes to man through recurrence, that is to say, precisely as that which makes him act as Other than himself and which determines his real relations on the basis of relations between Others? We have seen how *price* stabilises as a result of recurrence, and how it immediately imposes itself on everyone without having been wished as such by anyone; we have also seen how the concrete relation of the buyer to the seller is relegated to being an inessential appearance: entering the shop, saying hello, asking the price, haggling, hesitating, and buying something: all these supposed moments of the act are no more than gestures; the exchange is settled in advance, the price imposes itself; it is *things* that determine the relations of men. If, as Marx has often said, everything is *other* in capitalist society, this is primarily because atomisation, which is both the origin and the result of the process, makes social man an Other than himself, conditioned by Others in so far as they are Other than themselves.

In so far as the worker is a product of capitalism, that is to say, in so far as he works for wages and produces goods which are taken from him and uses industrial machinery which belongs to individuals or to private groups, the negative common object of the working class in the first half of the nineteenth century was, as we have seen, its total national production, that is to say, machines as capital requiring the worker to produce, through them, an expansion of capital. We have also seen that the common interest of the class can only be the negation of this negation, that is to say, the practical negation of a destiny which

95. On the other hand, the same machine *as such* may yield information about contemporary means of production, about techniques and, *in this way*, about certain ossified structures which worked matter establishes amongst its servants. But, in so far as the means of production are the same everywhere, these inert structures are everywhere the same. It is at the level of the group that one can tell whether a common *praxis* has returned to these structures and made them more flexible, or balanced them in other areas (reduction of working hours, organisation of leisure, cultural activities, etc.) or whether they have been left to fend for themselves.

is suffered as common inertia. We must therefore recognise that practical organisation, *as human exigency*, is, in itself, and even in the practico-inert field, a constitutive structure of relations amongst workers (this will become clearer in the next chapter). And this organisation is both a means and an end, since it presents itself *both* as a means of struggling against destiny (that is to say, against the men who in a particular system make *this* particular destiny out of the machine), *and* as the future reinteriorisation of the practico-inert field and its projected dissolution within a perpetually active social organisation which, as a concrete totality, will govern both the means of production and production as a whole.

The worker will be saved from his destiny only if the human multiplicity as a whole is permanently changed into a group *praxis*. His only future, therefore, is at the second degree of sociality, that is to say, in human relations as they arise in the unity of a group (and not in the disunity of the gathering-milieu). This is what Marx meant when he spoke of the sociality of the worker. Yet it should be noted that this sociality appears as the *joint* negation of two reciprocal aspects of the practical field: a negation of the common object as destiny and a connected negation of multiplicity as seriality. In other words, sociality as a still individual project of transcendence (in the organised group) of the multiplicity of individuals reveals seriality itself as a link of impotence; this seriality is the being-to-be-transcended towards an action tending to socialise the common object. On the other hand, this sociality, in so far as it was determined in everyone by the very structure of the collective in which he produced himself, and *in so far as it initially produced no result* (that is, during the first quarter of the nineteenth century and, basically, right up to the revolt of the Lyon silk-weavers) or was limited to the creation of reciprocal relations, appeared in everyone as a structure peculiar to his own project and thus decomposed into a multiplicity of identical projects, before producing active organisations through itself. Thus it emerges as a process of isolation *precisely to the extent that* it is fundamentally a transcendence of plurality towards unity. This means, quite simply, that the organising project *in everyone* begins by being negated by that which it transcends and negates, that is to say, by seriality as a link of impotence.

When we look at it more closely, we can see that the *necessity of some common action* can arise only out of an existing link between men and can present itself only as the transcendence and inversion of this fundamental link. If it were possible to conceive real (but abstract) individuals in a pure state – and I do not mean the social atoms of liberalism – in so far as they are united by bonds of reciprocity, and if one could abstract from the object's transformation of reciprocity into a link of alterity, it would be impossible to understand how the infinite dispersal of human relations could of itself produce the means of pulling itself together again. This conception is completely inapplicable to human history, but it retains some sense as a logical possibility, provided the idea mentioned above of living organisms, which depend on the universe, but are not affected by the contraction which is caused by *scarcity* as a fundamental, contingent characteristic of our History, is consistent. In the practico-inert world based on scarcity, however, the object brings men together by imposing the violent, passive unity of a seal on their multiplicity. And in the very moment where this object is a threat (for the colonised, or the exploited), in the very moment where this object, as positive interest, is threatened (for the colonists or the exploiters), the unity of impotence transforms itself into a violent contradiction: in it, *unity* opposes itself to the impotence which negates it. We shall discover the intelligibility of this moment later. For the time being, what needs to be emphasised is that impotence, as a force of alterity, is *primarily* unity in its negative form, *primarily* action in the form of passivity, and *primarily* finality in the form of counter-finality.[96]

Thus, as we have seen, there is a sort of *common mode of behaviour* amongst the white minority in a city where the majority are black: quite simply this behaviour is common in that it is imitated by everyone but never *adopted* by anyone (not counting the creation of organisations). All the same, the practical unity of men can never arise or originate in the domination of worked matter over man, from such unity itself. In this sense, *the common class-being* of the workers in 1830, in the presence of Machine-Destiny and of the organs of oppression and constraint, was the seriality of their relations of reciprocity, in that this profound impotence *was also a unity*. In fact, the existence of a labour market created a link of antagonistic reciprocity between workers, in which separation was lived as opposition and alterity: in the negative ensemble of individuals selling their labour power, we have seen everyone featuring both as himself and as Other. It is also clear that labour itself, according to the mode of production,

96. I see these three notions as *socialities*. It has been obvious from the beginning of our dialectical investigation that the original foundation of unity, of

engenders relations either of positive reciprocity or of dispersal. Although in the nineteenth century capitalist concentralisation tended to bring workers together, dispersal remained a crucial factor (the dispersal of industries throughout France, the dispersal of residential groups, etc.). Yet the worker tended to become aware of the objective characteristics which made a worker of him and which defined him by his labour and by the type of exploitation to which he was subjected. He gradually became aware of his objective reality and, thus, of that of his comrades. But their common characteristic of being the product of their product and of the society which was organised around this product, however apparent it may have been to some of them, could not create anything more than an abstract, conceptual identity amongst them, *unless* it was lived in action.

By this I mean that this common characteristic was manifested each day in the reciprocal and contradictory double link of antagonism on the market and of solidarity in labour, and above all on the occasion of local retaliatory actions, through their first failures and surrenders. In these early days of the workers' movement, when resistance was spontaneous, impotent and rapidly repressed, the defeated realised themselves *in this impotence* and lived it as the serial dispersal of men in their condition; but this objective condition realised itself through their everyday relations with their comrades, and it was this that held back all their efforts to take common action. This indefinite plurality of contradictory relations is both what defined their condition as workers (in particular, the fact that they competed with their comrades) and what created *class* as an indefinite series whose serial unity lay everywhere in the impotence of the individuals who composed it, just because this impotence derived from their separation. Exploitation was revealed as the passive unity of all (and not simply as an identity of condition), in so far as everyone lived the isolation of Others as his own isolation and their impotence through his own. Class as a collective became a material thing made out of men in so far as it constituted itself as a negation of man and as a serial impossibility of negating this negation. This impossibility makes class a factual necessity: it is un-

---

action, and of finality is individual *praxis* as the unifying and reorganising transcendence of existing circumstances towards the practical field. But we also know that this individual *praxis can no longer be recognised* at the most concrete level of the practico-inert and that it exists there only *to lose itself*, to the advantage of the maleficent actions of worked matter.

changeable destiny. It is not a practical solidarity but, on the contrary, the absolute unity of destinies brought about by lack of solidarity. Every worker feels himself confirmed in his inertia by the inertia of all the Others; every small organised group feels its own class as a universal flight, which neutralises all its efforts. For this proletariat in the process of formation, the Other is primarily the serial totalisation of Others (in which he features as an Other), that is to say, of all those, including himself, who represent for everyone the possibility of being out of work or of working for lower wages; in short, it is himself as Other, in so far as his serialised and totalised antagonisms manifest themselves in the fact that on the labour market he is his *own counterfinality*, who emerges as the Other who forces demands to be lowered.

This serialised antagonism, or negative seriality (which, for reasons of space, we have not examined thoroughly except in relation to the market) constitutes an initial structure of alterity, based on the reciprocity of antagonism, and constitutes every worker for every Other as *himself* in so far as he is his own enemy. But in the same moment *the serial unity* of these oppositions posits itself as a contradiction of the same and of the Other demanding a unifying *praxis*. Now, paradoxically, but very logically, it is not these antagonisms as such which make *unity-praxis* so difficult; on the contrary, as we shall see, their truth lies in the transcendence which integrates them in the common unity of demands. What made the workers impotent, in the first half of the last century, was alterity as spatial and temporal stratification. At the level of positive reciprocity in labour (which is the structure of alterity which contradicts the former and creates the true practico-inert tension of class), it is in effect dispersal which creates impotence. At this level, in fact, everyone's objective grasp of his *class-being* as the practico-inert reality of his own *praxis* (which was examined above) implies a reciprocal grasp of his comrade in his particular class-being; this was achieved *practically* (and not theoretically, at least at that time) by friendship, mutual aid, work relations, etc. And, in so far as this reciprocity spread through France in constellations and chains of constellations (including, through their relations with other groups, the villages from which some of the proletarians came and the political groups of the republican petty bourgeoisie), class posited itself – as the indefinite seriality of class-beings – as a *milieu*.

But this milieu was not *an objective representation of the worker*: it *constantly realised him* as practical impotence. If he learnt that a workers' newspaper had been founded, as a practical determination of class action, he would produce himself as directly affected by this group, which, from within the practico-inert, affected him in his being as an imperative order[97] to negate the structure of impotence and separation in this being. But, at the same time, because this limited undertaking was constituted *at the horizon* (he did not work in the town where it was constituted, a comrade from there told him about it, showed him a copy of the paper), it produced itself as a negative determination of itself and of everyone: in itself, it was in fact a proof that the totalisation of the milieu by class-action was always possible, and that it is the profound truth of the passive totality. But, by the same token, it defines itself as *not being this totalisation*, as being nothing in relation to class-totalisation and in a way as negating it through the simple fact, which is in any case inevitable, of *positing itself for itself*: it therefore refers back by itself to the class-gathering as an inert unity of multiplicity. As for the worker in Lyon who, in a moment of defeat, learnt of the initiative of his Parisian comrades, he himself was constituted as inertia, as rooted in impotence by sheer distance (connected in fact with *everything*), which prevented him from joining them and by circumstances which meant that the moment to imitate their action had not yet arrived at Lyon. At the same time, in this period of uncertainty, he remained hesitant about the content of the initiative: he has not completely thrown off Christian ideology, and he knows that his Parisian comrades are not entirely free of it either, so that his relation to the object produced (the newspaper, the ideas it supports, its propaganda, etc.) remains *indeterminate*. Here again it is common class-being which realises itself in this contradictory relation: in this collective, in effect, if a group, however small, constitutes itself, and if this group becomes known, then the unity of the group is lived negatively by everyone as a sort of intermediary between serial inertia and the active organism: everyone is united with the Others, passively but directly, in so far as he is determined as a moment of a total totalisation by the movement of partial totalisation which, *somewhere else*, and through a few people, negates the class-gathering as everyone's inert being-there. Between him and the groupuscule, through the inert density of the milieu, a synthetic link of univocal interiority (which proceeds *from the group* to the individual) establishes itself; but at the

97. Clearly the *imperative* character which collective action presents to someone who has not joined the group is the only way in which human freedom can manifest itself as other in the practico-inert field of materiality.

same time, both his own indeterminacy and the thorough indeterminacy of the group action, mean that this relation remains indeterminate
(neither negative nor positive), so that the bond of synthetic interiority allows itself to be absorbed by the serial bond of common membership of the milieu.

On the other hand, through the failures of local attempts which had
not been supported and followed through, or sustained and continued,
every group saw *active* class solidarity as an inert exigency of the class-
object on the basis of the rediscovery, in the defeat of negative solidarity, of destiny as serial flight. What was at stake here was not a
conflict of interests between workers, but rather their separation.
Faced with this indefinite milieu which needed to be *agitated* by serial
methods, the group became aware of its smallness, its impotence and
its fragility. In other words, it came to be seen as a fragile mode of the
common substance and, by the same token, it produced itself in its
vacillating activity as the relation of a 'micro-organism' (I am not using
this term in an organicist or Gestaltist sense) to the substance which it
determines, and which gives it its depth and fragility. Naturally, *class-
being* manifests itself as a temporalised separation, not only because any
political education and agitation presupposes a *hysteresis* originating in
the 'passivity of the masses'; that is to say, in the seriality of the class-
gathering, but also because the workers are at different levels of poli-
ticisation and liberation depending on their individual histories and
because spatial dispersal is reinforced by temporal dispersal.

In any case, in so far as the historical reality and specific structure of
the class had been defined in certain men produced by the mode of
production through the relations of production, it derived its general
structure and intelligibility from the fact that its common object constituted it as a serially structured milieu and that other classes, through
the contradictions which opposed them to it, through the same practico-
inert ensemble, made the negative unity of alterity into *the leaven of its
organising praxis*. In the example of the archaic proletariat, the worker
is in the class in so far as he is conditioned by Others, that is to say, to
the extent that he is himself, for himself, always Other, and that his
labour power, as a commodity, is Other than him, that is to say,
alienated. He is in the class in so far as his own inertia is based on the
inertia of Others and becomes the class itself in everyone as the inertia
of the Other as Other. And this class-being is normally expressed in
the serial, negative practices of abstentionism, defeatism, demoralisation or surrender. These practices in everyone are seriality as a whole.

In this way, common-class-Being manifests itself in all its rigidity in periods when workers are 'on the defensive'; on the basis of the contradictions of the individual, and of the material conditions of his life, it becomes, in everyone, destiny producing itself as the Other-Being of the worker in relation to himself and to all the Others. In this sense, common-class-Being as an interiorised common object is *neither* a totality imposing itself on its parts but differing from them, *nor* a word connoting the indefinite repetition of particular class-being as a universal reproduction of the identical, *nor* a way of designating the set of conditions common to everyone and which are sometimes called the 'condition of the working class'. At the most superficial level of the investigation, everyone is *in* the class, in so far as the indefinite series of relations is realised as a milieu by the human terms between which these relations hold. But at first this milieu as such is no Other than men and their objects making themselves into the milieu of man or, in other words, it is reciprocity as a relation amongst workers making themselves through things not only *humanity* but also a homogeneous, inert container of all. But in any case, at a later stage of the investigation the milieu will dissolve and reveal serially structured multiplicities of multiplicities. At this moment, *common class-being* is no longer, for everyone, *being-in-the-milieu-of-class*: it is, in fact, everyone's *being-elsewhere* in so far as he is constituted as *the Other* by the progressive series of Others, and as the Other-Being of everyone in his position in the series in so far as he constitutes the Others. Class exists as a totalised series of series.

This is why it is not really very significant to find (or to think one can find) continuous transitions from one class to another, intermediaries, and unclassifiable groups: if class were to be treated as a total, synthetic form, enclosing its members, it would indeed be highly embarrassing to admit those imperceptible passages from one class to another which bourgeois economists are so happy to describe, and the aporias which this new scepticism claims to have found (and whose logical structure resembles that of the old arguments about the bald man, etc.). But, if class is a serial totality of series and if the ensemble of these series corresponds roughly both to the worker's class-being and to his Other-Being, it does not matter if these series finally disappear, decompose or become Other; on the contrary, it is of the essence of seriality (as a determination of the practico-inert) to be infinite or indefinite; thus it is of the essence of class-being, as the absolute elsewhere of impotence, to disappear at the horizon and to allow itself to be determined in its Other-Being-to-infinity, by the Other-Being of other individuals belonging to other classes. These mediations do not affect the true weight of class and are practically ineffective: in cases of tension (which is to say, permanently), alterity sticks at the level of mediation, and nothing gets through any more, or the intermediary explodes and the two freed series define themselves by their struggle. Conversely, if one could define precisely the historical reality of a class and if this definition could be applied to all its members and to them alone, the series would still be infinite, because they would be circular.

But the seriality of class makes the individual (whoever he is and whatever his class) into a being who defines himself as a humanised thing and who, in the practico-inert universe, is strictly interchangeable, in given conditions, with some material product. And what finally characterises the working class (this being our example) is that the organised *praxis* of a militant group originates in the very heart of the practico-inert, in the opaque materiality of impotence and inertia as a transcendence of *this* materiality. Thus the other form of class, that is to say, the group which totalises in a *praxis*, originates at the heart of the passive form and as *its* negation. A *wholly active* class, all of whose members are integrated into a single *praxis* and whose apparatuses organise themselves in unity rather than conflicting with one another, is realised only in very rare (and revolutionary) moments of working-class history. Even without going into the question of the development of the working-class experience and of its objective organisation (which are one and the same thing), it is therefore clear, from the point of view of the intelligibility of the practico-inert, that the proletariat, in so far as it is both Destiny and the Negation of Destiny, constitutes *in its very form* a changing and contradictory reality, or in other words, that it is *always*, to a degree which is determined by the historical situation, a group *praxis* (or, usually, a multiplicity of group activities) which erodes the inert unity of a common-class-being. It is therefore a class which produces itself as a contradictory double unity, for the inert-being-of-seriality, as the basis and material of every other combination, is really the unity of workers in their being and *through Being*, in so far as their destiny owes its rigidity to their dispersal,[98] and

98. The *dispersal* of which I speak here has no historical connection with the process of concentration, although the latter can help to decrease it by increasing contacts; dispersal is fundamentally only the impotence of alterity in so far as it is lived by a necessarily dispersed plurality, although the field of dispersal may be more or less extensive.

increases it; whereas an active organisation constitutes itself against Being, and its unity is purely practical; in other words, *praxis*, as the organising transcendence of inert being towards the reorganisation of the social field, is the unity of the multiple as a perpetual labour.

However, a number of points should be noted. First, that collective *praxis* can occur only on the basis of a fundamental common-being; secondly, that it will remain structured by the being which it transcends and which determines it up to its limits and efficacity (as we saw, trade-union practice about 1900 was structured in its very temporalisation by the practico-inert characteristics of the proletariat as they had been produced under the pressure of universal machines); thirdly, that it stands in a relation of alterity and, through antagonisms, of seriality to other organisations independent of it and that the *conducting medium* of this new seriality is the class as a collective; fourthly and lastly, that any organisation, as we shall see, is in constant danger of dissolving into seriality (the bureaucratic nature of certain unions in some countries) or of falling straight back into the inertia of common-being, while, at the same moment, the class-collective, *as worked matter*, with all its inertia, supports the practical unities, which have become unities-of-being and inert meanings, as a seal. Thus, whether or not organisation has progressed beyond the series, the working class in its contradiction represents the most resolute and visible effort of men to reconquer themselves through one another, that is to say, to *rescue themselves from Being* to the extent that it gives them the statute of a human thing amongst other human things which are their inanimate products; and the field of practico-inert being is constantly closing up or threatening to do so; Being petrifies their actions in full freedom. This new moment of the investigation shows us that the practico-inert field is no more than a still abstract structure of History; indeed, it cannot constitute itself unless the world of alterity produces as a serial *unity* the condition and principle of its own transcendence. We must now examine this transition from being to organisation. Having grasped the dialectical intelligibility of individual *praxis* and of the passive activity of the collective, we must now grasp and fix that of collective *praxis*.

6 Collective Praxis

We have traversed the practico-inert field with the intention of discovering whether this place of violence, darkness and witchcraft *actually* has dialectical intelligibility or, in other words, whether some strict rationality underlies the strange appearance of this world. It is now clear that it does: not only do all the objects and processes which occur there obey rules of dialectical development, thus making *comprehension* always possible, but also the structuration of the experience in the practico-inert field realises itself through the appearance of *necessity within certainty* (*évidence*) and, therefore, necessity at the heart of free individual *praxis* presents itself as the *necessity of the existence of this field of inert activity*. In other words, in the practical experience of a successful action, the moment of objectification presents itself as a necessary end of the individual practical dialectic – which is submerged in it as in *its object* – and as the appearance of a new moment. And this new moment (that of the practico-inert or of fundamental[99] sociality) comes back to the total, translucid dialectic of individual *praxis* and constitutes it as the first moment of a more complex dialectic. This means that in every objectified *praxis* the practico-inert field becomes *its negation* in favour of passive activity as a common structure of collectives and worked matter. Thus the moment of objectivity defines its dialectical necessity as organic activity which has been *transcended and preserved by inertia* precisely to the extent that, both for the individual agent himself and in the apodicticity of the investigation, it presents itself as the transcendence of individuality, in this agent and in everyone, *by a suffered original statute* of reifying sociality. And we have carried the study of this sociality far enough to discover in it, through a new kind of investigation, the principles of an inversion, which refers from necessity to a different freedom (that of unification) as a third moment.

But this dialectical movement, as I have described it – and as it superficially appears – has *no intelligibility*; or rather, if we were to neglect its real conditions, we would fall back into an external dialectic (*dialectique du dehors*). Only Magic or Fate could explain how individual *praxis*, absorbed in the object, could be the source of a new negation by which it transforms itself into the first moment of a dialectic of collectivity, if we really had to accept that the intelligibility of the practico-inert field and of its negation by the group resides in the action of a dialectical force expressed *through* free *praxis* and developing

99. As I have already observed, the word 'fundamental' does not refer to any historical *a priori*.

through changes in the field and different kinds of action. The intelligibility of individual *praxis* as translucidity cannot in any way be the same as that of the practico-inert field, and, similarly, it would be absurd or idealistic to imagine that individual *praxis*, inert activity and common action are the three moments of the development *of a single force* conceived as *human praxis*, for example. In reality, there are *two* quite distinct dialectics: that of individual practice and that of the group as *praxis* – and the moment of the practico-inert field is in fact that of the anti-dialectic. It is, in effect, contained between two radical negations: that of the individual action which meets it in itself, in so far as it still adheres to its product, as *its negation*; and that of the unification into groups which occurs in collectives as a practical rejection of seriality. If one can nevertheless apply the term 'dialectical' to this material field of the anti-dialectic, it is precisely because of this double negation. In this field, everyone's action disappears, and is replaced by monstrous forces which, in the inertia of the inorganic and of exteriority, retain some power of action and unification combined with a false interiority. And conversely, the simple movement of unification, as it developed in the working class in the course of the last century, was sufficient to constitute the class, far beyond its precarious, limited initial unifications, as an impotence which was haunted by an invincible human power, as the serialisation of a fundamental totality.

The intelligibility of practico-inert processes therefore rests on a few simple, clear principles which are themselves the synthetic contraction of the obvious characteristics of the univocal relation of interiority as a basis of individual *praxis* and of the plurality of agents within the practical field. In fact, objectification always directly involves *alteration*. When they say that, in a socialist society, man will be his own product instead of 'the product of his product', Marxists mean that if man is his own product, he will be his only objectification (in himself and in Others); thus objective being will be homogeneous with the practice of objectification. But if the individual's reality lies in a material object, an anti-dialectic starts: sealed inorganicism appears as man's being. Now, this very special situation obviously depends on the multiplicity of individuals co-existing in the field of scarcity. In other words, only the free *praxis* of the Other on the basis of material circumstances, through some worked matter, can limit the efficacity and freedom of my *praxis*. In this sense the explanation of classes in *Anti-Dühring* is correct, although it hardly has any historical value. But, paradoxically, it is correct as a dialectical schema of intelligibility rather than as a reconstruction of a particular social process. Engels claimed in fact that classes (that is to say, the collective as a practico-inert type of sociality) begin to constitute themselves in an agricultural community when the products of labour become commodities. I have shown that his examples are all irrelevant, because they concern communities disintegrating under the impact of bourgeois societies which surround them or which have commercial relations with them.

But *from the point of view of intelligibility* these examples are adequate: for the characteristic of being a commodity comes to the product of peasant labour from the outside. Engels assumes that the land is common property and that every peasant produces in order to feed himself and his family, and we shall make the same assumption. At this moment of rural labour, the product is neither an aim nor an objective limit: it is the aim of labour only to the extent that it is a means of getting food. It is on the basis of exchange – and in particular of exchange as practised between bourgeois societies and under-developed societies – that *objective demand*, as a moment of a free *praxis of the Other*, constitutes the product *as Other*; that is to say, it removes it from the closed circle of the 'production/consumption' cycle and posits it in itself as an independent object, which has absorbed labour and is capable of being exchanged. Of course, this is not some ideal structure conferred on the product by the mere desire of the future purchaser; these changes occur in the course of a common action (colonisation, semi-colonisation, and an overall movement to enclose the community, and turn it into an enclave) performed by bourgeois groups, and through a set of serial processes which effect the disintegration of the village through a society which trades with it. The product *really* becomes a commodity. But the important point here is that this transformation imposes itself on free individual *praxis*: objectification becomes production of the object in so far as it posits itself for itself; in this case, the product becomes the man and as such the product. But this transformation is wholly intelligible. If we ignore for the moment the serial processes and transformations of the practico-inert field, two things remain. First, a *praxis* (that of a buyer or a group of buyers) has appropriated the freedom of the producer: it is as *the object* of this free enterprise that the producer will find himself to be producing commodities rather than objects of immediate consumption. Objectification becomes *other* because it produces its object in the free field of another's action. It is freedom limiting freedom. But secondly, two practical freedoms can confront one another only in the practical field and through the medium of materiality as a whole. If circumstances enable *one praxis* to appropriate the meaning of *the other praxis*, this only means that the object in which the latter objectifies itself takes on a different meaning and a counter-finality (for its producer) in the practical field of the former and through a reorganisation of this field.

The original situation therefore presents itself as follows: the univocal relation of interiority enables the buyer *to manipulate* the peasant's practical field; in effect, the peasant's relation to his environment – that is to say his labour – is an interiorisation in so far as *praxis* is a unifying organisation and in so far as the organism has its being-outside -itself in Nature. But *of itself* produced materiality cannot transform anything since it stands in a univocal relation with the producer. On the other hand, as soon as it is given *another meaning* for the producer *by an other* whose relation with it is also a relation of interiority though in a different way, a false relation of reciprocal interiority establishes itself between the product and the producer, because the former *signifies* the latter and because the producer behaves as *signified by his product*. Now, all this is perfectly clear, because, through this product and in so far as he is this product, a human *praxis directs itself* at the worker and tends to make him work for others when he is still working for himself. On the other hand, it is no less clear that the product, in becoming a *commodity*, allows itself to be constituted according to the laws of its passivity: it is its very inertia which sustains its new unity, and which transforms the *praxis* of the buyers into an *exigency* in so far as it becomes its own independent meaning (*signification*) *against* the worker. And it is *through this independence* (as an absence of human relations, lived in interiority as a synthetic relation of inhumanity) that, as a product which posits itself for itself as a commodity-exigency it becomes that which the worker has made, and therefore what he is, in the world of the object and as an object. Destructive power is simply a structure of *praxis* as individual dialectic; but the confrontation of freedoms, by the double constitution of the intermediate object, cannot become an objective, material contradiction unless the inertia of the object makes the two unities which are conferred on it into real, inert negations, that is to say, into passive forces.

This simple example contains all the conditions of the intelligibility of the practico-inert field: the only practical dialectical reality, the motive force of everything, *is individual action*. When a field of scarcity determines the confrontation of real agents, a new statute is imposed on *the worked Thing* by the activities which confront one another. In everyone's practical field (in so far as it is everyone's), it takes on secret, multiple meanings which indicate the directions of its flights towards Others; and as means and end of a particular undertaking (that of transforming the freedom of the Other into a docile means to my own freedom, not by force but by manipulating the practical field), it converts the *praxis* of the one who is winning into an *inert and fascinating hold* over the practical freedom of the loser. In the univocal milieu of interiority it *re-exteriorises* the *praxis* of the conqueror as the interiorising synthesis of the practical field. And as signification-exigency it reflects *his being* to the producer as *the inert exteriority of a slave* in the milieu of interiority. But, by mortgaging the worker's freedom by its imperative inertia, it transforms, through itself, the free *praxis* which confronts the worker into a mere inertia of exigency. And, in a way, every freedom, both in the milieu of the Other and in its own milieu of interiority, experiences its own inertial limit, that is to say, its necessity. As soon as multiplicity becomes *indefinite* (in the practical and serial sense), the multiplication of actions and responses is unified in the object which posits itself for itself as a negation of everyone by everyone (and, later, as a common object). And when I say that the object, as inorganic, sealed inertia, posits itself for itself, I mean this literally, although we are grasping the process in its full intelligibility: the fleeting unity of the object which affirms itself in opposition to everyone is in reality the negation of everyone, and of everyone for everyone in everyone's practical field, in so far as it becomes a negative, inert unity *in the object* (for example, everyone's impotence revealed *in the object* and through every attempt to change its structures).

The ensemble of living structures must, therefore, be recomposed in each case, according to the rule of the particular process, if we are to reach the schemata of intelligibility we are looking for: first, the univocal relation of interiority within free *praxis* as the unification of the field; second, the equivocal relation of a multiplicity of practical activities each of which tries to appropriate the freedom of Others by the transformations which it imposes on the object (practices are *both* negative reciprocal relations, and therefore relations of interiority, *and,* through the mediation of the inert object, indirect relations of exteriority); third, the transformation of every free *praxis* (in so far as it is absorbed and returned by the object) into an *exis*; fourth, the inevitable transformation of every *exis* of worked Things into a passive activity by the free *praxis of an Other*, whoever he may be, whose projects and overall point of view *are other*; fifth, the transformation of everyone into active passivity by the passive activity of the object, not through some metamorphosis of his organic and human reality, but through his relentless transformation of himself into an Other, effected by and under his own hands when he produces the object (in so far as the multiple meanings of the object, its exigencies and the meanings (*significations*) it gives its producer are prefabricated by other activities or by other objects produced by these activities).

From this point of view, it must be pointed out both that the practico-inert field *exists*, that it is *real*, and that free human activities are not thereby eliminated, that they are *not even altered* in their translucidity as projects in the process of being realised. The field exists: in short, it is what surrounds and conditions us. I need only glance out of the window: I will be able to see cars which are men and drivers who are cars, a policeman who is directing the traffic at the corner of the street and, a little further on, the same traffic being controlled by red and green lights: *hundreds of exigencies* rise up towards me: pedestrian crossings, notices, and prohibitions; collectives (a branch of the Crédit Lyonnais, a café, a church, blocks of flats, and also a visible seriality: people queueing in front of a shop); and instruments (pavements, a thoroughfare, a taxi rank, a bus stop, etc., proclaiming with their frozen voices how they are to be used). These beings – neither thing nor man, but practical unities made up of man and inert things – these appeals, and these exigencies do not yet concern me directly. Later, I will go down into the street and become *their thing*,[100] I will buy that collective which is a newspaper, and suddenly the practico-inert ensemble which besieges and designates me will reveal itself *on the basis* of the total field, that is to say, of the Earth, as the Elsewhere of all Elsewheres (or the series of all series of series). It is true that this reality, which tells me, *from Elsewhere*, my destiny as a petty bourgeois Frenchman, is still an abstraction – although, depending upon the case, it will either crush me or ensnare me. But we must be absolutely clear: it is an abstraction in so far as groups are constituted in it and against it, in order finally to try to dissolve it; it is an abstraction *in that* a total experience must involve the conscious striving for a unity which, most of the time, is not *directly perceptible*, or which remains masked by seriality. But if, from the point of view of totalisation, and taking the practico-inert field in its totality, there is such a thing as a group

100. It goes without saying that while I am in my flat I am the thing of other things (furniture, etc.).

intelligibility as the transcendence of necessity towards a common freedom, if, indeed, the dialectical origin of the group lies in the passive unity of alterity in so far as it negates itself as passivity, then, apart from assessing their concrete situation and their history within totalising History, there is no way of telling whether given individuals or gatherings will emerge from their abstract condition as practico-inert beings. In other words, for *some* men and *some* multiplicities, in so far as both of them are concrete realities, the possibility of remaining, within the limits of one life or of a set of lives, under the statute of *Being* and of *passive activity*, is itself a real, concrete possibility. There is no guarantee that a given bureaucrat or clerk will one day, by integration into a group, cease to be an Other both for himself and for Others. At this moment, manipulated by things (his *office*, as a collective, his boss as an Other), he is for other men a factor of alterity, of passivity and of counter-finality, as if he were a thing (a Spanish ducat) circulating through men's hands. There is no guarantee that, in itself and for him, this situation contains the seed of a contradiction.

This contradiction would be inevitable, however, if the freedom of practice came into conflict with constraints, with interiorised exterior prohibitions, *in everyone*. Such cases do occur: but they are not relevant to our present concerns. Mystification, in fact – as a real process rather than a concerted undertaking – is unfortunately so deep that the reified individual remains in possession of his free *praxis*. Or rather: to be alienated, or simply altered, a man must be an organism capable of dialectical action; and it is through free *praxis* that he will discover necessity as a transformation of his product, and of himself by his product, in the Other. The constraints of need, the exigencies of the worked Thing, the imperatives of the Other, and his own impotence – his *praxis* will reveal all these to him and interiorise them. His free activity, in its freedom, will take upon itself everything which crushes him – exhausting work, exploitation, oppression, and rising prices. This means that his liberty is the means chosen by the Thing and by the Other to crush him and to transform him into a worked Thing. Hence the moment of the free contract by which, in the nineteenth century, the isolated worker, a prey to hunger and poverty, sold his labour power to a powerful employer who imposed his own rates, is both the most shameless mystification and a reality. It is true that he has no other way out; the choice is an impossible one; he has not the ghost of a chance of finding better-paid work and in any case he never even asks himself the question: what is the point of it all? He goes and sells himself at the factory every morning (in the good old days, they made one day contracts to keep workers), by a sort of sombre resigned *exis* which scarcely resembles *a praxis*. And yet, in fact, it is a *praxis*: habit is directed and organised, the end is posited, the means *chosen* (if he learns that there will be a lot of workers offering themselves for hire, he will get up an hour earlier in order to be there before the others); in other words, the ineluctable destiny which is crushing him moves through him.

It would be true to say – and I said it above – that the semi-automatic machine dreams through the women workers, lost in some day dream and moving in a rhythm *external to them* – which is everyone's work itself *as other*. But, at the same time, these dreams are quiet, private behaviour, carrying out the machine's sentence by pursuing its own ends (the valorisation of the *physical person* against devaluation by the alien universality of exigency, etc.). And *as for this rhythm*, which is so alien to the personal rhythms of her life that for the first few days it seemed absolutely unendurable: the woman worker *wanted* to adapt herself to it, she *made an effort*, took advice from her friends, and invented a personal relation of interiority applying to herself alone (given her height, strength, other physical characteristics, etc.); and this, one might say, is the best means of individual adaptation. It is *perfectly clear* that this involved giving herself to the machine, and that the latter, as the work of Others in the negative unity of a destiny, took possession of her work and made it other: ultimately, the total adaptation to semi-automatism meant the destruction of her bodily rhythms and the interiorisation of a rhythm which was absolutely other. But the moment in which the girl emerged as the *object of the machine* – that is to say, when mystification revealed itself in objective alienation – was also the moment in which her adaptation was accomplished (within the narrow limits assigned her). There is nothing in this that she could have avoided (except, perhaps, by failing to adapt and getting herself eliminated, first of all from the labour market, and then, as surplus population, from society, through sickness): the initial constraints (the fact that her family could not survive without at least *three people* working at the factory); the constraints which put her in the factory, on the production line, etc., are ineluctable, and they reinforce one another. But these constraints derive from things only in so far as things become transmitters of human actions lying behind them. There is the multiplicity of workers and their false unity through the factory – that is to say, through a destiny which they have to negate and suffer together; and in any case these are not so much purely material constraints as *exigencies* in so far as a free *praxis* defines itself according to these stony voices.

In other words, freedom, in this context, does not mean the possibility of choice, but the necessity of living these constraints in the form of exigencies which must be fulfilled by a *praxis*. The family situation (the illness or unemployment of some of its members) may constitute itself, in the practico-inert field, as the impossibility of ensuring the survival of all its members *unless* a particular woman or old man resumes work. This family situation, as such, can be described by a simple quantitative study, as a functional relation between, on the one hand, the family structure, family size and the members' chances of survival, and, on the other hand, the number and character of its active members (in a given society, at a given moment, and for a given branch and sector of production). Nevertheless, for the old man who resumes work, this situation is first manifested *as a specific and quite specifically qualified danger* (the dangers are more definite for children or invalids and, consequently, appear to him through his human relations and preferences), which *only* he, the old man, can avert (since the others are out of work, or sick or already employed). And, in so far as the danger is *avoidable*, its negation constitutes itself, through the particular relations of the old man with the members of his family (and once illnesses are manifested in behaviour or as the *exis* of some members of the family in the restricted field of the home) *as exigency*. This characteristic of exigency in the actual context of individual *praxis*, is, as a matter of fact, entirely useless: the collective *praxis* of the family group (eroded at the same time by an internal seriality), one might say, comprises in its very development the possibility of a moment in which it will develop through the work and action of this old man. He knows this, everybody knows it and, in a way, his initiative in offering himself for hire did not involve any individual decision (in the classical sense of the term: hesitation, weighing of arguments for and against, etc.). Indeed, this is precisely what characterises free individual *praxis*: when it develops as an undertaking which temporalises itself in the course of a life, motivations are never 'psychical' or 'subjective': they are things and real structures in so far as these are revealed by the project through its concrete ends and on the basis of them. Thus there is normally no *act of consciousness*: the situation is known through the act which it motivates and which already negates it. But *precisely* because others are involved through things, and because their freedom confronts my freedom as Other – that is to say, as a freedom-thing or as the freedom of a given thing – the structure of the situation is nevertheless still *exigency*.

The importance of this authoritarian structure of passivity varies. It is negligible in the present case, but, in certain cases, it is crucial in that the free *praxis* of the individual reactualises it in constituting itself by surrendering its own sovereignty to this piece of matter – which, as we have seen, turns it against itself and converts it into inertia because of the impossibility of transcending it. But this inertia itself reaches *praxis* in so far as it is *praxis*: it confers its statute as a thing on a free activity, rather than on another thing. Similarly, if the exigency of a *thing* confronts another *thing* (tuberculosis slows down production = production demands the disappearance of tuberculosis) this can only be through the medium of free *praxis*. Between these *things*, as we have seen, the *praxis* of Others constitutes the individual's activity as a mediation, that is to say, as a means (essential as a means, but inessential as *praxis*). But it constitutes it as a *praxis*, that is to say, as an activity which organises a field in the light of certain objectives. It is *really a means*, in so far as the objectives of the practical agent are manipulated in exteriority in such a way that they give way to other material objectives and that they may never be attained: thus the manual worker steals from himself and produces the wealth of Others at the expense of his own life in the very work he carries out *in order to support his life*. But all these manipulations, which make freedom into a curse, presuppose that the relation of men to matter and to other men resides above all in *doing*, as synthetic creative work. And the *being* of man, as inorganic passivity, comes to him *in* his action from the fact that every individual undertaking is forced by its dialectical freedom to interiorise a double inert materiality: number, as the material statute of inert exteriority which characterises human multiplicity (*abstract* quantity which is revealed only through the set of relations which we have examined); and worked matter, as the inert meaning of the worker. Number can be regarded either as the absolute abstraction of man or as his absolute materiality in the abstract; and it is in this abstraction that worked Things designate him individually (as a general individual in a population). But if he can reinteriorise this reciprocity of materiality as the *untranscendable being* of his activity, this is because other activities have already interiorised and re-exteriorised it *as other*. In other words, the materiality of the multiple remains indeterminate as long as it is not itself revealed in a practical system.

(Demography, for example, is necessarily the study of both an *exis* and a *praxis*: number appears as the product of a certain mode of production and of the institutions it produces, and also as the movement of production, and its exigencies produce demographic differentiations between different sectors of the population. And these conditions are interiorised for everyone through their individual practices – birth control, or the Christian prohibition of it.)

From this point of view, for an isolated individual – that is to say, for every one of us, in so far as we receive and interiorise the statute of isolation – the consciousness of our *praxis* as free efficacity remains, through every constraint and exigency, our own constant reality in so far as we are the perpetual transcendence of our ends. And the individual does not recognise that it is in direct contradiction with his Other-Being because this untranscendable Other-Being reveals itself in *praxis* itself, either as a motivation of this *praxis* (in exigency or in value systems), or as an object of a possible transcendence. It is clear, in fact, that the Other-Being of the individual as the common structure of the collective derives its being for everyone *from its untranscendability*. But precisely to the extent that it is freedom which reveals untranscendability as a necessary structure of alienated objectification, it does so in the milieu of freedom as transcendable untranscendability. Indeed, for an exploited man who, in a period before any important developments of proletarian organisation, became aware, through his own *praxis* as *his* own reality, of his fatigue, of his occupational diseases, of price rises, of the obsolescence of his trade through machinery, etc., as the statute which defined him in his sub-humanity, the reality he grasps is simply the set of his impossibilities (the impossibility of living *humanly* or, perhaps more radically, of living at all). Clearly this reality of his Being is precisely that of his impotence; it defines itself, in and through the series of exploited men, as alterity or as an index of separation in negative unity. But in so far as everyone perceives his own impossibility (that is to say, his inability *to change or reorganise anything*) through his *praxis* (which posits itself in its dialectical structure as a permanent possibility of transcending any actual circumstances), this impossibility inside freedom appears to him as temporary and relative.

Of itself, no doubt, *praxis* does not occur as a concrete, material transcendence of impossibility towards a particular reorganisation: this, indeed, is what proves that the statute cannot be transcended. But the mere exposure of the impossibility makes it confront itself as the pure, abstract, and ideal negation of every given by a transcendence towards an end. Confronted with the real impossibility of living humanly, it affirms itself in its generality as human *praxis*. This affirmation is neither *more* than nor *other* than the action itself in so far as it transcends the milieu in order to reproduce life: and its affirmative power is simply the material power of the organism striving to change the world. But for lack of any real objective and of real means of attaining the end, the *praxis* reveals itself as a pure negation of negation (or of affirmation) *universally*; and, to be more precise, what it immediately grasps is not its formal structure, but, *in the reality which crushes it*, the impossibility of the impossibility of man. In fact, the impossibility of man is given as an individual determination of life; but the *praxis* which reveals it cannot see it as *its own impossibility*: it sees it in action – which is, of itself, an affirmation of man as an impossibility which is in some way impossible. In fact, *praxis*, as the *praxis* of an organism which reproduces its life by reorganising the environment, is man – man making himself in remaking himself.

To make oneself and to produce oneself on the basis of one's own possibility are one and the same thing; but it is at the level of the practico-inert, in the real production of man, that the impossibility of man reveals itself as his being. This impossibility refers to pure, formal transcendence as an affirmation without an object. 'It is *impossible* that this should continue; it is *impossible* that it should be unchangeable; it is *impossible* that there should be no way out, that I should continue to live like this.' Such formulas, which insist on the objective structure of possibilities, are very common. And there are also ones which refer to the subjective moment: 'I'll find a way out, I'll find a solution somehow', etc. After all, the contradiction would be in danger of exploding if it opposed two homogeneous moments. But the individual *will change his reality, he will transcend it*: he will occasionally have a chance to improve his lot. Thus the untranscendable comes to be transcended. But it is only an appearance: he has simply realised his being – the very thing he cannot change – in slightly different circumstances; and these superficial differences make no difference to the Being which has been actualised. A particular worker leaves a factory where the working conditions are particularly bad and goes to work in another where they are a little better. He is merely defining the limits within which his statute allows a few variations (themselves due to general circumstances of production: manpower requirements, wage rises in a particular sector, etc.), but at the same time he is confirming *his general destiny* as exploited. A rise in wages in a particular branch of production occurs only *in the general context* of the search for profit and it is to be explained in terms of the historical totalisation and of the present conjuncture. He may, therefore, *vary* the implementation of the verdict, but he cannot *transcend it.* Concretely, however, things are not so simple: provided he breaks his bonds of impotence but avoids replacing them by union, he will be able to acquire, in a still indefinite society, a society which remains indeterminate in spite of serial structurations (and because of them), the efficacity of an imponderable, that is to say, of a disintegrated individual.

In certain circumstances, in certain historical moments and in certain societies, there may be real possibilities of moving from one class to another. And these possibilities vary from sector to sector, and from country to country. In the patrician Venice of the sixteenth century, the bourgeois had absolutely no possible access to the patrician class; elsewhere – in France, for example – they were able to 'betray' their class and enter the *noblesse de robe*, and sometimes even slip into the *noblesse d'épée*.[101] Thus, at this level, an individual may avoid being a class individual, and may sometimes transcend his class-being and thereby produce for all the members of the class he has left the possibility of individually escaping their destiny. However, *in fact* – though it took him a great deal of intelligence, work and patience to transcend the common destiny – all he has done is to realise, in his person, one of the possibilities in the structured field of his class possibilities. In other words, if he moves into the petty bourgeoisie or gets his son to do so, he practically realises – at the same moment as several other individuals – a possibility (statistically determinable and conditioned by the whole historical process) *of his class of origin*: in the structured social field of his possibilities and impossibilities (as destiny), this class, at a particular moment and in definite conditions and sectors, is also determined by the possibility that a definite proportion of its members may move into another class (return to the peasant class, move into the bourgeoisie, etc.). This can be called class *viscosity*. Thus the worker who becomes a bourgeois demonstrates the *viscosity* of his class: by thus escaping the untranscendable in his

101. The *noblesse de robe* owed their patents of nobility to administrative or legal posts which they or their ancestors bought. The *noblesse d'épée* was the old nobility. [Ed.]

quality as an atom, he helps to constitute in its reality the structured impossibility which produces itself as the common-class-being of his comrades and himself. Thus untranscendability as destiny relates to the free isolation of a molecular *praxis* when the individual lives it as an *impossibility of remaining at one with his class*; we shall see shortly that this same practical freedom, positing both impossibility and the impossibility of this impossibility as the common-class-being which is to be transcended by the class itself, will posit a new type of transcendence, namely the group. But the important point has been to show that this impossibility can only be revealed through practical, directed activities, and also that it reveals *praxis* to itself in the abstract as the sovereign affirmation of the possibility of man.

It would be quite wrong to interpret me as saying that man is free in all situations, as the Stoics claimed. I mean the exact opposite: all men are slaves in so far as their life unfolds in the practico-inert field and in so far as this field is always conditioned by scarcity. In modern society, in effect, the alienation of the exploited and that of the exploiters are inseparable; in other societies, the relation between master and slave – though very different from what Hegel described – also presupposes a reciprocal conditioning in alienation. And the master of ancient times was alienated from his slaves not because they were his truth (though they were that too), nor because of their labour (as free *praxis* expressing itself by operating on the material environment), but *above all* because the cost of a slave tends constantly to increase whereas his productivity constantly tends to decrease. The practico-inert field is the field of our servitude, which means *not* ideal servitude, but real subservience to 'natural' forces, to 'mechanical' forces and to 'anti-social' apparatuses. This means that everyone struggles against an order which really and materially crushes his body and which he sustains and strengthens by his individual struggle against it. Everything is born at this line which simultaneously separates and unites huge physical forces in the world of inertia and exteriority (in so far as the nature and orientation of the energy transformations which characterise them give a definite statute of improbability to life in general and to human life in particular) and practical organisms (in so far as their *praxis* tends to confirm them within their structure of inertia, that is to say, in their role as convertors of energy). This is where the change from unification as a process to unity as an inert statute occurs; and where inertia, as a moment which has been transcended and preserved by life and practice, turns back on them so as to transcend them and preserve them in the name of their dialectical unity, precisely to the extent that, in labour and through instrumentality, it identifies itself with the practical inertia of the tool.

These transformations are wholly *material*; or rather, everything really takes place in the physico-chemical universe and the organism's power of assimilation and of strictly biological selection exists at the level of consumption. But one will never understand anything of human history if one fails to recognise that these transformations take place in a practical field inhabited by a multiplicity of agents, in so far as they are produced by the free actions of individuals. Serial plurality, as the inorganic unity of inertia, comes to this multiplicity only through the mediation of worked matter in so far as it transforms individual labours into the negative unity of counter-finality. Thus *praxis alone*, as it appears between the inert (and abstract) multiplicity of number and the (equally abstract) passive exteriority of the physico-chemical world, is, *in its dialectical freedom*, the real and permanent foundation (in human history up to the present) of all the inhuman sentences which men have passed on men through worked matter. In *praxis*, multiplicity, scarcity, exteriority and the improbability of the continuation of life are interiorised and humanised as the *internal inhumanity* of the human race; through it, these same characteristics of the inorganic take on the practical and directed aspect of *Fatum* and their simple non-humanity becomes counter-finality or anti-humanity. Of course, it is possible to reverse the terms completely, and, as we did at a more abstract moment of the dialectical investigation, show worked matter in its primacy and inorganic materiality as governing men through it: this view is as correct, or perhaps more so, in so far as it refers directly from the non-organised physico-chemical world to the number of individuals as the inorganic materiality of the social; but it will remain abstract as long as the development of the investigation fails to show clearly that any relation between things, in so far as they mediate between men, is strictly conditioned by the multiple relations of human actions in so far as they mediate between things.

From this point of view the problem of *negation*, as stated at the beginning of this chapter from a simple practico-inert point of view, is also completely explained. Our problem, in relation to the origins of the 'iron and coal complex', was to explain how it was that the discovery of techniques, which made the exploitation of fabulous wealth possible, *took the form of* a negation for most members of a nation (the gradual elimination of the English peasantry by expropriation and proletarianisation). We were acquainted with the historical *explanation* and it appeared obvious, *provided* it was based on an intelligible structure of the practico-inert field; that is to say, provided we could see its dialectical skeleton as matter constituting itself as the practico-inert negation of the *praxis* which works it and uses it in the context of multiplicity. We more or less know this much: that free *praxis* is the negation of every particular given, in the course of a particular action, and that it *negates matter* in so far as it reorganises it in its passive being in terms of a future objective originating in the satisfaction of needs. In fact, it is neither the presence nor the possible instrumentality of matter which is negated by the project, but simply its 'co-efficient of adversity', in so far as inertia presents it as a factual impossibility. And in its first moment, that is to say in its elementary structure, negation is a practical, univocal relation of interiority which man derives from matter through the need which explains it, and which matter derives from men in so far as the present material *state* (and not materiality) is always what has already been transcended. Thus in the practical field of man, as an individual worker, there appear tools which he himself made, or acquired in exchange for his labour, and these material tools are a practical, solidified negation, which is borne by matter and which refers to certain states of materiality in their passivity (that is to say, adversities, or counter-finalities). Thus, from the tool as a solidified product of past labour and a solidified inscription of future labour, to the Thing (which might itself be a tool – for example, one which needs to be mended), *a negative signification* establishes itself as solidified passivity. The future comes to objects through the tool, as a necessity that some material combinations should be realised and that others should disappear. In fact, it comes through freedom to the practical field in so far as it is already unified by need. But the negative structure as a relation of the worked object to nature and of tools among themselves nonetheless appears, in the field of scarcity, as a definite *intra-material* tension. Destruction, and destructability as a negation of man's materiality and of his goods, come to matter through man; they are designated and negated (wholly or partly) by the presence of the human tool. It is obvious that the tool has *some* positive, creative function, and that it is this function which *initially* characterises it.

In the next chapter we shall see the positive aspect of *praxis*: at present what interests us is that, even in productive labour, tools are *the inert as a negation of the inert* (combined with the permanent possibility of the organism acting in exteriority by becoming the tool of its tool). It is at this level that the matter *to be worked*, as passive resistance, makes itself a negation of man in so far as man negates *the existing state of affairs*; *fatigue* is *being* in so far as it is distinct from knowledge and from *praxis*, in so far as its inert capacity can be reduced only through an *expenditure of energy*. It is the inertia of exteriority interiorised in the organism in so far as organic *praxis* exteriorises itself as the seal applied to the product. Negation is there in these fundamental relations of need and labour and in so far as, *in* the *practical field*, they constitute materiality as the negation of its own passivity as much as of human activity. It comes to matter in *praxis* and, through the development of this *praxis*, it turns back against the individual in so far as it becomes a double negation solidified by inertia (the ambivalence of the tool). It is obvious, however, that the relation between two human activities is *of itself indeterminate*, as long as we have not defined the material conditions on the basis of which it arises. It is not true that 'each must aim at the death of the other'[102] – or his life, for that matter. Material circumstances as a whole (the set of tools and goods in the context of scarcity) settle it. In a word, *if* some free *praxis* becomes the negation of another *praxis*, this negation, which comes to them as a reciprocity of antagonism, produces itself in everyone as primary inertia, because it is the interiorisation of an exterior negation. It is in this sense that there was competitive antagonism between workers on the labour market, at the beginning of the century, *even before* they had made it a moment of practice or rejected it in the name of unity of action. Thus, *praxis* as a fundamental relation of man to the environment structures the practical field as a set of inert, intra-material relations of negation. Negation as a force of inertia is a human inscription in the inorganic world. And the multiplicity of activities is constituted *in its being* as a multiplicity of negative relations (antagonisms) because every *praxis* re-actualises for the Other, with all its signifying power, the inert negation of a particular part of the field by the Other in so far as this negation refers to the statute which makes one man the inert negation of an Other (in definite conditions and in a determinate form). Indeed, it might be said that *negation* comes to inert matter from individual labour and that *negations* come to men through worked matter as the matrix and receptacle of all passive negativity, through the inert numerical statute of their multiplicity. In counter-finalities,

---

102. *Phenomenology of Mind*, trans. Baillie, p. 233. [Ed.]

praxis inscribes itself in inertia and inertia returns as inverted *praxis* to dominate the very group which has objectified itself in this worked matter. Thus *not only* do individuals and groups receive their statute in inertia through *matter-negation*, in this inversion of action and passivisation; in addition, this very matter, in the development of dispersed actions, becomes *their unity* as the pure negation in everyone *as Other* both of himself and of all Others, in the name of an *alterity* which might, purely metaphorically, be called *the perspective of the inorganic on man*.

These few observations enable us to elucidate one final point. We have claimed, in effect, that everyone has the practico-inert experience in his work and in his public life (and, to a lesser degree, in his private life) and that it is, in fact, characteristic of our everyday life. We also saw that it remained abstract because this inert bond of sociality *does not explain* the group, as an organised plurality, but that the universe of passive-activity was still, for particular individuals (depending on their function, their class, etc.) a field which they could not leave. Yet, at the same time, we saw that everyone's free *praxis* remained his translucid experience of himself, not in so far as it was the Other but in so far as it was produced by dialectical *praxis* – in the regulated change which it produces – as the same as itself (or as 'changing so as to remain the same'). It seems therefore that, for all of us, there are two contradictory experiences. In other words, although the critique of dialectical Reason can and must constitute the second as a negation of the first, but as deriving its intelligibility from it, in everyday reality our remarks might imply that the practico-inert field is not a synthetic blossoming and a reunification of the fundamental abstraction and its contradiction. Something is negated *in misfortune*; which means that negation itself is diverted and that all activities lose themselves in the practico-inert to the advantage of false, anti-human unities. How, it will be asked, is one to conceive of this duality of experiences, which is *always possible for everyone?* Can we just pass from the translucid consciousness of our activity to the grotesque or monstrous apperception of the practico-inert, according to circumstances? My answer is not only that we can but also that we constantly do. There can be no doubt that at the moment of labour, and in so far as there remains, even in the case of a small section of work, the simple necessity of a control or, in the total subservience of the individual to specialised machines, a need for *an eye* or *a hand*, prior to automation, the action still appears – *at least* – as an adaptation of the body to a demanding situation. Similarly, if some worker agreed to work extra hard and thus to contribute to raising the norms, this result, from which he must necessarily suffer, will at first present itself to him as an almost unbearable work rhythm, which nevertheless he bears by a decision which anticipates the exigency of machines, that is to say, by a choice which may be disapproved of by his comrades. In this sense, the moment of freedom as unifying, translucid practice is *the moment of the trap*. By positing itself as free individual *praxis*, it contributes for its part, in itself and for all, to the realisation of the world of the Other. And this is precisely the practical moment in which it apprehends itself and sees only its reality.

The terrible constraints which matter forces on both the factory worker and the agricultural worker never allow them to remain for long at this level of abstraction; but there is nothing to prevent a member of the middle class, in certain favourable circumstances, from fortifying himself within the consciousness of his individual *praxis* by using an interior monologue on freedom as a kind of solder. However, it is through the experience of alienation as *necessity* (that is to say, as the real, social being of one's being), that the practico-inert field is revealed. It is for this reason that simplistic Marxists have calmly eliminated the moment of individual *praxis* as an irreducible experience of the dialectic or, in other words, as dialectic realising itself in practical experience. They have not seen that unless the fundamental reality of this moment is preserved the reality of alienation will have to be rejected. Their only excuse – and it is a feeble one – is that the moment of necessity throws experience into the universe of alterity. From the moment in which impotence becomes the meaning of practical power, and counter-finality the deep meaning of the aim pursued, when *praxis* discovers that *its* freedom is the means chosen elsewhere to reduce it to slavery, the individual suddenly finds himself back in a world where free action is the fundamental mystification; he no longer knows it except as a reality which is negated at this stage of the experience, absent or forever fleeing, and as the propaganda of the oppressors against the oppressed. But it is important to see that this experience is no longer that of the action, but that of the materialised result; it is no longer the positive moment in which one *does*, but the negative moment in which one is produced in passivity by what the practico-inert ensemble makes out of what one has just made. It is the moment, for example, when the worker who wished to raise *his own* work norm finds that *this* norm has become a general exigency and, thereby sees himself signified as an Other, that is to say, in this case, as his own enemy, as the agent of the employers and of exploitation.

In this sense, the discovery of sociality as *passive being* containing worked matter is not a plenary experience, comparable to the individual's experience of the action of his activity as a dialectical development. It occurs as *a fleeting discovery*, precisely because, through alienation as a passive result inscribed in social (worked) matter, it is the discovery of sociality as series, and because this series is flight (normally indefinite or infinite). Similarly, when anyone discovers his other-Being in so far as it is constituted by the serial absence of Others, he can *realise* it only as a negative, abstract meaning whose content he can express in language though he cannot hold it in a plenary intuition. The Being of this being is that it should be elsewhere. I do not mean by this that the alienation and the Other-Being which are manifested in it are essentially *probable* beings (as given to experience). It may, of course, happen that the otherness of my act remains obscure and probable for me: this depends on the circumstances of my experience and on the type of act in question; nevertheless alienation is the object of a necessary discovery, in the sense that the passivising reflection of objectified *praxis* is always given as necessary, even though the particular meaning (*signification*) of the alienation may remain confused and blurred. This means that the experience of alienation is not an instantaneous intuition – this would be meaningless – but a process which temporalises itself and which the 'ways of the world' can always interrupt, either provisionally or definitively, from outside and within by the intervening transformation of the conditions of the experience. But, in the context of a shorter, uninterrupted experience, Other-Being may also manifest itself in its own content as *necessary-being*. In short, it is possible to have a precise knowledge of it as the necessity that a given action will actualise a particular Other-Being. This knowledge, however, does not realise anything: the Other-Being which I am is *in principle* incapable of living in the dialectical development of *praxis*; it is the fleeting object of consciousness rather than consciousness itself; an abstract and precise limit of knowledge rather than a concrete presence to intuition. In this sense, my everyday experience of the Other-Being of Others realises itself as concrete experience only in moments when the necessity of the discovered alienation and the flight of alterity incite me to pursue this Other in his flight to the Others, for example, to realise my alterity through the serial impotence of the members of the series.

But, this shifting, indefinite experience of the practico-inert field reveals the Elsewhere to me as a spatial structure of alterity, and shows me my Other-Being in this Elsewhere, fleeing from one to the other, as the Other to Others, that is to say, to reified man as Other than man, as well as to the worked Thing as Other than the Thing (as the anti-human being of man). This fleeting experience reveals its unity only in the form of *common impotence* as the negative cement of all the beings in a series or as the *development to the limit* (that is to say, the practical, abstract affirmation of a totalisation to infinity of the series by a re-current, infinite transcendence). In this experience, which is constantly eluding itself, it is *true* that worked things come to us *as men* in the most everyday moment of life. (And the theatre has made great use, in melodrama, of the frightening effect produced by a door which opens by itself in an empty house, or – and this amounts to the same thing – of a door which slowly opens and which we know to conceal the criminal, and which becomes the door-being of the criminal, etc.) But this is true only in so far as man has become, for us, pure flight, in us and in objects – in so far as the inanimate relation of a thousand-franc note to some absolutely necessary article may be altered *at a distance* by the serial ensemble of serialities (an alteration of my being-outside-myself) just as my human relation to a comrade or to a member of my family may be alienated everywhere, in the ensemble of series which constitute my class – so that there is, in the end, a unity and fusion of all the meanings of practico-inert objects (men, things, relations of things, and relations of men) to the infinity of every Elsewhere.

In this first form, as the limit which separates *praxis* from passive, alienated activity (that is to say, from the individual of sociality) *necessity* provides its own intelligibility, that is to say, the *Reason* of its being. We have seen that it could not even *appear* in individual *praxis* or in human relations of reciprocity (with or without a 'third party'). But, in the same way, nobody, except by conceiving of natural laws in terms of a Platonic conceptualism, can imagine that such laws are *a priori* rules which impose themselves on matter and inflexibly govern transformations of energy. To the extent that scientific laws rest on experience, which constantly returns to them and modifies them, they are both *statistical* and *contingent* (at least for us and at this stage). In fact, we can now see that necessity is a particular meaning (*signification*) which links human action to the material thing in which it objectifies itself, on the basis of a univocal link of interiority between the organism and the environment. This is the moment where, through the very freedom which produces it, the Thing, transformed by other freedoms, presents, *through its own characteristics*, the objectification of the agent as a strictly predictable but completely unforseen alteration of the ends pursued. In this case, the characteristics of the object become the necessary foundation for any explanation of this alteration, because the action of other freedoms puts them in relief and manifests them: 'You should have realised that if you did this with that instrument, the result would be such and such, etc.' But the fixed characteristics (exigencies, instrumentality) of the instrument are precisely those of *worked matter*.

Thus, as one might say, necessity is freedom as the *exis* of worked matter, or worked materiality as the freedom-*exis* of Others in so far as it is revealed within a free operation. And, from this point of view, we can conclude that necessity manifests itself neither in the action of the isolated organism, nor in the succession of physico-chemical facts: the reign of necessity is the domain – the real, but still abstract domain of History – in which inorganic materiality envelops human multiplicity and transforms the producers into its product. Necessity, as a limit within freedom, as blinding obviousness and as the moment of the inversion of *praxis* into practico-inert activity, becomes, once man has swung back into serial sociality, the very structure of all processes of seriality, that is to say, the *modality* of their absence in presence and of their empty obviousness. It is the shifting ensemble of unlucky materiality in so far as it is simultaneously affirmed and stolen away, for everyone and in any free act, by all free acts as Others; that is to say, as forging our chains. This is the only possible relation between practical organisms and their milieu and, through the milieu, between them, in so far as they have not achieved a new practical unity. It would be easy to show how so-called 'scientific' necessity – that is to say, the modality of certain chains of exact propositions – comes to science *through* practice and *by it* as the limit-negation, through exteriority, of the dialectic, and how it appears by means of free dialectical research as its real and always Other objectification. But this is not our present concern.

What we must retain from all this is that the practico-inert field is not a new moment of some universal dialectic, but the pure and simple negation of several dialectics by exteriority and plurality. This negation, however, operates not by destruction or dissolution, but by deviation and inversion. Thus this second moment *of the investigation* (*l'expérience*) (but not of the dialectic) appears in itself as the anti-

dialectic or, in other words, as the inorganic simulacrum, in and outside man, of the dialectic as free human activity. Thus, just as the
dialectic transcends material conditions in preserving them in its very
negation, so materiality as the inflexible necessity of the practico-inert
transcends everyone's free *praxis*, that is to say, the multiple dialectics
in their development, so as to preserve them in it as the only means of
setting its clumsy machinery in motion.

We have seen that the practico-inert field, considered in general and
a priori, cannot, by any of its contradictions, occasion the form of
practical sociality which we are about to study, namely the group.
Groups always constitute themselves on the basis of certain particular
contradictions which define a particular sector of the field of passive-
activity, while one cannot have any *a priori* assurance that the same
applies everywhere. When such contradictions occur, then, as we shall
see, the dialectical *praxis* of the individual puts itself on trial at the heart
of the anti-dialectic which appropriates its results, and invents itself *in
another social space* as the totalisation of multiple actions in, for and by
a totalising objective result. This new approach is both reflexive and
constituent: each *praxis* as a free individual totalising dialectic places
itself at the service of a common dialectic whose very type is modelled
on the synthetic action of an isolated worker. Thus the original dialectics are transcended towards an other dialectic, which they *constitute*
on the basis of the anti-dialectic as an impossibility which cannot be
transcended. In this sense, we might be said to be passing here from
the nature-dialectic, as an original relation of interiority between the
organism and its milieu, to the culture-dialectic, as an apparatus constructed against the power of the practico-inert. In other words, individual dialectics, after having created anti-physis as the power of man
over nature and, in the same act, anti-humanity as the power of inorganic matter over man, create their own anti-physis by unification
so as to construct human power (that is to say, free relations amongst
men). It is at this level and on the basis of previous conditions that men
totalise, and totalise themselves, in order to reorganise themselves into
the unity of a *praxis*: in other words, we are approaching the third and
last moment of our investigation (*expérience*) – that which totalises the
human world (that is to say, the world of men and their objects) in the
historical undertaking. This new structure of the investigation presents
itself as an inversion of the practico-inert field: that is to say, the nerve
of *practical unity* is freedom, appearing as the necessity of necessity –
in other words, as its inexorable inversion. Indeed, in so far as the

individuals in a given milieu are directly threatened, in practico-inert necessity, by the impossibility of life, their radical unity (in reappropriating this very impossibility for themselves as the possibility of dying humanly, or of the affirmation of man by his death) is the inflexible negation of this impossibility ('To live working or die fighting'); thus the group constitutes itself as the radical impossibility of living, which threatens serial multiplicity. But this new dialectic, in which freedom and necessity are now one, is not a new incarnation of the transcendental dialectic: it is a human construction whose sole agents are individual men as free activities. For this reason, in order to distinguish it from constituent dialectics, we shall refer to it as the constituted dialectic.

Book II

From Groups to History

I

The Fused Group

The group – the equivalence of freedom as necessity and of
necessity as freedom – the scope and limits of any realist dialectic

1 The Genesis of Groups

As we have seen, the necessity of the group is not present *a priori* in a
gathering. But we have also seen that through its serial unity (in so far
as the negative unity of the series can, as abstract negation, oppose
seriality) the gathering furnishes the elementary conditions of the
possibility that its members should constitute a group. But this remains
abstract. Obviously everything would be simpler in a transcendental,
idealist dialectic: the movement of integration by which every organism contains and dominates its inorganic pluralities would be presented as transforming itself, at the level of social plurality, into an
integration of individuals into an organic totality. Thus the group
would function as a hyper-organism in relation to individual organisms. This organicist idealism is often to be seen re-emerging as a
social model of conservative thought (under the Restoration, it was
opposed to liberal atomism; after 1860, it tried to dissolve class formations into a national solidarity). But it would be a mistake to reduce the
organicist illusion to the role of a reactionary theory. Indeed, it is
obvious that the *organic* character of the group – its *biological* unity –
reveals itself as a particular moment of the investigation. As we approach the third stage of the dialectical investigation, we can describe
the organic structure as *above all* the illusory, immediate appearance of
the group as it produces itself in and against the practico-inert field.

In two remarkable works[1] Marc Bloch has shown how, in and even

1. Marc Bloch, *Feudal Society*, two volumes, (1939–40). English translation by
L. A. Manyon, Routledge and Kegan Paul, 1961. [Ed.]

before the twelfth century, the nobility, the bourgeoisie and the serfs – to mention only these three classes – existed *de facto* if not *de jure*. In our terminology we would describe them as collectives. But the repeated efforts of rich bourgeois, as *individuals*, to integrate themselves into the noble class caused this class to close up: it moved from a *de facto* statute to a *de jure* one. Through a common undertaking, it imposed draconian conditions on anyone wishing to enter *knighthood*, with the result that this mediating institution between the generations became a selective organ. But this also conditioned the class consciousness of the serfs. Prior to the juridical unification of the nobility, every serf had regarded his situation as an individual destiny, and lived it as an ensemble of human relations with a family of landowners, in other words, as an accident. But by positing itself for itself, the nobility *ipso facto* constituted serfdom as a juridical institution and showed the serfs their interchangeability, their common impotence and their common interests. This revelation was one of the factors of peasant revolts in later centuries.

The point of this example is simply to show how, in the movement of History, an exploiting class, by tightening its bonds against an enemy and by becoming aware of itself as a unity of individuals *in solidarity*, shows the exploited classes their material being as a collective and as a point of departure for a constant effort to establish lived bonds of solidarity between its members. There is nothing surprising about this: in this inert quasi-totality, constantly swept by great movements of counter-finality, the historical collectivity, the dialectical law, is at work: the constitution of a group (on the basis, of course, of real, material conditions) as an ensemble of solidarities has the dialectical consequence of making it the negation of the rest of the social field, and, as a result, of occasioning, in this field in so far as it is defined as *non-grouped*, the conditions for an antagonistic grouping (*on the basis* of scarcity and in divided social systems).

But the most important point here is that the non-grouped, on the outside, behave towards the group by positing it through their very *praxis* as *an organic totality*. Thus every new collective organisation can find its archetype in any other older one, because *praxis* as the unification of the practical field objectively tightens the bonds of the object-group. It is striking that our most elementary patterns of behaviour relate to *external collectives* as if they were organisms. The structure of *scandal*, for example, is, for everyone, that of a collective taken as a totality: in a theatre, everyone, in confronting each speech of a scene which he finds outrageous, is in fact conditioned by the serial reaction of his neighbours. Scandal is the Other as the formula of a series. *But as soon as* the first manifestations of scandal have occurred (that is to say, the first acts of someone acting for the Others in so far as he is Other than himself), they create the living unity of the audience against the author, simply because the first protester, through his unity as an individual, *realises this unity* for everyone in transcendence (*la transcendance*). Moreover, it will remain a profound contradiction in everyone, because this unity is that of all the Others (including himself) as Others and by an Other: the protester was not revealing or expressing popular opinion; rather, he was expressing, in the objective unity of a direct action (shouts, insults, etc.), what still existed for everyone only as the opinion of the Others, that is to say, as their shifting, serial unity. But once the scandal has been reported and discussed, it becomes, in the eyes of those who did not witness it, a synthetic event which gave the audience which saw the play that night a temporary unity as an organism. Everything becomes clear if we *situate* the non-grouped who discover themselves to be a collective through their impotence in relation to the group which they reveal. To the extent that, through the unity of its *praxis*, the group determines them in their inorganic inertia, they conceive its ends and its unity through the free unifying unity of their own individual *praxis* and on the model of the free synthesis which is fundamentally the practical temporalisation of the organism. Indeed, in the practical field, all exterior multiplicity becomes, for every agent, the object of a unifying synthesis (and, as we have already seen, the result of this synthesis is that the serial structure of gatherings is concealed). But the group which I unify in the practical field produces itself, as a group, as already unified, that is to say, as structured by a unity which in principle eludes my unification and negates it (in so far as it is *praxis relegating me to impotence*). This free active unity which eludes me appears as the substance of a reality of which I myself, in my practical and perceptual field, have unified only its multiplicity as the pure materiality of appearance; or, to put it another way, I do not attribute inertia – which must constitute the real foundation of the group (as inertia which has been transcended and preserved) – to the active community; on the contrary, it is my *praxis* which, in its unificatory movement takes responsibility for it. And the common action, which eludes me, becomes the *reality* of this appearance, that is to say, the practical, synthetic substance, the totality controlling its parts, entelechy, life; or, at another level of perception and for other groups, a *Gestalt.* We shall encounter this naive organicism both as an immediate relation of the individual to the group and as an ideal of absolute integration. But we must reject organicism *in every form.* The relation of the group, as the determination of a collective and as a perpetual threat of relapsing into a collective, to its inertia as a multiplicity can never in any way be assimilated to the relation of the organism to the inorganic substances which compose it.

But if there is no dialectical process through which the moment of the anti-dialectic can become by itself a mediation between the multiple dialectics of the practical field and the constituted dialectic as common *praxis,* does the emergence of the group contain its own intelligibility? Following the same method as we have used so far, we shall now attempt to find in our investigation the characteristics and moments of a particular process of grouping from the point of view of the purely *critical* aim of determining its rationality. In our investigation we shall therefore have to study successively the genesis of groups, and the structures of their *praxis* – in other words, the dialectical rationality of collective action – and, finally, the group as *passion,* that is to say, in so far as it struggles in itself against *the practical inertia* by which it is affected.

I will begin with two preliminary observations. First, I have claimed that the inert gathering with its structure of seriality is the basic type of sociality. But I have not meant this in a historical sense, and the term 'fundamental' here does not imply temporal priority. Who could claim that collectives come before groups? No one is in a position to advance any hypothesis on this subject; or rather – despite the data of prehistory and ethnography – no such hypothesis has any meaning. Besides, the constant metamorphosis of gatherings into groups and of groups into gatherings would make it quite impossible to know *a priori* whether a particular gathering was a primary historical reality or whether it was the remains of a group which had been reabsorbed by the field of passivity: in either case, only the study of earlier structures and conditions can answer the question – if anything can. Our reason for positing the logical anteriority of collectives is simply that according to what History teaches us, groups constitute themselves as determinations and negations of collectives. In other words, they transcend and preserve them. Collectives, on the other hand, even when they result from the disintegration of active groups, preserve nothing of themselves *as collectives,* except for dead, ossified structures which scarcely conceal the flight of seriality. Similarly, the group, whatever it may be, *contains in itself* its reasons for relapsing into the inert being of the gathering: thus the disintegration of a group, as we shall see, has an *a priori* intelligibility. But the collective – as such and apart from the action of the factors we are about to study – contains *at most* the mere possibility of a synthetic union of its members. Lastly, regardless of *pre-history*, the important thing here, in a *history* conditioned by class struggle, is to explain the transition of oppressed classes from the state of being collectives to revolutionary group *praxis*. This is particularly important because such a transition has *really* occurred in each case.

But having mentioned class relations, I will make a second observation: that it would be premature to regard these classes as also being groups. In order to determine the conditions of their intelligibility, I shall, as with collectives, take and discuss ephemeral, superficial groups, which form and disintegrate rapidly, and approach the basic groups of society progressively.

The upheaval which destroys the collective by the flash of a common *praxis* obviously originates in a synthetic, and therefore material, transformation, which occurs in the context of scarcity and of existing structures. For organisms whose risks and practical movement, as well as their suffering, reside in need, the driving-force is either danger, at every level of materiality (whether it be hunger, or the bankruptcy *whose meaning* is hunger, etc.), or transformations of instrumentality (the exigencies and scarcity of the tool replacing the scarcity of the immediate object of need; or the modifications of the tool, seen in their ascending signification, as necessary modifications of the collective). In other words, without the original tension of need as a relation of interiority with Nature, there would be no change; and, conversely, there is no common *praxis* at any level whose regressive or descending signification is not directly or indirectly related to this original tension. It must therefore be understood *at the outset* that the origin of any restructuration of a collective into a group is a complex event which takes place *simultaneously* at every level of materiality, but is transcended into organising *praxis* at the level of serial unity.

But however universal the event may be, it cannot be lived as its own transcendence towards the unity of all, unless its universality is objective *for everyone*, or unless it creates in everyone a structure of unifying objectivity. Up to this point, in fact – in the dimension of the collective – the real has defined itself by its impossibility. Indeed, what is called the *meaning of realities* is precisely the meaning of that which, in principle, is forbidden. The transformation therefore occurs when impossibility itself becomes impossible, or when the synthetic event reveals that the impossibility of change is an impossibility of life.[2] The direct result of this is to make *the impossibility of change* the very object which has to be transcended if life is to continue. In other words, we have come to a vicious circle: the group constitutes itself on the basis of a need or common danger and defines itself by the common objective which determines its common *praxis*. Yet neither common need, nor common *praxis*, nor common objectives can define a community unless it makes itself into a community by feeling individual need as common need, and by projecting itself, in the internal unification of a common integration, towards objectives which it produces as common. Without famine, this group would not have constituted itself: but why does it define itself as common struggle against common need? Why is it that, as sometimes happens, individuals in a given case do not quarrel over food like dogs? That is the same as asking how a synthesis can take place when the power of synthetic unity is both everywhere (in all individuals as a free unification of the field) and nowhere (in that it would be a free transcendent (*transcendante*) unification of the plurality of individual unifications). Indeed, let us not forget that the *common object*, as the unity of the multiple outside itself, is above all the producer of serial unity and that it is on the basis of this double determination that the anti-dialectical structure of the collectivity, or *alterity*, constitutes itself.

2. Obviously it is not under a threat of mortal danger that anglers form their association or old ladies set up a system of swopping books: but these groups, which in any case respond to some very real exigencies and whose objective meaning relates to the total situation, are superstructures, or, in other words, groups which are constituted in the general, permanent regroupment activity of collectives (class structures, class against class, national and international organisations, etc.). From the moment that the stage of the dialectical regroupment of dialectics has been reached, totalising activity *itself* becomes a factor, a milieu and a reason for secondary groups. They are its living determination and therefore its negation; but, at the same time, they contain it entirely within themselves, and their dialectical conflicts take place through it and by it. In this way, as we saw in *The Problem of Method*, it is possible to study them either horizontally (and empirically) in so far as they determine themselves in a milieu in which the group structure is already objectively given, or vertically in so far as each of them in its concrete richness expresses the whole of human materiality and the whole historical process. Thus I need only concern myself here with the fundamental fact of grouping as the conquest or reconquest of the collective by *praxis*.

But this last observation may help us. If the object really produces itself as the bond of alterity between the individuals of a collective, then the serial structure of multiplicity depends, basically, on the fundamental characteristics of the object itself and on its original relation with each and all. This is how the set of means of production, in so far as they are the property of *Others*, gives the proletariat an original structure of seriality because it produces itself as an indefinite ensemble of objects whose exigencies themselves reflect the *demand* of the bourgeois class as the seriality of the Other. Conversely, however, it is possible for the investigation to consider the common objects which constitute by themselves, and in the *practico-inert field*, an approximation to a totality (as the totalisation of the multiple by the Other through matter) and to try to discover whether they too must constitute the multiple in question as seriality.

2   The Storming of the Bastille

After 12 July 1789 the people of Paris were in a state of revolt. Their anger had deep causes, but as yet these had affected the people only in their common impotence. (Cold, hunger, etc., were all suffered either in resignation – serial behaviour falsely presenting itself as individual virtue – or in unorganised outbursts, riots, etc.). On the basis of what exterior circumstances were groups to be constituted? In the first place (in temporal order) the existence of an institutional, practical group, the electors of Paris, in so far as they had constituted themselves in accordance with royal decrees and *in so far as* they were in permanent session, in spite of, or contrary to these decrees, designated the inert gathering of Parisians as possessing, *in the dimension of collective praxis*, a practical reality. The electoral assembly was the active unity, as the being-outside-itself-in-freedom, of the inert gathering.

But this totalisation was not enough: indeed *representation* consists in defining, by some procedure, an active group as a projection of the inert gathering in the inaccessible milieu of *praxis*. For example, in bourgeois democracies, elections are passive, serial processes. Each elector, of course, decides how to vote as Other and through Others; but instead of deciding in common and as a united *praxis* with the

Others, he allows it to be defined inertly and in seriality by opinion. Thus an elected assembly represents the gathering *as long as* it has not met, as long as its members are the inert product of an inert alterity and as long as crude multiplicity, as a numerical relation between the parts, expresses the relations of impotence amongst collectives and power relations in so far as these forces are forces of inertia. *But as soon as* an assembly gets organised, as soon as it constitutes its hierarchy, and defines itself (by party alliances) as a definite group (characterised by the permanence of a majority, by a complex play around a shifting majority, by the complicity of all the parties against a single individual etc.), this real *praxis* (in which the passing of laws, votes of confidence, etc., now have only the *formal* aspect of the original election as an infinite alterity of isolations, but express numerically and *symbolically* the agreements, disagreements, alliances, etc., amongst the groups in the majority) presents itself both as the faithful representation of the gathering – which being *organised*, it cannot in any way be – and as *its dialectical efficacity*. But the very fact of penetrating the gathering with a false totalised unity[3] ('Frenchmen, *your* government . . . etc.') relegates the gathering to its statute of impotence. France as a totality realises itself outside it through its government: as the free totalisation of the collective which is the nation, the government relieves individuals of the task of determining their inert sociality in a grouping. So in so far as class conflicts and social conflicts did not, through the struggles of new groups, set the gathering against the legislative body and the executive power, the existence of these bodies was necessarily a mystification which relegated the collective to inertia: powers were delegated through serial passivity, and the affirmation of our unity *there*, in the Council, condemned us *in all cases* to infinite alterity. In this sense, those 'electors of Paris' were not necessarily a factor of practical unification, indeed, they probably feared the violence of the people even more than that of the government. However, *provided that* circumstances indicate a unification *elsewhere*, they can become a *representation*, but this time as a unity which is to be reintegrated as a unifying *praxis* in the gathering itself and as a negation of impotence.

The government constituted Paris as a totality from outside. As

---

3. I am not considering the problem at the real historical level and there is no need at present to know whether the government is an organ of the dominant class. I am merely discussing its formal relation as a *representing praxis* with the 'represented' gathering.

early as 8 July, Mirabeau had reported to the National Assembly (and his speech immediately became known to the Parisians) that 35,000 men were divided between Paris and Versailles, and that 20,000 more were expected. And Louis XVI answered the deputies thus: 'I have to use my power to restore and maintain order in the capital. . . . These are my reasons for assembling troops around Paris.' And on the morning of Sunday 12 July, the city was full of posters 'by order of the king' announcing that the concentration of troops around Paris was intended to protect the city against bandits. Through these notices the city was designated for and within itself. Thus the place, as the practico-inert tension and *exis* of the Parisian gathering, was constituted by an exterior *praxis* and organised as a totality. And this totality as an object of *praxis* (the city to be besieged, disturbances to be prevented) was by itself a determination of the practico-inert field; the city was both the place, in its totalised and totalising configuration (the threat of siege determining it as a container) and the population designated in the form of materiality sealed by the military action which produced it as a confined crowd. The *rumours*, the *posters*, the *news* (especially that of Necker's departure) communicated their common designation to everyone: *each was a particle of sealed materiality.* At this level, the totality of encirclement can be described as being lived *in seriality*. It was what is known as enthusiasm: people were running in the streets, shouting, forming gatherings, and burning down the gates of the toll houses. The bond between individuals was, in its various real forms, that of alterity as the immediate discovery of oneself in the Other.

Imitation – which I have described elsewhere – is one manifestation of this alterity of quasi-reciprocity. This structure of alterity constitutes itself through the action of *common fate as a totality*[4] (that is to say, as the practical objective of the royal armies[5] – in this case it is a totality of destruction, in so far as individuals were designated by their identical

4. Destiny as a common danger to the working class (in its structure of seriality) is not totalising because the class is not the object of *one* organised, totalising undertaking: exploitation is a process which occurs both as the deliberate practice of a particular group and through the dispersal of group antagonisms.

5. Furthermore, the government does not seem to have had any very precise plans. It did not really know either what it wanted or what lay in its power. But this is not the important point: the deployment of troops and the beginning of the encirclement bore their objective meaning in themselves, that is to say, they designated the Parisian population as the unique object of a systematic and synthetic extermination campaign. It is pointless to say that no one at court wanted there to be any killing: it became, of itself and in the relation between the general

membership of the same city) *on the basis of seriality as inert flight.* By threatening to destroy seriality through *the negative order of a massacre,* the troops, as practical unities, provided the totality, which was experienced by everyone as a negation, or a *possible* negation, of seriality. This was how, through the coexistence of the two structures, the one being the possible and future negation of the other (and at the same time the negation of all in everyone), everyone continued to see himself in the Other, but saw himself there as *himself,* that is to say, in this case, as a totalisation in himself of the Parisian population, by the sabre blow or the rifle shot which would kill him. And this *situation* established what is sometimes, and improperly, called contagion or imitation, etc.: in this behaviour everyone sees his own future in the Other and, on that basis, discovers his present action in that of the Other; but, in these still inert movements, *imitation* is also *self-discovery* through doing one's own action over there in the Other, and through doing the action of the Other here, in oneself, fleeing one's own flight and that of the Other,[6] launching a single attack both through the Other and with one's own fists, without either understanding or agreement (it is exactly the opposite of an understanding), but realising and living alterity on the basis of the synthetic unity of an organised, *future* totalisation of the gathering by an outside group.

This was followed by some incidents in Paris itself, at the barricades and in the Tuileries Gardens, between military detachments and imitation gatherings (*rassemblements d'imitation*). These resulted in a new wave of serial, defensive violence, and arsenals were looted. This revolutionary response to a constantly deteriorating situation has of course the historical significance of an organised common action. But that is just what it was not. It was a collective action: everyone was forced to arm himself by others' attempts to find arms, and everyone tried to get there before the Others because, in the context of this new scarcity, everyone's attempt to get a rifle became for the Others the risk of remaining unarmed. At the same time, this response was constituted by relations of imitation and contagion, everyone finding him-

---

function of an army and this particular situation, an immediate possibility which no longer actually depended *on the intentions* of the leaders.

6. A person runs when he sees someone running: this is not because he learns *what he must do:* he discovers *what he is actually doing.* And, of course, he discovers it *only by doing it.* We encounter the same law in the group relation but with exactly the opposite meaning.

self in the Other in the very way he followed in his footsteps. These violent, efficacious gatherings, however, were entirely inorganic. Certain unities were lost or rediscovered, but this had no effect on what one might – like Durkheim but in a quite different sense – call the 'mechanical solidarity' of their members. Besides, there was an imminent danger that they would fight among themselves (the collective breaking down into reciprocities of antagonism) over the possession of a rifle. If the meaning of this passive activity is revolutionary, this is mainly because, as a result of an exterior *praxis*, the unity of impotence (inertia) had, *by sheer weight of numbers*, transformed itself into a massive force. For this crowd, which within itself was still structured in alterity, found, in its very disorganisation, an irresistible mechanical force for destroying sporadic resistance at the arsenals.

But the other factor – which was soon to create the revolutionary *praxis* of a group – was that the individual act of *arming* oneself, in so far as it was in itself a complex process whose aim, for every individual, was the defence of his own life, but whose motive force was seriality, was reflected, both *of itself* and in its result, as a double signification of freedom. In so far as everyone wanted to defend himself against the dragoons – in other words, to the extent that the government was attempting a politics of force and that this attempt at organised practice determined the entire field as practice – both as what might *help* this policy and as what might oppose it – the result, *in the field of praxis*, was that *the people of Paris armed themselves against the king*. In other words, the political *praxis* of the government alienated the passive reactions of seriality to its own practical freedom: indeed, from the point of view of this *praxis*, the passive activity of the gathering was taken from it in its passivity and inert seriality reappeared on the other side of the process of alterity as *a united group which had performed a concerted action*. This applies not only to the army leaders, who were well aware of it, but also to the Parisian population, which re-interiorised this knowledge as a structure of unity. Here again, their unity was *elsewhere*, that is, it was both past and future. It was past in that *the group had performed an action* and that the collective had recognised this action with surprise as a moment of its own passive activity: *it had been a group* – and this group defined itself by a revolutionary action which made the process irreversible. And it was future in that the weapons themselves, in so far as they had been taken for the sake of opposing concerted action by soldiers, suggested in their very materiality the possibility of concerted resistance.

The uneasiness of the electors was to create institutional groups inside gatherings, as *negative unities*. They actually decided to re-establish a militia of 48,000 citizens to be provided by the various districts. The avowed aim was to avoid disturbances. In this new moment, the future militia appeared both as raised from the gathering and as designed to fight it, whereas most of the population had no fear of 'disturbances' and, quite rightly, saw no real danger except in the deployment of troops around the capital. In so far as the districts did seriously try to form militias, these groups in formation, unlike the representative groups, helped to unify the gatherings. 'Representation', in fact, presented itself as the gathering itself in the dimension of organised *praxis* and therefore, as we have seen, tended to maintain it in its inertia. The militia, on the other hand, was an organised body designed to bring about the practical negation of the gathering: it would prevent public assemblies and disarm the citizens. In this way, it helped the gathering to perceive its reality as an organised being. For it had to forcibly prevent the development of the organised being *which armed itself* yesterday and *which would defend itself* tomorrow. Or, to express it differently, these pre-fabricated groups were anti-groups which appeared to the gathering as having the task of keeping it in its structure of serial impotence. Through them, something was manifested as *that which was negated, and had to be prevented* and every member of the gathering, in so far as he was imperatively designated in his inertia,[7] saw profound unity both as an absence beneath seriality and as a fundamental possibility. At the same time, the militia, as pre-fabricated groups, themselves represented, though negatively, a synthetic determination of the gathering. And the fact that they had been defined within the gathering externally, by institutional or semi-institutional organs, manifested itself – in so far as it was a negated negation – as what had to be destroyed by means of a unification produced internally by the gathering itself. The violent contradiction between the militia and the people, occurring within the people, produced the possibility of an internal unity as the negation of the external unity. In so far as the militia was still a *seal* applied to a multiplicity, it could contradict and dissolve itself only in a *free organisation*.

7. 'Any private person found with rifles, etc., shall take them to his own district without delay.'
'. . . Citizens are warned not to form assemblies.' (Decree of the General Assembly, 13 July.)

Freedom – as a simple positive determination of *praxis* organised on the basis of its real objectives (defence against the troops of the Prince de Lambesc) – was manifested as the necessity of dissolving necessity. On this basis, a dialectic established itself at the Hôtel de Ville between the constituted authorities, which did not wish to hand out weapons, and which equivocated and found pretexts, and the crowd, which was increasingly threatening, and which, through the behaviour of the electors, of the provost of merchants, etc., revealed itself as a *unity-exis*. When rags were found in the boxes of arms promised by Flesselles, the crowd felt that it had been *tricked* – in other words, it interiorised Flesselles' actions and saw them, *not in seriality*, but in opposition to seriality as a sort of passive synthesis. The process of *trickery*, in fact, belongs in the context of an antagonistic relation of reciprocity. In tricking the crowd,[8] Flesselles gave a sort of *personal* unity to the flight into alterity; and this personal unity was a necessary characteristic of the anger which expressed and, for the gathering itself, revealed it. Everyone reacted in a new way: not as an individual, nor as an Other, but as an individual incarnation of the common person. There was nothing magical in this new reaction: it merely expressed the re-interiorisation of a reciprocity.

From this moment on, there is something which is neither group nor series, but what Malraux, in *Days of Hope*,[8a] called the Apocalypse – that is to say, the dissolution of the series into a fused group. And this group, though still unstructured, that is to say, entirely *amorphous*, is characterised by being the direct opposite of alterity. In a serial relation, in fact, unity as the formula (*Raison*) of the series is always *elsewhere*, whereas in the Apocalypse, though seriality still exists at least as a process which is about to disappear, and although it always may re-appear, synthetic unity is always *here*. Or, to put the same point in another way, throughout a city, at every moment, in each partial process, the part is entirely involved and the movement of the city is fulfilled and signified in it. 'By evening,' wrote Montjoye, 'Paris was a new city. Regular cannon shots reminded the people to be on their guard. And added to the noise of the cannon there were bells sounding a continuous alarm. The sixty churches where the residents had

8. It appears that he had acted in good faith, but this is not very important. It is not that the crowd *thought* it was being duped: but that it *was*.

8a. André Malraux, *L'Espoir*, Paris, 1937, translated as *Days of Hope*, London, 1938.

gathered were overflowing with people. Everyone there was an orator.'[9]

The city was a fused group. We shall soon see how this differs from seriality. But first we must make it clear that it would congeal into a collective if it were not structured in a temporal development, the speed and duration of which obviously depend on the circumstances and situation. A fused group is in fact still a series, negating itself in re-interiorising exterior negations; in other words, in this moment there is no distinction between the positive itself (the group in formation) and this self-negating negation (the series in dissolution). It can be shown that the initial structuration (in so far as it comes from the group itself) affected *one district*, as a part of a fluid whole, *with its practico-inert structure*. The Saint-Antoine district had always lived *in the shadow* of the Bastille: that black fortress was a threat, not so much because it was a prison as because of its cannons. It was the symbol of repressive power, as the boundary of a poverty-stricken and unsettled district. Moreover, skirmishes and repressed uprisings – in particular the bloody repression in April (the Réveillon affair) – had remained inside the gathering itself as an *exis* (a collective memory was passing into the common structure – a point to which we shall have to return).

For the moment, I am not even taking into account the explosiveness which this *exis* might derive from the energy released by the dissolution of bonds of impotence. The important point as far as the genesis of an active group is concerned, is that this *exis actually* structured a route; it was primarily a hodological determination of the lived space of the district. And this route was negative: it was the opportunity for troops to enter the district by coming from the west and the north-west in order to massacre people there (as in April).[10] In other words, the practico-inert unity of the field was determined at the

---

9. In *L'ami du Roi*, third edition, p. 70.

10. The Réveillon affair also proves that the different districts were opposed and already limited by a certain *social tension*, that is to say, by class conflicts. It was the practice of Réveillon, one of the precursors of the nineteenth-century French industrialists – a tough, rapacious, and arrogant man – that provoked disturbances among the workers. Conversely, newspapers owned by 'middle' bourgeois like Hardy show that the *military* isolation of the district (always liable to be cut off from the others and subjected to looting or massacre) was based on social isolation: 'The Parisians,' wrote Hardy, 'are frightened of some kind of popular insurrection, even to the point of shutting their shops in some areas . . . A considerable portion of the so-called workers of this suburb, stirred up by bandits against a very rich manufacturer of furniture paper, named Réveillon . . .'

moment in which seriality was in the process of dissolution, as the possible act of penetration by the Other, that is to say, by free hostile organisation. At the same time, this possibility actualised the threat of the Bastille: it was the possibility that the district's inhabitants would be *caught in the cross-fire*. And this possibility refers back to its fundamental social separation (which I have mentioned in the last footnote), which was also its negative unity. Of course, all this was still merely lived in anxiety during the first few days of July. But as soon as the news of the intervention of the troops at the Tuileries arrived in Saint-Antoine, it actualised the possibility of a special massacre in the district. In fact, the news, reported by Others and

---

The configuration of the place was a perfect expression of the social condition of its inhabitants. However, the district was not constituted *solely* of the poor, for the structures of a great industrial city did not yet exist. But the *workers* (in so far as they were working in the first factories, and had therefore been uprooted from the craftsman class by the new conditions) were much more numerous there than elsewhere and, generally speaking, most of the residents belonged to the less fortunate classes. It should also be noted that the Réveillon riots are cases of serial violence. At the beginning, there was not even any violence and workers could be seen crossing Paris in companies of five or six hundred men. In these regiments of hunger, *unity* as a negative determination of the whole could already be detected. But at the same time they were still gatherings of inertia: there was no structuration (no differentiation of functions), and no *common* action. For the individual troop, the procession of workers involved neither some particular action, nor a determination of plurality as such: two hundred more or less would not make any difference. Their number was pure exteriority and was not defined by the group in accordance with its *praxis*, and it therefore remained in a state of absolute materiality: pure quantity. Naturally, the unity of the gathering on the march, in so far as it was its real reason, was *seriality*. Even if, from the depths of the initial and contagional march, negative unity as a future totality was already occasioning *being-together* (*être-ensemble*) (that is to say, everyone's non-serial relation to the group as a *milieu of freedom*) as a possibility which was perceived in seriality and which presented itself as the negation of seriality, *the objective* of the march was still indeterminate: it appeared both as seriality itself as a reaction to the situation, and as an equally serial attempt at *display*. Everyone agreed that these groups were perfectly peaceful and that they *never resorted to violence*; yet everyone carried a stick. The Other (the petty bourgeois who was made a comprehensive witness by this passive activity) was presented with the contradictory character of the condition of the working-class: when he saw the gathering go past, he could see both their poverty and their strength. But this strength, which still derived from their number, and this poverty (whose characteristic of repetition in identity, or alterity, will strike the Other), consequently make the gathering on the march, in its practico-inert structure, at best a sort of serial exploitation of seriality.

believed in so far as it was Other, had to be perceived, in the practico-inert, as the truth of the district as Other, that is to say, in so far as it presented itself through Others as an other event, affecting Others. But this very alterity was a sign: this clash in the middle of Paris was simply a determination to take repression to extremes in so far as it was a sign – that is to say, as the first action in the district least exposed to this kind of action. Thus the *real* (but future) *meaning* (*signification*) of the Tuileries affair was the destruction of the Quartier Saint-Antoine, defined by the recent schemata of the Réveillon affair. Or, to be more accurate from the serial point of view, the Quartier Saint-Antoine was exterminated in the future by the Prince de Lambesc.

Of course, what we encounter here is, once again, the designation of the district by things and by its topographical configuration, as these would be used in the organised action of an exterior enemy, as the particularisation of a general development. However, there is a considerable difference. In so far as things, in this case, presented themselves as destiny (as instruments of the organised action which was going to destroy the district) and in so far as the individuals in the gathering were obliged to negate them as such, they defined themselves for everyone within this negation – violent, but still purely subjective (*passionnelle*) – as an instrumentality capable of being turned against the Others by a free, organised *praxis*. This means that their instrumentality for the enemy, once negated, revealed itself as a counter-finality for the enemy. But this counter-finality, as a pure abstract possibility, required a free, common organisation in order to be actualised and developed. From the point of view of this still unactualised aspect of destiny, organised by the Other and negated, what is new in relation to the characteristics already discussed is that the practico-inert structure of the district, as a negated destiny, realises synthetically, and as a material exigency (which only practical freedom can bring out) an objective relation of differentiation within the fused group. In other words, the practico-inert structure not only makes the fused group, through everyone, the unity of all, but also makes it a *structured* unity; materially and in inertia it suggests an initial differentiation of functions, a division of labour; that is to say, it presents everyone with the condition necessary for preventing the fused group from relapsing into a gathering. In fact, *suffered* destiny shows us the gathering caught in cross-fire, that is to say, subjected to the *combined* action of the two forces of extermination situated at either end of the district. Turned back into negativity, it points to the unity of this interiorised duality as a double movement of struggle *within the unity* of an organisation defined in its practice both by the place as passive activity and by hostile organisation in so far as it is negated. Armed men would be needed to defend the district against the royal troops, and others to defend it against the Bastille. And the Bastille, in turn, in the context of scarcity, revealed the primary exigency of common freedom: if the district was to be defended against the soldiers, they would have to get some arms; there were not enough *in the district*, but there were plenty in the Bastille. The Bastille became the common interest in so far as it *both could be and had to be* not only disarmed, but also made a source of supply of arms, and, perhaps, be turned against the enemies from the west – all in a single action. The urgency then was due to scarcity of time: the enemy was not there but he might arrive at any minute. The task defined itself for everyone as the pressing revelation of a frightening common freedom. Naturally, the action itself had its own weight, its schemes and even a model derived from the past: it appeared through the ambivalence of the relations between the Parisian population and the constituted bodies. The practice of the crowd in front of the Hôtel de Ville during the past few days had been partly solicitous and partly threatening, and, to this extent, the objective to be attained (getting arms wherever they could be found) defined itself through a predetermined operation. Yet the social structure of the group in formation (and the character of the repression it had already suffered), in addition to that of the hostile group (soldiers, some of them foreigners, and commanded by a noble officer) helped to give the operation a more uncertain character; that is to say, these two structures, in their synthetic relation, defined a limited field of possibilities in which the explosion of the still passivised attitude (demand-exigency) and the appearance of organised action *as violence* appeared as the probable future of the ambivalent task.

This example shows a group being constituted by the liquidation of an inert seriality under the pressure of definite material circumstances, in so far as particular practico-inert structures of the environment were synthetically united to designate it, that is to say, in so far as its practice was inscribed in things as an inert idea. But in order that the city or section should become totalising totalities – when, in other circumstances, the same realities might be lived as 'collectives' – they had to be constituted as such by the external action of another organised group. The population would constitute itself as a defensive organisation in so far as it was threatened through things by an organisation which aimed at its negative totalisation (through annihilation). Should we therefore say that groups in the process of constitution are determined as the liquidation of a serial structure in so far as this self-determination is conditioned by the transcendent (*transcendante*) action of one or more already constituted groups? The answer is both yes and no. The proposition is true – it conforms to practical experience – in so far as it suggests a sort of serial conditioning of groups in the domain of the Other. And as we shall see, the moment of this infinite conditioning does exist. Of course, very often – as in the example we have been discussing – a collective derives its possibilities of self-determination into a group from its *antagonistic* relations with an already constituted group or with a person representing this group. Nevertheless, the unity of self-determination through all the relations described comes to the collective through the Other in alterity as an *other structure* (*structure autre*) of the gathering, and as needing to *be realised by self-determination*. In fact, it was not the intention of the two reciprocal actions to constitute a group; the objective was always other and the antagonism was based on the conflict of needs, interests, etc. Thus the developing group is not constituted intentionally by the *praxis* of the Other and it is led to self-determination through this practice (which may, for example, be one of extermination) and *through* reorganisation of the environment by the Other, in so far as *the unity of the other praxis* conditions it as the negation of its own unity (or as totalisation through systematic destruction). In this sense, though the unity of the group is its own product and is always here, wherever its members act (at least abstractly and in theory), it is also characterised by a structure of flight, since the induction (*l'occasion inductive*) proceeds from the outside inwards without being either necessarily or generally desired by other groups.

But the structure of seriality, as *one* of the relations between groups, should not detain us any longer. It was only necessary to observe that synthetic self-determination is frequently the practical reinteriorisation, as the negation of the negation, of the unity constituted by the other *praxis*. The reason for using the example of the Fourteenth of July is that it shows how a new regroupment dissolves a habitual seriality into the homogeneity of a fused city: the constituted reality had ceased to exist long ago and for a time the violence of the danger and the pressure (what Jaurès called a historical *fever*) overcame social heterogeneities. Nothing had been foreseen which might constitute the unity of the city (except as a feudal 'good city'), no organ of unification, no instrument had been left at the disposal of the future group. On the contrary, it was intended to prevent it from existing as such. The Versailles Assembly had to be put at the mercy of the aristocracy by being isolated from the city. But the very precautions taken against the possible unity became a future of projected and shunned unity for the gathering, and therefore a negative ferment. Unity proceeded from one to another as an alienation of necessity to freedom, that is to say, as *Other* than the enemy's project and as an *other result* (*resultat autre*) of his *praxis*. This type of group (a homogeneity of fusion) produces itself as its own idea (we shall see what this means later): it is (by totalising extension) *the sovereign nation*.

In this conception of a fused totality, *combined with the old conception of electoral assemblies* (parasites of the electoral body as a practico-inert thing), we will find the origin of the contradictions which split the ideology of the Constituent Assembly and, particularly, of its theoretician Sieyès. But we might have explained the formation of other groups by self-determination, no longer as negatively defined by a *praxis* which, from the outside, makes them the antagonists of certain Other groups, but as induced to determine themselves by the marginal existence of a multiplicity of organised groups, whether institutional or not, as determinations of the practico-inert field by a common action. In this sense every group to constitute itself is singled out as a group through seriality by the synthetic relations amongst other groups, *even* if these relations do not affect it directly. Of course a group will constitute itself only on the basis of specific circumstances, directly or indirectly connected with the life or death of organisms. But the practical movement of organisation, in so far as it transcends its conditions towards its objectives, actualises an external determination, which the gathering has already interiorised as a fantom possibility of producing itself in the field of freedom.

3 The Third Party and the Group

Thus groups usually come to gatherings from groups; they may also arise within a larger group, as the recapture of unity in a partial or generalised petrification. However, it should be observed that worked matter, in so far as it mediates between the most varied activities (individual, collective, or common), may spontaneously present itself in the practico-inert field as a counter-finality, with the appearances of a negative totalisation of human multiplicity, although no concerted *praxis* presided over the configuration. In this way, it defines the place and time of self-determination negatively and in multiplicity. In fact, it almost always happens like this, *at least in part*; for example, the characteristics of materiality (as topographical configuration, as sociality of inertia, as transcended past or as *exis*) did, as we have seen, amplify and divert the vacillating, dangerous policy of the government (that is to say, they gave a character of brutal force to what in reality could only be a policy of weakness – even if the objective was violent oppression). In other words, it is always possible for materiality, as a worked Thing, to posit itself as essential through the inessentiality of separated men, and, in the seriality of inert-men, to constitute an imperceptible and omnipresent structure of free practical unity. Basically this means that scarcity itself, as a tension of the polyvalent practical field, at the same time as constituting man as the other species, determines, in the same field, an undifferentiated (valid for any kind of grouping) possibility of unifying synthesis. And, from this point of view, we encounter what we found before: there is one level of reality at which unity comes to the group through groups as the interiorisation of a practical process of revelation and of the serial unity of multiplicities of groupings; and there is another level at which the unity of the group is reflected to the gathering on the basis of the inert unity (or passive synthesis) of worked matter, that is to say, the level at which the unity of the individual *praxis*, joined with other unities in the object, is reinteriorised by the gathering as a possible structure of common unity. Of course, this possibility of the designation-exigency of a group by worked matter arises in specific conditions (which may, in turn, require the marginal co-existence of other groups). In other words, the *historical* problem of the priority of the group over the gathering (or of the gathering over the group) is, in this context, a *metaphysical* problem, devoid of meaning.

In fact, however, this is not the real problem. And, in order to determine whether the transition from a gathering to a group possesses a dialectical intelligibility, it is not necessary to know whether the group derives its unity of self-determination as its *own possibility* from the practico-inert synthesis as a conducting medium for other common actions, or as providing in itself a model of a practico-inert community of action on the basis of the dispersal of the individuals who transform it. We have established that a group only arises if it is *designated* through the field of passive activity. But this designation *is received by a gathering*, which can receive it only in seriality (that is to say, in the flight of the Other Elsewhere). The real problem of structural intelligibility, therefore, is this: what are the conditions for a series, on the basis of given circumstances, to actualise a structure of practical unity which, though really determining it, as a material meaning (*signification*) (or the unitary *praxis* of a group), must in principle elude it, in so far as milieux of seriality are structured so that they can refract unity only in the infinite flight of the facets of recurrence, as the absolute Elsewhere, that is to say, as the Other or as a series totalised in the abstract, by a passage to the limit? It is not enough that unity is possible: it is also necessary that the instruments for wresting it from recurrence should be present in the collective itself. And this is the second, and more important, point which we must examine.

As we have seen in relation to class, it is possible for unity, as an empty, formal totality which negates identity, to enter, under certain conditions, into contradiction with the seriality of impotence. We are not talking about concepts here, and it must not be supposed that the concept of unity will, through its opposition to the concept of alterity, develop from being abstract and negative into a concrete notion of positive unification. This simply means that the *exis* of serial unity is lived through multiple relations of reciprocity (comradeship of labour, bonds in the residential collective, the close links of small groups which are themselves thrown into seriality, families, societies, etc.), which tend through their own free development to produce it as a synthetic foundation of all concrete relations (labour, belonging to the same class, etc., form the basis of friendships; in this way, the unitary basis arises *in these relations* as the mirage of a free foundation for all choices). But, at the same time, confronted by Destiny and the Exigencies of the practico-inert field, the same unity as a serial structure of alterity is revealed as fundamental impotence (*assuming* we can ignore synthetic organisations) and reciprocity is encountered again, as the fleeting, inert dependence of everyone on the series, and of everyone, in his place in the series, on everyone else. This contradiction cannot take us very far, since unity arises here only to dissolve as an illusion; *in practice* it does not much matter whether, at least as a moment of illusion, it has a place marked out for it in serial experience. Unity cannot present itself, at least initially, as the objective possibility of groupment (that is to say, as the possibility of negating itself as gathering) because, at the moment where reality is *impossible*, the inert gathering presents itself as a concrete truth whose unity is an abstract appearance. Apart from this, the structure of this unity is indeterminate, since it does not present itself in terms of a practical objective, but rather as fundamental class-being, in so far as individual relations of free reciprocity cause it to appear as the foundation of individual choices.

The importance of the contradiction we are describing lies elsewhere: its function, in effect, is to lead us, in our dialectical investigation, back from the moment of the constitution of groups, to the ternary relations of free, individual action, of free reciprocity, and of the mediating third party. In other words, those relations which appeared to us as self-mystifying freedoms in the field of passive activity, are the only possibilities of making intelligible the appearance of a constituted *praxis*, in and against the passive field. Mystified, alienated, and cheated, these free, practical developments, the source of individual, serial impotence, are still actual synthetic actions, and are still capable of unifying – from the individual point of view, admittedly – any multiplicity that appears in the practical field. And though I claim that the totalising totality of the environment indicates a possible unity as the self-determination of every individual, it is true that it indicates it in the milieu of seriality, but it does it for everyone's free, dialectical actions in so far as they are for themselves dialectical translucidities. But the fact of everyone being affected by the possibility of union with all would have very little importance if this designation affected people only in their isolation or their relations of reciprocity. Indeed, unity could not appear as the omnipresent reality of a seriality in the process of total liquidation unless it affected everyone in his third-party relations with Others, which constitute one of the structures of his existence *in freedom*. In fact, as we have seen, everyone is *also* a *third party* in relation to reciprocal relations between other individuals, and this means that he totalises this relation in his *praxis* on the basis of material meanings (*significations*) and indications, uniting the individual terms of the relation as *instruments* serving a partial end. The third party is submerged in seriality, being structured *a priori* as the Other, and therefore as Other than everyone and Other than us, so that his internal-external relation of free alterity in relation to reciprocity gets lost in serial alterity. Nevertheless, it *does* exist – it is every one of us – as alienated freedom revealing itself in lived alienation as inessential.

Now, by constituting the worked Thing as a totalising totality, *the common danger* does not at first eliminate seriality, either at the level of the isolated individual, or at that of reciprocity: it tears everyone away from his Other-Being *in so far as he is a third party* in relation to a certain constellation of reciprocities; in short, it frees the ternary relation as a free inter-individual reality, as an immediate human relation. Through the third party, in effect, practical unity, as the negation of a threatening organised *praxis*, reveals itself *through* the constellation of reciprocities. From a structural point of view, the third party is the human mediation through which the multiplicity of epicentres and ends (identical and separate) organises itself *directly*, as determined by a synthetic objective. However, according to circumstances, this object will either fall outside the practical ends of the third party, or partially overlap with them, or contradict them, or harmonise with them, or subordinate them to itself, or subordinate itself to them. But if the practical unity of surrounding materiality constitutes the multiplicity, externally and negatively, as a totality, the objective of the third party produces itself for him as a *common* objective, and the plurality of epicentres reveals itself to him as unified by a *common* exigency (or *common praxis*), because it *decodes* serial multiplicity *in terms of a community which is already inscribed in things*, in the manner of a passive idea or a totalising destiny.

As the possibility of repression in the Quartier Saint-Antoine appeared increasingly probable, residents of this district, *seen as third parties*, were directly threatened. However, this threat did not apply to them as 'accidental individuals': they were not being sought for their individual activities (like a criminal in hiding). On the other hand, no one wanted to kill or imprison them as *Other*, that is to say, as general individuals (in the way that price rises threaten every wage-earner in a given category *as* a wage-earner of that category). Rather, they are threatened as *a moment* of a punitive campaign which will develop dialectically, as a free organised action, whose successive moments are foreseen by the enemy. In other words, it was their political and social activity, their condition, the location of their homes (in relation to the *military exercise*), the urgency, from the enemy's point of view, of beginning 'flushing out' somewhere, the importance of their neighbours, their activities, etc., which had been or would be synthetically united by a single totalising process which would be realised in its dialectical unity by realising the progressive and synthetic unity of the district *by annihilating it*. At this level, everyone, as a *third party*, became incapable of distinguishing his own safety from that of the Others.

This was not an issue of altruism and egoism; such behaviour, in so far as it exists in this very schematic form, constitutes itself on the basis of existing circumstances and it preserves human relations which are engraved in the practico-inert field, in transcending them. It is easy to see how a neo-positivist might interpret the new statute of the third party: in a situation of looting, disturbances, and sporadic riots (he would say) the 'accidental', 'serial' (in pseudo-generality) or universal individual might still have a chance of defending himself on his own; but if he was *concretely* threatened as a certain moment of a repressive campaign which unified the district by the development of totalising action, he would no longer have any such opportunity. He would have to defend himself as a concrete part of the totalised totality, that is to say, no one would have any hope apart from the totalising negation (through the union of all) of the destructive operation. But this kind of rationalism is not dialectical, and, though Marxists sometimes make use of it, its analytical, utilitarian origins are quite apparent. The truth is not that the campaign of repression linked individual risks to the risks run by everyone; it is that, for every third party, it constituted a statute (which we will define below), by producing his own possibility of being killed or imprisoned as a specification of the common danger, that is to say, as a foreseen and controlled element of the programme of extermination.

We must be quite clear about this: the totalisation which the third party receives from outside determines him through a new contradiction. His original structure as a third party expresses, in effect, simply the practical power of unifying any multiplicity within his own field of action, that is to say, of totalising it through a transcendence towards his own ends. As such, it can therefore serve as one moment of the mediation we are looking for: in his own activity (as a shopkeeper, worker, etc.), every resident of the Quartier Saint-Antoine district totalised his district in principle ('the customers', 'the comrades', etc.). But, at the same time, his *real membership* of the district was serial in character and manifested its inertia of alterity. In this connection, it is easy to make the mistake of believing in the homogeneity of their statutes on the ground that they concern the relations between *one* man and *one* multiplicity. He actually totalises the district in so far as he is not part of the totality, and the district serialises him in so far as he lives in it. But if the totalising power of the third party produces, as the revelation of an objective possibility, the perception of the district as *now* being a totality in danger, he will find himself thereby designated by this threat as integrated into the totality which he has totalised. But this requires mediation: to begin with, in fact, the free organisation of the practical field presupposes a transcendence and it is impossible for this transcendence itself to feature in the field as transcended; then, as I have said, the threat is perceived in Others as totalising, but at first it affects his *being-resident*, and does so as *panic*, in his serial impotence. The contradiction between contagious processes as a serial realisation of the common threat and the perception of the human totality as unified negatively (*en creux*) by this threat, therefore resides in everyone (since everyone *is also* the third party).

The contradiction can be transcended only in action. This is the reason which caused the Parisians to go out on to the streets in the critical hours of the Revolution, and to constitute gatherings, anywhere, anyhow. These gatherings, which were still serial but already quasi-intentional[11], were to become groups through their internal tension, and in a passive activity which changed, in accordance with strict rules proper to each event, into a common action. In other words, the third party, designated by the situation, which he revealed through the unification of his practical field, as an integral part of a whole, realised this whole without integrating himself into it and uneasily discovered his own absence in it as a risk of death. The object of the gathering was to overcome this malaise by *practically* integrating everyone by *praxis*. But no one could determine this objective clearly, since everyone joined the gathering *both* as Other, as the sovereign organiser of the practical field, *and* as a part required by a totality. Now, as we shall see later, seriality does in practice *tend* to effect an initial integration. We have already seen how the direct action of the totalising totality (the hostile group as a threat) on the practico-inert gathering immediately produced contagious reactions, that is to say, passive actions realising themselves through the free activity of individuals in so far as it was alienated, and in so far as they were subjected, by the necessity of freedom, to the laws of the Other. We should remember one of the most common episodes in these gatherings: a march,

---

11. People did not come out to meet particular individuals, or to obey some order, or to carry out some definite task: they went to a particular public place *in the knowledge* that they would find a lot of other people there who had come under the same conditions and whose objective was otherwise indeterminate.

followed by panic, flight, and regroupment (followed perhaps by an organised struggle). The panic was both the new practical incarnation of the Other and a practico-inert process realising itself through the alienation of free reciprocities. Everyone freely fled the flight of the Other, which means that the Other was embodied in everyone as imperative flight.

But as well as being Other, everyone is also a third party: as a third party, he organises the constellation which surrounds him, he attributes a free, totalising meaning to flight, as the violence of inertia on the basis of the overall situation. In so far as he becomes a third party, he can no longer grasp the serial structure of flight: he perceives the panic as the adaptation of a totality to a total threat. For him, it is neither Others, nor a few individuals, who flee: instead, flight, conceived as a common *praxis* reacting to a common threat, *becomes flight* as an active totality. But this simple unification would only be abstract, external and theoretical, if, for example, he observed these events from his window. Here, seriality helps: at the moment in which the third party grasps the flight, from outside, as an organised reaction, he lives it through himself, in serial imitation and as alterity. The two contradictory aspects of the Other and of the third party are now directly opposed in the indissoluble unity of a *praxis*. And the materiality of his membership of the series and of his passive activity gives the individual a statute which prevents him from unifying the multiplicity from outside; the movement of practical integration as freedom returns to him, a human thing in flight, and *signifies* him; the synthetic movement which starts from him cannot really enclose him, but at any rate it designates his integration as a *task to be done*. In the context of this new task, every third party as such will seek in himself the dissolution into free common activity of his serial being. The activity of the group turns back on his passive activity; for him, flight, which began as a contagious phenomenon, becomes a common, organised action, through his individual *praxis*, and in so far as he has unified the group in his practical field, with its own objective and, therefore, having to *regulate itself*, to adjust the means to the end, etc. For example, it may become a limited retreat leading to an offensive comeback etc. And this transformation would not be a change in knowledge or perception; it would be a real change, in himself, of inert activity into collective action. At this moment, he is *sovereign*, that is to say, he becomes, through the change of *praxis*, the organiser of common *praxis*. It is not that he wishes it; he simply *becomes it*; his own flight, in effect, realises the practical unity of all *in him*. This particular structure derives from the particular link which unites the third party to the gathering which is being destroyed, and it makes him both the transcendent synthetic unification (over which everyone is supreme in the practical field) and a term which is *signified* in immanence by the circular movement of its own totalisation. Transcendent, because the unification of all by the agent does not come to an end with his real integration into the totality; and immanent because the serial contagion can dissolve in him only in favour of the unity of the whole. On the other hand, his *praxis* is no longer in him as that of an Other, any more than it is his own reality for Others: in so far as seriality as contagion is liquidated in the resumption into freedom of the passive movement, his *praxis* is *his own* in himself, as the free development in a single individual of the action of the entire group which is in the process of formation (and, consequently, of everyone in so far as common unity serves as a mediation between everyone and the third party). It is on this basis that his own action as sovereign (simultaneously unique and shared) lays down its laws in him and in everyone merely by its development. Just now, he was fleeing because *everyone else* was fleeing. Now he shouts, 'Stop!', because he is stopping and because stopping and giving the order to stop are identical in that the action develops in him and in everyone through the imperative organisation of its moments.

It must be understood that, at this instant, the third party unifies the gathered multiplicity and makes it a totality, as when he unifies the Others in his practical field, as, for example, to take a readily intelligible case, when, in my perceptual *praxis*, I see the gathering of people waiting for the bus *as a group*, and consequently say to myself, 'There are too many of them, I'll take the underground.' (Thus this group-object, seen in relation to my own aim – finding a way of getting to work – and defined in these terms, becomes in its turn an objective motivation, that is to say, in the unity of my immediate project, it tends to counteract the slight preference which I have always had for travelling by bus.) The difference is that the group of passengers appears to me as an object, as a totalised totality. In effect, my project totalises them through its transcendence: to notice roughly how many there are, or to estimate it according to the density of the gathering, is to define it in my practical temporalisation by its co-efficient of adversity, that is to say, to define it in terms of how long I would have to wait before getting a seat on a bus. Besides, as we have seen, I pass from the illusion of polyvalent unity, as an initial synthetic perception, to the discovery of seriality, because the serial order which will force me to join a queue and perhaps arrive late outlines itself within my very perception of the group.

On the other hand, I have sometimes had the experience of *group-subjects*, which may be either terrifying or helpful, and for which I am an object to be preserved, or destroyed; and I have a sense of being transcended by their untranscendable transcendence (*transcendance*). This is what happens to the soldier who suddenly finds himself alone in the midst of the enemy, or to a half-dead mountaineer being carried down the mountain on a stretcher by a rescue team. Here, the unification is effected in the same way and in *my* practical field. But this unification does not disappear when confronted with passive seriality: on the contrary, on the basis of the common action of the group, it has the effect of revealing to me a unifying unity which does not depend on my own unification and which, suddenly, by its *numerical* strength, invests, penetrates and metamorphoses my own practical field, to the point of putting my own freedom in question (not in its inalienable existence, but in its ever changing or alienable objectification). This group is not an object in any way and, in fact, *I never see it*; I totalise it *in so far as it sees me*, in so far as its *praxis* takes me as a means or an end.

There are also some intermediate forms: an emperor's pretorian guard might, according to circumstances, be either his worked Thing, his human tool or, if he is afraid of being assassinated, a community-subject concealed behind simulated objectivity. Any transition from one form to an other is possible. But the gathering transformed *by me* into *my* group does not have either of these two forms; nor does it have any of the intermediate ones. However, it is easy to see how it presents itself: as a sort of synthetic transcendence of the group-object and the group-subject of the practical field. If, on this basis, I perceive *flight* as a common activity, totalisation will take place: the immediate structure of membership of the fused group is the real totalisation of all these movements by *the same which is in me*. In simple terms of perception, I can *see* the flight *of the group*, which is *my* flight, because, in the dialectical development of my *praxis*, I unite and co-ordinate similar or reciprocal actions (people *helping* one another to flee or to defend themselves). There is, therefore, something resembling one object fleeing on these hundred pairs of legs. And it really would be an object if I did not flee from its flight. But in fact, to the extent that I discover it through *our* flight, it is necessary that my synthesis should, in the end, turn back on me and integrate me entirely as a part of it. But this is impossible, because a totalising *praxis* cannot totalise itself as a totalised element. Thus, through the group, I indicate myself as a *necessary culmination* of the totalising action; but this operational indication never actually has its effect. (We shall deal with this fundamental structure at greater length later.) Thus I am neither totally integrated into the group, which has been revealed and actualised through *praxis*, nor totally transcendent (*transcendant*). I am not a part of a totality-object and, for me, there is no transcendent (*transcendant*) totality-object: the group is not in fact *my* object; it is the common structure of my action. In material terms, this is often expressed by the fact that I cannot really effect a total (for example, perceptual) synthesis of the group in so far as it is my environment: I can see my neighbours, or, turning my head, the people behind me, but I can never see them all *at once*, whereas I synthesise the marching of everyone, both behind and ahead of me, through *my own marching*.

Thus one thing which the group has in common with the group-subject of which we spoke earlier is that the synthetic totalisation which I effect in *my* field through *my* praxis reveals to me an interior unity independent of this totalisation itself, that is to say, a unity which has constituted (or is constituting) itself spontaneously and outside it. Flight, as the unity of the group, is a unity independent of an objectifying totalisation: it is simply revealed through it. But, conversely, I could not take the group as a community-subject of which I am the object (the means, for example): I have discovered that its flight, in it and in me, is the same; in other words, the practical unity which my totalisation reveals and which negates the objectivity of the group thereby negates my own in relation to the group, since this practical unity is *the same* (not in me *and* it, but *in us*). In the same way, if the pure, formal totalisation of multiplicity in my perceptual field revealed nothing but a practical unity which eluded it, this would be because this unity was in fact based on some deeper *praxis*: I come to the group as its group activity, and constitute it as an activity in so far as the group comes to me as my group activity, as my own *group existence*. The characteristic of the tension of interiority between the group (apart from me) and *myself inside it* is that in reciprocity we are simultaneously both quasi-object and quasi-subject, for and through each other.

4   *The Mediation of Reciprocity: the Transcendence-Immanence Tension*

But it is a common error of many sociologists to stop at this point and treat the group as a binary relation (individual-community), whereas, in reality, it is a ternary relation. Indeed, this is something that no picture or sculpture could convey directly, in that the individual, *as a third party*, is connected, in the unity of a single *praxis* (and therefore of a single perceptual vista), with the unity of individuals as inseparable moments of a non-totalised totalisation, and with each of them as *a third party*, that is to say, through the mediation of the group. In terms of perception, I perceive the group as *my* common reality, and, simultaneously, as a mediation between me and every other third party. I say *every third party* deliberately: whatever relations of simple reciprocity (helping, training a new neighbour or comrade, etc.) there are within the common action, these relations, though transfigured by their being-in-a-group, are not constitutive. And I also say: the members of the group are *third parties*, which means that each of them totalises the reciprocities of others. And the relation of one third party to another has nothing to do with alterity: since the group is the practical milieu of this relation, it must be a human relation (with crucial importance for the differentiations of the group), which we shall call mediated reciprocity. And, as we shall see, this mediation is dual, in that it is both the mediation of the group between third parties and the mediation of each third party between the group and the other third parties.

First moment of mediation. – Consider a regroupment behind some shelter, after a flight. Some individuals will not take part in it: the action of the enemy will have cut them off completely from any synthetic community. For them, seriality itself, which began in panic, has culminated in molecular exteriority: the individual, alone, cut off from Others, continues his flight, loses his way, hides in a cellar, gives himself up, etc. But we should not suppose that he *has revealed his cowardliness*. Cowardliness is a serial feeling, and, in isolation, the absent Other still determines it. But in any case – and this is the important point – every one of the third parties who are regrouping knows that the group will be less numerous than the gathering. This knowledge might be derived from experience, and in any case with certainty from his immediately preceding perception: the third party has seen the practico-inert field from which he has torn himself away reforming itself at the horizon through the flight of certain Others who will never return. When he goes back to join those who are planning to resist, his fate depends on the number of the resisters and is revealed to him by a rough estimate of this number. It is in the same way – though, as we shall see, in an entirely different structure of being – that everyone calculates the duration of his wait by the density of the serial gathering waiting for the bus. At most, the *praxis* may negate itself: this is what happens, for example, if the resisting forces are objectively excessively inferior to the enemy forces. And *the risk* run by the third party in his organic, personal reality reveals itself in objectivity as directly connected to the risks of failure which threaten collective *praxis,* and as inversely proportional to its perceived *density* (as the initial estimate of the multiplicity as power).

But, while I am on my way to join up with the central core of resisters, who are sheltering behind some building, I happen to be in the practical field of another third party, who is coming out of another street and approaching the same group with the same purpose. And the arrival of this third party at the group has real, objective links with my own approach: for me he increases the multiplicity of resisters, thereby increasing the chances of success and diminishing my personal risks. This is the joyful surprise which all the assembled demonstrators feel when, on the occasion of a demonstration which has been forbidden by the police, they see individuals and small groups converging from every direction, *more numerous than they had expected,* and representing *hope* to everyone. On the other hand, I am *for them exactly* what they are for me. This newcomer joins a group of 100 *through me* in so far as the group which I join will have 100 *through him.* Serially (or, as we shall see, from the point of view of the organisers, if there are any), we arrive at the group as *two* units. Through us, there will be 100 rather than 98. But for each of us (both me and the other third party) we are, reciprocally, each by the other (and, as we shall see, by all the Others) the 99th. To put it another way, each of us is the 100th of the Other. Thus it is clearly a matter of reciprocity. I see approaching me the number which I form by adding myself to the group and I see it through the arrival of the Other; at the same time, *because of this,* the group is increased in me and in the Other, by me and by the Other, in me through the Other and through me in the Other. And this reciprocity is mediated, because the action of each of us is the counterpart of that of the Other through his numerical objectification in the group. Thus the group is the mediation.

We have already discussed certain mediations *by an object*: in work, there are reciprocities which are mediated by the tool and the object to be produced. My act takes on meaning, in inert materiality, only if the act of the Other has already informed this materiality, has given it some initial meanings. If, however, we have not emphasised the mediating character of the practico-inert field, this is because its mediation is *passive*: it is the pure milieu in which actions meet. But the mediation of the third party by the group is of a different kind: first, of course, the bond between the worker and the material field is univocal; my bond with the group (as the link of the other third party) is one of interiority. When I approach it to join it, I am already *part of it*. We have seen in what sense: as a limit of totalisation, as an impracticable task which has to be done. And, from this point of view, the present multiplicity of the group (to the extent that it has been roughly estimated) constitutes me objectively as a member of a tiny group of desperate men[12] who will get themselves killed on the spot, either as members of a huge invincible demonstration, or as taking part (as is more usual) in some intermediate formation. This internal, synthetic constitution of me by the group is simply totalisation returning to me to give me my first *common* quality over the collapse of seriality. And it gives me this quality as *power*. Thus the third party comes to the group which already possesses him, as a *constituent and constituted power*; that is, he receives the power he gives, and he sees the other third party approaching him as *his* power. For, in the group, the other third party, in so far as I totalise him with the Others, is not for me a *third-party-object*, that is to say, a third party transcendent (*transcendant*) to me. As an individual, he transcends (*transcende*) me towards his projects in so far as I transcend him: this is simple reciprocity. Integrated into the group by totalisation, he is *quasi-transcendent* through the mediation of the group, since I am in fact to integrate myself with him into the community, and since the task is indicated and since I remain *in tension*, at the limit of immanence and trans-

---

12. I am not claiming that *number* alone makes me desperate: whether I am desperate depends on *the total situation*. It is simply that although I may behave with desperate tenacity in some circumstances, I will have neither the opportunity nor the time, nor even the desire, to behave like this in the event of a popular tidal wave effortlessly breaking down all resistance, such as, for example, an unprotected body of police.

cendence. My link to him is therefore new: if we were to collaborate *in the group* in some action which would involve only the two of us, we would encounter strict relations of reciprocity-transcendence again; but in so far as he himself signifies in and through my totalisation *my being-in-the-group* as a task realised *over there* and not here by me, he is transcendent-immanent to me; or rather his immanence refers back to my (totalising) transcendence in so far as, as we shall see later, his transcendence can determine my immanence. Through the mediation of the group, he is neither the Other nor identical (identical with *me*): but he comes to the group as I do; he is *the same* as me. The characteristic of this new, crucial structure of mediated reciprocity is this: that I *see myself come to the group in him*, and what I see is merely the objectification of what I realise at the same time as him; he is my lived objectivity. We know that up to now the objectivity of an act appeared *to Others* or was reflected for me in the object produced. In the fused group, the third party is my objectivity interiorised. I do not see it in him as Other, but *as mine*.

Now, the reason for this new structure (which lies at the origin of all so-called 'projective' actions or actions 'of projection') resides precisely in the fundamental characteristics of mediation. For the mediator is not an object, but *a praxis*. The group which I go to is not the inert gathering of these hundred people. Its inertia is merely an appearance – and one that does not even exist for me. It is, in fact, an action: we *are waiting* (to become sufficiently numerous, or for some information, or for the enemy to be off guard, etc.). And the truth is that I try to integrate my *praxis into the common praxis* (that is to say, the plan to counter-attack, for example). This *praxis* is immediately given as the comprehensible meaning of the regroupment, and if this meaning is comprehensible it is because it appears to me through my own *praxis*, which *is already*, in itself, a regroupment (of myself with Others), and is conditioned by the common regroupment. On the other hand, the group is constituted in its compact nucleus by several men huddled close to one another, but who, for me and for the third party who comes to the group, are simply third parties. The apparent *exis* of everyone (his being-there, immobile, in-the-midst-of-the-group) is revealed to me as *my praxis* both in me and in him: the dislocation of temporality makes no difference; being in the group, in effect, consists in having come to it, as I come to it, and in staying in it (that is to say, *coming to it constantly*) just as, for me, to come to the group is to be already in it, in that its structures and forces determine me in my very reality. Thus both the third party and myself are mediated by the action of every third party, in so far as this action *produces multiplicity* and makes each of us the hundredth for the Other – in other words, in so far as this unity of practical self-determination penetrates the freedom of our reciprocal actions and makes them *the same* for each of us in being common to all. There is nothing magical or irrational about this: on the contrary, the transformation of free action into common free action by the free *praxis* of the group is absolutely intelligible. The unity of the *praxis* is conditioned by circumstances: from the moment that I, as one of its members, unify the group which is in the process of unifying itself, the unification, in so far as it may be effected by any third party, inside the common movement, is not only conditioned, in its freedom, by free action, but also conditioning, as my own freedom (that is to say, as my own project) within my own *praxis*. And this conditioning of me by every third party, that is to say, by the *same movement everywhere*, whether it is manifested in my *praxis* positing itself as regulatory, or in the reciprocity of my action and of that of a particular third party, is precisely my own freedom recognising itself as common action in and through my individual action. It is this synthetic enrichment (apprehended in me here and in the third party over there) which makes my simple action, which comes to me *as the same* (and simultaneously as realised here), produce in reciprocity a *common* result ('There are a hundred of us! Here's the hundredth!', etc.), which could not be envisaged *in itself* (at least not at the rudimentary level of the fused group) and which operates *through me* in objectivity as the inversion of alienation.

We have already seen how, on the market, my mere presence is alienating, how I am already for myself *the Other*, and how bewitched quantity causes the stock-piling of precious metals in Spain, for example, to lead to devaluation – so that to appear is, in itself, at least in the abstract, to force up prices. In this example we can see seriality and alienation as the other objectivity of my objectification. But in the present case, by contrast, what I discover is action as human, and quantity as instrumentality. Within certain limits, to be *more numerous* is to be *more powerful*. My appearance in the group eludes me in so far as the number depends on everyone: but this objectivity of my objectification suddenly becomes my objectivity *for me*. Through me, the number is increased; I am no longer the Other who comes to Others, endangering myself by my mere material presence; I am now my own action in the *praxis* of the group in so far as its objectification belongs to me as a common result. A *common* result: it is new, but it is mine in so far as it is the multiple result of *my action multiplied everywhere*, and everywhere *the same*; at the same time, this multiplied action is a single *praxis* which overflows in everyone and into a totalising result. For the moment we can set aside the example of the regroupment: it was only meant to provide a graphic model. Of course, it is obvious that the relation of every third party to every Other *in the group and through it* is a mediated reciprocity. And reciprocity within the group *produces the group* as a container to precisely the extent that the group *allows* this reciprocity by becoming a mediation.

But I mentioned *a second mediation*: every third party tends to become a mediation, as such, between the group and any other third party (or all of them). This is because I am not in fact alone in carrying out the totalising operation, that is to say, in integrating the ensemble of individuals into the group and in revealing, through my action, the unity of a *praxis* which I produce and which produces itself. This operation is the individual and common *praxis of every third party* in so far as (failing to effect his real integration) he designates himself as free, common action becoming regulatory through him. From this point of view, I am, for every third party, a free human agent, but engaged (with other third parties and inside the group) in a constellation of mediated reciprocities. I move from the position of totalising sovereign in relation to everyone to that of totalised sovereign. At other (more abstract) levels of our investigation (*expérience*), this totality may be both the result and the source of violent conflicts. But this cannot be the case in this initial moment of the group, because the Other, by totalising the practical community through his regulatory action, *effects for me* the integration which I myself should have realised but was unable to. Through him, in fact, my being-in-the-group becomes immanence; I am *amongst* third parties and I have no privileged statute. But this operation does not transform me into an object, because totalisation by the third party only reveals a free *praxis* as a common unity which is already there and which already qualifies him.

In practice, this means that I am integrated into the common action when the common *praxis* of the third party posits itself as regulatory. I run with all the others; I shout: 'Stop!'; everybody stops. Someone else shouts, 'Let's go!' or, 'To the left! To the right! To the Bastille!' And everyone moves off, following the regulatory third party, surrounding him and sweeping past him; then the group reabsorbs him as soon as another third party, by giving some order or by some action visible to all, constitutes himself as regulatory for a moment. But the order is not *obeyed*. Who would obey? And whom? It is simply the common *praxis* becoming, in some third party, regulatory of itself in me and in all the other third parties, in the movement of a totalisation which totalises me and everyone else. I can recognise this totalising regulation as such only in so far as my action is *the same* in the totalising third party. On the basis of the common future adumbrated by the common movement (flight, charge, etc.), that is to say, on the basis of my future as the common meaning of my regulatory and totalising *praxis*, the order gives me my common, future possibility. It reveals this possibility as a means within my project. In this way I can, as *being-in-the-group*, myself become a means of the common *praxis*, that is to say, an instrument of my own *praxis*. ('Get back, you lot! Let the others move ahead!' – initial differentiations, almost immediately re-absorbed, according to the circumstances and the outcome.) I execute the 'command'; I am the 'order', in so far as, through the third party, it accomplishes the integration which I cannot accomplish myself. This integration is *real* (and as we shall see, it will become more real as the group becomes more differentiated). And it is really the constituent whole which achieves practical unification through the order. In the extreme case, no regulatory third party even appears: orders circulate. Of course, they originated in some individual third party, or sometimes in several third parties at once. But distance, and the impossibility of *grasping* the group when one is *inside* it, and many other reasons all mean that it is only the word which reaches my ears and that I hear it *in so far as it comes from afar* (in so far as my neighbour *repeats* it without changing it). The words circulate from mouth to mouth, it might be said, like a coin from hand to hand. And, in fact, discourse is a sound-object, a materiality. Furthermore, as they 'circulate', the words take on an inorganic hardness, and become a worked Thing. But this is far from meaning that we are going back to collectives. This thing is the vehicle of sovereignty: in short, it *does not circulate*. Even if it 'comes from afar', it is produced here as new, in so far as wherever it is, every place in the group is the same *here*. This object which is apprehended, understood, and reproduced in the immediate trans-cendence of *praxis* is merely totalisation itself in everyone, in so far as it can be achieved only by a sign. I decode the sign by my action, by conforming to the maxim produced; and the absence of the first *signifier* (of the third party who was the first to shout the words) makes no difference to the structure of my *praxis*: the authorless words, repeated by a hundred mouths (including my own) do not appear to me as the product of the group (in the sense in which this might be a hyper-organism or a closed totality) but, in the act which comprehends it by actualising its meaning, I apprehend it as the pure totalising and regulatory presence of the third party (as *the same as me*) in so far as it accomplishes my integration where I am and *through my freedom.*

But it should be noted that this regulatory totalisation realises my immanence in the group in the quasi-transcendence (*transcendance*) of the totalising third party; for the latter, as the creator of objectives or organiser of means, stands in a tense and contradictory relation of transcendence-immanence, so that my integration, though real in the *here* and *now* which define me, remains somewhere incomplete, in the *here and now* which characterise the regulatory third party. We see here the re-emergence of an element of alterity proper to the statute of the group, but which here is still formal: the third party is certainly *the same*, the *praxis* is certainly common everywhere; but a shifting dislocation makes it totalising when I am the totalised means of the group, and conversely. In other words, everyone has, for each and for all, a possible dimension of *escape* or of tyranny, in so far as integration, though a free, practical unity, refers everyone who has been *integrated* back to an 'immanence-transcendence' tension which is in danger of breaking into transcendence (or into a false immanence which conceals a dominating transcendence). In any case, we shall call the individual's being-in-the-group, in so far as it is mediated by the common *praxis* of a regulatory third party, his 'interiority' or 'bond of interiority' in relation to the group.

This alternation of statutes (everyone passing from interiority to quasi-exteriority) must appear as the very law of the fused group. Everyone is *distanced* from all, as the transcendent (*transcendant*) agent of the union and as merged with everyone by a totalising third party; this alternation is characteristic of temporal actualisation, but it temporalises a basic structure, or in other words, a set of structural determinations. In historical reality the event conditions the actualisation. In fact the number of regulatory third parties, even if it is fairly high, is always limited, and concrete circumstances select them, or lead each of them to select himself from the group as its spokesman. At the Palais-Royal in 1789, the first person to have got himself heard, on some historic day, was probably one who happened to be close to a bench or chair and who could therefore get higher than the Others, in the spatial materialisation of all the dialectical characteristics which we have enumerated, *within* the group, but *separating from it* in order to totalise it and therefore establishing a dialectical relationship with the crowd and then being reabsorbed by it and reintegrated by the speeches of some other orator emerging a little further on. At this level, there is no longer any leader. In other words, the crowd *in situation* produces and dissolves within itself its own temporary leaders, the regulatory third parties. But a dialectical inversion can already be detected here. For we have seen practical community coming to individual action and structuring it in the movement of disintegration of seriality. But we can now see in this orator, addressing the upturned faces and shouting, 'To the Bastille!', a *common individual* (that is to say, one whose *praxis* is common) who gives the entire crowd the biological and practical unity of its organism as the rule of common unification: and in fact we shall see below how common unity, as a developing totalisation, attempts to realise itself as individuality.

5   The Intelligibility of the Fused Group

We have now observed the formation of a fused group and described its structures. Now we must define the *mode of intelligibility* of this new *praxis*. I must remark to the reader that this appearance of the group as an undifferentiated totality does not correspond, at least not necessarily, to a historical anteriority of the Apocalypse. (On the contrary, for me, the Apocalypse presupposes the existence of serial gatherings and institutionalised groups). We are discussing it first because its historical *reality* is undeniable: in certain circumstances, a group emerges 'hot' (*à chaud*) and acts where previously there were only gatherings and, through this ephemeral, superficial formation, everyone glimpses new, deeper, but *yet to be created* statutes (the Third Estate as a group from the standpoint of the nation, the class as a group in so far as it produces its apparatuses of unification, etc.). Sieyès' question[13] about the Third Estate, which was *nothing* (and therefore a pure

13. 'What is the third estate? Everything! Up to *now*, what has it been in the political system? Nothing! What does it seek? To become something in it!' See Albert Soboul, *1789: 'L'An un de la liberté'*, Paris, 1950, p. 64. [Ed.]

multiplicity of inertia, since it existed as nothing) but could be *everything* (that is to say – as certain people then thought, including Sieyès himself, by an abstraction from which, as a liberal bourgeois, he soon recovered – the nation, as a totality perpetually reshaping itself, the nation as permanent revolution) shows clearly how *through the troubles of 1788–9 and the groups which formed* sporadically (which up to that time were called *riots*) the bourgeois even more than the worker in the cities (though work was *really* done by the workers) glimpsed the transition from an ossified, cold world to an Apocalypse. This Apocalypse terrified them; in order to avoid it, the members of the Constituent Assembly would willingly have become accomplices of the aristocracy if only it had been possible. But it was France as the Apocalypse that they discovered through the storming of the Bastille. And through this people's battle, they learnt not only what the inert words of this speech suggested to them: its 'power', the contradictory 'necessity' of governing both through it and against it etc.; they sensed that History itself was *revealing new realities*.

This was not highly significant; but what is important is that this form constitutes itself in reality at certain moments of the historical experience and that it then forms itself as new – irreducible to the gathering, to the mass statute, etc., and also to organised, semi-organised, or institutionalised groups, and that its novelty is of itself an allusion to a more radical and deeper novelty: free *praxis* becoming through society as a whole and through the conflicts of antagonistic groups the *developing statute* of all the social structures of inertia. For our purposes, this is enough: its real, dialectical existence and its emergence from the liquidation of petrified forms are sufficient reasons for taking such a *historical reality* as our starting point. Indeed, from the point of view of critical knowledge – that is to say, from *our* point of view – this formation is more absolutely simple than any other (since groups develop by differentiating themselves) and, therefore, more legible. I shall now go back over my earlier descriptions and examine them from the point of view of practical dialectical rationality. Is there an *intelligibility* of the fused group? And what intelligibility? And what can intelligibility mean in *this* conext? These are the questions which we have to turn to now.

The centre of the problem is the question of the shifting unity of syntheses, of the multiplicity of the unifications, etc. It is at this level that we must ask ourselves: can *several* syntheses produce *one* synthesis? Is the synthesis useless? etc.

What we have seen emerging, at the expense of the collective, and under the pressure of circumstances and through a hostile *praxis* which expressed its project of totalising destruction through the synthetic significations of the practico-inert field, is not an actual totality, but a shifting and ceaselessly developing totalisation. But this group did not constitute itself *for itself*; whatever enthusiasm and joy may have been felt by the petty bourgeois who ran through Paris, addressing complete strangers and exhorting one another, the deep motivation was Terror; that is to say, as project and motivation are one, it characterised the project in so far as it was transcended and preserved; and union was created *on the basis of a number of objectives* which gradually became more definite and converged into a single one: the defence of Paris (and, in the case of the Quartier Saint-Antoine, the defence of the district). Furthermore, to precisely the extent that the structure of the group anticipates differentiation, it comes to the group, as we have seen, precisely from the gradual definition of the objective (for example, the need to defend the district by fighting on two fronts). It will be said that the same applies to an organism, and this is true – with two crucial reservations. The possibility of an action, whether individual or common, arises at a certain stage in the development of organisms and *through their organised structure*; the organism which has satisfied a need by some practical activity survives the disappearance of this activity: it survives *as an organism*, that is to say, through the unified variety of its functions. Although the group, as an evolved and differentiated reality, is also characterised by a hierarchised and unified plurality of functions, the completed action (local – that is to say, entrusted to a group or common organ) refers the group to a certain type of practico-inert being which we shall describe later. In short, the organism is both totalisation and totality; whereas the group must be a developing totalisation whose totality lies outside it in its object, that is to say, in the material totality which designates it and which it attempts to appropriate and turn back into instrumentality. In this sense, the objective and the danger are two stages of a single process which designates the developing totalisation from the outside: objectification (or the conquest of the objective) becomes the transcendence and domination of the common danger through transforming material destiny (topographical configuration, etc.) into an instrument. But to precisely the extent that the totalised totalisation achieved by the surrounding matter (occasioned, for example, by *an other praxis* on the part of some *other* group) is reappropriated by the group and reinteriorised as its internal and univocal relation to a particular instrumentality, this totalising totality, *within the group*, and as an *instrument in use*, becomes the very condition of all structural transformations.

It is chiefly in this sense that we should understand the intelligibility of Marxist descriptions which show the *object* at the basis of the group as conditioning its internal turbulences and the overthrow of its relations with the others. In one sense, therefore, and provided one remembers that work – not only as a free organic dialectic, but also as wear and tear, as expenditure of energy, and as real but particularised efficacity (which, as such, is *stolen* or integrated into an active group) – *is a material, concrete reality as a process*, as a *transformation of energy*, only at the level of individual *praxis*, it can be said that the *praxis* of the group is constantly to reorganise itself, that is to say, to interiorise its objective totalisation through the things produced and the results attained, to make of it its new differentiations and its new structures, and thereby to transcend this rearrangement towards new objectives – or rather, to make *this internal rearrangement*, as structures which have to be transcended (because *attained*) the transcendence of old objectives and of interiorised instrumentality. In this sense, a group might define itself from the outside on the basis of the common objective imposed on men by a totalising structure of the surrounding materiality (and perhaps of another *praxis* examined in its objectivity). If the group happens to *posit itself for itself* in its most differentiated forms (and, for example, with antagonistic bonds with some other group); even if the group happens to be able *in itself* to present itself as the real, total meaning of each and every individual life, as is the case whenever a national community (which, as we shall see, is a complex ensemble of antagonistic groups, of provisional alliances and of serialities) goes through a crisis of nationalism; and if, finally, *being-in-the-group* becomes, as a regulatory objective, a structure of the human relations which are to be constructed out of the liquidation of bourgeois atomism, the fact remains that the concrete group, in its elementary forms, is a practical organisation required by certain situations through every third party. In other words, it constitutes itself *as a means*: but this in no way implies that it must *remain* a means. Here, in fact, the dialectical investigation (*expérience*) shows us at once that it is a means of the third party to the extent that he is a means of the group. In particular, because it is free, practical relations between individuals which produce the group, it must be recognised that the group undergoes a dialectical evolution of which we must provide an account. The point is to show the (dialectical rather than historical) basis of all groups (including ones which posit themselves as essential through the inessentiality of their members), that is to say, to display their practical instrumental reality. Certain situations pose urgent questions to individuals, as multiplicities in the practical field – questions which already transform them in their reciprocal relations and which can be resolved only by a rearrangement of their relations, that is to say, by the interiorisation of multiplicity and the liquidation of alterity.

From this point of view, the danger of the organicist illusion having been finally removed, it should be noted that this reshaping of human (and non-human) relations takes place in the same mode as the transformations of an organism: individual action is perpetual adaptation to the objective, that is to say, to the material configuration; the body interiorises the surrounding materiality in its *attitudes* and *postures* and, less noticeably, in its internal reactions and even in its metabolism. In this sense, the basis of intelligibility, for the fused group, is that the structure of certain objectives (communised or communising through the *praxis* of the Others, of enemies, of competitors, etc.) is revealed through the *praxis* of the individual as demanding the common unity of a *praxis* which is everyone's. The structure of synthetic unity is, therefore, even at the level of the univocal relation of interiority, directly derived from the grasp of a unitary (and passive) structure of the surrounding materiality through the synthetic unity of a dialectical, individual *praxis*. Unity is reactualised *practically* by the individual, both over there as the community of the objective, and in his own action, here, in its present moment either as the exigency of being common *praxis* or as the first realisation in him and in every third party of this community. On the other hand, if the urgency of common action appears (whether rightly or wrongly, that is to say, whether in accordance with a real actualisation of objective exigency or in accordance with mistaken calculations) only to one individual, or to *several* members of the gathering, then this intelligibility relates only to a possibility which is negated as soon as it is posited. If the 'order' is not followed, if the individual who advances towards the enemy remains alone (either because there has been no liquidation of seriality, or because the group has constituted itself against him and by another *praxis* suggested by Others), then the constitution of the common *praxis* manifests itself in this individual *praxis* as a negated possibility. Of itself it liquidates itself in favour of isolated action or, on the other hand, of immediate reintegration into the gathering. The individual *who no one follows* may, in case of extreme anger, throw stones at the attacker or the police, *alone*. Alternatively, he may suddenly turn round and seek refuge in the infinite milieu of circular seriality.

The reality of the *praxis* of a (fused) group depends on the liquidation (either simultaneous or subject to temporal dislocations which can be ignored) of the serial, both in everyone and by everyone in everyone, and its replacement by community. This reality (which sometimes produces itself and sometimes does not) must therefore be comprehended in its intelligibility. But this intelligibility is defined *precisely* by the practical relation of the hostile *praxis* (through the material object) to the free action by which the third party unveils this *praxis* by opposing it. It is *through* the individual discovery of common action as the sole means of reaching the common objective, in fact, that the historian demonstrates and evaluates the urgency, the imperious clarity, and the totalising force of *the objective* (that is to say, of the danger which has to be avoided, of the common means which has to be found). Since every action, *here*, is the same, we must concentrate our attention primarily on the *praxis* of the third party, wherever it may be, in so far as it is conditioned in its free development by a common future (either to be realised or to be avoided). It is the tension of this future in the practical present, and the progressive and regressive decoding of this fundamental relation, which furnish the first elements of intelligibility. We must investigate not only how the threat – or the real action, already begun – of the enemy *affects* the third party, but also how this developing future transforms his statute, and with what urgency it appears (an urgency which, as an objective relation between the enemy action and that of the third party, may turn out to be very different from *real* urgency, that is to say, from the urgency which the historian will be able to demonstrate *after the event* as a meaning of the entire process). And conversely, on the basis of a common action adumbrated by the third party, we must investigate what possibilities are defined through and for this action, and what chances of success reveal themselves in the object itself through the adumbration of the *praxis*, etc. From this point of view, it may be that the problem is not to understand why a given initiative accompanied by a particular order was not taken up (in a historical reconstruction, the explanation might be, for example, that the group would have run into disaster if it had followed the order, and that it must have known this, given the material configuration of the place and all the other circumstances) but, rather, to interpret intelligibly the fact that *in such circumstances* a few individuals might have believed they could dissolve the gathering by inventing a common *praxis*.

This problem – though a negative one – concerns certain secondary disciplines within anthropology (in particular those which deal with the individual as such) and it refers us back to the abstract statute which we went through in the first moment of our dialectical investigation (*expérience*). The failure of this attempt relegates the individual to isolation and is to be explained in terms of his negative relation to the third party, that is to say, of a relative non-integration (or maladjustment, the word does not matter) which in turn is to be explained, in the context of the totalising movement and of History, in terms of the circumstances of his personal life. Precisely because of this, the transformation of the gathering into a group, wherever it occurs, includes, for the historian, its own intelligibility: that is to say, it is to be interpreted positively as the most concrete relation of the third party to circumstances and to circumstantial objectives, in so far as this relation manifests itself without being either obscured or determined by the specific behaviour of every individual *as such*. But it is obvious that such individual circumstances (which, as we have seen, may be his *position*; or which may also be his personal qualities – intelligence, courage, initiative there are plenty of these rather vague words) will produce one individual rather than an Other as the first regulatory third party. But these circumstances are 'general particularities': they determine the third party in relation to the group and the group in relation to the third party without telling us anything about the past or the transcended-being of the individual, and indeed, even without our really knowing[14] whether this rapidity of initiative was produced in him by his free *praxis* as one of his *group qualities*, that is to say, as an

14. I say, 'even without our knowing', not because, *a priori*, there can be no means to settle the question, but because, in fact, most of the spontaneous regulations, directly emerging and directly absorbed, elude the observer and moreover the historian who, in any case, is seldom obliged to study them. He would, however, if, for example, he was dealing with the event known as the 'September Massacres', simply because, ever since the first meetings of the Convention, the Girondins brought up the problem of responsibility in relation to this very subject. But it is clear that later historians will seek for the action of an anonymous Third Party only if they are trying to establish the responsibility of particular organised bodies (the Commune) or politicians. The Third Party in so far as he is *the same*, a little ahead of *the same*, is not their concern: only *the Third Party as a group* (simple totalised-totalisation, immanence-transcendence relation) can be of interest to them.

exis which can be neither interpreted nor understood outside his collective *praxis* and his *being-in-the-group*; and without our even knowing whether it manifested itself on *this occasion* and inside this particular gathering.

Nevertheless, the first moment (first from the point of view of *the investigation (expérience)*: the Apocalypse may be the liquidation of a *seriality of old groups* in favour of the amorphous homogeneity of a new fused group) suggests a number of observations. In so far as the group *is* – simply and primarily – a common *praxis*, the community of *praxis* is still expressed in the appearance of a group as the interiorisation of multiplicity and the reorganisation of human relations. We should therefore examine the immediate characteristics of a fused group such as, for example, *Paris* in 1789, or the *population of the Quartier Saint-Antoine* on 13 and 14 July, in connection, of course, with the situation and the objectives which alone give it meaning, but in so far as the group presents itself in its *praxis* as a developing reality. From the outset, in fact, we can understand that the group is a directed process: we must *fight*, save Paris, *seize weapons wherever they can be found*, etc. Nothing will prevent this objective, once attained, from suddenly revealing broader, more distant objectives (or for that matter, imminent dangers) which will necessitate the continuance of the group and its reorganisation. Indeed, there is nothing to prevent a consciousness of this possibility from existing in some way (we shall have to investigate how) in the group itself.

What is important for us at this moment is that this directed process constitutes itself only to be annihilated in its objectification. The insurrection of 1789 (unlike, for example, the revolutionary 'days' of June 1848 or of 1917) was purely defensive (in an *objectively* revolutionary context): the purpose was to restore order, that is, to repulse a threat. Once this had been done – that is to say, the negation having been negated – the group would dissolve into the inertia of seriality. But in fact this is never what happens; after the storming of the Bastille, Paris *could never again* be the Paris of June 1789. New organisations arose on the ruins of the old; new alarms led to new differentiations; and the struggle between group and inertia continued. Nevertheless, it is true that the realisation of its objectives led to a dissolution of the group *as such*. The 'Conquerors of the Bastille' as such were now united only by a past action which was engraved in Being, and also by a desire to exploit it for their own purposes or in support of a particular policy: it was no longer either the same group or the same men. The fused group should therefore be characterised as an irreversible and limited process: the reshaping of human relations by man had temporalised itself in the practical context of a particular aim and *as such* would not survive its objectification.[15]

In this sense, a group defines its own temporality, that is to say, its practical speed and the speed with which the future comes to it (on the bases of a threat, for example, which itself externally defines *an urgency*, that is to say, which makes time an objective exigency and a scarcity; the practical speed of the group is the reinteriorisation and embracing of urgency). Joseph Le Bon, a member of the Convention and representative of the people at Arras, said, from his prison, after Thermidor, that no one – not even himself – could really understand or judge events and actions which had occurred at *an other speed*. But this problem of temporalisation refers us back precisely to the real structure of the group, that is to say, to its own type of reality. The problem is to understand what, in a fused group, is signified by *unity* (which the description immediately confers on it: *the* group *does* this or that, etc.) as a synthetic unification of the diverse.

What is really involved, as we have seen, is in fact a synthetic relation which unites men for and by an action, and not those vague interpenetrations which an idealist sociology sometimes tries to resuscitate in some form or other. But – and this is where the question of structural intelligibility arises – our comprehension of the individual dialectic has made us see synthesis as the unifying unity of a unique *praxis* which integrated diversity through work. The univocal relation of interiority linked inertia as diversity to action as the unifying negation of this diversity. Within the group, as we have seen, diversity arises not at the level of the individual agent, or even at that of relations of reciprocity: it appears *at the level of the syntheses*. In other words, every third party, in so far as he is himself and not another, effects the unification of all, and by the mere actualisation and practical interiorisation of the totalising designations through which other groups single out the inert gathering as a negated totality (or a totality to be negated) indicates that his integration is a task to be done. Is this not just another example of serial commutativity? It would seem that alterity

---

15. I shall deal with institutional groups and groups of repetition later. It is obvious that their structure is more complex, since they define themselves both by the dissolution of serial inertia and as materiality sustained by the passive syntheses of seriality.

is to be found quite simply at the level of totalisations and that every totalisation is, for everyone, that of the Other, in him and in the Other. These questions at least have the advantage of defining the problem: if there is any doubt as to the intelligibility of the group, this is not because of any *lack* (that is to say, the question is not, and never has been, as some have believed, how separate particles could constitute a totality). On the contrary, it is because of an *excess*: the difficulty is due to the fact that we are acquainted with *praxis* as a synthetic activity, that we have observed every third party in action liquidating seriality and unifying the gathering into a group; thus we seem to be faced with *an excess of unifications*. Can we call this reality with a thousand centres a *unity*, when we have already discovered, in the case of reciprocity, a relation with several epicentres, which, for this very reason, was unable to unify its terms?

But, in fact, the question has been badly formulated. We are not really trying to find out whether the group, as a multiplicity of individuals, possesses an inert statute of unity, whether the men who compose it can be stuck together as organisms by some kind of gelatinous glue, or whether some 'collective consciousness', a totality irreducible to its parts, imposes itself externally on each and every consciousness, as the Kantian categories impose themselves on the multiplicity of sensations. We have seen, in fact, that the unity of the group was *praxis* (when it was *hot*; we shall observe other possibilities later). The important thing, therefore, is to find out how far the multiplicity of individual syntheses can, as such, be the basis for a community of objectives and of actions.

But these syntheses themselves, as we saw when we discussed them above, realise the substantial unity not of men, but of actions. In effect, every synthesis is *both* the *practical* constitution of common action, subject to reciprocal conditioning, *and* the revelation of this action as already existing. And in effect we have taken the third party at the moment when he was still in the gathering, and engaged in a passive, disordered activity. And we have seen how, by dissolving his seriality, he is able to see the original contagion disappear and how he constitutes not only his behaviour as free activity (by *giving* it a meaning), but also serial violence as common action, through his own activity (which he constitutes as the rule and meaning (*signification*) of the *common* praxis). This 'discovery', in fact, is itself an action: at first, as we have seen, the third party, by his exhortations, his orders, etc., acts on passive activity and helps to transform it in Others into a *praxis*;

and thus he makes himself a free rule for the liquidation of passivity in all. On the other hand, on the basis of existing circumstances (in particular, on the basis of the negative unity signified by a hostile *praxis* through the passive syntheses of the environment), this movement of actualisation of the common *praxis* occurs at about the same time in *all the third parties* as such. It is the moment in which orders circulate. Now, in this moment – for example, in the moment already mentioned, where a gathering, broken up by the police, regroups against it and becomes a demonstration – the multiplicity of individuals is still not transformed into substantial unity. Yet a regroupment does occur: something exists as a totality. But this totality is quite simply the demonstrators' attack on the police. And *this* is the first thing for us to explain. Now, it is obvious that, in the case of gatherings which, as in 1789, are unorganised, the transition from flight to regroupment does not originate in any particular order, issued by any particular individual; or at least, such an order was not very important. If the first order was 'obeyed', this was actually because everyone gave it. But here, it seems, we have that plurality of syntheses which would seem to be incapable of constituting a true unity. However, let us look at it more closely: in the moment where the demonstrators regroup, everyone rediscovers his *praxis* in the Other emerging from the other street and joining the group in formation; but, in so far as each of them was the free origin of his new behaviour, he would find it in the Other, not as his *Other-Being*, but as *his own freedom*. Here we encounter once more the mediated reciprocity which will turn out to be the essential structure of the organised group. But we can now see that this regroupment in formation, towards which everyone is advancing, and seeing himself advance in the person of his neighbour, serves as a mediation between third parties: this means that for everyone it is an ensemble to be totalised and a group to be expanded by his own presence; and through him, in fact, everyone perceives the movement of the third party who confronts him as his own movement and as the spontaneous expansion of the group of which he is about to become a part. Thus my *praxis* appears to me not only as myself, *here, now*, but also as myself approaching me through my neighbour, and as sustained by its own totalised effect on my neighbour and myself. (By acting in the same way and by making myself the same as him, I encounter him in the group as a totalising increase of its strength, which by totalisation determines me through the group itself: his individual action which is mine gives me, through the expansion of the whole, a greater security). Now, from the beginning of the regroupment, and during the ensuing fight, the plurality of totalisations by third parties does not cease to exist; there is nothing but hundreds of individual syntheses. However this multiplicity negates itself in every one of the acts which constitute it. Indeed, in so far as each of them constitutes the whole as common *praxis*, he presents himself as the regulator, that is to say, as the *praxis* of the whole in himself. And in so far as he recognises himself in each individual *praxis*, he sees each of them as the presence in a third party of the total *praxis*. But, at the same time, by liquidating seriality, he has produced his own *praxis* as a free, dialectical determination. Thus when he tries to attack the police, he carries out an action which only the existence and practice of the group make possible; but, at the same time, he produces it as his free practical activity. Thus the action of the group as total *praxis* is not initially *other action* (*action autre*), in him, or alienation from the totality; it is the action of the whole in so far as it is freely itself, in him and in any third party.

This requires further explanation. We must show in what way every *praxis* is a free individual development and in what way it could only be what it is as the *praxis* of a totalised multiplicity. The second point can be easily established by means of an example: alone or with a few comrades, a particular demonstrator would never even have tried to attack the police – simply because the impossibility of such an attempt would have been inscribed in the facts. His behaviour was therefore determined in itself as collective, that is to say, as an action which could be carried out only by a multiplicity of individuals. But for the first time we are encountering this multiplicity in the form of a *means*, that is to say, as a reinteriorised multiplicity. We have seen how the mass, by its sheer quantity, is weight, efficacity. But it is also clear that the efficacity of masses as such produces *the other effect* (*l'effet autre*); that is to say, the effect necessarily produced by inorganic materiality in the practical field. Here, in contrast, the individual joins the struggle *as a multiple*, that is to say, multiplicity is already in his action as a means which has been integrated by a free *praxis*. He joins in the attack neither as *isolated* nor as a *hundredth*, but as the free utilisation of the power he gets from *being*, here and everywhere, *the material strength* of the number one hundred. Number, as a structure of the action – that is to say, as an element in everyone of the decision of the third party – is merely an elementary kind of weapon. Everyone possesses it in its entirety, just as everyone can possess a pick or a pistol (that is to say, *the* pick or *the* pistol). But, at the same time, everyone sees it around him, and finds himself in it, just as several soldiers may find themselves together in some military machine and manoeuvre it together. For instance, *as well as* being his own guarantee, it may be his protection (or, in other circumstances, a negative element – people separate and divide; but this will become clear later). In this sense, number in *this* particular third party and in others does not appear as an *other-being (être-autre)*, but as the interiorised reality which multiplies individual effectiveness a hundredfold (not by giving the third party a hundred times his own strength, but by allowing him, for example, to disintegrate the hostile group by fighting against *one* of the individuals who compose it, instead of suffering their undivided action in separation). *Addition*, therefore, instead of being a mere inert summation of the units, becomes a synthetic act for everyone: everyone joins the group *in order to be more numerous* and hence the increase of the group becomes everyone's practice.

The other question can now be answered directly: free totalising *praxis* allows itself to be conditioned in reality and in practice by the totalisation it has just brought about. Its dialectical rationality has revealed the threat to it, in totalisation, as the negative unity of the group and of itself as totalised by the enemy; again, its dialectical rationality, by transforming the passive totality of the future victims of the repression into the active totalisation of resistance, has, in and through the group, appropriated a practical structure of interiorised multiplicity. In and by his *praxis*, the third party affirms in the group the lack of distinction between the individual and the common action. Earlier we said that the series was nowhere, that it is always *elsewhere*; the group, in contrast, is always here and in so far as we know it to be elsewhere too, it constitutes this elsewhere *as the same here*. This is how its circularity is to be understood. The circularity of the series is a circularity of flight; it destructures every *here-and-now* by disqualifying it through *the Others* here-and-now. The circularity of the group comes from everywhere into *this* here-and-now so as to constitute it as the same everywhere, and, at the same time, as free, real activity. My *praxis* is in itself the *praxis* of the group totalised here by me in so far as every other myself totalises it in another here, which is the same, in the course of the development of its free ubiquity. Here there appears the first 'us', which is practical but not substantial, as the free ubiquity of the me as an interiorised multiplicity. It is not that I am myself in the Other: it is that *in praxis* there is no *Other*, there are only several *myselves*. In fact the free development of a *praxis* can only be total or totally alienated. Thus the synthetic unity of the group is, in everyone, freedom as the free, synthetic development of the common action; for the demonstrators fighting the police, it is *the battle* (though not for Stendhal, the provincial officer or for Fabrice, a mere witness, in that it was always *elsewhere* and that *its elsewhere was its unity*), but to the extent that it is everywhere *the same* and that everyone becomes *in it* the same as all, namely *self-objectifying freedom*.

Later, when the group has cooled off and become permanent, its members will be *chronically* separated, and the struggle will remain their unity – their only unity – as a practice: but freedom here, in so far as it is that of all in everyone, may regain an *imperative* character. This is because, as we shall see, it is not only the same but also, as such, already, affected by alterity. But in the spontaneous *praxis* of the fused group, free activity is realised by everyone as unique (*his own*), multiple (interiorised multiplicity, and force realised *in the individual result* as a multiple result) and total (as the total developing objectification). Obviously this is not a matter either of co-operation, or of solidarity, or of any of the forms of rational organisation which are based on this first community. The original structure of the group derives from the fact that free, individual *praxis, can objectify itself* in everyone, through the totalising situation and in the totalised object, as free, common *praxis*. The *battle in progress* is, for everyone, an absolute reciprocity, *in the object* and *seen in the object*, between the group, as a multiplicity which has been reinteriorised because of the regulatory third party, in so far as it allows the individual a *given initiative*, and the individual, in so far as his *praxis*, as a total, regulatory *praxis here* (as being *the whole battle*), allows the totality in everyone, and everyone as a free totality, to objectify itself, or himself, in the common objective.

This objective, of course, is discovered as the process continues (we have only been examining the case of the fused group) according to the possibilities which present themselves. But it is revealed in its development in so far as *anyone*, as a regulatory third party, exhibits the common possibility in the particular. The street and the little wall will appear to everyone or anyone, and thereby to all, as a temporary shelter: to signify this is to create a group. Whoever signified was the group, since he saw the possibility with *common* eyes; but he *made* the group (advanced its integration, avoided rout) by *designating*. But everyone *already* transcends this designation: it is no longer a possibility (actualised by some designation but already materially present in the structure of the common environment), but by the time the other third parties *realise* that the little wall is a possible shelter, they are already regrouping behind it. The sovereign third party who freely designates is no different – precisely because he is everyone's own freedom – from a mere sign-post bearing a practico-inert message (*signification*) which is to be transcended by *praxis*. To say: 'Let's shelter behind this wall' is to make oneself a free meaning freely transcended everywhere *including here*, since for the third party who points it out, indicating it and running are the same thing.

We should notice here that, in a case of panic, the mere fact of the Other's running reveals my action to me in the milieu of the Other, and that running to hide behind the wall emerges as a contagious propagation. In any case, in so far as the group is *in the process of* constituting itself by liquidating seriality in all, where seriality does remain it may help the common action by caricaturing it, simply by local panics. The basic difference between serial activity, which – though counter-finalised and passive – does have its *teleological reason*, and group *praxis*, in this case and wherever it occurs, is not the freedom of individual *praxis*, since contagious panic, as much as a deliberate attack, realises itself through everyone's *praxis*; it is that in the first case, freedom posits itself only to reveal its alienation in the passive activity of impotence (I discover myself in the Other as hunted, and the alienation culminates by transforming itself and passing from the discovery of necessity to the submission by the other to the reign of necessity), while in the second case, in the group in the process of constitution, the leader is always *me*, there are no others, I am sovereign and *I discover in my own praxis* the orders which come from the other third parties. When demonstrators are questioned about the origin of this or that common *praxis* (either when their action was 'wild' or, quite simply, when it took place on a local scale and without being foreseen), they often cannot decide whether *someone* (that is to say, anyone) gave a *practical sign* to direct the common activity or whether, as they all say, in fact: 'We did this because it was the obvious thing to do, because there was nothing else to be done', etc. They have – especially if they are questioned in a trial, by hostile judges – a clear, active awareness of their solidarity with *any* of the demonstrators: if someone *actually* did shout, attack or fire first, etc., they will not give his name or, if someone has been caught in the act and is shown to them, they will say (and this is an active *praxis* of a militant group)

that they do not know, that they are *all* responsible. Thus, at this first
stage, there is no leader, or, in other words, the situation may *by
accident* be such that *a single third party* designates, signifies and
adumbrates the initial action; but *after* that for one reason or another,
and in any case because of the circumstances of the struggle, there was
no longer any common signification, the developments of the skirmish
forced every individual or small group to adapt to the *praxis* of the
enemy without being able to co-ordinate with the other parts of the
original group – but with each individual still fighting as the *free
totalisation in action* of the demonstration.

But it is remarkable, too, that when he is questioned, the demonstrator does not relate to the group, either as to a transcendent (*transcendante*) synthesis or as to a single quality in everyone's action. Whether
he is responding in a hostile way to the representatives of an oppressive
government or establishing the facts for themselves, he will interpret
the action as a free development, the objectives and means as free,
practical certainties (*évidences*). And this means that he presents the
situation as revealing itself to *praxis as it does in simple, individual
activity*. Quite simply, the accounts (and the emergence of the dangers
which themselves designated their demonstrations, or of objectives
which produced their risks and their finality, as each individual
describes them to us in his evidence) *necessarily* presuppose that every
participant was *the same praxis* as the totalisation *here* of the free,
common development by and through the free totalisation of the
practical field by an individual *praxis*. Thus, in contrast to the rout as
seriality, this flight – which already projects itself obscurely as a means
of regroupment – has everyone as its sovereign agent *here* in so far as
it is common; and everyone *produces* the common meanings (*significations*) which come to him from everywhere either as certainties, by
transcending them, or as free choices of means and ends. Of course, in
the fight itself, the offensive or defensive activity may involve certain
beginnings of differentiation which constitute a structure of alterity
(some – others). But since this alterity *is a means* (*some* people are to
attack the soldiers or police from the street behind, while *others* charge
them head on), it *is produced* in the free development of *praxis* as
invention. For everyone, of course, this involves reinteriorising a
given (in fact this 'given' will turn out to be simply the earlier statute
of seriality). But, for precisely this reason, he is subordinated to the
common unity of the *praxis* and every 'same' *becomes other*, both here
and over there, in so far as he is the same everywhere (that is to say, in

so far as the elementary, spontaneous organisation is half-produced by, and half-imposed on, every third party by objective circumstances and by the tactics of the enemy). Similarly, the *interiorised number* remains a quantity; but in so far as it conditions (as a means) the development of action, this quantity without parts presents itself in everyone as an *intensity*, that is to say, as the same degree of power (in all third parties) against the enemy. In this sense, the relation to the neighbour is both interchangeability and unicity (of me and him) as the absolute presence of the entire *praxis* everywhere: everyone is a hundredth in so far as everyone freely *becomes a hundred*.

In the methodologically simplest case (that of victory; for example, the taking of the Bastille), the unity of the result (as in individual *praxis*) becomes the objective reality of the group, that is to say *its being*, in so far as it can produce itself only in inert materiality. It may be objected that the result is not always inert: but this objection is based on regarding the inorganic as a certain statute which defines a particular kind of materiality, rather than, as would be correct, as a condition which, in particular circumstances, may characterise any kind of material entity. If, for example, the prisoners taken by the crowd, on 14 July, are a material and inorganic result of the common action, this is because they represent the objectification of the people's victory as the destruction of an organised fighting group and as its replacement by a multiplicity of impotence (by re-exteriorised quantity as the only possible relation amongst the prisoners). It goes without saying, of course, that the result – as a group objectified in its practice – is *in itself* capable of being alienated. This problem must be studied quite closely and we shall return to it. But this alienation – even if it is a new encounter with necessity – does not necessarily appear in the moment of victory; it may continue only much later, through thousands of different circumstances and practices. Indeed, in this respect, collective practice resembles individual practice: everyone can, now or later, discover his alienation as necessity, dependent on activities and circumstances. However, as we have seen, this alienation shows through in every moment of daily life, in that, for example, every attempt by the exploited to escape their condition individually inflexibly confirms their class-being in objectivity. The action of the group is necessarily new in so far as the group is a new reality and its result an absolute novelty.

The people have taken the Bastille. This public fact cannot be interpreted in the same way as the significations which it has just overthrown. This is why alienation – if it occurs – generally reveals itself *much later* and through confrontations. Thus the moment of victory presents itself to the victorious group – except in exceptional circumstances – as the pure objectification of freedom as *praxis*; and its character of irreducible novelty reflects for the group the novelty of its unity. And no doubt everyone sees the objectification as the result of his free *praxis*, in so far as it is the whole developing here through free individual action; but it is striking that this perception by everyone of total objectivity occurs in the milieu of third parties, as common behaviour. It is the constant procession of Parisians in the passages, halls and staircases of the Bastille which is the real actualisation of the people's victory. For isolated individuals (such as an armed bourgeois on guard at night) the common objectification has now become simply an abstract signification and their exultation – if they experience it in isolation – is a spiritual exercise rather than a way of living victory. (Besides – as we know from contemporary accounts – the dominant feeling amongst the bourgeois guards was fear. Absorbed by a *worked thing* which was too large for them, the common action transcended and crushed them, and manifested itself – wrongly – with its counterfinalities, and perhaps even, in an illusory way, as alienation. In the absence of all, it became the Other Action (*l'Acte Autre*), which might lead to catastrophes, merciless repression, etc.) In short, as long as the victory was still alive, the total object appeared to everyone only through a total practice, that is to say, in so far as everyone was with everyone else and realised *here* the actual presence of this totality. Thus its inorganic materiality, as the first alteration of the objective *praxis*, remained temporarily concealed: in so far as every visitor to the captured Bastille interiorised the multiplicity in his 'public visit' the synthetic unity of the object as a practical organisation revealed itself and the plurality of inertia was itself subjected, *in this object*, to unity. The unity of a group had, to some extent, come to the gathering from the hostile object which designated it as the unity of a process of annihilation (in so far as a group *praxis* actualised this threat). At present, the common action of everyone in the milieu of all expresses the victory by producing the total unity of the enemy object, and reduced to impotence. What, from a certain point of view, is already no more than a historic château, a ruin, produces itself through the group as hostility crushed and bound, but still dangerous.

In short, the multiplicity of syntheses cannot be defined in the *practical* group (or the fused group) as the inert co-existence of identical processes, connected by mere relations of exteriority. Nor can it be described as a serial link of alterity uniting the syntheses as others. Yet it does exist, since everyone acts and develops his actions on the basis of circumstances which condition him. It is also true that there is no synthetic unity of the multiplicity of totalisations, in the sense of a hypersynthesis which would become, in transcendence (*la transcendance*), a synthesis of syntheses. What actually happens is that the unity of the all *is*, within each actual synthesis, its bond of reciprocal interiority with any other synthesis of the same group, in so far as it is *also* the interiority of this other synthesis. In short, unity is the unification from within of the plurality of totalisations, it is *from within* that it negates this plurality as the co-existence of distinct actions and affirms the existence of the collective activity as unified (*unique*). From within: from the inside of each synthesis in so far as it affirms itself *here*, in freedom, as *the* developing totalisation and constitutes all the others, through practice, as *itself* (either by positing itself as regulatory, or by accepting its rule from some third party, that is to say, by producing it freely *here* as the same and unified).

On the other hand, the interiorisation of practical unity involves, as we have seen, that of the multiplicity which becomes the *means of the common action*, and, therefore, the means of unification from the point of view of total objectification. This reinteriorisation of multiplicity, as a transition from discontinuous quantity to intensity, results in the dissolution of *number* as a relation of exteriority between discrete elements (between individual totalisations). *Being a hundred, being a thousand*, as much for the group as in the eyes of the enemy himself ('There are *too many* of them, we'd better leave them alone,' etc.), is a possibility of counting or being counted which immediately reverts to being a free unity-means. Thus, in so far as it reabsorbs number, the group is a non-quantifiable multiplicity. This does not mean that its quantity is eliminated as inorganic materiality; it means that its quantity must be conceived in it as instrumentality. And, of course, this also applies to the characteristics of *masses* (weight, etc.), in so far as, in the elementary fight we are considering, they are all interiorised and controlled exteriority. Here, the inorganic characteristics of the group are means of acting in the practico-inert field, just as the practical organism in its individual action acts as a source for transforming energy in the physico-chemical field of exteriority (that is to say, in so far as it uses and controls its being-in-exteriority as an inorganic structure transcended and preserved by organic structures).

Now it is clear that the intelligibility of this new (and possibly unexpected) structure, that is to say, of unity as ubiquity within each and every synthesis, depends entirely on the two following characteristics: this ubiquity is *practical*: it is not that of a being or of a state, but that of a developing action; and it can be conceived only as the ubiquity of freedom positing itself as such. I have already stressed the first characteristic: if the problem were to place the unity of the group *in its substance*, everything we have just said would be pure logomachy or sophistry, for the substantial unity of a totality exists in every part only in so far as the whole is distinct from each part and produces itself as a transcendent (*transcendante*) totalisation of them all. But we are dealing with a *praxis*, and we must realise that here, in contrast, all the synthetic determinations we have described *really create* the common action in so far as each of them makes it exist both in itself and everywhere (for example, the order which springs from any mouth and which is executed by a hundred arms is a real process of totalisation). Besides, the substantial being of such a common action lies *outside it and in the future*, in the common objective (which is the first designation of the group by the enemy in so far as the group constitutes itself as the negation of this negation); and it objectifies itself as *common* by the common realisation of the objective which itself and by itself (outside it) has already constituted itself as common. For example, the flight of the adversary is *common* in itself (and not only as produced by the common effort), in so far as the common practice of the enemy appears as turned back but still common. Even the prisoners, as the destruction of a threatening unity which has been reduced to passive multiplicity, have meaning only by reference to a previous meaning (to the negative common *praxis* which has been destroyed). But the essential characteristic of the fused group is the sudden resurrection of freedom. Not that freedom ever ceased to be the very condition of acts and the mask which conceals alienation, but we have seen how, in the practico-inert field, it became the mode in which alienated man has to live his servitude in perpetuity and, finally, his only way of discovering the necessity of his alienations and impotences. The explosion of revolt, as the liquidation of the collective, does not have its *direct* sources either in alienation revealed by freedom, or in freedom suffered as impotence; there has to be a conjunction of historical circumstances, a definite change in the situation, the danger of death, violence.

The silk-weavers of Lyon did not unite *against alienation and exploitation*: they fought in order to prevent the constant lowering of

wages, that is to say, basically, for the restoration of the *status quo.*
(But of course, their very practice prevented this restoration in any
case. After the revolt, society was no longer the same, the pre-history
of the French proletariat had given way to its history.) But against the
common danger, freedom frees itself from alienation and affirms itself
as common efficacity. Now, it is precisely this characteristic of freedom
which produces in each third party the perception of the Other (the
former Other) as *the same*: freedom is both my individuality and my
ubiquity. In the Other, who acts *with me*, my freedom is recognisable
only as *the same*, that is to say, as individuality and ubiquity. It is
freedom, therefore, as the dialectical structure of action, which prevents
the third party from letting himself be determined by the third parties
as Others: in fact, in our example of running away and regrouping,
freedom dissolved alterity by positing itself, simultaneously, as a first
synthesis, in the third party and in everyone, and as a transformation of
passive activity into freely directed action for a common objective. And
the totality as *praxis* came to *my* freedom through the totalisation of all
(that is to say, through the transformation of the gathering into a group
unified by action). Thus, through the presence of the free actions of
which it made itself regulatory, my own action took on a dimension of
interiorised multiplicity. But if this interiorisation of the inorganic did
not reintroduce alterity into the agent in the form of an inertia of the
totality, or of an infinitesimal distance between the practical totality and
the individual *praxis*, this was just because the interiorisation was only
an instrument chosen by my free action in so far as it was chosen everywhere by the free *praxis* of all.

Thus the common *praxis*, as the totalisation and struggle against a
common *praxis* of the enemy, realises itself in everyone as the new, free
efficacity of his *praxis*, as the free intensification of his effort; every
freedom creates itself laterally as the totalisation of all freedoms, and
totalisation comes to it through the others as a lateral dimension of its
individuality, in so far as it is freely individual for them. This has
nothing to do with the radical transformation of freedom as individual
praxis, since the statute of this freedom is to live the very totality of
the group as a practical dimension to be realised in and by its individuality. But it is true that there is a new relation between freedoms
here, since in every totalisation of the group, the freedoms acknowledge themselves to be *the same*. This relation, which differs from
ternary relations of reciprocity and from third-party relations, is a
reciprocal recognition between third parties in so far as it is mediated

by the developing totalisation of all the reciprocities; and this recognition is neither contemplative nor static: it is simply the means required by a common emergency. It is for this reason that common action, at the elementary level, is not essentially different from individual action, at least in its practical aspects, except in its results, which are obviously greater. A single individual freedom, inflated by a totalised multiplicity, and emerging anywhere, identical, always controls, in a plurality in action, from *here, from the centre*, wherever it manifests itself, a first use of the multiple and of its strength, a first differentiation of functions. And the unity of this freedom beneath the shifting multiplicity of the syntheses is itself, and fundamentally, the relation between a negative unity of all (totalisation through annihilation by the enemy) and the negation of this negation to the extent that it is *occasioned* as totalising and that it *produces* itself freely on this basis.

Of course, this theoretical description is never completely applicable: it is not true that freedom, emerging everywhere and everywhere the same, communicates the common project through everyone to all and through all to everyone. Conflicts occur precisely to the extent that the liquidation of seriality is a temporal process which may be late *here* and early *there*; the remnants of alterity represent, for the freedoms themselves, as totalising, a threat of seriality. The group must act on itself in order to hasten these liquidations: we shall come back to such common, internal action. Moreover, we have supposed for convenience that the individuals who compose it are *homogeneous*, or (to put it differently) we have considered them only from the point of view of the threat which hangs over them. In fact, each comes to the group with a *passive* character (that is to say, with a complex conditioning which individualises him in his materiality); and this passivity – in which we should include biological as well as social determinations – contributes to the creation, even apart from seriality, of a hysteresis which is capable of occasioning a new *series*. For these and other reasons, the theoretical schema which I have sketched does not apply in reality: there are procrastinators, oppositionists, orders and counter-orders, conflicts, temporary leaders who are quickly re-absorbed and replaced by other leaders. But the essential point remains, through this *life* of the fused group (which is in fact only its struggle against death through passivisation): namely, if the group is really to constitute itself by an effective *praxis*, it will liquidate alterities within it, and it will eliminate procrastinators and oppositionists. This means that the common freedom will create itself in everyone *against them* until in the end the orders which circulate really are the orders which everyone gives himself in himself and in all, until the homogeneity of anger, courage, and the determination to fight to the end, manifesting itself everywhere, reassures every demonstrator, and shows him that the danger of defeat or indecision will no longer create, over there, as an anxiety, the possibility *of an Elsewhere* and instead constitutes him from everywhere as the practical reality of the group *here*. This is the heart of the matter: I depend on everyone, but through freedom as practical recognition I am *guaranteed* against this dependence. They will fight *my* fight, with my determination; *over there* is no more than a *here*; I am no more in danger 'over there' than they are here; I *expect* nothing from them (alterity), since everyone gives everything both here and 'over there'; thus my own action – even when the conditions of struggle prevent me from seeing them – is *regulatory of theirs*; it is practical freedom in me which sets its own limits in them; thus in driving my tenacity to the limit, I produce this tenacity everywhere.[16]

16. In fact, aggravating surprises, stampedes, and routs do occur. But for the moment we are discussing the group without taking into account the hostile *praxis* (if the hostile group decides to throw in all its strength at a particular point, it will break down the homogeneity of the group from the outside). But for the moment, this does not concern us: in effect, the group is not a metaphysical reality, but a definite practical relation of men to an objective and to each other. If certain circumstances of struggle lead to stampede and if this stampede is not followed by regroupment, the group is simply dead, and contagious panic restores the domination of the practico-inert.

The Statutory Group

1 The Surviving Group: differentiation

The intelligibility of the fused group depends, therefore, on the complex ensemble of a negative designation of its community, re-actualised in the negation of this negation, that is, in the free constitution of individual *praxis* into common *praxis*. At this level, there is group behaviour and there are group thoughts in that the common *praxis* is self-elucidating; and the essential structure of these practical thoughts is the unveiling of the world as a new reality through a negation of the old reality of impotence, that is to say, through the negation of the impossibility of humanity. The fact that the origin of the grouping was Terror is not actually very significant; every *praxis* constitutes itself as an opening made in the future, and sovereignly affirms its own possibility – simply through the emergence of the undertaking itself – that is to say, it makes success into a structure of practical freedom. As the freedom of revolt reconstitutes itself as common violence against practico-inert necessity, its future objectification becomes, for it, the free violence of men against misery and impossibility of living. But this structure of the common project – which derives from its synthetic character – does not settle the real issue, at least not alone.[17] However, it does make intelligible for us the complex dispositions that are to be found amongst the demonstrators, during the insurrectional days of the French Revolution – especially, the transcendence of Terror towards Hope and the double structure of sovereignty and violence which characterises freedom as a common

---

17. It settles it in so far as it occasions inflexibility in the combatants. But then everything depends on other factors; and inflexibility may simply lead them to extermination.

praxis. It is, in effect, not only a practice of defensive violence against the violence of the enemy but also, as sovereignty, *violence against necessity*, that is to say, violence against the practico-inert field in so far as it is constituted by Thing-destinies and by enslaved men. Just as, as the investigation has shown, in this field of alteration, necessity is an imperative limit which imposes itself on freedom from within (in so far as it is expropriated by the outside), so the reversal of the practical movement and its reappearance as a negation of necessity constitute themselves as the violent destiny of necessity itself, in so far as it produces itself for man through men and things.

But, at the same time, this violence, always ready to attack any re-emergence of inertia within the group, dissolves itself in pure, unanimous sovereignty, in so far as, through the active member of the group, sovereign freedom is always *here* and *now*. However, as violence is always going on, whether against an external enemy or against insidious alterity within, the behaviour of a revolutionary, on 14 July as on 10 August, appears contradictory: he not only fights for freedom (that is to say, for the practical realisation of a concrete objective), but also realises sovereign freedom in himself as unity and ubiquity; at the same time, however, he commits violence on the enemy (in fact this is simply counter-violence) and he uses perpetual violence *in order to reorganise himself,* even going so far as to kill some of his fellow members. But there is not really any contradiction here: this common freedom gets its violence not only from the violent negation which occasioned it, but also from the reign of necessity, which it transcended but preserved in itself, and which constantly threatens to be reborn as a disguised petrification, that is to say, as a collapse into the inertia of the gathering. Freedom as the sovereignty of individual *praxis* is not violence: it is simply the dialectical reorganisation of the environment. Freedom as alienation unmasked becomes the structure of its own impossibility in the form of necessity; finally, necessity as confined and self-confining freedom in passivity becomes the qualification of the practical negation which transcends it in so far as this practical negation has to destroy a dimension of freedom in it. As ruthless destruction of freedoms buried in practico-inert necessity (and which, as slaves, exhaust themselves in imparting to it its movement of infinite flight), this freedom constitutes itself *a priori* as violence. The only contradiction between the characteristics which are so often opposed to one another by reactionary writers – Hope and Terror, sovereign Freedom in everyone and Violence against the Other, both outside and inside the group – is a dialectical one. And indeed, these are the essential structures of a revolutionary group (not only in its most undifferentiated reality but also, and to an even greater degree, as we shall see, in its most complex forms). And it will be easy to show that these supposedly incompatible characteristics are indissolubly and synthetically united in every action and declaration of the revolutionary demonstrators. I mention them in passing here in order to show, as I have done in previous chapters for other levels of the investigation, that the practical and ideological determinations of a fused group are a single structure dependent on its morphology and the dialectical laws of its movement.

But this definition of the fused group in terms of common *praxis* does not determine the structural relations which hold between third parties in primary interiority, in so far as the group is a means of common action. We have seen that the ontological relations of the group's members cannot be characterised in terms of common membership of a totalised totality. But at this level of our investigation we can in fact define the group as a perpetual reshaping of itself, in accordance with objectives, with exterior exchanges and with internal imbalances. We have still not established anything about History, or whether it is really a totalisation of totalisations. But – apart from the dialectical syntheses which constitute individual action and which totalise the whole of the practical field rather than the organism – fused groups have presented us with the (methodologically) most simple form of totalisation. A group *is not* (or at least it dries up and ossifies, the more being or inert materiality it contains): it constantly totalises itself and disappears either by fragmentation (dispersal) or by ossification (inertia). This totalisation does not produce itself – in the simple case I have discussed – through differentiated organs: it occurs everywhere and through everyone; wherever one is, it happens *here*. So we must now define the relation between individuals (as totalising and totalised, rather than as the presence *here* of the total *praxis*). In short, does common activity not condition a *being-in-the-group* for everyone? And how should this term be interpreted?

We have already observed that totalising syntheses have two moments: in the first, I produce myself as the third party by effecting the totalisation of the gathering; and indeed, I produce this totalisation *in so far as I form part of it* and in so far as the inertia tends to dissolve in me, along with my bonds of alterity. Yet, as I have pointed out, I cannot effect a *real* integration of myself into the group. To the extent that I produce the synthetic unity, this unification cannot figure in the totality as a unified unity. But this does not in any way mean that the unified individuals are passive objects in the synthesis: the unification is practical and I can recognise my own action in the common action. But the common action, which is free in so far as it is common, this flight, for example, is constituted by my unifying *praxis* as a *grouped flight*, that is to say, as a unification of the diverse in one *praxis*; and the movement which reveals this group to me in its action refers me back to the same action, performed by me in the group, and as a member of the group; but at this moment the movement stops and designates me as needing to be integrated in my organic reality into the ensemble which I have just constituted. In short, my integration becomes a *task to be done*; in so far as I am designated abstractly in my membership of the group (as *one* of its members) and in so far as I am really unified by my *praxis* as common *praxis here*, I become a *regulatory third party*, that is to say, my action presents itself as *the same* in the very slight dislocation which derives from the non-realisation of membership; and as it is freedom, this infinitesimal (but impassable) distance produces it as the free reflection here of the common action, that is to say, as the possibility for all of grasping the common action in myself and of consciously regulating it. But, conversely, in so far as every third party does the same and issues some order, he becomes the rule of my freedom in me and therefore really integrates me into the totalisation, which returns to him without closing. Through him, an interiority creates itself as a new type of milieu (a milieu of freedom) and I am in this interiority: if he stands on a chair, or on the podium of a statue, or if he harangues the crowd, then I am *inside*; and if I in turn climb onto the podium which he chose, I am, again, inside but my interiority is stretched to the limit, and the slightest jolt could make it into an exteriority (for example, if I make a mistake about the common action, if I propose to the group an object different from its own).

Thus, in the simple case of the fused group, my being-in-the-group is my integration into it through all the regulatory third parties in so far as it is *the same* free support of a common action within the interiorised multiplicity; and at the same time, or alternatively, it is my belonging to the totalisation which I effect, and which is *the same*, in so far as I cannot totalise myself. It is this presence-absence, this belonging which is always realised for the Other who is myself but unrealisable for me, who am nothing other than him, it is this contradiction, this abstract separation within the concrete which characterises me in the individual tension of my being-in-the-group. Of course, this tension exists in everyone as a third party. But we should be quite clear about this: the group is not a reality which exists in itself *in spite of* the 'transcendence-immanence' tension which characterises the third party in relation to it. On the contrary, the 'transcendence-immanence' of its members creates the possibility of the group as common action. Pure immanence, indeed, would eliminate the practical organism in favour of a hyper-organism. Or, quite simply, if it were possible for everyone to effect his own integration, every action, in so far as it was common, would lose any possibility of or reason for positing itself as a regulatory action and the group would no longer conceive itself in its *praxis* through innumerable refractions of *the same* operation. In other words, the action would be blind, or would become inertia. Pure transcendence, however, would shatter the practical community into molecules related only by bonds of exteriority and no one would recognise himself in the action or signal of some atomised individual.

Altogether, these observations enable us to attempt a critical assessment of rationality (as a rule of understanding) at the level of the group. Common *praxis* is *dialectical*, from the most basic level on (that of the fused group): it totalises the object, pursues some total aim, unifies the practico-inert field and dissolves it in the synthesis of the *common practical field*. If common *praxis* is to be a form of rationality, it must be dialectical rationality. And, since it is always intelligible, we are compelled to recognise the existence of this form of rationality. Moreover, it should be noted that in itself it does not display the specific characteristics of the *individual* dialectic as the free development of a practical organism. Although – as we have seen, and as will soon become clearer – a dialectical relation may insert itself between a common *praxis* and an individual's *praxis*, a common *praxis* is not in itself a mere amplification of the *praxis of* an individual. As we have seen, the interiorisation of multiplicity is one of its essential characteristics. And the organism is undoubtedly comparable in some ways with interiorised inertia. But, when applied to the organic individual, these words have only a *metaphysical* and uncertain meaning in relation to its biological being, in so far as it eludes apodictic, dialectical investigation and manifests itself, beyond reach, in the milieu of the transcendental (*transcendentale*) dialectic. In fact, dialectical investigation shows us the action of the individual as unifying itself in the unifying synthesis and in the transcendence of the practical field, but it *never* reveals it to us as *unified*. The practical organism is the unifying unity of unification; thus the investigation refers us (as if to its first, most abstract intuition, and as if to its limit) to man as the *biological unit* on which every *praxis* is based (and which every immediate *praxis* realises as a temporalisation towards an end). The interiorisation of multiplicity, however, is a moment of collective action and the group constitutes itself *by it* (as by the other factors already mentioned) as the means of the common *praxis*. In this simple form (the fused group), we are in fact forced to admit that the group is initially a *means*, in which the organism is agent, end and means all at once.

In our example, the grouping, still in a primitive state, is the *invention of everyone* in so far as everyone is personally threatened by a danger which presents itself as common. And everyone can invent this new instrument *in so far as* the practical organism can already totalise multiplicities in a practical field, recognise the *praxis* of developing common totalisations and create a group as a reinteriorisation and practical inversion of a totalising signification of negation (the *praxis* of total annihilation). Thus the practical creation of *means of defence* is a resumption in freedom, as a new relation with men, of an exterior unity, or a dissolution of the serial relation of impotence by the free affirmation (through circumstances) of freedom as a human relation in a new *praxis* (which comes to the same thing). This does not mean, however, that *either* the interiorisation of the multiplicity in me, *or* the affirmation here of *my* freedom as a recognition of all *our* freedoms, *or* totalisation as the constitution of a *means* for *praxis*, *or* the synthetic and common character of the original urgency and of *our* objectification in the victory, are capable of constituting a new statute of hyper-organic existence, as *being-in-the-group* – any more than the specific characteristics of common action (in particular, the utilisation of multiplicity and the differentiation of functions) succeed in making it a hyper-dialectic whose intelligibility lies in its synthetic transcendence of individual dialectics.

We have shown in fact that the unity of the group is immanent in the multiplicity of syntheses, every one of which is an individual *praxis*, and we have emphasised the fact that this unity has never been that of a created totality, but rather that of a totalisation which is carried on by everyone everywhere. Thus the intelligibility of the group *as praxis* depends on the intelligibility of individual *praxis*, in so far as individual *praxis* is lost and then rediscovered in the practico-inert field. A rupture occurred, as we saw, at the stage of alienation (and not the creation of a new moment of the dialectic) and the groups we have described are a new determination of every *praxis, beyond impossibility, in so far as* it is determined *by itself coming to itself as the same* and in so far as it *comes to itself everywhere as the same*. This dialectic of the group is certainly not *reducible* to the dialectic of individual labour, but it is not autonomous either. Thus its intelligibility, as will become clearer later, is that of a *constituted reason*, of which the dialectic of free individual *praxis* is the *constituent reason*. Although they present themselves to our investigation as specific realities, and although they are, in effect, specificities whose very obviousness implicates a range of factors which they unite in an original synthesis; and although they presuppose as their foundation, their danger, their means of action and the servitude which they are transcending, the practico-inert field which as such eludes the synthesis of the individual organism, their own certainty (*évidence*) is based on the translucidity of the *praxis* of an organism and to the extent that, as we shall see, dialectical investigation displays group structures and group behaviour as *certainties* (*évidences*) *which lack translucidity*, their specific contribution can be described as a new aspect of *object-being* (and, as we shall see, of seriality), in so far as a certain passivity masks the translucid certainties of constituent *praxes* but nevertheless bases itself on them. The difference between constituent Reason and constituted Reason can be concentrated into two words: the former is the basis of the intelligibility of a practical organism, while the latter is the basis of the intelligibility of an organisation. Thus our investigation will lead us from the fused group to the organisation and thence to the institution.

This is not a matter of *genesis*. I am explaining organisations in terms of the Apocalypse; but it could be done the other way round. This order *is not untrue*; but the reverse order is possible. I am adopting it because it leads from the simple to the complex, and from the abstract to the concrete. Now, we have already seen certain as yet fluid differentiations occurring within fusion under the pressure of circumstances. It would be instructive to examine how such a relatively homogeneous group (setting aside the presence of the French guards) creates its differentiations in action, on the basis of objective structures, by investigating the various stages of the taking of the Bastille, under the guidance of Flammermont and Lefebvre; but such an examination would take too long. In any case, this differentiation originates in the fact that the whole group is always *here* in the *praxis* of *this* third party, and that *for this third party* it is also over there, that is to say, *here* yet in the *praxis* of another third party. Consequently, the action which I perform here against some enemy, though its particular structure depends on the enemy, the place, etc., is, through and for me, *the common action*; it is so in so far as the activities of Others, by individualising themselves under the pressure of circumstances, help to *render* mine possible and, to this extent, *require it*. In a way, each individual holds down part of the hostile forces by his struggle. Mediated reciprocity is the basis for the intelligibility of the differentiation which arises in the context of the struggle and as a response to the hostile *praxis*. The action of the other third party remains *the same* as mine (whether what we are combating is a natural scourge or an enemy), beneath a differentiation which produces itself as purely circumstantial, in that the common *praxis* is defined in and through the regroupment with its common objective, which remains *the same* in every individual *praxis*. But in a fused group, a mere means to common security, these differentiations, however advanced they may be, do not survive action. Even if they are free adaptations to enemy action, they are nevertheless originally induced by it. Any *spontaneous innovation* (such as that of the combatants who try to scale a wall in order to lower the draw-bridge of the Bastille) is – as in individual *praxis* – a transformation of a practico-inert structure into practical activity; or, to put it differently, it is the practical reading of a possibility inscribed in matter, and which reveals itself (or constitutes itself as a means) on the basis of the total project. Once the total result is achieved, the group can read its unity as a totalitarian synthesis *in its objectification*. Thus it can, in principle, relapse into non-differentiation.[18] The differentiation of functions – as a very general structure of which the division of labour is a concrete particularisation – appears as the statutory reality of the group only in so far as the group itself becomes the object of its totalising *praxis*.

In particular, whatever the origin of the group may be, the permanence of the dangers may require it to persist between the moments of real activity, as a permanent means of resisting the enemy. I take this example (the enemy have withdrawn, they may attack tomorrow) because it is an extension of those we have just examined: but I must repeat that we are not trying to reconstruct a genesis. The new exigency comes to the group to the extent that the third party reveals it, or in other words, in so far as individual *praxis* interiorises the

---

18. In fact, memory, roles one has played, successes won, etc., create a particular *exis* for certain individuals *as members of the group*. And this is already a first return of Being in so far as the past is transcended-being.

objective permanence of the common danger in the form of a common exigency. But this new state of the group (which manifests itself historically in every revolutionary situation) is defined by new characteristics, conditioned by new circumstances. The unity of the fused group lay quite simply in real common action, that is to say, in its own undertaking as much as in that of the enemy, and in the violent, dangerous, and sometimes fatal attempt to destroy the common danger. There was nothing ideal about the totalisation of the group: it was done by sweat and blood. It objectified itself in destruction, and perhaps in the slaughter of enemies (for example the summary executions after the taking of the Bastille). At the same time, though constituting itself as a means of acting, the group did not posit itself for itself: it posited the objective and it *became praxis*. If, however, the grouped multiplicity is to survive the realisation of its immediate objectives, the urgency diminishes. Of course, the offensive return of the enemy troops is always possible; in some cases, it is probable, even *highly probable*. Faced with this threat, extending from the possible to the virtually certain, the common watch (the refusal to sleep, or to yield to fatigue), continually being armed, etc., cannot be regarded as belonging to what I called *exis*; these are really *actions* – especially as these actions (whose development we shall examine later) transform themselves into organised and organising behaviour. But the *imminence* of the danger should not be allowed to conceal its *absence* from us. This absence of the enemy is not a non-being: it is a relation to the group which fears its return. And this relation – at least as far as we are concerned – manifests itself as *practical deconditioning*. The differentiations of the group, during the skirmish, its transformations and its real intentions, occurred under the almost unbearable pressure of the enemy group and were determined as negations of this pressure. It is in this sense that they can be called 'adaptive behaviour': the structure of the fighting group is also that of the enemy *taken negatively* (*saisie en creux*). In absence, the new differentiations are, of course, determined in close relation to the totality of objective circumstances. Nevertheless, the group determines itself in accordance with a future unification (unification through the return of the enemy) and a past unity (its group-being as transcended past, or, in other words, its practical reality in so far as it *has been*, and in so far as it has objectified itself in materiality). This means that it has no way of acting on the enemy, tomorrow or even tonight, other than by immediately acting upon itself.

This structure of common action was already implicit in the fusion, since the initial differentiations were, in effect, internal transformations of the group. However, the active and the passive were so closely intertwined that it was often impossible to tell whether the group differentiated itself through its struggle or whether it was differentiated by an enemy manoeuvre.[19] On the other hand, when the enemy does not realise itself as a controlling force, differentiation becomes, within the group, an action of the group on itself. In other words, by becoming its own immediate objective, the group becomes a means of future action. We may speak here of *reflection*, in the strictly practical sense: the group, waiting for the attack, looks for positions to occupy, divides itself so as to man all of them, distributes weapons, assigns patrol duties to some, and scouting or guard duties to others, establishes communications – even of the crudest sort, a mere warning shout – and in this way, in the free exploitation of places and resources, it constitutes itself for itself as a group. Its objective is indeed a new statute, in which individuals and sub-groups take on various functions in, by and for it, and so intensify its power, and strengthen its unity. It is impossible to deny that it *posits itself for itself* once it has survived its victory. Or, to put it another way, there is a new structure to be explained: *group consciousness* as the transcendence by every third party of his *being-in-the-group* towards a new integration. We must examine the dialectical problem of unity and differentiation in this light. Are these two *practices* initially incompatible? Or does one arise as a transcendence and strengthening of the other?

Furthermore, the problem of the *surviving group* (for it begins by surviving its original *praxis*) suddenly becomes connected for us with the problem of *being*, that is to say, of *permanence*. So far we have seen only two sorts of permanence, the first being the inert synthesis of the inorganic, the second, biological integration. Can the group transcend both? Or will it be constructed on the model of one or other of them? From the moment in which the pressure drops, the chances of dispersive massification increase: every third party can see behind him his common action, and can also perceive it ahead of him in a produced object (or in the ruins of a destroyed object); and, as we have seen, this

---

19. Or by *tactical mistakes*: in thoughtlessly attacking one part of the group, without seeing the other elements emerging from other streets, the body of soldiers or police will constitute these new arrivals as *encirclers* or define them by the opportunity it offers them of attacking *from behind*.

perception of common objectification is a group structure (*the crowd visits its conquest, the Bastille*). But as the urgency disappears, group behaviour may also be broken. For the common perception of objectification is neither necessary (for every third party) nor urgent: besides, all it does is relate the group's past-being to its present totalising practice as its sole *reason*. The group comes in order to *see itself* in *its* past victory; that is to say, it takes itself as its own end, first of all implicitly (seeing the Bastille conquered, the fortress finally reduced to impotence) and then explicitly (the lowered draw-bridges, the prisoners, the free movement in the courtyards and halls, all reflecting, in the practico-inert, the action which changed their statute). To this extent, then, reflexivity comes to the group from its past *praxis*, in so far as the produced object designates the group to itself as a group – to precisely the extent that this object appears only to an unfolding group *praxis*. But this object designates it to every third party in a synthetic opposition of two statutes: outside, past, inert, inscribed in things, the group is already made of marble and steel; its object-being (the Bastille) is the real preservation of its past-being (practical struggle and victory) in so far as this past being is in itself inertia (transcended being).[20]

But in so far as its *praxis* of disclosure is common, and in so far as the common object refers of itself to this community, the practical link appears as *developing disintegration*. Indeed, from one point of view, the only *reason* for the regroupment here is the common object, in so far as it has to be perceived in common. Thus the immense pressures which caused the liquidation of seriality have temporarily disappeared; in this way, the regulatory third party has practically nothing left to regulate: the 'order' no longer has any meaning simply because there is very little left to *do* apart from reactulising the common objectification. The people may be united to one another by an immense

20. It would be impossible to devise a theory of individual and group memory here. This problem is central in any study of groups, whatever its purpose. But it lies beyond the range of the present investigation. It should however be observed that the *structure of inertia* of the past (as transcended being) is not its only determination: it derives *a practical structure* from the transcendence itself in so far as it *preserves* it in its movement. It would also be necessary to describe the past as *exis* both in the practical organism and in the group. Organic *exis* is itself the object of a transcendence (there is no habit which is not also an adaptation to the present on the basis of the future); the *exis* of organisation, as we shall see, can be transcended, but need not necessarily be so. In any case, it is sufficient here to note that I consider the group in its relations to *a certain structure* of the past rather than to the past as a complex reality within the dialectic.

collective pride (or any other common conduct), but this is not very relevant: the behaviour of the third party always manifests itself as *the same here* as anywhere else in the group, but it no longer has *practical efficacity*. Multiplicity remains interiorised (*we* visit the site of *our* struggle), but it does not have any real effect. (Though it may have an effect on the group itself: *we* come in large numbers to inspect *our* victory, therefore *we* still hold fast. Or again: we can feel confident, etc. This is an example of what I shall call propaganda as immediacy: a finality without an agent and without a project.) Certain actions can be regarded as true regulations: someone dares to push open a door and go into a dark room; then some other daredevils follow on his heels: but the real aim – such as free access to the conquered Bastille – is not directly connected to these initiatives; even if the door had not been pushed open, the crowd would still have enjoyed its great victory. And even at the time there is no way of telling for certain whether these *unnecessary* (*si peu exigées*) actions, which are already dispersing, are totalising and common actions, or whether they are contagious or quasi-serial. In short, the being-of-the-group is the unity of all outside themselves in the produced object and the group *praxis* is weakened by the very movement by which it tries to *appropriate the object*.

Total disintegration (which would mean the disappearance of the common object as such) does not actually ever occur, because everyone is still linked to the object by other practices of appropriation unfolding through other third parties as the same: one person climbs on to the battlements, and another plants a flag. All these slightly differentiated practices run through the common object (like shivers), and so it is revealed to me *by them too* and therefore appears to me – illusorily – as a still developing objectification of the common action. No matter: this tension within *survival* expresses for every third party the double danger which threatens the group: being incorporated into a passive synthesis of the practico-inert field (a 'monument to the dead') or dissolving into a new serial gathering. This tension, lived by the third party, is in fact a sudden flash of awareness, to the extent that it reveals *the group in danger* and that it transcends itself – by revealing itself – towards a new end, that is to say, towards the preservation of the group, as a free practical unity, against this double danger. In particular, this aim will appear in urgency, when struggles threaten to begin again, or when a surprise attack is expected. The group becomes the common objective in everyone: its *permanence* must be secured. But the tension which we have just explained posits a common exigency:

the permanence of the group cannot be either the loosening of the common bond, threatening to tip the group back into seriality (either suddenly or gradually), or the practico-inert inertia of objectification, which is simply a being-outside-oneself, and which by its very structure contradicts freedom itself as a common violation of necessity.[21] In other words, the group as *survival*, between a completed action and an imminence in absence, posits itself for itself as an immediate objective, both from the point of view of its practical structure (differentiation and unity) and from the point of view of its ontological statute. Of course, it is still a mere *means*; but it is a means to be worked on – in the same way that a tool must be an immediate aim to the extent that essential ends depend on its manufacture.

2   The Pledge

It will be immediately obvious that *initially* the ontological statute is the most important: in a first moment of the dialectic, in fact, the relation of unity to differentiation depends on permanence. If *the existence* of the group in itself resists the forces of dissolution, divisions into sub-groups according to the needs of the struggle and of work will not pose any threat to its unity. But in a second moment, as we shall see, unity as *praxis* will become the very foundation of the ontological statute.

In the first moment, the group, positing itself for itself through the third party and by the *reflection* of transcendent unity as inertia onto totalisation in interiority as *praxis* in the process of dispersal, requires a contradictory statute, because the group desires permanence in the form in which it derives it from inertia and from free totalising *praxis* or, to put it differently, because it desires that totalisation in its very freedom should be subject to the ontological statute of inert synthesis.

21. This practico-inert being-outside-itself effectively threatens to subject the common action in its objective result to a new alienation: the alienation of the group itself as a group in the alienated world. We shall see that it cannot avoid it. But the spontaneous movement is *to avoid it*: simply because it perpetuates itself in freedom.

It is the actual conditions of survival which drive it back into this contradiction: the common *praxis* is freedom itself doing violence to necessity. But if circumstances demand the persistence of the group (as an organ of defence, of vigilance, etc.), while people's hearts are untouched by any urgency or hostile violence, which might occasion common *praxis*; if its *praxis*, turning back upon itself, in the form of organisation and differentiation, demands the unity of its members as the pre-existing foundation of all its transformations, then this unity can exist only as an inert synthesis within freedom itself. This moment of the fused group, in which everyone is *the same, here*, in some exhausting and dangerous action, which itself becomes the universal measure of everyone's action, must perpetuate itself for everyone in separation and in waiting and perhaps in isolation (in the case of a guard, for example); any particular sub-group must be able to retain in itself, in so far as it becomes regulatory, a free but *given* link with every other third party as regulatory and as totalised. This opaque *elsewhere*, which congeals around it and isolates it (night, silence, the special dangers of the situation), retains the fundamental structure of a *here*, despite all the appearances of alterity; in short, the *really other* action of the sub-group (which is on patrol, while the others are behind the barricades or at the windows of houses) is designated from its very foundation as *the same*, here and everywhere. But since in fact its alterity is real, this determination of unity can come to it only from the group as a lived permanence which imposes itself through dispersal.

This ontological structure of the group therefore involves an inversion. Of course, it is always a means in relation to the final objective (which is complete victory). But in relation to the *praxis* of differentiated waiting, it has to posit itself as a pre-existing agent. *Praxis* is the only real unity of the fused group: it is *praxis* which creates the group, and which maintains it and introduces its first internal changes into it. In the moment of the *praxis* of organisation and anticipation, it is the group which guarantees that every separate action is a common action or, to put it differently, it is the group as a reality which produces the unity of the common *praxis*. My courage and endurance, during my lonely watch, will be proportional to the permanence within me of the group as a common reality.

The dialectical exigency which I have just explained reveals itself to everyone, in the moment of survival, as a *practical exigency*: in fact, to the extent that the distribution of tasks determines itself on the basis of a near future, it entails mistrust of the future; it is in it, as a possibility of dispersal, that the dissolving action of separation and of inactive activity first come to be feared. Suspicion appears within the group not as a characteristic of human nature, but as the behaviour appropriate to this contradictory structure of survival: it is simply the interiorisation of the dangers of seriality. (Interiorised multiplicity was *really* present in everyone as an immediately given power in the earlier skirmish; and this multiplicity remains; it is always instrumentalised, and it is what makes it possible to post guards, patrols and combat groups everywhere. But, *at the same time,* it passes over to a statute which is more concrete, in that it is diversified and structured, but less immediately understood, since it coins itself in isolation. Separation as the rational use of number is an inversion of immediate union, or a mechanical use of quantity. One does indeed turn out to be multiple, but in a situation which appears to have all the characteristics of the isolation of impotence). Besides, the possibility of free secession manifests itself as a structural possibility of every individual *praxis*; and this possibility reveals itself in every other third party as *the same* in so far as this particular third party, here, reveals it in them.

Thus the ontological statute of the surviving group appears at first as the practical contrivance of a free, inert permanence of common unity in everyone. When freedom becomes common *praxis* and grounds the permanence of the group by producing its own inertia through itself and in mediated reciprocity, this new statute is called *the pledge (le serment)*. It goes without saying that pledges can take very different forms, from the explicit act of swearing an oath (for example, the Tennis Court oath; an oath as the synthetic link between members of a medieval commune) to the implicit assumption of a pledge as the already existing reality of the group (for example, by those who are born into the group and who grow up among its members). In other words, *the historical act* of making a pledge in common, though it is universal and *always* corresponds to a surviving group's resistance to the divisive tendency of (spatio-temporal) distance and differentiation, is not the only possible form of the common pledge, in so far as the pledge is a guarantee against the future, inertia produced in immanence and by freedom, and the foundation of all differentiation. If we examine it in its explicit reality as a historical act – for example, the communal bond in the Middle Ages – this is only because this posits itself *as such* and shows its structures more clearly.

A pledge is mediated reciprocity. All its derivative forms – for example a witness's oath in law, an individual swearing on the Bible, etc. – derive their meaning from this basic form of pledge. But we must be careful not to confuse this with a *social contract*. We are not trying to describe the basis of particular societies – which, as we shall see, would be absurd; we are trying to explain the necessary transition from an immediate form of group which is in danger of dissolution to another form, which is reflexive but permanent.

A pledge is a *practical device*. It cannot be presented as a possibility *for the individual*, unless it is assumed that the possibility is social and that it appears only on the basis of groups which are already bound by a pledge. As we have seen, the abstract experience of the practical organism, in so far as its *praxis* is a constituent dialectic, can give us only the translucidity of an action which is defined by its objective and which exhausts itself in its objectification. But, in so far as it is the group itself as *praxis*, this invention is the negation of some exterior circumstance which defines it negatively (*en creux*). In other words, it is the affirmation by the third party of the permanence of the group as the negation of its exterior negation. And exterior negation must not be confused with the danger of extermination by the enemy (or by a cataclysm); it only involves the possibility that certain tasks involve the re-emergence of the multiplicity of alterity or of exteriority, and this re-emergence does not directly imply the annihilation of the individuals as such. In this sense, the pledge is an inert determination of the future: that is to say, this inertia is above all a negation of dialectic inside the dialectic. Regardless of subsequent developments of *praxis*, of the event, or of the developing totalisation (up to and including the level of historical totalisation), one element will remain non-dialectical: every member's common membership of the group. The group will enter into new dialectical combinations which will transform it as such, but this will not affect its common unity, that is to say, its interior statute as a group.[22] The act of swearing an oath therefore consists in freely presenting the dispersal of the group in the future as an inert impossibility (as a permanent negation of certain possibilities within the field of possibilities) and, conversely, in bringing the future group to the present community as the limit to all possible transcendence. Here again we encounter the dialectical law which we met at the beginning of this investigation: the re-exteriorisation of inorganic inertia is the basis of instrumentality, that is, of the struggle against the

22. I refer to the *intended objective* rather than to the real effect of historical developments on the group under consideration.

inertia of matter within the practical field. The group tries to make itself its own tool against the seriality which threatens to dissolve it; it creates a factitious inertia to protect it against the threats of the practico-inert.

The device itself, that is to say, behaviour as immediate *praxis,* appears in the schema of intelligibility elucidated earlier. There is mediated reciprocity; whether or not it is spoken, the order: 'swear' certainly represents the invention as the regulatory action of the third party in the existing group. But it should be observed that in the milieu of *the same,* the third party fears dispersive dissolution *in the other third party as much as in himself*: the possibility of his being isolated may come to him from the third party, but only to the extent that it can come to the third party from him, or even, to the extent that it can come to him through himself. This negative possibility is therefore in every-one and *here* the same, and the reverse of the *praxis* of the fused group *as ubiquity.* And it is the possibility in everyone of becoming *other* through the other third party, and for him, through himself and for himself. Thus, in the order: 'Let us swear', he claims an objective guarantee from the other third party that he will never become Other: whoever gives *me* this guarantee *thereby* protects me, as far as he is concerned, from the danger that *Being-Other may come to me from the Other.* But equally, if he were to swear alone (or if everyone swore except me), then I alone would thereby take responsibility for bringing alterity to the group. But in fact the act of making a pledge cannot be anything but common: the order is 'Let us swear'. This means that I also make myself, both in and for him, a guarantee that alterity cannot come to him through me (either directly, as would happen if I were to abandon him in the middle of a joint action on behalf of the group, or through the mediation of all, as would happen if, within the majority, I abandoned the struggle with them and fled or surrendered).

This reciprocity is *mediated*: I give my pledge to all the third parties, as forming the group of which I am a member, and it is the group which enables everyone to guarantee the statute of permanence to everyone. A given third party can pledge the permanence of the group against alterity only in so far as this permanence depends on him, that is to say, in so far as the other third parties have assured him, on their account, of future *unchangingness.* For how could he guarantee that he will never be the Other, if he does not begin with the assurance that alterity will not come to him from outside and in spite of him (or unknown to him)? Indeed, it is characteristic of alterity to come to everyone through *the Other*. Thus my pledge to the third party receives at its source a dimension of *community*; it comes to touch everyone directly and through all. This common action of the third party realises itself as an objective structure of interiority and characterises the group as such. The pledge is not a subjective or merely verbal determination: it is a real modification of the group by my regulatory action. The inert negation of certain future possibilities is my bond of interiority with the sworn group to which I belong, in the sense that for everyone the same negation is conditioned by mine, in so far as it is *his* behaviour. Of course, it must be added that my own behaviour is itself conditioned by everyone else's. But this is not the most important point to emphasise: what appears at first, indeed, is that the guarantee of permanence provided by the oath of the Others produces itself in me as the objective impossibility (in interiority) that alterity should come to me from outside; but, at the same time, it is the possibility that I should make myself Other (by betraying, fleeing, etc.) which is underlined as a possible future coming from me to the Others. Now, this possibility may realise itself in the free development of my action: I may freely decide to abandon my post or to go over to the enemy. It goes without saying that the word 'freely' – here and elsewhere in this work – refers to the dialectical development of an individual *praxis*, born of need and transcending material conditions towards a definite objective. Betrayal and desertion, brought about by fear and suffering, are, therefore, from this point of view, free *praxes* in that they are organised behaviour *in response to* exterior threats. It is also clear that the fear of being afraid – for example, of letting the side down, of being the one through whom the group changes through panic into an inert mass – may be important for an inexperienced young combatant. He is afraid of this fear as an irresistible impulse and, at the same time, he rejects it as a free preference for his own safety over that of all. In this sense, my pledge becomes my surety for myself in that it is me offering myself, in every third party, as everyone's guarantee of not relapsing, in my person or through my conduct, into serial alterity. Thus, in making a pledge, the first movement is to swear so as to make the Others swear, through mediated reciprocity, that is to say, so as to guarantee oneself against the possibility that they will disperse. The second moment of the operation is to swear in order to protect oneself against oneself in the Others. It should also be noted that the second moment cannot be that of the totalising action of a regulatory third party: when I make a pledge, in fact, or when *I swear* or perform some equivalent act, I remain in a relation of transcendence-immanence to the group as a whole, and through my behaviour I effect a totalising synthesis which does not actually integrate me into the whole. My making the pledge thereby reveals itself as common freedom, but not as the inert negation of my possibilities. In other words, I unveil my future behaviour and its objective, which is the permanence of the group; but I unveil them in freedom, that is to say, the description expresses an *untranscendability* which freedom, as practical transcendence, cannot produce of itself. To put the same point another way, by becoming a freedom which swears, it reproduces itself as a freedom to transcend (to change, to betray) the pledge if circumstances change. On the other hand, *the pledge which I have made* returns to me from the third party and re-integrates me into the group, in so far as it is a constitutive structure of his pledge: it is the third party who, by his pledge, reintegrates me into the group as a third party whose immutability is an objective condition over there of the pledge of another third party. The act of swearing, when performed by the third party, becomes in turn a regulatory and totalising *praxis* and I am synthetically united with Others in the community of a quasi-object. Now, this quasi-object is reinteriorised by the third party, who makes a pledge as the sworn permanence which can alone give meaning to the pledge. My 'sworn faith' is reflected to me *as a surety against my freedom*, through that of the third party: in fact it is this which gives him a real possibility of swearing, since it is because of it (and, of course, because of everyone else's) that the possibility of relapsing into alterity no longer depends on him alone. (How could he *for his part* pledge the permanence of the unity, if this permanence were not constituted everywhere else except in his own freedom, if it was in danger of being broken at every point and at every moment?) Insured against my possible betrayal, he is in a position to affirm to all that he will not be the one through whom betrayal comes.

But this totalisation is also the moment in which a new sort of alterity emerges. In so far as, with the others, I am a common condition of the pledge for the third party, I already am permanence. My pledge is not a mere free act or a mere set of words describing my future behaviour and its possible developments: in so far as a third party constitutes it as such by basing his own pledge upon it, it is already the untranscendable, and therefore inert, negation of any possibility that I may change, regardless of the circumstances. And when the third party addresses me (and, as we have seen, he does this both indirectly and directly) his regulatory pledge is addressed to everyone who has already assumed permanence or, to be more precise, he constitutes me as such simply by transcending my pledge through his. Thus I turn out to be Other than myself within my own free *praxis* simply because its untranscendability comes from the other third party, that is to say, in fact, from *all the third parties* who have sworn, are swearing, or are going to swear, although I entirely accept my pledge. For the guarantee which I give to a particular third party is guaranteed by everyone and it is also *the same* (in the totalising synthesis of the third party) as that of all; it therefore turns out to be, for the regulatory third party, my common-being as untranscendability. And in this way it returns to me through everyone's pledge; that is to say, the group to which I belong becomes, in me, the common-being as Other-Being as a limit of my freedom: in fact this limit as untranscendability is different from free *praxis* and can come to it only from the Other. Or, to put it differently, it is this common Other-Being, which I am for *the same, here* (anywhere), which is the basis of his pledge to remain the same in so far as his oath is *the same* as mine.

It may be objected that my action here, in the fused group (work or combat), already allows and conditions that of the Other (of the same in that Other over there). And this is true: but *the action conditions it* in and through the object. It is the enemy held down and the task completed (by me, or us) which objectively determines the possibilities of action for a given third party. Similarly, everyone features as a unit in the interiorised multiplicity: but in everyone's act of interiorisation every third party figures (through mediated reciprocity) chiefly as a transcendence of this inert separation by the interiorisation of the multiple. In other words, in the fused group, the third party is never other: he produces his action in the object as the objective condition of my own action or, through the mediation of the group, his free *praxis*, in its real living development, conditions mine *to the extent that it is the same* (that is to say, a free dialectical development) and that it is conditioned by it. Besides, the results of this reciprocity of conditioning are to be read in the group as an objective reality (its growth) rather than in the free action of every individual. Free reciprocity in the regroupment so arranges things that *we come* to the group *as two*. But 'two' characterises neither my act of going to the group nor that of the third party, although both reinteriorise the quantity. On the contrary, the pledge is an act which refers to free *praxis* as such and tries freely to limit this freedom, *from within*. It would be absurd to suppose that an individual freedom could be limited *by itself*, except through some form of unpredictability (that is to say, the opposite form from that of the pledge: if circumstances were to change in some way or other I would be unable to predict sincerely what I would do), since *praxis* is the transcendence of conditions, it is adaptation to transformations of the practical field. This does not mean, of course, that we are uncertain, that we lack basic projects, acquired structures of predictables: quite the reverse.

But even if these conditions, transcended and preserved by freedom, did enable us to predict everything (as with an agent who is completely contained within the practico-inert field), they are exactly the opposite of a pledge: through a pledge, freedom gives itself a practical certainty for cases in which (because circumstances vary) future behaviour is unpredictable. This is possible only in so far as freedom is *other* for itself – that is to say, in so far as it is no longer simply the transparency of an urgent adaptation to the exigencies of need and to the dangers of the field. And this *alterity* can come to freedom only from the *Other*. If, however, we do not relapse (at least not yet) into seriality, this is because the Other is being regarded here *in* his practice, that is to say, as power and as freedom; and this activity affects me as a hardening against the world of impotence and seriality. In short, the third party remains *the same* for me (he freely does what I do, when I do it: his pledge, like mine, is regulatory in mediated reciprocity); but through the practical activity of the third party, *in so far as it is the same*, I come back to myself as the unshakable common condition of his possibility. The deep reason for this completely formal, negative alterity is that the group takes itself as its own objective. Thus every action of every third party must have every other third party (and all) as its objective, and as its means and agent (in so far as he takes it up or transcends it and organises it for Others); and, instead of transcending itself towards the object, every action turns out to be in an object which manifests itself as homogeneous. Thus, by appearing *as an aim* and revealing itself as a *common praxis* which has to be sustained, the group reveals every *praxis*, *in formalism* (if not in inaction, since there is such a thing as an activity of surviving communities), as the condition and means of every Other, in so far as this Other is the same. In *practical reflection*, everyone returns to himself in so far as he positively conditions the free action of every third party by negatively limiting his own. But the project of limitation returns to him (through a freedom which makes a pledge) as an exigency in him for everyone's freedom, that is to say, both as his freedom as an Other and as the freedom of the Others. The moment of making the pledge is – in spite of the words that are spoken – only a project which announces itself with an urgency and affirmative force which are conditioned by the real organism, by need, by danger, etc.; or rather it would be, if it could be separated, for *one* individual, from the common pledge. But if this moment is, *also*, that of all the pledges returning upon mine, I become in everyone *the transcended condition of free praxis* (sure of myself and of the Others, no one need concern himself with anything outside his specialised task) and, in so far as this free common *praxis* returns to me as a condition of *my own freedom* (I, too, must rely on them in performing my task, either on my own or in a sub-group), it constitutes the untranscendability of being-in-the-group as *an exigency*.

Exigency, as we saw in our discussion of the practico-inert, is a claim made on some *praxis* by an inorganic materiality (and, of course, through some other *praxis*). Exigency, in this context, has the same characteristics, but it is the agents themselves that are inorganic inertia. To the extent that the permanence of my membership of the group is my own free project, this permanence is for my action an objective situated in the future, and coming to me on the basis of future dangers. But this project of itself makes a claim on every member of the group, in that it can be carried out for and by everyone only in and through the permanence of the group, *everywhere*. In so far as the same project becomes, through my free pledge, a complete response, deliberately given by me, to this claim in the third party, it returns to me through the third party: as faith sworn to the Other – and in the Other – it is, therefore, a limitation on my freedom. Now this limitation conditions the possibility of his free pledge, that is to say, of that free limitation which I need in order to be free. Thus my project returns to me as its own negative, inert condition: for me to be able to rely on the group in separation, everyone must be able to rely upon me; I can claim that they will sustain the limitation of their own possibilities (of betraying, of disbanding, of slackening their activity, their work, etc.) as an impossibility of changing only if I yield to their claim on my freedom, for example, as the necessary condition of the calm with which they will carry out a dangerous task, certain that everyone everywhere is doing everything to guarantee their maximum security. Yes, in *this dangerous mission* which may save *us*, or save me in the totality, I exist in everyone as his trust and courage, that is to say, as the immutability of all the Others; through every concrete action performed elsewhere, the future negative therefore appears in my action as my exigency upon myself in so far as it is the claim of all the Others on me (and on all the Others). The inorganic, in this context, is the rigid, non-dialectical future, and this future is posited both as an impenetrable framework and as the basis of any dialectical *praxis*: a framework because whatever my acts may be, they cannot destroy the permanence of the group; and a basis, because as long as the group still has an urgent objective, any activity must tend to sustain the powers and practical efficacity of the group. On the basis of this *untranscendability*, I will set myself tasks (or be given some), which can be achieved only through free, practical development. This triple character of untranscendability (the exigency, framework, and basis of any *praxis*) may have given the impression that the reflected group becomes the basis of a new dialectic (as *praxis*), whereas it is really constituted by the original dialectic, of which *permanence* is simply a negative determination.

For clarity, I have distinguished two moments: that of the project being announced, and that of the pledge of the Other which returns to me. But it goes without saying that this purely formal distinction was intended to explicate the structures of the pledge. In other words, *the project* (as the dialectical transcendence of material conditions) is still the fundamental movement. But it is obvious that for everyone, even before the Others make their pledge, *it is already a pledge*. My point has simply been that it could be so only *through the Others*. A pledge necessarily involves the following: (1) the characteristics of an order, of a regulatory action, whose (*reflected*) aim is to involve third parties: I offer myself so that they can offer themselves; the offer of my services (my life, etc.) is already *the same* as theirs. At this level, my commitment (*engagement*) *is* a reciprocal commitment, mediated by the third party. (2) The characteristic of a manipulation of myself: to swear is to give what one does not possess in order that the Others shall give it to you so that one can keep one's word: I define the permanence of the group as *my* untranscendability in a practical movement of all which, through the totalisation of pledges, must *confer on me* this untrans-cendability as a negative limit and as an absolute exigency. These two characteristics are indissolubly linked; in so far as each of them is a claim made upon the other third party or myself, through the mediation of the third party, these claims are immediately satisfied by the pledges of all the Others. In fact, although the actual giving of the pledges may be successive (each representative of the Third Estate in turn signing the proceedings in the Jeu de Paume) and thus involve a quite formal seriality, the entire real moment of the common action is contained in the order 'Let us swear' – that is to say, in the common decision to swear. At the moment of the decision, the pledge still lies in the future, but its signification – as an immediate objective of the group and as a *means* of maintaining the permanence required by certain more distant objectives – presents it to everyone as a common operation, or, in other words, as the group acting on itself *through every member*. Thus even if the pledge of one third party is given before that of others (for example, in the serial order of signing), it can never fail: it temporalises itself in an already limited temporality which contains in advance the pledges of all. In a sense, to say 'Let us swear' is to swear: the possibility of a disagreement about this is in fact normally purely formal. If the pledge is *recreated*, this is because objective circumstances already constitute it as the group's only reflexive means of preserving its unity. It should be defined as everyone's freedom guaranteeing the security of all so that this security can return to everyone as his *other-freedom* so as to ground his free, practical membership of the group as an untranscendable exigency. Indeed, after the pledge, as before, the third party *makes himself* a member of the group through his common *praxis*, and therefore in freedom: this means that his very action develops in dialectical freedom, either within a sub-group or as the common *praxis* of an isolated individual. The pledge is simply the coincidence, at the source of his practice, of the security of the absent third parties (which he guarantees) and of his own security (guaranteed by the third parties). Exigency and untranscendable permanence as an inert negation of possibilities reveal themselves under the influence of definite conditions (actions of the enemy, for example, such as terror, torture, or separate offers to negotiate, etc.).

3   *Fraternity and Fear*

At this level of description, it is at last possible to pose the question of intelligibility. In fact, we shall discover the intelligibility proper to the pledge if we can solve two problems. First, since the pledge comes to the surviving group through third parties and in mediated reciprocity, our investigation must grasp the dialectical continuity (that is to say, the free development) which always constitutes the re-creation of sworn faith. In other words, the individual project and the common *praxis* of the fused group are *comprehensible* realities; our investigation must establish whether the re-creation of the pledge is a dialectical process, capable of being understood on the basis of concrete circumstances. Secondly, the structures of the common pledge, as elucidated here, at first appear to have a sort of abstract ideality: the reason for this is that the pledge as an action of the group on itself does not at first appear as a modification by the effort (by work and combat) of the material statute of the group, but as an immobile contraction of its bonds. Of course, language is materiality, action is effort. But neither the repetition of orders by a hundred mouths, nor the raising of hands, can be compared with the exhausting work of construction or of combat. In our descriptions of the fused group, meanings (*significations*) corresponded to the creation of a common *praxis* both as a *real consumption of energy* and as a directed modification of the environment. Thus the group *really constructed itself* as a whole produced by work, through sweat and toil, to precisely the extent that its common effort inscribed it in Being. Compared with this enormous dialectical event, which can also be seen simply in terms of energy transformations, the moment of the pledge appears as a moment of ideality. Moreover, the unity of the fused group derived its materiality from the intolerable pressure of the enemy group; *it was* the interiorisation and inversion of this pressure (of this totalising destruction). The unity of the pledged group, by way of contrast, in so far as it comes from it alone and from a *possible* but not yet actual attack, seems to be a mere play of signs and meanings; nothing *material* really unites me to the third parties. And if the pledge were simply a reciprocal determination of discourse, it would not explain the adhesive force which causes me, while isolated and under enemy pressure, to have the feeling of being a member of the group. In the case of differentiated dispersal, in fact, the action of the enemy tends (directly or indirectly, and whether deliberately or not) to accentuate isolation (in contrast to what happens in a fused group). In the face of death or torture, common interest is in danger of giving way to immediate necessity (avoidance of death or pain): it would be almost impossible to believe that the operation described above could, on its own, constitute the untranscendability of the group in these circumstances as an irresistible force of inertia.

These two problems are really identical; we will solve them together and through each other. For, though we have described the internal structures of the pledged group, we have not grasped the true, immediate meaning of the pledge as freely re-created by the third party.

The origin of the pledge, in effect, is fear (both of the third party and of myself). The common object exists; indeed it is common interest in so far as it negates a community of destiny. But a reduction of enemy pressure while the threat persists, entails the unveiling of a new danger for everyone: that of the gradual disappearance of the common interest and the reappearance of individual antagonisms or of serial impotence. This reflexive fear is born of a real contradiction: the danger still exists (it may even be objectively *more serious* – the enemy may have obtained reinforcements), but it becomes distant, and moves to the level of *signification*, and does not arouse enough fear. Reflexive fear, for the third party, is born when no one – not even him – *is sufficiently afraid*. The change of state which characterises the surviving group is its very vulnerability: assuming it does not disintegrate, there is no guarantee that attack would give it back its statute as a fused group. Reflexive fear is lived entirely *in the concrete*, through real facts: one man being exhausted, another wounded, and a third asleep, myself having an argument with a fourth, and so on. And the transcendence of this developing dissolution by the third party can occur only through the negation of the circumstances which condition it, that is to say, by the negation of the absence of fear.

The fundamental re-creation, within the pledge, is the project of substituting a real fear, produced by the group itself, for the retreating external fear, whose very distance is deceptive. And we have already encountered this fear as a free product of the group, and as a coercive action of freedom against serial dissolution; we have seen it appear momentarily during the action itself; and it is called Terror. Terror, we said, is common freedom violating necessity, in so far as necessity exists only through the alienation of some freedom. Through the third party who reveals the group as threatened by death in his own person and in that of the Others, transcendence reaffirms the group as a threat of immediate death for any *praxis* which tried to become individual again and relapse into seriality. *The group as action upon itself*, at the level of survival, can only be coercive. The regulatory third party reveals that the diminishing fear of danger is the real threat, and that it must be counteracted by an increasing fear of destroying the group itself. The aim is the same: to protect the common interest. But, in the absence of any material pressure, the group *must produce itself as a pressure on its members*. And this re-creation is in no way idealist, for it presents itself concretely as a set of real means (accepted for everyone by all) of establishing in the group a reign of absolute violence over its members. It does not matter much whether statutes are laid down, and organs of supervision and policing created (as in some developed groups) or whether the pledge simply gives everyone, as a member of the group, the right of life and death over everyone, either as an individual or as a member of a series. The essential point is that the transformation lies in the risk of death which, as a possible agent of dispersal, everyone runs within the group. On the other hand, this violence *is free*: for present purposes, it is irrelevant that, historically and in particular circumstances, some elements of the community may have usurped it for their own advantage: we shall return to this point. What matters is that no usurpation of violence (or conquest of power) can be intelligible unless violence is initially a particular, real, practical bond between freedoms within common action – in other words, unless this violence is the kind of action on itself of the pledged group, in so far as this action is re-created, carried out and accepted by all.

But *this* is precisely what a pledge is: namely the common production, through mediated reciprocity, of a statute of violence; once the pledge has been made, in fact, the group has to guarantee everyone's freedom against necessity, even at the cost of his life and in the name of freely sworn faith. Everyone's freedom demands the violence of all against it and against that of any third party as its defence against itself (as a free power of secession and alienation). To swear is to say, as a common individual: you must kill me if I secede. And this demand has no other aim than to install Terror within myself as a free defence against the fear of the enemy (at the same time as reassuring me about the third party who will be confirmed by the same Terror). At this level, the pledge becomes a material operation. The first moment, 'Let us swear', corresponds to the practical transformation of the common statute: the common freedom constitutes itself as Terror. The second moment – the successive or simultaneous giving of pledges – is a materialisation of Terror, its embodiment in a material object (swearing on the sword; signing the text of the common pledge or creating organs of coercion). Thus the intelligibility of the pledge derives from the fact that it is a rediscovery and an affirmation of violence as a diffuse structure of the fused group and that it transforms it reflexively into a statutory structure of common relations. In fact, to precisely the extent that the relations of the third parties are mediated, that is to say, to the extent that they pass through all, the character of violence cannot be detected in them: they are the free common relations of members of the group as such. But as soon as the danger of disintegration appears, every third party produces himself for everyone else as the one who passes sentence in the name of the group and who then carries out the sentence (or, conversely, as the one on whom the sentence will be executed by everyone else). But, at the same time, everyone has constituted himself as demanding to be defended against himself and as accepting the sentence, whatever it may be. And Terror comes to everyone – even before any particular risk – from his structure of immanence-transcendence: at the very moment when the synthetic, totalising operation of his *praxis* becomes a pure designation of the totalising third party as a *third party to be integrated*, the real danger of falling out of the group is lived in practice in and through this *impossible integration*. The material force which unites the sworn parties is the force of the group as a totalisation which threatens to totalise itself without them (if they lost sight of the common interest) and this force as the coercive power of a hostile totality is, for everyone, directly and constantly, the possibility of losing his life. In this sense, being-in-the-group as an untranscendable limit produces itself as the certainty of death should the limit be transcended.

From this point of view, it does not matter whether the pledge, as a material operation, involves some transcendent (*transcendant*) being (the Cross, the Bible, or God himself) or whether it remains in common immanence. In either case, transcendence (*la transcendance*) is present in the pledged group as the *absolute* right of all over every individual: in other words, the statute does not present itself as a mere practical formation which is provisionally adopted because it is best suited to the circumstances; it is posited by everyone's freedom as demanded by it and all the third parties, against it and against any failings of the Others. Its transcendence (that is to say, its permanent, absolute right to manifest itself in a sentence of death for anyone) is based on freedom's affirmation of itself as justified violence against the practico-inert. Thus God, or the Cross, do not add anything to this character which is, so to speak, for the first time, the positing of man as the absolute power of man over man (in reciprocity). But, conversely, when the pledge, in a profoundly religious society, is given under the eye of God and calls for divine punishment of anyone who violates it (damnation, etc.), this commitment to God is only a substitute for immanent integration. God becomes responsible for executing the lofty tasks of the group; he is, as it were, a substitute for the executioner. It might even be thought that damnation takes the place of capital punishment (since it is taken to be real and has the same function as death); but in fact, if the pledge is betrayed, divine sanctions in no way prevent the group from executing the traitor: the right of life and death – however linked to the transcendent – is the very statute of the group.

A free attempt to substitute the fear of all for the fear of oneself and of the Other in and through everyone, in so far as it suddenly re-actualises violence as the intelligible transcendence of individual alienation by common freedom: that is what pledges are. They are completely intelligible because they are the free transcendence of *already given* elements towards an already posited objective in so far as this transcendence is conditioned by concrete circumstances which prefigure it negatively (*en creux*) (a destiny to be negated). But the structures of freedom and reciprocity which we examined at the beginning, far from disappearing, take on their full meaning when they manifest themselves in the practical material movement of terror. It is still true that my pledge is a guarantee for the other third party; but the meaning of this guarantee is precisely violence. The third party is guaranteed against my free betrayal by the right which I have granted everyone (including him) to eliminate me in the event of my failure, and by the Terror which the common right establishes within me and which I have demanded; and this guarantee – which deprives him of any excuse in the event of dispersal or betrayal – means that he can freely guarantee his own solidarity (freely demand Terror for himself).

Thus I encounter Terror within myself as exigency. In other words, the fundamental statute of the pledged group is Terror; but, if circumstances are not specially restrictive, I can remain at the level of exigency and untranscendability. For the pledge is a free relation of free commitments. At this level, I perceive the exigency only as my committed freedom in the other and as the exigency of *myself* towards *the Other*. If the pressure increases, the same relation reveals itself in its fundamental structure: I have freely consented to the liquidation of my person as free constituent *praxis*, and this free consent returns to me as the free primacy of the Other's freedom over my own, that is to say, as the right of the group over my *praxis*. Here again, it does not matter whether this right is conceived as a duty towards the group (that is to say, concretely as an imperative negation of a possibility: this obviously has nothing to do with *morals* or even with *codes*) or whether it is conceived as a power of the group, consented to by me, of taking my life if I do not act in accordance with a given directive. *For us*, and *in this moment of our investigation*, this makes no difference: these different forms of behaviour are in fact conditioned by circumstances and they

constitute themselves *in their situation*. The important point is that
within itself, and implicitly, the concrete duty contains death as a
possible destiny for me; or, conversely, that the right of the group
determines me, in so far as it is *agreed*.

This statute of the pledged group is, in any case, crucial: indeed, it
might be said that our dialectical investigation has led us to elucidate
the original *practical, and created* (and constantly re-created) relation
between active men within an active community. The group as
permanence is, in effect, *an instrument constructed* in concrete circumstances, on the basis of a fused group (or at least, this is how it appears
in our dialectical investigation). And this construction, which is
common, or effected by every third party as a common individual, can
never be reduced to 'natural', 'spontaneous' or 'immediate' relations. It
occurs, in effect, when external conditions have occasioned a reflexive
praxis within a surviving group: the nature of the danger and of the
task implies that the group – in so far as it is threatened with dissolution
– posits itself as a means of its *praxis* and a *means to be consolidated*.
Thus the relations between members of the group establish themselves
in a community which is *acting on itself*; they are pierced by this subjective *praxis* and conditioned by it. However, we have already seen
that the coercive character of the group derives from the fact that it
does not have *existence* (like an organism) or *being* (like a material
totality). At this level, the group, as a reality, is initially no more than
the impossibility for everyone of abandoning the common *praxis*. To
put it differently, its *being* is for everyone a pledge of death as the inert
negation of any possibility of strictly individual action.

This *being* is, as we have seen, an *Other-Being* for every free *praxis*.
But still we do not relapse into seriality, since, for each third party, this
Other-Being is *the same* Other-Being as for his neighbour. In this sense,
violence is everywhere Terror as the first common statute. But this
Terror, as long as unity has not been destroyed by circumstances, is a
terror *which unites* rather than a terror which separates. Indeed, in so
far as these men have constituted themselves by their pledges as
common individuals, they find their own Terror, in one another, as *the
same*; *here and everywhere* they live their *grounded* (that is to say,
limited) freedom as their being-in-the-group, and their being-in-the-
group as *the being* of their freedom. In this sense, Terror is their primary
unity in so far as it is the power of freedom over necessity in everyone.
In other words, being-in-the-group is, for everyone, an intermediary
between free common *praxis* (for simplicity, we assume that the action

has not yet begun) and the statute of serial impotence. It is the statutory guarantee, freely demanded, that no one will relapse into the practico-inert field and that individual action, *in so far as it becomes common*, as such escapes from alienation (even if the total *praxis* of the group relapses into it). As a reflexive construction, this guarantee is everyone's solicitude for everyone, but this solicitude is a bearer of death. But still, it is *through this mortal solicitude* that man as a common individual is created, in and by everyone (and by himself), *as a new entity*; and the violent negation of certain future possibilities is, for him, indistinguishable from this statute of created novelty. In the pledged group, the fundamental relation between all the third parties is that they created themselves together from the clay of necessity. It is on this basis that their immediate relations of reciprocity established themselves. Everyone recognises violence in the other third party as the agreed impossibility of turning back, of reverting to the statute of sub-humanity[23] and as the perpetuation of the violent movement which created him as a common individual. But, of course, this recognition is both practical and concrete. It is *concrete* because every third party recognises the members of the group not as abstract men (or abstract instances of the genus), but as sworn members of a particular species – a species which is connected with concrete circumstances, with objectives, and with the pledge. It is *practical* because it is the pledge itself renewing itself through some particular act of reciprocity (he helps me, does me a good turn, etc.) and presenting itself as its fundamental structure. This is particularly evident in the case of public or clandestine mutual aid groups, but this case is more complex than those we are examining here. And as every pledge is conditioned by that of all, since ultimately it is that of all which provides the basis in everyone, *in his inert-being*, of the freedom of the common individual, recognition is simultaneously recognition in everyone of his freedom (in a double form: committed freedom and the freedom of free practical development following commitment) through the freedom of the other, and an affirmation *of membership of the group*.

Totalisation, in this context, is simply the reactualisation of the statute everywhere (that is to say, in everything *here and now*). It presents itself both as having been performed once and for all and as

23. I use this term without giving it any definite content and because it seems to me to mark, at every stage, the relation between a group which posits itself for itself and the passivity of the practico-inert field.

having to be constantly reactualised. In the act of constructing the pledge, in fact, an object is created (in the 'historic' moment in which the decision was taken): this material object retains in its materiality the historical pledge as an untranscendable past. The objectification of the fused group (a fortress taken and dismantled, etc.) is not abandoned; on the contrary, it becomes the material realisation of an archaic unity, the moment of common rising. But it is another, earlier mode of reality: the signed agreement and the actual place where the pledge was made appear, at the level of the pledged group, as the group's *force of inertia*, as the perseverance of the being-in-the-group in its being against internal and external threats. It is the indissoluble reciprocity of significations between, on the one hand, the inorganic materiality of the fact, revealing *here and now*, on the basis of every future-project (*avenir-projet*), its *present-being* as a constitutive structure, and, on the other, past human fact as the immediate link with the future (the fact of swearing was, in both its immediate and its profound reality, a precaution against the future), but as an *untranscendable* link, and so as the eternity *of presence in the future*. The pledged group produces its objectification as a particular material product *in it* (the written pact, and the very hall in which it was signed, which was formerly a container, become, after dispersal, an interiorised product, a material mediation between the members). But this interior objectivity (which produces itself for everyone as an impossibility of going back beyond a certain past date, as an irreversibility of temporalisation) is not the objectification of the group as *being*; it is the eternal, frozen preservation of its rising (of the reflexive, statutory rising through the pledge). It is the origin of humanity.[24]

In becoming for everyone an imperative nature (by virtue of its character as an untranscendable permanence *in the future*), this beginning therefore directs recognition to the reciprocal affirmation of these two *common* characteristics: we are *the same* because we emerged from

24. Let there be no misunderstanding: I am not talking about those few great revolutionary moments in which contemporaries actually have the feeling of producing, and being subjected to, man as a new reality. Every organisation which has the reciprocity of the pledge is a new beginning, since it is always the victory of man as common freedom over seriality, whatever it may be. In fact, this victory is already won at the level of the fused group, but it is through the pledge that the group posits itself for itself, no longer as the implicit means of a common *praxis*, both produced and absorbed by it, but as a means of attaining a more or less distant objective, and *therefore* as its own immediate objective.

the clay at the same date, through each other and through all the others; and so we are, as it were, an individual species, which has emerged at a particular moment through a sudden mutation; but our specific nature unites us in so far as it is freedom. In other words, *our common being* is not *an identical nature* in everyone. On the contrary, it is a mediated reciprocity of conditionings: in approaching a third party, I do not recognise my inert essence as manifested in some other instance; instead I recognise my necessary accomplice in the act which removes *us* from the soil: my brother, whose existence *is not other than mine* approaches me as my existence and yet depends on mine as mine depends on his (through everyone) in the irreversibility of free agreement. Indeed, everyone lives *group-being* as a nature: he is 'proud' *to belong to it*, he becomes *the material referent* (*signifié*) of the uniforms of the group (if there are any) – *but* as *the nature of freedom* (it is its frightening force of inertia, in so far as it comes to me as exigency). Thus the relations of common individuals within the group are ambivalent links of reciprocity (unless they are governed by the resumption of the struggle and the total objective): he and I *are brothers*. And this fraternity is not based, as is sometimes stupidly supposed, on physical resemblance expressing some deep identity of natures. If it were, why should not a pea in a can be described as the brother of another pea in the same can? We are brothers in so far as, following the creative act of the pledge, we *are our own sons*, our common creation. And, as in real families, fraternity is expressed in the group by a set of reciprocal and individual obligations, defined by the whole group on the basis of circumstances and objectives (obligations to help one another in general or in the particular and fully determinate case of an action or a concrete task). But as we have just seen, these obligations in turn express only the community of fundamental exigency and, in addition, past self-creation as an irrevocable mortgage of practical temporalisation. From this point of view, fraternity is the real bond between common individuals, in so far as everyone lives *his being* and that of the Other (whether in simply being there, close to the Other, or in the resemblance-solidarity of black rebels, or of whites on the defensive) in the form of untranscendable reciprocal obligations. Indeed: the colour of their skin, taken as a pure, reciprocal obligation by the black rebels of San Domingo, and, at the same time, as everyone's material, inert guarantee against the possibility of being alienated, the colour of their skin being taken, in and by everyone, not as a universal physiological characteristic, but as a historical characteristic based on the *past unity* of a free *promotion* –

this is fraternity, that is to say the fundamental, practical structure of all the reciprocal relations between the members of a group. What is later called comradeship, friendship, love – and even fraternity, using the term in a vaguely affective sense – arises on the basis of particular circumstances and within a particular perspective, for a given reciprocity as a dialectical, practical enrichment, as a free specification of this original structure, that is to say, of the practical, living statute of the sworn members. The constituted group is produced in and by everyone as *his own birth as a common individual* and, at the same time, everyone can grasp, in fraternity, his own birth as a common individual as having been produced in and by the group.

Furthermore, this fraternity is *the right of all* through everyone and over everyone. It is not enough to recall that it is also violence, or that it originated in violence: it is violence itself affirming itself as a bond of immanence through positive reciprocities. This means that the practical power of the bond of fraternity is simply (in immanence[25]) the free transformation of the fused group by everyone, for himself and for the other third party, into a group of constraint. This lack of distinction is particularly evident when the sworn group proceeds to the summary execution or lynching of one of its members (suspected, rightly or wrongly, of betraying the group). The traitor is not excluded from the group; indeed he himself cannot extricate himself from it. He remains a member of the group in so far as the group – threatened by betrayal – reconstitutes itself by annihilating the guilty member, that is to say, by discharging *all its violence* onto him. But this exterminating violence is still a link of fraternity between the lynchers and the lynched in that the liquidation of the traitor is grounded on the positive affirmation that he is *one of the group*; right up to the end, he is abused in the name of his own pledge and of the right over him which he acknowledged in the Others. On the other hand, lynching is a *praxis* of common violence for the lynchers in so far as its objective is the annihilation of the traitor. It is a bond of fraternity aroused and accentuated amongst the lynchers, in so far as it is a brutal reactualisation of the pledge itself and in so far as every stone that is thrown, every blow delivered, is a new affirmation of the pledge: whoever participates in the execution of the traitor reaffirms the untranscendability of group-being as a limit of his freedom

25. Indeed, it goes without saying that, down to its last member, the group is characterised by its transcendent relation to the other group, that is to say, to the hostile group; we shall return to this.

and as his new birth, and he reaffirms it in a bloody sacrifice which, moreover, constitutes an explicit recognition of the coercive right of all over every individual and everyone's threat to all. Furthermore, in the developing *praxis* (that is to say, during the execution) everyone feels at one with everyone in the practical solidarity of the risks run and of the common violence. I am a brother in violence to all my neighbours: and it is clear that anyone who shunned this fraternity would be suspect. In other words, anger and violence are lived both as Terror against the traitor and (if circumstances have produced this feeling) as a practical bond of *love* between the lynchers.[26] Violence is the very power of this lateral reciprocity of love.

This enables us to understand how the intensity of the group's actions arises from the intensity of the external threats, that is to say, from danger; and if this intensity no longer manifests itself as a real pressure but the danger itself still exists, then it is replaced by the artificial substitute of Terror. Terror is a real *product* of men in groups, but it still depends, *in itself* and for its degree of intensity, on hostile violence (that is to say, both on suffered violence surviving in people's memories, and on expected violence, as in the case, for example, of a counter-attack). The creation of Terror as a counter-violence engendered by the group itself and applied by common individuals to every particular agent (in so far as he contains a threat of seriality) is, therefore, a use of common strength, hitherto used against the enemy, in order to reshape the group itself. And *all the internal behaviour of common individuals* (fraternity, love, friendship, as well as anger and lynching) derives its terrible power from Terror itself. In this sense, everyone is, for everyone, the same in the unity of a common *praxis*; but, precisely because reciprocity is not integration, and because the epicentres, though dissimulated, are still in mediated reciprocity, and because I cannot be both a totalising and a totalised third party, and because the Other me who approaches me also exists in me as myself become Other (and limiting my freedom), the possibility of constraint or extermination is given *simultaneously* in every reciprocal relation. This has nothing to do with *mistrust*: mistrustful behaviour occurs in groups of constraint when they are already eroded by divisions, and therefore at a quite different moment of the common temporalisation

---

26. I am of course referring to the execution of traitors rather than to the kind of racist lynching which, in America, provides recreation for a member of another group.

and in different circumstances. The possibility of loving a traitor is given in fraternity itself and as a condition of it: and this means that any concrete and practical relation within the group is necessarily addressed through the common individual to the organic individual, and thereby helps to give him a real existence which common solidarity must either negate or pass over in silence. And this possibility that fraternity with a given person may suddenly change, through the betrayal of the brother, into lynching and extermination, is given in fraternity itself as its source and limit: we fraternise because we have made the same pledge, because everyone has limited his freedom by the other; and the limit of this fraternity (which also determines its intensity) is everyone's right of violence over the other, that is to say, precisely the common, reciprocal limit of our freedoms. However, as can still be observed today in authoritarian parties, fraternity is the most immediate and constant form of Terror: traitors, in fact, are by definition the minority. It is *really* the reciprocal translucidity of common individuals (which is capable of leading organic individuals into friendship): no 'milieu' is *warmer* than an authoritarian party which is constantly subject to external threats (and which is authoritarian *because* it is threatened). But, whatever the fraternity, in the event of deviation, heresy, or betrayal, it cannot survive violence (except in the form described above: the link between the executioner and the condemned man); and it cannot oppose it either; not, as has too often been said, because it would be weak and ineffective *against* Terror, but quite simply because it is violence itself lived as violence-friendship (as a violent force within relations of friendship). This violence, born in opposition to the dissolution of the group, creates a new reality, the act of treason; and this act defines itself precisely as that which transforms fraternity (as positive violence) into Terror (negative violence). Thus, if I am a member of a constraining group, the violence of my fraternisation rests on the practical certainty (which is not, or need not be, explicit) that this fraternisation will become either a lynching, *in its own name*, or a pitiless condemnation, if my brother behaves as an Other and if the group sees in him a threat of dissolution.

The immediate bond of freedom and constraint has produced a new reality, a *synthetic product* of the group as such. My application of the term 'right' to this reality may seem premature, since, ultimately, all institutions are grounded on the pledge, which is not in itself institutional. It would be better to say that this reality, in this abstract moment of our investigation of the group, is simply the diffuse power of jurisdiction. But we must be quite clear about this: I use the word *diffuse* only to make a contrast with specialised organs; in fact, the common individual's pledge gives him juridical power over the organic individual (in himself and Others). Freedom which has been freely limited forever by his other-being is each person's *power* over all in so far as it is in everyone an accepted mutilation. It is impossible to derive juridical power either from individual freedom, which has no power over reciprocal freedom, or from a social contract uniting several entities, or from the constraint imposed on the group by some differentiated organ, or from the customs of a community in so far as they appear to involve an *exis*. As for the circumstances which explain the particular content of this power (that it is exerted as a *particular* prohibition, as a *particular* exigency, etc.), they may show us, in fact, that a given risk run by a given group in particular circumstances gave birth in this group to a given common decision, but by themselves they cannot explain repressive power as a practical form of the decision in question.

However, we are not in any way attempting to describe the historical genesis of the power of jurisdiction: and we shall see below that such an undertaking does not even have any sense. But our dialectical investigation involves us in the re-creation of this power in a surviving group which is attempting to become a statutory group. Juridical power appears here as the creation of a community which realises that it neither is nor ever will be a totalised (and totalising) totality; it is therefore a new form of totalisation intended to compensate for the impossibility of completing the totalisation, that is to say, of its appearing as a form, a *Gestalt*, a collective consciousness above all the members, and, therefore a guarantee of their permanent integration. This new statute of totalisation is Terror, and Terror is jurisdiction: through the mediation of all, everyone agrees with everyone else that the permanent foundation of every freedom should be the violent negation of necessity, that is to say, that, in everyone, freedom as a common structure is the permanent violence of the individual freedom of alienation. And everyone demands that everyone should both guarantee him the inert structure of common freedom and make himself, as violence and terror, the inert negation of certain possibilities.

It would be dangerous to assimilate this diffuse juridical power to the simplest form of the sacred: this would take us too far and the examination of these matters is not part of our task. It will be sufficient to note that in our investigation and at this level of abstraction, for groups which have defined themselves in combat and by the liquidation of the old seriality of impotence, the Sacred constitutes the fundamental structure of Terror as juridical power. The Sacred is manifested *through things*; it is freedom producing itself in worked matter, both as absolute sovereignty and as thing. It is, so to speak, freedom returning to man as a superhuman, petrified power. This has nothing to do with the exigencies of the practico-inert field, which, although they do indeed express the freedom of the Other, absorb it entirely and do not show it, so that an inert thing could of itself be an exigency. In the case of the Sacred, freedom manifests itself in a thing, upon its very destruction (through explosive disintegration)[27], but by affirming itself in opposition to the thing it becomes an inert-power over man. And *revelation, prayer* and other practices in relation to this power constitute it as sacred in its very contradiction: freedom, in human relations, does not intimidate; it is the same in the agents of a relation of reciprocity; it defines itself for everyone by its homogeneity. In the present case, however, it manifests itself to individuals *over the total submission of matter* (disintegrated or pierced by rays or directly modified, without labour, by mere sovereign will), but it does so as heterogeneity, that is to say, as an untranscendable negation of their possibilities. In this sense, its *power* has the possibilities which are negated in everyone as its fundamental structure, as the inertia of every freedom. To put it differently, it constitutes everyone, within his freedom, as received (and accepted) passivity. And worship consists precisely in free *praxis* which recognises the inert limitation in it of its possibilities as an absolute gift and a creation which proceeds from inert freedom as a sacred power. This simply means that any pledged group, as a diffuse power of jurisdiction, manifests itself for every third party, and in the totalisation performed by the other third party, as a sacred power. It serves no purpose if the sacred assumes a specifically religious or cultural form: it is (at least in general: circumstances determine cases) simply a character proper to Terror as inert freedom and negative power and its relation to everyone's other-freedom in so far as it negates certain possibilities. This relation manifests itself as sacred when a coercive and unanimous totalisation reveals itself *through the common object*. This is the origin of *ceremonies*, to the extent that materiality (vestments, stereotyped actions, objects of veneration, the

27. This disintegration keeps the thing (Moses' tablet, etc.) intact as a material entity. At the same time, it does not stop producing itself.

inert commemoration of the past, the inflexible and invariable order of actions etc.) expresses inertia in them, and also that their conventional and teleological aspect embodies freedom-power. And the Sacred, with its rituals and its ceremonies, derives, like juridical power, from a non-being of the group, that is to say, from the fact that any real community is a totalisation or, to put it differently, a totality which is perpetually detotalised. It is through a fundamental contradiction, in fact, that the act of totalising, in so far as it is performed by everyone, is *also* the essential factor of detotalisation.

However, as we have already noted, the possibilities of dissolution, for the group, even when enemy pressure is relaxed, would be less close and less threatening if its members could remain united, in one place, in the square, etc. For unity in everyone, as a synthetic determination of multiplicity, would be the interiorisation of the real, visible and tangible promiscuity of the people in the group. We have seen that the group posits itself for itself in a reflexive practice and becomes its own immediate objective *not only* when circumstances require it to be permanent, but also when the diversity of its tasks requires that differentiation take the place of the fluid homogeneity of fusion. In this way, in fact, a risk is incurred that distance will make everyone isolated and separate, or that new conflicts, arising from the differentiation itself, will produce new antagonisms in the community. Through the pledge, the group ensures an ontological statute which will mitigate the dangers of differentiation. As I have already said, this pledge is not necessarily a real operation or an explicit decision: in reality, when the group posits itself as its own end in and by every third party, and when this practical reflexivity defines, if only implicitly, the common reception of Terror, it is enough that violence, both in its negative forms (the liquidation of the uncommitted, and the suspect) and in its positive forms (fraternisations) manifests itself in such a way that the statute of permanence becomes an immediate certainty for every totalising third party. So, whether or not a pledge was really made, the organisation of the group becomes the immediate objective. It was this organisation, as an ulterior objective, which necessitated the creation of permanence; and again it is this organisation which the permanent group now sets itself as its immediate aim. And the unity of the group is nowhere but in everyone, *as a pledge.*

This pledge, whether implicit or explicit, defines everyone as a *common individual*, not only because it concerns his being-in-the-group, but also because it is only through the mediation of all that it can take place in everyone. But this has nothing to do with inorganic products or with an inertia of exteriority: in this sense, Terror does not inflexibly define the permanent limits of freedom for everyone. In fact, it merely *raises the threshold* at which untranscendability will become transcendable; or, to put it differently, it makes it *less probable* that one will abandon one's post, go over to the enemy, etc. Treason, as a new form of human action, is nevertheless always a concrete possibility for everyone; its probability is a function of the synthetic complex of historical circumstances (including everyone's individual history). This means that the group is *also* – negatively – the totalisation of its points of possible rupture, and that for each point there is a certain threshold above which the rupture may occur; and these thresholds are extremely variable.[28]

28. This does not in any way mean that for certain individuals their being-in-the-group is really untranscendable. But this has nothing to do with either courage or fidelity: the best may fall into a trap, the most devoted may become the unwitting instrument of the enemy. It is therefore perfectly legitimate to consider the group *also* as a multiplicity of points of rupture; *the more so* the more differentiated it is. However, we shall see that from another point of view differentiation is a unifying link.

3

The Organisation

1 Organised Praxis and Function

In so far as *organisation*, as the action on itself of the statutory group, is directly relevant to a critique of dialectical Reason (whether it is a matter of differentiation in combat, or of the division of labour in a particular case), there is no need for a formal enumeration of its possible forms (or for tracing the *historical* movement of the division of labour or of the transformations of the army on the basis of weapons and of combat techniques). Our sole problem is dialectical rationality. We are acquainted with two types of intelligible actions: the translucid (but abstract) *praxis* of the individual, and the rudimentary *praxis* of the fused group. To the extent that the second is relatively undifferentiated and that action in it is everywhere *the same*, everywhere *common*, everywhere governed by orders coming from all sides, but which a single third party might have uttered one after the other, we can take it that *non-differentiated praxis* retains the characteristics of individual action and amplifies them. It is alive in so far as it is, in everyone, both total and the same; no doubt it multiplies, but we have seen that an individual becomes a member of a group by interiorising multiplicity. Through the relation of mediated reciprocity, he spontaneously and concretely benefits in his own activity from the activity of the Others. *Inertia, control,* and *complex organisations* are nowhere to be found: this means that *praxis* is everywhere plenary, that it is everything it can be everywhere and that, ultimately, reciprocal conditioning manifests itself through the object and through objectification, but that the *operation*, in so far as it is very close to the operations of a practical organism – though separated from individual *praxis* by the whole practico-inert field – retains a sort of translucidity. *Organised action*, however, involves a system of relations, and of relations between relations, such as to make one wonder *what type of praxis* manifests itself in it – comparing these combined structures with the constitutive dialectic of individual action – and whether this *praxis* is still dialectical, and what kind of objective it sets itself, what kind of reshaping of the practical field it performs, what internal development characterises it, and, finally, how far it is *really praxis* (that is to say, freedom) and how far a constituted instrument.

The word 'organisation' refers both to the internal action by which a group defines its structures and to the group itself as a structured activity in the practical field, either on worked matter or on other groups. People say both: 'We have failed because the organisation (distribution of tasks) left a lot to be desired' and 'Our organisation has decided that . . .', etc. This ambiguity is important. It expresses a complex reality which might be described in the following terms: the group can act on a transcendent (*transcendant*) object only through the mediation of its individual members: but the individual agent performs his action only in the definite context of the organisation, that is to say, in so far as his practical relation with the thing is directly conditioned by his functional relation to the other members of the group, as *already established* either by the group (as a plenary meeting of its members) or by its representatives (however they have been chosen).

Organisation, then, is a distribution of tasks. And it is the common objective (common interest, common danger, common need assigning a common aim) which defines *praxis* negatively and lies at the origin of this differentiation. Organisation, then, is *both* the discovery of practical exigencies in the object *and* a distribution of tasks amongst individuals on the basis of this dialectical discovery. In other words, the organising movement settles the relation between men on the basis of the fundamental relation between group and thing. Depending on the nature of the circumstances and on the characteristics of the *praxis* (in fact, according to the whole historical conjuncture), this can lead either to a voluntarism which defines the task of the individual on the basis of the exigencies of the aim without reference to everyone's individual possibilities, or to an unprincipled opportunism which *reduces* the common *praxis* (common in its aims, intensity, and complex organisation), in accordance with empirically given limits of individual *praxis* (limits which, on closer examination, might show themselves capable of being pushed back by some action of the group upon itself, without the workers, combatants, etc. suffering it *in their individual organisms*). Depending on the ensemble, one can equally well find organisations (generally very close to the simple pledged group) in which function is always (or sometimes) defined in terms of the task to be carried out and of the particular capacities of each person (in so far as he is *known* by Others: for example, in a very small combat unit, a particular mission will be assigned to a particular soldier because of his exceptional strength).

I have presented these various possibilities not because they occur historically in disorder or in an arbitrary order, but because, as far as *our* problem is concerned, they are strictly equivalent: voluntarism and opportunism are characterised, in the organisation, as the action of the group on its members. The group acts on the object, indirectly, only in so far as it acts upon itself; and its action upon itself – which as we shall see is its only action *as a group* – defines itself on the basis of a *praxis* (which is either already *established* or gradually revealing itself).

The group defines, directs, controls and constantly corrects the common *praxis*; it may even, in some cases, *produce* the common individuals who will realise it (through technical education, for example, etc.). But this set of operations presupposes differentiation: for example, the distribution of tasks (or of weapons or supplies) pre-supposes an earlier distribution, that is to say, the creation within the group of *specialised apparatuses* (misleadingly called *organs*: directive organs, groups for co-ordinating, mediating or distributing, or regu-lating exchanges, administration, etc.). This first moment of differenti-ation – which has nothing in common with the appearance of *com-mand*, although, as we shall see, it is the basis of it – is, therefore, funda-mentally an action of the group upon itself. And, to precisely the extent that this differentiation remains very abstract (there is the service which prepares the work and *the other* common individuals), it corresponds to a still very abstract conception of *praxis*: the group, united in a common, but still inadequately determined project (a combatant community, a vigilance committee, a team of technicians or an association for buying and selling property on the moon) pro-duces its first differentiation in order to give itself the means of pro-ceeding to this determination. And there should be nothing to surprise us in this differentiation, in itself, since it is simply a pledged statutory group acting on itself – a group, that is, whose internal relations have been explicitly constituted so as to respond to the demands of the situation and to make differentiations possible. In other words, our problem is not to explain any particular division: the internal *praxis* of the pledged group or (and this comes to the same thing) the possibili-ties which reveal themselves to the action of every third party in the group, are simply the *unveiling of its tasks through its morphology*. The establishment of any particular differentiation is only a concrete modality of a more general structure: through the pledge, the statutory group *becomes capable of differentiation*; to put it differently, it makes itself such that *not only* do differentiations not destroy its unity, but also practical problems *can reveal themselves to it through differential problems*. And since *the thought* of the group, that is to say, its practical idea of the Universe, is simply the transcendence (*dépassement*) of the practical idea which it has of itself towards the transcendent (*transcendant*) object; and since the practical idea which a group has of itself – the schema which it uses to resolve its internal problems – cannot be separated from its internal constitution (both as its action on itself and as its objective structure), differentiation, which is the abstract thought of the statutory group, becomes the concrete thought of the organised group: it appears, in fact, as the creation by third parties of an increasingly precise differentiation and thus the thought of the transcendent object expresses the increasingly concrete and differentiated structure of unified multiplicity. (I shall return to this point shortly.)

Thus individual differentiation is of little importance, at least for our purposes, and its appearance, though *new*, is immediately intelligible. But *the intelligibility of organised action* is a completely different matter: the problem is what type of unity and reality can be attributed to *praxis* in its new form of *organised praxis*, and what meaning it can have. What we are interested in, therefore, is the relation between *the action of the group on itself* and *the action of its members on the object*.

We shall study the different moments of this relation step by step and by deepening our investigation (*expérience*). We must first specify what *the task* is when it appears in the group as the objective of a process of organisation; this will lead us to a new definition of the common individual, since his statute in the organised group is of itself a determination (and therefore a limitation) and a concrete enrichment of the statute of the pledged member (inertia in freedom, right, etc.). Then, having explained *function*, as the statute of the common individual, and its two aspects (a *practical task* in relation to the object, and a *human relation* in so far as it characterises the being-in-the-group of the third party), we shall have to examine the foundations of a logistics of organised systems (as the multiplicity and unity of inverted and mediated reciprocities) and describe *the structures* as such, that is to say, as they arise in the group in opposition to the passive activities of the practico-inert; and then we shall find in them a new human and social product: *active passivity*. Only then can we approach our two essential questions: in fact we shall have to rearrange all our conclusions into a synthetic movement which will itself produce the intelligibility of organised *praxis* and reveal in it a new apodicticity – that is to say, a radically different necessity from the first. This will enable us to examine the ontological statute of the organised group as a concrete reality given in the dialectical investigation (*expérience*) or, in other words, we shall discover whether the organisation should be regarded as practical existence or as being.

At the level of the fused group, the common individual appeared to us as an organic individual in so far as he interiorised the multiplicity of the third parties and unified it through his *praxis*, that is to say, in so far as unity determined multiplicity through him as an instrument, a force. This characteristic of synthetic unity posits itself for itself in the statutory group when the situation demands separations which endanger the community for everyone in the person of every third party and in the possibility of his breaking the unity, and relapsing into the statute of massified isolation. The *common* characteristic of the individual (or his being-in-the-group) becomes everyone's juridical power over organic individuality in himself and in every third party. But this power is still abstract: its abstraction is a measure of that of the group and of the common *praxis*. At the level of *organisation*, this abstract and fundamentally negative power (as the free inertia of freedom) is concretised and changes sign: in fact, it defines itself for everyone, in the context of the distribution of tasks, by a positive content. It is *function*. As such, it remains an inert limit of the freedom of the third party, and, therefore, its basis is still Terror. And Terror can always re-emerge as a relation between pledged members when the conjuncture and the particular history of the organisation compromise the functions of the third party (or render them useless or parasitical) and reveal, from below, the danger of dislocation. The organisation then reverts to the less differentiated stage of the statutory group; and functions appear as little more than abstract significations with no reality. That is why, in certain historical conditions, Terror can appear as a regression and simplification.

But in the normal exercise of organised activity, *function* is a positive definition of the common individual: either the group as a whole or some already differentiated 'organ' *assigns* it to him. It is a determination of individual *praxis*: an individual belongs to the group in so far as he carries out a certain task and *only that task*. In simple Terror,

however, the inert limit of possibilities remains abstract and purely
negative: it is freedom freely renouncing the right to dissolve the group
relation in *any* case of separation. Function is both negative and
positive: in the practical movement, *a prohibition* (do not do *anything
else*) is perceived as a positive determination, as a *creative imperative*:
do *precisely that*. But in the milieu of the pledge, *doing that* is the right
of each over all, just as it is a right of all over each: the definition of
power, in so far as a concrete function particularises it, is that for
everyone it is the right to carry out his particular duty. Thus, he must
actualise everything that *predetermines* his function (the common
objective, practical problems, the conjuncture, the state of techniques
and instruments) *in inertia* (as an inert possibility defined by discourse,
for example, and which it realises in repetition), in the milieu of
sovereignty over things (the dialectical freedom of organic *praxis*) and
of *power over men* (social freedom as a synthetic relation based on the
pledge), in short, in *freedom*.

If a football team is being formed, the function of goalkeeper, or
forward, etc., appears as a predetermination for a new young player.
He will be recruited by one of these functions; it will select him on the
basis of his physical qualities (weight, height, strength, speed, etc.):
but in so far as it designates him in his free *praxis*, that is to say, in so
far as it produces a determination of inertia at the basis of his freedom,
it is already power, and he lives it as exigency: *the exigency of training*,
for example. The team in which he has been *signified* by this function is
then obliged to raise him to a (physical and technical) level at which he
will be capable of performing the actions which the group requires.
This may also signify his right to refuse excessive training, badly
organised and exhausting travel, matches played in bad conditions,
etc. And it is *as a common individual* that he has these negative rights:
in other words, his *praxis* freely reappropriates the exigencies of his
function.

At this level, there is no difference between rights and duties. The
classical distinction – which tends to make duty into a right of other
third parties over me, and to make right into the duty of other third
parties towards me – was still valid at the previous level; but once the
positive content of function has been defined, the distinction ceases to
exist. There is no ground for stating *a priori* that the diet involved in
the training of a *particular* sportsman is either a right of the Other (of
the other members of the team) or his own right. If, as an organic
individual, he were to *resist* following the diet, the Others would

impose it on him (either because he needs to lose weight, or because he has a wrong attitude to his 'job', or because he eats too much, or eats indigestible food) because each of them, as a function, in the *praxis*, requires every member of the team to reduce himself to his own function. On the other hand, if he adopts the prescribed diet without qualification, then, for the administration of the sport group (the 'organisers') this is simply their duty to keep it for him as long as necessary; as a function of the group, he will require his fellow team members not to deflect him from his duty, or even help him to carry it out, and if necessary to force him to do so. It is clear that each formulation indicates only more clearly the increasing inextricability of right and duty. If one member of the team makes this exigency (to keep fit, to persevere with the training) into a *power* over another player or over the group, then it acquires a juridical and dialectical structure which is the complex organisation of all forms of imperative.

Suppose that I am integrated into a group, and that there is another common individual, M, defined by a certain function. I require that M should receive from the group the necessary subsistence and training, etc., to enable him completely to fulfil the requirements of his job. Now, I require this not only *for the group* (that is to say, from the point of view of the common *praxis*), but also *from the group* (since it is the group which distributes the functions).[28a] I require it for my own function, that is to say, for the guarantee which each and every member must freely offer me, and I also require it for everyone as a particular third party, and for *anyone* (both because member N or Z as such will require that I require this guarantee for him: it is he, for example, who has most to lose *in his functions* through the failings of M – and because, for example, I am more seriously threatened *through N or Z* by these failings); lastly, I require it because M himself, in the name of the pledge, requires of me (as a limit-power) that I require it of him. Now, all these abstract moments of concrete exigency are given together in my way of acting, of realising my function through my action and of basing my action on my powers: the right which the group has through me over all, and the duty towards the group as defined by all, the reciprocity of right (I have the right that you should assert your rights),

28a. Of course, the group requires it of the group through me in so far as it has provided itself with a representative (team captain, manager, etc.). When conflicts are still masked or undeveloped, therefore, the group as a milieu of regulated heterogeneity realises itself through tension between functions; its internal structure is *facetted* (*à facettes*).

that of duty (my duty is to remind you of yours), that of right and duty
(I have the right that you should allow me to do my duty), that of duty
and right (I have the duty to respect your rights) – the infinite complication of these reciprocities (in the context of the complex reciprocities
which we shall examine shortly), all these lines of force constitute the
web of what might be called power as reality lived in and through
praxis. According to circumstances, one or other of these lines of force
may appear, as a form, against the synthetic background of all the
others; but if they are not all present, the group will break up.

For the sake of simplicity, let us consider the abstract case of an
organisation which is not directly conditioned in its internal structure
by exploitation (it may constitute itself either for the exploitation of
Others or against the exploitation of its members by Others, but there
will be no relations of exploitation *between* the third parties who
comprise it) and a particular function of which consists in a certain
operation performed with a particular tool and with some definite
technique. The technique and the tool define the moment of the
historical process in so far as it produces, penetrates, sustains and
totalises this particular group within this developing totalisation. But
the common individual perceives techniques and tools as *his sovereignty*
in the practical field, that is to say, as an extension of his individual
praxis. In this sense, tools and techniques (which are really one and the
same object) are the group itself in so far as the common individual
perceives it as his own social power over things. In other words,
acting with tools reveals his dated historicity to him (it can *also* be
defined as an *inert negation* – but from the abstract point of view of a
diachronic totalisation) as practical sovereignty (over inorganic matter).
It is at this level that the tool is a practical unveiling of the world to
precisely the extent that the practical organism is a tool. By this I mean
both that it changes the world by a reorganising transcendence, and
that in this very transcendence it reveals it to be a world in the process
of being reshaped.

These themes have been discussed many times by many different
authors: I shall only refer to the first technical agent to grasp, and fix
in experience, the social moment of unveiling the world by a *praxis*
involving tools: Saint-Exupéry and his book *Terre des Hommes.*[29] The
astringent power of the aeroplane (as an instrument which reduces
travelling time) is not only *produced* by a technician using an object

29. Antoine de Saint Exupéry, *Terre des Hommes*, Paris, 1939. [Ed.]

which has already been worked by men, but also, and inseparably, *revealed* as a real movement of contracting space. But this real movement in itself is revealed as a *means of control*, and can never be a matter of contemplative perception (except for the inert passenger who is being transported from one city to another). It also determines the speed of the operations to be carried out (*including* thoughts, as hypothetical actions and as constantly corrected syntheses of the practical field). In the context of the practico-inert, we saw how worked matter produces its own idea. Here, it is the other way round: activity involving tools defines itself through the instrument of society as a practical power (structured by the tool which it uses and transcends) *of thinking the development of the world*. This power comes to the third party through the group which produces (or acquires) the tool and defines the function. But though this enriching limitation may limit possibilities – as abstract determinations of the social future – it must also *concretise* them, that is to say, multiply the practical options by creating, through the task and the tool, differentiated structures amongst the possibilities or in other words, by defining *sub-possibilities*. It is obvious that the options do in fact impose themselves on the basis of real objectivity, or of the developing process; but the instrument, as practical perception, creates the permanent possibility that certain sub-possibilities will inscribe themselves in *praxis* from the outside, and require an immediate option. The speed of the danger and of the defensive action, for example, are just as much a function of the speed of the plane, as of the nature of the possible dangers. But these imperative options present themselves to the agent (the pilot, for example) in terms of the world soliciting his own power; and the final choice[30] expresses his sovereignty.

Here we encounter the organic individual as an isolated agent in the first moment of his concrete truth. It will be recalled that he was presented, in his pure abstraction, at the beginning of our dialectical investigation; we find him now in his complex relations with the

---

30. It would be completely wrong to give the word 'choice' here an existential interpretation. It is really a matter of the concrete choices which present themselves to, for example, an airline pilot trying to save the passengers in his plane, two of whose four engines are out of action, which is losing fuel, etc. It would be taking Pavlovian obstinacy to the point of total blindness if one denied the specificity and irreducibility of these choices. The part played by routine is undeniable, but in cases of danger it is not sufficient; it is necessary to innovate or to take risks.

common individual. He loses himself through the pledge so that the common individual may exist (as an enriching limitation of the field of possibilities) and then he finds himself again at the level of concrete *praxis*, in relation to the common individual, that is to say, to the task (with the available instruments). And by 'organic individual', here, I do not mean some given individuality which distinguishes everyone from everyone else (individualities, as we have seen, are historical individualisations of material conditions; and in any case they do not concern us here); I mean free constituent *praxis* in so far as it is finally only signified by function; in fact, to the extent that the determination of the sub-possibilities becomes richer and richer in the context of function under the influence of tools, functional predetermination appears as a schematic adumbration of a sector of activity: in this sense the common individual, as function, remains mostly undetermined. To be a pilot, of course, is *to be nothing but* a pilot. But, in the course of the job, the variety of *exigencies* (revealed by the tool and in action) is so great, their urgency so evident, that it would be impossible to realise one's *being-a-pilot* as a totalised ensemble of practices confined within strict limits. A *praxis*, however, though completely unintelligible unless defined in terms of tools and techniques, of the common objective and the material circumstances, is only a free organisation of the practical field *on the basis* of the enriching limitations which have produced us. Of course, the individual action of a practical organism no longer has anything in common with that of another practical organism which possesses rudimentary tools and less developed techniques: *it is true* that the conditions of sovereignty are social.[31] Everyone knows that the power of the plane is not that of the pilot. On the other hand, in so far as this power can be practically realised only through the specialised *praxis* of the pilot, that is to say, through the *transcendence* of inertia and the *use* of forces of exteriority, everybody also knows the opposite – that airline pilots, though identical as common individuals, are at the same time differentiated, *for the group itself,* by what is stupidly called their individual qualities, which is, in fact, simply the history of their technical choices as free dialectical agents. For an airline pilot in mortal danger, what is excluded is a set of possibilities, which are in any case completely unserviceable (to negate the common individual in him, the responsible individual, the

31. This is why, truth being circular, we shall find the organised group relapsing into the practico-inert field and dissolving into a new inertia.

sole master on board, all of whose initiatives must be aimed at saving the plane, and to relapse into fear, isolation and the irresponsibility which is characteristic of isolation located *beneath* any group-being). What is required, meanwhile, is to transcend the pure inertia of common-being by some action (if action is still possible) or to choose between two techniques, both tested, both of which have their defenders: thus, in function, the practical individual (as a constituent dialectic) reasserts himself by transcending common inertia in a *praxis* which preserves it by using it (which, as I have said, amounts to transcending the inertia of the instrument). The individual as organic *praxis* is *below* the common individual in so far as he grounds him with a pledge, and *beyond* him in so far as he is his practical individualisation. But in this new moment of his reality (still abstract, because we have not yet run through the moments of alienation and of the practico-inert in the reverse order), he is no more than the common *praxis*, in so far as it has to be actualised through individual acts which transcend it.

It goes without saying that the common individual, in so far as he is *produced by* the group, is something more and something different than he at first appeared. For his function is a technical bond with a particular instrument. And of course the technique is the instrument itself in so far as it ha; been invested with meanings (*significations*) (mediations between t'ıe agent and the thing) by the labour of Others. But, of course, it is also the becoming-instrument of the specialised agent. Through training, professional instruction, etc., the instrument exists as an *exis* in the practical organism of anyone whose function makes him use it. Or, in other words, the *exis* of the specialist must correspond to the signifying inter-connections of the parts of a machine (or tool), as an inter-connection of assemblies. However, we are not at the level of alienation here: the group constituted itself in opposition to it and has not yet relapsed into it. And this inter-connection should not be seen as an inert instrumentality of man tied to the inert humanity of the machine. In fact, *praxis* is the temporalisation of *exis* in a situation which is always individual (or rather *which always threatens to be so*); this means that action defines itself here as the simultaneous transcendence of assemblies by the tool, of the tool by assemblies, and of the whole by a directed process which future possibilities have occasioned in the distant future. There can be no *exis*, no *habit* without practical vigilance, that is to say, without a concrete objective to determine them in their essential indetermination, and without a project to actualise them by specifying them. Thus *exis*, as an enriching limitation of the common individual, manifests itself concretely only in and through a free practical temporalisation. Routine opposes initiative, of course, but this contradiction occurs at another level: it has meaning, in fact, only in the context of a complex historical conflict which opposes new means of production to old ones, forces of production to relations of production, etc. As such, routine corresponds to a total situation and expresses the overall attitude of particular groups and milieus (that is to say, it manifests itself in terms of a political and social alliance between these milieux and the conservative class). But, to take a routine practice (that of a Tennessee peasant in 1939 who refused to use electricity) as a particular action and in its positive relation to a specific objective (ploughing, sowing, breeding etc.), there is no difference between its structure and what we have just been describing: regardless of whether he uses electricity, votes for the Democrats or Republicans, and of whether (because of his lack of technical education) he is hostile to elementary forms of co-operation, the peasant, with his work tools, defines his practice in terms of a few concrete and constantly renewed objectives; he effects a real transformation of the practical field by adapting himself to difficulties with the means at his disposal.

The main purpose of my examples was to show how the *common* is transcended in work itself. They were not intended to take us back to the simple groups which we were studying before. In effect, these were characterised not only by their integration, but also by the strictly common character of their objective and, consequently, of their *praxis*. However else they may differ, a football team and a group of armed rebels have one thing in common, from the present point of view: that the real objectification of the action of each member lies in the movement of common objectification. In the case of a football team, the action of every player is predetermined as an indefinite possibility by function, that is to say, in relation to a future objective which can realise itself only through an organised multiplicity of technical activities. Thus, function is for every member a relation to the objective as a totality to be totalised. In the match, every common individual will, in the light of the group's objective, effect a practical synthesis (orientation, schematic determination of possibilities, of difficulties, etc.) of the field in its present particularities (mud, perhaps, or wind, etc.); in this way, he tries to make himself generally prepared for the specific characteristics of the match. But he will realise this practical synthesis – which, ultimately, is a kind of mapping, a sort of totalising survey – not only for the group and on the basis of the group's objective but also on the basis of *his own* position, that is to say, in this case, of *his* function. From the moment when the real struggle begins, his individual actions (though they require initiative, daring, skill and speed, as well as discipline) no longer appear meaningful apart from those of the other members of his team (in so far, of course, as each team is also defined by the other) – not only in the abstract, in so far as each function presupposes the organisation of all functions, but also in the very contingency of the concrete, in so far as a particular player's slip or clumsiness at a particular point strictly conditions the movement of another player (or, of all the others) and gives it a teleological meaning which can be understood by the other players (and, though this is incidental here, by the spectators).

Thus no particular movement, pass, or feint, is entailed by the function itself: function only defines the abstract possibility of making *particular* feints, and performing *particular* actions in a situation which is both limited and indeterminate. The action is irreducible: one cannot comprehend it unless one knows the rules of the game (that is to say, the organisation of the group on the basis of its objective), but it can never be reduced to these rules; it cannot even be understood on the basis of them unless one can also see the whole field. Thus, this particular act is contradictory. In itself it is in fact a complete individual action (it has a *partial aim*: to pass the ball; an assessment of the developing situation *in terms of the future*, a calculation of chances and a decision – which may be modified by new developments), which can either fail or succeed and whose success defines it as a self-sufficient dialectical process. In other words, if we assume that this particular individual had this particular objective (to pass the ball to the member of his team whom he thinks best placed to use it for the benefit for the entire group), the action, as a constituent *praxis*, irreducible to function, is completely intelligible. But in fact the impossibility of stopping at this partial objective is revealed to us in our investigation by the fact that the permanent reorganisation of the group continues (in accordance with general rules and with the particular exigencies of the situation) and that it absorbs every particular moment which conditions it. Thus the *meaning* of the particular undertaking – even if, as such, it is successful – lies in the use made of it elsewhere in the undertakings of other members of the team. And it may be worth remarking the *practical justification* of this past activity lies in the future: only the opening, the try, and possibly the goal will provide a definite justifica-

an objectification which eliminates it[32] as an active organisation in tion of the daring with which a particular individual tactic was adopted at a given moment. Thus individual *praxis*, as its transcends the common individual through its concrete temporalisation, is retrospectively modified by every other *praxis* in so far as they are all integrated into the development of the match as a common process. But is this a case of *alienation?*

It will of course be noticed that the individual practice of the player integrates and objectifies itself in the real, living development of a common tactic (or in some cases, strategy); every practice, solicited by a moment of the common development, becomes engulfed in the moment which it helps to produce on the basis of the first. As we have seen, its justification and truth lie in the completed process. But as this validation is produced through successive mediations, that is to say, through successive suppressions of third parties in favour of the practical totalisation (*one* initiative is justified by *another* which it has enabled another player to take, but this initiative, in turn, will be mediated, in relation to the whole, by other initiatives), the objectification, as a mediation by the other and the mediation of this mediation etc., could be seen as a process of serial alienation. In this way we would come back to the schema of the moment of necessity: the action of the practical organism in objectifying itself is revealed as *other* both in its practical essence and in its results.

But in fact, this alienation (at least at this level) is only apparent: my action develops, on the basis of a *common power*, towards a *common objective*; the fundamental moment which is characteristic of the actualisation of the power and the objectification of the *praxis* is that of free individual practice. But it determines itself as an ephemeral mediation between the common power and the common objective; in *realising itself in the object*, not only does it annul itself as an organic action, in favour of the common objectification which is in the process of completion, but also this annulment-towards-the-objective *reveals the common praxis* to it – not *in it*, as the ontological structure of the constituent project (in which case we would be back with some organicist magic), but outside it, as something whose developing objectification dissolves all individual work (that is to say, every individual objectification). But this common objectification is, in fact, simply the realisation of the objective: the group temporalises itself in

32. Either definitively (they separate) or temporarily (the winning team remains compact until the next match, but *in an other way*).

favour of the result as a produced reality. And this totalising elimination towards and in favour of the common objective is the common undertaking of every third party, in so far as it is lived as the indissoluble unity of right and duty. This common undertaking manifests itself in the individual act which actualises function on the basis of concrete circumstances and it is through this act that the undertaking advances to its end. Thus, the individual *praxis* is a *self-suppressing mediation*, or a mediation which negates itself for the sake of being transcended by a third party. But its unique and total aim is to produce a particular result as a means which has to be transcended towards the common end. He therefore produces his action in the light of the common objective, mediated by the future actions of the other members of the team, and, inseparable from the long term end, so as to dissolve in the common objectification. In fact – in a football match, for example – his action has a common past – namely the perpetual reorganisation of the field by the players – and this common field is precisely what, at a certain moment of common temporalisation, rouses him in turn, as a common individual, *to action* (indicating the common danger, the common possibilities, the weaknesses of the present organisation, etc.). This common individual, with his powers, his tools, and his acquired abilities suffers, in *praxis* itself, an alienation to freedom: he cannot, in fact, set himself a common aim without it immediately metamorphosing into the individual aim of a free constituent *praxis* (passing the ball, conceived in terms of the whole organised field and as a means of offensive reorganisation, becomes the occasion for combining the positions and movements of the individual organism in his individual relations with the ball, in terms of the individual tactics of an opponent who is trying to intercept him; the essential moment of the action becomes that of *individual struggle*. Even before passing the ball to another member of his team and seeing the outcome of his decision gradually emerging, the individual must have triumphed, *through his personal qualities*, over another individual, in the other team, who has the same function and who has therefore benefited, in principle, from the same training, etc.). But this transformation of practical power into isolated freedom is only a moment of the metamorphosis which leads up to the disclosure of common objectification; and this culmination is *precisely the meaning* of the transition to isolated freedom; this freedom is expressly designated as a mediation between the common individual (who is nevertheless defined fundamentally by an inert limit, to be reactualised in freedom) and the common objectification which realises itself *at the same time* as the individual action (a reorganisation *around* the passing of the ball) and reflects the common objective back to the common individual. Through the mediation of everyone's individual *praxis*, the common individual *objectifies himself* as a common individual in the common objectification which produces him and which is produced by him. The moment of freedom has to be passed over in silence, since it would negate the team if it were to posit itself for itself.

This indeed is what happens if one has no 'team spirit' – which is rare in sport, work or research, but frequent in some contradictory activities such as theatre. The 'great' actor, the sacred beast, has no team spirit: this does not mean that he relapses into his own individuality (that he arrives late, that he rehearses when it pleases him, or that he refuses to perform and pretends to be ill, etc.), or rather, since this does sometimes happen, it does not necessarily mean this. But it *must* mean that his free *praxis* posits itself for itself as an *individuality from beyond*. On the basis of the common aim, the common undertaking, the common organisation (every character being a function defined by actions, and speeches, which are strictly conditioned by the reciprocal organisation of times and places), he affirms himself *alone*. This already gives a hint of what is, as we shall soon see, *usurpation*: it changes the fixed places, the times of speeches, the order. Now, in individuality as *power-beyond*, this is not a return to seriality, but a confiscation of power for the sake of a single individual. He is not back in isolation; he is the group's actual unity. And in serving the common undertaking (*Macbeth* or *Lear*) everyone turns out to be *serving him*. We shall dwell on this point later.

However, it should not be supposed that 'team spirit', that is to say, the strict interdependence of powers in connection with the common objective, results in the concrete agent being reduced to his function. This could not occur unless the situation – by its everyday banality – could itself be assimilated to an abstract generality (the weather is fine, not too hot, the wind has dropped, the local team is playing at home against another team from the same region, a team which it knows and which is clearly inferior). As soon as unexpected emergencies arise (which, in a sense, is normal) individual initiative takes on considerable importance; in the final objectification, that is to say, in the totalisation of the undertaking by its result, the group as a past totality defines itself not by the order of its functions, but by the real integration of individual actions into the common *praxis* and by the hierarchy of individual initiatives in the context of the 'general' struggle. However, every third party appreciates the importance of a particular third party ('It's lucky you were there . . .', 'If you hadn't been fast enough to . . .', etc.) *in the total objectivity*, that is to say, on the basis of the match as a totalisation which *was developing* and which has eliminated itself *in an object* (victory). This transcended totalisation (*totality-in-the-past*) is the concrete reality of organised *praxis* in all its contingencies and material accidents (due to accidental features of the environment), that is to say, of its historical temporalisation.

By way of contrast, function (at the beginning of a match, for example) is, for everyone, a common and partially indeterminate signification of possibilities. So after his action, the individual manifests himself to the group as a concrete moment of the past totality, as a structure of irreversibility in its temporalisation, and therefore as a *common individual*. But this common individual is defined as a historical and concrete individual in so far as his action was an unforeseen (and, on the basis of function, unforseeable) moment of the common undertaking – or, to put it differently, of the reshaping of the group by the group. What is revealed as *common* by the group is the *individual* particularity of his action (in so far as his initiative was justified by subsequent developments). In him, the group becomes aware of having saved its common undertaking by a risky but successful manoeuvre. In other words, every third party becomes aware through him of practical freedom (the constituent freedom of *praxis*) as *creative freedom in the common individual*. This retrospective illusion is nevertheless a common structure: the group-totalisation turns back on itself as a transcended totality and, *in this transcended totality*, it perceives the free *praxis* of a given third party as the practical superiority of a given common individual. *So-and-so*, for example, *is a good goalkeeper*: he *is good* because on several occasions he has saved his team by his individual actions, that is to say by a transcendence of his powers in a creative practice. But if it is possible to speak of class-being, for example, in the practico-inert field, the reason is not hard to see: the complex system of alienations means that individual *praxis* realises its being in trying to transcend it. But it must be emphasised that in this case the opposite applies: the individual transcends his common-being in order to realise it; and being a goalkeeper or half-back is *not* like being a wage-earner. Function, as common-being, is an indeterminate determination which temporalises itself as a positive enrichment in circumstances which present themselves as concrete imperatives requiring concrete choices; so, as soon as the common individual 'makes' one of these choices, he transcends himself as a common individual in order to lose himself in the common objectification. What will later be called *the* goalkeeper, *the* centre-forward, etc., in the organised group ('We have an excellent goalkeeper, but our backs are not that good', etc.), that is to say, *the common individual in so far as his function is determined by his past acts* (and, therefore, is characterised by his future possibilities: the team will *count* on the goalkeeper, will *rely* on him for a particular operation) possesses only *past being*. This being, who is the object of a non-temporal designation (even though the process is temporalised), reveals himself to the practical, retrospective perception of the common undertaking; but in the moment of temporalisation, he is not: he is free organic *praxis* transcending function so as to become annulled in the common objectification but who, in particular circumstances, appears as an irreducible signification of the transcended, structured totality. Function is abstract imitation, inertia transcended and preserved by the action, in the moment of temporalisation; or it is, so to speak, the particularity of common individuality in so far as the action, in the past, is confined within the limits it prescribes (not so as to have been incapable of realising anything but its own power, but so as to have deliberately set itself this realisation as an objective). In the organised group, in moments where the practical tension relaxes (though the group does not dissolve), the common individual perceives his function as his common individuality: the *past meaning* of his present is both his task as a prescription-pledge and his *actions* as actualisations of his task, transcended in the course of earlier undertakings; the *future meaning* of this same functional present is the determination of his power (in future undertakings) by concrete possibilities which define themselves simply as the projective transcendence of past actions and their metamorphosis into a future beyond of the right-duty couple: *a good goalkeeper* is individualised as a common individual in so far as he produces himself in the future through his past actions as capable of *doing more* than is expected of everyone at the normal level of organisation. He becomes *capacity*. Now, this *capacity* as determination of the possible future is simply the practical, constituent freedom of the organic individual lived as the free future individuality of the common individual; it is past, transcended *praxis* in so far as the member of the organised group lives it as the individualisation of his being-in-the-group; lived as *future exis*, it is past freedom. By allowing his free *praxis* to be absorbed by the common totalisation, the common individual reappropriates his being-in-the-group as a free determination, beyond the task and the pledge.

2 *Reciprocity and Active Passivity*

We have now grasped, for the first time, the complex relation between the practical organism and labour, and the common individual as function. But this investigation teaches us that the efficacity of the common individual, as an integrated member of the group, entirely depends on the mediating moment of organic *praxis*, even if this *praxis* in itself makes use of common instruments and reveals, through them, the common field defined by the group. This means that organisation is a real operation which the group performs on itself as a distribution of tasks in accordance with the common *praxis*. The common *praxis*, on the other hand, is the mutual or successive conditioning of functions in so far as a multiplicity of individual actions concretely inscribes them in a definite situation. The only direct and specific action of the organised group, therefore, is its organisation and perpetual reorganisation, in other words, its action on its members. By this, of course, I mean that common individuals settle the internal structures of the community rather than that the group-in-itself imposes them as categories. But the important point here is that, from this point of view, function defines itself both as a task to be carried out (an operation defined in terms of the transcendent object), and as *a relation* between each common individual and all the Others. This is not a pure, logical, formal relation; indeed, it is clear that it must always be some determination of the 'right-duty' tension which provides the objective and internal bond of a community in the process of organisation. In other words, the *relation* is originally synthetic and practical, since it specifies everyone's power over each and all; it must be defined as a human relation of interiority. But, by introducing this specification under the pressure of circumstances, the group being organised has to pass from fluid homogeneity (everyone being *the same*, here and everywhere) to a regulated heterogeneity. Alterity reappears explicitly in the community. Its origin may be transcendent (*transcendante*): if the community becomes differentiated, this is because, in the unity of a single threat, the danger and means of defence (or attack) *are always other* and vary according to spatial and temporal determinations. But the source of the differentiation may be internal: precisely to the extent that the instrumental complex which characterises a group (in its evolution) can be regarded as the immanent common object of this community; in this case, the objective of the distribution of tasks is either a better use of technical equipment or else a response to the pressure of new inventions and new tools. In any case, the important point is that the group reinteriorises alterity the better to struggle against it: either to dominate the complexities of an immanent object; or to confront a transcendent (*transcendante*) diversity. In the organised group, the alterity of the members is both induced and *created*. Following the pledge, in effect, every third party remains *the same* as the other third parties, even though the pledge is made with a view to a differentiation (still abstractly foreseen). In other words, the third party undertakes, by means of his pledge, to commit himself to negating any possibility of alterity, arising either from his own action as a practical individual, or from any *exis* whatever. (The young pledged member of a combat group is given a new *exis* by the situation: for example, he is the one who has never fought before, who has not known war, etc. That which, in the moment of civil peace, was only an abstract and purely logical determination, in *praxis*, through enemy pressure and through the common objectives, becomes an *exis* – a complex of negative possibilities, of being unable to shoot, of being afraid, etc. – and this *exis* distinguishes him from, for example, the old soldier who is making the pledge next to him; he is *other* than the old soldier. But by his pledge, the young fighter swears to put this alterity in brackets, and to render it accidental and negligible).

But, in the dialectical development of a statutory group and in its transition to an organised group, it is clear that the function of the pledge (to exercise terror over the Other and, making a clean start, to establish the dictatorship of the Same in everyone) is to serve as the basis for the reintroduction of alterity. As Lévi-Strauss would say, it is suppressed as Nature, and reinteriorised as Culture. Alterity-Culture becomes a creation of man and a free means of preserving the free group when the group is able to make an indissoluble connection between the following two approaches: both affirming the radical lack of differentiation and strict equivalence of its members as common individuals (through the pledge); and itself producing functional alterities on the basis of this perfect equivalence – producing, that is, alterities which define *the Other in the Same* by his task.³³ Thus, to the extent that the group has so decided, everyone is Other in the group, just in so far as this alterity is a relation defined by a rule, in conformity with a *praxis* and in so far as this relation, to the extent that it has been *established*, is capable of being the object of practical understanding. As a member of a series, I do not understand why my neighbour is other; serial alteration reinforces accidental alterity (birth, organism) and renders it unintelligible; as a member of a living organisation, I understand that the Other is a practical and signifying creation of *us-as-the-same* (*nous-les-mêmes*). From this point of view, another team-member's *relation to me* is entirely comprehensible: he is, so to speak, the means, the object, and the principle of all practical understanding in the organised group. He is other *because it is necessary* (from the point of view of the common objective and of the common *praxis* which he indicates at the horizon) that this or that should be done, to allow the completion of some other task, which conditions the possibility of me carrying out mine.

And the teleological link between these functions is immediately given in the functional action: there is no need to explain it in words or to take a contemplative view of it (which would in any case be impossible). Action and comprehension are one. In comprehending my own aim, I comprehend³⁴ the aim of the Other, and I understand both – and those of all the Others – in terms of the common objective. And,

33. In fact, as we have seen, the real process is often more complicated than this, because the statutory group, when it is incomplete, develops and organises itself by creating functions in accordance with nature-alterities. 'The strongest person will do this,' etc. But it is sufficient simply to note this fact. Beneath the surface, the process is the same: it is just that in this new case, the common use of a natural difference suppresses it as nature (accident, chance, the negative and serialising influence of the individual past or of individual organic characteristics) and consecrates it as culture. A particular strong man becomes function and his power is his strength: the group consecrates it in him; and this is the original meaning of: 'Give away everything and everything will be rendered unto you.' This imperative is typical of the group, and means: negate negative alterity in yourself, cast it off to the common benefit of positive alterity (negate your youth, your fear; give away your vigour and agility), and you will be reborn as a common individual produced by the group *without negative alterity*; as for positive alterity, it is a power which the group has created and consecrated in you and, as such, it can be amplified (physical strength by training, by weapons, etc.). I note this in passing, but concentrate on simpler facts in order to grasp their intelligibility better (though more abstractly).

34. I hope no one will raise as an objection the *much more frequent* case in

to precisely the extent that the group restores individual 'qualities' as a consecrated power, differences of training or physical strength which benefit some Other receive, so to speak, a statute of intelligibility: it is as if the group had at some point produced the strength and the brains it required. Hence my relation to this brain or these muscles will be primarily social, based on the ubiquity of the pledge and the equivalence *of everyone who is the same* (*des mêmes*). He is not primarily a stronger man than me; he is primarily a reinforcement of the common defences in a particular place which is more liable to attack than any other. But the express condition of this practical reinforcement is egalitarian fraternity; it is merely a special form of it: the pledged relation of fraternity is channelled by a functional relation. In fact, in small organised groups (without any direct relation to the appearance of command), the limits of everyone's powers, what falls within the competence of one third party and what into that of another, is always carefully and exactly determined. Conflicts within the group frequently arise because competences have remained indeterminate in some respect or other, or because some new circumstance, by creating a new problem, produces a provisional indeterminacy in certain functions (and therefore in the relation between men).

Thus freedom, as common *praxis*, initially produced the bond of sociality in the form of the pledge; and now, it creates concrete forms of human relationship. Every function, as a relation between me and a particular Other or all the Others, defines itself *negatively* as a reciprocal (direct or indirect) limit of competences, and positively as the action which makes my action both necessary and possible. But function is the common individual, or everyone's being-in-the-group. At the level of the organisation, being-in-the-group is no longer an abstract, polyvalent determination of human relations; it is the organised relation which unites me to each and all. But this *human relation*, by concretely expressing a *being*, receives an inert rigidity from it. In fact it involves reciprocities of powers based on the pledge, that is to say, on the free negation of certain possibilities. In fact, the relations between common individuals, in so far as these relations present themselves as a tem-

---

which, within a particular group, the common individual no longer understands the function of the others, or fails to understand that a particular function is fulfilled by an *Other* rather than by him. I would ask the reader to be patient, and recall that a dialectical investigation is circular. We shall get to it when the investigation leads us there.

poralisation of their 'being' within definite limits, aim to leave nothing indeterminate. (This is clear when, for example, the first meetings of a society establish its office, secretaries, treasurer, committees, etc.; and still clearer when the relations are hierarchical). The determination of competences, being *a distribution of tasks*, implies that a given functional individual can never have a certain type of relation with another: this is the negative meaning of all 'rules'.

In the organised group, human relations involve their own freely accepted limits. But, as we saw above in connection with the task, the concrete limitation of statutory relations corresponds to a positive enrichment: within the limits of hierarchical relations, for example, numerous sub-possibilities differentiate themselves, whereas in a pledged group, the only possibility, in its total abstraction and complete indeterminacy, was for everyone to preserve the group from all kinds of external and internal threats. It was the same thing (in a negative sense). But the hierarchical relation of superior to inferior, for example, consists precisely in avoiding internal ruptures (insubordination or slackness) by positive and adapted actions (a joint rejection of voluntarism and obedience, etc.). The aim of the parties to the pledge, on the other hand, was urgent but still vague: the Tennis Court oath is an example of this. Faced with a still imprecise threat, but with an increasing hostility from the aristocracy and court, the deputies of the Third Estate swore *not to allow themselves to become divided*. They did not know what their tactics should be. And in fact it was the people of Paris who resolved the problem. The unification of an organised group, in contrast, is always defined by its objective, which is *concrete*. The relations between common individuals must, therefore, be constantly created within the limits laid down by a concrete task and solely with a view to the successful completion of this task.

Now, this relation is no longer the simple, indeterminate relation of each to each, with and through all: it is primarily a particular mediated reciprocity which unites an X to a Y (or to several Ys); the mediation is effected by the whole group as a developing totalisation (rather than as a complex of units), that is to say, as a common *praxis* laying down its own laws; and it is through the mediation of new reciprocities – this time uniting the Ys to the Ms, and thereby the Ms to the Ns, etc. – that the common term X relates to each and to all. Thus every common individual is specified, and his direct and indirect relations within the group are necessarily specific and established with specified other individuals. Furthermore, in this concatenation of specific relations which unite an X to the Ys, then, *through the Ys*, to the Ms, and through the Ms to Ns, etc., the group intervenes, as a totalising *praxis* defined by its objective, in every new relation, in order to perform the mediation. However, the structure described here is too simple; and in fact, it complicates itself of itself. In fact, it should be noted that there is always a concrete possibility that the mediated relation between X and N will arise, *at the same time* and *in the same connection*, both by an indirect chain of specific relations *and* directly. If this possibility were realised, two sub-possibilities would remain: either the direct and the indirect relations between X and the Ns will not differ in their specification (the general has his orders transmitted to soldiers through the hierarchy, but in certain circumstances he may be in direct contact with a fighting unit and give them orders personally), or the specifications of the direct and indirect relations are different. (*In principle* – and setting aside for the moment the question of what actually happens – the hierarchical and indirect relation of a Soviet manager with 'blue-collar' and 'white-collar' workers is mirrored within the Party, of which the manager and many of the workers will certainly be members, by a direct relation in which the hierarchy is dissolved and replaced by another hierarchy. It is possible – though this is a purely *logical* hypothesis, and never actually happens – that the manager might indirectly command a local leader of the Party and, as a member, directly obey him, and find himself directly under his orders.) In fact it often happens that the two cases occur together and define the same power in relation to two different sub-groups. An X has direct and indirect relations of identical specification with Ms; and direct and indirect relations of different specifications with Ns. These various relations may be established with the distribution of tasks; and it is not rare for them to be specified in the course of common action. And it should be added that, if the group is numerous and relatively dispersed, indirect relations tend to disperse into indefiniteness; or else the limitation of competences may, for a whole interior zone, fail to determine the common relation which is to unite common individuals to specified powers: in either of these cases the original 'Terror-Fraternity' relation reappears in all its starkness, generally in its positive form; the common individuals whose existence I am aware of, who work in the common *praxis*, and whom I cannot touch directly, are *my brothers*. But fraternity, as the affirmation that every Other is the Same, does not eliminate heterogeneity. Each of the workers, of the sportsmen or combatants is my brother *in so far as by his differentiated function* he commands me and enables me to fulfil *my function*. Fraternity reveals itself as the immediate and fundamental relation which subsists in its abstract starkness between heterogeneous individuals in the absence of any specified relation. In direct or indirect functional relations this fundamental link subsists, as the synthetic bedrock on which all relations are built; but it does not allow itself to be grasped in its abstract strength, precisely because it is there to serve as a basis for differentiations. Thus two common individuals within a sub-group may well abstractly designate the bond between them as fraternity: but in fact – except when the historical conjuncture dissolves all specifications without breaking up the group – this is only a verbal determination. It is in their reciprocal action, in their function, in their specific relation as mediated, that they actualise the fundamental bond and transform it by affirming it. But at this level of *praxis*, discourse is practical and concrete: it is used to give orders or to name everyone's respective function.

Furthermore, in arbitrarily considering 'an X' in his relation with the Ys, I have, for brevity, presupposed an absolute beginning. This has no importance provided we re-establish the true procedures of dialectical investigation, but it would be a mistake to stop at this way of classifying or of thinking: indeed, if it were necessary to begin arbitrarily with the sub-group of the Xs or the Ys or with any other sub-group in order to conceive the ensemble of mediated relations, one would have to admit that there was at least one case in which all functions are *independent* of each other: the case in which the group and its structures are explained in terms of any one of them. In fact, the relations of X to the sub-groups of Ys, Zs, etc., have meaning only in the *true milieu* of the organisation, that is to say in *circularity*. For the possibility of beginning the explanation of specific relations anywhere and everywhere really means that every relation is double: X has a functional link with Y and Z only in so far as the specific relations, both direct and indirect, of all the individuated powers of the group turn back on him and specify his power. In other words, I can, *a priori*, determine the powers of X on the basis of Y as well as those of Y on the basis of X. Of course this is a logical determination: actual *praxis* emphasises subordinations and co-ordinations, either temporarily or definitively. But if the practical structure of an organised group has an orientation, and if, *practically*, it is this orientation which I have to find ('Who is responsible?', 'Who must I speak to?', etc.), this vectoral reading does not destroy the circular structure: this structure, in effect, is simply the determination of the milieu of 'Fraternity-Terror' *by mediated reciprocity*.

In our investigation we have discovered that, whatever the organised group may be concretely, it is a complex circularity of mediated reciprocities, both direct and indirect. In this respect, it merely determines and enriches the reciprocity which we have seen to constitute the original bond of the fused group. But we cannot go any further unless we examine this new type of reciprocity – which is born of fundamental reciprocity, and is a construction of the group, and, in fact, a product of its work on the original relation.

Now, the first effect of this work is that it inverts the fundamental relation. In the fused group, mediated reciprocity emerges from *praxis* itself as a relation of convergence between two third parties who come together in the generating movement of the group: I see the advent of myself in the other (the same) in so far as the other sees the advent of himself in me, and, through this very movement of regroupment, everyone becomes in turn a constituent and a constituted third party. Reciprocity is a direct, convergent, lived relation. As we have seen, the vicissitudes of action and the transformations of the situation gradually produce the diversity of tasks. Even at the level of the fused group (*elsewhere* is always *here*; but *elsewhere*, the enemy is other and behaves otherwise), this diversity is interiorised; and it is as a defence against the dangers of differentiation that the group recreates its unity in the freedom of the pledge. But the pledge itself, as a fundamental relation between agents, is *reciprocity*. Only reciprocity can produce in me a free limitation of my freedom: as I have already shown, I rediscover myself in myself as Other-Freedom in so far as, for the Other, I am his guarantee of always being the Same as myself; and in so far as the Other's pledge is for me a guarantee of being the Same as him. There is reciprocity here but, in so far as it allows practical freedom to be affected by inertia, it is already a *worked* reciprocity. The pledged member uses mediation by the group so as to entirely transform the free spontaneous relation which appeared at the beginning of our investigation. As soon as the pledge is given, reciprocity becomes *centrifugal*: instead of being a lived, concrete bond, produced by the presence of two men (with or without mediation), it becomes *the bond of their absence*. In his isolation, or in the milieu of the sub-group, everyone derives his guarantees and imperatives from the inertia which affects common individuals whom he no longer sees. In this sense, reciprocity is no longer the living creation of bonds; it is, on the contrary, reciprocal inertia. Through the pledge, man rebels against the separating power of inert materiality (spatio-temporal distances, obstacles, etc.), but at the same time, he interiorises it; and reciprocity, as an inert limit of freedom, comes to man from outside, as exteriority against exteriority, and it exists in him as *worked matter*. This very inertia, still in a crude state, is what is refined in everyone by functions, and transformed into precise tasks, into practical relations with instruments, with places, with enemies or with things.

Since this inert reciprocity is established to serve as a basis for powers as alterity reappearing inside freedom, it is important to understand an apparent paradox: the heterogeneity of functions (even in a hierarchy) is simply a determination of inert reciprocity. I call this an apparent paradox because, at least from the point of view of positivist logic, relations which unite two heterogeneous terms and refer to them in their heterogeneity seem vectoral, that is to say univocal, relations. Between one common individual and another, it is possible to establish a double system of directed relations (in opposite directions). But their differences of function apparently make it impossible to merge the two systems into a single, two-directional system. A doctor treats the deputy mayor; and he votes for him in the municipal elections. Thus there is a set of relations proceeding from the doctor to the patient (treatment, the practical knowledge of his body and its deficiencies), and of others proceeding from the patient to the doctor (trust, fees, etc.). Now we can add another relational system: administrator → administered, elector → elected. Of course these circumstances all interact and the relations condition one another. Nevertheless, reciprocity seems to be excluded *a priori*: it would be absurd to say that the doctor is to the patient what the patient is to the doctor, and perhaps even more absurd to say that the doctor is to the patient what the administered is to the administrator.

But this is because we have deliberately taken our example from a social situation which is not characterised (at least not necessarily) by the individuals belonging to the same organised group. Thus heterogeneity is to some extent (we shall see later how much) based on suffered, serial alterity. It may be that the doctor is treating the deputy mayor because they belong to the same political group (they met during an electoral campaign, etc.), but it is not true that he became a doctor in order that the other should become deputy mayor – nor conversely. In an organised group, however, heterogeneity derives from the needs of *praxis*; it is created on the basis of reciprocal sureties and is a determination of mediated reciprocity. Sometimes it is in-correctly called interdependence. But interdependence, as we have seen, can be suffered in serial alterity: in an inert gathering, everyone depends on the others in so far as they are Others and in so far as he is himself an Other. But here, interdependence is a free overthrow of serial interdependence: everyone depends on the Other in so far as they are both *the same*. The mediation of functions is the common *praxis*: the group produces me as the power to realise a certain detail of the common *praxis* so that this *praxis* can be realised in its totality and differentiate itself (*se détailler*) in objectifying itself; by performing this function, and through the development of the common action, I allow every particular function to differentiate itself, and to realise itself as another detail of the objectification.

Thus the reciprocity of two radically heterogeneous functions re-mains unintelligible as long as they are not mediated by the practical group, but its full intelligibility emerges as soon as both functions are understood in terms of the common *praxis*. But this should not be taken to mean that *every* organised group, or *every* agent, is indispens-able. This obviously depends on the objective and on the circumstances: indeed the common individual has, as it were, a marginal utility, because, according to circumstances (lack of finances, of weapons, or of men), functions are eliminated *in a certain order*, which varies according to the *praxis* and its aim. But though such a reorganisation is always possible, in accordance with some scarcity, it is in fact the creation of some other group, with other means and, often, a more limited objective. The problem is not to determine *who* is and *who* is not indispensable to the common action; or rather this problem is practical rather than critical. The important point, for us, is that in a group in action, the organisation of powers and tasks creates a concrete internal milieu with its own structures, tensions, and immanent rela-tions; and this internal milieu, in so far as it defines itself in relation to a transcendent objective, is the practical reality of the group, its physiog-nomy and internal objectivity. In so far as every function maintains this objective reality through particular events, and for a given multi-plicity (and in fixed or only slightly variable conditions: budget, means of communication, etc.), it is the reciprocal counterpart of the others. That any particular function may atrophy or disappear when the situation is transformed is obvious: but this will only occur if the group proceeds to a rearrangement and modifies the internal relations of its members, and therefore its structure. Functions are reciprocal in that all of them, in reciprocity, help preserve a particular internal physiognomy of the group in activity, that is to say, in so far as they have been defined by *a practical plan* which is the guiding schema of the action.

A political group which undergoes a purge and survives it thereby demonstrates that the purged members were not indispensable to it: but, at the same time, it becomes other and the new statute which it gives itself defines it irreversibly. But most of the time, all functions are initially all equally indispensable: this is because they are established on the basis of certain techniques and instruments which themselves helped to define a particular type of action. Later, this action may appear wasteful and ineffective, but only from the point of view of other techniques and instruments. It is therefore impossible ever to make an absolute hierarchy of functions (which define themselves in a dated temporalisation). *On the contrary*, the fundamental character of an organised group is that all these functions are conditioned and guaranteed by the mediation of the developing common *praxis*. Hence every function becomes the signification of the other in so far as it is itself signified by the *praxis*; and every function contains the other in its practical activity. This is particularly evident in small, highly disciplined groups, like sports teams, in which every movement of a fellow member, seen *in its functional differentiation*, is decoded in the very movement which it occasions in another fellow member, as a differentiated function, through the practical field defined by the action of the group and as a function of all the other movements.[35] Mediation, for a given goalkeeper or centre-forward, is the pitch itself in so far as their common *praxis* has made it a common practical reality to be occupied or traversed with a variable co-efficient of instrumentality and adversity; and every developing reorganisation of the team on the field constitutes it *through the pitch itself* as *functionally situated* (in relation to the ball, to a particular opponent ahead of him, etc.). But as soon as he takes up this spatio-temporal situation and transcends it by his *praxis* (in accordance with his function), the common situation of the whole team is *reciprocally* modified. For a spectator, to understand a match is precisely to decode the functional and individualised

---

35. In fact, in a football match, everything is complicated by the presence of the opposite team. The positive reciprocity between members of a team is closely connected with a negative and antagonistic reciprocity. But this complication does not alter our problem in any way.

particularisations of mediated reciprocity as a perpetual totalisation on the basis of a known objective.

But *inert reciprocity* as reciprocal inertia cannot be reduced to the simple forms just described. Of course, it is and remains centrifugal, and affirms itself in opposition to the void and to separation. But we have just seen its original structure: it is necessary for A to do what he does for the common *praxis* in order that B can do what he does, and conversely. This structure becomes complicated under the pressure of circumstances simply because it becomes a sort of inorganic materiality of freedom. Thus, in a way, through inert reciprocity, inorganic materiality again becomes the mediation between practical agents, like the worked thing (precious metal, etc.) in the practico-inert field. This means that the group acts constantly on itself in order to modify its possible counter-finalities and that it can act only by creating new reciprocities. In fact, *organisation*, as internal *praxis*, can neither produce nor preserve itself in the milieu of reciprocity unless it becomes a determination of this reciprocity as a free, inert relation of synthetic interiority.

So far, we have always described organised groups as if they were composed of relatively homogeneous individuals or of ones who differed only in respect of some qualities whose very diversity corresponded harmoniously to the differentiation of their functions. But this would hardly apply even to selective groups, carrying out their own enrolment according to definite rules. But the organised group is a very broad genus of which the selective group is only a small species. In fact, organisation takes place on the spot, with whatever means and men are available (at least in most cases and in the living moment of *constitutive activity*). Thus the synthetic bond of unity and the rule of reciprocity – which distinguish the group from other multiplicities, into a particular, hitherto inert, multiplicity – positively reveal, within the resulting interiority, as a function of these bonds of interiority, differentiations which, *outside the group*, were simply inert relations of exteriority, and inside the group become *involuntary reciprocities*.

An example may make this clearer: throughout this investigation we have maintained that a nation is not a group. Consequently the proportion of young and old in a nation depends on complex processes (which, as we shall see, alone represent the absolute concrete – that is to say, the perpetual conflict between group *praxis* and practico-inert processes, the presence of common structures even in seriality and of seriality even in organised groups) which, *taken as a whole*, cannot correspond to any *praxis*. Amongst these processes, in fact, the demographer will attempt to designate, as immediate factors, sexual behaviour in the different classes of a particular society, progress of domestic hygiene and of medicine – in other words, medical technique in relation to the infant and old age mortality rates. And these data will be taken *from* a society which is already defined by the relation of its children to its old people, that is, a society which bequeathes to its new generation a certain demographic structure on the basis of which the demographic tendencies arising from new conditions will partially modify this inheritance. Of course, as Marx indicated in a passage quoted in *The Problem of Method*[36] 'population' is an abstraction: its variations refer us to all the material conditions and to the historical process. Thus the rise in the French birth rate after the Second World War is a process whose development can be studied without any complete understanding of its signification. (At first it was thought to be a temporary phenomenon, common to all post-war periods. But it has persisted and stabilised, which is somewhat paradoxical since it is, at least in some respects, peculiar to France.)

But as soon as economic (or social, technical, or political) research turns to French *production* – or the redistribution of national income or the demographic demands of economic progress, etc. – and, using some constantly revised working hypothesis, decides to treat the active population, or various groups of workers (defined as primary, secondary or tertiary, or by class, or according to any other synthetic project) as a unified group, the relations of pure exterior contingency which *apparently* unite an Alsatian adult, living and working in Paris, to some old man born in Paris and to a fourteen-year-old boy from Nantes who passes them in the street, suddenly appear as *structured in reciprocity*. *Within the group of producers*, in effect, the old man and the boy become non-productive elements who have to be fed. However, for society, the child is an investment: society spends money to make him a worker. The old man is more or less a dead weight (it goes without saying that I am looking at these relations strictly from the point of view of contemporary economists and demographers). On this basis, we can see how adults (who, even in primitive society,

---

36. *The Problem of Method*, p. 49. 'The population is an abstraction if I leave out, for example, the classes of which it is composed. These classes in turn are an empty phrase if I am not familiar with the elements on which they rest. E.g. wage labour, capital, etc.' See Marx, *Grundrisse*, trans. Nicolaus, Penguin Books, 1973, p. 100. [Ed.]

confuse death and birth, childhood and old age: not *primarily* in the name of mysterious intuitions, but because they are *useless mouths*) are engaged in a double reciprocity: regardless of the social system, part of their product will in fact go to the child, and part to the old man. In the case of the child, the reciprocity is that of capital invested with interest: he is maintained so that one day he can take over and maintain others in turn; and he allows himself to be kept, controlled, and produced with a view to this future. The other reciprocity refers back to the past; it is a temporal reciprocity. The contract or pledge, without ever having given rise to any particular act, goes back to the period when the old man was an adult at the height of his powers and the adult of today a child. Thus we encounter the original situation again, though we live it in its consequences and thirty years later; and this shows that functions, as reciprocity, *can succeed one another*, the second appearing when the first no longer exists. But this is not what concerns us here. The important point is that if one totalises, then differences will be interiorised and lived as special characteristics of the common *praxis*, that is to say, as the internal physiognomy of the group. The French community considered as a productive group has its present structure, and a different future, because of the proportion of the young (under 15, for example) to the old (over 60), that is to say, because of the proportion in it of *useful work* (production of goods, of future workers) *to sacred work* (pledged reciprocity, the maintenance of old workers). In reality, *for the sake of simplicity*, demographers, sociologists and economists *choose* to treat the active community as if it were an organised group: and this is quite justified as long as they see it merely as a heuristic hypothesis or a method of exposition and do not allow themselves to be taken in by it.

But this example shows clearly to what extent, in the common act of pledged association and through the synthetic structure of reciprocity (the only fundamental structural bond of the group), the practical unification of a multiplicity into a group gives rise to heterogeneities which produce themselves in serial inertia as *non-reciprocal* but which, in the common *praxis*, have to be lived as reciprocities. This means that in the milieu of mediated reciprocity nothing can happen except in the form of reciprocity; but this means too that the *heterogeneity constructed* and sustained by the pledge reveals non-constructed and non-functional or pseudo-functional heterogeneities (that is to say, heterogeneities which determine themselves in this functional unity as functions or as counter-functions). Mediated reciprocity, as a free determination of the common *praxis*, is constantly traversed and is always in danger of being modified by secondary reactions of reciprocity developing from the distribution of tasks. These secondary reciprocities have the same structures as primary ones: they are mediated by the common *praxis* and through this mediation every individual characteristic becomes functional. In the case under consideration, for example, the totalisation of productive forces makes age a characteristic of the common individual. In this way, it helps give the group its physiognomy; *praxis* would be different if the proportion of old and young varied. But though these secondary reactions may be favourable to the common activity (it is not *logically* impossible), the fact that they arise from the pledge does not mean that their origin does not lie in the practico-inert. Thus, the possibility that they may impede, or slow down, or divert *praxis* is also present *a priori*. Besides, it is not out of the question that they will endanger the group even when they constitute an internal factor of acceleration.

It is well known that Rakosi set out to liquidate the Hungarian petty bourgeoisie and proletarianise it. But a number of workers in Budapest were former members of the petty bourgeoisie, and *as petty bourgeois* they were deeply opposed to the régime. At the time of the rising, when the workers organised demonstrations, this group, through its common action, developed in reciprocity its internal contradiction. The proletarianised petty bourgeoisie accelerated the insurrectional movement and, in certain places and in certain cases, gave it a counter-revolutionary aspect. This did not in any way correspond to the action of the true workers (that is to say, workers of working-class or peasant origin), but it was used later as a pretext for justifying Soviet intervention.[37] In so far as factory work could not escape the practico-inert, it was incapable of opposing the two groups of workers to each other. In short, these two groups did not exist and, given the temporary impossibility of even imagining an insurrection, the origin of a worker remained an accidental matter for the Others. In the unity of a *praxis*, however, the workers – who as alienated producers were all *really* members of the working class – grouped themselves as a class and

---

37. I did not take account of this in my article *Le Fantôme de Staline* (Les Temps Modernes 129–30 [1956–7]; reprinted in *Situations* VII; trans. *The Spectre of Stalin*, London, 1969. [Ed.]), because I was unaware of it. It was later – some weeks afterwards – that I learned of it from reliable witnesses. Need I say that this correction makes absolutely no difference to my conclusions and my position?

thereby caused class conflicts to reappear inside their practical community. The majority remained working-class, but the minority revealed itself to be petty bourgeois and demoralised. The violence of the hatred and despair produced a ferment; it triumphed, in so far as it was lived in reciprocity. But it also *denatured*. It is known that the insurrectional committees arose partly in order to struggle against this denaturing. Nevertheless the whole group had to live the contradiction of its minority, in which *the condition of the workers* opposed *the class-being of the petty bourgeoisie*. In other words, the group could not exclude by violence pledged members who were pursuing the common aim or at least seemed to be doing so, and perhaps believed they were too; but it was too late to do any effective rearrangement or reorganisation: there was not enough time, and the second intervention interrupted the reorganisation when it began.

For a group which is organising itself in the reflexive awareness of its practical unity, the problem is not so much the neutralisation or elimination through violence of reactive reciprocities, as their re-appropriation and their *retrieval* in the light of a consciously pursued objective. But although the abstract possibility cannot be ruled out *a priori*, and many examples of it could be cited, such reciprocities are not usually dissolved in freedom; as a rule, freedom tries, through the action of all common individuals, including those through whom a reciprocal counter-finality is manifested, to provide them with a foundation as free, created functions. Indeed, at this level, Freedom-Terror itself comes to be respected as a free, diversifying integration: when counter-finality presents itself as a movement towards some more total integration, it is respected for showing the face of unity. This is why – particularly in combat groupings – sectarianism and all forms of violence initially manifest themselves in the form of respect, and then get the upper hand (for the point of view of a totally adapted *praxis* imposes itself only gradually). On the other hand, in so far as secondary reciprocities appear to threaten *praxis* with paralysis (or to threaten the group with serial dissolution), Terror, as the liquidation of interiorised differences, attempts the exclusion of third parties and the liquidation of pseudo-functions. In any case, these abstract considerations can only be meaningful in the context of a historical study of a particular group. I refer to them here simply in order to indicate the nature of the perpetual work which the group must perform upon itself. In fact, in so far as this work tends to transform interiorised alterities into functions, which is the usual case and the one which concerns us at present, it is bound to effect this integration on the basis of the aim and of the primary reciprocities. But this immediately shows not only that the true work of organisation is the synthetic production and the distribution of tasks, but also that it must constantly effect the synthesis of the mediated reciprocities which arise in different layers of the common reality. The organised group cannot be practical and alive except as a progressive synthesis of a plurality of reciprocal fields. In other words, all common organisations are *pluridimensional*. In fact, as the task becomes more complicated and the volume of the group increases, systems of simple reciprocities are replaced by systems of composite reciprocities. In particular, the appearance of commutation (which is often destined to compensate for reactional alterity) introduces a successive system of temporalised reciprocities the function of each of whose intermediary relations is simply to mediate mediations between the initial and the terminal relation. This is not the place for an abstract logistical study of reciprocities, though such a project might tempt a mathematician. A *calculus of reciprocals* would obviously leave out of consideration practical totalisation as the mediation and foundation of this original, social relation; but, on the other hand, it would provide a rigorous elucidation of the typical organisations of the reciprocal, of their developments and interactions – and of substitutions of terms and transformations of elements in so far as these modifications of individuals leave the structures of the system intact.

But if it really is possible to devise a theory of reciprocal multiplicities in organised groups,[38] independently of all concrete, historical ends and of any particular circumstances, do we not immediately collapse in the face of an inert ossature of the organisation? And do we not abandon the terrain of liberating *praxis* and the dialectic and revert to some kind of inorganic necessity?

3   Structures: the Work of Lévi-Strauss

The entire question of the intelligibility of organised *praxis arises at this level*. There can in fact be no doubt that reciprocal relations can be

38. In fact, this theory is adumbrated by cybernetics.

treated by the 'exact sciences': and they are *already* present, as a foundation, in the administration of a school when it decides the timetable for a particular class or in the strict arrangement (by the management of French Railways for example) of the train timetable of a particular network for the winter or summer period. But, on the other hand, it should be noticed that these calculated determinations nevertheless refer to actions (in railways, for example, they involve not only finished, 'crystallised' work – machinery, rails, etc. – but also the actual work of the railwaymen, from engine drivers to ticket-collectors). Thus the peculiarity of this 'ossature' seems to be that it is both an inert relation and a living *praxis*. It should also be added that the permanence of the relation as such does not in any way imply the immutability of the terms or of their positions; there may be considerable changes, provided they take place in such a way that the specific determination of reciprocity is preserved. This has been explained admirably by Lévi-Strauss in his work on *The Elementary Structures of Kinship*. We should note in particular how his study of matrimonial classes led him to this crucial conclusion: 'These classes are much less conceived of in extension, as groups of objectively designated individuals, than as a system of positions whose structure alone remains constant, and in which individuals may change position, and even exchange their respective positions, provided that the relationships between them are maintained.'[39]

But above all Lévi-Strauss's work makes an important contribution to the study of those strange internal realities which are both organised and organising, both synthetic products of a practical totalisation and objects always susceptible of rigorous analytical study, both the lines of force of a *praxis* for every common individual and the fixed links between this individual and the group, through perpetual changes of both of them, both inorganic ossature and everyone's definite powers over everyone else, in short, both fact and right, mechanical elements and, at the same time, expressions of a living integration into a unitary *praxis* of those contradictory tensions of freedom and inertia which are known as *structures*. Function as lived *praxis* appears in the study of the group *as objectivity* in the *objectified* form of structure. And we shall not understand anything of the intelligibility of organised *praxis* as long as we do not raise the question of the intelligibility of structures.

39. C. Lévi-Strauss, *Les Structures Elémentaires de la Parenté*, Paris, 1949, trans. von Sturmer *The Elementary Structures of Kinship*, London and Boston, 1969, p. 113. [Ed.]

But let us quote Lévi-Strauss, one of whose examples will be helpful to us:

'Suppose there are two patrilineal and patrilocal family groups, *A* and *B*, united by the marriage of a *b* girl and an *a* man. From the viewpoint of group *A*, the *b* woman represents an acquisition, while for group *B*, she represents a loss. Thus, for group *A*, which benefits, the marriage is expressed by a change to a debit position, and for group *B*, which is decreased by the loss of one female member to the profit of group *A*, by the acquiring of a credit. Similarly, the marriage of each of the men of group *B* and of group *A* represents a gain for his respective group, and thus places the group in general, and the family involved in particular, in the position of debtor. By contrast, the marriage of each of the *a* or *b* women represents a loss, and thus opens up a right to compensation. . . . Each family descended from these marriages thus bears a sign, which is determined, for the initial group, by whether the children's mother is a daughter or a daughter-in-law. . . . The sign changes in passing from the brother to the sister, since the brother gains a wife, while the sister is lost to her own family. But the sign also changes in passing from one generation to the next. It depends upon whether, from the initial group's point of view, the father has received a wife, or the mother has been transferred outside, whether the sons have the right to a woman or owe a sister. . . .

'Each couple bears a $(+)$ or $(-)$ sign, according to whether it results from a woman being lost to or acquired by line *A* or *B*. The sign changes in the following generation, the members of which are all cousins to one another. . . . It is now only necessary to look at the cousins' generation to establish that all those in the relationship $(+ +)$ or $(- -)$ are parallel to one another, while all those in the relationship $(+ -)$ or $(- +)$ are cross. Thus, the notion of reciprocity allows the dichotomy of cousins to be immediately deduced. In other words, two male cousins who are both in the credit position towards their father's group (and in the debit position with regard to their mother's group) cannot exchange their sisters, any more than could two male cousins in a credit position with regard to their mothers' group. . . . This intimate arrangement would leave somewhere outside not only groups which did not make restitution, but also groups which did not receive anything, and marriage in both would be a unilateral transfer.'[40]

The interest of the proposed schema, which is in fact a deliberately

40. *Ibid.*, pp. 130–1.

abstract summary of several concrete studies, is that it displays the structure as a complex reciprocity of credits and debts. These credits and debts, of course, depend on a basic dichotomy: they are reciprocities which unite two groups. But, from our point of view, there is no difference between groups-united-by-a-system-of-matrimonial-relations and sub-groups.[41] Now, we can also see that a debt pre-supposes a power, a right acknowledged by the individual or the family and appropriated by some individual or family of the other sub-group, the system being a mediation *between* the two parties. Of course, this is a mediated reciprocity and, in a sense, a concrete relation between a *demand* (in the name of the common pledge) and a free will which has freely deprived itself of the freedom to refuse. In short, the debt of family group *A* (which has just acquired a daughter *b* by marriage) is a debt which is *lived, created by actions*, and accepted or even undertaken, though certain complex circumstances of family histories may cause it to be cancelled (hence violent conflicts between groups). In spite of this, the debt is capable of being represented by an algebraic sign associated with a symbolic designation of the group (A) or of the individual (a), and the same applies to the credit which corresponds to it. And their mutual, symmetrical relation can be expressed by an exact proposition: in the matrimonial system of 'cross-cousins', no individuals who (as a result of the system of filiation) possess the characters $(+ +)$ and $(- -)$ can be united; marriages can take place

---

41. The abstract point of view of *critique* can obviously *never* be that of the sociologist or the ethnographer. It is not that we are denying or ignoring the concrete distinctions (the only real ones) which they establish: it is simply that we are at a level of abstraction at which they have no place. In order to connect with them, one would need the set of mediations which transform *a critique* into a *logic* and which, by specification and dialectical concretisation, redescend from logic to the real problems, that is to say, to the level at which real History, through the inversion which is to be expected of this abstract quest, becomes the developing totalisation which carries, occasions, and justifies the partial totalisation of critical intellectuals. In the very moment in which the ideologue (as we shall see) recognises his investigation as *dated* (1957, here and not elsewhere or at any other time), History takes back and transcends, but does not remove, the dialectical schemata which it has always had, but which he has only *signified*, and which designate him as a moment, as their passed signifier, and then allow him to sink into Being, while they become dialectical schemata, the intelligibility and objective rationality of the totalising movement, that is to say, the rational foundation and rule of development which illuminates concrete processes, but appears *in them* only in the form of *the poorest* and *most removed* layer of signification.

only between individuals who bear opposite signs (+ —), that is to say, between cross-cousins. Here we have, as it were, the embryo of a strict proof (in the sense in which we have seen necessity intervene in demonstrative experience): Lévi-Strauss has already defined cross-cousins: 'Members of the same generation are divided into two groups: on the one hand, cousins (whatever their degree) who are kinsmen descended from two collaterals of the same sex . . . (parallel cousins), and, on the other hand, cousins descended from collaterals of different sex . . . (cross-cousins).'[42] This is a matter of the strict, universal definition of the constitution of a class (in the logical sense of the word). And the passage we have quoted offers us a deduction of a mathematical *kind* (mathematical not in its content but in its apodictic certainty) which from definitions produces two groups (+ + or — — and + — or — +), and which thereby makes us see, in the alienating experience of necessity, that one group (+ + or — —) is strictly identical with the group of parallel cousins, while the other group (+ — or — +) is identical with that of cross-cousins. But this demonstration — however rigorous and alienating, and therefore non-dialectical, it may be — is no more than a mediation. Lévi-Strauss actually attempts to determine the true nature of marriage between cross-cousins. 'In the final analysis, therefore, cross-cousin marriage simply expresses the fact that marriage must always be a giving and a receiving, but that one can receive *only* from him who is obliged to give, and that the giving *must* be to him who *has a right to receive*, for the mutual gift between debtors leads to privilege, whereas the mutual gift between creditors leads inevitably to extinction.'[43] Obviously this is not a matter of a common *praxis*, organised 'in the heat of the moment', like the one we have just studied. Later we shall see what kind of comprehension applies to this type of behaviour (common and individual). What is crucial for us is that in spite of everything these practices relate to a single aim: the exchange of women organised in such a way as to combat, *as far as possible*, scarcity and its consequences for the social ensemble. In opposition to privilege and extinction, every family, in the milieu of the pledge (the meaning of this will become clear later) claims its rights and recognises its duties in a single movement; and, as we have seen, these amount to the same thing.

But at this level of *power* and of *right*, a strict formulation is *both possible and necessary*. The two (imperative) formulae of the exchange

42. Lévi-Strauss, *op. cit.*, pp. 98–9.   43. *Ibid.*, p. 131. My italics.

of sisters and of the marriage of cross-cousins can be defined in these terms: '*A* is to *B* as *B* is to *A*; or again, if *A* is to *D* as *B* is to *C, C* must be to *D* as *B* is to *A*.'[44] Here we encounter some well known aporias (but ones which lack real consistency, and which the sociologist is right to ignore): right cannot be deduced from fact, fact cannot produce right, and right (as the ensemble of juridical practices, whether codified or not) is fact (it is *a fact* that one gets married in a particular society in one way rather than another), fact engenders right (in the organised community and when it takes place in accordance with juridical laws: a particular marriage between a man from group *A* and a woman from group *B is a fact*; they *did* get married, yesterday or last year; but this fact is lived by group *A*, for example, in the form of a complex of obligations, that is to say, of exigencies which come to it from the future). But in the perspective which the work of Lévi-Strauss has opened up, these superficial aporias are merely *characteristics* which are indissolubly linked and which constitute the intelligibility of the structure. Let us try to see them in their true relations.

(i) Structure and Function

The persuasiveness of Lévi-Strauss's rigorous demonstrations is due to more than the necessity of their conclusion; as a determination of our knowledge this necessity can have no basis except in a *practical necessity*, the necessity which makes a man from group *A* who marries a woman from *B*, for familial or personal reasons, into a debtor of *B* and which constitutes through him the whole of group *A* as debtor. We have already anticipated that in organisations we would encounter an apodictic experience on the part of the agent and that this would, at first sight, resemble that of alienation. The married man from group *A* constitutes himself as an other in relation to group *B* – and not as any other, but as a common individual designated by a new function (his debt). And we must go further, since the act of marriage will have the effect of constituting every child in a 'creditor-debtor' relation to the groups in question, and because, through him, this relation will strictly determine his future marriage possibilities (but in *common*, leaving his individual possibility undetermined). The son is born with an untrans-

44. *Ibid.*, p. 132.

cendable future, that is to say, with an untranscendable limit to some of his possibilities: he is *designated* on the basis of a free action of the previous generation (the father chose one woman or another *from among the b women*), and as a result of a concatenation of determinations which can be treated by a sort of ordinal algebra.

Is this *really* alienation? Obviously not: the free choice of a wife, in the first generation, effectively involves, as a freely accepted condition, the inert negation of certain possibilities (in other words, the acceptance of the inert necessity of exogamy in some form or other) and this negation is itself based on the free production of a particular kind of mediated reciprocity. Obviously these characteristics (inert negation, inert possibility, lived reciprocity) are not, or need not be, explicit. In the very freedom of choosing a wife, they are reactualised and sustained. And *debt*, as a relation which constitutes a man *a* in relation to *B*, is the free production, *through this choice*, of a mediating function between *A* and *B*. Through *a*, *A* and *B* – debtors and creditors – are linked, and to some extent, the power of *B* over *a* is the power of *a* over *A*. Thus he has the right to require the group to keep the undertaking given by the common individual who, in his person, married a *B* woman.

Thus these are genuinely free human relations (undertakings, pledges, powers, rights and duties, etc.). And if the son of an *ab* marriage is constituted with a double character *even before being born and regardless of who he may be*, this is because, even before his mother becomes pregnant, he is primarily a *determinate* possibility of the father and mother – that is to say, a limit which is as yet still only *their* limit, and which will remain *theirs* as long as the future child is no more than their own possibility. From birth onwards, the arrival of the child in the milieu of the pledge is the equivalent for him of making a pledge; anyone who arrives within a pledged group finds himself to be pledged – not as a passive object receiving his statute from outside, but as a free common agent who has been granted his freedom (the real function of baptisms, initiations, etc., is to reinteriorise the pledged function as a free pledge[45]). Later, we shall discuss this point at length: for this

---

45. This explains the strange attitude which is current amongst many lukewarm or sceptical Catholics (or even free-thinkers). I call them Catholics because of their origin rather than their faith; but if a married couple in this category has children, they will have them baptised as a result of the following line of reasoning: 'They must be left free: they can make their own choice when they come of age.' For a long time I was surprised by this; I thought it concealed some

second pledge has special characteristics which need to be elucidated and, most importantly, is infinitely more widespread than the first.

What is certain is that birth is a pledge to precisely the extent that the pledge is a birth. If birth is reproduced *artificially* (in an initiation, the group takes responsibility for it) then the young initiate will no longer distinguish between his social birth, his bodily birth, his powers and his pledge: in fact, initiations were originally associated with trials and ordeals; and at the same time, were expected and promised. The organic individual freely bore the expected ordeals in order to achieve the statute of the common individual (that is to say, in order to have and to exercise practical powers); and this undertaking – manifested by

---

sort of conformist timidity, some fear. But in fact, *from the point of view of the group*, the reasoning is valid. As someone who had been baptised, but who had no real links with the Catholic group, it seemed to me that baptism was a mort-gage of future freedom (especially as these same arguments often lead to the child being given a religious upbringing, going to his first communion, etc.). I thought that total indeterminacy was the true basis of choice. But from the point of view of the group (to which the lukewarm or unbelieving but respectful Catholics still belong, the cousin possibly being a seminarist, the maternal aunts being pious, etc.), the opposite is true: baptism is a way of creating freedom in the common individual at the same time as qualifying him by his function and his reciprocal relation to everyone; he interiorises common freedom as the true power of his individual freedom. He is, as it were, moved to a higher potential of efficacity and capacity. Thus the parents wish to place him at this higher level so that he can, with all his power and in complete knowledge, decide whether to remain in the group, whether to change his function (lukewarmness) in it, or whether to withdraw. It seems to the Christian non-believer that 'the born atheist' is only an individual and that he is unable to *rise* to the level of faith as common freedom, so as either to choose or criticise it, whereas the believer will have both the experience of religious power in the Christian community and also, through his doubts, if he has any, the experience of the lower level of isolation. I now realise that neither my own reasonings nor those of the respectful free-thinker were correct. Whatever one does, in fact, one *prejudges*: in the eyes of Christians, atheists are isolated, and characterised by a simple negation; but atheists also form a group (with different statutes, looser bonds, etc.) and a child must submit either to the baptism of atheism or to that of Christianity. The truth, which is very hard for liberals – but then any truth is hard for tender liberal souls – is that it is necessary to decide the meaning of faith (that is to say, of the history of the world, of mankind) on behalf of the child, and without being able to con-sult him, and that whatever one does, and whatever precautions one takes, he will bear the weight of this decision throughout his life. But it is also true that it can mark him only to the extent that he has freely interiorised it and that it becomes the free self-limitation of his freedom rather than an inert limit assigned to him by his father.

his very endurance – is precisely the second pledge. There can be no doubt that the individual lives it as an acquisition of *merit*: but it is equally certain that adults see it as an indication of commitment. It is as if, on the basis of this commitment, they were reserving the right to punish him if he should wish to leave the group – on the basis of this commitment; as if they wanted to be able to say to him: 'Your impatience for the initiation, your courage during the ceremony committed us to you, and you had the right to ask us to install you as a common individual in the community. But, *reciprocally*, in committing us so wholeheartedly, you were committing yourself to us: your enthusiasm was a free determination of your future and you took upon yourself the burdens (exogamy, etc.) which have weighed upon you ever since your parents' marriage.' Thus rites of passage, like marriage, are bi-lateral, symmetrical ceremonies: they actualise a reciprocity. It is therefore impossible for the child not to interiorise this *future anterior* which has been constituted for him *a priori* and not to interiorise it *through positive acts* (initiation procedures, choice of a wife, military prowess or, where appropriate, the struggle for power). This is still the meaning of the very true and constantly repeated sentence, 'No adult can say, "I did not ask to be born" '. Thus, ultimately, the organic individual grasps his contingency in every movement of his life. This means that he is not his own product; but as a common individual, his birth is indistinguishable from the arrival of his freedom and its determination by itself. To be born is to produce oneself as a specification of the group and as a complex of functions (burdens and powers, debts and credit, right and duty). The common individual produces himself as a new pledge within the group.[46]

But in the case both of the original pledge and of the secondary one, (in fact it is *always*, except in emergencies, a matter of secondary pledges), function depends on a veiled inertia, on what I just called the inorganic materiality of freedom. And the aim of the common individual within the group is to preserve the permanence of relations through changes in the position of individual terms; which means that

---

46. It goes without saying that what we are considering here is the abstract case (or the elementary group) in which problems of exploitation or class struggle do not appear. We are proceeding slowly, and at the end of the journey we shall encounter the concrete, that is to say, the complex collection of practical organisations interfering with the practico-inert and the alienation of common action taken up by the passivity of the series. Only at this level will class struggle, exploitation, etc., take on their true meaning.

he modifies his *praxis* (and acquires new characteristics) in so far as other third parties (or all of them) are themselves led to change either by *praxis* or by the pressure of external circumstances. Thus the relation remains fixed in so far as it is preserved. And if, through a directed action, a system in movement is invoked, that is to say relations which produce one another, then these relations will arise as mathematical relations rather than as the moments of a dialectical *praxis*. As functions, in fact, they are still the condition for the *praxis* (of the common individual and of the totalising group), but they are not the *praxis* itself; on the contrary, it is their inert instrumentality (as the limitation of their possibilities) which conditions everyone's efficacity. This is how the efficacity of a goalkeeper, as well as his personal possibility of being good, very good, or excellent, depend on the set of prescriptions and prohibitions which define his role. The match would no longer have any meaning, and would become a form-less scuffle if the goalkeeper could, as he wished, also play the role of half-back or centre-forward (and conversely). Once functions have been distributed, therefore, it is not a matter of them dialectically modifying themselves simply through belonging to the same whole (which is, however, the characteristic of *actions* in so far as they are produced by individuals – within certain limits, as we shall see). *In fact*, the creation of the functions was dialectical, although it was produced in the light of the multiplicity of agents and exigencies. But, although always capable of being rearranged, the functional organisation has to be put in question by the whole group, either through a *reflexive* attitude of each of its members, or by some specially differentiated organ, in order to realise the co-ordinations, modifications, adaptations, etc., when they come to be necessitated by the totalising *praxis*.[47]

---

47. What is deceptive today is the acceleration of History, due, as we know, to the internal contradictions of the capitalist system. The need to reduce costs in order constantly to create new outlets entails the constant transformation of the means of production; industry, from this point of view, is in a permanent state of revolution, which leads to a constant rearrangement of capitalist organisations and, rather more slowly, a perpetual transformation of trade-union organisations and of their *praxis*. But these transformations take place in spite of everything on the basis of reflexive totalisations (coming either from the base or from the sum-mit), that is to say, on the basis of the questioning of the whole of *praxis* by the common individual (the unions will be described as 'failing to adapt to the new directives of the employers' policy'), rather than by a sort of interpenetration of activities, or, to put it differently, by a spontaneous reorganisation of all detailed action by all the others, under the pressure of new circumstances and beyond

We shall therefore call these structures, in so far as their inorganic materiality has been freely interiorised and reworked by the group, the necessity of freedom. This means that the inert (that is to say, different reciprocal limitations) comes into contact with itself in the group, and through the profound relations of interiority which unite each to all in mediated reciprocity, but that this contact of inertia with itself necessarily takes place according to the laws and the intelligibility proper to this sector of materiality; and this means that the conditioning of functions by each other (once their synthetic, reflexive determination is complete) takes place in exteriority, as in the physical world. However, it is important to recognise that this skeleton is sustained by all the common individuals and that it is always possible for the group, as totalising action, under the pressure of new circumstances, to dissolve it entirely. It should therefore be noted *both* that it is the free attachment of each individual to the community in so far as it is the inorganic-being of each member *and* that this necessity, as exteriority structuring interiority, is simply the obverse of the practico-inert: the latter effectively appeared as passive activity, whereas the former constitutes itself as active passivity. Everyone's *inorganic-being*, as we have seen, involves a considerable measure of indeterminacy: it is the foundation of my *praxis*, and it frames it and circumscribes it, it channels it and gives it everyone's guarantee along with the instrumental spring board it needs. But *praxis* itself, when completed, cannot be reduced to this skeleton: it is more and it is different; it is the free concrete realisation of a particular task.

We should not be surprised by the opposition of these two necessities: the second is the interiorisation of the first and its negation by organising labour. We have seen how the group acquires inertia in order to struggle against inertia; it absorbs the passivity which enables matter

---

reflexive questioning. In other words, an organisation (whatever it may be) will, given an acceleration of the historical process, live its inertia as a perpetual dislocation which must always be compensated. But these rearrangements can occur only in the light of new functions which also owe their efficacity to the exact determination of their limits. In short, the action of reorganisation is *praxis* in so far as it redistributes tasks with a view to achieving the same total objective in varying circumstances. The same applies to the organic action of each common individual. But even if function were modified every day, it would, as a statute defined by the reflexive attitude and assumed by the effective action of the worker or fighter, remain a structure of inertia, and an object of logical analysis, and, as such, capable of being studied as a mechanical system.

to sustain the passive syntheses which it needs in order to *survive*; but it is *precisely* not, in itself, a passive synthesis, and its passivity sustains the active synthesis which is *praxis*. The practical comprehension of active passivity is given to everyone – regardless of his group – in the behaviour known as 'freely agreeing to discipline'. The only error – which in any case is not so frequent as one might suppose – is due to language: there is a danger that the words will give the impression that the only effect of free consent is to bring behaviour into line with prescriptions. But in fact everyone discovers in his action that discipline affects him in his very freedom with a kind of being, that is to say, with a certain form of exteriority which, paradoxically, sustains his bonds of interiority with everyone else. But this means that exteriority as such, as the foundation of the action, is always external, or rather that it is at the extreme boundary which separates transcendence (*la transcendance*) from immanence: in the heat of battle, a soldier obeys the order of a superior in freedom, because he recognises its importance, because he transcends it towards the common aim; in a sense, therefore, this is a free reciprocity. Yet the hierarchical bond between the lieutenant and the private is entirely contained in this relation; in other words, the inert reciprocity of command underlies concrete action. The complex structure of this organised connection actually comprises three signifying layers which it is necessary to describe: the first is concrete *praxis*; this includes the second, which is *power* (freedom-terror) and function (right-duty); and this in turn includes the third, which is an inert skeleton. And the inert skeleton is in fact the most abstract of the three layers. The organising sub-group could not determine it – as a set of elements in a symbolic calculation – except on the concrete basis of a differentiated pledge, of rights-duties, of functions and of everyone's relation to the common objective. From the moment when, for example, an organisation selects its 'cadres', a problem immediately arises, one of whose aspects is purely quantitative – namely that of the numerical relation of cadres to militants (of officers and NCO's to privates) in a particular situation, in the light of specific objectives and on the basis of quite definite instrumental and technical resources (for example, in a state of international tension in which, as at present, there is an opposition between 'blocs' each characterised by a given level of armaments, presupposing a certain industrial capacity). And calculation enters into this quantitative problem as if all the relations involved were relations of exteriority. It should also be added that the creation of these cadres, if it takes place, may lead to a qualitative change in relations of interiority (for example, a tightening of authority). But there would be no sense in working on the inertia of the group if it were simply a matter of rearranging inertia which has already been produced, as interiorised exteriority, in so far, that is, as it is sustained by relations of power, of rights, etc., which were differentiated through the pledge and which perpetuate the pledge which produced it.

(ii) Structure and System

In this sense, we can describe structure as having two sides: it is both an analytical necessity and a synthetic power. Power certainly constitutes itself by producing in everyone the inertia which is the basis of necessity. But, conversely, necessity is only the external appearance of this freely created inertia; it is, in other words, the index of this inertia seen in exteriority, either by an observer who does not belong to the group, or by a specialised sub-group which uses analytical methods and symbols for dealing with certain problems of apportionment and distribution, because the multiplicity which they treat (the group as plurality in circumstances of scarcity, scarcity of cadres or provisions, etc.) is only the external appearance of an interiority which *alone* makes the problem possible (not in its solution, but in its very formulation). Even to think of regarding individuals as organisms which have to be fed, in order to enumerate them, to establish the relation between provisions and the number of mouths to be fed, to establish provision centres or to bring the existing ones closer to the front etc., the army must already be a practical totalisation, a combat. But even this is not sufficient; certain functional relations and powers and discipline must be presupposed, so that, at a particular practical level, execution can be relied on. To say that the bases are too far away means that the Quarter-master is doing everything possible, and is not to be blamed. To say that they can be brought nearer (by a certain distance) means: we are increasing the power of the supply services; their efficacity will therefore increase accordingly – in short, they are entirely devoted to their functions.

The other aspect of structure is, in effect, that of a mediated reciprocity. Furthermore, we have seen that this mediation is quite simply that of the totalising group. Thus, while structure is revealed, in exteriority, as a mere skeleton which can be examined and reworked in itself on the mere tacit presupposition of the whole – that is to say, *by silently ignoring* the practical totalisation as the support and reason for the inertia at the moment of the combination of terms – it is, in interiority, an immediate relation to the totalisation. In fact the totalisation is closer, at each term of the reciprocity, than everyone is to each other, since everyone is linked to the other through it. Pouillon is right in saying: 'The idea of structure is . . . profoundly different from that of order. Only structure makes it possible to transform the vicious circle of which Pascal accuses Cartesian knowledge into, so to speak, a true circle. In a structure, each element is the particular expression of the totality immediately and totally reflected in it, rather than an intermediate stage in the constitution of the whole. There is no other way of avoiding the paradox of the simultaneous autonomy and dependence of an element in relation to the whole or of conceiving the synthesis of the heterogeneous.'[48]

But it is important to realise that what we are dealing with here is not a totality but a totalisation, that is to say, a multiplicity which totalises itself in order to totalise the practical field from a certain perspective, and that its common action, through each organic *praxis*, is revealed to every common individual as a developing objectification. In other words, the mediating group is already, in itself, a complex dialectic of *praxis* and inertia, of totalisations and already totalised elements. In fact, this is where the reflexive structure which is characteristic of the organised group as such needs to be more securely defined. It does not mean that a particular, collective illumination inhabits the group (a consciousness *of* collective consciousness), but only that every common individual (*already* common: through the pledge or the first action of the fused group) adopts practical behaviour which takes the group as its immediate objective on the basis of some distant objective. These practices produce the group *as a quasi-object* for its members. (For non-members, not only contemporaries, both enemies and allies, but also, subsequently, historians and sociologists, it is an object in any case and whatever its structure, *but* it is a practical and signifying object, which produces its own instrumentality around certain instruments.) The group has an *internal objectivity*; that is to say, the group exists through every common individual in two

48. Jean Pouillon, 'Le Dieu caché ou l'Histoire visible', *Les Temps Modernes*, 141, p. 893.

radically distinct forms: prior to any functional determination, it *is*, for everyone, the security of each and all, which is once again present in him as the Other-Being of his own freedom.

We have seen that, as the organisation becomes formed and constituted, this inertia, which can affect freedom only by *using* other freedoms, appears decreasingly as a negative limit and increasingly as the basis of powers. But obviously this unity of inertias will not *of itself* produce change *in anyone* except through someone's real, free *praxis*. The group as a totality or an objective reality does not exist; *on this level* it is simply the fact that the free production of inertia is *the same* and determines itself as such intentionally or, to put it differently, that there is a single pledge. And this does not mean that *this pledge on its own* is the transcendent unity of the pledged agents; on the contrary, it means that, in each common individual, there is no *principle of individuation* for the act of swearing: thus the individuals are diverse but their pledges – however distinct as spatio-temporal acts – are, through everyone, *the* pledge, an individual act of the common individual (in that it consolidates or produces this individual). But in the common decision to swear there is a presentiment of the exigencies of differentiation; and it is precisely the unfolding of these exigencies before the pledged individual which shows him the group as a means, and therefore as an end and an object. Every means is an end in the practical moment in which it has to be found or produced so that another means, and thereby the end, can be accomplished. And the *group-means* is revealed *through circumstances*: they indicate certain possibilities in the multiplicity in so far as it is subjected to and controlled by unity through each individual unification.

Thus the creation of forms of differentiation treats the group as a transition from homogeneity to a calculated heterogeneity or, more commonly, from a less differentiated state to a more differentiated one. And, in so far as it reveals itself to the practical action of the organising third party, the group appears as a *developing* (or still to be achieved) *totalisation*, rather than as a completed totality. Nevertheless, it is an object; and this means that its *instrumentality* can be modified by work; through organisation, the organising third party produces or maintains tools (like a worker who whets or repairs his tool). And once again, for everyone, this practical object cannot be any more than a *quasi-object*, since it is both the matter which is to be differentiated by functions and the unity of the pledge which founds heterogeneity as the free, controlled use of multiplicity, and allows it to be reintroduced.

In other words, through the individuated practice of the common agent, the group is an object *in one form* and the foundation of the act (as pledged inertia) *in another form*. And this produces reflexivity as quasi-objectivity. (Individual reflexion also involves a single consciousness, but in so far as its relation to itself never allows it to be either one or two.) But it should be noted that once the organisation already exists and needs to be rearranged (possibly from top to bottom), the relative autonomy of functions (that is to say, of the limits of competence), by threatening to posit itself for itself in the individual function, accentuates the *object* character of the unified multiplicity and tends (without ever wholly succeeding) to simulate the impossibility of a total objectifying duality.

In any case, radical duality is still out of the question: it is *the same* (the pledge as non-individuated in the common individual) which recurs practically as the still undifferentiated unity of this multiplicity. Even if he belongs to a specialised group, the organiser derives his power to organise from this relation of the group to itself (and to its end); if he tends to conceal his membership of the group in his behaviour, this is precisely to the extent that his work makes him treat structures and common individuals in exteriority (that is to say, as a numerical multiplicity and a relational skeleton which have to be rearranged). But in an organised group, the act of organising is only a means – often entrusted to specialists – of efficacity; and the essential practical relation is that of the individual agent fulfilling his task with the external object in which he realises the common objectification. It is at this level that function, as a relation to a given sub-group or – directly or indirectly – to all, is mediated by the group. And it is clear what *group* must mean here: a practical relation between the pledge as *the same* in everyone and the already unified multiplicity which it allows to become differentiated. This reflexivity determines every common individual in so far as he understands the utility of his task and the necessity of his *being organised*. This means that every functional differentiation, regardless of which individual or sub-group chose it, is reaffirmed in pledged freedom; in short it is adopted (*assumée*). In this sense, although every common individual may be transformed, disqualified, requalified, silenced, or displaced by new reorganisations according to the common objective, he can never produce himself, in his actions and his active passivity, as purely and simply an object of the group. It may in fact be true that the group treats him (or can treat him) as an object: his activity may be chosen (and subsequently changed) according to a strict calculation. But, in so far as every pledged member is always *the same*, the organiser makes his decisions in so far as he *is the same* as the organised, and the organised adopts the decision in so far as he *is the same* as the organiser; this means that he sees his own common decision as a moment in a common, already differentiated process.

A given activist, sent into a particular factory or collective farm, in order to explain a decision of the Soviet government to a group of workers must treat himself both as the inert object of a choice (his deployment does not necessarily take his capacities into consideration), and as an element in an immense *process* which realises itself in *divergence* (at the same moment thousands of activists are spreading out in order to go and perform the same act everywhere) and whose deep convergence of *praxis* will temporalise itself in the common objectification (the unification of reactions in all milieux everywhere). But he cannot grasp himself in his inertia and in his being as a discrete element of an objective process unless, *by himself* and in free, individual *praxis* he realises all the moments which affect him in this process (from the moment when *he presents himself* by some prescribed means of communication at his place of work to the moment when, on the basis of a set of principles, explanations, and unchanging evaluations, he produces the individual reply which he must give to a particular individual question). And it is precisely the free realisation of the common process which refers him back to the other free realisations of different propagandists and which reveal his localised action to him (he has persuaded people *here*, in a given town or province) as the common objective of a common *praxis*. In other words, structure as the exteriority of interiority is reinteriorised by functional activity *without being dissolved* by it. The agent conceives it, in his very activity, as the intersection of two planes: on the one hand, the work of instrumentalisation which the group performs on its multiplicity and, on the other hand, his own inertia as a free pledge and as a free adoption of his character as a discrete quantity on the basis of an indissoluble common unity. For him, exteriority signifies interiority and the multiplicity of inert relations is simply the practical determination of the common unity.

This example still does not get us to structure, since essentially it concerns a very rapid event which is quickly reabsorbed into its objective: the propaganda which accompanies and follows a policy change. Nevertheless, if it is examined more closely, it becomes evident that it presupposes structure as an expression of the totalisation and as the inorganic skeleton of organisation. It should be noted, in fact, both that any young activist, taken individually (that is to say every one of them) was *produced* by the Party, or by certain specialised organisations, to perform tasks of agitation and propaganda and, at the same time, that this productive action, performed by a sub-group (as an expression of the whole) over very young boys can temporalise itself only in reciprocity, that is to say, it must *also* be adopted and interiorised by the individual. He is the product of a given administrative group in so far as he is his own product and vice versa. If his mission is to train a group of workers and to increase output (as a team leader and Stakhanovite) he still has to make himself capable of raising norms by his own work. Conversely, if the administration selected him, this is for a set of aptitudes, linked to his loyalty to the régime and revealed *through his praxis*; and in any case, his selection can always be revoked. These two indissoluble actions, which together require that the product of the free, common organisation should, as a common individual, make himself his own product, eventually, in their reciprocal development, achieve the double, equally reciprocal result of producing the activist as an inert determination of multiplicity and as an individual expression of the developing totalisation. *Then* a particular mission will constitute him as a power-object, that is to say, as a unit which has to be transported to a particular place by a particular means of transport in order to make contact with specific sub-groups and as a real *right-duty* who *may* require of the local authorities or of certain individuals the means to carry out his duty. It is therefore *the exercise of a function* which develops in this particular event: and this function is *structure* in so far as it is seen as the potential and power of the group of activists. On the other hand, in this relatively simple case, and other things being equal, everyone *is the same as everyone*, and since every propagandist is conditioned in his very power by the interiorised multiplicity of his sub-group,[49] and, finally, since the group does not possess the metaphysical existence of a form or a *Gestalt*, of a collective consciousness or a

49. The size of the regions to be covered, the number of meetings to be held, and, ultimately, the very efficacity of his work – as determined by his own fatigue as well as by the slowness of communications – are determined (at a variable level of the organisation, sometimes at the apex, from the outset, sometimes at the base, in the course of the operation) on the basis of the simultaneously quantitative and reciprocal relation (in definite circumstances and with definite instruments) of the multiplicity of the sub-group of activists and of the social ensemble which is to be 'agitated' or persuaded.

created totality, each individual, as a common individual, is *in himself* the propaganda sub-group as a statutory unit of the interiorised multiplicity and his own activity is an expression of the totalising organisation. (The 'totalising organisation' here means the synthetic ensemble of governmental and administrative services which have created these 'organs' of agitation in the light of a certain objective, of certain mediations between the apex and the base, and of certain relations with the masses.)

It is obvious – and we will come back to this at length, later in our investigation – that suffered inertia has infiltrated this ensemble, which includes a régime, in the form of revived seriality. But, at the present abstract level of our investigation, this inertia does not yet appear: it will emerge later, in dialectical circularity. The important point is to define the moments of the investigation *in their purity*, even if it is only logical, so as to avoid the danger of attributing to constituted realities characteristics which confused and hasty observation reveals to us, but which really belong to another moment of the dialectical process. It is therefore particularly dangerous to speak here of bureaucratic seriality, although it is obvious that in our example it affects everything, and *primarily* the creation of propaganda sub-groups. We shall also see that this seriality transforms, but certainly does not eliminate the character of *practical expression* which is concealed by function in the common individual: it extends this transformed expressiveness and produces the *common* as a signifier-signified in relation to society as a whole.

At present, taking the sub-group and the totalising organisation in their pure state (that is to say, in the concrete struggle against a given, particularised threat of serial dissolution), there can be no doubt that *this* particular young activist, in his individual way of realising his powers, is not only *autonomous*, as Pouillon noted, but also a simple, detailed, practical expression of the total operation (and of the complex organisation which has foreseen and planned this kind of operation *for a long time*). He is *autonomous* simply to the extent that concrete circumstances (he is speaking to an audience defined by particular interests and jobs, by a particular culture and particular *habits* – in the sense of *exis*) are the other side of untranscendable inertia, that is to say, in so far as they always require him to mediate between the abstract determinations of his task and the particular difficulties he encounters. He is *expression* in so far as his whole undertaking is incomprehensible except from the point of view of a certain transcendent relation between the leaders and the masses, which involves the social and political system of the USSR as a whole. From this point of view, tactical differences are themselves expressive since they never cast doubt on the basis. A kind of authoritarianism (which we need not define here) lies at the basis of their mission and their common-being (in so far as these products of the organised group produced themselves). And from the structural point of view it does not matter whether this authoritarianism manifests itself as a structured characteristic of the individual (which is sometimes incorrectly called a character trait) or whether it appears through a tactic which is apparently flexible and conciliatory but which really has no other aim than to *realise* the centralised authority while concealing it. Or rather, tactical differences do not reflect differences in the structure unless they arise at two different moments as two attitudes of the sub-group (rather than as individual variations). If the operations of the activists, as a unified multiplicity, are carried out in voluntaristic arrogance, they will, in one way or another, simply express the activities of the government and administration.[50]

We shall therefore refer to the function of the sub-group or of a member of the sub-group as *structure*, in so far as its concrete exercise through the free *praxis* of the agent reveals it as a specification of the totalising rearrangement of the whole by itself. It should be clear that the word *expression* here refers to a fundamentally practical relation, that is to say, a reciprocity of constitution: free, individual *praxis* realises the previous totalisation as a positing of limits; it pursues the totalising operation by concretely objectifying itself in a concrete result which *signifies* the totalisation of results which are in the process of being objectified. Meanwhile the organised totalisation designates and solicits individual action, as function, as its inevitable concretisation; it constitutes a power and an instrumentality for it. *Structure* is this double constituent designation, in its two simultaneous and opposite orienta-

---

50. This does not mean that the arrogance of the activists necessarily signifies a return of central organisations to some form of dictatorship at any particular moment. On the contrary, it may – in concrete circumstances – signify a lack of coordination between organisations or a stubborn resistance to new policies from the structured past amongst the young activists. The ensemble determines the signification, as an expression of the totalising and totalised totality. My point is simply that this expression – which always appears *in experience* – is a necessary presence of the totalisation in the totalised part since the totalisation *for this part* is no more than function, that is to say, structure.

tions, either at the level of mere abstract potentiality (the level of *power acknowledged* by common individuals), or at the level of actualisation. It is obvious that this relation between the individual and the group (as an interiorised multiplicity in each and all) existed even in the fused group where, indeed, we laid stress on it. But one cannot yet speak of a structured relation, for the simple reason that the reciprocal bond has not yet been specified. Structure is a specific relation of the terms of a reciprocal relation to the whole and to each other through the mediation of the whole. And the whole, as a developing totalisation, exists in everyone in the form of a unity of the interiorised multiplicity and *nowhere else.*

(iii) *Structure and the Group's Idea of Itself*

In the reflexive context of the group, however, this structural relation must also arise as reflexive knowledge: in other words, the individual action of the common agent cannot realise itself as a determination of the indeterminate without conceiving function negatively in the transcendent object as exigency and as a negative adumbration (*esquisse en creux*) of behaviour and, positively, in interiority, as duty and power. The moment of mediation through organic *praxis* is also that of knowledge, that is to say, of the co-presence of all reciprocal implications; but of course this does not mean that this knowledge is explicit or thematised. But, if we consider all the characteristics, already enumerated, of knowledge in the organised group, we can immediately see that the organic individual produces and is aware of himself as a common individual: first, in so far as the object reflects the group to him as practice and as practical knowledge, that is to say, *both* on the basis of the common objective as the future revealing the present situation in the practical field *and* on the basis of conceiving one's work on the object as a particular detail of the common objectification; and, secondly, in so far as the whole, as a practical totalisation which is also performed by him, forces him, in functional determination, practically to conceive the transcendent object as common and the practical field as a common situation to be modified. Thus structure, considered, by way of abstraction, as knowledge, is simply the idea which the group produces of itself (and of the universe in so far as it is practically determined as a field of objectification). And the content and foundation of this reflexive idea is simply the common organisation as an objective system of relations; or rather, the organisation conditions it and becomes its internal norm. At this level of abstraction and purity (that is to say, in the absence of serial determination) the idea of the group is *without alterity*: it is the same everywhere as a pure expression of the *here and now*; and there is nothing surprising in this since it is a particular actualisation, under the pressure of specific exigencies, of structure as a relation of reciprocal expression between the part and the whole. But, at the same time, at this level of non-differentiation, it remains purely practical, that is to say, it is still both an organising reflexion and a pledge; or in other words, both the *truth* of the group as practical experience and its *ethic*, as the constitution of common individuals by imperatives and rights based on pledged inertia, are absolutely not differentiated and, indeed, the principle of their indissoluble unity lies in the very urgency of the common tasks. The idea of man, in an organised group, is simply the idea of the group, that is to say, of the common individual, and fraternity-terror, in so far as it is expressed by specific norms, derives this particular colouring from the real objective, that is to say, from needs or dangers. The material organisation of the group is indistinguishable from the organisation of its thoughts; the system of logical relations which constitutes the untranscendable principles of every mental operation for everyone is indistinguishable from the system of inert worked relations which characterises functions in exteriority. Invention and ideational discovery – as individual *praxis* – occur as free, reflexive action *on the basis* of an organised specification of freely adopted inertia; and it is one and the same thing to be unable to transcend a given practical organisation, or a given system of values or a given system of 'guiding principles'. However, the idea of man which is produced by the group as an idea of itself cannot be compared to the idea which is produced by the gold coin in the practico-inert field.[51] This in fact supports the ideas of the Other by its fundamental inertia; and so it cannot change. The idea of the group, on the other hand, as a structural determination of the indeterminate, must be invented, and remains infinitely variable within certain limits.

But the double character of structure (an inert object of calculation when seen as ossature without taking account of totalisation, or an effective power actualised by the *praxis* of each and all) implies a double character in the idea. In one sense, it is the free comprehension *every-*

51. See above, p. 171. [Ed.]

where of functional activity in everyone in so far as its heterogeneity relates to the homogeneity of pledges on the one hand, and to the synthetic unity of the transcendent end on the other. It is at this still practical level that the group has a silent knowledge of itself through each common individual: but this understanding (*évidence*) is not available to those who do not share its objectives. As practical individuals, they may perceive these ends in the common action as it unfolds before them, and carry out a correct reconstruction of the *praxis*: but they will never perceive the common relation to the end concretely as an inter-individual relation, that is to say, as a milieu specified by organisation. It is at this level that complex knowledges may disconcert a sociologist or ethnographer who encounters them in underdeveloped societies, because they conceive them as theoretical knowledges derived from observation of an object, whereas they are really practical structures which are themselves lived in the interiority of a common action. Ethnographers have stressed the logical flexibility of primitive thought. Deacon has written about a matrimonial system: 'The native is capable of pretty advanced abstract thought.'[52] But this is not a good way of formulating the question; the point is not to discover whether they are capable of abstract thought in general, as if this thought were a universal capacity which everyone possesses to a greater or lesser degree, but to show within the investigation whether or not they are capable of comprehending the abstract structures of their matrimonial or kinship systems, which is perfectly clear today. In other words, we should avoid putting the cart before the horse by claiming that primitive people understand the abstract relations which constitute the organisation of their group because they are capable of abstract thought; on the contrary, we should say that their capacity for abstract thought is determined by the abstract relations which structure their society, that it is simply these relations themselves in so far as every common individual has to *live them all* in order practically to realise his relation to all in the unity of a common objective. In fact, functional relations determine not only the level of abstraction of thought but also the limits of its application: this relational system as the instrument and limit of ideational power constitutes itself as a generalised system of logical relations, which means

---

52. A. B. Deacon, *Malekula: A Vanishing People in the New Hebrides*, ed. C. H. Wedgewood, London, 1934 (George Routledge and Sons), p. 132. Quoted in Lévi-Strauss, *op. cit.*, p. 127.

both that it can be applied to a certain number of similar cases, well defined and forming part of the social, everyday life of the natives, *and* that its existence – as inertia – is by itself a sometimes invincible resistance to the elaboration of any other system. In this sense, in effect, truth is normative because fidelity to logical 'principles' is only a form of fidelity to the pledge.

But, apart from this implicit understanding – which is simply a structure *of power* – there is, at least for certain specialised organs, a knowledge which is equally practical and reflexive, but which is of a logistical and combinatory kind, directed at function as inorganic inertia, that is to say, *the relational system as ossature.* I shall not dwell on this since I discussed it above: it is clear that totalisation as a pledged milieu which sustains this inertia is passed over in silence in the moment of calculation. But it should be noted that, although the totalisation is invisible, it occurs at the level of the organisers and calculators in that they know and acknowledge their right and power to calculate only to the extent that it is their specialised function: the basis for the calculation of discrete elements is, therefore, the lived comprehension of structure as the reciprocity of the whole and of the part (that is to say, the comprehension we have just been describing) in so far as it arises in the *praxis* of the organisers and in so far as it gives meaning to this *praxis.* The organiser therefore has an immediate, practical comprehension of the structures in all their complexity and this is the basis of the abstract analysis which he then performs on these structures as skeletons. In fact, the natives of Ambrym 'gave Deacon demonstrations, using diagrams'.[53] They drew lines on the ground, and these, according to their length and position, represented one or other of the spouses, their sons, their daughters, etc., seen, of course, from the point of view of a complex matrimonial system. In this case, it is important to realise that in producing these relations in the domain of the absolute inert (earth or sand) and of perfect exteriority, they were not copying some model which they carried in their heads; and it would be equally incorrect to say that they project their synthetic practical consciousness of themselves and of everyone into the analytical milieu of the inanimate: such a projection, in fact, is impossible, since it would involve – roughly speaking – two distinct orders of rationality.

I have shown that analytical rationality can be transcended and integrated by synthetic rationality, but it is also clear that the opposite is not true: a dialectical proposition would lose its meaning and dissolve into relations of exteriority if it were 'projected' into the milieu of logical or mathematical calculation. In fact, the decision to make the kinship system into a fabricated, inorganic object (lines made on the ground) corresponds, for the native, to a practical attempt to win the support of inorganic materiality in order to produce the structures in the form of inert abstract schemata. The reason for this is that he is explaining them to a stranger who is *situated in the exterior*, and who therefore thinks in terms of exteriority: he therefore expresses pledged inertia not as an interiorised exteriority, but as a pure determination of universal exteriority. But in establishing this *minimum* schema, that is to say, in reducing structure to ossature, he is guided by the synthetic understanding which defines his membership of the group. Thus his task is not a matter of projection or transposition: he is simply creating an inert object which presents in exteriority, to a man from the exterior, a set of passive characteristics which retain only the inertia of these structures and which, indeed, falsify this inertia by presenting it as an elementary, suffered condition (whereas in fact it is produced by the pledge).

It is obvious that this construction is not a thought: it is a piece of manual work controlled by a synthetic knowledge which it does not express. But this example enables us to understand *the other work in exteriority*, performed by a specialised sub-group on pledged inertia as an exteriority of structure, in and for the group. This work is also guided by a dialectical thematic and a comprehension of the whole which it does not seek to project or 'render', and it cannot, in the first instance, be regarded as a thought. It becomes one only through practice: the organiser creates analytical thought (and the rationalism which corresponds to it) with his hands; it is born within his hands because every *praxis* explains itself in terms of the objective and the object. Thus, at the level of calculation and redistribution, the 'transformations of ossature' which are performed on the basis of a functional and totalising power develop a set of guiding schemata which are simply the laws of inertia transformed into practical laws of organisation. Practical knowledge unfolds simultaneously on two planes and according to two types of rationality; and this is not surprising, especially in modern societies, where it is almost impossible to find the solution to a practical problem if the question is not treated at several levels *simultaneously* (in fact, as we shall see, the practico-inert field reintroduces itself at the moment of the true concrete so producing a new complexity). But this does not constitute an unintelligibility or a split in thought, since dialectical Reason sustains, controls, and justifies all other forms of thought, because it explains them, puts them in their proper place and integrates them as non-dialectical moments which, in it, regain a dialectical value.

The Constituted Dialectic

1 Individual and Common Praxis: the Manhunt

In the course of these preliminary observations we have not encountered any major difficulties. This is because we are trying to determine the meaning and scope of dialectical Reason. Now, at the level of these first approximations, we have not encountered any critical problems which are really new. True, the new necessity produced and sustained by organising freedom had to be analysed and elucidated; and the relation between the two aspects of structure (system and function) has had to be discussed in some detail. But, on the one hand, this has, on the whole, involved a very simple dialectical progression, which merely united into new syntheses factors which had already been discussed (the pledge, terror, inertia, reciprocity, objectification, reflexion, etc.) and, on the other hand, at the level we were occupying we rediscovered constituent organic *praxis* as the indispensable mediation between the common individual and the common objectification of the *praxis* of the group. So since *praxis*, when considered at the level of each function, is still individual action and, as such, a moment of the constituent dialectic – regardless of readjustments and the relation of common individuals elsewhere; and since the organised group acts only upon itself (in order to make everyone better able to carry out his share of the common task), and since this very action is done through the mediation of individual *praxis*, the real new modifications which have arisen before us have not raised the question of *constituted* intelligibility. In other words, the kind of dialectical intelligibility which we explained at the beginning of our critical investigation was sufficient to explain the practical relations of individual functions within the organised group. But this is because we ourselves were taking an insufficiently synthetic view of such groups. This was necessary in order to explain its structures, but it meant postponing the real critical question: what type of existence or being characterises the common action of the organised group *in so far as it is common* (rather than in so far as it can be resolved into a multiplicity of functions)? What kind of intelligibility does this action define? What is a constituted dialectic?

What we have been studying, in fact, is the conditions of common action, rather than common action itself. This action can in fact be referred to by certain determinations of language: the people of Paris have taken the Bastille; the rebels have seized the radio building; the team has won a match; we have put a new locomotive into production, etc. In all these sentences, the subject is plural (or unified but multiple) and the action is *singular*, seen either as a temporalisation ('They *took*, they are taking') or in its common result: *The* storming of the Bastille, the people *have taken . . .*, etc. Now, we have explained the interiorisation of plurality, but this gives us no guide to *praxis* as a common temporalisation or common objectification of the group. We have seen, in effect, that through the organisation it is realised through the mediation of organic individuals and of the individual dialectic. But, in opposition to this, it has a concrete unity, which implies an organisation of means in the light of the end and a realisation of the synthetic end through labour. Everything would be simple if, corresponding to *praxis* as the concrete, living temporalisation of the group, there was a living, concrete group – in short, a *Gestalt* or an organism or a hyper-consciousness – which temporalised and objectified *itself*. In fact, it is clear that the group, 'united' around an instrumentality or 'contained' in appropriate locations, does not exist anywhere except *everywhere*, that is to say, it belongs to every individual *praxis* as an interiorised unity of multiplicity. And the ubiquity of the *heres* corresponds to the real practice of negating plurality. This totality does not circulate, it is not elsewhere; it is always and entirely both *here* and *the same*. But if we abandon every magical or mythical interpretation, then it is clear that this ubiquity does not mean in any way that a new reality is incarnated in every common individual, like a Platonic Idea in indivi-duated objects; on the contrary, it means that there is a practical determination of everyone by everyone, by all and by oneself from the point of view of a common *praxis*. The proof is that this unified multiplicity re-emerges as inert exteriority within the group itself, that is to say, as *ossature*. However, the action is *one* as individual action, the objective is *one*, and the temporalisation and the rule it gives itself are *one*; so everything is as it would be if a hyperorganism had temporalised and objectified itself in a practical end, by unifying and unified labour of which every common individual with his constituent mediation would be a completely inessential moment. The thing seems even more paradoxical at the real level of action, that is to say when it is split, within the group itself, by deep conflicts of interest, by local (or generalised) revivals of seriality, or by accidents. Through all the well known incidents, disorders, accidents and misunderstandings the Parisian crowd *stormed the Bastille*. But though we are still only at the level of abstract purity, this synthetic signification of *praxis* at first appears paradoxical: the *praxis* is not in fact the temporalisation of an organic unity, but a negated and instrumentalised multiplicity which temporalises and unifies itself in the common *praxis* through the mediation of individual temporalisations. In other words, the only unity is practical unification, that is to say, the unity of every particular labour with all the Others. But then what is this unity of local, heterogeneous temporalisations? What kind of reality does it have? And what kind of intelligibility? Of course, everything is *already organised*; but is the common *praxis*, as a synthetic temporalisation of this organisation, *organised* or *organic*? And since its signification (its temporalisation as diachronic signification, and its final objective as synchronic signification) is and can *only be one*,[54] should its unity be regarded as homogeneous with the significations of individual, organic *praxis* or should we recognise that a signifying synthesis performed by the organised group is absolutely *of a different order* than an individual synthesis? If it is *of the same order*, how are we to explain the fact that the group produces a *praxis* which is individual and organic in character (even if it is distinct from individual actions in scope and power)? And if it is *of a different order*, shall we have to accept a hyper-dialectic, which means either regarding the group as a hyper-organism, or making the dialectic into a transcendent law imposed on the object? In fact how does it come about that *I* understand the meaning of a group action? Of course, I may be mistaken or mystified: but the existence of historical science is sufficient to convince me that it is possible, in the long term and given sufficient information, to understand a common signification in the course of individual research. The historian, as a solitary worker, can grasp the precise aim of some political action, that

54. Of course, I am speaking from the abstract level of purity. I do not yet have the means which, later, will enable us to reveal *a new alienation* as a new apodictic experience and a new incarnation of common *praxis*.

is to say, the end pursued by a given organised group, *even if this end* was not realised. Scholars debate and disagree about *the* declaration of war in 1792 and about *the* behaviour of the Girondins. Sociologists like Lévi-Strauss grasp the functional signification of *the* incest taboo in certain societies, although this signification is normally hidden. Is there, therefore, any homogeneity of knowledge between the moment of individual *praxis* and that of the common project as a temporalisation which unifies the organised multiplicity? And what if there are structures and practical sub-reactions whose teleological signification must, *a priori*, escape me because the practical thought of the individual researcher is of a different order and, *a priori*, of a lower degree of complexity than the signifying action of the group? All these secondary problems are simply special ways of formulating the fundamental question of the constituted dialectic and its rationality.

Now there is a false aporia which can be quickly disposed of: if I have a real understanding of the common activity of a group of which I am not a part, this must be because it does not transcend my possibilities as a *practical individual*; but, conversely, it is also because I approach it with the powers and in the function of a *common individual*. I mean by this that the historian is a product of a group, that his instruments, techniques and powers, as well as his knowledge, define him as a member of a research community and that he will understand the common undertaking of a historical group in so far as he himself belongs to a historical group which is defined by a particular common undertaking. And if he were a solitary researcher – which is really senseless unless it simply means that he is not a member of a university or does not have a degree – he would still be integrated into *other groups* (economic, cultural, political, religious, etc.) and would therefore be a common individual, capable of understanding any common *praxis*.

But the reciprocity between historical knowledge and its object postpones the problem rather than solving it. Since organic constituent *praxis* is an indispensable mediation between the common individual (as a limitation of possibilities in the light of a common objective and as the unification of a multiplicity by mediated reciprocity) and the practical exercise of a common function, how can this moment of pure practical individuality carry within itself a comprehension of the *common scope* of that which is realised by the individual organism? This can also be expressed from the point of view of historical research: the historian, of course, is function, power, and ability; but all this has to be reactualised by a synthetic invention, that is to say, by and in a synthetic, individual decoding of the practical field: now, the practical field, in this case, is constituted by certain documents and monuments through which a *common* signification must be rediscovered. Thus it is clear that the historian would not have the capacities necessary for comprehending a common historical action if he were not the social product of an organised group. This implies that his experimental invention, as an individual mediation between his function and the object (the past group which he is reconstructing), must involve a double comprehension: that of the common function of the scholar and that of the common *praxis* of the past group. These observations point to the following conclusion: there is always a permanent possibility, even if it can occur only in the context of organised functions and powers, of the practical organism comprehending the *praxis* of an organisation.

But as I showed in *The Problem of Method*, comprehension is not a faculty, or some kind of contemplative intuition: it is reducible to *praxis* itself to the extent that it is homogeneous with every other individual *praxis* and that it is *situated* by reference to any action performed in the practical field, and therefore in an immediate practical relation to it. This implies, therefore, that common action and individual *praxis* exhibit a real homogeneity. The individual would be unable to understand either his own common action in terms of the totalising *praxis* of the group, or that of a group external to himself, if the structures of common *praxis* were of a different order than those of individual *praxis*. If the objectives of the group had a hyper-individual character, then the individual would never be able to grasp them. This does *not* mean that the common action is an organic synthesis of the members of the group but, *on the contrary*, that the group, far from having hyper-individuality in its action, sets itself objectives of an individualised structure and can achieve them only through common operations which are individual in character.

But there is a danger of very serious confusions if we do not explain these conclusions at once. The common aim is in fact always doubly common: it is the aim of everyone as a member of the group, and its *signifying content* is necessarily common. *In any case*, there is an interest which defines the group itself, which is valid only for the group and which is accessible only through it, and this is equally true for a group of rebels organising to resist government forces and for employers reaching an agreement against the workers' unions, etc. Indeed, a group is often established as a last resort on the basis of individual recognition of impotence: the history of industrialisation in France shows a bitter resistance by family capitalism to all forms of capitalist association. In particular, the first mining companies appeared when it became absolutely impossible for landowners to exploit the sub-soil individually. In the same way, the *common means*, that is to say, the distribution of tasks and powers, the division of labour, the organisation of functions, are constituted by the transcendence of seriality, massification, individual antagonisms and isolations. And, as we have seen, it is circumstances, external pressures, which dissolve seriality in *third parties* and make it *emerge in the group*, that is to say, in a milieu of freedom and terror which they were unable even to conceive. In this sense, the group statute is indeed a metamorphosis of the individual. And the practical moment of the actualisation of the powers constitutes him, in himself, as fundamentally *different* from what he was on his own: adopted inertia, function, power, rights and duties, structure, violence and fraternity – he actualises *all these reciprocal relations* as his new being, his sociality. His existence is not, or is no longer, simply the temporalisation of organic need in a project: it arises in a field of violent but non-antagonistic tensions, that is to say, through a web of synthetic relations by which it is profoundly and fundamentally constituted as a mediated relation, that is to say, as terror and fraternity for all and for itself. Thus sociality comes to the individual through common totalisation and initially determines him through the curvature of internal social space *here*.

But these essential reservations only serve to underline the fact that the formal structure of the objective and of the operations is still typically individual, in the original sense of the term, that is, in the sense in which the organic individual is characterised as a constitutive *praxis* and rearrangement of the practical field by an individual totalisation. If the objective of the group is, by definition, incapable of being *realised* by an isolated individual, then it can be *posited* by such an individual (on the basis of need, of danger, or of more complex forms). Although groups founded in this way seldom have much historical importance, it is quite common for an individual to conceive a common aim, and thereby to discover a community which ought to be formed and try to constitute a group because he also realises that he is unable to realise his undertaking on his own. Such isolated cases occur naturally in complex societies which present inert serialities, collectives, various groups, etc., alongside one another; and the very project of founding a group is conditioned by the real existence of similar groups. But the fact remains that practical action in this case is the individual's determination of a group which ought to be constituted for a common objective which he discovered on his own.[55] It may be added that he already belongs in some way to other organised groups: this is certainly not false. But though he may be a common individual *in these groups*, he discovers the end as an isolated or serial individual. If an individual senses the need to start an international health organisation, then it can in fact be said that it is *in his sociality*, that is to say, in his relation to the society in which he lives, that he is affected by the external imperative. But he goes beyond this sociality towards a larger integration, because his membership of a given national community cannot *by itself* show him an international objective. On the contrary, this practical movement of disclosure can occur only in connection with his attempt to *de-situate* himself (to remove himself from a restricted situation and enter a broader one). This does not mean that everyone is always capable of grasping every common objective: that would be absurd. On the contrary, the problems arise in terms of objective contradictions. And, as we have seen, they can appear to all the Others in a series in the dissolution of this alterity. But here too what matters is that, through mediated reciprocities, through the play of the regulatory third party and of immanence-transcendence, the movement of comprehension appears in everyone as the individual transcendence of seriality towards community. There is no common aim that an individual cannot set himself, *provided* that, in the unity of the project, he tries to constitute a group to realise it.

And precisely because the decision to group or to regroup is occasioned by the common objective as the exigency that it should be pursued and realised in common, it also appears that the constitution of a group is a means which is accessible to individual *praxis*. In fact, it is clear that the abstract individual whom we encountered in the first moment of our investigation perceives *the Others* as a multiplicity in his practical field. And we have also seen that his sovereign *praxis*, as a perpetual reorganisation of the field in the light of needs, realises the

---

55. Obviously this objective must answer some need of the society under consideration and appear as an exigency in the historical circumstances which define the moment. Normally, there are individuals in different places who are unaware of one another but who are pursuing the same aim. But this does not mean that they are not individually subjected to a common exigency; and even if, as often happens, they eventually unite, they do not discover the social object as common individuals.

practical unity of this objective multiplicity. This unity may appear as mere serial alterity; but if there is an exterior group then, as we have seen, it reveals itself as a group to the extent that unification by the individual, though effected from outside, turns out to display an internal unification, realised in practical autonomy. But above all the practical agent performs totalising actions in relation to organic individuals as well as to inanimate objects: to flee from a marching crowd is to totalise it, to turn it into a group when it may have been only a series. Thus the action of *forming a real group* is already given in organic *praxis*, and given *precisely to the extent* that there has always been a possibility of unifying a discrete multiplicity, whatever it may be (whether inert or constituted by organisms). This possibility contains an indeterminacy because it is not yet settled whether the group is to be constituted from the outside (this can occur in the construction of a trap as the totalisation of an already constituted group as well as in a practice which defines a seriality – children, the sick, etc. – as a unified, receptive group which can be the object of my generosity) or whether it is to be constituted as a wrapping produced by the agent in order to envelop both himself and the others. But clearly this indeterminacy is *logical* rather than real. Practical priority is initially given to the group-object which is totalised from outside, since the primary movement is the sovereign reorganisation of the objective structures of the practical field. And anyone who tries to constitute a group in order to realise a common objective, useful to all, sees it initially, in the abstract moment in which he begins the undertaking, as *his* means of achieving *his* objective. It is only the progressive constitution of the community which gradually reveals to him that he is *necessarily integrated into it*. But this makes his comprehension of multiple activity even clearer and more obvious to us: in the moment in which he is still staying outside the group (which is as yet unconstituted or in the course of being constituted), he already grasps the unity of an interiorised multiplicity as a specific means from the point of view of an individual *praxis*. In fact, he also organises material objects: in the dialectical unity of his *praxis*, he creates material quasi-totalities whose elements interact in such a way that, for example, they can transmit and amplify a movement which he makes at one point of the system to the intended objects. The transcendent, organisational movement is not in principle different when it is men who are being grouped; the difference emerges in the undertaking itself (and, in fact, there is no need for it really to begin: the abstract schema of the synthetic movement is sufficient) in that the projected unity immediately appears as perpetuating itself through everyone's activity.

This initial disclosure reveals two contradictory characteristics: the passivity of the inert object maintains the unity that has been forged, but it also covers up an infinite dispersal. On the other hand, the activity of a group in formation realises true unity *as praxis*, but thereby emphasises the real multiplicity of the pledged members as a multiplicity which is constantly being overcome by a *produced* inertia. On the other hand, the original difference between a group which is united from outside and a controlled mechanical system is not basically a matter of complexity and simplicity; the human system is a practical arrangement which produces its effects through itself. Thus, when the sovereign individual undertakes to *rearrange* the human multiplicities of his practical field *as a group*, he tries to produce an instrumental system whose elements are united and governed in accordance with a practical rule, and whose organisation differs from inert systematisation in one essential respect: autonomy as productive of passivity and of specifications. And the complexity of organised groups is generally connected with the complexity of the mechanical arrangements which the agents are capable of at that historical moment.

These remarks are, of course, not intended to emphasise the individual as the producer of the group (this accidental case is of limited interest). They are only intended to show that the organic individual, simply in his movement to organise the practical field, develops a comprehension of the group-object as an instrumental construction. Anyone who can shelter behind rocks can also shelter behind those other masses – men. On this basis, if these men, for some reason, assume the task of protecting him, he will be able to comprehend that these new kinds of rocks *make themselves* into rocks by their reciprocal pledges and that they arrange their gathering as rocks by means of a reciprocity of functions. This means that they behave as though they were animated by his own will, and *at the same time*, that his will branches through them and produces innumerable divergencies, so as to converge, and that, complete everywhere, it opposes itself everywhere in order to recognise itself as the same. But these constantly resolved oppositions do not disconcert him from outside. Neither *the ensemble* (the group-object, integrated into his personal undertaking as a *specific means* and, consequently, illuminated by the objective itself), nor detailed rearrangements (the transformation of a simple musical notation into a chord, the amplification of the plan and its plural realisation) can disconcert him. When danger threatens, the Pretorian guard *arranges itself* around the sovereign; but the danger threatens *him*, and the group-object, which is simply the means of avoiding the danger, is to be decoded in terms of the fears of the exalted personage, and it provides reassurance in so far as it rules them out as impossible; the sovereign 'fears' doors, windows, and everything that opens onto the outside world; his fears, diversified by the diversity of the practical field, are embodied in one instant *as precautions* in the diversity of the guards who go and position themselves at every possible entrance. In this moment, they become active and functional (inertia as active passivity, power in so far as it is defined by the objective constitution of the entrance to be guarded, etc.); and the individual who is being protected understands them as, for example, the simultaneous realisation of the actions which are required by the object and which, if he had been on his own, he would have had to perform successively.

It is here, in fact, that the novelty of the group-object resides for the individual – here rather than in the *praxis* (of each and all) as such, for *praxis* is in fact always *understood* through *praxis*, at least as regards its formal reality (since what is involved here is precisely the comprehensibility of certain material supports). In its origin, the transformation lies in the possibility of realising in simultaneity, on the basis of reciprocal relations, what the individual would have to realise successively. But, apart from the fact that the basis for comprehending this simultaneity is given in the *praxis* of the organism itself (the simplest operation, *for the individual*, is the organisation of simultaneities: I hold the handle of one lever and push it with my right hand; and I pull another with my left hand; at the same time I bend or reach out, etc.), and apart from the fact that an adumbration of a practical redistribution of the group, in its objective interiority, is schematically provided by the organic *posture* and that this involves a comprehension of every practical, spontaneous metamorphosis of an object in response to a situation, the most important point to emphasise is that the arrangement of an instrumental (and inert) ensemble by one person involves, as an essential aim, the compression of a given practical temporalisation into simultaneity, so that the agent can transcend this flattened duration by a new temporalisation.

This is what is called 'making time', and it is an exigency of time itself in that, in the world of scarcity, everyone's time is scarce (although it is no more than practical temporalisation). In this way, one puts the auxiliary tool 'within reach', another tool, to be used later, a little further away, near the object on which it will be used; and in this way, as I have said, inert interdependencies are constructed so that *individual* practical movements can be absorbed, divided, and distributed in several directions at once. In short, there is no visible contradiction – at least in elementary forms of sociality – between the group-instrument and the inert instrument. To the person who gives it its tasks, the main characteristic of the group-object (slaves, for example) appears to be its ability to absorb the *praxis* of the individual and to make it into its temporal and practical unity. For primitive societies and techniques, the inert instrument retains a magical, double residue of individual *praxis*: the past labour of the tool-maker and the past labour of its user coincide in the tool; and it has been established that in such societies, the maker and the user of the tool are generally the same person. For the primitive, therefore, this magical character derives from the fact that his own future *praxis* appears to him as a power inscribed in inertia and as an already given transcendence of this passivity towards the future. (Obviously the two moments – creation and use – inter-penetrate in the indifferentiation of passivity.) Now, the instrument itself is not an *indeterminate force*: it is an organised reality (for example, it has a blade *and* a handle). So at this elementary level there is a homo-geneity between, on the one hand, the group-object as it reinteriorises an individual's project and *praxis* and so becomes, as a means, his *relation* to the objective, and, on the other, the inert instrument as it absorbs a *praxis* which produces and constitutes it as a mediation between its owner and his aim. This is illustrated by the native's magical tendency to attribute *mana* to his weapons or tools (that is to say, a *power* as potential *praxis* and a mortgage against the future) and by the opposite tendency, in the outsider, to treat the organised group as a material object endowed with powers. In the extreme case, *in the practico-inert field*, the sanctified instrument and the totalised group are equivalent.

Conversely, an individual who is tracked down in the practical field by a group organised for a man-hunt – and, specifically, for a hunt for *him* – experiences this organised *praxis* as the free project of an indivi-duality which is wider, more flexible, and more powerful than his concrete individuality, but homogeneous with it. The practical field appears to him to be undermined by this freedom; it becomes the other meaning of every object in the field. And this other meaning becomes practical truth: the truth of a given exit (a gate or path) is no longer that of an exit, but that of a trap set by the group. The individual cannot attempt to break out of the circle unless he manages to reinteriorise his objectivity for the group, that is to say, to decipher his own acts in terms of the common freedom of his enemies: the action I am about to perform is precisely what they expect of the object that I am for them, etc. Thus he is immediately given an understanding of the common aim, since this common aim *is himself.* And on the basis of the objective that he is, he can reconstruct in practice and in prospect the operations of the group (of which he is the negative and totalising unity)[56] and thereby assess his own action objectively from the practical point of view of escape or flight. *Dialogue* (in the sense of rational antagonism) is possible between the individual and the group that surrounds him. And both of them − he in his isolation, and the other either through each and all or through differentiated organs − can foresee, with some variable margin of error, how the other will act by treating *for his own part* his own acts as objects.

We need to go beyond this and note that the hunted man realises in practice the truth of the group: except in the special case where he knows the names and characters of all his hunters (which can only apply in a very restricted multiplicity), he realises the group not as a hyper-organism, but as ubiquity in each structure and in everyone's *praxis.* Meanwhile the hunted man sees or guesses at human presences behind a door or trees and regards these presences as *all the same*; he sees their ruthless ferocity as *transforming every elsewhere into a here.* For him, the differentiation will depend entirely on the practical situation: the *group* is up there on an eminence so that it controls a whole region; *the group* is down there, behind some trees whose function it is to hide it, but which may also, by way of counter-finality, conceal certain presences from it. Thus, through the practical interiorisation of his objectivity for the group as practical freedom, he

---

56. We have already seen how either a hostile extermination group or a 'natural' danger can constitute themselves as the negative totalisation of a given group, via the destructive process which unites all the members in a common (and non-serial) extermination. But here the negative totalisation is different: by discovering himself as an *objective* and reinteriorising this objectivity, the individual becomes the outside-being (*être-dehors*) of the group which is pursuing him and, in so far as he is threatened with the danger of being killed, he sees death approaching him as a possibility which belongs to the enemy group and as the possibility that the success of the group will be realised (the annihilation of the individual) as a negative objectification (the result is an inert disappearance) and as a disruption of unity (the lynchers disperse after the lynching).

reveals the truth of the function. By deciding to go behind the curtain of trees rather than cross the field without cover, he differentiates these *sames (les mêmes)* by means of the real situation, that is to say, through function: in *these* common individuals, behind the trees, the group is closer to him, but not so well placed to see him; in the person of those lying in wait on the hill, the group is further away but it can see further by means of an instrument (the hill is being *used*). And this differentiation of functions does not by any means prevent the fugitive from being trapped: and therefore function, reciprocity and structure are also revealed by the flight of the hunted man as the physiognomy of a freedom which is organised for extermination. In other words the hunted man, in the tension of being surrounded, sees *those behind the trees* as the same as *those up on the hill* in so far as both of them deprive him of the possibility of escape by their reciprocal positions; and the common *praxis* appears to him as a *here* in both places to the extent that the danger up there and the danger down there are a function of one another. But in the deliberate action of the man-hunt he sees this reciprocity everywhere as an intentional structure of the common *praxis* in every member of every sub-group. He acts, in fact, in the light of the ubiquity of the enemy's co-ordination: those up there are directly connected with those down there. If he is seen by those on the hill, they will *force* him towards the sub-groups who are concealed in the plain, etc.

It is not necessary to develop this example any further. It must be admitted that, as moments of the dialectical investigation, these examples still do not show that the formal structure of the common *praxis* is the synthetic unity of the individual *praxis* – and this formulation is inaccurate anyway. But they do at least prove that an individual's understanding of *praxis* can remain of the same kind whether applied to the *praxis* of a group-object, to that of a group-subject or to that of a practical organism. In each case, the common end is practically conceived as that towards which the group transcends what is given; and this practical perception is itself an individual transcendence (*dépassement*); and in each case, the actions are decoded in a movement from the future to the present and each of them reveals itself in this regressive unity as a means, unified by the common objectification, to the end.

There is nothing surprising about this: it is true that the objective of the group is *common* in so far as it appears only through each common, that is to say pledged and structured, individual; but it is also true that the practical moment is realised through organic *praxis* and that this constitutes itself as the comprehension of *its* individual task in so far as *the* common task objectifies itself in it. This shows that the final, common objective can manifest itself only through individual action and as its common beyond, and that structure, as a relation to the totality, is lived as the deep meaning (*signification*) of the task being performed. Certain determinations of action *in effect* come to the individual from the group, as a new statute which, in his individual isolation, he could not have produced or even understood – in particular, and fundamentally, the pledge as a free limit of freedom. We have seen, in fact, that a *praxis* reduced to its individual translucidity cannot in any way commit an indeterminate future (that is to say, a future in which all the conditions of *praxis* are different); my own freedom turns against me as Other in so far as it is other for the Others. Thus the *modality* of action, its normative aspect, often eludes those who are not grouped, even if they live it themselves as members, in different circumstances, of another group.

What people call *fanaticism*, *blindness*, etc., is really fraternity-terror as experienced in another group and in so far as we, *as individuals*, treat it as an emotional occurrence *in individuals*. But, on the one hand, a pledge is not produced by a hyper-dialectic; it is an incarnation of the inter-individual relation of reciprocity. And on the other hand, even if the *modality* of action eludes the non-grouped individual externally, it is still lived in the group through the mediation of individual *praxis*; and this means that power and the imperative, far from producing and qualifying this praxis, are adopted and interiorised by it in so far as they occasion it. In the process of concretely unfolding and adapting to circumstances, free *praxis* produces its own inertia, its own limitations, and keeps these determinations in Being. Moreover, individual *praxis* is immediately reciprocal, as we saw at the beginning of this investigation. And this reciprocity is the basis of the worked product – of freedom interiorising multiplicity – which we have called the pledge. The pledge is the practical comprehension of reciprocity as a means of constituting a group inertia in the same way that pledged *praxis* implies a common understanding of the group objective and of the pledge. From this point of view, apart from modality (it is still necessary to establish dialectically the formal conditions in which a non-member of the group can recognise it in the group member), there is *always* a possible reciprocity between the member of the group and the non-member; it may be difficult for the first to explain the conditions of common life to the second (but this difficulty appears *a posteriori*; the soldier will find it easy or difficult to explain the interior milieu of his unit to the non-soldier, depending on what type of war he is fighting), but he can always reveal his *aim* to him. In other words, they can communicate in so far as there is a formal homogeneity between the following three comprehensions: the comprehension of the group-object by the subject who is not grouped (in the sense of being a subject of the individual, grouping action); the comprehension of the group-subject by the non-grouped as an object (that is to say, by the very process which interiorises its objectivity), and the comprehension of the group-*praxis* by each of its members, as a mediation of function and objectification.

2   Spontaneity and Command

But, far from making our task easier, the homogeneity of individual *praxis* and common *praxis* at first presents us with difficulties; it involves a kind of aporia, or impotence of the dialectic. Given that the group as an interiorised multiplicity is so profoundly different from the organic individual, that, in other words, we have avoided treating the group as an organism, except metaphorically, how can the group produce, in common, actions whose fundamental structure is the same as that of individual actions? It might be said that a limit is given *a priori*. Not a limitation adopted as pledged inertia, nor for that matter a limitation experienced and suffered as the insurmountable resistance of some inert materiality to a given undertaking: but rather a kind of breathlessness of the dialectic reproducing its original movement, regardless of the internal constitution of the agent who realises it. This involves a new kind of untranscendability, and it is necessary to explain it. In order to do this, we must make a closer examination of the process of organisation, not as a real constitution of a being-in-the-group based on the pledge, but as a distribution of tasks.

It is common – for example, in periods of revolution – to contrast a centralising, authoritarian tendency coming *from above*, that is to say, from the elements who hold power for the time being, with a democratic, spontaneous tendency which grows from the base. The first is supposed to realise the organisation of the masses into hierarchised action groups *from outside* or, at least, on the basis of a frozen immanence-transcendence; and the second is supposed to realise groups through the free, common action of the multiplicity upon itself, and as such to represent true democratic self-determination *in interiority*. The difference between these kinds of organisation is supposed to be qualitative and radical; they are treated as two *essentially* opposed realities, only the second of which can really constitute the group as common self-creation. The implication of this fundamental contrast is that truly common objectives, operations and thoughts are produced in the autonomous process of the demassification of the masses by themselves and of their spontaneous organisation.

This conception has political and ideological foundations which cannot be discussed here. I am not denying that *politically* it is of the greatest importance whether organisation is imposed from above or produced from below. Similarly, I admit that the social, ideological, ethical (and, *primarily*, material) consequences of a movement will be completely different depending on whether the popular movement produces its leaders as a temporary expression of its *praxis* and reabsorbs and transcends them through the development of this *praxis* or whether, on the contrary, a group detaches itself from the masses, specialises in the exercise of power and arranges the tasks in an authoritarian manner in the light of its own conception of the people's objectives. Of course it is obvious that the régime itself will be different in the two cases, as well as the relations of reciprocity between individuals. But the important point here is, *quite apart from any political considerations*, that the mode of regroupment and organisation is not fundamentally different according to whether it depends on centralisation from above or on a spontaneous liquidation of seriality within the series itself and on the common organisation which follows. In short, this is not and cannot be an issue about Blanqui, Jaurès, Lenin, Rosa Luxemburg, Stalin or Trotsky. And, just as a premeditated crime and an act of justified defence may, in spite of all the practical and legal differences between them, involve the same muscles and be realised in the same basic actions (the differences emerging at a higher level and from the point of view of a different *praxis* – that of a police investigation or a trial, for example), so, in the same way, the type of formal intelligibility and rationality can be the same with organisation from above as with organisation from below.

It should in fact be recognised that the habit of speaking of dialectical transformations of the masses is always metaphorical. For example, when Trotsky emphasises the qualitative transformation (especially from the point of view of revolutionary potential) caused by the first meetings of workers and soldiers, he is perfectly right. And today, when other writers take up these remarks and develop them in order to show the revolutionary character of the Hungarian rebels, showing that a truly revolutionary situation is characterised both by specific circumstances and by the constitution of insurrectional groups including workers, students and soldiers, they may be right historically, that is to say, at a level whose concrete determinations no longer fall within the area of our research. But we should avoid following certain historians or Marxists (whether Trotskyists or not) when, before or after the event, they give what is really a 'Gestaltist' description of these 'typically revolutionary' meetings, as if an organic synthesis arose spontaneously out of them – based, of course on the quantitative relations of the three social groups involved, but transcending the quantitative relation towards a new *qualitative* differentiation. (For, as we have seen, Engels permitted every consistent Marxist to reveal the transformation of quantity into quality in the name of the external dialectic.) *In fact*, even if soldiers and workers do constitute the first organising committees of the rebellion (not only in Paris in 1789, with the encounter of the residents of the Quartier Saint-Antoine and the French guards, but also in Germany in 1918 and Russia in 1917), these relations are *too universal* and have to be specified in each case: universality is hard to find and define in a dialectical process.

Whereas for analytical Reason this is concrete reality, as a relation which is indifferent to its terms, in a dialectical investigation it appears, as we shall see, either as an immediate, abstract appearance, as the first delusion to be dissolved, or else as the concrete, hidden conclusion of the entire investigation, and, as it were, as the totalising but ultimate foundation of rational development. And if, without prejudging the nature of a 'typically revolutionary' organisation, one imagines these groups in a particular concrete historical situation, for example, *either* St Petersburg in 1917 *or* Berlin in 1918, but not in both cities at once, then a concrete relation of reciprocity will re-establish itself. For the workers, given the situation in the country and the city at the time, and the special characteristics of the Navy and the Army, here and always, either the soldiers *or* the sailors (and each case must be examined separately – Kronstadt is not St Petersburg, etc.) are practical, irrefutable evidence against the government, and a defence against its attempts to smash the rebellion, a direct or indirect relation to other classes (in particular, to the peasant class in so far as the peasants who had been mobilised outnumbered the rest, and also in so far as these war-weary, discontented servicemen were a mediation between the workers, the ex-peasants, and the countryside, of which the fighters in fact represented the most advanced section) and a proof of the collapse of the régime, a beginning of universalisation: these other exploited men appeared to them as representatives of all exploited people. But above all 'the soldiers are with us' took on, for and in everyone, a special meaning because ever since 1905 (not to mention earlier times) the soldiers had been, in spite of themselves, instruments of repression. Conversely, for a soldier who rejected external discipline, the workers represented the only possibility of integration and of fighting-discipline; the workers, indeed, unlike the soldiers, knew that insurrections required practical organisation even more than strikes.

These relations of *reciprocity* are exactly the reverse of the suggested 'Gestaltist' syntheses: they establish themselves through a *practical recognition* within action, on the tacit basis of the pledge. And the *given* heterogeneity, which presides over the encounter, becomes a pledged homogeneity which guarantees a created heterogeneity. On the other hand, it would be absurd to deny the practical end of such organised groups: in each case there is a danger, and it is necessary to secure defences, to maintain vigilance, etc. And above all, whether one likes it or not, one has to go back to the truths established by the historians: the organisation selects its organisers. It may reject or reabsorb them, but it is undeniable that, generally speaking, it preserves them in their role by means of the pledge which supports function by adopting passivity. Historians of the French Revolution have established, for example, that there was a category of popular agitators, some of whom have been identified and traced, who, between 1789 and 1794, were present at every important event, and whom the 'common individuals' of the sections regarded as *their organisers* and whose function, preserved by reciprocal inertia between the popular 'days', maintained a kind of passive organisational ossature in the everyday dispersal: the organisation would reform around them in moments of tension. These popular agitators *were not leaders*: it is primarily in this respect that their power differed from that of the actual leaders. They did not issue orders: but the group reconstituted itself around them, exalted them and communicated its power to them; it gave itself orders through them. They were in fact simply regulatory third parties whose regulatory activity became function on the tacit basis of the pledge. For this reason it would be absurd to use them as an argument against the democracy of the popular organisation.

But two important points should be noted. On the one hand this democracy is really *fraternity-terror*, that is to say, it is actually based on violence. For this reason Guérin is wrong to contrast it with the violence of authoritarianism from above. Although circumstances may, in fact, produce violent contradictions between the base and the apex, the only possible basis for violence from above is violence from below. But as we shall see, violence tends to become purer as it moves away from its origins, and what disappears is fraternity. On the other hand – and this is what is most important for us – by virtue of the pledged inertia of function, the organiser-agitator will remain, for some time, the means through which the group defines its *praxis*, and creates its own organisation. This does not mean that the organiser can impose a particular action or forbid another: he would immediately lose his power if he tried to issue orders. He is a medium and he knows it; and if he acts (some of them are corrupted) it is through the group, and in secret. But since the orders of the people issue from his mouth, since the reorganisation has to be carried out through his individual *praxis*, and since his exhortations and gestures indicate the common objective, we have to conclude that popular *praxis* is essentially capable of being created, understood and organised *by an individual*; which means, in other words, that the group can define its common action only through the mediation of an individual designation. In the tension of immanence-transcendence, the 'leader' proceeds to the reorganisation of the group as a quasi-object and distributes quasi-objective functions in accordance with the objective which he thereby defines. In this way, he constructs a practical device in quasi-objectivity which will preserve itself as it is through assumed inertia, just as an instrumental system in the inorganic world is given an organisation by individual *praxis* and supports it with its passivity. Of course, things are not really so simple: he is interrupted or warned, his invention is anticipated by someone else, a few people organise spontaneously in connection with everyone, and others suggest some rearrangement to him, etc. As I have said, he is, in a sense, a mediation. But the important point is that this mediation is necessary as long as the group itself, because of this mediation, is not finally constituted along with its organs of control, distribution, etc. And clearly, *even then*, whatever the system of self-administration (Soviets, revolutionary committees, etc.), the mediation of the individual will simply have been institutionalised. For example, if one votes one will be voting for one motion and against another, for one amendment and against another, in short, for an individual, practical determination of discourse.

The difference between a regulatory third party and a leader is that one is in charge and the other is not. We will come to the question of command shortly. But – except when contradictions become acute – it should not be supposed that the 'transcendence-immanence' tension disappears. In fact, what distinguishes the leader from the agitator – apart from the coercive nature of his power – is, frequently, the number of mediations which separate him from the group. But in each case we come up against a strange limit of the dialectic: the organised group obtains results which no individual could achieve alone, even if his strength and skill were doubled; moreover, organisation as practical being is normally constituted in a more complex and better adapted way than any organism. To resemble a guard in a square formation, one would have to have eyes all round one's head, and arms in one's back; to resemble a combat unit which is protected by guards at night, one would have to be able to sleep and watch at the same time. Thus an organisation does not *reproduce* an organism, but is meant to be an improvement on it by means of human invention. It takes the practical unity of the organism as its ideal (though as we shall see it does not achieve it), but it dissolves the facticity of the living being. But these transformations do not extricate it from the inflexible necessity *of being situated*, that is to say, regardless of its instruments, of being designated as a practical point of view, as an anchorage defined by the very world it is trying to modify. And in order finally to achieve these supraindividual results, it must allow itself to be determined by the unifying unity of an individual *praxis*. Thus the individual cannot achieve the common objective on his own, but he can conceive it, signify it, and, through it, signify the reorganisation of the group, in the same way as he would carry out a rearrangement of his individual practical field. The individual integrates himself into the group and the group has its practical limit in the individual.

3   *Disagreements in Organisational Sub-groups*

No doubt it will be objected – quite rightly – that most organised groups entrust planning, the distribution of tasks, supervision and administration not to individuals but to specific sub-groups. In such communities, everything is a common task and the individual as such apparently dissolves in a small sub-group; and then reciprocities exist only between sub-groups. But if the individuals of the organising sub-group sink into anonymity, the sub-group still does not transcend the framework *of an individual conception* in its common *praxis*. In other words, it is still impossible to determine *a priori*, that is to say, on simple inspection, whether the plan adopted is the work of one person or several: for, in order to construct it, several became one.

Of course, disagreements within the organising group are inevitable and may even be violent. And the plan gets organised through these disagreements. In the most complex groups, rent by class struggles, by conflicts of interest or of point of view, and partly infected with seriality, it will no doubt be claimed that the several organisers, if they have been carefully selected, represent the diversity of tendencies – which no individual could do. But, apart from the fact that a synthesis is not usually achieved and that compromise proposals reflect in some form the deep impotence which results from divisions, such decaying or dis-united groups do not belong to the present level of our investigation. People in a technical office or managerial department, etc., normally belong to the same class and milieu, share the same interests and have had the same technical training: however violent their disagreements may be, they are not a direct result of social conflicts and it would be ridiculous psychologistic scepticism to attribute them to personality conflicts or secret rivalries, although, of course, such conflicts and rivalries may be expressed in the contradictions which divide them.

In fact, these contradictions are really just objective structures of the practical problem that has to be resolved. And when experts are trying to find a solution to a problem like traffic in a city, they are faced with a set of *given*, material incompatibilities, whose origins may be extremely varied: the constantly rising number of cars, the insufficient number of garages, the relative narrowness of most of the main roads, the neces-sity for car owners to use their cars for getting about and to have parking places, which is in itself contradictory since the number of cars lining the streets necessarily limits the speed and volume of traffic. The solution, if there is one, obviously has to transcend and resolve all these material conflicts; and it must emerge in a framework of scarcity, since the budget of the city (or state) does not permit any large expenditure. Any conflict between the members of the group will, in fact, be due to the fact that in trying to transcend the objective contradictions everyone is, unintentionally, simply favouring one of the terms of the contradictory proposition in a false synthesis. One solution ignores the interests of *traffic flow*; another makes parking in the city impossible, and so makes the car useless and threatens to impede the expansion of the motor industry; and another, which revives an old plan of building wider roads, simply ignores the limitations of available resources. Each of these solutions is individual: by which I mean not only that it was proposed by an individual, but also that it determines and defines an individual in the group; if he favours one solution rather than another, it is not impossible that this is the result of certain pressures, or if he has discovered this solution amongst all the others, this may be because his fundamental project cleaves to certain possibilities and rejects all the others. But such practical 'predispositions' can do no more here than define an approach to the problem: the contradiction is in the object; it manifests itself spontaneously and it explodes in the final synthesis all the more violently if the synthesis neglects one term in favour of an other. Of course the contradiction may strike other experts, especially ones who are themselves proposing a partial synthesis, that is to say unintentionally *expressing* one contradiction while meaning to transcend others.

Each of the solutions is an individual reality – an objective, individual failure – in so far as the mistake has to be attributed to individual limitations: a part was mistaken for the whole. But the limitations are themselves individual: by this I mean that people are limited here in relation to other individuals, better equipped than themselves, rather than in relation to the group or to mankind. However, this individual reality (in the ancient sense in which the individual is characterised by the degree of nothingness which he has interiorised) reveals, *through false discourse*, an objective, material contradiction which *produced* the false synthesis which favoured one term and neglected another. In other words, it represents the objective possibility of serving some interests while neglecting others (possibly *in the same person*); and this possibility is a structure of the problem in so far as it is *really* already expressed in the practice of certain groups of car users, garage owners or traffic police. Through them, one term attempts to destroy the other and impose itself; by lending the support of its common strength, the municipal authority may allow the attempted solution to 'hold', at least for a while. But since the contradiction would remain, with one term being favoured, it would reappear even more violently in some other form and the whole problem would recur. Thus, what a particular individual becomes responsible for is the contradiction as it exists *in the practico-inert field*: it is in this field that the increasing number of cars (a strictly serial phenomenon) comes up against the rigidity of urban structures (inorganic and serial inertias); and this contradiction, by becoming a structure of a technical problem, detaches itself from the milieu of seriality: it is at the centre of the practical field.

But it should also be noticed that, *as an individual*, the expert serves a purpose, in that his own solution becomes his ideological interest, his being-outside-himself which he defends in the same way as he would defend himself, and because *it is* himself. Thus the conflicts between different solutions reactualise the contradictions as a permanent conflict, *outside*, of material forces. Every solution is really just a veiled attempt to make one term dominate the other. And the inter-individual violence of the conflict is inconceivable outside an organised group. In the milieu of the pledge, *the Others* must become *the same* again, for otherwise the calculated alterity of functions becomes a suffered alterity. Thus, above all from the practical point of view of finding a solution, the conflict between two individuals (a reciprocal antagonism) occurs as having to end with the destruction of one in favour of the other, or of both in favour of a third or of their reabsorption by the group. For these serene experts, of course, there is no threat of physical liquidation or of brain washing; but though their individual lives are not in danger, their *social being* may perfectly well be annihilated (either in the form of *this* individual solution, or, less determinately, as *their reputation* with others, both of which define their being-outside-themselves-in-the-group. And this being-outside-themselves is not to be confused with the *constitutive relation* of the common individual: reputation is really the specification of power in so far as this specification arises as a common result in the interiority of the group and is functionally connected with the concrete exercise of this power). Thus the mediation of the individual was necessary in order to carry the objective contradiction into the group; but the common-being-in-the-group was necessary in order to restore the virulence of the contradiction through personal conflict. In fact, it is obvious that everyone has been aware of all the givens of the problem for a long time and that, in the course of a given session, the first reports will once again enumerate the difficulties, aporias, objective conflicts, etc. But these oppositions cannot manifest themselves in their truth as long as they are the object of a pure enumeration or of a strictly verbal description (I include diagrams, statistics, etc., under this heading). This is because the organising sub-group stands in a relation of immanence-transcendence to the surrounding group: a quasi-separation (or quasi-negation) conditions the relations between them in inertia (we shall return to this shortly) *as long as* the lived contradictions of the surrounding group (in the relations of its members in so far as they need to remain the same but are in danger of being disunited by the object) cannot be reinteriorised by the organising sub-group and lived at a level of abstraction and specialisation which is precisely that of the sub-group.

Thus any expert, if he is a car-owner, can experience for himself the contradictions suffered by every member of the *seriated-group* (the meaning of this term will become clear when we examine it concretely) which is the Parisian population (in so far as some of its members are car-owners). But *at this level*, he either *suffers* or avoids the problem by some special expedient which is incapable of being generalised. In short, his own misfortunes determine his reactions as a Parisian, but they have practically no effect on his attitude as an expert (an individual defined by his power), though he may use them as examples or illustrations in his arguments. But his practical point of view is formed within a community of experts (or else in isolation, but only in so far as this isolation is simply one mode of being-in-the-group: for example, when working on his report in his office). Thus car accidents, impassable streets, traffic jams, etc., are reproduced in all their violence within the specialised sub-group when conflicts of material interest are taken up by individuals in the form of ideological interests. As a mediation of an antagonistic reciprocity, the sub-group controls its tension and defines the urgency of transcendence. Thanks to the fact that individuals are endangered in their being-in-the-group, and that the sub-group makes their conflict both possible and inevitable, the objective problem develops (or *can* develop) all its contradictions at the level where it *ought to be possible* to find a solution (of course there may not be any solution *in present conditions*). Besides, these inter-individual conflicts may become common conflicts, in so far as the individuals who suggest the solution become, for others, the regulatory third parties of an organising action which they had already guessed at though without seeing it quite clearly.

But what *purpose* is served by this virulence? – To raise the question in all its forms and in all its complexity, or, in other words, to effect the becoming-question (*le devenir-question*) of the sub-group. The maximum tension will be realised when the group, at its own level and in accordance with its functions, becomes *the traffic of Paris*. Now this complexity bristles with contradictions and cannot sustain itself as such: it is a way of interiorising the problem, but as long as they remain divided, the common individuals will be paralysed; the moment of the interiorisation of the contradiction, in so far as it transforms those who are *the same* into *others*, must be transcended towards synthetic unity. The more integrated the sub-group, the more sensitive it is to the profound contradiction of the same and the other through all its members, and the more tempted it is to reach a solution through terror, that is to say, through requiring support for one of the proposed theses. In this case, it is not important whether or not a vote is taken: what matters is the elimination of the minority as such. And, *above all*, it must be made clear which thesis is being supported; if, as often happens, this is a thesis which has already been proposed, one which has just been explained, then, if one refuses to submit to the law of alterity, one is bound to give an arbitrary advantage to one or more of the terms of the objective contradictions, to the detriment of the others. There is no *thought*, in the sense of an 'organising practice', which selects a best (if not actually good) solution by a synthetic transcendence of the contradictions.

The common action (or power to determine a reorganisation) therefore becomes defined as a *common adoption* of an individual proposal (made by a common individual). *If thought does take place*, however – that is to say, if someone proposes a best, if only temporary, solution – then it will *obviously* manifest itself as a regulatory *praxis* and through the regulatory third party. (It does not matter here whether there is one third party or several, or whether the solution is 'found' by several people at the same time; what is important is that everyone, in so far as he is a common individual mediated by organic practice, produces it as a free dialectical movement of his thought). What is involved, in fact, is a dialectical transcendence through a practical project: and it therefore presupposes a synthetic grasp of all contradictions, in short, a living reunification of the [sub-]group by the third party, taking the dissensions themselves as an instrument of reunification. The sub-group then becomes simply the synthetic unity of its own divisions, that is to say, it realises, through its dissensions, the objective contradictions which the whole group derives from its situation. And, by finding a solution, the individual posits himself as a regulatory third party, that is to say, he exhibits his solution as the opening to a possible future and to a field of action which is conditioned by a new objective (in the short term, since the fundamental objective remains unchanged). And this solution presents itself both as an objective transcendence of objective contradictions and as a possible reorganisation of the sub-group itself in interiority. When the solution is adopted, factional divisions (in the most general sense) organise themselves into a structure of positive reciprocity: within the new unity, the contradictory terms are preserved as indissoluble elements of the new arrangement, and their mediated contradiction becomes an adopted heterogeneity.

It does not matter in the least whether the solution was found in the course of meetings of the sub-group or through isolated work, since, as we have just seen, isolation is a particular functional relation between the individual and a sub-group to which he belongs. What is important, on the other hand, is that the practical development of the contradictions can and must take place through the regulatory third party: in so far as these contradictions realise themselves in the unity of the divided sub-group, he grasps them both within himself, and outside himself, in the common field, and in so far as he is a common individual (just as a footballer perceives the moving organisation of the practical field as it conditions and transforms him and so realises itself through him); and since these internal contradictions are the interiorisation of objective contradictions, he perceives them in the indissoluble unity of *praxis* as a problem of the objective organisation of the whole group in so far as the solution of this problem must effect a reorganisation of the organising sub-group. In other words, he *not only* sees the solution as necessarily involving a reorganisation of the sub-group, but *also* sees the reorganisation of the sub-group as having to be effected on the basis of a possible solution.

And the practical conception is *thought*: which specifically means that it is a practical transcendence of the group's relations to the world and to itself and of the sub-group's relations to itself and to the group, in so far as these relations are the inert, pledged ossature of the community or, in other words, capable of being seen as the inert exteriority of interiority. Its thought is based on these relations, *even* if it has to modify some of them in the name of the whole; it is structured by them, and it preserves them by synthesising them through a project which transcends and uses them. *At the same time*, they lie before it in quasi-objectivity as the inert matter of an ordinal mathematics. Thus the structure and instruments of thought are common, but thought as *praxis* is a mediation of the practical organism and of the free, constituent dialectic between these inert relations and the final objectification. Finding a solution is the synthetic, individual relation between structures brought together in living syntheses and the structural relations rearranged in response to this synthesis, in a practical field rent by contradictory exigencies. Since the discovery of a solution arises as a regulatory *praxis* of the third party, and since comprehension is this discovery in so far as it occurs in the other third party as regulated *praxis*, the action, as the unity of the reorganisation of the subgroup and of the new organisation of the group, occurs everywhere as *the same, here, now*.

This is the crucial point: what we are touching on here is that essential structure of communities which epistemological idealism calls *an agreement of minds*. There are no such things as minds – any more than there are souls. This is already established. But the word 'agreement' is also misleading. Agreement presupposes, in effect, that different individuals or groups, with different horizons, and with characters and habits of totally different kinds, realise a contractual agreement in reciprocity *on a minimum basis*. Idealist optimism may then claim that this minimum will rise to a higher minimum, this minimum to another, so that, finally, agreement will reign in the whole of human knowledge or activity: but this is a philosophy of History. It is still always the case that the new agreement is the minimum for the given situation, even if it is based on previous agreements. At a given moment of its history, science can bring about the agreement of individuals who differ in age, sex, social condition, interests, language, nation, etc. (We shall come back to this later.) And these individuals will agree, for example, on Fresnel's theory or on the laws of thermodynamics and their proofs. At the same time, the object of the agreement becomes external to each of them: a communist physicist and an anti-communist physicist can agree on some experimental results and their interpretation, without any change in their sociality or organic individuality.

And, in a way, this is what actually appears to happen; but this is because it involves a more complex structure than what we are examining at present: but what is really involved is a resurrection of unity through seriality and the creation of groups in the serial milieu *without the dissolution of alterity*. In fact, such induced unity is the degraded product of small, active groups whose activity, as we shall see, is refracted in seriality. The contradiction in the idealist conception is due to its assumption that truth can be the same in the other as Other. And it would be impossible to claim that scientific agreement between two others is an example of basic human reciprocity (and that, consequently, alterity in its social and political forms, etc., is merely a secondary modality which will ultimately dissolve) without making an *a priori* judgement on the whole of History and, for example, simply rejecting class struggle and exploitation. For intellectual agreement about a scientific truth is always possible between an employer and one of his workers (all that is necessary is that both of them should have the desire and the opportunity to learn, which depends mainly on circumstances). But if a welder and the owner of a shipyard are both convinced of the truth of Archimedes' principle, each of their convictions is an *other* conviction, because it exists in a divided society and, as it were, at the two ends of an exploitative system. Here, an agreement about science *is quite unimportant* (just like an equally real agreement about the weather or the temperature). One might even say that it has no concrete reality, simply because the two individuals are such that a confrontation in knowledge is extremely unlikely, and would, in any case, be pointless. They are in fact two individuals whose concrete relations are governed by the mode and the relations of production and who, each for himself within a homogeneous group, reproduce the movement of thought of a given strict proof. In short, when individuals or groups are fundamentally *other* (and therefore inevitably opposed), 'an agreement of minds' as a permanent possibility of reciprocity remains abstract and quite inessential: after all, the artillery of two enemy armies will be in complete agreement about ballistics.

On the other hand, both in organising and in heuristic groups (which includes active groups of scientists concretely working together), the appearance of a solution commits everyone much more totally and much more concretely than any 'agreement'. An agreement, in effect, realises at one point the exterior unity of the Others as Others and thereby decomposes into a dust of identities: all the Others are identical at this particular point. When a solution is produced as the practical conduct of a regulatory third party (for this is what primarily it is: a determination of discourse, graphic proofs, the reproduction of experiments, etc.) and when it *also* reproduces itself through the *praxis* of every other third party, then it is in fact the temporalisation of everyone as the same in the ubiquity of a *here*. This means that comprehension is creation (and amongst such scientists or experts, it may happen that, as soon as the first words have been spoken the field of possibilities becomes illuminated, that the future immediately appears, even more clearly than the regulatory action had intended to determine it); but it also means that the free creation does not occur in an Other as such but in a common individual who, momentarily *altered* (by the contradictory divisions) *reconstitutes himself as the same* by his practical activity in so far as this is one and the same thing for the whole of this interiorised multiplicity.

Thus we have two descriptions of the act in question (a third party explaining a solution to his peers); and both of them are inadequate. The first is implicitly organicist: it presupposes that there is a synthetic act (the demonstration by the proposer) and that this single act realises itself through the audience as the unity of integration. This interpretation amounts to submerging all but one of the people involved into indistinct inessentiality and to constituting the originator as a totalising hyper-consciousness; it is based on superficial syntheses of perception which make the ensemble of listeners appear as a background from which the author stands out. The second interpretation, by contrast, is based on analytical rationality: it eliminates the group, replacing it by its multiplicity of exteriority, and resolves the act of understanding into a definite number of identical processes occurring in different organisms. The proposer's demonstration is then itself a process every term of which is governed by the preceding one and it serves as the inducer of identical reactions in external units (listeners, spectators).

The concrete truth is much simpler than the two mistaken interpretations between which we constantly vacillate: the actual process of discovering the solution – even if it slightly precedes that of the exposition – still belongs to the process of common division: in fact it is, inevitably, primarily the appearance of one solution amongst others; and each of the false contradictory solutions has really been lived as a totalising reorganisation and has been realised as a new internal contradiction, dividing the group and signifying its author *in his individuality*. When it comes to trials, the truly synthetic solution realises itself as a restructuring of the group. The trial may be experiment or calculation – as isolated work – or, in different circumstances, it may consist in the explanation of the solution. In any case, an isolated trial, however severe, is still inadequate: the truth is *both* a controlled, practical decoding of objectivity *and* a determination of sociality in interiority.[57]

57. There is no reason to expect these two operations to occur together or to follow one another in quick succession. Nevertheless, the first fixes certain abstract conditions for an integration which is the only possible source of its concrete meaning.

Thus the operation is not the property of the regulatory third party any more than the storming of the Bastille was the responsibility of the first individual to shout: 'To the Bastille! Run!' It is performed by everyone, in three ways: a practical chain of abstract arguments (that is to say, of inert necessary relations whose necessity appears to everyone in all its persuasiveness, in so far as it is understood through the same relations united in the living structure); liquidation, through a totalising rearrangement, of their ideological separatism; and the realisation of the common practical field by and around them and by all in a strict and novel operation. This constructive liquidation takes place through three temporal ex-stases: past and future are mutually determining and the practical present, already illuminated by a global understanding (that is to say, by the future already prefigured as signification) occurs as a regressive determination of the mediations which unite this future to the past. It can therefore be said that the operation takes place *everywhere*, that the only way in which explaining is superior to comprehending is that it has the abstract privilege of regulatory action over regulated actions, that this operation – explaining and comprehending – is *an individual praxis* of the liquidation of practical contradictions on the basis of common structures: and that this individual *praxis* can never reproduce itself in the form of identical processes in each third party since it actually presupposes two mediated reciprocities: that between each comprehension and explanation through the medium of the developing totalisation (that is to say, of the rearrangement as everywhere) and that between everyone and everyone else and between everyone and all through the regulation of the third party (the solution being explained).

But the synthetic bonds of reciprocity are here reduced to their simplest expression: reciprocity designates the comprehension of the other as the same as mine in so far as mine is the same as his. The abstract link simply amounts to a reinteriorisation of multiplicity and to its strict subordination to the different forms of synthetic unity. In fact – and this structure was explained above – there is not *one* comprehension, or *ten*, or *thirty*: this comprehension, everywhere *the same*, has no numerical determination. It is neither the explanation by the third party realising the group in the form of a totality-unity, nor a numerical plurality of acts. It is not the synthetic action of a hyperorganism; nor is it the individual, localised action of a particular practical organism: it is the action of a practical organism without any determination of individuality, to the extent that it mediates between function and objectification and *that it arises as ubiquity* in the organised milieu. My comprehension is mine only in so far as it is that of my neighbour: and the multiplicity of identity disappears *in so far as* every understanding implies all the others and realises them; ubiquity is the reciprocity of unity as, with a single movement, it excludes both the multiple and the identical. This double exclusion is perfectly conveyed by language with the first person plural, when it expresses the interiorisation of the multiple: in the *we*, in fact, the multiple is not so much eliminated as disqualified; it is preserved in the form of ubiquity. True, one can say, 'We are two', just as one says, 'They are two'; but in the second case, the enumeration is real, and expresses commutativity (either may be the second unit) whereas, in the first case, this commutativity is the non-explicit content of reciprocity.

Thus before becoming an objective reorganisation, the discovery of the solution is an individual moment whose *here* is everywhere and which determines itself reciprocally by its reciprocal presence in every *here*. Of course, this is an abstract interpretation: as soon as seriality enters the group – however slightly – multiplicity tends to reappear. But there are intermediaries between the non-multiple or ubiquity and numerical multiplicity, and the latter really exists as such only when the group is completely dead: and then there will not even be any comprehensive construction of a solution, or if there is, it will no longer have the power to break the serial inertia. But for us the most important point is that the moment of synthesis is still that of individual performance; quite unlike a universal objective realising an agreement of minds while preserving their diversity, the individual performance realises nothing, but *everyone realises himself as the same by realising it*. The truth in its original sense, therefore, as sociality and within an integrated group, is the elimination of all alterity; it realises integration through the mediation of a regulatory third party. But this leads to an absolute impossibility of distinguishing between the truth as an individual performance and as a common one. This lack of differentiation through ubiquity between *one* and *all* finds expression in the fact that science will both name a law or principle after its discoverer – Ohm, Joule, Carnot, etc. – and also allow constructive work to develop anonymously. Not only is it impossible for common operations to transcend individual operations in their practical structure; in addition, as we shall see, the individual operation appears to the group as a practical ideal which it can never entirely achieve.

But we must return to the organising sub-group. Let us suppose that a schematic solution to its problem has been found. A solution has been outlined, and it is now necessary to consider matters of detail, concrete modalities of application, etc. At this level we encounter the heterogeneity of freedom once again: and it is based, in effect, on the common adoption of the regulatory plan of the solution, which has now assumed a new character: common structure. On the one hand, it is a *comprehensible and pledged* inertia; it is obeyed, and no one should try to question it. Thus, in itself, it represents a synthetic relation of omnipresent inertia. In everyone it is entirely *the same*, as a common basis, and it does not reside in anybody in particular, or even have any special position in its originator. On the other hand, as an organising schema (which controls the new organisation of the group through the sub-group), it defines the limits and powers of organising *praxis*: precisely because they are integrated, because everyone is the same and bases his own activities on the same overall plan, it is possible for any individual to create his own heterogeneity by means of a detailed proposal which presupposes, and contains, as its ossature, the inert relations of the overall plan. In the extreme case, everyone will make himself heterogeneous through his free, enriching proposal, while constituting this invention in the object as a moment of the totalising objectification which will have to be transcended. The progressive work of adapting the schema to the concrete therefore develops under the control of the plan, through heterogeneous moments each of which preserves and transcends the previous one.

At this level (at least in theory, that is to say, at the level of abstract purity which we are now occupying), the contradictions do not affect the group itself; they are temporalised and surmounted in the light of a possible future unity, of the common *praxis* and the group itself. But, from the point of view of intelligibility, it should be recognised that the harmonious development of heterogeneity on a basis of unity again refers us to the practical unity of the organism. Even if the entire process were the product of different operations, performed by different individuals, every proposal that was suggested, contradicted, transcended along with its contradiction, and preserved, might, *a priori*, be a position that was transcended and preserved in the free, dialectical *praxis* of the organism. The only difference is that the constituted dialectic rests on a non-dialectical moment: that of adopted inertia. This inertia, in fact, makes common *praxis* possible in so far as it lays down untranscendable limits to the constituent dialectic. And of course every practical organism contains a structure of inertia – this is why it can be the instrument of any instrumentality – but this has nothing in common with the inertia of freedom. In fact, free, organic transcendence is always a transcendence of material conditions; but the limits of action are prescribed by historical circumstances as a whole, rather than by a pledged inertia produced by *praxis* itself.

This inert negation, however, is the necessary condition of common action: it is through it that the common individual exists as power, function, and structure; and dialectical *praxis*, as the mediation between the common individual and the object to be worked, itself differs from the free isolated *praxis* of an organism, in so far as it transcends, preserves, and actualises inertia, power and function – in short, the common individual. There is a synthetic, constitutive relation which, in the group itself, is the definition of each individual (in relation to everyone and to all); and the common individual, actualising himself through individual *praxis*, arises in a field of incredibly violent forces which form and deform him and involve him *everywhere*. In this sense, the concrete individual in the group is radically different from the organic individual and the common individual. At first sight, this makes it even more paradoxical when the group in action 'relapses' into its common *praxis* at the level of individual *praxis*, if not as regards the power and the efficacity of its action, at least in its formal structure. But the paradox disappears when one remembers that the group is an 'antiphysis', that is to say, an undertaking, a systematic operation on the fundamental relations which unite men, and that the overall plan of this operation could only be the dialectical movement which produced it. In other words, the practical aim is not the group, but the common objective; the group organises itself in order to achieve the objective in common, but organisation constitutes it dialectically as an amplifier of dialectical *praxis* – in fact not only *as* a very powerful organism, but also *as* an organism which eliminates the contingencies of its constitution by a careful division of labour and a systematic differentiation of functions.

Now these new characteristics do not prevent it from being situated and, consequently, they do not prevent external transformations from giving rise to contingency in its organisation (that is, to contingent limitations of its foresight). Nor do they mean that the plan of action cannot be the same for the group as a product of human labour and for the labour which produced it, except that the group as an object of labour must retain its determinations, as a worked thing, by a certain inertia, or that the only unity which a group can give itself – since the hyper-organism is an illusion of idealism – does not oscillate between the false unity of worked matter (a coin which has been struck) and the synthetic, living unity of the organism. So we are now in a position to assert that the dialectical rationality of common *praxis* does not transcend (*ne transcende pas*) the rationality of individual *praxis*. On the contrary, individual *praxis* goes beyond it. And its special complexities, its knotted relations, and the formal concatenation of its structures derive precisely from the fact that the second rationality is *constituted*, that is to say, from the fact that the group is a product.

In other words, the group constitutes and organises itself in response to the pressure of necessity in order to produce a dialectical action. And if it succeeded in *becoming an organism*, the organic unity of its action (assuming a hyper-conscious unity, etc.) would be different in kind and would have a different intelligibility: each organism might have some comprehension of the hyper-organism as a structure connected to the *whole*, but this would be very different from ours, which, in the organised group, aims at totalisation. In any case, the conjecture is so vague that it is impossible to settle whether this comprehension would apply to the hyper-organic whole, or to its hyper-action (which is itself a rearrangement), or to the one through the other, or whether there might be no comprehension at all. But precisely because it fails to become a totality, that is to say, to transcend individual *praxis* by a practical hyper-dialectic, it falls short of the level of the *praxis* which alone could provide it with a model of active unity, just as the organism itself provides its totalisation with a model and schema of ontological unity (a point to which we shall return). And the paradoxical tension which constitutes the *praxis* of a group is that it is in itself a metamorphosis conceived as the ubiquity of the individual through all the others, and *therefore*, in a way, a new statute of existence (*power* and 'violence-fraternity') and that its action – which is the very reason and law of its constitution – does not differ from what can be projected by an organic individual who uses a group-object in order to carry out the project. But this factual untranscendability (which is not a *necessity*, but a permanent certainty of the investigation) necessarily refers to the impossibility of being a hyper-organism, which is the limitation of the group; and this impossibility itself is primarily simply the impossibility of acquiring an organic unity. The untranscendable connection between the group and the practical organism as Idea (Idea not in the sense of a determination of discourse, but as an unrealisable task which becomes regulatory by constantly positing itself as capable of being realised the next day) is the changing signification of a perpetually rearranged and perpetually unsuccessful totalisation.

The group is haunted by organicist significations because it is subject to this rigid law: if it were to achieve organic unity (which is impossible) it would therefore be a hyper-organism (because it would be an organism which produced itself in accordance with a practical law which excluded contingency); but since it is strictly forbidden this statute, it remains *a totalisation*, and a being which is subsidiary to the practical organism, and one of its products. In short, since the organic level cannot be transcended, it cannot be attained; and the organic state, as a threshold which would have to be crossed in order to reach hyper-organic unity, remains as the ontological and practical statute which serves to regulate the group. Similarly, the group constitutes itself through labour as a tool for producing a dialectical *praxis*, though this dialectic, forged through organisation, is constituted by the free dialectical actions of the organic individual and is modelled on them. The result is not only that the common action is capable of being recreated by a single individual (the *leader*, the *'organisation-man'*, etc.), but also that the intelligibility of the constituted dialectic is weighed down and degraded in comparison to the full intelligibility of the constituent dialectic.

4   Praxis as Process

We must now seek to explain why, though – as we shall see – it is still intelligible, common *praxis* lacks the translucidity of individual *praxis*. First of all, it is obvious that the fundamental reason is its adopted inertia: however extensively adopted it is, it will still come to everyone as his *other freedom* and consequently from the third party as Other, even though alterity arises here in its formal purity. If I run up against my own limits, against certain untranscendabilities (the fact that I have one function in the group rather than another), then I can obviously provide *practical* interpretations of them (recognising the reason for my function in circumstances and my abilities) and, rediscovering my original pledge, whether it was implicit or explicit, I can reproduce it in the urgency of the resuscitated past, and on this basis run through the dialectical sequence which leads to this present, to this task. But negation and limitation as such cannot be dissolved even if I comprehend them, as I must, in terms of their instrumental function. And I can always rediscover the dialectical movement within the group, which produces all the determinations which are based on these – rights and duties, powers and structures – though they do not have the translucidity of my own pure organic *praxis*. Both my right and my duty appear with a dimension of alterity. Of course, these are relations with others, but still, translucid human relations do exist, and I spoke of them at the beginning of this work: I mean immediate reciprocities. What we have here is worked reciprocities. Right and duty, in their non-transparent certainty, appear to dialectical investigation, and to practical consciousness, as my free alienation from freedom. But, in fact, we know the aims of the pledge: the problem was to struggle against *our* multiplicity by interiorising it, that is to say, by constantly subjecting it to unity. Thus the problem of dialectical rationality as constituted Reason arises at the most basic level of integration, that of common action against multiplicity.

Taking our investigation to a lower level of abstraction and purity (though it is still wholly abstract), we can immediately observe that the interiorisation of multiplicity constantly has to be redone, and is never successfully completed: this is due primarily to the actual circumstances of struggle and action, that is to say, not only to the totalising historical process, but also to the objective and the instruments. To begin with the latter, it is striking that, provided the group is not itself the whole of society (that is to say, practically always), *the other* intervenes in so far as the instrument of the group is the product of his labour. And worked matter, from within the group which is constituted upon it, thereby impregnates all interior organisations with a certain alterity. Whichever group is *considered today*, it takes no more than a strike affecting the post office (or telecommunications) for practical unity to be temporarily broken. Now, this unity has meaning only in the movement of action and in the urgency of the situation: if it is disrupted, this will not break a pledged fidelity between common individuals; it will simply force everyone to carry out his task in very unfamiliar circumstances, since he will be deprived of the information, instructions and orders which the group normally provides. The common individual subsists; he is the pledge and *habits* in everyone; but in the new situation he tends to reduce himself to a purely negative determination, a handicap of inertia: the organic individual is no longer a mediation between, on the one hand, a common-being which is *alive* (that is, sustained and nourished by the common milieu, by the given and maintained powers), though limited by inertia, and, on the other, the objectification of common *praxis*. Isolated, he identifies himself as a practical organism with the group, that is to say, he gives the group the statute of dialectical spontaneity which characterises his own organism. (As we shall see, this sudden isolation as rupture is not lived in the same way as those continuous functions which characterise the being-in-the-group of the individual *as isolation* and which, consequently, produce isolated individuals as useful, necessary members who live their isolation as their practical community statute.)

But it is obvious that this identification of the group with oneself contains two specific and opposed possibilities: sacrifice to the group, in spite of the unreliability of orders and information, and the use of the group by the individual. The danger that common individuals will dissolve, in this case, is not prior to the pledge (fear, 'private interest', etc., in so far as they threaten a group with disintegration), but subsequent to it: the group dissolves in the individual when he keeps the powers of the group and, in the absence of links, embodies the group *in himself alone*. Thus the problem of links (*liaisons*) is inseparable from that of organisation; or rather, it is a special aspect of it: the problem of the links of organisation is inseparable from that of the organisation of links. And if the developing organisation, through the general form it assumes, determines the general type of links, then conversely these links, depending on the difficulties they present (cost, relative slowness, scarcity of men, danger, etc.), act on the organisers and make them alter their plans. The connection between forms of government and administration and the possibilities of communication (that is to say, the real techniques and means of communicating) is revealed to us in its inflexible rigidity by the whole historical reconstruction.

But, for us, the problem has two aspects: this dependence really gives the group, whatever it is, *the depth of the world*; which means that it is united to the serialities of the society in which it was engendered through the mediation of worked matter. It may be said that the individual also depends entirely on the social ensemble, that is to say, on the social circumstances of his materiality. This is true. And, ultimately, his class situation and, for example, the state of medical techniques, in so far as they reflect production as a whole, and affect him through the refractive index of his class, determine his *practical* possibilities in so far as they condition his organism *from inside*. But this is only a superficial analogy, just because biological reality is one. Certainly, there are linking organs (nerves, blood, endocrine secretions, etc.): and illnesses – occupational or other – may destroy some of these links while certain medicines may re-establish them and even, in certain cases, *improve them*. The differences must lie elsewhere, even if one imagines progress in medical techniques making it possible gradually to transform the organism. It is in this respect that the biological links are established through and between biological functions and in the biological milieu. The organism produces its own ways and these ways are themselves functions; the inorganic appears in it either as a substance which has been integrated into the whole or as a product of a secretion, but not as inert distance or as an inert vehicle whose speed is a function of some exterior operation. Within the organism, distance itself is organic; it allows itself to appear in its inorganic reality only through the degradation of the living being (slow reflexes in the sick and the old, etc.).

With groups, however, the inorganic (as worked materiality) is an inert mediation between the functions of the community. This leads initially to the presence of an internal alterity not produced by the group and which, depending on circumstances (but independently of the objective, or, at least, without any practical link to it, established by the agents) appears as practically negligible or threatens to tear the community apart. ('Our supporters are not turning up, or are coming in smaller numbers because we are meeting too far from where they live, because transport is too expensive', etc. A particular revolutionary movement, which needs to manifest itself at several places in the country at the same time, may fail because links cannot be established.[58] A particular fighting group may be wiped out because its links with the army to which it belongs have been broken.) Such internal conditioning causes a reappearance of interiorised multiplicity; and, so to speak, re-exteriorises it in interiority. The group has eliminated facticity by setting itself a transcendent aim and by eliminating the organic hazards of its *praxis*; but then it encounters it again, within itself, in the form of a dispersive limit to its unification. But it should be noted that this facticity, unlike basic facticity, does not present itself as a special biological determination of unworked materiality, but rather as a contingent determination of the practico-inert field. This

58. This is only an individual event: if fundamental contradictions produce an exigency for Revolution, the failure will only be incidental.

determination is said to be *contingent* not because it lacks either strictness or intelligibility (given the practico-inert field on the basis of which the group arises, it is inevitable that the problem of links should present itself to the common practice in some way or other), but because it is external to the practice in so far as it organises the group in accordance with a particular objective.

The second aspect of this dependence is of even more concern to our inquiry than the first: in so far as the group wishes to struggle, with contemporary techniques and tools, against the dispersive force of the practico-inert field, it must produce within itself apparatuses of mediation, supervision, and inspection, whose essential function is to put the sub-groups into relation either with one another (as with a federal structure, for example) or with the central apparatus (with a centralised structure). The active function of such mediators – whether they are *missi dominici*, timekeepers in a factory or inspectors in secondary education – is to unite two inertias as such. And these inertias were not produced by pledged freedom; they came to the group through dispersal in exteriority and the mediating apparatus *constitutes* them as inertias which have been transcended and mediated by its mediation: and without this mediation the central administration would have no power over the local executive and *vice versa*; the mediating apparatus may of course be produced by the administration, but as soon as it has been produced, the administration is dependent on it, as well as the local executive. In such cases, a control body is often created to supervise the mediating organ. Of course, these remarks would be even more appropriate and complete in relation to a hierarchical group subject to controls. But we have not yet examined such a structure. But in any case, the link reveals and develops the inertia of exteriority while struggling against it by rearranging pledged inertias. The peculiarities of organised *praxis* are that it is constituted by a pyramid of inertias, both external and internal (through the exteriorisation of the inertia of interiority and through the interiorisation of the inertia of exteriority) and that the object of any apparatus (the sub-groups which have to be linked together) appears as an external-internal inertia and must be treated as such, while in its relations with other co-ordinated organs the same apparatus is treated as inertia by subordinate apparatuses.

But means of communication are only one example of the separation of interiority. Depending on the task and the circumstances, it may also find expression in temporalisation: each particular task in its particularity may be completed and be separated by a time-lag from the particular task which it makes possible in the development of the common action. In an industrial complex (either a socialist *Kombinat* or a capitalist organisation: we are not directly concerned with exploitation here, but rather with technical necessities which are the same everywhere, east and west), the extraction of raw materials or the manufacture of intermediate products (blast furnaces and forges; iron and steel, etc.) is objectified in a certain object (such as crude oil, or steel ingots) which absorbs labour just like 'commodities' and allows it to crystallise in it. The process will be resumed, the oil refined, the steel transformed into a crank-shaft, a drive shaft, etc., somewhere else (possibly nearby) and in a third process it will be enabled to perform its functions directly (the machine will be assembled out of its separate parts, etc.).

But it is clear that the *praxis* of every sub-group is absorbed as an inert seal of worked materiality and transcended by a new operation. From the point of view of the economy of the firm, it is very important that workers, premises, organisers and managers should be integrated into a single complex. But to the sub-group which produces blast furnaces it is of very little importance whether the treated raw material was mined by a sub-group belonging to the complex or whether it was transported by train from some distant region. In the second case, the fact that the so-called 'raw material' is *already worked* (the fact that men have laboured in common to extract the mineral) is practically irrelevant. Even if the worker in the forge belongs to the same class as the miners, this class solidarity is not a structure of the group as such, at least not directly, and, besides, it affects the members of the class (whether they belong to the group or not) rather than the members of the group. For the worker, in fact, the inert exigency of the object may refer to those who have produced it, but, as we have seen, it may also be perceived as a sort of inhuman function of materiality. At this moment, it separates more than it unites, or rather it unites in seriality. But still we have not relapsed into seriality: the group loses its abstract purity, but it still has its efficacity and its structure of interiority. But the important point here is that in the technological complex under consideration, the task of the preceding agent is perceived – owing to the time-lag (the transportation of the product from one workshop to another, or from the mine to the forge, etc.) – as inverted and turned back into passivity by its basis of inert passivity. It becomes a mortgage of the future of the new worker, a limitation of his possibilities to which he must submit, *whether it was done outside the group* by others as Others *or whether it was the result of an undertaking which was common to certain members who are invisible in so far as they are the same.* There are many ways in which this reorganising correction can occur: the mediating sub-group may improve integration by increasing contacts between workers in different sectors; it may ensure that everyone understands the common *praxis* by giving theoretical instruction to enable every worker to see the meaning and importance of his own function and also to learn to recognise the meaning of other tasks; or it may institute a system of rotation which puts everyone into each of the different jobs of the ensemble in the course of three or five years, etc.

I am not mentioning these practices because of their social efficacity, but simply to show their common character: they take up organisation at the 'neutral' point at which it was left by temporal dislocation; and they treat the isolation of each sub-group or individual in relation to other individuals and sub-groups as an inert negation which has to be dissolved, and they treat each worker as a massified unit who has to be won back from emerging seriality.[59] By means either of a real re-arrangement (rotation of jobs) or of a verbal action (teaching, explanation), they have a material effect on inorganic materiality. It is true that this work is intended to replace a cloud of isolations (such as time-lags) by a functional unity; but in terms of the common *praxis* of organisation, it shows that concrete organisation is a perpetual negation of the negation, that is to say, a practical, effective negation of the developing disorganisation. From this point of view, the heterogeneity of functions in a totally and abstractly pure group is, as we have seen, a creation of freedom. In a complex group, however (in which spatial distances and time-lags are constant sources of massifying dispersal), and from the point of view of totalisation, it is clear that differentiation, if it is determined *both* by the organising apparatus and by spatio-temporal 'lag', can collapse, in a moment, into a statute of accidental heterogeneity (of exteriority). In an effective, practical, but real group, there is a constant danger that the current will cease to flow.

And, as we have seen, what is true of the elements which are mediated by the apparatus is true also of the apparatus which mediates. The

59. Obviously these mediating activities are inspired by different principles in the East (the humanism of labour, and political propaganda) and in the West ('Human Engineering'). But this has little importance here.

group uses up part of its energy (the energy of its members, its numerical strength, credit, money, etc.) in maintaining itself in a state of relative fluidity. Thus by a scissiparity of reflection (which is highly intelligible since it involves mediating sub-groups and mediators between these sub-groups, etc.), the group as interiority, that is to say, as a developing totalisation, is in danger of being resolved (and will in fact be resolved) into a hierarchy and circularity (both of them, for reasons we shall discover later) of unifying actions which take actions and agents of a lower level[60] as inert quasi-objects, or, conversely, into a hierarchy of quasi-objects deriving their statute from an Other (a sub-group, or an individual considered as a quasi-subject) as a quasi-transcendent determination of their suffered, adopted inertia. At this level, the group tends to have more in common with the kind of complex which is constituted by a machine and by the workers who use it for a particular job than with practical organisms which dialectically transcend every inert moment of the worked object, every inert organisation of the practical field; and this occurs without the moment of passive negation and arrest being directly produced by *praxis*, but, on the contrary, in so far as it returns from the worked object to the work as a limitation of the developing objectification which is immediately transcended by the inorganic statute of materiality. In fact, even if it is true that the group never relapses to the level of the machine (even that of a 'feedback' machine as has been suggested), and if it is also true that it can never raise itself to an organic status, this is because it is actually a human product, that is to say, an instrument made by men in accordance with laws which make it possible to create automatic devices on the basis of the inorganic, and because it is simultaneously constituted by the free, dialectical *praxis* of human individuals, in so far as it acts in interiority on every member, and in exteriority on the common object.

There can never be a social machine, because it would resolve into a massified plurality of organisms as soon as every practical organism received a suffered statute of inertia in relation to the group; on the other hand, its operations become more *machine-like* as integration advances, that is to say, as the group, through the organisation of its structures, increasingly produces itself as a function of the practical organism (as a regulatory schema of the constructed relations of

---

60. Inferiority, like hierarchy, being determined arbitrarily, that is to say in accordance with the conjuncture and the common *praxis*.

interiority). This in no way implies that this *organisation*, as an impossible mediation between the organic and the inorganic, is of itself unintelligible. But it does mean that it is a constituted dialectic; that is to say, there is no dialectical *praxis* here to realise the unity of individuals but, on the contrary, there are individual, constituent dialectics inventing and producing, through their work, a dialectical apparatus which encloses them and their instruments and which is determined in accordance with the aim. Within the apparatus, everyone is transformed with and through all the others, and the common individual as a structure of the totalisation appears as the highest level of integration which the group is capable of realising in its attempts to produce itself as an organism; but the group can be comprehended only as a particular dissolution of the practico-inert field at a certain degree of depth; and as such, it preserves the dissolved field, at least in the form of a constant danger of the resurrection of seriality and its very complication leads it towards the passive statute of inert things, of worked products. As I have said, even this is provisional: later, we shall examine the avatars of the group and what becomes of them when the group is reconquered by seriality. The important point here is that the common *praxis is both an action and a process.*[61]

Since every moment of the action, in so far as it is everywhere the same, is produced as a finished action by a practical organism as the mediation between function (common individual, structure) and objectification (inscribing the common work on the object), in common *praxis*, there is a common aim, objectification, labour, transcendence, reciprocal adaptation, etc., just as there is in individual *praxis*; and every partial result must be grasped in its constituent intelligibility as a free, practical realisation of one detail of the common aim. But the common aim itself, whether regarded as present in the structure of individuals or as the reflexive rule which governs the reorganisation of the whole by means of a differentiated apparatus, appears as a determination of the future by a project on the basis of concrete circumstances. At this level, the individual dialectic actually transcends itself towards another form of intelligibility, since it can already reproduce and comprehend the specific modalities of the group – which would be unknown to an isolated individual, if there could be such a thing – that is to say, structure, being-in-the-group, function, power and, ultimately,

61. This is, of course, *before* any description of *alienation* an an avatar of the group-*praxis*.

the pledge. The pledge, in fact, as a determination of mediated reciprocity, is incapable of being produced, or, therefore, comprehended, by an isolated freedom. And if everyone understands the group in this way, in so far as it appears to transcend itself towards a new form of integration, this is because membership of the group is given to concrete experience at the same time as practical-individual existence; thus there are not two separate moments of comprehension here, but rather two types of activity (practical and theoretical) which are always possible, either separately or together.

But, as we have seen, at the moment in which the group transcends itself towards the organism through its individuals, it is still inoperative. It can go no further: being-in-common can produce new relations with others (and therefore with oneself) in everyone; but it cannot produce an integrating and integral organism; the totalisation cannot become a totality. And if the group is to remain an effective power to produce particular results, it will clearly be necessary that the number of readjustments and mediations in it should increase; that is to say, it should become within itself a practical multiplicity of points of view perceiving it in all its forms as an inertia which has to be transcended. This second procedure is simply the result of the failure of the first: since, at best, integration leads to the transformation of multiplicity into ubiquity, but never succeeds in replacing it with a new unity, this multiplicity without parts inevitably reproduces itself as a quantitative, discrete multiplicity, within the group itself, under other relations and through the mediation of the practico-inert.

Circular recurrence does not yet establish itself on this basis, but the circularity of passivity always does, for the mediating organ must itself be mediated and it turns out to be split by the separations it mediates. Now, in this circular ensemble – and even when we introduce, as we soon shall, the functions of authority – everything occurs *also* as an autonomous result, positing itself for itself in the inertia of isolation, while its practical Reason lies in the mediation of a sub-group of reorganisation. At this level, passivity is given first – as an effective but isolated process (as the work of *one* machine in a group of machines) – and teleological activity is simply what comes, from above, to break up isolation and to restructure functions; totalisation constantly breaks down and is always re-established by others (who are now no longer quite *the same*); its free, practical reality *comes to everyone* as a passive recovery of his common individuality. From this point of view, which is *also* that of the interior practice of the group (and which tends to dominate as the difficulties increase), the common action becomes *a directed process*.

What difference is there, then, between process and *praxis*? Both are dialectical: they are defined by their movement and their direction; they transcend the obstacles of the common field and transform them into stepping-stones, stages, steps marking and facilitating their develop ment. Both are defined in terms of a particular determination of the field of possibilities, by which the meaning of their different moments can be explained. Both are violence, fatigue, wear and a constant trans formation of energy. But *praxis* is directly revealed *by its end*: the future determination of the field of possibilities is posited at the outset by a projective transcendence (*dépassement*) of material circumstances, that is to say, by a project; at each moment of the action, the agent *produces himself* in a particular posture, accompanied by a specific effort in accordance with present givens in the light of the future objective. I have called this *praxis free* for the simple reason that, in a given set of circumstances, on the basis of a given need or danger, it creates its own law, in the absolute unity of the project (as a mediation between the given, past objectivity and the objectification which is to be produced). The process is comparable *neither* to an avalanche or flood, *nor* to an individual action: it actually retains all the characteris tics of individual action, since it is constituted by the directed action of a multiplicity of individuals; but at the same time these characteristics receive in it the modification of passivity because, through the resur rection of the multiple, every *here* presents itself as a passivity (and implies passivity as ubiquity in every *here*) and activity appears as *the evanescent elsewhere*, that is to say, as the dissolution *here* of suffered inertia in so far as this activity of the Other must, in another elsewhere and for Others, be an inertia which has to be dissolved by activity. In the group as common *praxis*, the pledged inertias are the forever concealed and veiled mediation between organic activities. In the group-process, practical activity, as an ungraspable, fleeting event, serves as an organising mediation between suffered inertias (in so far as it dissolves them temporarily).

There cannot be any question of determinism in either case, since the development is concrete, and directed, and grows richer with each transcendence, and defines itself in terms of a particular future end. In the first case, that is to say when the group is manifested in its abstract purity as a living organisation, comprehension is quite simply the production of the member or of the transcendent (*transcendant*) spectator by himself in his being-in-the-group: this act is always possible because the organic individual is always a common individual. This understanding is *richer* than inter-individual understanding, because implicitly or explicitly it reproduces new dialectical structures as the pledge. And this pledge is still intelligibility, although it is, in everyone, other-freedom, because in itself it is a free operation performed on the fundamental relation of reciprocity. However, *translucidity* is effaced as a function of complexity: structures, law, and terror contain no mystery; these new determinations do not contain any opacity, and it is both possible and necessary to produce them dialectically in the explanation. However, in so far as they arise on the basis of a relation *to the third party who I am not* – and who, of course, appears as *the same, here* – and in so far as reciprocity bases them on *inertia pledged by the other*, that is to say, on abstract alterity as an inert pledge never to be other than myself, the certainty of the structures is based on an empty relation, whose *other term* is active in me in so far as it is not me and in so far as it denies itself the possibility of being totally itself in isolation. The action is intelligible because *it is the same* as my own; but I consider it in a vacuum because, in the ubiquity of the pledge, *the same*, everywhere, is not myself. We are therefore confronted with a negative limit of transparency rather than with a positive limitation (as by some irrational effusing of common manifestations).

Apart from these two differences (comprehension is *richer* from one point of view, and *poorer* from another), a common action is intelligible to me as organic action, that is to say, through some graspable end which totalises us (or the group, if I am situated outside it) negatively. The totalisation of a multiplicity, whether this multiplicity is inert, living or practical, is effectively a fundamental operation of *praxis* as dialectic. And common *praxis* in its purity is understood on the model of organic *praxis*, that is to say, as the individual action of a community in the light of a common aim. For understanding, common *praxis* appears precisely as a mediation between the practical community and the common aim by the singular, just as the action of the individual organism is the constant mediation between the common individual and the common objectification. There should be nothing surprising in this comparison: the common *praxis* actually reveals itself through an organised multiplicity of free, individual undertakings (within the limits of functions and powers) and each of these presents itself as exemplary, that is to say, as the same as all. Thus the schema of intelligibility is not provided by some super-individual undertaking, but, on the contrary, by the dialectical (and perfectly comprehensible) relation between pure, simple, individual action (modified by the relations mentioned above) and a common aim. Individual *praxis* is the synthetic mould into which common action must be poured.

In the second case, the process manifests itself as an object. This does not mean that we perceive it as a totality; on the contrary. But, whether I am in the community or outside it, the movement which animates it is not of the kind that I can produce, as a practical organism; it belongs to the category of those which I suffer in so far as I have my being-outside-myself-in-the-world. In other words, it reveals itself as a reality in relation to which I shall always be outside, even if it envelops me and leads me on; and which will always be outside me, even if, with everyone, I help to produce it. This reality is structured in interiority (for, in spite of everything, whether they are inert or isolated, functions subsist and function together), and yet it does not have interiority. It does not produce in immanence its own determinations: on the contrary, it *receives* them as a perpetual transformation of its inertia. But as these received determinations are themselves synthetic and 'internal', since they are always directed to a future end, and they represent a constant enrichment and an irreversibility of time, they proceed not from analytical Reason or the laws of exteriority but, if one is not to prejudge them, from an external law of interiority.

This law might of course be referred to as destiny, since an irresistible movement draws or impels the ensemble towards a prefigured future which realises itself through it. But it is more interesting to see it as the celebrated external dialectic which was criticised and rejected at the beginning of this essay. Indeed, it is precisely this which appears as a transcendent law of interiority, and which is given as the movement of constituent reason and as destiny or fatality. And if one becomes its dupe, it makes 'processes' appear not as temporalisations, but as temporalised realities. And it is because of it that all projective and teleological structures are reabsorbed by necessity. The process develops in accordance with a law from outside which controls it in accordance with earlier conditions; but this necessity is still directed, the future is still prefigured, and the process retains its finality, though it is reversed, passivised and masked by necessity.

But this conception of human activity as *process* takes rather different forms – especially non-dialectical or aberrant ones – in the work of many American sociologists. Lewin's *Gestalt* is based on a vision of *praxis* as process; there is destiny, totality (as an external law of interiority), and the synthetic passive organisation of results. The works of Kardiner and Moreno, and the studies of the culturalists are always based on the directed, irreversible, and overblown passivity of an inert fatality which we have just seen; and the group-process is, from one point of view, a constant reality of our own investigation. Its characteristics are not their invention; they have not chosen to see only it and to study it at the level of its complete unintelligibility.

This unintelligibility is simply a moment of intelligibility: it is the first appearance which certain groups display. Moreover, it becomes intelligibility at a level of greater complexity, which we shall soon reach, at the level at which the group interferes with the series. For the moment, it is better to present process as the permanent obverse of common *praxis*. Its intelligibility, taken on its own, comes from the fact that it can be dissolved and reversed; in fact, it simply represents the moment where the interior action of the group intensifies so as to counteract the multiplicity which begins to erode it. Everywhere reabsorbed by the inert, at every level, it tries to dissolve it everywhere; and if it escapes or flees, it is through its own negative character. It appears parasitical though it is in reality practical reality itself. And as long as the group, with its control mechanisms, remains effective and active, its fundamental truth is still *praxis*. However, we must retain this first aspect of *process* if we simply wish to mark the concrete limits of *praxis*. As long as one isolates it from the world in order to study it in its abstract purity, it will yield its intelligibility without transparency as an individual and common practice. When it is considered *in the world* without relation to anything except time and place, it will display new aspects: separations, scleroses, useless survivals, local wear, stratifications, the inertial force of apparatuses, fragmentation of the group, tendencies, antagonisms of function (carefully defined competences cease to be so as *praxis* develops, because of the need to adapt to new circumstances). And the negative *praxis* of mediating apparatuses which attempt to dissolve these callosities and knots is essentially in danger of being simply an ever *anterior* liquidation, a preparation for common action, a restoration of instrumental functions without any other positive connection with the *praxis* of the group in the common field.

Thus, while continuing its real development, the group *also* appears as an object which is constantly being repaired and the teleological aspect of the repairing is lost through its very negativity: it appears to be subordinated to the inert structures which have to be maintained.

The possibility of the group being seen inside out as an enormous, passive object, being dragged towards its destiny, and expending its energy in internal reactions, absorbing the human conduct of its members and subsisting by a sort of inert perseverance is still no more than an abstract limit of dialectical intelligibility. It simply shows that the group is *constructed* on the model of free individual action and that it produces an organic action without itself being an organism; that it is a machine for producing non-mechanical reactions and that inertia – like every human product – constitutes both its being and its *raison d'être*. And when we say that, considered as a process, it represents the limit of intelligibility, we do not mean that it is unintelligible in the depths of its inertia, but, on the contrary, that this fundamental inertia must be inserted into its very intelligibility; in other words, that the *praxis*-subject of a pledged community maintains itself in being as a process-object, and that this is its own materiality. The materiality of the group is suffered in so far as it is forged, and forged in so far as it is suffered: the pledge is a function of distance (becoming correspondingly more weak or inflexible); distance (as a reciprocal path which cannot be entered without difficulty, and an expenditure of strength and wear) is created by the pledge; and in the form of this double conditioning of inertias, it makes it possible to indicate *the state* of the group.

By this, I do not mean either its *being*, which we shall come to shortly, or its constitution (as a structured ensemble: an exogamous system, or an administrative apparatus), but simply the relation between constituted inertia (suffered and pledged) and *praxis*, at any given moment. It is at this level that explanations will be found of such matters as the *ageing* of one part (that is to say, both the decline in recruitment and the stratification of the controlling organs) and the effect of scarcity on the possibilities open to a group (scarcity of men – empty classes, etc. – being either a national circumstance in the light of which the group determines itself, and which determines its density, or an event proper to the group itself and to its modalities of recruitment, renewal, etc., or an objective relation – both internal and external – between the objective of the group and the objectives of other groups or serial individuals in the society under consideration).[62] At this

62. Scarcity of money is crucial and bound up in many ways with scarcity of men. (A shortage of money may be due to a shortage of men, and equally, a shortage of men may be due to a shortage of money. And this second meaning is

level, too, one can speak of softness, or, on the other hand, of hardening, of routine or of a frenzy of innovation; at this level it is possible to
explain the difficulties of a given group in new circumstances, by
showing, for example, that whereas all its structures were organised
with a view to a defensive *praxis*, the conditions of struggle are forcing
it to go on the offensive, etc. Examples could be multiplied indefinitely;
it will be sufficient to remark that *the state* is not inertia as an inert
foundation, as a sclerosis of structures, etc., but inertia as a condition
of *praxis*, to the extent, that is, that it acts as an untranscendable limit
(in which the suffered and the pledged are mingled and bound together
in an indissoluble reciprocity) of any action which tries to negate it.
It is at the level of the state – and we shall return to this – that the group
is totally conditioned, in a form for which it was not prepared, by the
practico-inert field which it attempts to modify: a particular action, in

---

duplicated: (1) the men do not come because we do not have the means to pay
them, (2) they come in large numbers but we turn them away because we cannot
give them work – we are short of weapons or machines.) My reason for not discussing this here is that my purpose is not to study the concrete conditions of the
'functioning' of a group, which would involve taking a real group at a given real
time and tracing its historical evolution from beginning to end. But this work,
however important and desirable it may be, goes well beyond the limits of the
present problem. Money necessarily depends on the system of production, and on
the relations which arise on the basis of it. The statement 'there is no historical
group without money' (such as Labiche's *La Cagnotte*) means: there is no group
which does not reflect the true condition of man in *that* moment of History; there
is no group of exploiters, for example, which did not arise in a milieu of exploitation and signify it in its very organisation, whether the aim of the organisation
is to set up an amateur orchestra or a circulating library. I also admit that the
investigation of a group in which there is no scarcity of money is in danger of
being completely abstract. Nevertheless, a group of exploiters (as long as no
crisis threatens their property) may be assured as a group that its expenses will be
automatically covered by fees as long as they stay within reasonable limits: this
applies to clubs (whether English or American). This amounts to saying that for
certain groups in the exploiting class – and when the means of the members are
far in excess of the needs of the group – money is no problem; it does not represent suffered inertia or restriction, but, on the contrary, power. It is for this
main reason that I have not taken scarcity of money into account – that is to say,
because, at least in theory and in certain special conditions, it *may* not be an essential and negative factor. There is another reason: this is that a group cannot exist
in a pure state and that we shall shortly arrive at the concrete, that is to say, at the
line of intersection of the group and seriality; and that, *at this level*, we shall once
again encounter the real problems of a society, that is to say, *precisely* its
system of production.

a particular locality, may be aimed at intimidating, at improving wages; but it may appear inopportune, instructions may be ignored *because* the dangers which have to be avoided are not yet sufficiently clear and above all because the workers in the biggest firms are about to begin their paid holidays.

We seem to be on the point of encountering seriality again. And in fact we shall encounter it. But, for the moment, it is sufficient to *comprehend* the group as constituted *praxis*. In it, through the determination of its members, the contradictory tension which opposes totalising *praxis* to the multiplicity of the agents can be seen arising *as a dialectical conflict.* However, it must be recognised that both the dialectical structures and the synthetic movement which produces the opposition proceed from organic *praxis* and that multiplicity is a factor of dialectical intelligibility only in so far as it manifests itself as untranscendable inertia, that is to say, as the explosive exteriority of the interiorisation of number. The group at work is individual *praxis*, initially exceeded and reified by the seriality of actions, and everywhere turning back on the amorphous multiplicity which conditions it in order to extract from it the serial, numerical statute, so as to negate it as *discrete* quantity and, in the same movement, to make it, *in practical unity*, a means of achieving the totalising objective. *Praxis* remains fundamentally individual because it is constituted as *the same*, that is to say, as the directed exploitation of multiplicity without parts. In this first moment, *praxis* does not treat *this* multiplicity differently from the inorganic gatherings of the practical field (when it combines them to make an instrument), but the crucial difference is that, after the pledged agreement, every detailed action (in so far as it is both the same and differentiated) turns out to make use of *its own multiplicity*, which becomes an interior feature (power, structure) of the individual unit. When, for the second time, this interiorised multiplicity is placed in exteriority, this does not mean that it has escaped common control, or removed itself from the multiple unity in everyone, so as to reconquer its quantity: this would be inconceivable except on the assumption that it had a dialectical power of its own. But the suppression of multiple inertia and of relations of exteriority has, quite simply, occurred *practically*, that is to say, in and through practical objectification, and yet the ontological statute of multiplicity (the plurality of organisms) is not affected by this. Under fire, the unit replaces dispersal with practical organisation; it encloses its multiplicity in itself. But first the unit is counted; and before long, it will count its wounded and its dead;

and the enemy, if they have observation posts, can always count the able-bodied soldiers it still has at its disposal. And this inertia as the ontological limit of integration (we shall see that there are other limits) is not a theoretical given of some passive knowledge: it is, in fact, the objective field of the unforeseen; through it, indeed, the passive action of the practico-inert is reintroduced into the free group which is organised to combat it; and this passive action reappears not as the action of an interior force but as an interior danger of dispersal; this pure exteriority is, so to speak, lived in interiority as a permanent threat and a permanent possibility of betrayal. Thus multiplicity is reactualised in its untranscendable objectivity by the practico-inert and the practico-inert is simply the activity of others in so far as it is sustained and diverted by inorganic inertia. Thus a passivised form of activity reactualises discrete multiplicity, and the group, as dialectical *praxis*, perceives it in its very dispersal as an internal danger, that is to say, as a dispersal produced *by the unity of an action*. (This action is passive activity, seen, through the unity of the *praxis* which it contradicts, as an active negation of this *praxis* by a directed counter-*praxis*. It is at this level that Manichaean explanations, in terms of English gold, the plot of the aristocrats, counter-revolutionary activity, etc., appear.) And it is in opposition to this action – which reactualises in itself discrete multiplicity as the ubiquity of the possibility of betrayal – that is to say against itself, that the organisation reorganises itself, breaking up old frameworks and, through mediating organs, etc., trying to reduce the passive act of multiplication to a simple, multiple, discrete inertia, ineradicable, but negligible from the point of view of action. Thus we rediscover organic *praxis* everywhere, in so far as it acts on its inert multiplicity; and this multiplicity manifests itself *initially* at every level of reflection as sustained by passive activity, in so far as it is the point at which practico-inert forces act.

But we have seen that the practico-inert field is in itself a caricature of the dialectic and its alienating objectification. Thus, common *praxis* is organised at every level against the anti-dialectic, first by jointly settling the objective and the means of attaining it (dissolution of seriality), and then by perpetual rearrangements of its structures. And the internal life of the group manifests itself through the positive and negative consequences of these rearrangements, that is to say, through new determinations of the practico-inert in the interiority of the organisation and through the practical (and dialectical) reaction of the organising *praxis* to the common consequences of these determinations; but, at the same time, every partial reinteriorisation of the multiple is a way of introducing it at another level as inert quantity and separating force. In this sense, the hostile group, if there is one, determines the enemy both as *praxis* and as process. It cannot actually be unaware of the enemy *praxis* as such; it must comprehend and anticipate it on the basis of its aim; but at the same time, if it wishes to prevent it from being achieved, it must strike the enemy at the level at which *praxis* is also the development of a process (destroying its supply-bases, cutting its lines of communication, etc.). And the group which is under attack, in so far as it anticipates the enemy, must appear to itself, in action, in the form of a process: this is the basis of reflection.

The complex intelligibility of the constituted dialectic therefore arises from the fact that organic *praxis*, in everyone, works, with all, on multiplicity as a practico-inert determination so as to make it an instrument allowing action to become *common* while remaining individual. And, as work is the paradigm of dialectical activity, the group in action has to be understood in terms of two kinds of simultaneous activities, each of which is a function of the other: dialectical activity in immanence (reorganisation of the organisation) and dialectical activity as the practical transcendence (*dépassement*) of the common statute towards the objectification of the group (production, struggle, etc.). The object which is realised is (if we temporarily ignore the dangers of alienation) the expression in transcendence (*transcendance*) of the organisation as a structure of immanence, and conversely. There is, therefore, no *ontologically* common *praxis*: there are practical individuals constructing their multiplicity as an object on the basis of which everyone can perform his task in the free, agreed (and pledged) heterogeneity of common function, that is to say, by objectifying themselves in the common product as necessary details of the developing totalisation.

But this does not mean that constituted intelligibility demands the dissolution of every common *praxis* into individual actions: such a dissolution would imply, in effect, that there was no intelligibility apart from constituent intelligibility; moreover, it would blind us to the real metamorphosis which the pledge causes in everyone and to the 'fraternity-terror' relation as the foundation of all subsequent differentiations. On the contrary, there is such a thing as comprehending common *praxis* as such, that is to say, in so far as it is related to the group as a practical subject (in the sense in which one speaks of a 'subject of History') rather than to the individuals who are integrated into it. It is simply a matter of regarding the group as a product of human labour – that is to say, as an articulated system – and of seeing the common action as a determination in passivity (through the constructed instrument) of individual *praxis*. These precautions will make it possible to comprehend group *praxis* in terms of this reciprocity of inertia: the instrument as a positive and negative image of activity, and the final product as a definition-exigency of this same activity by the future.

On this basis it will be possible to grasp the synthetic connection between the two permanent actions – reorganisation and production – in so far as each is the condition of the other; but the limit and specification of the constituted dialectic and of its intelligibility is that in it action is defined and carried by passivity and that the modifications of the common action occur in everyone. Originally, therefore, we can understand any common *praxis* because we are always an organic individuality which realises a common individual: to exist, to act and to comprehend are one and the same. This reveals a schema of universality which we can call constituted dialectical Reason, because it governs the practical comprehension of a specific reality which I shall call *praxis*-process, in so far as it is the rule both of its construction and of my comprehension (that is to say, of my production of myself, on the basis of the common, as a developing *praxis-process*.) Both as object and as subject of the constituted dialectic, the group produces itself in complete intelligibility, since it is possible to see how every determination in inertia transforms itself, in it and through it, into a counter-finality or a counter-structure (and, also, in the best cases, into structure and finality); this intelligibility is dialectical because it shows us the free, creative development of a practice. But its specificity as a constituted dialectic means that freedom is not the free activity of an autonomous organism but, *from its origins*, a conquest of alienation; moreover, the specificity of the object demands that freedom be sustained, channelled, and limited, both in interiority and in exteriority, by a pledged and suffered inertia which is simply the free determination – direct and indirect – of the field of passivity.

The whole of this practical development produces undeniable results; in other words, it constitutes the first abstract determination of History as such – in relation either to the taking of the Bastille or to the silk-weavers' revolt; and these results – though directly susceptible to alienation, as we shall see – represent *in reality* the objectification of a community as such. In other words, the constituted dialectic, as the ubiquity of the same *praxis* penetrated with inertia, transcends itself – in the case of a practical success – in its result: the objectification really is common, to the extent that the objective was common. But as an organising, effective *praxis*, the untranscendable limit which it encounters is that of organic, practical individuality, precisely because this constitutes it and because, as a constituent dialectic, it is the regulatory schema and untranscendable limit of the constituted dialectic.

It is at this level, I think, that it is possible to grasp the strange circular conflict, where all synthesis is impossible, which is the untranscendable contradiction of History: the opposition and identity of the individual and the common. I would like to illustrate this conflict and this lack of distinction by means of an example. The one I have chosen is certainly neither pure nor abstract and it scarcely concerns the group (at least as homogeneity), because it was conditioned by the capitalist mode of production and the class struggle, and it occurred towards the end of the nineteenth century, on the eve of the second industrial revolution. But this has very little bearing on the formal researches which we are conducting. What I wish to show, in effect, is the identity of individual action and group action, of group action and mechanical action, in short, the organic *praxis* as the regulatory *praxis* of the group and of machinery, and at the same time the irreducible opposition between the individual and the machine.

5 Taylorism

Taylor was without any doubt the first of what we now call *organisation-men*.[63] His aim was to increase output by eliminating wasted time. If a worker's task comprised five successive operations, then five operators, each performing one of these operations five times, would take up less time than five workers each performing one complete action. The ingenuity of the organiser here consists in replacing temporalisation by passive temporality. An action is a temporalising *praxis*. And, in a way, every elementary operation is also temporalised (in fact, it too is an

63. In English in original. [Ed.]

action, complete in its realisation, and incomplete in the common signification of its result). But what makes the living totality of the action disappear is that the five operations are separated both spatially and (at least) by a time-lag which is the time of waiting. (For operation 2 to begin, it is necessary and sufficient that operation 1 should once have taken place.) Thus every operation is passive in relation to the succeeding one, because it does not form part of the same temporal development, but each is separated from the other by a determination of time (and, incidentally, of space) through the negative exteriority of inertia. Moreover, every operation, in itself, in so far as it has been timed and in so far as its 'normal' duration has been established by means of a determination of exterior time (that is to say, of the non-dialectical time of inorganic materiality, in so far as it is defined by specific practices of measurement), reintegrates a passivity into its free, practical realisation. Instead of being conditioned by the result which had to be achieved, and by the free organism in action, it temporalises itself dialectically by preserving, as its internal ossature, the passive temporality defined by the workshop clock.

Thus the action is now constituted by five practices which are determined by the interiorisation of a passivity and separated by the passive flow of time (that is to say, by the abstract ossature of *the time of Others*: employers, other workers, customers, etc.). It disappears as an organic action; and, in isolated – and differentiated – work everyone is thereby *disqualified* as an individual practical agent: his operation is no longer an action. But at the same time he still becomes a common individual (but in alienation – this goes beyond the cases considered above) in so far as his operation depends on the first two, for example, and conditions the other two *at a distance*. In so far as he lives his labour and his solidarity as a member, with his comrades, of an exploited class, this interdependence *may* become power and function (but this is not very relevant here). In any case, clipped and mutilated and torn from his hands and muscles by an exterior rhythm, the operation is still *his* practical operation and, despite its determination in inertia, it realises itself dialectically through him, if only at the most elementary level. The important point is that the skilled job, destroyed by Taylor, expropriated from skilled workers and distributed to the four corners of the factory, regains objectivity in its totality as a *manufactured product* of five separate workers. The only difference is quantitative, so it must be taken as a simple determination of exteriority: five specialised workers, each performing a single unchanging operation, produce *n* objects in a given period of time, while five skilled workers each performing the whole task from beginning to end will produce *n–x*. The reification of work is undeniable; it is simply a consequence of exploitation. What is striking is that this reified labour, *in so far as it is the praxis of everyone*, regains its synthetic character as a free determination of the practical field *in inorganic matter*. If we know that a particular product can, *a priori* (and given a certain level of technique), be made either by a single skilled worker, with years of apprenticeship, or by five unskilled workers, who have had apprenticeships of only a few months, there is *no* way of telling, without some other source of information, whether a given sample of the product was constituted by a multiplicity of actions, external to one another and determined in passivity, or by a single totalising process.

This first moment of the example shows the absolute homogeneity between a dialectical action which composes itself, and an alienated, decomposed operation, between free temporalisation and expropriated temporality. This homogeneity does not manifest itself in the concrete moment of labour – which is very different in the two cases – but in the synthesis of objectification which is effected in the inertia of the product. The inorganic product, in effect, has this double character: by its passivity, it sustains but inverts the synthetic action which is inscribed in it, and endows it with a hidden exteriority; by its false unity, it holds together, and integrates into a single seal, various different operations, coming from different points in time and space; in it, the unity of a *praxis* becomes a *false unity*, and this false unity becomes a false integration, outside themselves, of an objective diversity of operations.

This observation suggests another: no action is *a priori* incapable of being decomposed into several operations; these operations are passivised and can be grasped by analytical Reason. And some of them, such as the ossified structures of the group, can become the object of an ordinal mathematics. No analytical treatment of these operations is even conceivable if the synthetic point of view of the objective totality is not retained, that is to say, if they are not integrated *in advance* in the produced object as their totalisation: in the same way, analytical Reason *can conceive* a universal combinatory of functions in a given group; it will have the concrete ability to construct it only in so far as it is a special case of dialectical Reason, that is to say, a function produced, directed and controlled by it. There is no action so complex that it cannot be decomposed, dismembered, transformed, and infinitely varied by an 'electronic brain'; it would be impossible to construct or use an 'electronic brain' except within the perspective of a dialectical *praxis* of which the operations under consideration were merely a moment.

But it should be remembered that the deskilling brought about by Taylorism is soon followed by a second moment: that of specialised machines. For in so far as each operation becomes mechanical, each machine can perform an operation. And of course if this operation is performed by a man, it will be *praxis*; but this is because the practical organism has no reality apart from organic *praxis* and because it realises everything it does *in praxis*. By itself the operation already has no specific character. Piling bricks into a truck is a human action if it is done by a man and a mechanical action if entrusted to a machine. Specialisation passes from man to machine, and a worker who is tied to his machine after an apprenticeship of a few weeks, sometimes a few days, is aware of his interchangeability. Finally, through automation, the individual operation, *combined with all the others*, becomes the task of the machine or of the complex of machines; in the end, human action is completely absorbed and re-exteriorised by the passive instrument. However, the product does not change, or at least not much: it presents itself in the synthetic unity of an instrument which is constructed by men, and appropriated by them for the needs and ends of other men. Its inert unity reflects to the consumer the creative power of human labour. And rightly so: for automation itself presupposes an analytical Reason which is sustained and guided, both in the inventor and in the producer, by a dialectical Reason; and also because the new machines, far from eliminating human tasks, merely distribute them differently.

But there is still the objective interchangeability, as it can be observed in the product, of individual *praxis*, of the passive addition of common operations, of production by specialised machines and of automatic machines as a substitute for practical autonomy. From our point of view, this *at least* means that the original *praxis* of the organism serves as a model equally for machines and for groups. Constantly decomposable, and constantly deskilled, it remains untranscendable, and there is no other constituent schema, whatever the type of efficiency being sought. In automation, however, *praxis* becomes pure process, and, with Taylorism, it becomes semi-passivity. These transformations are crucial, but they always occur *below the level of* the final objectification; they must be regarded as *infra-transformations* which leave the goal and the distant ends unchanged as determinations of the field of possibilities. The individual schema contains within itself everything that comes to man through man (with the exception of seriality); it is the practical category *par excellence*. And it is in it, and through its mediation, that the equivalence between the specialised group and the automatic machine can be affirmed.

But, in addition, this example also shows that this practical category guides the analysis of tasks and the construction of instruments, but that it is necessarily negated by this analysis or by this construction – and also by the work of the pledged group on itself – in so far as neither the group, nor the addition of tasks, nor automation can of themselves realise the immediate integration of an action which gives itself its own rules by revealing them as exigencies in the object. Thus, in the case which concerns us here – and the only one which is relevant to the dialectic – the group both seeks and negates *in its being* the only translucid unity of active integration, that is to say, the unity of which the only example is the organism. It both seeks this unity and negates it, by the very means which ought to establish it, and at the same time it realises it by this very means in its objectification (construction, discovery, victory). Now this practical, dialectical, unity which was the group and which causes it to negate it in its very effort at integration, is simply what we have elsewhere called *existence*. The final problem of intelligibility arises on this basis: what must a group be *in its being in order to negate existence in and of itself* and in order to realise its own common ends in the object as the amplification of ends which have been freely posited by practical organisms as free dialectical existences?

5

The Unity of the Group as Other: the Militant

The group derives its unity from outside through others,
and in this initial form its unity exists as other

A group, as the erosion of a seriality, the practical unity of a developing objectification, and the manifestation, immediately suffered by the other, of a specific (positive or negative) efficacy, determines a negative, practical totality in external seriality: *the totality of the non-grouped.* And the not-being-grouped of every Other is the common relation of serial individuals to the grouping totalisation and to every non-grouped Other (as such) within the series. In other words, the Other is *also* determined, as Other, as a *common individual.* Obviously only the particular circumstances can determine, for a given historical group, whether the totality induced in seriality is just an abstract signification or whether the relation between the serial non-grouped and the grouped is a practical, concrete relation. The practical constitution of pigeon-fancying or numismatics clubs, if it occasions any negative unity among the non-grouped, does so in a very abstract way. This is a case of a logical determination. On the other hand, the organised constitution of a fascist militia which specialises in surprise attacks may, according to circumstances, be the occasion of the negative unity of the unarmed population (fear), or even of positive anti-fascist regroupments.

But, above all, when an institutionalised or quasi-institutionalised ensemble (in a few pages we shall see how the group leads to the institution) appears to have some public utility (given a more or less developed division of labour, where it takes on a given task, so relieving Others of it *in so far as they are serial*), it will produce a totality of dependence in the serial flight of the Other; in other words, it will determine its *consumers*. These consumers may remain in a state of recurrence (the customers of the post office, for example) or else – in circumstances which we have already described – the inducing group may occasion an induced group (the state's quasi-monopoly of education induces a Parents' Association corresponding to the practical community of secondary education).

In considering this new practical category, that of the non-grouped practically engendered by the group, we must recognise that it can take various concrete forms: the volunteers who march past with their arms, after the first victories of an insurrection, and who display themselves to the people who have not been fighting (but who, for the most part, support them) as 'those who defend, or liberate *them*', produce a *lateral totalisation* whose structure actually involves other groups: 'the king's army', or 'the bandits', are in fact the true inducing groups, having already totalised the population of a district or town (by attempting extermination). On the basis of this inducement, a group constitutes itself on seriality. But the passive ensemble (women, children, etc.) turns out to be designated by a double contradictory *praxis*: the enemy (at least this is the aim which is interiorised by the concrete certainty of the people, which, indeed, is always true – in a sense that will become clear later) totalises through a vacuum: the *whole* town will be razed to the ground; the group which resists the enemy totalises *by the negation of a negation*. But at the same time, as a totalising negation occasioned by and resisting the external negation, it *reconstitutes* the negative totality of the non-combatants into a seriality of impotence, in opposition to the exterminators; they will be *those who are defended*, but their relation within the town will still be either an inert gathering or molecular isolation (both these statutes exist, one when the housewife – whose husband is on the ramparts or the fortifications – is queueing for food, and the other when she tries, in her home, to preserve her family in conditions which become more difficult day by day). However, this seriality, haunted by a passive, induced unity, is thereby subject to a certain modification: the proof of this is that, if circumstances deteriorate, a new section of the population may be incorporated into the defence group and other sections may be organised to back up the first (a health committee, a supply committee, etc.). The initial unity of the non-combatants is *the unity of those who suffer their seriality*; and this seriality, conceived as *suffered*, as socialised impotence, amounts to the beginnings of a recognition of recurrence and of alterity.

The post office, on the other hand, as a public service which functions smoothly and permanently, initially constitutes *its customers* as a serial exigency, although its complex, totalising work becomes, for the 'public', a common interest, that is to say, the basic possibility of totalising itself so as to protect or control the functioning of this organised group. In any case, whatever the induced relation, as a tension between seriality and unification, may be, the totalisation of the group is an inducer for the social ensemble (which, for the moment, we are treating as a set of groups and serialities). It is so as a purely formal determination, in so far as the group leaves the unity of the non-grouped outside itself by a negative totalisation; and it is so above all as a practical determination in so far as this same group has practical relations with the non-group; and lastly it is so – as we shall see later – in so far as the group – on the basis of a certain social volume, which varies according to circumstances – expresses in itself the society as a whole, in the form of a totalisation. Through this totalising relation of transcendent (*transcendante*) multiplicity, the group realises itself as the first historical mediation between the practico-inert and practical freedom as sociality. But it is not from this point of view that it concerns us at present. We are describing its effect on seriality only in order to explain how modified seriality reacts on the community which modifies it.

Indeed, from the moment in which the group becomes a mediation between the non-grouped, they become – either in the individuality of each, or in the alterity of the collective, or in an initial developing totalisation – a mediation between the members or the sub-groups of the community. If I am a postal clerk, with the task of registering postal orders or parcels, my relation to my bosses passes through the mediation of others, of those who queue in front of my counter (seriality). And each of these individuals perceives the totalisation of the group as a completed, fully functioning totality; this totality is constituted, of course, as a totalisation of functions and instruments; and the serial individual's serial thought expires in the practico-inert field and implicitly conceives common individuals as instruments, and inorganic instruments as living functions, as absolutely equivalent. When a customer hands a registered parcel to a post-office clerk, or puts an express letter in the special box for such letters, he sets in motion an operation which begins, in the one case, with a relation between men (though not necessarily with a human relation) and, in the other case, with a relation to inorganic instruments. But in both cases the entire operation presupposes both instruments and men to use them in a particular perspective. And for the customer the practical character of the juridical exigency is that the user makes no distinction between the instruments and the men. Ought we to say that in this respect he is conditioned by his practico-inert field? The answer is both yes and no: his practico-inert thought, as an interiorisation of his impotence, certainly encourages him to perceive the group as a unity which seals an inorganic passivity. But, on the other hand, his relation as a user to the common instrument and to the common individual is a free juridical relation;[64] and, from this point of view, his individual operation is narrowly confined within the operation of the clerk as a common individual: the clerk reads, corrects, or recopies the forms which the customer fills in in order to send his parcel, etc.; a reciprocity is established which qualifies him from a certain point of view as *common* (a common beneficiary and a common starting-point, that is to say, communised by the common aspect of the operation, its pledged inertia becoming its own past guaranteed by the pledge of the others and by a form or receipt which is handed to him).

There is, therefore, a certain practical homogeneity between the customer and the clerk, to precisely the extent that the initial operation creates a practical reciprocity *across* the real limits of the group (and material ones, in the inorganic sense: for instance, the counter) and by connecting the exteriority of the customer to the interiority of the clerk. Now, from the point of view of this practical homogeneity (that is to say, from the free point of view of pledged faith), the customer will discover, as such, the active unity of men and instruments in the 'service'. On this occasion unity is created in another sense, as the dissolution of instrumentality and multiplicity in the act. This is what one feels whenever one performs one of those everyday actions which involve a public service: *posting a letter*, in one sense, for a particular Parisian, is to put it in his uncle's letter-box in Marseilles, or, in other words, to put it into a hollow pipe which sucks it up like a vacuum cleaner and finally deposits it on the table of the addressee; and it is also – since circumstances vary, for example one may learn that a

---

64. Right and power grow from the pledge and from function, and consequently *inside the group*. But *on the basis* of free, pledged inertia and in the context of a common *praxis*, the group acquires the ability to give a power over itself to non-grouped individuals or to external groups, either in the form of contractual reciprocity (through inertia pledged in the Other from outside), or in any other form.

particular letter-box was closed in a particular part of Paris without the users being told and that hundreds of letters therefore went astray – to entrust an important message to the many hands of a free, pledged, but fallible organisation. The post office is *my instrument*, it is an extension of my arm, like a cane, a spade or a broom, or it is a free, pledged action which gives me a power but which may also fail me. What is involved here is not the two opposed terms of a dilemma, but rather two limits between which there are many possible intermediaries. And, in a sense we encounter once again process and *praxis* as we defined them above.

However, precisely to the extent that the original relation is *a power* (of the customer over the group, or of the organised group over the inorganic gathering), those who are not grouped still recognise both aspects (or the synthesis of them) on the basis of a pledged inertia which constitutes for their practice the interior of the group. Whether instrument or organisation, the group must be responsive to the exigency of the customer (or the massified individual to the exigency of the group): if the instrument alone is visible (the plane for its passengers), it *must* function as a free common function; and if men appear in their mediated inertia, they must respond to the exigency. This *second* freedom is not transparent, individual *praxis*; it is common freedom, determined by its limits, grasped by a freedom which is *common* to every user (despite its preserved seriality). And this common freedom defines the character of the common *praxis* for the customer in so far as it is expressed by a tension which affects the whole group (the *whole* postal system and the whole of France is penetrated by the pledged *praxis* which carries a letter from Lille to Nice). Thus the Other (the customer) posits the grouped totality as a *practical object* whose *exis* is pledged freedom; he posits this totality as producing totalising actions and as manifesting itself as a whole in these *practical expressions* of itself. At the same time, the customer posits the individuals who compose it (and the instruments which are in them) as inessential particularities. Or rather: as he proceeds from need to the practical power which the group confers on him, and from this power to the apparatuses which the group produces to give him satisfaction, he sees each person (as a common individual) as an *a posteriori* specification produced by the group in the course of its development. And this is not untrue, for the common individual is a product of the pledge; but at the same time the organic individual remains indeterminate for him: he sees the clerk as a human generality specified and signified by the total group and does not (or not necessarily: in fact, very rarely) know the details of the individual and his free *praxis*. He does not see this *praxis* as an individual mediation between function and concrete result, but as the free production of a preliminary operation by the group through an individual organ: the phrases and letters which correspond to the recording of a number of parcels, and which are specified in contact with the individual parcel which is to be recorded, are traced as the group-*praxis* through the otherwise indistinguishable hands of these particular clerks. Generally speaking, individuality will be grasped as pure negativity (clumsiness, slowness, lack of intelligence or courtesy), in short as the brute resistance of matter to freedom. Furthermore, this is another case of a reciprocity (usually based on scarcity, and particularly on the scarcity of time), for in the moment at which the operation-exigency of the customer constitutes me as an inessential product of the community and treats function, in me, as an essential line of force of the totality as such, I, as the clerk, treat him as an interchangeable member of a series, who exists for me only as a support of a precise, general exigency (or as an inessential member produced by a grouped totality: for example, for me, as a teacher, or a representative of the Parents' Association). Of course the relations between the administrator and the customer can become individualised: this happens, for example, if the reciprocal operations take place frequently. But this individualisation reveals a free reciprocity with no practical relation to their practical, functional bonds.

Thus by the mere juridical exigency of the customer, the user, etc., the Other dissolves me into my group as a part into the totality and dissolves my free practice into the juridical freedom of common *praxis*. He then constitutes this totality, which digests and transforms external solicitations, and responds to it with a totalising and totalised operation as a *being in interiority*. In effect, the structure of the group, which must correspond to the power of the user, cannot be anything but pledged inertia, and consequently *Being* – but *Being* conceived as a *norm* (as the counterpart to a power). Thus, from the outset, we see the identification by the Other *of Being and of having-to-be* and this radical identity will constitute for the Other the ontological statute of the organised group. But this *required-being* is constituted through certain relations of interiority, since the customer understands the group, through his own action, as a synthetic operation defined by its aim and by the unity of its means. In this way, the 'being/norm' contradiction is resolved: for the Other, Being as pledged inertia arises in the form of totality (or, so to speak, the totality-object can exist only if inorganic inertia, seen as an *invariable being*, sustains it), but this inert totality is structured in interiority. So its inert being is produced in interiority as a norm of common freedom. On the basis of this norm, the totality produces its differentiations not as totalising efforts, but as diverse expressions of the totalised whole. The being of the whole, lived in interiority, becomes a normative scheme which occasions the production of total operations, and these operations, as interiorised practices, produce their own men and instruments. For the user, the public service is an object with an *interior*, that is to say, an internal milieu with its own tension, its index of refraction, its web, its spatio-temporal directions, its structures and its reflexivity. What is involved is, therefore, what might be called practical intersubjectivity as a milieu of the totalised totality. And this intersubjectivity does not relate to any abstract or 'collective' consciousness: it is quite simply the reflexive structure of the group as seen by the user.

Now the member of the group, that is to say, the common individual, the clerk, realises himself practically in the reciprocal operation which unites him to the customer or user as an inessential product of reflexive intersubjectivity: this means quite simply that the determination of inessentiality comes upon him on the basis of *the Other* and that he has to assume it through his operation itself. In short, I produce myself through the Other and for myself as an inessential, passing mode of the intersubjectivity of my group in so far as I operate with and on the Other on behalf of this group. And in the practice itself I perceive myself as an objective expression *for the other* of a totality, whereas the internal movement of the community which is not mediated by strangers is given reflexively as a simple developing totalisation.

This will appear still more clearly when the other mediators between the members of the group become for each member, not only through their actions but also *through their material density*, the real factor of his separation, of his isolation; when their resistance (either inert and serial or organised) conditions the possibilities of his communicating with his comrades in the group. This happens very often: however close the internal bonds may be, it is rare for a group to be constantly actualised, that is to say, gathered together in its entirety in a particular place. Besides, in many cases, these plenary meetings are *a priori* impossible: for example, the sheer size of the group may preclude any real gathering; political parties hold *conferences* in which each individual is the representative of several others. Thus each member of the group is temporarily or permanently set apart from the other members by the forest of humanity. For example, a militant in a non-underground party is constituted – as a common individual – by his fidelities (the pledge) and by his practical functions (which assign him a given place of residence in a particular town). But at the same time the forest of humanity which surrounds him is, like Macbeth's, active and alive. Its density is material and practical: the human environment treats him (whether with favour, contempt, hostility, trust or mistrust, etc.) as a party militant. That is to say, the serial or common practice of the Others constitutes him *on the basis* of the political and social programme, of the present action and of the past history of his party. His individual practice – with its style and colour, its skill or incompetence, etc. – intervenes only *a posteriori* and lacks efficacity and therefore reality except within a very narrow framework (for example, in relationships with other militants or sympathisers or with a layer of sympathisers who hesitate to join). But in the first instance the overt militant is constituted in his being as a normative inertia in so far as, in a period of political tension, for example, the positions of Others are adopted, harden, and become unshakeable.

However, it would be a mistake to think that these attitudes of trust or hostility are directed towards him as *a particular* Communist, for example, or *a particular* Socialist. The force or violence of these practices of themselves signify that they are directed at the Party through any inessential individual. When fascist terrorism or lynchings are directed against *one* Communist, in sole charge of some office, it is to the Communist that they are directed: that is to say, they are directed at the Party as a present and essential totality through an inessential individual whom they never consider in his individuality. But, to take a simpler and more everyday case, the political discussions between a given opponent or enemy and a particular militant are not aimed at convincing him, but at refuting the Party in his person; and the interlocutor systematically ignores the personal limitations of the individual (slowness, lack of education, lack of aggression, or poor projection: someone else might have given a better answer, or routed the enemy): in any case, his reactions are those of the group as a totality which is embodied in each of its temporary modalities. Conversely, the militant finds himself constrained by this *practical separation*, to which he is subjected by the human environment, to interiorise this relation between the inessential and the essential and between the part and the whole. He constitutes himself as a *signifier* to precisely the extent that he appears to all as *signified*. In effect, it becomes extremely important for the common practice that it is impossible either to confound his free individual practice with the *praxis* of the Party as such, or to judge the latter in terms of the former. And since the ordinary manoeuvres of the entourage consist either in penetrating the acquired characteristics of the individual without seeing them in order to go straight to the Party as his sole profound reality or, on the other hand, in taking individual characteristics, and isolated weaknesses, and making them into the common reaction of the political group as a totality, the isolated militant tries to dissolve personal characteristics in himself so as to make himself merely the local presence of the Party in totality. It is irrelevant that the militant is fair-haired, and has a stammer, or that he is intelligent or stupid: he makes himself *for all* what all make him, namely, the *non-specified* embodiment of a centralised mass revolutionary Party, etc., which gets six million votes at each election and which takes up and elaborates the exigencies of its electors and members. He becomes *exigency-being, accusation-being;* and he *learns the common thought* both as a determination of memory and as a pledge, in such a way as to make certain that this normative inertia will be reproduced in him as *the same* as in all the other mouths of the Party.[65]

But this transformation, which happens concretely under the pressure of the Others, is not an individual initiative: it expresses what the group – through its organs of mediation, liaison and direction, and through each particular sub-group (cells, committees, or sections, whatever they may be called) – requires of each of its members in so far as they are all isolated and besieged. However, the formal rigidity of the identification with the whole is accompanied by complete confusion as to its material content. In so far as he has imprinted certain functional relations on himself, the militant has at his disposal an ideology which enables him always to take stock of the situation and which, through his mouth, gives the common interpretation of the historical situation by the militant totality as a determination of discourse.[66]

65. This is not a stratification of discourse in memory, but a stratification of the relations which determine discourse.

66. This interpretation will have been devised by leaders in a specific sub-group, taking account of all the circumstances and, amongst other things, of the implicit exigencies of the practical community. These leaders may be perfectly competent; they may have public confidence and they may deserve it. But nothing can prevent a radical transformation when a militant who is isolated (or in an embattled minority) takes up – as a thought produced by the totality of 'the

But, at the same time, individuals – through the indefinite recurrence of the serial – or enemy groups – by systematically appropriating his action – divert or dissolve the *significations* which he gives to his practice and to the course of things, both here and for every *same* in every other *here*. Refracted by a dark density, bristling with projects and actions which elude him, these significations become indeterminate objects or – and this comes to the same thing – objects with thousands, or hundreds of thousands, of facets. When the militant publicly re-affirms the abstract, schematic determination of discourse, he immediately reveals, to everyone, the Party as a group-totality. But it remains schematic, and the more it identifies him with the group, the more it cuts him off from reality. It should be clear that what we are discussing here is not the political difficulties of any particular situation: I am simply trying to show that the forest of humanity – as materiality and as the *praxis* of isolation – must, for the militant, be interiorised as the *ubiquity of the group*. But we have seen that this ubiquity – which, despite the pledge and the heterogeneity produced, remains fluid as long as the relations of common individuals are direct – freezes and ossifies as soon as it is affirmed in opposition to the practice of the non-grouped. At the moment in which the group as a totality-object becomes an abstract schematisation for the militant, he becomes unable to comprehend either his own organic *praxis*, or that of the others, or the concrete course of events. But, at the same time, he refers to what he realises as his common reality constantly and for his every decision, that is to say, to the Party as a normative inertia and a completed totality, as pure objectivity and inter-subjectivity (that is to say, possessing an interiority), in short, as a substance which is total everywhere and which recreates its own instructions everywhere.

But it should not be forgotten that this new constitution comes to the member of the group *through Others*. This means that it arises *in the milieu of alterity* and that he adopts it in accordance with his functional relations to the non-grouped. Thus this structure, as the practical instrument of his operations, represents in everyone his Being in the milieu of the Other and the practical reinteriorisation of the Other-

---

Party', that is to say, as a totally *expressive exis* of this totality – a practical decision, taken by a few common individuals (in the name of all in virtue of their powers, of course) and reinteriorised in a practical movement of reorganisation by every common individual, that is to say, by each inessential embodiment of the group as an essential substance.

Being of the group. For it is in its objectivity for the Other that the group can superficially appear as a totality.[67] And it is clear that in itself, as an internal relation, it becomes a totalisation. On the other hand, the structure of embodiment (the inessentiality of the individual, and the present essentiality of the whole) is not lived by the organised member for and in itself; he does not grasp it in the reflexive unity of an organising action which has the totalisation of the group as its direct objective: he produces it through the mediation of the Other as the controlling schema of his relations to the Other. Thus it is important to recognise that the practical and theoretical object, for the person in the group, is the Other and that he does not grasp his own reality as an inessential embodiment except as an implicit rule of action and as a signification which is discovered and projected onto the Other in the course of the antagonistic reciprocity of combat or of argument. This univocal relation to the Party or to the Group (his being-in-the-group being lived as the dissolution of the part in favour of the whole) can never be either the *aim* of his action or the *object* of any intuitive, practical certainty. Nor is it ever explicitly formulated, unless it is first formulated by others. It is an empty knowledge, and also an inertia which is received and suffered, but interiorised into an abstract pledge and re-exteriorised into stereotyped actions (or rather actions whose relational structures tend to be stereotyped) and a sort of regressive intentionality aimed at relating every particular circumstance, as a pure accident, to the totality as a substance which digests and dissolves all concrete reality (as inessential). And, in a way, if one is careful to avoid equivocations, one can say that the *praxis* of the militant – when he is connected to other third parties by the mediation of the forest of humanity – brings a certain alienation to the group; this is because he experiences, as a bond of interiority to the totalising organisation, a relation of exteriority to the group-object (as an *exterior* object) which is

67. It is worth recalling what was said above: that any grasp of a group in the practical field is a totalisation by the individual who is not grouped, and that this totalisation formally engenders a totality-object. But if the group is given in its actual operation, then, as we have seen, this totality proclaims itself as an appearance in so far as it makes it possible to perceive the object as a *totalisation* independent of the individual synthesis. The *totality* remains as what calls a halt both to investigation and to *praxis* when the group gets too large, too ramified, or too complex to offer itself in its entirety. Thus the sub-groups which are present, though they are totalisations, appear as inert embodiments of a totality which is referred to in a vacuum.

precisely the relation of the Other to the inert totality which he has reinteriorised as a defence.

Nevertheless, he is constituted by a complex relation, composed of two opposite mediations: the Other's mediation between the common individual and the group-object; and the group-object's mediation between the common individual as an agent and the Other as the object of his action. And the abstract meaning of this relation – as an empty, inert, and formal intention – is still fundamental: going back through the everyday practices of the agent in relation to pledged inertia, this relation indicates the immanence of the individual in the intersubjective totality, that is to say, the dissolution of the mode into the substance or, in other words, the fusion of individual organisms into a hyper-organism, as *the future which has to be realised* once the group as such is fully assembled.

6

The Institution

In the interiority of the group, the movement of mediated reciprocity
constitutes the unity of the practical community as a perpetual
detotalisation engendered by the totalising movement

1 Mediated Reciprocity in the Group

When, at a Party conference or demonstration, the militant is put back
into the midst of the group, or when the clerk, ceasing to communicate
with his colleagues through the medium of the customers, turns back
to them and rediscovers the direct bonds of the organisation, their
expectations are disappointed and their relation to all is metamorphosed: for they rediscover the real milieu of immanence, to precisely
the extent that it is impossible for them to dissolve into it; and, to
precisely the extent that alienation to the group-object disappears with
the Other, they rediscover a community which could never become a
totality-subject. At this level, in effect, where the organisation takes
itself as an immediate objective in the light of a transcendent aim,
being-in-the-group is no longer, for everyone, mediated over there by
the Other; instead it is mediated here *by the same* (by the negated
multiplicity of *every same*). It would be pointless here to enumerate and
describe the intermediate mediations which actually give the being-of-
the-group its inconceivable complexity: for example, I may, through
the absent, abstract Other, communicate *with the same* (*avec les
mêmes*) in a concrete, reciprocal relation (there have been complaints
about a particular clerk and he has to explain his behaviour, etc.). It
will be sufficient to contrast the two extreme, opposed relations: on the
one hand, alienation to the totality and the false bond of interiority
which constitutes the group through everyone as an inter-subjective
substance whose Being is defined both by inertia and by having to be
(*le devoir-être*); and on the other hand, the relation of true interiority

through mediated reciprocity, the practical recognition of functions, of sub-groups and of individuals through totalising reorganisation.

But if we examine this being-of-the-group in immanence more closely, we will discover a new statute of intelligibility. We have seen that organisations are based on a pledge. Everyone pledges himself to remain the same. This pledge occasions a first contradiction in that it becomes the basis of the heterogeneity of functions. And this contradiction produces another, since it is free individual *praxis* which, through individual action, realises the detail of the common objectification. Thus the urgency of danger and of need is reflected not only in 'fraternity-terror', as a relation of indissolubility and violence, but also in more complex structures whose necessary effect is to allay terror and mask fraternity. This would be unimportant; but as we have seen the fundamental integration of the third party into the group is performed through mediated reciprocity. And by fundamental integration, we mean both the individual's *coming-to-the-group* (as the initial movement of grouping) and the permanent act of totalisation which is carried out by and for everyone in various forms and through the complex evolution of the group in action. Now, this mediated reciprocity, despite mediation, retains its original structure as a detotalised duality (with a double centre); and this detotalised duality manifests itself here, within the movement of integration, and through a temporal dislocation of the totalisation, as reciprocal *praxis*. Indeed, when describing the fused group, we noted the main features of the *regulatory third party*, in particular what we called his relation of immanence-transcendence to the group of which he was a part. Let us return to this point, now that we are more familiar with common structures, and describe it more fully. And, in order to concentrate on one example, let us imagine that two individuals, A and B, in the course of a common action, totalise themselves reciprocally, both with and in the group, through mediated reciprocity.

This totalisation is practical. We are not concerned here with ritual recognitions, which have no objective aim other than to preserve the bonds of interiority; we are concerned with reciprocities which are already organised and functional: the concrete relation between two powers which come together in order to produce a given result in the objective. In this sense, every function integrates the other into the differentiated totalisation through their heterogeneity seen as reciprocal. The regulatory act performed by A – that is to say, his practical behaviour as defined by the common individual A – does not arise in

B as such (unlike what happens in fused groups). But, through the reciprocal grasp of the common field, the act remains regulatory because it occurs in a signifying totalisation, the meaning of which is known to both agents, and because the two agents are themselves reciprocal products of the organisation: they have been formed, trained and equipped in such a way that B could see a forecast of his future action in that of A. (Thus in the common field of the football match, on the basis of the common game and the given conditions, each movement of each back is regulatory for the actions of the goalkeeper.)

Now, the structure of the regulatory act is complex: it is, in a sense, a limited affirmation of sovereignty. By sovereignty, in effect, I mean the absolute practical power of the dialectical organism, that is to say, purely and simply its *praxis* as a developing synthesis of any given multiplicity in its practical field, whether inanimate objects, living things or men. This rearrangement – in so far as it is performed by the organic individual – is the starting-point and milieu of all action (whether successful or unsuccessful). I call it sovereignty because it is simply freedom itself as a project which transcends and unifies the material circumstances which gave rise to it and because the only way to deprive anyone of it, is to destroy the organism itself.[68] In conditions in which this rearrangement of the diverse into a totalised field is also realised by action as material transformation of this field in its internal configuration and real content, sovereignty is not only *absolute* but also *total*. Now, at first sight, this regulatory action – whether it occurs in a fused group or in an organised group – resembles the exercise of absolute, total sovereignty. The play of A practically totalises the group: in fact, for its part and in this moment, it defines the orientation of the *praxis* and the momentary organisation of all; through individual readjustments and owing to the power of each over all, a particular run or breakthrough will arrange the entire team in a certain practical order (the meaning of which, for example, may be both to support the manoeuvre and to anticipate a counter-attack). Through this totalisation of the team and by means of it (*for* it) B will be inte-

---

68. But it is very important not to conclude that one can be free in chains. Freedom is a complete dialectical development, and we have seen how it can become alienated or bogged down or allow itself to be caught by the traps of the Other and how simple physical constraint is enough to mutilate it. But still even the most oppressed slave, simply in order to be obedient to his master, both can and must perform a synthesis of the practical field.

grated into the structured whole: he will realise this practical integration by determining his own position on the basis of the present state of play, of the tactics being used, of the order adopted by all and of his own special function. Thus, A's sovereignty will define the mode of integration of B into the group in his operation; and A will totalise B, C, D, E, etc., by means of his regulatory action.

But if the exercise of sovereignty were complete, the sovereign would have to be external to the group and to totalise it as totality-object in his practical field. We should then encounter a type of relation which we have already defined: *either*, in its crude, fundamental form, the univocal synthetic bond between the agent and the (material and human) environment *or*, in an elaborated form, the relation, *both* in interiority *and* in exteriority, of the *customer* as Other to the clerk. Now, we are aware of the limit of this sovereign synthesis: it is that the bond is not univocal but reciprocal, that the regulatory third party integrates himself into the group in so far as his regulatory action succeeds in integrating me into it. *His* practical field, and *mine*, and *ours*, are one and the same. Thus sovereignty is limited by its very reciprocity; everyone is sovereign: but it should not be inferred that no one is. On the contrary: since each is sovereign over the sovereignty of all, at the same time as being the organised object of each practical synthesis in interiority, he ought to be described as quasi-sovereign and quasi-object; and the group itself, in so far as it is totalised by the practice of a given common individual, is an objective quasi-totality and, as a negated multiplicity of quasi-sovereignties, it is in a state of perpetual *detotalisation*. In fact, the dislocation which, in the practical temporalisation, separates the moment where A becomes the regulatory third party from the moment in which B in turn is a regulator, constitutes B's being-in-the-group, as well as A's, as an ambivalent statute of interiority. In so far as B *adapts himself* to the initiative of A, he defines himself practically as a restructured element of this collective materiality (suffered and pledged inertia) which each third party, as a third party, reunifies in his quasi-sovereignty. His objective, practical truth (that is to say, the action to be performed, as *signified* in interiority by other third parties) therefore comes to him through A as quasi-sovereign, through common mediation; he grasps it through his action, which submissively realises the regulatory signification. But, by submitting – and in conformity with intentions which have come from outside, by means of the Other and interiorised by himself – B tries to realise the unity of immanence as the fusion of the mode into the substance; but in fact, this unity is destroyed by the simple fact that his action, as a free mediation between the common individual and the common objective, by a practical organism, realises the synthetic objectification of the group in the worked object by negating his interiority of immanence in and by his dialectical development, that is to say, by negating his being as an inessential mode in relation to the essential substance. Wherever the action develops freely, he posits himself as essential (if only as a detail) through its very development. At one and the same moment, therefore, B not only manifests his being-integrated-into-the-group as a practical and objective integration based on his inability to integrate himself *ontologically* into a substance, but also, at the same time, in the mediated reciprocity which harnesses his actions to the regulatory action of A, he sees himself by and through A as an integrated element of a quasi-objective totalisation performed by a quasi-sovereignty.

But this ambivalence – which is simply a developing contradiction – also refers B to his own sovereignty; in becoming the third party through whose mediation B will rediscover himself *over there*, merged and organised with the others in the inter-subjective substance, A forces B to *recognise* him, in a new movement of reciprocity, as the third party who has the power to integrate (and not as the abstract sovereignty of the individual organism), and therefore as a member of the group. In other words, B has to see A as a simple modality of inter-subjectivity (a definite function as the specification of the substance by itself), and this will force him, *in A and in all*, to snatch himself away from the common substance – that is, away from the integrating operation – so as to become a mediation between the individual A and his common-being-in-the-group. A therefore becomes not only, for B (and by means of B), an *alter ego* (the same – positive reciprocity) but also an *excluded third party* (as a quasi-sovereignty: a quasi-exile, the tension of immanence-transcendence); and B, by means of A and in the same conditions, also becomes an *excluded third party* and an *alter ego*. Everyone can and must be determined *over there* in his inessentiality in relation to the group through the integrating sovereignty of the other – who becomes the provisional *subject of the group*. But in order for this operation to take place outside him by means of the *alter-ego*, everyone must posit himself in his irreducible essentiality as the one who (with all the others) guarantees the Other's membership of the group by means of his pledge, his powers and his action.

Thus, in the pledge with which B becomes, through his practical subjection to the regulatory action, the object of an integration which is mediated over there in A, he constitutes the group as detotalised (or helps to do so): through his obedience he produces A as a quasi-sovereign, and therefore as quasi-excluded; and in the moment in which he grounds this quasi-sovereignty by a mediated recognition of A's powers and functions – that is to say, of his concrete membership of the group – he produces himself as regulatory (either for A or *for Others*; as when he acts as a guarantor for A and declares to the Others, in the name of his own powers: he must be followed, helped, obeyed, etc.), and so realises in his person the quasi-exile of quasi-sovereignty. However, it cannot be denied that the interiority of relations, my common being's intimate membership of the whole, the inessentiality of my own existence (in so far as *we are the same*) and the essentiality of my function as a structured relation to the totality, are all practical truths: and the proof of them is that, in a living group, they are realised and verified every day by concrete action; discipline, self-sacrifice, etc., are practical affirmations of all these truths. But in fact, in the living milieu of interiority, these truths, as determinations of my ontological statute, appear only in a perspective of flight and as a *quasi-transcendent* meaning of immanence. My real membership of *this* particular group as a transcendent rule of my concrete life is realised in me as a lived impossibility that my *group-being* should merge with those of other members in an undifferentiated ontological totality. From this point of view, each of my regulatory actions appears as a false totalisation, detotalised, in fact, by the surety which all the Others give me; and my guaranteed sovereignty never becomes transcendent sovereignty; and none of my regulated actions ever succeeds in submerging me in immanence since it is itself a surety for the regulatory action which occasioned it. *Being-in-the-group*, in interiority, is manifested through a double, agreed failure: it is being unable to leave and also unable to integrate oneself into it; in other words, being unable either to dissolve it in oneself (pledged inertia), or to dissolve oneself in it (practical unity being the absolute contradiction of ontological unity). However, *the being-one* of the group does exist: it is pledged inertia, *the same* in everyone, that is to say, one's own freedom become other through the mediation of the Other. But apart from the fact that this *inert-being* (*être-inerte*) resolves itself, on examination, into a tight web of inert, mediated reciprocities (and thus loses its appearance of unity), it cannot be regarded as the real ontological statute of the group, since it is in fact a means of producing practical differentiations. To reduce the being of the group to the set of its inertia-means (*inerties-moyens*) is to transform this basically practical organisation – which exists only through its action – into a skeleton of relations capable of being treated by an ordinal calculus. But the illusion remains as an essential structure of any community, for two fundamental reasons.

First, the violence and coercive force of *fraternity-terror* as a true relation of interiority between the members of the group are based on the myth of *rebirth*; they define and produce the traitor as absolute evil to precisely the extent that they define him as the man who destroyed *the previous unity*. In other words, both terror and the pledge relate to the deep fear of a dissolution of unity. They therefore posit it as the essential security and as the justification of any repressive violence. But the basic contradiction of the group – which is not resolved by the pledge – is that its real unity lies in common *praxis* or, to be precise, in the common objectification of this *praxis*. When the community affirms itself as the reign of common freedom, it cannot in fact – whatever it does – either realise the free interpenetration of individual freedoms or find an inert *being-one* which is common to all freedoms.

Secondly, for those who are not grouped and for other groups (rivals, enemies, allies, etc.), the group is an object. It is a living totality. And, as we have seen, it has to interiorise this objectivity. It would be pointless here to examine the dialectical relations between groups and show how they are determined through their oppositions, each in relation to the others, and how they are transformed by interiorising their being-for-the-other and even, in certain circumstances, the being-for-others of the other, as their own immanent being. This has already been done many times – though never very rigorously. The only point that has to be remembered is that, as we have seen, the group is seen in its totalised unity by the ensemble of the others and that this pressure is so strong that even in its relations of pure interiority it interiorises this unity as its *being-from-behind* (*être-de-derrière*), that is to say, in the last analysis, as the material but synthetic source which sustains and produces it. Thus, in its developing reorganisation, it perpetually refers to its deepest interiority which is in reality only its most abstract exteriority. There is a *being-X* of the group – as its transcendental reality – and this is produced at an infinite degree of compression and gathers together the totalised ensemble of its structures, of its past and of its future in so far as they are externally the common object of the ignorance of Others; and this *being-X* as the pure abstract object of a regressive intention becomes the interiorisation of the ignorance of Others, that is, the meaning and historical destiny of the group in so far as they are the object of its own ignorance.

2 *Purges and Terror*

This untranscendable conflict between the individual and the common, which oppose and define each other and each of which returns into the other as its profound truth, is naturally manifested in new contradictions within the organised group; and these contradictions are expressed by a new transformation of the group; the organisation is transformed into a hierarchy, and pledges give rise to institutions. This is of course not a historical sequence; and indeed we shall see that – on account of dialectical circularity – any form can emerge either before or after any other and that only the materiality of the historical process can determine the sequence. The only purpose of arranging them in a series is to indicate the complex characteristics which are to be found in most concrete groups; our investigation proceeds from the simple to the complex because it is both formal and dialectical and it does so as it proceeds from the abstract to the concrete.

If we look at it closely, we can see that the basis of terror is the fact that the group has not, and cannot have, the ontological statute which it claims in its *praxis*; conversely, it is that each and all are produced and defined in terms of this non-existent totality. There is a sort of internal vacuum, an unbridgeable and indeterminate distance, a sort of malaise in every community, large or small; and this uneasiness occasions a strengthening of the practices of integration, and increases with the integration of the group.

It should be realised, in fact, that the conflict between the essential and inessential is not at all theoretical: it is a permanent danger both for the group and for the common individual. In fact the *pledge* posits the inessentiality of the organic individual by making it impossible for him to dissolve the group in himself; besides it is obvious that, in every structure, the presence of the developing totalisation in the individual part also indicates the importance of every part and their interchangeability; finally, the Other treats the organic individual as a general reality which can be ignored, and tries simply to approach the group through the mediation of the common individual; and as we have seen, this inessentiality of exteriority is also interiorised. It is at this level that the group-individual is defined by the practices of all the members, within the community, as a common individual. He is a determinate function, power and competence: the practical relation with this contradictory being (freedom becoming a legal claim through the transcendence of free, pledged inertia) is *juridical* and *ceremonious*: even outside action, each relation within the group is a reciprocal recognition of attributions and of the system of 'rights and duties'.

Attempts have sometimes been made to base the transition from the repressive to the restitutive, from violence to contract, from contempt for life to respect for the human person, on the historical differentiation of functions. The individual, as such, is presented as a product of the division of labour. But these arguments are senseless: they only express the common wish to reduce the practical organism to its social function. Now, conflict occurs precisely *at this level*; in relation to the common operation, each function has a *relative* importance and therefore the common individual is inessential or relatively essential; but in relation to carrying out *this particular social task*, the practical organism is *an essential mediation*. Of course this does not mean that any particular individual, as a specific product of History, is indispensable for the task which the group has assigned to him. This may happen in makeshift organisations, but in a group which itself produces the workers it requires, this dependence is automatically eliminated. But this means that – irrespective of the individual and even if he could be immediately replaced – the moment of *praxis* – *that is, the essential moment* – is always that of the free, individual dialectic and of the sovereign organisation of the practical field. No individual is essential to a group which is coherent, well integrated, and smoothly organised; but when anyone realises the mediation between the common individual (who has no real existence except through the organic life of the agent) and the object, he reaffirms his essentiality *in opposition to the group*. And this essentiality has nothing to do with the historical individuality of the operation (or not necessarily), but rather with practical freedom as an indispensable moment of any operation, even in the practico-inert field of alienation. The individual agent has not transcended or betrayed his pledge; he has executed his mission, performed his function; and yet, in a way, he has created a new isolation for himself, as beyond the pledge, as a bracketing of inertia (whether suffered or pledged). In short, through the powers and responsibilities which have actually transformed him, through the instrumentality which increases his power, he has returned to transparency and can realise his fidelity in the group only through a transcendence which removes him from the common statute and projects him into the object outside. However it is lived, this contradiction will be objectively expressed as a permanent danger of exile, or even as real exile. And the fear of being exiled, in reciprocity, gives rise to the fear that the group may be dissolved, as inessential, in the essentiality of individual actions. This is not the fear which, in the fused group, occasioned the pledge: the fear then was that the group might be dissolved *by default* (negative behaviour, rout, abandonment of post, etc.). What is feared now is dissolution *through excess*, and a pledge has no power against this new danger, since it arises precisely *from* pledged fidelity.

But although the structure in reciprocity already extends it to all, even if it is lived in the particularity of individual labour, the contradiction between the inessential and the essential would be no more than a simple cause of disquiet unless it were taken up and amplified by the relation between the regulatory and the regulated action. The counterpart of the integration of each third party into the group is, as we have seen, reciprocal exile; but as each member of the group is the third party through whom integration is effected, it follows from this that the practical realisation of this integration has as a counterpart a shifting exclusion, a circular succession of exiles for each and all. Through the permanent practice of integration and ritual recognition, the group resists the dangers of seriality. But it is precisely these continuous operations which, for everyone, occasion a way of living one's own being-in-the-group as a constant but masked separation, and the being-in-the-group of other third parties as a perpetual danger of secession. Particularly in the case of groups which can meet together or live in a particular place which gives material support to their unity, a contradiction emerges here between geographical position and real relations: if the group is protected by a wall, for example, then I may see myself as *being really in it*, but this only means that I identify its being with that of its container.

In one sense, such an identification is legitimate, since the container (in so far as it has been chosen, defined, and worked, and in so far as it occasions special conduct, etc.) clearly represents the practical materiality of this interiorised multiplicity. But, at the same time, in my relations with the third parties I realise my own tension of immanence-transcendence as the truth of our human relations, and this truth is either that I am not really *in* the group or that my *being-in-it* cannot be taken in a naive way as a relation between content and container. Thus *the interior of the place* as such acts as a basis for my human relation and it aggravates my exile in interiority in so far as membership of the material whole, as a support and expression of the totalisation, is no longer lived as a security, and becomes secondary and slides towards annihilation, although *being-in-the-group*, as the practical interiority of relations, does not emerge in intuitive experience and as a new security: what is realised in everyone is interiority as a spatial bond between the container and its contents *in its inadequacy* and as an anonymous mystification. I am *inside* but I am still afraid that I may be outside. In other words, everyone grasps his quasi-sovereignty (which is nevertheless an indispensable moment of the reorganising re-totalisation) defiantly, as if it threatened to designate him as *essential*: in effect, the synthetic operation of regulation *indicates him* as the final term of the integration, but without integrating him: it therefore isolates him. This did not matter in the moment of the fused group, because differentiated functions had not yet been produced. But when quasi-sovereignty is realised as the exercise of any kind of concrete power over Others and as an individual practice which eludes the pledge (not by transcending it, but through being its basis), the regulatory action is revealed in all its contradictoriness: *intercession-secession*.

And once freedom – seen as the free, organic negation of common freedom and as the free dissolution of deposits of inertia in everyone – becomes afraid of itself, and discovers in anguish its individual dimension, the dangers of impotence and the certainty of alienation which characterise it, and the regulatory third party has become a regulated, integrated, third party, integration by the Other will be revealed to it by dislocated reciprocity both as a danger to sovereignty (through the reification of the group within the practical field of a single individual) and as a danger of exile (which means a danger of being killed – for the third party seen in his implicit secession – as well as a danger of betrayal). What emerges at this level is that mediation by all is itself reciprocity between third parties, each of whom is, in himself, the perpetual explosive contradiction which we have called quasi-sovereignty. In this sense, mediated reciprocity relates to circularity in so far as the relation of the powers A and B depends not only on their reciprocal recognition but also on a series of sovereign recognitions each of which may, depending on concrete circumstances, be either essential or inessential to the unity of the group. (The power relations between two organising sub-groups actually depend on how those who are being reorganised acknowledge the powers of the two 'organs'; on their giving one of them precedence over the other – even if the order of precedence has been fixed the other way round; or on their rejecting them both).

Thus the *being-one* of the group (both as an abstract, ontological aim and as the concrete reality of the detailed objectification) depends on my individual freedom – that is to say, on the movement which constitutes exclusion, physical liquidation and betrayal as real possibilities for me – in so far as my *being-in-the-group* eludes me and constitutes itself in the shifting circularity of regulatory actions (in so far as these *can*, in themselves, and as far as I can tell, become the liquidation of the group or the petrification of the community into an inorganic object).[69] *Separation* as suffered inertia which comes to reinforce pledged inertia increases the tension between sovereign exile and impotent dependence: if the group goes beyond the boundaries of the place or of the container (or if, for some reason, relations within the place, the camp, or the city, are *penetrated* by distance, as happens, for example, with a clandestine action: the work of the enemy police, as the common action of a hostile group, is equivalent to being conditioned by spatiality as practico-inert extension), the quasi-sovereign third party is still *my brother*, but he is also almost or completely unknown. Yet his action does not cease to be regulatory: through the organs of mediation, I may learn that a particular common initiative has begun elsewhere in the spatio-temporal destiny of the practico-inert field, and with others who are present I will define our action as a sub-group *in relation to this initiative*. And of course *elsewhere* is still *here*; but it is a *here* whose special characteristics are essential (because I am anxious to know them) and whose universal ubiquity is an inessential abstraction.

By this shifting flight of reciprocities, everything is finally put in its place, and thus the organised group can, through its own freedom, develop *a circular form of seriality*. And, though it may seem surprising, this appearance of the Other does not present itself as an alienation of

---

69. This second possibility cannot correspond to any real operation; and it manifests itself to everyone as an expression of the freedom of the third party in so far as, through his own practical affirmation, it is a negation of reciprocities in and by a reciprocal act.

praxis to the practico-inert (though this alienation must occur else-where), but as the rediscovery of free individuality as the sole means and the sole obstacle for the constitution of an organised group. In fact, it is the new reaction of negated multiplicity.

Of course, what we have been describing are dialectical possibilities of a purely formal order. By themselves and in their structural for-malism, these implicit contradictions, which relate to *structures common to all groups*, do not and cannot give rise to a revival of seriality within unity, to betrayal or repression by Terror, or to the liquidation of the group. In fact, whatever happens, they *have* to be lived and produced, because they define the intimate contexture of the organised group, and because neither actions nor members can be produced in their concrete reality except through the internal curvatures proper to the groups which produce them. But it is the historical process as a whole and, in a totalising context, particular circumstances, the aims of a group, its past history, its relations with other groups, etc., which will settle how the reciprocal, serial connection of exile-secession will be lived in the concretely differentiated zones of a particular practical community. For example, it is obvious that a relatively small group, which organises the complexity of its apparatuses through a victorious *praxis*, cannot even live its reflexive contradictions in the form of uneasiness: real unity is transcendent and practical, it imposes itself from the future in real modifications of the common object, in the structures of the future revealed by the object (*possibilities* reveal them-selves, *facilities* which absorb action like real exigencies, *crevices* in which *praxis* becomes lost, *short-cuts*, etc.). For the easier, the more urgent and the more glorious this objective future, the more it abridges the mediating behaviour of reflection inside the group: if the organisa-tion can be clearly decoded in the object negatively (*en creux*), if it presents no difficulty in itself, and is indistinguishable from the trans-cendent operation, then it becomes a lateral interaction of reciprocities in the development of a common action. No doubt it will be necessary to sanction and reorganise it; but, for us, the important point is that, when successful, the object provides the ontological unity of the group, at least as the quasi-certainty of each of its members. And this quasi-certainty is not a subjective determination: it is the character and modality which everyone's action has for him, in so far as he sees it *produced as common* in his hands. Failure or – to take a less extreme case – the difficulties of a slow, disappointing action, obviously give rise to reflexion (by raising the question of reorganisation) and make every individual or sub-group live separation as defiance: 'We here are doing what we can . . ., etc.'. In the moment of free individual *praxis*, action displays its contradictions precisely to the extent that its individual success *here* is no longer immediately absorbed by the common success. In itself, personal, localised success tends to posit itself for itself as an essential moment all the more when common success seems compromised or more distant. And separation occurs in each individual agent to precisely the extent that the local success of his action produces in the object an incomplete determination which signifies nothing (since the true, intelligible meaning of the action, of the complete development of the practical individual, lies only in common realisation) and which *demands* (objective exigency) that the common object should adopt it and integrate it through broader modifications produced by the labour of all.[70] Above all, everything depends on a complex ensemble which connects the members of the group, their multiplicity, their means of communication, their techniques, their instruments, the nature of their object and their aim in a single historical movement. For example, a group whose aim is a synthetic, unifying action (agitation, propaganda) and whose object is serial gatherings which go beyond it in every direction will find it easier to interiorise the objective seriality against which it struggles; thus one can see balances being established (generally damaging to the developing action) between the seriality-object which is in the process of dissolution and the group-subject (in the practical sense) which is in the process of serialisation. But it is sufficient to mention these well known examples. What is important is the relation of the common structures to their historical content (that is to say, to the temporalising temporalisation of the group by its individual *praxis* in relation to its temporalised temporalisation by the *praxis* of other groups); and this

70. It goes without saying (though the example does not concern us here – in relation to the dialectical development, it appears *accidental*) that separation is seen more violently and in all its irrepressible negativity when a given individual in a group which is succeeding in its undertaking realises his own action as a failure (of detail). But all this has often been described by psychologists and novelists. I refer to it only as a reminder. Suffice it to say that the individual-failure becomes a pure object of common repression. The terror exercised over him is a common action (mediated reciprocity) aimed at destroying in him and with him the possibility, which is proper to everyone, of transforming suffered separation and revealed circularity into secession or exclusion. In a traitor, everyone finds – in reciprocity (for himself and for everyone) – his own permanent possibility of betraying and being betrayed, and believes he is destroying it for ever.

relation can be expressed as follows: circular serialities, as structures of secession-exclusion, cannot be *a priori realities* or reflexive determinations independent of History; they realise themselves as a temporalising-temporalised moment of the life of the group, under the pressure of particular circumstances and in particularised forms (factional struggles, terror, internal anarchy, absenteeism, discouragement, etc.). But historialisation, in the form of internal conflicts – whether masked or explicit – of circular seriality as a proper product of the group, only temporalises, through the action of specific factors, the contradiction proper to communities; and this basic contradiction – which is to be found both beneath and beyond the pledge – is that their practical unity not only demands their ontological unity but also makes it impossible. Thus the group creates itself in order to create and destroys itself by creating itself.

And being-in-the-group is a reality which is in itself complex and contradictory, because it is, in the past, the co-emergence in the group of pledged inertias through reciprocity and, in the temporalisation towards the future, the reaffirmation of this common emergence through organic, free, regulatory action which thereby transposes it into transcendence-immanence and *negates* it by living it as the contradictory and simultaneous impossibility for the individual of being either completely inside the group or completely outside it. Thus being-in-the-group is an inert 'being-in-the-midst-of-the-group' seen as an untranscendable past and realised by a movement of integration neutralised by a movement of secession. And everyone's concrete operation, as a free adoption of pledged untranscendability, manifests itself in its full positivity as *having been able* to be a refusal to take up the pledge and as having freely reproduced this past inertia. Hence, to the extent that it replaces the pledge as a vivid opacity within the transparent freedom of commitment, it constitutes for it, in the future and simultaneously, both the pledged non-possibility of being transcended and the permanent possibility of dissolution. And, no doubt, it is my freedom *as Other* which swore in me: but any action, both as a concrete expression of my translucid freedom and as mine, re-establishes the priority of the constituent dialectic over the constituted dialectic and, precisely to the extent that it is subjected to my *other-freedom* (*liberté-autre*), it indicates that behind this, in the past, there lies a moment of free transparency which, in a word, is the basis even of *the other freedom* (*l'autre liberté*). In fact, this moment was real because we experienced it as the *reciprocal decision to pledge*.

The group reacts to this permanent danger, appearing at the level or organisation, with new practices: it produces itself in the form of an *institutionalised group*; which means that 'organs', functions and powers are transformed into institutions; that, in the framework of institutions, the community tries to acquire a new type of unity by institutionalising sovereignty, and that the common individual transforms himself into an institutional individual. But, since the new internal constitution is intended to combat a re-emergence of seriality by strengthening inertia and even, as we shall see, by exploiting recurrence in order to consolidate pledged passivity, the interference between these two inorganic movements tends rather to produce degraded forms of community. 'Degraded', here, does not, of course, have anything to do with a system of values, even the ethical affirmation that freedom is the basis of values: I merely mean that the group – whose origin and end reside in an effort by the individuals who are gathered together to dissolve seriality in themselves – will, in the course of its struggle, actually reproduce alterity in itself and freeze into the inorganic so as to struggle against it *within*, so that it gradually gets closer to the 'collective' statute. In other words, our dialectical investigation makes a turning here and goes back towards the practico-inert from which Freedom-Terror removed itself a little earlier: it is beginning to appear that the movement of the investigation may possibly be circular.

There can be no doubt, in fact, that the new recurrence is perceived by the members of the group in and through the struggle which they wage against it. It is sufficient to recall the rising tide of mistrust within the Convention from September 1793 on, that is to say, from its first meeting. We can certainly see increasingly violent conflicts of interest emerging within this regularly constituted group. And these conflicts, which reflected the real conflicts which divided the country, inevitably split the elected Assembly. But still it is worth noting that the parliamentary system is established for the purpose of resolving conflicts within groups of electors or elected: the majority decides. This is a serial organisation, but this determination and the preservation of unity by action on seriality are nonetheless an organisation. Now, on the whole, past and present circumstances as well as the immediate future practically relegate the system of conciliation by vote to the level of pure pretext and replace it by integration-terror. This presents itself in fact as an exigency for unanimity and a rejection of opponents as traitors: the formal system of voting will be retained (and in certain moments it may regain decisive power), but the Convention's real action on itself will occur in the heat of the moment, through violence, with the strength of the armed people.

Besides, there can be no doubt that, if the Girondins ended up by representing the interests of the conservative bourgeoisie or even, unwittingly, of a section of the aristocracy, the differentiation of the groups (in particular of the Girondins and the Montagnards) was a slow process, involving a complex evolution whose moments have been well described by Lefebvre: in the beginning, questions of federalism, of hostility to Paris, and of social and political views did not arise. Everything was constituted in the course of the struggle and through irreversible episodes. The irremediable split in the Convention was a legacy of the Legislative Assembly: in fact everything – their social origins, their milieu, the professions they were engaged in before the elections of 1792, and their education – tended to give real homogeneity to the deputies *of both Assemblies*. So it would be a mistake to regard the Convention (and still less the Legislative Assembly) as primarily and fundamentally divided by social struggles, even class struggles, rather than as a homogeneous Assembly the overwhelming majority in which was constituted by petty-bourgeois intellectuals, and whose irremediable contradictions were the result of a slow past evolution, which gave each of them – in relation to his group, to his electors, to the nation, and to hostile groups – a *pledged untranscend-ability*. Every day, each of them adopted an inert alterity by repeatedly pledging himself to be *other* than those Others, those enemies who, frozen in inertia, regard him *as the Other*.

Let there be no mistake: we are not dismissing the Montagnards and the Girondins together: the Girondins were entirely responsible for the violence of the conflict, first for having thrown the revolution into war, that is to say, for having produced Terror as the sole means of government, and secondly for having been *the first* to take an inflexible line, which inevitably led them to become representatives of particular interests; and lastly, the Girondins were bad politicians and the Montagnards good ones: they embodied the movement of a revolution which was being radicalised by the pressure of circumstances; the Others embodied the bourgeoisie which was attempting to put an end to the revolution. It was not a matter either of politics or of day-to-day tactics; and in any historical situation violence is a result of pledged inertia. Nevertheless the Montagnards made themselves, and were made, into *pledged* enemies of the Girondins through the development of the revolutionary process and through the pledges of the Girondins themselves. There can be no doubt that the essential aim of the 'May 31st revolution' (of 1793) was to re-establish homogeneity within the Assembly, by eliminating the twenty-nine most prominent Girondins. The new, purged Assembly would be able to set up its own apparatuses of control, supervision, administration, etc.

Now, this situation of false homogeneity is precisely what concerns us here. For the homogeneity of the renewed Convention was false: in the first place, as has been clearly shown by Georges Lefebvre, the majority of the deputies would never forgive the Montagnards for the humiliation of 2 June; secondly, there were still many Girondins sitting in the Assembly; and lastly, new circumstances were to create deep divisions among the Montagnards. The difference comes to this, and this is what concerns us: before the first purge, the antagonistic groups in the Convention based their irreconcilable heterogeneity on the irreconcilability of their political actions; whereas after it, the ruling apparatuses gradually produced the unity of the common *praxis*. But this practical unity was scarcely sufficient to conceal an imperceptible, but irreconcilable heterogeneity which, this time, concerned individual people. This heterogeneity was not based either on individual practice or on organic individuals as factors of numerical multiplicity: it originated in the violence of the past (31 May, 2 June) in so far as this was connected, as suffered inertia, to the pledged inertia of the representative of the nation, that is to say, in so far as *power* as an untranscendable and pledged statute transmitted a statute of untranscendability to them (violence against power becomes violated power which has to be re-established in its purity by violence). In fact what we learn from historical experience, especially in recent years, is that though purges are intended to re-establish an internal homogeneity, they actually replace a quasi-structured heterogeneity (the function and powers of opposition) by a diffuse heterogeneity. Thus Terror begins after the purge.

Once those who are *the same* again (they vote the same way and are committed to the realisation of the same policies) have become simultaneously and secretly *Others*, alterity becomes the secret truth of unity for everyone. Whatever the direct relations between each deputy and the Committee of Public Safety, other relations established themselves – if only through the necessity of living in the same district – between the deputies themselves. And these relations – which are normal while homogeneity is guaranteed – appear as *other relations*

(*relations autres*) which determine everyone in his alterity: in so far as he is *other than* his pure integration, that is to say, than his direct relation with the organising axis, he enjoys the relations of a free, practical individual with his neighbour in so far as this neighbour is other; and the reciprocity which is established between them is defined as a reciprocity of alterity in relation to the developing totalisation. And since these reciprocities are, or may be, mediated (since they establish themselves inside the group in activity), this means that everyone, in so far as he has no direct relation with his neighbours (but only relations of function, or of power, passing through the ruling apparatus and defined by it), comes to be determined in his common activity, and in his ability to carry out his task, and finally, in the depths of his *being-in-the-group*, by the direct or mediated relations between his neighbours. Hence a contradiction arises for everyone, as a member of the Assembly, between the undertaking of practical totalisation, which eliminates particular individuals in favour of an individualisation of functions, and circular seriality, which, in the form of the developing totalisation, constantly anticipates the *same group* relapsing into a collective. Unification as an organising *praxis* continues to elude everyone – in so far as he is a unifying agent – because of the *other* relations which the Others have with this unifying synthesis (are they not using them to lay a trap for him or for some Other? etc.).

Far from *realising* its unity through its committees' efforts to unify it, the Convention *became an object* at precisely the point when totalisation broke against recurrence.[71] In fact there was *one* Convention because, in this practical group, the absence of an ontological statute for common individuals allowed the ontological statute of circular seriality to establish itself, as an indestructible foundation of impotence. There was *one* Convention in so far as the foundation of its unity was always based on the Other, that is to say, in so far as this

71. The unspoken antagonism between its two ruling apparatuses – the Committee of Public Safety and the Committee of General Security – was necessarily a mediated, though negative, reciprocity. This relation actually presupposed that each sub-group opposed the other *in so far as* the deputies as a whole recognised its powers. But each apparatus therefore produced the entire Assembly as other for the other 'organ', and, for the entire Assembly, everyone was both positive and negative, at once the same and other. Thus the *other-being* of each of the Committees lay in the reciprocity of the deputies, when this reciprocity was mediated by the other Committee, as an other determination of unity.

unity fell outside the practical and was, in fact, simply the impossibility, *endured* by everyone, of either pursuing integration or escaping it. At this level, everyone was *inside*, to precisely the extent that all the Others were outside: the tension of immanence-transcendence was again degraded and passivised in the collectivised group; *the collective object is me-in-the-group-without-me*. In it, I feature as Other, and become the object of actions and determinations of which I am unaware; I either become the passive victim of projects which are concealed from me or, without being aware of it, I become involved with conspirators or with suspects through an interdependence which they frame without telling me, and perhaps without knowing it themselves; and it may be that within it I become an object of fear too; certainly as a means and possibly as a (relative or immediate) end.

But it is impossible for me even to determine this imposed alterity in the abstract without effecting a synthesis in mediated reciprocity of the social field which passes through the mediation of the organising axes and which, at the same time, proclaims me in my own eyes as suspect: this practical synthesis is in fact a regulatory action. Hence, in the tension of immanence-transcendence, I find, in indissoluble connection, not only my being-outside-myself-in-the-group as an alterity of impotence, but also my impossible integration as a danger of exile-secession. In the purged Convention, the 'collective' manifested from below the impossibility of the group being a subject (contrary to what Durkheim believed) and its degree of reality was directly proportional to this very impossibility. It is on this account that it had its own structures, laws and rigidity; it was on this account that it acted on its members – not as a consciousness, nor as a *Gestalt*, but as *a real object*, that is to say, as a structure of exteriority limiting our attempt at interiorisation, as an indirect counter-unity which is merely the negation of subjective unification and its inverted image; and lastly as the mark of the *impossible integration*. (If this was not even attempted, we would be back with the pure collective of dispersal – prices, the market, etc.; and if it were completely carried out – which is impossible – the group could no longer be an object for itself).

However, in so far as everyone attempts to realise the group as a unified *praxis*, and in so far as he reveals the other-reality of the community as an unpredictable serial deviation to which his own regulatory action will be subjected in this milieu of alterity, he must strive to liquidate the Other as a factor of dispersive inertia and circular deviations; and as the Other is everyone *as Other*, fraternity has to be imposed by violence. This means that everyone must risk being radically destroyed in so far as he supports any particular embodiment of the Other. The contradiction is blatant: integration-terror is supposed to eliminate the other; but the Other is indestructible. The Other is simply a particular relation which manifests itself in precisely those circumstances which also engender the attempt to destroy it; besides, everyone is Other in the Other. Thus terror would be a pointless circular course unless it did, *in fact*, suppress individuals in so far as they are *themselves*, that is to say, in so far as their free practical undertakings designate them as excluded regulatory third parties, always capable of lending themselves to the Other.

Of the two negations of the group – individual *praxis* and seriality – the first, as we have seen, is accompanied by the realisation of the common undertaking; it is both an ontological negation and a practical realisation. The second is definitive and it was in opposition to it that the group originally constituted itself. Yet it is individual *praxis* which appears suspect to the apparatuses of terror. But this is because terror itself is suspect in its own eyes: in so far as it actually becomes the function and power of certain sub-groups and common individuals (public prosecutors, juries, judges in the revolutionary tribunal, the Committee of Public Safety, etc.), it is produced not only through deliberations and decisions which themselves create recurrence but also through processes which are realised in the tension of transcendence-immanence. Through a purge – of whatever sort, whether exclusion or execution – the purger constitutes himself as suspect and as always liable to be purged; he produces himself as such *in his own eyes* and it is therefore the freedom of the regulatory third party which he everywhere pursues, confusing it with elusive alterity. And this free practice is undoubtedly capable of regrouping the opposition, of constituting a conspiracy, etc.: as such, in the moment of Terror, it appears to the apparatus as intolerable. And if it is at this moment – rather than earlier or later, when the régime is more relaxed – that it seems intolerable, this is because, on the basis of well defined exterior circumstances (invasion, disturbances in the provinces, the revolt in the Vendée, social unrest and the danger of famine),[72] terror established itself as the only means of governing. And, whatever the historical context in which we consider it, it always arises in opposition to seriality, rather than to

---

72. I am not putting these factors in any particular order but simply enumerating them.

freedom. In fact, both in its origins and in its manifestation, it is freedom liquidating the indefinite flight of the Other, that is to say, impotence, through violence.[73] In the Convention, Terror was born of the objective contradiction between the necessity for a common *praxis*, free and indivisible, and the objective but inconceivable – and, indeed, unformulated – divisions of a governing Assembly which remained chaotic and which was *altered* by the violence it had suffered. In this fundamental atmosphere free *praxis* was suspect: seriality mediated by freedom appeared as passive alterity, and practical freedom was

73. Concerning this event (which, as we know, began on 14 July 1789), I repeat what I have mentioned at various points in this book: there is no Platonic Idea of Terror, but only different Terrors and if the historian wishes to identify characteristics which are common to them, he will have to do it *a posteriori*, on the basis of careful comparisons. What I am trying to describe here is not the development or the factors of the Terror-process (which does not exist either 'in itself' or 'in the mind'); nor is it some long historical sequence which people have chosen to call Terror (the Terror of 1793, the White Terror, the Red Terror, etc.). The Terror of 1789 to 1794 is inseparable from the Revolution itself and has meaning only within a totalising reconstruction effected by historians. All I want to do is to use an abstract example to show the connections between free *praxis*, the pledge, violence and recurrence inside organised groups. I am not attempting to set out the essential relations, even reduced to the utmost simplicity, which might constitute an *essence of Terror*: there is no such essence. I only wish to describe certain conditions – the dialectical chain of abstract determinations (*infinitely indeterminate except at a particular point*) – which is necessarily re-alised by the being-in-the-group of a common individual when Terror occurs as a historical development in specific circumstances. The plurality of Terrors even during the revolutionary Terror (1789 to 1794) seems to me so obvious that I have chosen for my example a limited and induced terror (the circular Terror in a homogeneous group which was being eroded by seriality), whereas the primary phenomenon (Terror as a fundamental relation between the French people and the Assembly as the government) was created in order to combat *non-circular*, indefinite seriality. In 1793, given that the first invasion had taken place, that several towns had precipitously surrendered to the enemy, and that the enemy occupation of border areas resulted in fraternisations in various places, and given that the idea of a nation was new whereas that of international solidarities between aristocracies was very old, the frontiers did not in any way make Frenchmen into a multiplicity contained in one place. At the frontiers there was the danger of treason as an anticipation of indefinite seriality (with a sudden or imperceptible transition – through treason – from *being-French* to *being-German*). The re-fraction of an order – as a synthetic process of organisation – in a case of mortal danger, into indefinite seriality gave rise, *by itself*, to the practical necessity (the free necessity) of breaking seriality by violence (like breaking ice) to give a synthetic milieu of execution to the synthetic order.

therefore denounced for generating alterity. All this could be lived as the diffuse reality of the group (integration refused *to the newcomer*: in the confined milieux of prisons, detention centres, houses of correction, etc., Genet has suffered and defined the permanent experience of terror; fraternity realised itself in only one form: against him). The experience can also be had if one *experiences in oneself the praxis* of specialised apparatuses (surveillance, police supervision, threats, arrests, etc.). In any case, everyone is both purger and purged, and Terror is *never* a system based on the will of a minority; it is the reappearance – in specific circumstances – of the fundamental group relation as an inter-human relation; subsequently, differentiation may or may not create a specialised organ whose function is to govern according to terror.

In a terror-group, my bond with my brother is terror: the regulatory action by which he unites me to all gives me a respite *for myself* because I am constituted in the group and because my exile dissolves; but he thereby determines it as lying at the limit of interiority and thereby shows the infinitesimal gap between the regulatory movement (that is to say, his quasi-sovereignty in the common *praxis*) and the true sovereignty of the absolute Other (enemy group or individual) whose synthetic activity may gather us together *from outside* as a herd-object in *his* practical field. We are united, but *we* are threatened by him.[74] Thus as an arbitrary member of the group, I perceive, in the two forms of my *praxis* (regulated and regulatory), freedom, the *non-being of the future* which has to be made, as an indication of *group non-being*. And my individual terror behaviour consists in consolidating inertia within myself in so far as this reciprocal practice of consolidation is also realised in the other third party through the mediation of all the others. At this level, the pledge appears as a necessary but insufficient basis for common unity; it is the foundation stone on which unity as *inert-being-everywhere* has to be based.

However, this inert unity – at least as everyone can realise it in himself and, through himself, in others – must be very different from serial inertia since it is the struggle of freedom against an internal revival of seriality. This systematic petrification, that is to say, the

74. These indeterminate possibilities are concretely determined both in trust and in defiance in the totalising situation: but trust – which is immediately connected with defiance against others – is here only a mode of terror. It is a trust-menace and a trust-exigency which controls and controls itself: at the slightest divergence, it is replaced by *suspicion*.

struggle of inertia against inertia, ought to be described as an inorganic, created, counter-seriality. There would be no point here in describing in detail the well known process by which everyone tries to expel from himself and from others the regulatory moment of immanence-transcendence, in order to be able to identify himself purely with the common producer of regulated action. The fundamental modification consists in transferring *the common-being-of-the-group*, regulatory freedom and impossible ontological unity to the *praxis* of the group as such. Since it is this, and this alone, which creates common unity and since the group requires the ontological statute in proportion as a revival of seriality threatens to dissolve it, everyone's reciprocal work consists in projecting ontological unity into practical unity: *praxis* becomes the being and the essence of the group; in *praxis* it will produce its men as inorganic instruments which it requires in order to develop. And freedom resides *in the praxis*, rather than in each individual action. This new structure of the group is not only the practice of Terror, but also a defensive reaction against Terror. It consists in a double relation of mediated reciprocity: everyone construes himself, through the Other and through all, as an inorganic tool by means of which action is realised. Everyone constitutes action as freedom itself in the form of terror-imperative. This new structure gives a certain amount of vicarious freedom to its tools. But this vicarious freedom is not disturbing; it is the reflection of the common freedom onto a particular inorganic object rather than the practical freedom of an individual agent. It is at this level that the institution is defined; or – not to abandon our guiding thread – it is at this level that certain practices which are necessary for the organisation acquire a new ontological statute by institutionalising themselves.

3 Institutionalisation and Inertia

In the living moment of the group (of fusion in the first stages of organisation), the common individual is not inessential because he is the same in all, that is to say, the ubiquity of the group as multiplicity negated by a *praxis*; it would be better to say that everyone comes to everyone, through the community, as a bearer *of the same essentiality*.

But, at the level of the degraded group, the individual, in his terrorist and terrorised negation of his own freedom, is constituted as inessential in relation to his function. Functions and powers are, of course, nothing but concrete determinations of the common individual. But, in the living group, a temporary balance was established between the common individual as a social product and organic freedom as the adoption of this individual-power and as the free execution of the common task with the common means. Through the undertaking of the pledge and through the concrete determination of the future, through pledged inertia, it *actualised* the power and sustained it in the milieu of freedom – thereby producing common freedom as constituted freedom – and, through its mediation (between the group and the object) it produced the common, here, as individual. On the other hand, freedom, conceived as a common transcendent subject, denies individual freedom and expels the individual from function; function, positing itself for itself, and producing individuals who will perpetuate it, becomes an *institution*.

These purely abstract descriptions may give the impression that this is a matter of the idea working upon itself. But the changes we have described are, in fact, a product of real, concomitant transformations, one of which is *suffered* as an inorganic force while the other is a real act of differentiation.

(*First transformation.*) An institution cannot result from a free determination of practice by itself. And if practice readopts the institution as a defence against terror, it does so in so far as its petrification is a metamorphosis which has been induced, and whose origin is elsewhere. And we are familiar with this origin: it is *precisely* the re-emergence of seriality. For the institution has the contradictory characteristic, often remarked on by sociologists, of being both *praxis* and thing. As *praxis*, its teleological meaning can become obscured; but this is either because the institution is a mere carcass or because those who are institutionalised have a real comprehension of its aim but cannot or will not communicate it: in fact, whenever we acquire the means to decode it (for example, whenever we examine the institutions of a contemporary industrialised society), we discover its teleological characteristics, that is to say, a frozen dialectic of alienated ends, liberating ends and of the alienation of these new ends. On the other hand, however, the institution, as such, has a considerable force of inertia, not only because it is part of an institutional whole and is incapable of being modified unless all the others are modified too, but also, above all, in itself, because it posits itself, in and through its inert-being, as essentiality and defines men as the inessential means of its perpetuation.

But this inessentiality does not come either from the institution to the individual or from the individual to the institution: it is actually practice isolating itself in so far as it is produced in a common milieu defined by new human relationships. These relationships are based quite simply on serial impotence: if I regard the institution as basically unalterable, this is because my *praxis* in the institutionalised group determines itself as incapable of changing the institution; and this impotence originates in my relation of circular alterity to the other members of the group. Terror is practised against sub-groups – chiefly against those which might form spontaneously under pressure of circumstances; and even, to a certain extent, against sub-groups which are organised and specialised by a common and reciprocal differentiation of the entire group (or against people who, as we shall see, are constituted by the *authorities* as the legitimate 'organs' of the entire community). And this, as we have seen, is simply because pledged heterogeneity, when merged with suffered separations, in the irreversibility of temporalisation, produces alterity as a revival of the practico-inert *in interiority*. When a group is *invaded* in this way, everyone lives mistrust as a reciprocity of impotence: I become suspect if I ask another third party to modify some structure, power, or practice, by joining with me and with others: what separates is not in fact the object to be changed so much as the possibility of founding a faction in the group as a negative determination, negated by the developing totalisation. Thus I do not dare make a proposal (take the initiative of the regulatory action) or, if I do make one, my proposition will elicit no response. Besides, I myself know that the other third parties are genuinely *others* and, with the possible exception of those who are closest to me, it is impossible for me to estimate how my regulatory action will appear to them, that is to say, I do not know with what alterity it will be affected: it will be deformed and diverted, and there is a danger that it will bring about results quite contrary to those I intended; it may damage the common object of the common practice (at least, as I discover it in my experience); or it may be turned against me to destroy me. And this very concrete reason always tends (according to the concrete conditions of this particular terror) to plunge me even deeper into silence. But still this is unimportant since it is only a matter of individual actions. But let us recall that *separation*, in whatever form, does a lot to raise

the threshold of communication between third parties; and consequently, it is objectively more difficult – if not impossible – to make
contact with them; and those who can be contacted might be unable to
reach others. In a degraded group, to sum up, every proposal is
'divisive', and its proposer is suspect – because he offers a glimpse of
his freedom – and a divider; and any local regroupment, provided it is
determined in interiority by the individuals present rather than by *the
others*, elsewhere, who hold power, is a faction, because the inertia of
the Others will make it into a separate group inside the group rather
than a sub-group; any concrete proposal from individuals will be lost
because – even if some Others are prepared to adopt it – the only
possible means of communication *with the Others*, in so far as they have
already been serialised, is the serial unity of the *mass media*:[75] *separation*
definitively eliminates 'orders passed on by word of mouth'.

This impossibility of changing the practice in a given domain and
adapting it to particular circumstances need not be directly perceived
by the individual as a thwarted or failed attempt to bring about some
particular change. His attitude to any given common activity, with its
powers and functions, may well be positive. If I have stressed the
impotence of the third party and treated it as the determining factor in
the transition to the institution, this is only because this impotence, as a
basic reciprocal relation between third parties in relation to a given
practice, necessarily results in a modification of the attitude of each and
all toward their operation; and this modification has as much to do
with adhesion as with refusal. Both attitudes are, in effect, lived in the
concrete mode of impotence. It is too bad if I do not agree: I shall have
to come to terms with it. And if I agree, so much the better: it is a fluke,
an accident, crucial for me but indifferent for the practice itself, and
might be expressed in these words: since it cannot be changed, it is
just as well that I am willing to go along with it. Whether it is an
internal practice of organisation, co-ordination, supervision, a struggle
waged within the group against scarcity (of men, of money, or of
communications), in short, a factor of integration, or whether it is a
detail of the common, transcendent action on the object or the enemy,
the practice becomes an institution as soon as the group, as a unity
which has been eroded by alterity, becomes powerless to change it
without completely disrupting itself, that is to say, as soon as everyone
comes to be conditioned by the shifting flight of the others. And this

75. In English in original. [Ed.]

metamorphosis does not in any way imply that it has become useless. Of course, it may be sustained either on the real basis of conflicts of interest between members of the group or, quite simply, as an integrating part of a practical group practice which gets older without being able to change (because of balances of opposing forces which reduce the ensemble to impotence in the midst of a society in the process of being transformed, etc.). But these different possibilities (which themselves refer from antagonism to alterity) should not be allowed to conceal the fact that the institution, as a detail of common action, can, *at the level of the institutional group*, retain its usefulness (either for the individuals as a whole – an exogamous system – or for a dominant fraction within the group). Similarly, as a detailed practice, it can and must realise itself through individuals who have been selected or produced by the group; it therefore presupposes powers, tasks, a system of rights and duties, a material localisation and an instrumentality. Thus it is characterised by the same features that enabled us to define organised practice: but, *in so far as it is an institution*, its real being and its strength come to it from emptiness, from separation, from inertia and from serial alterity; it is therefore *the praxis as other*.

We have considered active passivity both as the regulated production of pledged inertia and as a condition for common activity; and, in the practico-inert field, we have also investigated passive activity as a result of alienation. We must now consider the institution in a declining group as the *transition* from one to the other. There can be numerous intermediaries between active passivity and passive activity, and it is impossible to know the statute of a given institution *a priori*: this can only be determined by its entire concrete history. The important point is that – at least as long as it still has its finality – it can never be entirely assimilated to the practico-inert: its meaning is still that of an action undertaken in the light of a certain objective (regardless of what counter-finalities may have developed); but on the other hand, the presence of alterity in it as suffered separation makes it impossible for it to become identical with the inert (if slight) forms of active passivity which are based simply on the pledged untranscendability of certain possibilities. At this level, the group is still entirely practical, despite the seriality which eats away at it, and the institution (or rather the institutional ensemble as systems of solidified relations) is simply the modality of its *praxis*. And the institutional character which is concealed by the common action is the strongest bond between the third parties, because its being is based on everyone's impotence, in other words, on the beginnings of a circular massification whose origin is the community's *not-being-substance (non-être-substance)*.

The *being of the institution*, as the geometrical locus of intersections of the collective and the common, is the *non-being* of the group, produced as a bond between its members.[76] The unity of the institution is the unity of alterity in so far as it is introduced into the group and used by the group to replace its own absent unity. But its relation to everyone is one of interiority, though it may define itself as *praxis* in exteriority: in fact, it determines everyone both in inertia and in practical obligation. Indeed, it transcends everyone in so far as it resides in all the Others, and is unpredictable and other in them, and dependent on this unpredictability. On the other hand, as an institutionalised *praxis*, it remains either *a power over everyone* (in the name of pledged faith) or, if everyone represents and maintains it, *his own free power over the Others*. This free power is now being challenged: for everyone, along with his power, will appear to everyone in the contradictory unity of the same and the Other. Thus recognition is challenge, and challenge is recognition. Permanent trade-union officials will appear worthy of trust *if they are put to the test* (thus the Other relates to the same and, ultimately, to freedom; but if the freedom appears too manifest, defiance will immediately be rekindled: it is necessary to identify a man who is at the service of his function, but the function must always have precedence over the man). But supposing they had deserved and won such trust, they would lose everything and be in danger of possibly serious violence if they were so inept as to oppose some wild-cat strike (or to try to impose some unpopular course of action); but by their violent reaction the workers would be acknowledging the power that they were challenging: they would react less strongly to the protests of a non-unionised worker.

Thus the new statute of power emerges everywhere, even in the army, the archetypal institutional group. In the context of the organised group, we defined it as the right to do one's duty; but here it must be defined as the duty to do one's best in order to get one's right to do

76. Here too it is necessary to rebut an idealist interpretation: institutions are generally sustained by the 'forces of order', that is to say, armed sub-groups enforce order by violence. But since not only these sub-groups, but also – as we shall see – sub-groups of authority, are institutions, it is still the case that the institutional system, including the coercion which maintains it, depends on the original reciprocal impotence of every third party in relation to every Other and through his relations to all.

one's duty recognised. Institutional man has to get this *recognition* by means of two opposed and simultaneous practices: on the one hand, when his institutional power is not directly threatened, his general tactic will be to liquidate the Other in himself so as to liquidate it in the Others (the officer who lives with his men and models his whole life on theirs); on the other hand, in the moment of exercising his power, institutional man will immediately constitute himself as the absolute Other, by adopting certain behaviour and dress; and he will base the firmness of the power exercised and of the decisions made, on his *institution-being* (*être-institution*), that is to say, on inertia and the total opacity of the alterity which has become the particular institution's presence in him, and, hence, the group's presence as common *praxis*. At this level, in fact, mystification is very probable: with the institution remaining a practice and the group not being dissolved, the institution, in its negative being (which is really only the ubiquity of non-being) appears, in appropriate circumstances, as the ontological statute of the community. This means that it refers to the whole of the institutional system as a relational totality of the synthetic determinations of the grouped multiplicity. Through the power-man (*l'homme-pouvoir*) who reveals himself – through familiar rituals and dances – as institution-being, the organised individual believes he can see himself as integrated into the group through the institutional ensemble (and in fact this is what every citizen says and believes), whereas the institution can actually appear only at a particular moment in the involution of the group, and as an exact index of its disintegration. And, if the dance has been well done, if the power-man has, as he should, referred to the inorganic as *the fundamental human reality*, the order or decision will themselves appear as inorganic (unshakeable), and at the same time they will be obeyed in the name of pledged loyalty, that is to say, of pledged inertia. The freedom of the power-man, for the individual who *acknowledges this power*, is a pure mediation between the inertia of the institution and the inertia of the particular order. This is certainly a case of the abstract being transcended towards the concrete, but although this transcendence is acknowledged, it does not posit itself for itself, as in free practical labour: the mediation exhausts itself and disappears, remaining, for example, an inert determination of discourse, in that it is based on an inert, synthetic determination of human multiplicity and is addressed to the double inertia of organised individuals (pledged inertia based on serial impotence).

In this moment, freedom is completely hidden or else appears as the inessential and ephemeral slave of necessity. Necessity, on the other hand, is absolute in the sense that its free, practical form (necessity produced by freedom) merges with its form as serial alienation. The imperative and impotence, terror and inertia are based on each other. The institutional moment, in the group, corresponds to what might be called the systematic self-domestication of man by man. The aim is, in effect, to create men who (as common individuals) will define themselves, in their own eyes and amongst themselves, by their fundamental relation (mediated reciprocity) with institutions. More than half of this task is carried out by circular seriality: everyone systematically acting on himself and on everyone else through all, resulting in the creation of the strict correlate of the man-institution, that is to say, the institutionalised man. In so far as the ossification of the ossified *praxis* which is the institution is due to our own impotence, it constitutes for each and for all a precise index of *reification*. This does not necessarily mean that we suffer it as a constraint, but rather that it is our own inorganic inertia in the social milieu. But the moment of common degradation in which the institution emerges is precisely that in which everyone aims to expel freedom from himself in order to realise the endangered unity of the declining group as a thing. So at this level of involution (under the pressure of exterior circumstances), the common individual tries to become a thing which is held against other things by the unity of a seal; the model for the institutional group is *the forged tool*. And everyone is implicated as such in institutionality. But on the other hand this is also because they are its victims *even before they are born*. The previous generation already defines their institutional future, as their external, mechanical destiny, that is to say, as determinations of untranscendability (or as determinations *of their being*), even before they are born. 'Obligations' – military, civic, professional, etc. – constitute in advance an untranscendability deep inside everyone who is born into the group; and of course, it is necessary to *fulfil* these obligations (not 'play these roles' or 'adopt these attitudes' as the 'culturalists' would put it, indiscriminately mixing up material conditions with possibilities defined by the historical ensemble on the basis of these conditions and with institutional obligations). Being born into the group is a pledge (reiterated by rites of passage), and to make such a pledge is to take on the institutional inertia with which the others affect the child, in the form of a free commitment *to realising the institution*. From this point of view, institutional being is, in everyone, a prefabricated inertia of inorganic being, and will be transcended by a practical freedom whose pledged function will be to objectify itself in this same being as an inert determination of the future. The institution will produce its agents (organisers and organised) by giving them institutional determinations in advance, and institutionalised agents will then reciprocally identify themselves, in their relations of directed alterity, with the practical system of institutional relations, in so far as it is necessarily inscribed in a complex of worked objects of inorganic origins. Thus the institution as a stereotyped *praxis* (though, under the pressure of certain circumstances, its efficacity may reside in being stereotyped) adumbrates the future in its rigidity; and as the inert persistence of a reified organisation within a grouping which might well reorganise itself in any case, it constitutes itself as the elementary and abstract permanence of the social past *as being*, even, and above all, if the developing re-arrangements reveal the perpetual changes of this past *as signification*.[77]

4 Institutionalisation and Sovereignty

(*Second transformation.*) The institutional system as an exteriority of inertia necessarily refers to *authority* as its reinteriorisation; and *authority*, as a power over all powers and over all third parties through these powers, is itself established by the system as an institutional guarantee of institutions.

The foundation of authority is in fact sovereignty, in so far as, after the stage of the fused group, it is the quasi-sovereignty of the regulatory third party. Thus the *leader* emerges at the same time as the group itself and produces the group which produces him, except that at this elementary moment of the investigation, the leader might be *anyone*. In other words, everyone's quasi-sovereignty is one of the constitutive bonds of the group. We then pointed out that if certain individuals became regulatory third parties more often or for longer periods of time than others this was on the basis of particular historical circumstances, and, as such, initially of accidental ones. Lastly we pointed out

77. Which occurs whenever the institution is preserved while the common transformations around it give it another relation to all in the developing totalisation, *in interiority* and without even touching it.

that, in revolutionary periods, groups which appear and disappear within a day are organised and reorganised around quite specific individuals who may be trusted for long periods. Such 'agitators' are regulatory third parties, but they should not strictly be called leaders: they mimic or express for all the *praxis* which is implicitly defined everywhere, in the ubiquity of mediated reciprocity. At the level of the pledge and of the organisation, we have observed the emergence of powers. At that point we did not describe *authority* since powers (as reciprocal quasi-sovereignty) do not directly involve the specific power which is called authority. However, we did observe the emergence of a truly common relation of everyone to each and all – which is the diffuse power of life and death over the traitor, or, in other words, fraternity-terror as a basic determination of sociality.

This permanent living structure of coercion is a necessary determination of sovereignty as authority. From the moment in which a regulatory third party (or a sub-group acting as a regulatory third party) becomes a pledged holder of the power of regulation as organised function, and when this third party receives and concentrates the internal violence of the group as a power to impose his regulation, everyone's shifting quasi-sovereignty is immobilised and becomes *authority* as a specific relation of one individual to all. This relation may appear at the level of organised groups; but, in so far as the group is alive, and therefore constantly being rearranged, the relation itself moves and passes from one to the other, according to the requirements of the situation. *Authority* does not emerge in its full development except at the level of institutions: institutions, that is to say, a rebirth of seriality and impotence, are necessary for the consecration of Power and for ensuring its *de jure* permanence; in other words, *authority* necessarily depends on inertia and seriality, in so far as it is constituted Power; but, on the other hand, its real efficacity must, through its coercive strength, tend to increase the power and number of institutions, as products of recurrence and massification and as the only effective common weapon in the struggle against factors of dispersal. Or, to look at it from the other point of view, the institutional system presents itself, by a permanent mystification, in its inorganic-being as the real unity of the declining group. But if the system is simply revealed in itself, it will unfold as a multiplicity of diverse, *non-totalised* relations. We have seen in effect that the institutionalisation of functions occurs through the medium of a history, in otherwise disparate places, and that the diversity of circumstances and problems necessarily causes a local diversity of temporalisations. There are dislocations, delays, asymmetries: in one place the apparatuses of co-ordination will be directly established in an institutional form, while in another, mediating 'organs' will never reach the stage of institutionality (some disappear, and others survive). This kind of social solidification, therefore, does not present itself as a *praxis*, or even as a unifying process. Thus *authority* fulfils a definite function: as the synthetic power of a single individual (possibly, though not necessarily, as an expression of a united sub-group), it gathers up the multiplicity of institutional relations and gives them the synthetic unity of a real *praxis*. Institutions claim to be the inorganic being-one of the serialised community; the leader claims to be the dissolution and synthetic reunification of this external passivity in the organic unity of the regulatory *praxis*, that is to say, of the *praxis* of the group in so far as it is reflected to him as the common *praxis* of a person.

But this is the essential contradiction of authority: the individual reincarnation of the fused group and of Freedom-Terror – the leader – himself as such enters the institutional multiplicity, since he is a real product of an institution. Thus the leader preserves institutions to precisely the extent that he apparently produces them as an internal exteriorisation of his interiority, and he dissolves their inert-being in his historical *praxis*. But this historical *praxis* – as the reciprocity of the sovereign and of common individuals – is itself produced by the inert eternity of institutional relations. This dialectical movement must be examined more closely: through it and on the basis of it, the search for the intelligibility proper to the institutional group will be completed.

Now, the first point to notice is that, contrary to what is so often maintained, sovereignty in itself does not constitute any problem or require any foundation. The illusion that it does is due to the fact that the state of massification is normally regarded as logically and historically basic, and that the reified relationships which occur in societies based on exploitation are treated as the prototype of human relations. From the moment in which *absence of relationship* becomes the fundamental relation, one can ask how the type of synthetic relation known as Power can set itself up as the bond between the separate molecules. And all means of interpretation except two have been foresworn *a priori*. These two are, that Power emanates from God, and that Power emanates from certain intermittent metamorphoses which transform society into a totalised-totality, and that it expresses the constraints of collective representation, etc. Unfortunately, neither God nor the totalised group actually exist. If it were really necessary to find a foundation for sovereignty, we would be searching for a long time: for there is no such thing.

There is none *because* there is no need for one: sovereignty is simply the univocal relation of interiority between the individual as *praxis* and the objective field which he organises and transcends towards his own end. There is no place for a foundation for the right of *praxis* by which man reproduces his life by freely rearranging the matter around him: on the contrary, this dialectical transcendence, which shows the becoming-*praxis* (*le devenir-praxis*) of need is itself the foundation of all rights. In other words, sovereignty is man himself as action, as unifying labour, in so far as he has a purchase on the world and is able to change it. Man *is sovereign*. And, in so far as the material field is also a social field, the sovereignty of the individual extends without limit over all individuals: these material organisms have to be unified as his means in the total field of his sovereign action. The only limitation on man's sovereignty over all Others is simple reciprocity, that is to say, the total sovereignty of each and all over him. When this original relation is lived outside any institution, it just reconstitutes every person as an absolute for any other person, that is to say, as the untranscendable means of which everyone is both the means and the end to precisely the extent that every individual is the means to his own end and the end for every means. In this way, sovereignty is both the univocal bond already described and the basic relation of reciprocity (co-sovereignty).

Sovereignty within the group, therefore, does not have to explain its positive power, but rather the negative and limiting determinations to which it is subjected. In fact, we have seen how it became *quasi-sovereignty* in the tension of 'transcendence-immanence'. And from our point of view, this limitation is still the foundation of Power: the sovereignty of the leader can only be a *quasi-sovereignty*, since otherwise he would not be a regulatory third party and the bond of interiority would break. An Assyrian King who had his prisoners of war (members of the other army) executed was exercising total sovereignty over them, but, at the same time, it was impossible for him to treat them as men; his sovereignty could express itself only as a univocal relation of violence with a given multiplicity, invading his practical field from outside, which he had the material means to annihilate. On the other hand, his relation to his own soldiers is one of quasi-sovereignty *precisely because the relation of authority is no longer based on physical strength*. Let there be no misunderstanding: discipline could not be more strict, supervision more vigilant, the organs of coercion more numerous, or the 'forces of order' more powerful. But the 'forces of order' present themselves to the mutineers, or rebels, as *the same to the same*; the soldiers who shoot them are *the same* as those who are shot and there is no *a priori* way of assigning a given military sub-group to either of the two categories (marksmen, victims). Alterity makes them into forces of order, and this means that the primary relation of authority is a quasi-sovereignty of interiority, as violence creating its means, *with* sub-groups which – either through their interests or through the common interests of the group or through the specific connection between their interests and those of the group – define their coercive action as a function of its regulatory action. In the same way, the technical and instrumental superiority of the repressive group (in the service of authority) over the group as a whole is not always either obvious or necessary, especially to the army since the forces of order and the rebels have arms which are *a priori* similar. Of course, the 'forces of order' will always, as long as order reigns, have heavy, common weapons (whether horses, artillery, or planes), but this is precisely because their relation of violence to the rebels is a power over the majority of third parties, lived and acknowledged by the non-rebels as a whole as right-duty.

A 'public force' as the support of authority expresses itself as just violence only in the milieu of 'Freedom-Terror' and through the 'Freedom-Terror' which is in any case going to destroy itself. 'Freedom-Terror' becoming specialised function – this (and, as we shall see, the seriality of impotence) is the relation of interiority for repressive groups. And interiorised withdrawal is precisely the common milieu of the group which, as long as it remains the same, gives repression a regular victory. The defeat of a rebellion is settled in the precise moment where it discovers its own limits in extension: *this unity*, and no more. It is these limits which pass sentence: and the sentence comes from the group. By remaining entirely what it is – an institutionalised group – regardless of its sympathies and of the individual sympathies of other soldiers for the rebels, within itself it constitutes the group of insurgents as its radical negation. In fact, and precisely to the extent that the 'loyalists' resist any reorganisation of the group as a new totalisation proposed by the rebel group, that is to say, in so far as they see the group not as producing a new possibility for the future, but as negating their own future, purely and simply (that is to say, the rigid future of institutionality), these 'loyalists' constitute the group as a pure internal weakening of unity, as a negative, corrosive power, as a threat of seriality and an inert force of negation. So, as the 'majority', they are the party which is linked to the public forces of destruction: they *legitimate* this annihilation by means of their fidelity and, furthermore, they make it materially possible either by abstaining or lending their support.[78] Thus the bond between Power and the regulated third parties, *in spite of and above all because of* the failure to challenge the sovereignty of the leader, is based chiefly on the transformation of total sovereignty into quasi-sovereignty. This simply means that the leader, as a unifying, reshaping and repressive function, is inside the group itself. At the moment in which the group constitutes itself, under the pressure of circumstances, from the first stirrings of the crowd which liquidates its own seriality, to the last avatars of a group in the final stages of petrification, everyone makes himself quasi-sovereign and this determination in interiority of the regulatory third party, as a transition from the Other to the Same, is a fundamental structure of *praxis* as community.

No, it is not sovereignty which has to be explained, or even the initial limitation which gives it its efficacity. It is the second constitutive negation: why, on what basis, in what external and internal circumstances, to what end, etc., is the circular reciprocity of quasi-sovereignties suddenly halted, and why is the common individual (or the subgroup), which is the material place at which the blockage occurs, defined as *sovereign?*

The problem is often obscured by ascribing the sovereign's enormous actual power to him *from the outset* and by seeing it as a manifestation of some positive force (as if he were the incarnation or reflection of 'collective sovereignty'). To do this is to forget that quasi-sovereignty, like the mediated reciprocity of each to all, is characterised by its ubiquity rather than by some synthetic virtue

78. This does not in any way mean that the common individuals of the group support the policies of the leaders, the conduct of the war, etc. But it does *at least* mean that they regard the dissolution of institutional unity as a *much more serious* danger than any which might be incurred through the incompetence of the leaders. And in so far as this appraisal expresses the aberrant synthesis of the seriality of impotence and practical unity, it necessarily characterises the individuals who are institutionalised: once again, the meanings which are produced are basically structured by the relational statute of the group.

which combines all the 'powers' of the group. In fact, it is *the same* everywhere because it is always, for everyone, the possibility of defining a *here* and defining oneself as a regulatory third party. Quasi-sovereignty is not, and never can be, a totalised power of the group over its members, nor can it be the successive power of each over all. Power enters with the first limitation, that is to say, with the pledge. Quasi-sovereignty was originally the following simple contradiction: in every third party the synthetic power of reorganising the practical field manifests itself as his membership of the rearranged group, and, therefore, as *the same* in everyone, now; thus the common *praxis* is realised everywhere at the same time and it is both means and end. Thus every quasi-sovereign, as a regulatory third party, transcends the grouped ensemble by a head, without ceasing to be integrated into it, and, as a regulated third party, he allows himself to be transcended by a *himself* who has emerged in some arbitrary here.

The sovereign, by contrast, can be defined within the group by a statute peculiar to him, the basic reality of which is negation: no one can claim that he is outside the group, or that he has ceased to be a third party. Sovereignty-institution designates the common individual who exercises it as a non-transcendable third party, at least in the performance of his functions. If he is not transcendable, and if he still does not leave the group, his regulatory action (either actually performed or defined as an organised operation) is always determined as common *praxis* laying down its own laws before all. But untranscendability produces the untranscendable third party as the member of the group through whom this regulation *always has to be carried out*. Thus the existence of a sovereign is based negatively on the impossiblity (suffered or agreed or both: this has still to be determined) of every third party becoming directly regulatory again. This does not mean that every practical initiative, every attempt at reorganisation, every invention and discovery has to originate in the sovereign: it means that they must pass through him, be reinteriorised by him, and, through him, appear to the group as a new practical orientation. The sovereign can make use of the means of communication (whether roads or canals or the 'mass media') because he has sole responsibility for communication. We have seen how the group, in the process of organising itself, produces apparatuses of control and mediation. But whatever their importance, these apparatuses are always specialised: the function of the sovereign is to ensure the mediation of all the mediations and to constitute himself as such as a permanent mediation between the common individuals. But this mediation is aimed at more than the preservation of the unity of the group: it attempts to preserve it in the light of practical realisation of the common aim.

Now, the fixity of the mediation arises as both a result and a condition of certain expropriations which are suffered and accepted by common individuals: in fact it constitutes the negation of direct reciprocity and the alienation of indirect reciprocity.[79] The negation of direct reciprocity is centralisation, as the necessity that two given sub-groups whose practices are complementary should *go through* 'the departments' or 'the Council' in order to adapt their actions reciprocally. The alienation of indirect reciprocity is that mediation is itself a modifying action on this reciprocity. Mediated reciprocity, which is the constitutive structure of the group, is direct and free as long as the mediation is done through all, that is to say, quite simply, within common *praxis*. It becomes an uncertain, other object when the common *praxis*, embodied in a single, untranscendable mediator, works as an individual activity on the reciprocal relation: in fact, communication may always be broken (by a break of any origin) or altered; reciprocity may return to everyone in the form of a task laid down by the central power *on the basis* of reciprocal relations, that is to say, in so far as they are revised and corrected by a third party. Thus the relation of the same to the same returns to everyone as *Other*.

And this alterity is expressed in its new structure: it is either an order or a defence. The structure of 'Fraternity-Terror' and pledged inertia will no doubt already have determined a structure of alterity in each practical freedom, and this will have produced the imperative and power as structuring, structured relations of the statutory group and the organised group. But these free imperatives defined themselves through initiatives which were both assumed and controlled, and which were a direct function of the task to be done. But the stratified action of the sub-groups on the group as a quasi-object will already be marked by a certain passivity, through the multiplicity of rearrangements: it is this that transformed what was originally a pure common *praxis* into a *praxis-process*. But, in any case, the new mediation emphasises this movement. Thus the sovereign, being untranscendable, is *other* than everyone. It is no longer possible to say that all members

79. I am referring to the relations between representatives of powers as such rather than to free relations of reciprocity (although, in special conditions, the latter may be seriously altered thereby).

are the same or that every elsewhere is *here*. In effect, there is a common individual who, as a member of the group, is *other than all* because he cannot become *a regulated third party*. And this third party will of course be an institution, in that, like all the Others, he will be the inert, imperative, unity of all the institutionalised members. But, on the other hand, the paradox of this institution is that it has to realise itself through a free, organising *praxis* to which all are subjected by an Other. The *praxis* of the group becomes other in so far as it is manifested in a particular temporalisation and as an individual action: or rather, it becomes *other* in so far as the common project presents itself as *individual will*.

And so, for every third party, the imperative which defines his power returns to him as the will of an Other, which he obeys because of his pledge. It is a new structure (the individualisation in a sovereign Other of the common imperative) which constitutes the command as such. In obeying the Other as Other in the name of the common *praxis*, everyone becomes other in so far as he is the same. This is the basic structure of obedience: it is realised in the milieu of 'Fraternity-Terror' and against a background of violence: in everyone, inert pledged being is an untranscendable negation of the possibility of not carrying out the imposed action; refusal would effectively mean the dissolution of the group (both as an organised group and as a pledged group); but, in so far as action is, in this case, an interiorisation of an *other will* (*volonté autre*), it introduces an induced passivity into it, and comes to be occasioned by an untranscendable sovereignty with no reciprocity; and the refusal to dissolve the group in oneself, that is to say, the legitimation of common violence (as repressive terror) by readopting the pledge becomes no more than submitting to the individual decisions of the untranscendable third party and to his quasi-sovereignty as violence without reciprocity.

It is at this level that freedom in itself (and not only in its objectification) becomes alienated and hidden from its own eyes. Task and function, as imperatives, referred only to all and to the urgency of the job to be done: pledged inertia referred to everyone's free *praxis* (as other, admittedly, but formally, and not as the concrete freedom *of one* Other). Thus the imperative as such arose in the milieu of dialectical freedom and, in the completion of the task, revealed free organic action (as a mediation between the common individual and the object of the common *praxis*). Obedience to orders cuts out these references. But in spite of all the masks, organic *praxis* is still the only modality of action; the most disciplined soldier, when he shoots on command, has to take aim, *estimate* distances, pull the trigger at the right time (that is to say, as soon as possible after the order, *making allowance for special circumstances*). But the sovereignty of the untranscendable third party expresses itself as *an order* through the will of an Other; and the pledged (*and suffered*) impossibility of not adopting the order becomes an interiorisation of the other will as the real unity of the practical temporalisation. In the moment of *organic* mediation, the free project of the transcended third party arises, with its own comprehension as an *other project* (*projet autre*) (or *project of an Other*) referring every ensemble *not only* to the community, to reciprocal powers, and to the remade pledge *but also* to a free *praxis* which is not mine, and which imposes itself on mine as regulatory, that is to say – because of its own untranscendability – as an *individualisation of the common aim*. In developing the Other's project *in terror* (that is to say, both under the constraint of the sovereign's coercive forces and in the climate of fraternity-violence, the two being ultimately identical), I deny myself in my organic individuality, so that the Other can accomplish his project in me.

At this level, a double transformation takes place. (1) At the level of *the common individual*, my powers are conferred on me by all but only *through the mediation of the Other*; there is still reciprocal organisation, but it takes the form of a univocal rearrangement, without reciprocity; and common *praxis* manifests itself in the form of an untranscendable *praxis* of an individual in freedom. (2) At the level of my own individual activity, my freedom is stolen from me and I become the actualisation of the Other's freedom. This does not mean that I feel as though I were being subjected to some external or internal constraint; or that the Other manipulates me from a distance like a hypnotist; the specific structure is that my freedom is freely lost and divests itself of its translucidity so as to actualise, here, in my muscles, in my body at work, the Other's freedom *in so far as* it is elsewhere, in the Other, and in so far as it is lived, here, by me, as an alienating signification, as a rigid absence and as the absolute priority, *everywhere*, of interiorised alterity – everywhere, that is, *except*, in the untranscendable Other, who is other than all precisely in being alone in being able to be himself.[80]

---

80. Whatever the historical situation, there is a serious error which must be avoided. It would be absurd to define an order as an exigency in exteriority (the

master commanding the slave) based on force, and then to go on to derive institutional powers of authority from these initial relations. To do so would be completely to mistake the true structure of an order and of obedience, that complex dialectic in interiority, of the same and the other, of constraint and legitimacy. When a slave obeys his masters' orders, this does not in any way mean that he regards them as legitimate. Neither, of course, does it mean, *a priori*, that he denies their legitimacy: the relation is in fact quite indeterminate. A given slave may be reconciled to his fate; he may be privileged in relation to the other slaves, born in the *domus*, etc., and, especially if he has personal relations with the master, he may regard the master's authority as legitimate, that is to say, he may almost unconsciously betray his fellow-slaves. But another, who is deeply rebellious, and conscious of the injustice of his condition, may obey either cynically and out of mere prudence or, possibly, in the expectation of a revolt which he will join. If one sets out from this absolute indeterminacy it will be impossible to comprehend why obedience, as a *simple fact* (a surrender to constraint) may sometimes appear as pledged faith, as a permanent legitimation of authority, etc. The rational order is in fact quite strict: *authority*, as a complex relation between an untranscendable third party and the common individuals who legitimate his powers by obeying him – *this is what is given in the first instance*. And the violent integration of new individuals into the group (for example, the slaves in familial exploitation) takes place *in the name of this legitimate authority*. Obviously the mystification is complete. But it results precisely from the juridical structure of the community: newcomers are introduced into it with a certain statute, certain functions, etc., and the sovereign (for example, the *pater familias*) demands their obedience in the name of a pledge which they never made but which they accept in spite of themselves, for the other members of the group, because it is the synthetic basis of all common relations and because they are in fact (through either capture or birth) integrated into the community. On the other hand, when the historical development of the oppressed class is just beginning, while it is paralysed by impotence and seriality, while individual antagonisms make any common action impossible, and, above all, when individuals are *placed* (by birth, for example) into a juridical group which exercises 'fraternity-terror' on itself through the mediation of a leader, obedience legitimates the sovereignty of the exploiters in the eyes of the exploited. As the case of the Lyon silk-weavers proves, revolt is not born of systematic questioning of the system but rather, amongst men who still respect and acknowledge the employers' right to own machines and to govern, of the sheer impossibility of survival. It is revolt – as permanent *praxis*, initially blind, imposed by need, and by the danger of death – which gradually creates the illegitimacy of public powers and in the end reduces class relations to a new and basic truth: that of power relations. Except in a case of suddenly instituted tyranny, of military occupation, etc., it is not and never can be the illegitimacy of the powers which occasions revolt. In other words, cynical obedience to orders which are regarded as illegitimate is a historical moment in the evolution of authority: that in which conflicts which are initially spasmodic and disordered, in the process of becoming more ordered, create an objective situation in which it is possible to reduce the relations of exploiters to exploited or of oppressors to oppressed to mere power relations.

In the light of these considerations, it is possible to establish the original finality of sovereignty as an institution as well as the formal conditions of its possibility. The problem of its historical emergence in each case is not our concern.

We have seen how the group's common *praxis* can, through the institutional system, be conceived as its transcendent freedom and at the same time as its fundamental being. But we have also learnt that the institution is a practical relation (to the common object), based on impotence and separation, as the reified relationships between members of the group. Furthermore, we have observed that as soon as one tries to explain an institutional system, it tends to appear as an ensemble of relations in exteriority. Lastly, *praxis* as common freedom is no more than an index of the alienation of our individual freedom. However, the group remains effective and practical: the army may make use of the institutional relations which characterise it in order to define a local tactic or a strategy. Wherever common *praxis* retains its vitality and reality, the constituent dialectic – that is to say, organised practices – sustains the constituted dialectic, even beneath the thick stratifications of serial and institutionalised ensembles.

Now, the contradiction which is proper to institutional systems (and which derives both from the fact that they are produced as the only practical instruments in the circumstances and from the fact they are produced through the resurrection of serialities) is that, in themselves, they represent both the irresistible force of transcendent *praxis* and the permanent possibility that it will break up into serial relations of seriality. This danger is increased by the fact that a group's tendency to define itself in terms of its institutions is proportional to the importance of the serialities which penetrate it. In practice, this means that the group is constantly threatened by the danger that an increase in its level of seriality may lead each institution to function for itself, as a pure practico-inert *exis*, and that their practical unity may explode into a mere exterior dispersal. In this light, it is possible to discern the true function of sovereignty: it is the institutional reinteriorisation of the exteriority of institutions or, in so far as the latter are reifying mediations between passivised men, it is the institution *of one man* as a mediation between institutions. And this institution has no need for any group *consensus*; on the contrary, it is based on the impotence of its members. Thus the sovereign is a reflexive synthesis of dead-practices which were tending to be separated in a centifugal movement. Through his personal unity, he unifies them into a totalising project which *individualises* them; and this no longer has anything to do with relations tending towards the universal (like *the* taxation system, *the* military law, etc.), but instead with an individual historical ensemble of which every institution forms a part as an instrument of all, and whose totalisation is its practical employment for attaining the common objective. Of course, the sovereign and his *praxis* are products of the institutional system: in this sense, they participate in the exteriority of all the relations, in their analytical universality and in their inertia: not only is there an ensemble of laws specifying the mode of recruitment and professional training for the untranscendable third party, but also – since in himself he is no more than the institutional system lived in a reflexive synthesis of interiority – the limited field of his practical possibilities is simply a determination of his future by the unifying ensemble of institutional instruments.

But we have already seen that these institutions are themselves the practical relations between the institutionalised third parties and that they define them in reciprocity in the endlessly repeated movement of a single *process-practice*. At this level military service is an objective process which can be studied in exteriority: each year, at a given time, X young men of such and such an age are called up for X months or X years. It is also a finality in the process of being passivised: the national group must be able to defend itself by arms. Lastly and, from our point of view, most important, it is a determination in inertia of the reciprocity between the people in the group (conscripts, those refused admission, or called up, or recalled, or granted deferment, or released, etc.), and this reciprocity is naturally *practical* because it creates diversities both of passive functions (postings, technical abilities) and of interest.

Now, the institutional production of the sovereign represents the practical reinteriorisation of these determinations of exteriority. First, the passivised end of the military institution becomes a common objective and means of achieving some specific exterior end. The problem is really to keep the institution inside the framework of a concrete policy and as an indispensable means of maintaining it; if he is not prevented from doing so by his statute, the sovereign must be able (directly or indirectly) to modify the institution (increase the length of service, for example) in accordance with political needs, or to give an appearance of *practical reorganisation* to processes which are conditioned by external changes (the development of industry and of weapons, the reorganisation of the army around new weapons). But above all, the revival of free *praxis*, as untranscendable interiorisation, has the effect of referring this unified activity to the institutionalised third parties as the truth of their institutional being. Without the sovereign, it is impossible to dissolve their passivity: military service, in fact, becomes no more than a process. But free sovereign *praxis* presents itself as the meaning and the embodiment in freedom of the inert-being of the third parties. The institutional group, constituted reason, the dialectic imitated and already distorted by seriality, appears in the practical unity of the sovereign as constituent reason. Separation at the base remains necessarily what it is, but is transcends itself (*elle se transcende*) through everyone and returns to the apex, as a consequence of sovereign unity; impotence, as a relation of exteriority at the base, is conceived by everyone at the apex as a systematic and ordered deployment of the original synthesis. This is because, as we have seen, the institutional group alienates the practical freedoms of its members to the free *praxis* of the community. But this *praxis* exists only as the abstract, negative object of an empty intention. The institution of the untranscendable regulator has the effect of reinteriorising this common freedom and of giving it an ambivalent statute of both individuality and generality.

In so far as the sovereign is *one person* in pursuit of the common objective and realising quite specific activities, this untranscendable third party refers this common action to the institutionalised third parties – who perform it without recognising it in themselves – in the strict form of *an individual activity*. Such is the first relation between the third party and the sovereign: in one way, it is a relation between two individuals (the first, inert and impotent, finds individual action in the second and finds his own justification in him, in the Other). On the other hand, the sovereign is signified by sovereignty-institution as a general and indeterminate individual who simply has to respond to certain conditions (relating to his mode of recruitment). And his power, born of the institution itself, as a common product of the group as serial impotence, is in itself *common*; in other words, the sovereign is, so to speak, *a common individual* through himself, like any third party. From this double point of view, he tends in exteriority to flee historical, individual determinations and his authority will always appear to be the temporalisation of the eternal ('The king is dead, long live the king'). Lastly, as he is the product and temporary embodiment of an institution, his institutional-being is inorganic inertia – that is to say, the impotence of the Others. Thus he can reflect to each and to all the common, institutionalised individual as any arbitrary member of the group: his common reality is institutional-being (suffered impotence, pledged inertia), as producing its own power in inertia and freedom; and from this point of view, his actions always have a structure of generality: they apply to everyone, as an individual defined by his function, because they emanate from an individual who is himself defined by his function. The group rediscovers itself through everyone in the universalising power of their individual actions. Thus the sovereign-individual and the sovereign-institution are both present in every decision of sovereignty.

But the institution of authority cannot prevent the dispersal of institutions as such: in itself, it is strictly homogeneous with all the others. In fact, only the realisation of the universal *through an individual, historical action* can reinteriorise the centrifugal exteriority of inertia. Every action practically reinteriorises the institutional system by employing it in its entirety for a synthetic complex of historical operations; every individual practice realises itself as a temporalisation. This merely means that the group cannot perceive itself as *praxis* in the sovereign, except in that highly *suspect* moment of the undertaking, in which free *praxis* acts as a mediation between the common individual and the object. Only the sovereign can and must be free; he alone has to produce his actions as moments of a free dialectical development. There is only one freedom for all the members of the group: that of the sovereign. And this ambiguous freedom is both *the* common freedom (in its institutional origins) and *his* individual freedom in the service of the community. But it is an organisational freedom: it rearranges the group by issuing orders; and these orders, as we have seen, have the effect of detaching everyone's free *praxis* – buried beneath institutionality – and at the same time of alienating it, by realising themselves as *other* through it. Now, at the level of this alienation, the presence of the Other is produced as a substitute for the ubiquity *of the same*: the sovereign is present in everyone as Other in the moment when he is obeyed. And everyone thereby distances himself slightly from the statute of alterity in relation to the Others, because he *becomes the same* as a bearer of the universal Other and as mediated by him in his relations with everyone.

But the ambiguity of the obedient third party, in his relation to the Other will which he actualises, indicates sufficiently the function and, as it were, the failure of sovereignty as the practical reunification of an institutionalised group. The question whether the members of the group will be reunited *in a common praxis* rediscovered through particular orders and sovereign operations or whether they find their unity as organic individuality in the person of *their* sovereign, and then accept his own wishes as a common aim, cannot be settled *a priori*. Here again we encounter the absolute limits of the constituted dialectic: if the group seeks its common-being in the institution of sovereignty, its being will be dissipated in abstract exteriority; if it wishes to grasp its own ontological unity (which, as we have seen, does not exist) in the concrete, it will run up against an organic and untranscendable individuality; and this untranscendable individuality presents itself as a transcendence (*dépassement*) of every multiplicity of individuals (because it really emerges as *the* group, inside the group).

Embodiment, as a fact of sovereignty, the production of the group by the group in the form of *this* particular person, with *these* individual characteristics, *these* ailments, *this* irreducible physiognomy, and of *this* particular age, is the manifestation of a constitutional impossibility which we observed long ago: it is impossible for a multiplicity, even if it is interiorised in each of its members and negated, to produce itself for itself, in itself, under any ontological statute other than those of dispersal through inertia and organic individuality. The latter form of being, maintained by the institution as a common reality but utterly inadequate to the group, presents itself to every member of the group not only as *generality* (institutionality), but also as a practical individuality, homogeneous with every separate individuality (though superior in power, dignity, etc.), and as a condensation of the *common* by means of an immense pressure which is liable to transform it into *idiosyncracy*. The future leader, son of the present one, has just been born: the third parties worship the group which they and their sons will compose in the future, in the form of a child. In fact, when the mode of recruitment is defined as the inheritance of functions, the group is reborn, materialised, concretised, and produced as *the eldest son* by the leader; it is reborn *by the flesh*, recreated through the virility of one individual, and, within the reflexive structure, his inert-being comes back to him as transcended, and transformed into a living, physical unity. At the same time, he *is* the father, as an organic *praxis* with a common structure. The formal untranscendability of biological integration is concretely realised inside institutional groups by the untranscendability of the third party.

Thus, in a group which is eroded by serialities, the sovereign (in his quasi-sovereignty) emerges initially as an *organ of integration*. He is untranscendable, and his quasi-sovereignty places him above recurrence; living and one, he reveals common unity to the half-dead group as a symmetrical synthesis of the human body. He is a universal mediation, and he destroys reciprocity wherever it exists, and relations between transcended third parties cannot establish themselves except through his mediation. But in fact he emerges in the moment where these relations are on the decline. His instituted presence undoubtedly contributes to their decline: at least, he re-establishes them as *his own products* (in other words, he creates a concrete, practical reciprocity between given sub-groups or individuals, sovereignly and by order). This relation solidifies in so far as its reason lies outside itself in the *praxis* of the Other, and in so far as this is its only reason for preserving itself. But the institutional individual mistrusts the *free relations* which reveal the threat of everyone's freedom everywhere as a dissolution of the institutional monolith: he sees integration as a petrification by which alterity will be merged into an inertia of homogeneity (which he takes to be the rediscovered Being of the group). At times of mistrust, the untranscendable third party in the mediated relation is a surety for every third party for the other; and everyone appears to the other as a common project in so far as its details are defined by an individual will.

And when the sovereign organises new sub-groups – either directly or through official mediation – he is *the body* of the constituted body, his decree is the practical, imperative milieu in which every member of the sub-groups was reborn, from a point of view which is defined elsewhere, by the Other, and with powers which he derives from the group in so far as they are defined by the wishes of a particular individual. These reciprocities (and limits of competence, etc.), *as others*, are for everyone the concrete, or life itself, in so far as their still synthetic character and their alterity represent in and for everyone a protection against seriality (the victory of the inorganic over the practical organism), by the total and reciprocal alienation of all practical organisms to a single one. The last word is no longer *dust* (dust thou art and unto dust thou shalt return), but the living totality. And, in serial isolation itself, obedience to or reverence for the sovereign saves everyone from his sclerosis of inertia: unable to sustain relations with all or to realise the inessentiality of his person and the essentiality of the common being, everyone emerges – in respect, fear, unconditional fidelity, and sometimes in worship – as an inessential embodiment of the whole, that is to say, of the sovereign. Here the relation is inverted: the sovereign once embodied an impossible ontological unity as the organic, individual unity of all in one; and conversely, everyone can relate concretely to the all-sovereign of whom he becomes both a constituted part and an inessential embodiment – and these amount to the same thing though their logical orientations may be different. The alienation of an individual to the individual-totality represents a further decline of the group as common *praxis*; but, at the same time, it revives the *structural* bond in a bastardised form. This bond defined itself, in practical unity and in it alone, as a synthetic relation of the part to the totalisation; and it seems to reproduce itself here as an ontological relation between an element in the process of massification and the totality which reaffirms itself as already created.

But the practical perception of inessentiality comes to people when quasi-sovereignty, as untranscendability, constitutes them from outside as quasi-objects – not theoretically or through speeches or ceremonies (though there may well be some of these), but *practically*, through the perpetual rearrangements which the apparatuses of sovereignty make *by order* and which are carried out at all levels by the *manipulation* of each and all. Such a rearrangement should, in principle, advance the integration of the group in accordance with imposed transcendent objectives. It realises itself as a means within the closed world which is determined by the pencil of rays which unite the sovereign and the object (the exterior object which has to be produced, destroyed, etc.). Thus he encounters common *praxis* in both manipulation and command, but in the form of individualised will. But this does not matter: this will radiates from a single source, it is transmitted by specific apparatuses, and it determines a field of pure will in which every quasi-object recognises itself *in its quasi-objectivity* as a product, a point of application and transmitter of this *other will*. The important point for him is that this will should be *one*, that its practical development should simply be a temporalisation of the organic unity of the sovereign and, most important of all, that its immediate objective should be to impose (by his command, by constraint, and if need be by terror) biological unity at every level of dispersal, in opposition to the multiplicity of alterity and as the ontological statute of the totality.

The sovereign is produced by terror,[81] and he has to become the

81. It may be said that power is often far from bringing about a reign of terror. This is true and we shall see the reason for it. But what we are studying here is not sovereignty as it occurs in a historical *society*; we are considering it as an apparatus which constitutes itself inside groups which are institutionalising themselves.

agent responsible for it: everyone abandons mistrust in favour of the untranscendable third party, on the understanding that he will express everyone's mistrust of everyone. In fact, there is still recurrence, and the shifting mistrust grows deeper because it has become *power* (the duty to betray one's neighbour to the apparatuses of sovereignty, the sovereign power to liquidate anyone in particular); and, most important of all, serial circularity as a unity of flight becomes the object of a permanent, sovereign operation aimed at destroying it. The apparent progress of reflexivity here is due to the fact that the untranscendable third party, *from his elevated position*, believes that he has a synthetic view of the common field whereas, in fact, the means of transmission necessarily serialise his information (he thinks he can see but really sees nothing, apart from other, ready-solidified views, provided by others and originating at the common level). The politics of integration corresponds to these synthetic views: through his apparatuses, the sovereign tries to constitute the group not only as a practical object, but also as a living object. For him, as a product of mistrust and separation, who regards all plurality and alterity as suspect, and therefore as having to be liquidated immediately, the only non-suspect unity is his own practical unity and the ontological structures which develop in it: in short, the unity of the organism – his right hand trusts his left and no other.

Through an intelligible inversion of the contradiction, this power, which is institutionally defined as a permanent reinteriorisation of the group in exteriorisation, already represents, both in itself and ontologically, the impossibility of common-being; but in the name of its practical function, integration, it makes an authoritarian attempt (using violence if necessary) to realise the *organic-being* which actually indicates the impossibility that the common *praxis* should be based on a common-being, as the common-being of the group. In the practices of authority, the impossibility of giving oneself an ontological statute becomes, within the group, a violent and vain reduction of third parties by the regulatory third party to an *other* ontological statute, by definition unrealisable. This at least is what the sovereign 'believes' he is doing, and what he is 'believed to do'. But here we confront once again the contradiction between the two ontological statutes: the mixing and manipulation of third parties with the object of constituting organic unities, actually produce inorganic quasi-objects whose inertia receives sovereign orders just as the inertia of wax receives the seal. And the conduct of every third party, as a molecule of the quasi-object, moves from enthusiastic realisation of an other will to passive, resigned acceptance of this will. Thus the sovereign's *praxis* on the group, being both transcendent and immanent, is expressed, successively, or even, sometimes, simultaneously, in two kinds of determination of discourse. The goal may be expressed in terms of mechanical unity: the group is a machine which the sovereign sets in motion (*perinde ac cadaver*). Or the group may define itself as an extension of the sovereign, that is to say, as the arms, legs and eyes which he produces in order to realise the common objective. But, in fact, the second formulation relates to sovereignty-mystification, whereas the first necessarily reveals the function of the sovereign as dispossession, alienation and massification. The false unity of common quasi-objects (instrumentality) can in fact arise only on the basis of an accelerated process of passivisation; so that when constraint is relaxed, individuals revert to a molecular dispersal which separates them even more than their previous alterity.

Could it be said that the sovereign is the group's chosen means of maintaining its unity in specific circumstances? The answer is both yes and no. The emergence of a sovereign is in fact the result of a *process*. In circular recurrence, the slightest short circuit will create sovereignty: and such short circuits occur, in given conditions, as reinforcements of the differential by recurrence. In universal impotence, this recurrence will run up against a sub-group or individual with differential characteristics which make reciprocity less obvious, and which are produced as univocal bonds of interiority. In fact, regardless of what these characteristics are, they cannot extract a future sovereign from the reciprocal relation until the group is eroded by alterity. On the other hand, in a group which is in the process of being institutionalised, impotence, as a shifting separation of peers, makes the actual power of certain individuals appear as untranscendability – not only because serial paralysis prevents everyone from acquiring these characteristics for themselves, but also, and most importantly, because – whatever the characteristics may be – the group (still effective in its transcendent objective, though affected with inertia in its internal relations) does not in fact have any common power with which to oppose the strength of a particular individual. This is the process: the possible sovereigns are installed and there is nothing for the third parties either to accept or to support, since they are incapable of refusing anything. When the sovereign takes power, he establishes himself as the free, directed transcendence of common passivity: and this will mean the re-emergence of freedom as constituent Reason within the constituted group.

De facto power – in so far as it is consolidated by recurrence – is prior to *de jure* power. But in order that untranscendability should move from fact to right, power must become institutionalised. Here, through institutions, a kind of passive finality re-emerges: the need which everyone feels either to allow the institutional system to lose itself in exteriority, without surety or internal unity, or to reinteriorise it as an instrumental system *employed* in a unique, individual temporalisation. This is the exigency of institutional practices as practice-processes maintained in their being by everyone's impotence and freedom. This means, then, that the movement of institutionalisation involves the institutionalisation of the practical individual as such as its only chance of completion; or, in other words, the institutionalisation of the freedom of a single individual as an institution. With the emergence of free *praxis*, in fact, the whole movement of institutionality turns in on itself and reverts to being a practical field and an instrument. Thus authority, as the internal unity of institutions, is required by their very being (by the contradiction between their practical efficacity and the inertia of their dispersal). The expulsion of individual freedom by inertia would become the occasion for a relapse into the practico-inert, unless common, transcendent freedom were embodied in the free *praxis* of an institutionalised organism; through the institution everyone sacrifices his freedom for the sake of inert efficiency, but he gets it back at the apex in the double, undifferentiated form of common and individual freedom; the order reincarnates it in him as the freedom of an Other actualising itself through him.

The purpose of these last remarks is to show that the sovereignty of the untranscendable third party arises, in groups which are in the process of being institutionalised, when the empty, inert exigency of an institutional system in search of its unity coincides with an interruption of recurrence by some material, accidental superiority. There is an integration of *de facto* power with the generality of power and, therefore of a *process of impotence* which constitutes a given man or ensemble *from outside* as the strongest, or the richest, of *the Others* (or – as happened in the early stages of feudal authority – as the-man-with-a-horse) with a passive finality born in the institutional system of the still practical character of the institutionalised men. *De facto* power gives a practical content to the institution: for the institution of sovereignty does not designate the sovereign as the passive unity of the system, but as the unifying force which condenses, integrates, and changes it by making use of it. The institution, on the other hand, in so far as it preserves the exigencies of Terror and of violence, *demands* force and legitimates it. In the other functions, the *power* of each specialised individual may involve the right to call on force for support, though force itself is not the content of their power. On the contrary, the reunification of the institutional skeleton requires that the work done by the institutions (and if necessary against them) should be directly produced by sovereign force; unifying force is the immediate content of sovereign power. In this way, force is both the right and the duty of authority: it is the concentration in a single individual of Terror as the struggle against seriality. But this concentration would be no more than an idea or a material exigency of the system unless the regulatory third party *already had* the necessary strength. In short sovereignty does not *create* sovereign strength, but rather makes the sovereign's *pre-existing* strength sovereign.[82] However, this positive strength is tiny compared with the real strength which the group would have if it were to dissolve its emerging seriality. Thus the relation of untranscendability is originally that of a relatively small strength to generalised impotence.

At this level it is possible to discern one of the contradictions of sovereignty: the sovereign reigns through and over the impotence of all; their living practical union would make his function useless, and indeed impossible to perform. However, his proper activity is to struggle against the invasion of the group by seriality, that is to say, against the very conditions which make his office legitimate and possible. We have seen how the contradiction is resolved, in practice, by a new form of alienation: that of each and all to one person. In order to avoid relapsing into the practico-inert field, everyone becomes a passive object or an inessential actualisation for the freedom of the Other. By means of sovereignty, the group alienates itself to a single man so as to avoid alienating itself to the material and human ensemble; in fact everyone experiences his alienation as *life* (as the life of an Other, through his own life), instead of experiencing it as *death* (as a reification of all his relations).

---

82. Of course, this applies only to the original moment in which sovereignty constitutes itself in opposition to recurrence. Once the powers of sovereignty have been strictly defined by tradition, executive powers will be transmitted from one sovereign to the other.

However, the synthetic relation of the sovereign to all through institutions presents a new contradiction, due both to the 'immanence-transcendence' tension which produces a mere quasi-sovereignty in him and to his untranscendability which, though it does not remove him from the group, separates him from all the third parties. As it realises the integration, this quasi-sovereignty, being untranscendable, treats the group as a whole as a field of inorganic materiality or as an organised extension of his organs. The object of the exercise is to realise a *praxis*, to attain a transcendent objective; and the essential relation posits itself as that *between the sovereign and the object*. There is therefore no *a priori* answer to the question whether the practical objectification will be that of the sovereign by means of his group or that of the group through the mediation of the sovereign – whether, in other words, the aim is the object of the sovereign individual as such (in his practical individuality) achieved by *common* means (by setting to work a multiplicity of common individuals), or whether it is a common aim achieved by common action which has been planned, thought out, and organised by means of an untranscendable regulator. Is the object the objectification of *a reign*, or is it that of the men who have lived under it, maintained it, and created it? This indeterminacy is expressed in the phrase '*my* people', which means both *the people who belong to me* and *the people to whom I belong*. It would not help to claim that the sovereign is a specific product of given institutions and that he sets himself constant aims (defined by circumstances and by the constant possibilities of geopolitics: to defeat the house of Austria, etc.), which he can achieve only by using specific instruments, namely institutions. We have already made this point, but it is not relevant to the present problem. Nor is it sufficient simply to claim that the sovereign, as a product of the group (considered as a practical multiplicity of individuals), expresses the deep relations, the conflicts, and the tensions within the group, in spite of himself, and that his *praxis* can be no more than the practical reinteriorisation of these human relations.

But the problem is not so simple. To judge by the claims of those who wish to dispose of him, the sovereign apparently establishes his authority either over a fused group or over an organised group, that is to say, over free practical men, whose only inertia is pledged faith. If this were so, then the sovereign would effectively be no more than the medium of his group. But the sovereign does not exist at this stage of integration. Since his authority is based on serial impotence, and given that he exploits the inertia of internal relations in order to give the group the greatest possible external efficiency, it must be acknowledged that his power is not based on consent (as a positive act of adhesion), but rather that consent to his power is an interiorisation of the impossibility of resisting it. In other words, he imposes himself through the impotence of all, and everyone accepts him as a way of bartering inertia for obedience. This element of nothingness, this 'Devil's Share', is the true support of sovereignty. Everyone obeys in seriality: not because he directly adopts an attitude of obedience, but because he is not sure whether his neighbour has undertaken to obey. This is far from preventing orders from being seen as *legitimate*: in fact it prevents the question of legitimacy from being raised. So if the sovereign works on the inorganic, it is not that 'his' group is using him as a *reflexive medium*, but rather it is himself using 'his' group in order to achieve certain ends.

And of course the limits of his options and choices are indicated by institutions themselves, which are his instruments; that is to say, they are indicated by the petrified ensemble of institutionalised men. But, in the first place, within these limits, his power can vary according to institutions and circumstances; and this power may become quite large. But the most important point to grasp is that, in the course of the repressive Terror which he has to practise in the name of integration, certain stratifications, blockages, and regroupments constitute themselves, each of them calling a temporary halt at this level of Terror, that is to say, in more or less stable equilibrium, and which, as a whole, constitute a passive structuring of the group on the fringe of institutions – a sort of geological section which is nothing other than sovereign *praxis* maintained in its unity by the inertia of separation. And this structured ensemble which is dependent on the practice of the untranscendable individual is not only a material formation which he maintains and constantly engenders, and which will collapse when he dies, but also the ensemble of avenues and paths of his power: as he reigns the sovereign increases his power, because he produces the group in his own image. Naturally, the converse is also true: the group condenses into the indissoluble unity of an organism, and the sovereign dilates through the multiplicities of the group. Nevertheless, the group, through these acquired structures, performs an extra-institutional task on itself, and this is simply an inert extension of sovereign *praxis*. And these very conditions of sovereignty suffice to show that there is no *a priori* answer to the question. From the point of view of the group, the institutions, the circumstances, the common objective, etc., the sovereign posits himself either as the medium of the group or as its end. And, on the second hypothesis, and depending on the situation, he may either posit himself in his practical, free individuality as a goal of the community, or regard the institutional system as essential in so far as he himself has the institutional power to reinteriorise it (while the multiplicity of institutionalised members is inessential). Whether it is the man or the apparatus which posit themselves, a new alienation results for the third parties: provided that the goal of the sovereign really is the common object of the group, no one will have any aim other than serving the sovereign himself, and everyone will pursue the common aim, not because it is common, but because it is the object of free sovereign *praxis*.

This is the particular embodiment of sovereignty which is normally encountered in History. Its dialectical reason is simple, and we sum-marise it here only so as to reveal a few of the formal structures of sovereignty. And in fact our inquiry is leading to a new moment of our investigation: the institutional group coming into contact with the various serialities of the non-grouped. Several different objectives, in fact, are possible and logically definable; the aim of the group may be the production and reproduction of the life of its members, struggle against some other group, or direct action on collectives. This last category includes agitational and propaganda groups as well as publicity associations or groups of cadres, etc. Now, if a group which is still effective (though possibly eroded by seriality) really acts on serial individuals, its action on the series is due to its unity. At this level, we are now in a position to complete a description which we gave at an earlier and more abstract level of our investigation, where we spoke of newspapers and the radio as *collectives*. And this was not a mistake, since everyone reads or listens to the opinions of the Others. But our description missed another aspect of its reality: the fact that what is lived and used as collective by the serial flight of alterity is *also* an organised group (the newspaper) or an institutional group (the state radio) which, in a common undertaking transcends itself (*se transcende*) towards collectives and inert gatherings as their own objectives.

At this level, the group is capable of adapting to the collective: it has been through it; and each of its members is himself – in other moments, and in relation to other individuals – a serial being; besides, each of them, even inside the group, is already more than half serialised; and finally, experience in his job may have taught him the effect of a given item of news or of a given statement when it is reproduced in the privacy of a couple or of a family and appears as a collective opinion. At this level, group *praxis* (unless it is aimed at the dissolution of inertias of seriality in a given place) is, in itself and for all its members, a rational employment of recurrence. It is by starting from impotence and separation, in the knowledge that every thought in every individual is a thought of the Other, that they manipulate the inert material of their work. The group, as a practical totalisation, which organises itself in the unity of its directives through the practical thought which reveals and combines the elements of alterity outside it, becomes the free, synthetic unity of alterity as such, that is to say, it relies for the effectiveness of its action on the impotence and dispersal of its objects. An advertising project, or a film which has to be seen, or a view which has to be expressed, establishes itself in every *Other* with its own co-efficient of alterity which, as we have seen, shows that the other-thought (*la pensée-autre*), in seriality, *has to* reinteriorise and reactualise the thought of the Other. Thus a group which works on an inert gathering produces itself both in relation to this gathering and *in itself* as a sovereign in an institutionalised group, except that, in our examples, its action is not institutional in character. This does not mean that collectives can simply be manipulated according to one's wishes. On the contrary, as we have seen, these serial flights have inflexible laws. But regardless of his range of choice, even the sovereign cannot manipulate the group just as he wishes, any more than workers or technicians can do what they like with their tools and materials. This is not the issue: the important point is that the group is *active* and that the practico-inert man is its *passive object* – not as a practical organism, but as an Other. It is also important that the action which rearranges the practical field has both the result and the aim of working inert gatherings so that the force of the inertia should itself produce the intended result. In this way, an organised group can exercise *sovereignty* over collectives, since it treats them as an individual treats the objects of his practical field and because it acts on them in accordance with their laws, that is to say, by exploiting their relations of exteriority.

In this sense, in the case of an institutionalised group which has a sovereign in some form or other, he becomes the sovereign of the collective in so far as he is the sovereign of the group. But there is one all-important reservation: this sovereignty is not itself institutionalised. But this is not important. Hearst, the magnate of the conservative press in America, with his newspaper chains, over which he exerted authoritarian control, was sovereign and reigned over public opinion. Besides, an inert gathering is more likely to accept the institutionality of the sovereign when it thinks of him in serial impotence and through indefinite alterity – which means that he appears to every member of the series as a benefactor of the indefinite recurrence which is known as public opinion. The sovereign is both man and infinite; he is outside the practico-inert, and his freedom opposes the suffered alienation of alterity. The action of the group on the gathering has to be conceived synthetically on the basis of knowledge of the serial and it is realised serially through the directed and controlled serialisation of agents. But when, in a gathering, separate individuals rise from produced seriality (press, radio, etc.) to an individual who directs the operation, this Other, who is other than all of them because of his organic and practical unity and his power, seems to them to determine – and actually does determine – their indefinite flight, so as to occasion an abstract, totalising unity in it: the whole indefinite series of the newspapers and the *other* readers is condensed in him; and, in him, recurrence is free temporalisation; in him, public opinion is one individual, historical thought, a free determination of discourse, though without ceasing to be multiplied to infinity in the practico-inert.

All I have wanted to show by these formal remarks is that the unity of the sovereign, as the sole practical freedom of the group, occasions an abstract phantom of unity within the series, and that this relation is really no more than a degradation of his relation to the third parties of the community. For this reason, when an emergency threatens a concrete ensemble composed of a group and a gathering (the raw material of the group being the gathering), or when the division of functions makes some regulation necessary, the group may claim the power to distribute tasks to the members of the series, and the members can accept them, without escaping from seriality. In fact, it is worth remarking that the presence of constituted groups – except ones which are explicitly aimed at the dissolution of seriality – prevents the formation of fused groups out of the collective (or at least it makes it more difficult). Induced unity is sufficient; alterity is liquidated when there is no other means of struggle, and no other hope. When there is a group, orders are accepted partly from a simple inability to refuse and partly because the transcendent unity of the group creates an economy of dangerous unification for every other. The mobilising group may impose its institutions on the series because they are homogeneous with it in so far as they are still practices of impotence. But when they become serial, institutions decline a little further and they become suffered processes whose concrete meaning is dissipated in the milieu of exteriority. For every *Other* in the gathering, it will suffice to know that the institutional ensemble takes on a meaning for the sovereign. In this sense, collectives and inert gatherings never legitimate either sovereignty or institutions: they accept them out of impotence and because they have already been legitimated *by the Others* (in the group). In one way, in the milieu of alterity, the mere fact that a group exists outside them and in its synthetic unity constitutes a basis for legitimacy. Not for them, however: *for it*. The group is legitimate because it has produced itself by a pledge in the synthetic milieu of practical freedom, that is to say, in the milieu which rejects the gathering on principle.

In fact, through the other of alterity, the group *as such* (as its own production from the clay of seriality) is legitimate, because it both realises for itself and manifests for all (by determining impotence in depth) the action of freedom in opposition to necessity. This means that, through the group, the sovereignty of *praxis* over the practico-inert manifests itself to seriality as a basis for, and an impotent rejection of, passive activity. Free activity is manifested *elsewhere* to passive activity as the absolute reign of law. And this absolute reign, as a negation of the practico-inert, involves, at least as an abstract connection, the univocal power bursting open the chains of seriality in every Other. In this sense, although the collective has *no ability* to confer sovereignty, and no structure to enable it to do so, it can grasp it as a mode of existence proper to certain practical forms of sociality, and may even, with an institutional group, go back to the origin of totalisation, to individual freedom conceived as the will of all. And its relation to the group (unless the group has produced hostile groups, rivalries or competition, etc.) may be a capitulation to inertia, not only because the Other is manipulated in everyone and because every Other sees the group in and through the Other as freedom creating itself, its legitimacy, and all legitimacy, and, in the same movement, the gathering as in principle foreign to every statute of legitimacy (neither justified nor unjustified: the question of justification does not arise, *a priori*, as far as it is concerned). Besides, though manipulated both as an inert object and as an Other, manipulation does not change every Other; but the intention of producing an effect by transforming the whole series may occasion, in the very locus of alterity, a kind of transcendent unity *as Other*; the relation of exteriority, worked on in the collective by the group, takes on a synthetic, *impracticable* meaning for every other: in so far as the group deigns to use it for its unitary undertaking, this

index of separation becomes, *out there*, in untranscendability, a hidden
unity of alterity.

5   *States and Societies*

These remarks have nothing to do with the historical origins of
sovereignty, but only with entirely abstract logical and dialectical
relations, which must, however, be present as the intelligibility of any
historical interpretation. Within groups, sovereignty is in fact at least
relatively simple. But the ensembles in which sovereignty, in some
form or other, manifests itself in its full development and power are
societies. And we have already established that a society is not a group,
nor a grouping of groups, nor even struggling groupings of groups.
Collectives are both the matrix of groups and their grave; they remain
as the indefinite sociality of the practico-inert, nourishing groups,
maintaining them and transcending them everywhere by their indefinite multiplicity. Where there are several groups, the collective is
either a mediation or battlefield.

Society, which our dialectical investigation has, up to this moment
of its development, approached only very abstractly, thus yields up its
highly formal and indeterminate structure: in the material context of
needs, dangers, instruments and techniques, there can be no such thing
as society unless there are, in some way or other, human multiplicities
united *by a container or by a soil*, unless these multiplicities are divided,
by Historical development, into groups and series, and unless the basic
internal relation of the society – whether production (division of
labour), consumption (type of distribution) or defence against the
enemy (division of tasks) – is ultimately *that of groups to series*. And
among the many differentiations of this internal bond, one of the
easiest to grasp is the institutional ensemble, cloaked and reunited by
the sovereign institution, by the State, in so far as a small group of
organisers, administrators and propagandists take on the task of
imposing *modified* institutions within collectives, as serial bonds which
unite serialities. In short, what is known as the State can never be
regarded as the product or expression of the totality of social individuals or even of the majority of them, since this majority is serial

anyway, and could not express its needs and demands without liquidating itself as a series, so as to become a large group (which either immediately opposes authority or else renders it *completely* inoperative). It is at this level of the large group that dissolving alterity permits concrete needs and objectives to constitute themselves as *common* realities. And the idea of a diffuse popular sovereignty becoming embodied in a sovereign is a mystification. There is no such thing as diffuse sovereignty: the organic individual is sovereign in the abstract isolation of his work; and in fact, he immediately becomes alienated in the practico-inert, where he learns of *the necessity of impotence* (or of impotence as a necessity at the basis of his practical freedom). At the level of the series, juridical and institutional power is completely denied to human multiplicities by the very structure of their relations of exteriority. Thus, inert gatherings do not have the power or nature either to consent to or to resist the State. Sovereignty does not rise from the collective to the sovereign; on the contrary, sovereignty (as command, as a phantom of unity, or as the legitimacy of freedom), descends through the sovereign to modify collectives, without changing their structure of passivity. As for the institution as such, and the concrete power which fills it, it is clear that they arise *in the group* when it is institutionalised and that what ensures its efficacy is a *process-praxis* which also preserves a certain unity in the community which is being serialised.

Thus, within a given society, the State cannot be said to be either legitimate or illegitimate; it is legitimate within a group, because it is produced in a milieu of pledged faith. But it does not really have *this legitimacy* when it acts on collectives, since *the Others* have not sworn anything either to groups or to one another. However, as we have just seen, *the Others* do not claim that it is illegitimate, at least as long as they still do not themselves constitute a group. If they do not make such a demand, this is, *in the first place*, out of impotence: as a series, they have no means of either contesting or establishing legitimacy. *Secondly*, it is because the group, whatever it may be, appears to establish its own legitimacy in that it freely brings itself into being, when it is seen by the Other in alterity as the synthetic signification *elsewhere* of his bonds of exteriority and as the abstract and permanent possibility that the collective *too* should become a grouping.

Something like acceptance may therefore occur; but in itself this is ineffectual since it exists in every other only as an awareness of impotent recurrence. I obey because *I cannot* do otherwise; and in itself this confers serial pseudo-legitimacy on the sovereign: his power to command proves that he has a different nature from mine, or, in other words, that he is freedom. But if I were a member of the group I would somehow find my freedom in that of the sovereign and even, as we have seen, in the alienation of the third party to the living organism of the untranscendable third party. Thus I am in league with the sovereign, and I can pursue his ends as though they were common ends, and therefore as my own, even if, for me, he is already, as the pure unity of integrating violence, *my* untranscendable end. But, given that the institution maintains itself in the series as pure inertia, and given that – once a skilful practice has imposed it – it belongs to the world of practico-inert constraints; given that it presents itself as an exigency rather than as a synthetic signification within a totalisation, it produces itself within the collective (as inert repetition) purely and simply as a *reality* (a *de facto* constraint), while retaining a character of sacred exteriority in so far as it relates, through empty intentions, to the free fulguration which created it. It is the *realist* element which pre-dominates: resistance is futile and there is no point in trying to comprehend: 'That's how things are.' From this point of view all negations which reduce to impotence are assimilated to one another – whether alienations originating in seriality itself, impossibilities result-ing from the economic and social system in the conjuncture, or 'en-forceable' or sovereign orders. Reality, as Mascolo rightly observed – though he did not understand why it was so – is, for the exploited, the unity of all the impossibilities which negatively define them. The State is therefore *primarily a group* which is constantly reorganising itself and altering its composition by means of a partial, discontinuous or continuous, renewal of its members. Within the group, the authority of the sovereign is based on institutions and their exigencies, on the need to ensure the strict unity of the apparatus in the face of the dis-persal of series. In other words, this integrated group sets itself the aim of manipulating the collectives *without extricating them from seriality* and of establishing its power over the heterogeneity of its being and of serial being. The impotence of the series as alterity in flight is both the origin and the limit of state power: always living, always commanding obedience *here*, authority is always threatened *elsewhere*, and in the very moment when the Other who is *here* obeys it.

This radical heterogeneity of the State and of inert gatherings pro-vides the real intelligibility of the historical development of sovereignty. If classes exist (that is to say, if practical, historical investigation reveals them), then, in effect, the State institutes itself in their struggle as the organ of the exploiting class (or classes) and sustains, by constraint, the statute of the oppressed classes. In fact, as we shall soon see when we finally reach the concrete, classes are a shifting ensemble of groups and series; within each class, circumstances occasion practical communities which attempt regroupment, under pressure from certain specific emergencies, and which finish by relapsing, to some extent, into seriality. But if, as we have been assuming, such regroupments occur inside societies in which dominant and dominated classes confront one another, they differ radically according to which class they are in; if they occur within the dominant classes, then, whatever their aim, they necessarily participate in the process-practices of domination; and if they occur in the dominated classes, they will (*even* if, to Others, or in the light of subsequent developments, they may appear as complete betrayals) contain an initial, abstract negation of class domination as one of their basic determinations.

Of course, this does not mean that the problem of sovereignty cannot arise within exploited classes (at least when they reorganise in order to intensify the class struggle); but it does imply that the formation of a State, as a permanent institution and as a constraint imposed by a group on *all* serialities, can occur only through a complex dialectic of groups and series *within the dominant class*. A revolutionary organisation may be sovereign. But *the State* constitutes itself as a mediation between conflicts within the dominant class, in so far as these conflicts run the risk of weakening it in the face of the dominated classes. It embodies and realises the general interest of the dominant class over and above the antagonisms and conflicts of particular interests. This amounts to saying that the ruling class *produces its State* (that its internal struggles produce the possibility and the exigency for a group to arise to defend the general interest) and that its institutional structures will define themselves in terms of concrete reality (that is to say, in the last analysis, in terms of the mode and relations of production). In this sense, for example, the nineteenth-century bourgeois state reflected the unity of bourgeois society: its molecular liberalism and its programme of non-intervention were not based on the fact that the molecular statute of the bourgeoisie was really given, but rather on the exigencies of a complex process which developed industrialisation through the contradictions and antagonisms of competition. Order – *negative* here – is identical with the general interest of the capitalists as a negation of the powers of association and organisation of the exploited classes; they are realised in the relation of the dominant classes by means of a strenuous effort to subordinate the strength of the landed aristocracy to that of industrial and financial capital; lastly, within the most favoured class, they consolidate a hierarchy which has already been proclaimed – at least, it was in France before 1848 – and ensure the bankers' control of the country as a whole. This means that they absorb their *de facto power* as untranscendable third parties and transform it, through new institutions, into *de jure power*. Thus Marx was right when he wrote 'Only *political superstition* still imagines today that civil life must be held together by the state, whereas in reality, on the contrary, the state is held together by civil life'.[83]

Marx was right, *subject to the* qualification that there is a circular process at work here and that the State, being produced and sustained by the dominant, rising class, constitutes itself as the organ of the contraction and integration of the class. And of course this integration takes place through circumstances, and as a historical totalisation; but still, it takes place *through the State*, at least in part. Thus it would be wrong to see the State *either* as the concrete reality of society (as Hegel apparently wished to believe), *or* as a pure, epiphenomenal abstraction which merely gives passive expression to changes effected by the concrete development of its real society.

This is particularly important in so far as the State cannot take on its functions without positing itself as a mediator between the exploiting and the exploited classes. The State is a determination of the dominant class, and this determination is conditioned by class struggle. But it affirms itself as a deep negation of the class struggle. Of course, it derives its legitimacy from itself, and series have no alternative but to accept it. Moreover, they ought to accept it: it must appear to the dominated classes as their guarantee. It is absolutely wrong to ignore the fact that the government of Louis XIV, or of Hitler or of the Convention, claimed that it was the embodiment of the legitimate interests of the people (or the nation) as a whole. The State therefore *exists* for the sake of the dominant class, but as a practical suppression of class conflicts within the national totalisation. The term *mystification* is not appropriate to this new contradiction: in a sense, of course, it is a mystification, and the State maintains the *established* order; in class conflicts it intervenes to tilt the balance in favour of the exploiting

83. *The Holy Family* in Marx and Engels, *Collected Works*, Vol. 4, Lawrence & Wishart, 1975, p. 121.

classes. But, in another sense, the State really does produce itself as a national institution; in the interest of the privileged, it takes a totalising view of the social ensemble; it sees beyond antagonistic individuals, and may devise a paternalistic social policy which it will subsequently impose on the dominant classes, even though it is created *in their interest.* Lenin noticed this when he said that the State arbitrates whenever power relations tend to a state of equilibrium. But this means that it *already* posits itself for itself in relation to the class from which it emanates: this united, institutionalised and effective group, deriving its internal sovereignty from itself and imposing it as accepted legitimacy, tries to produce itself and to preserve itself in and through itself as an essential national *praxis*, by acting in the interests of the class from which it emanates and, *if necessary, against them.* One need only look at the policies of the French monarchy between the fourteenth and the eighteenth centuries to see that it did not confine itself to providing mediation when forces were evenly balanced, but rather created this balance by perpetual changes of alliance, so that the bourgeoisie and the aristocracy would control each other, so as to produce itself, on the basis of this deadlock (which was due partly to social evolution and partly to the economic policies of the government) as an absolute monarchy.

Thus, from our formal point of view, and regardless of the historical reasons for its development in any particular society, the State belongs to the category of institutionalised groups with a specified sovereignty; and if, amongst these groups, we make a distinction between those which work directly on an inorganic common object, those which are constituted to struggle against other groups, and those whose objectification demands the manipulation of inert serialities, etc., it is obvious that the State belongs to the second class.[84] Having emerged from a certain kind of seriality (the dominant class), the State remains heterogeneous with it, as with the dominated class, because its strength is based on its impotence and it appropriates the power of others (the dominant classes) over others (the dominated classes) by interiorising it and transforming it into right. It sets the unity of its own

---

84. In fact, the categories are always more complex: seriality, the inorganic, the enemy group, etc., are always present in some degree at the same time, as the example of supplying an army in enemy territory shows. But what is important to us here is the abstract and formal clarity of the schemata. One can encounter the complexity of the real for oneself and at leisure.

praxis in opposition to all classes, especially, perhaps (at least in capitalist societies), in opposition to employers who have long been paralysed by their mutual antagonisms, rather than to the proletariat, which is very ready to attempt to replace seriality by unity, that is to say, by its *autonomy*. And there can be no doubt that the most powerful private interests can always influence its decisions (as can the totalising evolution of circumstances). Coalitions of the privileged may destroy it or put it out of action, but on the whole its autonomy is preserved because, for the oppressed classes, it is the organ of legitimacy and because, in so far as they agree that it should be its own legitimation, the privileges and inequalities are also given a juridical statute. Whenever a ruling class has wished to attack the State, the ruled classes have quickly formed groups and carried forward the liquidating action against the classes which began it (the best known example being the aristocratic revolution which, in 1787, paved the way to the bourgeois revolution, which in turn led to the popular revolution).

In fact, the overthrow of a State normally takes place within the State apparatus, as a crisis of sovereignty. The rich bourgeoisie was able to halt the Revolution when the final consequences of the Terror had lost the Committee of Public Safety the support of the *sans culottes*. But 9th Thermidor was neither a surprise attack, nor a 'day' (*journée*) (unlike the 'days' of 31 May, 2 June, etc., which were popular and *as such* revolutionary): it was a legally and institutionally resolved crisis of authority within the government apparatus. Thus, there are many transformations of the possessing class, including ones which occur in the concrete domain of real society rather than in the abstract domain of civil society, which have to be publicly realised by the State acting on the citizens. And, until the exploited classes reach full revolutionary consciousness of themselves, this is because the passive legitimation of sovereignty by the popular classes becomes the State's guarantee against those who hold power. Though it is imposed by the exploiters as a cloak for exploitation, it is also guaranteed by the exploited. This position of autonomy, and heterogeneity of structure, and these possibilities of manoeuvre, lead it to *posit itself for itself* as the nation itself; it tries, as a sovereign institutional group, to become the creator of the objective which is common to all, the designer of the plans through which it will be achieved and the manipulator of all the series (each as a function of the others and simultaneously). This does not alter the fact that the supposed mediator favours one or more of the dominant classes (at the expense of the Others and of the dominated classes). And we are now in a position to add the crucial point that the institutional group, in so far as it aims to preserve its being (in the organic being-one of the sovereign), wishes to carry out its policy as a means of developing the milieu of sovereignty, rather than to put its sovereignty at the service of a policy. The real contradiction of the State is that it is a class apparatus pursuing class objectives and, at the same time, positing itself for itself as the sovereign unity of all, that is, in the absolute Other-Being which is the nation.

6   Other-direction: the *Top Ten*, Racism and Anti-Semitism

Having now reached the complex level where the group becomes a mediation between collectives and where collectives serve as intermediaries for groups, and where the immediate (or even absolute) goal of certain communities is the manipulation of series and of the masses as such (that is to say, of the practico-inert field in so far as men within it mediate between worked objects), we must now define, in their abstract intelligibility, the resulting new model of common *praxis* and the new long-term effects of this *praxis* on the sovereign group.

The principle of the new *praxis* (propaganda, agitation, publicity, the diffusion of information which is more or less misleading – or at least selected with a view to action rather than truth – campaigns, slogans, the muted orchestration of terror as an accompaniment to orders, 'stuffing people's heads' with propaganda, etc.) is to exploit seriality by pushing it to an extreme so that recurrence itself will produce synthetic results (or results capable of being synthesised). The sovereign will rethink seriality in practice as a conditioning of indefinite flight, in the context of a total undertaking which is controlled dialectically. Alternatively – and by now we should be accustomed to this contradictory tension which constitutes *practical thought* – he will define the operation on the series as a unity of action which is *serialised* in the synthetic context of a broader totalisation. Thus serial Reason becomes a special case of dialectical Reason. But this practical view of a transcendent series cannot arise in a dialectical context unless the non-synthetic unity of alterity is reproduced in the practical scheme with at least a formal appearance of synthetic unity. It must be possible to embrace this flight in the unity of a circular act. Now, this act is given in the group itself as a developing serialisation of the still efficacious *praxis*; effectively, the sovereign is born of circular recurrence and arises as an obstacle within it; and the relational system which constitutes the skeleton of his practical devices implies a constant incurvation of recurrence: it is by passing through blocked, circular recurrence towards indefinite seriality that he becomes able to see this seriality as the ubiquity of a circular, infinite recurrence whose centre is everywhere but whose circumference is nowhere.

In fact, however, this seriality is not really of this kind. Nevertheless, this is how institutional agents working under the orders of the sovereign will constitute it: on a basic foundation of alterity, they will give it an artificial statute. This statute will consist in the fact that through the mediation of a directed operation, everyone's alterity by and for everyone will present itself as the index of refraction of a *united* social milieu whose law is that each of its practical features is produced through the determination of every Other (in alterity and through all the Others) and conversely. To allow this unitary milieu to exist fully through recurrent dispersal, it is necessary and sufficient that every Other should make himself completely other, that is to say, that he should direct his free *praxis* onto himself so as to be *like the Others*. This is what various American sociologists have aptly called 'other-direction'.[85] The third party, in each of the groups under consideration, effectively presents himself as inner-directed, by which I mean that his powers and actions are determined for him on the basis of an interior limitation of his freedom. And, through reciprocity, the other (as the formal alterity of my freedom) certainly figures in my pledge as pledged inertia. But it is still true that my own *praxis*, in so far as it is strictly subordinated to the interests of the group, is produced from within, on the basis of *my own* limitations and powers. It is not necessary either to do or to be like the Others, but simply to remain the Same here, through differentiations imposed by action and interiorised. Manipulated seriality, on the other hand, has no common aim – which is appropriate since its metamorphosis into a group is necessarily and fundamentally the beginning of a revolution; it derives its inertia from its impotence rather than from a pledge, and people are involved in it only in so far as their actions and thoughts come from Others. The

85. See David Riesman, *The Lonely Crowd*, Yale University Press, 1950. [Ed.]

praxis of the sovereign group therefore consists in conditioning everyone by acting on the Others. But this is not sufficient to create the passive quasi-unity of other-direction. In order to realise it, it is necessary to fixate every Other on an illusion: the totalisation of alterities (that is to say, the totalisation of the series). This is the trap of other-direction: the sovereign intends to act on the series so as to extract a total action from it *in alterity itself*; but he produces this idea of practical totality as a possibility of the series totalising itself while remaining the fleeting unity of alterity, whereas in fact the only possibility of totalisation for the inert gathering consists in dissolving seriality in itself.

These considerations may seem very formal. I shall now give a simple example, which will illustrate two characteristics of other-direction: the mediating action of the group which conditions every other through all the Others, and everyone's practical fixation on the illusion of totalised seriality.

In 1946, when I was in the United States, several radio stations broadcast a list of the ten best selling records of the week every Saturday and, after each title, they played a few bars of the record they had just mentioned (usually the tune). A series of tests and comparisons revealed that this programme increased the sales of the ten records in the following week by between thirty and fifty per cent. In other words, *without the programme* at the weekend, the number of buyers for the ten records would have been between thirty and fifty per cent less. Thus the programme tended to preserve and perpetuate the previous week's result. But this result was itself statistical and serial. No doubt it was partly due to advertising campaigns: but these campaigns were in competition with one another, or at least – as when several bands belong to the same company – they served several records at once. Above all, they were attempts to determine a future action in everyone, that is to say, to define a possibility of his practical field. They did not *give* anything (everything was in the future: the record which *you will like*, etc.); or else they related to the action of some small group – the Top Record Prize, for example – and tried to persuade serials that the specialised group which awarded the prize was simply a channel for the expression of the opinion of all. In this case, there was already an attempt to establish an equivalence between a synthetic unity and alterity (the jury is the public). But the public does not really co-operate, except for a few prizes or choices whose legitimacy it accepts and is subjected to. In any case, its relation to the small group is complex and ambivalent: the decision of the group must signify both the judgement of the nation (as a seriality of serialities) and the decision of those competent to judge. In one way, the jury represents the great dispersals of alterity in the astringent milieu of the group; it establishes how one should behave. Thousands of people are prepared in advance to behave in this way: it involves buying, or giving, and it remains abstract in everyone (as a fleeting relation of reciprocity) in so far as it lacks an *object* (a means and end). The jury therefore appears *to live in symbiosis with serial alterity*, and, indeed, it *does have the power* to choose which record will be bought. It should be observed that this power – like all powers which relate to seriality – is conferred on it by a small group, namely the group which organised it; the public merely accepts it. No doubt the public could have remained in a state of negative inertia (neither challenging nor accepting this legitimacy, which was none of its concern). If it chooses serial docility *as Other*, this is on account of concrete historical circumstances which we need not go into here. Formally, this very symbiosis is the beginning of fixation and this is what gives it its hold over the Other in inert gatherings. It apparently gives two different statutes to the same act: buying *the* record, because one always buys *the* 'Prize Record', and giving it (because it is *the* New Year present for music fans). Here we have a set of alienated actions based on alterity (the 'Prize Record' is acknowledged by the Other – by later generations; and then someone will hear the record at a later date, as belonging to this year, and when we meet he will expect me to have heard it). This behaviour not only constitutes the prize as an Eternal Return (and a socio-natural one: it corresponds to the beginning of winter as a social season) by making it *return* every year in a new form, but also leaves open the purchaser's value judgement (a different act) concerning the object he buys. As an act, the Prize is other and indeterminate; it is the annual (and only) relationship between 100,000 persons and music, mediated by a small group.

And here we encounter the second characteristic of the group as seen by the series: it is a group of experts. This means that the evaluation of music is their profession. No one actually believes that the record is *really* the best of the year, but at least it must be 'worth listening to'. The quality of being an expert is sovereignty in the milieu of alterity (that is to say, it is transcendent of seriality): and this sovereignty, which is expressed in one specific act, flows into *one* object and becomes a *definite power* in it, a right over a certain category of serial individuals. Here we can see precisely the mirage in its elementary form: *the* record, in a shop window, fresh and new, unique amongst the other records, is the individual unity of interiority-objectification of the individual who produced it and of the small group which chose it. If I go into the shop, buy it and take it away, it is a record-seriality, a record which I must have because the Other has it, a record which I listen to as an Other, adapting my reactions to those which I anticipate in Others.[86] Mirage and metamorphosis: synthetic unity can manifest itself as an abstract determination, in a transcendent milieu, for individuals in an inert gathering; but once an object which has been produced in this way is introduced into the gathering, it acquires structures of alterity, and becomes, in itself, a factor of alterity.

But although this initial behaviour towards the object which is prized or acclaimed is totally alienated, it does not determine the actions of small groups or of practical individuals, in so far as these elementary units lie *below the level* of seriality. There is a kind of pleasure or displeasure in the listener which, apart from his alienated evaluations, expresses either his personal valuation (that is to say, his *power*: in so far as it relates to some group to which he belongs *elsewhere*, or in so far as his free practical activity turns to evaluation through the very alienation which takes it away from him) or, perhaps, that of his family group. At this level, the group's choice is never in dispute: in order to be able actually *to prefer* another record, one would have to have heard it; and the opportunity to read two or three potential prize-winning books, of trying to anticipate the decision of the academicians or to prepare oneself in advance to criticise it, is obviously confined to a very small social category (the liberal professions, certain housewives, etc.). But their pleasure or disappointment are expressed in their assessments in rather the same way as by lovers of Burgundy; there are good years and bad years; the Prix Goncourt, for example, is an annual product which exists in its raw state *before* December and which is worked as a result of December's activities; and the deep identity of this annual product (a product of vegetable spontaneity and human labour) is subject to the same yearly variations as Beaujolais. 'The Goncourt's pretty boring this year.' 'Oh, I quite liked it.'

86. If a book has not been socially *acclaimed*, it may unite a few isolated readers – but only spontaneously, by itself, by being interpreted by everyone and by referring, through this very interpretation, to the same who composed it, samely (*mêmement*), as a common object. But if a book is acclaimed, then, when I open it, it is produced by the other and as a serial formula of alterity.

This last observation brings us back to the example of records. The Prix Goncourt, the Prix du Disque, the Prix de la Chanson: these initial operations extend the group's *action at a distance* on series through the sovereign unity which it gives itself and which is not challenged (it could be challenged, in fact, only by other, more powerful, more numerous groups, etc.); and the fact that it *goes unchallenged* appears to serial impotence simply as a security: and the Other, as an alienated individual, is in any case incapable of making a challenge *in practice*. But if real practical groups are either neutral or in favour, sovereignty as a *causa sui* will radiate from itself, up above, at the level of the jury. But this initial transcendent unification is not a case of other-direction: it conditions the series by producing its possible unity in transcendence (*transcendance*), but it does not yet employ intra-serial behaviour as a unitary and fixating method of conditioning of other-behaviour in everyone. But with the radio programme, everything becomes quite different: the reflexivity whose only truth lies in the group (and then only at a given level of development) enters the series: an action-group (in this case concerned with advertising) *shows the series what it is doing* (of which it was necessarily unaware since every Other was lost in the milieu of the Others). In other words, the initial reaction of the series (to external and transcendent conditionings) is reflected back to it *through* the mediation of a group which is itself transcendent in its basic structure, and which is capable of establishing the fleeting series of actions by the means appropriate to seriality (statistics, averages, etc.) and of totalising them into one action, as far as its structure and its totalising function permit. The series becomes aware of what *it* has done. Thus it is produced as a whole (through the 'mass media') for each of the *Others* who compose it. Cardinal becomes ordinal; quantity, quality: the quantitative relations between the sales figures of two or more particular records suddenly come to indicate a *preference*, and the objective ranking of the records sold becomes the objectivity of a system of values proper to the group. The systematic transmutation of quantity into quality is completed by connecting the *name* of the work (usually a 'catchy' name) with its individual quality (the fragment of a theme) and with the names of the performers (singers, etc.): a given song has a certain indefinable objective quality which puts it at the top of an equally objective hierarchy. And everyone sees the hierarchy as an expression of collective choices and as a unified system of values. The two aspects complement one another; a serial action expresses and sustains a hitherto hidden hierarchy.

In reality, it is clear that the group is lying when it tells the truth. The figures are correct, but they have no validity except in the domain of the Other: of course they may result partly from various unities of preferential choice *in the individual cases* of particular individuals or small groups. But, apart from the fact that as such this choice is *the exception* (the *other*-choice forces itself on one as a choice of the *Other*, through circumstances and through the concerted action of organised groups, propaganda, etc.), the failure to make any comparison with total record sales for the week (for it is crucial to know whether the record which is placed first represents five or fifty-five per cent of all the records sold) deprives this exception (if indeed it can be considered in isolation) of any real, that is to say differential, significance. In fact, the result that is given has no more than the false appearance of interiority: it is neither the choice of the group nor the choice of the Others; it is the *Other as choice*. In other words, it is the negation of choice as such (as free choice), or alienation produced as freedom. And its totalisation is the result of the hidden work of an advertising group which gave it its structure of pledged inertia and of practical unity.

But, we should remember that this radio programme is addressed to *Others* in separation (as we noted above) and that it is aimed particularly at two categories of listeners: those who have not bought the 'top ten' records (or not all of them) and those who have bought them (or at least – depending on their resources, who have bought some of them). For the first group, the 'top ten' is an exigency: it indicates to the temporarily isolated individual that a broad social process of unification and agreement has taken place this week and that the listener at whom the broadcast is aimed has not taken part in it. This 'spontaneous' phenomenon is *over* (wages are received weekly in the USA, where the week is a unit of consumption: calculations are made by the week and not by the month); the week closes in on itself and displays the unity of the others to the non-buyer in this small individual exile (which becomes the expression of seriality for all exiles). In reality, the factors which prevented the purchase are purely negative: the man was sick, or absent, or busy, he did not notice the advertisements, etc. Or rather, the question has not arisen so far: his circumstances and behaviour presented themselves as a sort of positive process relating only to itself. It is because of the totalisation of serial results by the group that he now feels the need for an explanation: in relation to the number of top records sold, the words, 'I did not notice the advertisements' take on a negative meaning of quasi-interiority, whereas without the 'top ten', they would indicate a mere relation of exteriority. But now, hearing the first bars of this guaranteed music, the serial individual experiences the information as an accusation: he was out of touch (if he did not buy any records that week); he had no taste (if he bought others which did not get into the top ten); or he was unlucky (if he did not notice the advertisements). Fortunately, records last more than a week; their owners will not tire of listening to them within a week. The guilty party can still make up for his mistake on Saturday afternoon: he will buy one or more of the records mentioned, depending on his resources. It is true that this serial action is not in time with the 'spontaneous' ceremony of purchase: but the ceremony of *listening* – that Mass of alterity – is always possible and he can repeat it on subsequent days as often as he likes.

The contradiction here is due to the fact that the totalising power of the ceremonies comes from the mediated and actualised reciprocity of all the members in a group; but the isolated reactualisation of a unity which has never existed *except* in the concerted efforts of an advertising group, succeeds only in depicting unity and in realising alterity as separation: for the individual listens to the selected record through Others and through himself as Other. The 'Top Record Prize' leaves him a little more independence: of course, he is overwhelmed by the opinion of the experts, but as we have seen, his own reaction takes the form either of mute dissatisfaction or of wholehearted endorsement. The case of the 'top ten' is quite different, since here the mystification consists in offering him, once he has bought the records, *the other-choice* as though it were his own. There can be no doubt that the action of the advertising group produces in him the vague project of uniting with the Others by enjoying what they have enjoyed completely spontaneously in the depths of his own spontaneity; but the realisation of the project leads to total alienation, since the isolated ceremony consecrates him *as Other* even in his own feelings. This operation will trick him even in his social relations, because when he is in the office, or with friends, he will take himself to be communicating in reciprocity with some Other who has also bought the record, whereas – as we have seen – they are really just the instruments of well-organised collectives.

But what is important for us is the *praxis* of the group. Its goal is synthetic: to sell as many records as circumstances permit. The means is to manipulate the practico-inert field so as to produce serial reactions which will be retotalised at the level of the common undertaking, that is to say, reshaped and forged like inorganic matter. And the means to this means is to constitute the serial as a false totality for everyone. Recurrence, controlled from outside as a determination projected from everyone, through Others, into the false totality of a common field and, in reality, into pure reflexive flight, is what we shall call *other-direction* (*l'extéro-conditionnement*). This has two complementary aspects: from the point of view of the *praxis* of the transcendent group, it appears as a labour which transforms seriality into antiphysis; from the point of view of the serial individual, it is an illusory grasp of his Other-being as unifying itself in the totalisation of the common field, and the realisation of radical alterity (directed by the outside group) in him and in all the Others on the basis of this illusion. In short, other-direction takes alterity as far as it can go because it makes the serial individual do the same as the Others in order to become the same as them. But *by doing* the same as Others, he loses the chance of becoming the same, except in so far as everyone is other than the Others and other than himself. Now in the totalisation of the common field, lines of flight appear (as reflected by the 'mass media') as characteristics, or as habits (in the sense of *exis*), or as customs. Thus, by capitalising on their impotence everyone comes to be affected by these characteristics, habits and customs *in so far as* they are manifested, in the false unity which is given by the external group, as structures of totality. Thus his alterity for the Others is gradually constituted for him, and introduced to him: if he listens to the radio every Saturday and if he can afford to buy every week's No. 1 record, he will end up with the record collection of the Other, that is to say, the collection of no one. But the reflexive action of the advertising group, as it affects every other, gradually brings together no one's collection and everyone's collection. In the original state of recurrence, in effect, statistical results as such were not worked out systematically and had no tendency to perpetuate (or universalise) themselves; if figures for record sales in the United States *were not published*, then if one studied the annual figures there would be no *a priori* reason for supposing that the overall results should correspond to the contents of the majority of record collections: in fact it would be necessary to distinguish categories, levels of education, social contexts, fashions and the sectors where they were promoted, etc. Thus there would be several popular lists, and not just one; or rather, buying one record might appear incompatible with buying another, in a given social milieu. But the fact that a single list is constituted and carefully diffused every week has the effect of breaking down social and cultural barriers, of creating homogeneity (by a double movement, both upward and downward), and of gradually assimilating regional lists to a universal list. Ultimately, the record collection which is no one's becomes indistinguishable from everyone's collection – though without ceasing to be no one's.

The interest of this *praxis* is immediately obvious, at least in contemporary societies: transcendent action on seriality, in advanced capitalist countries, tends to constitute a distribution-pattern for the market (for everyone and no one, and therefore for every individual) and a control of consumption. Rivalries between advertisers then become irrelevant: at a national level the different sectors of industry and commerce reach a more or less tacit agreement to take advantage of rising incomes and to drive the masses (as inert gatherings): (1) to consume more, and (2) to adapt their budgets not only to their own needs or tastes, but also to the imperatives of national production. If a wage-earner, with long habits of prudence and, where possible, of saving (inner-direction) retains his thrift when wages rise, the techniques of other-direction will have to replace his inner directions by those of the Other. But this is not really possible unless the serial individual has been produced from childhood as other-directed. It has recently been shown, in fact, that in infant schools in America (and, of course, throughout the child's education), everyone learns to be the expression of all the Others and thereby of his whole social milieu, so that the slightest exterior serial change returns to him and conditions him from outside in alterity.

Everyone has seen the newspaper competitions in which the names of ten buildings, artists, or cars, etc. are listed in a random order, and the object of the competition is to guess the hierarchy-pattern (which really means the average hierarchy) which will be established by collating the replies of all the *Others*. The competitor whose list is closest to this list is the winner. In fact whoever wins – that is to say, is chosen, selected, publicly named, and rewarded – does so because he has been more perfectly Other than all the Others. His practical individuality, in the milieu of seriality, is his ability (at least in this particular situation) to become the medium of the Other as a unit of the flight of alterities. Should we say that he was already this mediumistic product of recurrence, or is it that *he made himself* a pure prediction of seriality? The answer is, both of them inseparably. The ambivalent statute of prophetic being and passive activity is simply that of every other-directed individual. This never arises at the level of production, even alienated production, even within an exploitative system, simply because work defines itself in terms of need as a free practical operation, in spite of, or even because of, the fact that it may confront the worker as a hostile force. But still it would be a mistake to suppose that this is confined to consumers in heavily industrialised societies. In any society which is haunted by the need to predict and mutually adjust production and markets from a particular point of view, other-direction plays an increasingly important part; it represents a real and new *statute* of the massified individual, namely the direct hold on the masses of control, management and distribution groups.

But to treat this new relation between the group and the mass as created *ex nihilo*, form and matter, would be a complete misunderstanding of dialectical rationality. What is new is the historical content and the circumstances which determine it; what is *actualised*, but permanent, is the synthetic form of unity which appears here. This formal link has in fact always been filled by a content; but what is apparent today, at *this* moment of History, in which the structures of other-direction are more manifest in and around us is, in fact, the crucial importance of these structures for the comprehension of historical events. There has been a regrettable tendency to see certain collective actions as the product of suddenly formed groups – of mass 'spontaneity' – or simply as the result of the more or less disguised activities of those in power. In many cases, both approaches are misleading. For example, there is the seriality of racism, which I have explained: it is always the attitude of the Other. But seriality – though it may cause lynchings or pogroms – is not a sufficient explanation of, for example, the active anti-semitism of the German petty bourgeoisie under the Nazi régime. Now some highly ingenious recent studies have shown that anti-semitism as a historical fact has to be interpreted in terms of the systematic other-direction of the *racism of the Other*, that is to say, in terms of the continuous action of a group on a series. And this action is defined primarily by its *reflexivity*: the group demonstrates racism to the series by producing within it practical signs of its hostility to Jews, or by causing them to be produced; these signs – caricatures, definitions endlessly repeated on the radio, in the newspapers and on walls, tendentious information, etc. – ultimately play the same role as the standard *list* for everyone and no one. In short (ignoring for the moment their deliberately Manichaean, projective and sadistic characteristics, etc.) they are both concrete designations of a particular monster and the *created formula of the series* as an indication of the masses as a totality. The hatred which these dummies excited in everyone belonged to the Other; but totalising propaganda constituted this hatred into other-direction as an exigency of a totalising ceremony. Then it depended on the government (that is to say, on the determination which it brought elsewhere to Others and which it then diffused as a possible unity of all through the 'mass media'), whether the circumstances for this totalising ceremony would be created, that is to say, whether the petty-bourgeois masses would become the practico-inert agents of an *induced* pogrom. Anyway, the arrest or execution of a Jew on government orders passively realised the same ceremony of alterity in the masses; every act of violence was irreversible, not only because it destroyed human lives, but because it made everyone an other-directed criminal, adopting the leaders' crimes in so far as he had committed them *elsewhere* and as an other in an other. Conversely, the acceptance of the sovereign's acts of violence, as an *exis* in the milieu of other-direction, may always, through the transcendent action of the directing group, be reconverted into a pogrom, as the passive activity of a directed seriality.

And this *exis*, along with the practical process which its reconversion may produce, remains a false unity for two essential reasons, both of which are dialectical in character. First, even the most enthusiastic consent only means the inability to offer resistance, and therefore separation.[87] Secondly, and most important, the serial acceptance of this irreversible other-direction *itself* increases separations, impotence and the real index of alterity. In fact, both with an approved action and with the practical process seriality re-emerges (in a moment of looting or execution for example) as a force for separation, simply because there has been no real resistance from a hostile group, and no practical totalisation through threats of extermination, to occasion, as real negations, the dissolution of the serial in the Others. On the contrary, looting and firing of undefended shops are in themselves dispersive acts of destruction: they have nothing to do with unity of agents (on the contrary, violence is engendered by disorder) and, from outside,

---

87. This does not mean that it is impossible for a particular individual's approval of the acts of violence to arise *also* on the basis of a possible challenge; but only that the practice of the sovereign group consists in intensifying separations in every domain, so that the illusion of unity (acceptance-pogrom) is manifested on the basis of a serial inability to realise any other unity. The pogrom becomes the only solution *in so far as* the police régime introduces mistrust as an additional factor of separation.

they make everyone into *the other who is responsible* for the maximum violence committed in the gathering *by an other*. At the level at which 'collective responsibility' is serial responsibility, its acceptance or rejection by a given other are simply two contradictory expressions (in discourse) of one and the same fact. And this serial responsibility – as the projection of a precise, totalising policy in the milieu of alterity – increases the power of the sovereign group to precisely the extent that it deepens everyone's impotence while sustaining the misleading scheme of the totalising ceremony.

With this example, I have tried to show what differentiates a racist *exis* (which is what is usually studied) from an anti-semitic *movement*; I have tried above all to indicate that the government apparatus and its sub-groups for constraint and propaganda are careful not to occasion what might be called *organised action* within inert gatherings. Every organisation disturbs them in so far as it dissolves seriality. Thus the real problem, at this level, is to extract organic actions from the masses without disturbing their statute as non-organised. At this point, the problem of 'organised spontaneity' (*l'encadrement*) is bound to be raised: modern societies, both East and West, provide the example of organised demonstrations. A procession – on 1 May, 14 July, 1 October etc. – gives a serial public the spectacle of strict organisation. An order is given: soldiers, workers, peasants, intellectuals march in Peking according to some pre-existing plan; there are leaders who regulate the march, its speed, the number of stops, etc. But these supposed groups, in which everyone does the same as all the Others, and regulates his action by that of the Others, and whose leading feature is sheer quantity, have nothing in common with the structures of communities. It is true that the march is regulated from outside; but the result of this trans- cendent action of a member of the sovereign group is precisely to keep them under the statute of other-directedness. These few examples, though very superficially studied, enable one to see – though the point cannot be developed or proved here – that the relation of the State to concrete society can never, even in the best of cases, transcend other-direction.[88]

88. Even if its mode of recruitment is 'democratic', it is still a matter of co-option: the sovereign group confronts series of series and it is *its organs* which determine them by reflecting their seriality to them in the form of standard lists. All kinds of electoral systems constitute the set of electors as a passive material for other-direction; and the election results no more represent *the will* of the country, than the top ten records represent *the taste* of the customers. The only

7   *Bureaucracy and the Cult of Personality*

Thus a sovereign group increases the inertia of collectives and governs by means of it. But, as I said above, it will be worth giving a brief account of how seriality reacts on the sovereign. There are already too many commentaries on it, so I shall not dwell on it for long. As we have seen the ensemble of the sovereign (sub-groups and constituted bodies) forms a complex system whose apparatuses, at the base of the hierarchy, are in direct contact with the masses and constitute what are variously called, very misleadingly, cadres, nuclei, liaison organisations, etc. In reality, these are inorganic instruments whose very inertia constitutes the surface which is in contact with serial inertia, and their role, defined by superior groups, is to manipulate the other-directedness of *Others*. I have already observed that these sub-groups are surrounded by series; and in separation, as I have shown, they in turn become serialised. Everyone becomes sovereign to himself alone; but, in the milieu of the Other, the sovereign *elsewhere* is other. On the other hand, other-directedness is based on the passivity of the masses; but this passivity conditions their own passivity: first, because for those who are other-directed they themselves become the embodiment of the standard lists, solidified exigencies, etc., and, in the unity of a single petrification, the representatives of the law – that is to say, of sovereignty-as-an-individual in so far as this produces itself as a universal power.

By this double petrification, they mean either to eliminate change or to control it, depending on the case. These sub-groups retain a *practical* appearance as long as they can *really* act as a mediation between the central authorities and the series. But such mediation cannot establish itself as a permanent function: a group may become the mediation between two groups, an individual between two communities; but mediation between the series and the sovereign cannot continue if the sovereign *praxis* is determined to keep the series in impotence and

---

possible manifestation of a 'will' amongst the masses is their revolutionary grouping against the inertia of institutions and against the sovereignty which is based on their impotence. As a passive means, elections may bring about changes – though insignificant ones – in the composition of the sovereign body; but they can *never* claim to modify government policy (unless the circumstances which accompany it are such as to modify it anyway).

alterity. Needs will be determined and, where possible, satisfied *from outside*, in so far as they can be measured by biologists, doctors, etc., but not in so far as they are the object of a genuine demand. This is because their serial structure prevents individuals from forming a group on the basis of a demand, and because the task of other-direction is constantly to raise the threshold for effecting regroupment. In the world of the Other (which is the world of government) violence, rejection, exigency and even riots, sometimes occur: but such disturbances, which are quickly repressed, *never* serve as a lesson, or as an indication of the depth of popular discontent, precisely because it is always the Other who rebels or makes a demand: the Other, the alien, the suspect, the trouble-maker. The notion of a *trouble-maker*, in particular, is senseless except for a member of the sovereign group, that is to say, for a functionary convinced that the only ontological statute of human multiplicities is other-directed passivity. He controls this passivity in the light of the general interest; and the trouble-maker is an anti-sovereign who controls the same passivity in the light of his individual interest (or some other sectional interest). At this point the leader who is criticising the trouble-maker makes a self-criticism on the back of an Other, that is to say, as Other.

Thus there can *never* be any such thing as popular discontent from the point of view of the sub-group which is immediately responsible for arrangements, and this is for the good reason that discontent is the practice and *exis* of a group and that the serial statute rules out the possibility of regroupment. The relation between sub-groups and series becomes *reified*: they no longer do anything but act materially on the series by means of the serial combinatory, that is to say, the schemes which arise from a serial constitution and make it possible to interpret actions of seriality. The difference between the local leader and the led individual is almost imperceptible: they are both serialised, and both of them live, act and think serially; but the leader thinks the seriality of the Other and acts serially on other-directed series. Thus nothing can be transmitted from the local level to the top because there is no longer anything being transmitted from the popular series to the leader whom they have serialised. It is precisely for this reason that, for his superior, the local leader is the object of a sovereign and univocal *praxis*. He is a tool for stirring the human material, and no more than a piece of inorganic matter. His autonomy and powers could give rise to reciprocity, if, in virtue of his function, he were to express the people's demands to his superior as human exigencies. But these demands and exigencies *do not exist*: which simply means that they are still the product of the living, suffering individual who is paralysed by alterity. If at some time in the future they do manifest themselves, it will be as those of a group which rejects all mediation and constitutes its own sovereignty; demands always become 'known' *too late*. This is either because they have no being, and emerge as revolutionary or because they remain unexpressed, depending on circumstances. For his superior, the local leader is an inert guarantee of the inertia of the masses and *he becomes such* because they do not offer him, nor does he accept, the counter-power of making demands to the sovereign on their behalf.

Thus, the multiplicity of subordinate agents appears, to the next level 'up', as a superior instance of seriality; and their passivity becomes a material to be worked by other-direction. But this by no means prevents everyone from being suspect, in that his operations could be carried out as a free, practical initiative, or, in other words, assert themselves as an individual's individual sovereignty over the serialities which fill his practical field. Both other-direction *and* terror have the aim, in relation to local leaders, of replacing real activity by the inert practice of worked matter at every level. Thus each level treats the agents of an inferior level as inorganic objects governed by laws, and loses their guarantee and their free support in relation to the superior level; it, too, becomes serial in so far as it is effective. This means that throughout the hierarchy, objects which are governed by laws of exteriority govern other objects which are placed beneath them, according to these laws and other [in-]organic laws; and that the combination of laws which, at each level, makes it possible to move the material on the inferior level is itself produced within the leaders on this level by a combination of *their* laws which was created above them. The paralysis of the system necessarily rises from the series which are led to the top, the sovereign alone (whether a small group or an individual) remaining unaffected. Or rather he is affected with passivity as a totalising individual; he becomes inorganic from below, from the depths of the hierarchy; but there is no superior who can transform him into a thing.

In this new constitution of the group, we can observe the following characteristics: at every level of the hierarchy, everyone is a *possible* sovereign over the agents of an inferior level or a *possible* regulatory third party (taking the initiative in agitation or in the formation of a group); but everyone *denies* these possibilities out of mistrust for his peers and fear of being suspect in the eyes of his superiors. Towards his peers, indeed, he adopts the attitude of the pledge and binds himself to inertia in order to be able to lay claim to theirs: separation and recurrence both encourage the re-emergence of the discrete multiplicity which he rejects. The shifting alterity of his equals unravels interiorised plurality into relations of exteriority. The exteriorisation of relations which we observed above is realised in the one who *is* the institution (and through all his peers). But the structure of sovereignty produces itself at every level as an institutional reinteriorisation; and so everyone, looking towards the superior level, demands perpetual integration from the sovereign; he dissolves his organic individuality in himself as an uncontrollable factor of multiplicity, and merges with his peers in the organic unity of the superior, finding no guarantee for his individual existence other than the free individuality of an other.

It is this triple relation – other-direction of the inferior multiplicity; mistrust and serialising (and serialised) terror at the level of the peers; and the annihilation of organisms in obedience to the superior organism – which constitutes what people call bureaucracy. We saw it emerge from sovereignty itself, when sovereignty was no more than an institutional moment of the group; and we now see it asserting itself as a total suppression of the human, except at a minute point at the top of the hierarchy, as a result of inertia at the bottom. Its form and dialectical meaning are obvious: the impotence of the masses is the support of sovereignty, and sovereignty undertakes to manipulate them by means of mechanical laws – that is to say, of other-direction – but this *voluntarism* (that is to say, the affirmation of the practical sovereignty of man over man and the concerted maintenance of the practico-inert statute at the bottom) necessarily implies the mineralisation of man at every level, except the highest. It asserts itself everywhere as the opposite of freedom and tries with all its strength to destroy itself. Thus the impotence of the masses becomes the impotence of the sovereign; it becomes impossible for the half-paralysed man or subgroup at the top to maintain the pyramid of mechanisms, each of which is supposed to set the other in motion. The historical conditions for a bureaucratisation of powers are of course defined in the course of the historical process and through temporal totalisation. But this is not our subject. What relates to the dialectic from the point of view of temporalisation, can be expressed in a few words. Where the State is an apparatus of constraint in a society divided by class conflicts, bureaucracy – the constant threat to the sovereign – is easier to avoid than in the building of a socialist society: tensions between classes, partial and more or less organised struggles, and groupings – as a developing dissolution of serialities – force the 'public powers' into a more complex action, and confront them with communities, however ephemeral, which challenge the sovereign. He has to define a flexible, living *praxis* towards them through the other-direction of Others: the scintillating life of the fused group will either reject the old worm-eaten sovereignty of the bureaucracy, or, if it has already manifested itself, as a permanent danger, it will prevent the sovereign from being constituted in the most bureaucratised form, namely, as police.

The omnipotence of police, as an absolute petrification of the functions of the sovereign group, is based on the separation of impotence; such separation must exist for the police-state to maintain and use: in a society which is 'hot' – in Lévi-Strauss's excellent phrase – that is to say, in a society in which all forms of class struggle are perpetually alive *in opposition to* the statute of seriality (among the oppressed *and* the oppressors), the action of the sovereign will be a *politics*. Repression, though always in the background, will not be used as much as antagonisms (other-direction will partially disappear and re-emerge in the classic form of 'divide and rule'), tactics and strategy will have to be worked out by apparatuses and the circulation of sovereignty will have to be ensured in both directions. The job of the subordinate functionary is not, of course, to *express* the demands of popular groups, but to *inform* on these groups and, in particular, on their demands. This will assure him a sort of *quasi-mediating* function; the permanent danger that seriality will dissolve around him may confront him with a vital hostile *praxis* whose menace and urgency demand immediate action. Even if no such thing actually happens, the subordinate agent is defined in his possibilities as *capable of taking* such an initiative. On the other hand, a particular contradiction sets the sovereign group, as the unity of the individual and the universal positing itself for itself, in opposition to the dominant class which produces it and sustains it (pays it) as its own apparatus. The dependence of the sovereign is, as we have seen, beyond doubt; but so too is the perpetual affirmation of autonomy with respect to every level. This leads to a tension, which varies with circumstances, and which can determine various methods of reconquest, in the power-groups of the dominant class: osmosis (regulated exchanges between government officials and economic groups), infiltration, influence (direct and indirect), etc. The sovereign group defends itself against these methods, which are in general aimed at altering its internal composition, by perpetual vigilance. But this vigilance, or white terror, does not have the paralysing effects of real terror, since, in this particular case, the problem is to defend the sovereign against the over-solicitous concern of his original allies. Of course, they dream of denying either his legitimate sovereignty or the correctness of his *praxis* in the long term; but they do try to set aside (or suggest) short-term objectives, to propose some operation, etc., or (if a rebellion has been crushed) to push for sharp repression. All this has to be *integrated* by the sovereign group: it may take over the proposals, dissolve them in its *praxis* while appearing to accept them, etc., but it can neither reject them *a priori* nor ignore them. This bond of interiorisation between the wishes and common demands of the dominant class (as expressed by pressure groups) on the one hand, and sovereignty as *praxis* on the other, represents, so to speak, the class existence of the sovereign. It requires certain subordinate agents to become real mediations between *at least* one serial ensemble and the top: and this serial ensemble is just the dominant class, in so far as pressure groups form within it in order to create – in opposition to the policy of the government – independent sectors of other-direction.

These remarks are not designed to prove the superiority of sovereign groups in bourgeois democracies, but rather to show that they derive their life from the social contradictions they express. When a sovereign group, with its implacable homogeneity, has integrated *every practical grouping* into itself, in other words when sovereignty has the monopoly of the group, and when this grouping of groupings defines itself in the last instance by its direct hold over passive serialities and its strict practices of other-direction, and when this sovereignty is not a class product (like a monarchical or bourgeois state) and is necessarily recruited by co-option, producing its legitimacy by and for itself, then the sovereign pyramid will turn on itself in the void, regardless of its transcendent tasks. It will elude the control of a dominant class (for example capital) and will have to struggle only against itself, that is to say, against the dangers of separation and institutionalisation; and it is precisely this struggle against itself which will lead to bureaucratisation.

No one today could believe that the first stage of a socialist revolution realises the dictatorship of the proletariat. But, in a perpetual state of extreme emergency, and in the light of well known gigantic tasks, a revolutionary group has institutionalised itself and as such has produced its own legitimacy as sovereign and, monopolising the possibilities of grouping, it has set in motion and arranged serialities by practices of other-direction. It should be understood, in fact, by means of dialectical Reason itself, that any creation by a sovereign institutional group of a supposed regroupment of serial individuals (whether trade unions or other regimented formations) can only be a new differentiation and extension of the group itself to the extent that its members are all bearers of the sovereign power and that regimentation, even at the lowest level, does not transform the Other-Being of serial individuals into being-in-the-group, but rather, by means of a false, fixating totalisation, defines a new sector of intensive other-direction. The limit on the real power of the most dictatorial State is that it cannot create a group outside itself: all it can do is, when circumstances permit, grow to some extent and differentiate itself (by producing new sub-groups). The only effect of the determinations which it directly produces within inert gatherings is that it transfers them – in a given place and situation – from the serial level to that of an 'other-directed zone'. Every group, in fact, in so far as its own totalising movement contains the abstract possibility of establishing its own sovereignty, constitutes itself *either* outside the State (even if it is more or less directly connected with it, through subventions, official encouragement, etc.), by positing the autonomy of its *praxis, or,* primarily in opposition to the State, as a denunciation and rejection of its transcendent sovereignty, through a practice of abstention, passive resistance, disobedience or revolt.

The internal contradictions of the socialist world bring out, through the immense progress that has been made, the objective exigency for debureaucratisation, decentralisation, and democratisation: and this last term should be taken to mean that the sovereign must gradually abandon its *monopoly of the group* (the question arises at the level of workers' committees). In fact, in the USSR at least, the destruction of the Soviet bourgeoisie was completed long ago. This means that the 'dictatorship of the proletariat' was an optimistic notion, constructed too hastily through misunderstanding the formal laws of dialectical Reason: there was once a time when it was *too soon* for such dictatorship in the USSR: the real dictatorship was that of a self-perpetuating group which, in the name of a delegation which the proletariat had not given it, exercised power over the bourgeois class which was in the process of being destroyed, over the peasant class and over the working class itself. From the point of view of the masses the sovereignty of this group was neither legitimate nor illegitimate: its practical legitimation was due to the fact that the sovereign constructed his own illegitimacy by his mistakes and crimes: this is the judgement of History. Today it is *too late*, and the problem which really arises is that of the gradual withering-away of the State in favour of broader and broader re-groupments of other-directed serialities.

And the reason why the dictatorship of the proletariat (as a real exercise of power through the totalisation of the working class) never occurred is that the very idea is absurd, being a bastard compromise between the active, sovereign group and passive seriality. Historical experience has shown quite undeniably that the first moment in the construction of socialist society – to consider it at the still abstract level of power – could only be the indissoluble aggregation of bureaucracy, of Terror and of the cult of personality. This first stage seems to be approaching its end, despite some terrible setbacks; and, in any case, *wherever* a new socialist régime is established today, the developing socialisation of half the world will produce this new revolution in a conjuncture and historical totalisation quite different from those which characterised the revolution of 1917. From our point of view, the impossibility of the proletariat exercising a dictatorship is formally proved by the fact that it is impossible for any form of group to constitute itself as a hyper-organism. Bureaucratic terror and the cult of personality are just another expression of the relation between the constituent dialectic and the constituted dialectic, that is to say, of the necessity that a common action as such (through the multiple dif-ferentiation of tasks) should practically reflect upon itself so as constantly to control and unify itself in the untranscendable form of an individual unit. It is *true* that Stalin was the Party and the State; or rather, that the Party and the State were Stalin. But his violence is an expression, in a specific process, of the violent contradiction between the two dialectics, that is to say, of the impossibility that the group as constituted *praxis* should transcend the statute of this organic indivi-duality which it contains within itself, and transforms and *transcends* in so far as it is, in common interiority, a function of multiplicity. However, the untranscendability of the ontological and practical statute of the regulatory third party is not a *de facto* and therefore unintelligible limit assigned to communities: we have seen how it arises, in the translucidity of the critical investigation, in the course of development of the constituent dialectic, as a free, organic *praxis* and as a human relation of reciprocity. In other words, the constituent dialectic, while producing itself as the *Reason of action*, and realising its structures in the light of temporalisation, already determines the possibilities and impossibilities of common *praxis*; it *naturalises* (*nature*) constituted Reason. Thus constituted Reason derives its very intelligibility – as the structured logic of common action – from constituent Reason: and if our critical investigation enables us to grasp the formal genesis of the second dialectic, in its double character as *praxis* and process, with its scope and its limits in terms of the practico-inert field and of dissolutions of seriality, this is enough.

Our investigation has now arrived at a shifting flight of elucidations: the practical unity of the group which organises itself lies in its object, in groups external to it; it passes momentarily through every participant in an undertaking as an 'excluded third party' (*tiers exclu*); and it resurfaces theoretically and practically in the activity of the sovereign. But it is never really given *inside* the group itself, in the way that the unity of the moments of an individual action lies in the unity of an active development. On the other hand, we can immediately see the true power of the group in the impotence of each of its members: this impotence endows functions with a material force of inertia, and turns them into hard, heavy organs which are capable of striking, crushing, etc. Thus the true efficacity of the group, as a *praxis* bogged down in matter, lies in its materiality – that is, in its becoming-process. But, in so far as *praxis* is process, goals lose their teleological character. Without ceasing to be genuine goals, they become destinies.

7

The Place of History

Dialectical investigation as totalisation: the level of the concrete, the place of history

1   The Reciprocity of Groups and Collectives

The group emerges from the more or less complete dissolution of collectives and in the unity of a common *praxis*. And the object of this *praxis* can be defined only in relation to other groups, which may or may not be mediated by series, or to an inert gathering, which may or may not be mediated by other groups, or to worked matter, which may or may not be mediated by series and groups.

But if the collective from which the group arises bears at least some superficial mark of its dissolving *praxis*, then the result of the common action, regardless of its other characteristics, must also be a determination of the collective and of worked matter. Thus, in a sense, the objective reality of the group (its practical objectification) is the collective and the inorganic. In other words, looking at the *praxis* of the group outside itself in the transcendent milieu of its objectification, we can see that it is defined by three principal characteristics.

(1) It practically realises new and unifying realities in the social and physical material which constitutes its practical field. In the friendly or hostile groups which are adjacent to it it *directly* produces certain modifications which are both *suffered* and readopted in the course of internal rearrangements. *Indirectly*, by its mere presence in the common field (as a practical field for every community at various levels), it produces transformations *at a distance*, that is to say, induced rearrangements readopted by distant groups through the totalising transformation of the field. Since the field is, effectively, a synthetic unity of practical totalisation, the distant appearance of another group as a non-

totalisable retotalisation of diversity (and as a totalising mutual re-conditioning of elements in a sort of formidable, fleeting autonomy) confronts each group with the permanent threat of a *radical alteration of all the internal references of the system* and thus of the modification of the group itself *through a retotalised totalisation* at least as an unrealisable signification. The question whether these practical results represent a partial failure or a success need not concern us at present. What is obvious is that the efficacity of a *praxis* is directly linked to its concrete objective and that the different actions which it performs here are all unified within the common field *at every level of investigation and by all groups present.*

(2) These synthetic results are necessarily *alienated*, although the moment where alienation appears is not necessarily that in which objectification occurs. The alienation of a free, isolated *praxis* – as it occurs in the practico-inert field – has to be immediate because this pseudo-isolation is already in itself a statute of impotence created through the mediation of the inorganic. But the objectification of common *praxis* can be an immediate, total success: since the group is the negation of impotence, its success is conditioned by the reigning relations of forces. An army may annihilate an enemy army and entirely occupy the defeated country. But in so far as this *objectification* is ultimately an inert object and an individual reality within the developing totalisation, it is necessarily appropriated and alienated. Even defeated groups in the practical field can manipulate this field itself, and endow it with a real polyvalence which deprives the object of any univocal, uncontested signification. In other words, the object which is produced is in itself pluri-dimensional and there is no guarantee that its different significations will not be contradictory. It is also clear that they present themselves to the group as unrealisable significations, related to an *elsewhere*. By means of an indirect, antagonistic reciprocity, the object returns marked by the developing totalisation of the totalising groups: the common field as a pluri-dimensional insecurity becomes the mediation between the object and the group. But since the truth of the group lies in its object, the practical plurality of the objective dimensions of the thing which is realised turns back on the active community and modifies it in turn, to precisely the extent that its own victory has modified other communities.

This does not mean that we have to return to historical scepticism – *on the contrary*; but we must recognise that these multiple significations can be integrated only from a point of view in which it is possible to integrate all the groups of the common field and all its practical determinations, that is to say, *from a historical point of view*. Nevertheless, even if the group survives *this* practical success, and even if it organises and maintains itself, we must abandon any idea of humanity historialising itself in the development of a single temporalisation which began with 'the first men' and which will finish with 'the last': the dialectical investigation establishes that here too, in the absence of a temporal hyper-organism, we have treated diachronic totalisation as though it were a free, individual temporalisation. Humanity treated as *one* Man: this is the illusion of the constituted dialectic. There are in fact *several* temporalisations; what I have in mind are those diachronic multiplicities known as generations. Each generation is a natural and social product of the previous generation; but each generation separates itself from the previous one and, as a *material condition of its praxis*, transcends the objectification of the previous *praxis*, that is to say, the being of the previous generation, in so far as this being becomes, through this very transcendence, an inert object which needs to be rearranged. Thus the temporal development of the objective process to which the group gives birth entirely eludes it as one moves further away from the moment in which it was realised by *praxis*: it becomes the condition for a new *praxis* within this *praxis* become object, the condition of a condition, material, etc. Of course this does not mean that new generations can, by their own *praxis*, arbitrarily assign it any signification and use, but it does mean that however rigorous its objective features, they will acquire their meaning only in the course of a process of dialectical development (of the totalising synthesis of various circumstances) which, *being dialectical*, must be not only inflexible but also, from the point of view of the first generation, completely unpredictable (at least given a certain time-lag, whose length will vary according to circumstances).

The plurality of temporalisations together with temporal unification (a synthetic unification of the antecedent by the consequent, a present unification of the new multiplicity through old frameworks) actually constitute the evolution of humanity as the *praxis* of a diachronic group, that is to say, as the temporal aspect of the constituted dialectic. Synchronic groups are a work of unification of simultaneous multiplicities in the light of a common objective. Diachronic groups are the result of the retro-anterogressive unification of temporalisations; thus the temporality of a nation, for example, as a created unity and a constituted dialectic is to the living temporalisation of the members of one generation what common *praxis* is to free organic practice. We shall return to this point. What is certain is that the result achieved by the original group (original in the sense of being first on this occasion, rather than absolutely) is a quasi-object for the young and passes progressively to the total inertia of the inorganic object; similarly, the living temporalisation (or rather the mediated reciprocity of temporalisations) which produced it is transformed by the transcending *praxis* of the newcomers into an inert and finished determination of temporality (as a created process and a diachronic unity). Produced by the *praxis* of their parents, children reinteriorise their *praxis*, divert it, transcend it and make it other through its new results: they *appropriate* it. And there is no reason to suppose that defeated groups will not produce, through the changes caused by their defeat, sons who will take advantage of it and wipe out their conquerors. Thus objectified *praxis* must necessarily allow itself to be modified by a double alienation (both synchronic and diachronic).

The costly French victory of 1918 was expressed on every level by a multiplicity of social transformations. Let me describe just two of them – perhaps not the most important – to illustrate these points. On the one hand, the first occurrence of total war (or national war, as it was called at the time) was expressed after the peace by a demographic fact which was (at least originally) of an almost mechanical nature: *empty class-rooms*. The *military practice* known as the 'strategy of a million' (*stratégie du million d'hommes*) re-emerged, alienated and passivised, as a simple *numerical relation* characterising the succeeding generations. But this numerical relation was itself preserved by the Malthusian practices of the survivors. These practices existed at the level of pure recurrence, being the object of religious and political prohibitions, but through the *alterity* of the collective they helped give the result an appearance of analytical necessity. The conditions of the war and of the post-war years – which were very different in Germany – led to an increase in the numerical superiority of the German population. Thus the victory of 1918 created in the common field of Europe the possibility of the defeat of 1940.

On the other hand, for the French children born between 1914 and 1920, the war lay behind them as a hideous object, a product of paternal madness. Most of them transcended it towards a militant pacifism or a dream of universal peace, precisely because it had ended in victory. The German defeat, in contrast, was transcended as a revolt against the defeated fathers and as a wish for revenge among young Germans *through the practice of Nazism.* This reversal, which is often remarked on, therefore expresses a double alienation (synchronic and diachronic) of the French victory. Thus group action is always doomed to synchronic alienation[89] except when the practical community is identical to all the individuals in the common field; then it is doomed without qualification to diachronic alienation. On this basis one can see counter-finalities re-emerging at the level of group *praxis*, and tearing up the common field (empty classrooms, in so far as they are produced with the mediation of Malthusianism as recurrence, manifest themselves as a counter-finality of total war and of victory, its objectification).

(3) But, apart from these interactions, group action is of itself a radical transformation of the common statute in so far as its results, without losing their synthetic unity, imprint themselves on inorganic matter or become the strict determination of a collective (or of any practico-inert concretion). The practical unity of the group and the free pledged inertia of its members are reflected to it as the inorganic passivity of a pure physical or human materiality which retains, in itself and in the exteriority of its parts, the false unity of a seal. The group was constituted in opposition to recurrence; and it becomes the means of determining a serial process through the knowledge and application of laws of alterity. We have seen how the paralysis of seriality rises from other-directed gatherings towards the sovereign. But the embodiment of powers is a special case. As a general rule, the group develops counter-finalities which elude it in so far as it acts on the inorganic, either directly or through the mediation of collectives, and in so far as it acts indirectly on groups and brings about a serial process in a gathering. Such, ultimately, are the limits of its *praxis*: born to dissolve series in the living synthesis of a community, it is blocked in its spatio-temporal development by the untranscendable statute of organic individuality and finds its being, outside itself, in the passive determinations of inorganic exteriority which it had wished to repress in itself. It is formed in opposition to alienation, in so far as alienation substitutes the practico-inert field for the free practical field of the individual; but it cannot escape alienation any more than the individual can, and it thereby relapses into serial passivity.

---

89. By this I do not mean that alienation must follow action immediately, but that it will occur in the historical temporalisation of the group and of its generation.

We have seen institutionalisation as petrified practice. But if we were to make a simple investigation of the social field around us, we would find plenty of examples of even more extreme petrification. In the extreme case, the group (as a *praxis* of other-direction) merges completely with its object; that is, it is not its *praxis*, but itself which passes entirely into objectified being. In particular, I would single out the studies of shop workers by American sociologists. Recent studies in the USA have examined the practical behaviour of such workers, as agents integrated into an organised economic group. Today they must undergo a real apprenticeship in order to learn techniques of manipulation: the customer (as a serial object) must be manipulated as a complex apparatus according to certain methods based on certain laws (which are also serial). But in order to manipulate his customers, the employee must first learn to manipulate *himself* (change his mood, put the customer in the right, etc.). The operation itself turns out to be the same: one manipulates *oneself* in order to manipulate others, or one manipulates Others in so far as one is manipulated oneself. For, ultimately, to manipulate oneself – as this study clearly demonstrates – is, *for the employee himself, and without any possible doubt, to have been manipulated* (apprenticeship) in such a way as to adopt practical self-determinations in particular circumstances and for a given aim. This manipulation, as a determination in *exis* of manipulative-being (*l'être manipulateur*) relates to two indeterminates of seriality, one vertical (the hierarchical group, manipulations of manipulations, etc.) and the other horizontal (the exterior series of the manipulated). But each of them relates to the Other, and ultimately manipulation, which was originally simply a technique of treating the Other as Other,[90] becomes the universal law of alterity. The only difference between the manipulating group and the manipulated series is that in the latter alterity is the constitutive law of the practico-inert field, and therefore a law which is obeyed in exteriority, whereas in the group it is the radical exteriorisation of a *praxis* which is organised in interiority, but which allows itself to be defined entirely by its object.

Of course, the group's reversion to the collective statute does not

---

90. The problem is to persuade the customer to buy what the Other is buying: *that object* which as a private individual he would reject. This 'privacy' has to be masked by treating him as an Other and, for this purpose, it is necessary to approach him as the Other. Manipulation consists in producing oneself as the Other in order to refer the customer to his alterity through the simple reciprocity of relations.

necessarily take any particular period of time. It is determined by the historical process as a whole and by the special features of the undertaking: nevertheless, if the group were not already dissolved, constituted temporality would tend to make the group as an inert instrument of passive action equivalent to an acted-on gathering as the end, reason and means of this practico-inert connection. It would be easy – but outside our subject – to show how the generalised practice of other-direction tends, in economically advanced societies, to constitute a new objectivity of the social object as an object of external, infinitely infinite conditioning, every part of which is itself induced in other objects by other conditioning. The absolute destruction, even in the conditioning groups (power-groups, propaganda-groups, pressure-groups, etc.) of common, totalising *praxis*, and its metamorphosis (through the sclerosis of the group and the multiplication of series) into a fleeting unity of alterity, have the effect of dissolving the unitary *praxis* of manipulation into the horizontal and vertical multiplicities of infinite seriality. At this level, the image of organic individuality as the untranscendable schema of the constituent and constituted dialectic either dissolves or remains as a crossroads of serialities. But the dialectical structure of action will also have inscribed itself in inertia as its law of exteriority: and the example of Taylor, as we have seen already, shows how a dialectical operation can be divided and redistributed between pure, inorganic inertias (specialised machines) through an analysis by positivist Reason. The total objectivity of man for himself, in so far as he is an *Other-Being* for and through the other, is not yet reinteriorised as a pure, transcended condition for a dialectical and unified act of integration: on the contrary, any employment of the *other field* (*champ autre*) transforms the group into an Other, that is to say, into a practico-inert unit of alterity. The historical and practical problem does not concern us here, though it is of crucial concern from the point of view of our real activity as concrete men. What concerned me was to lead the group through the triple character of realised *praxis* to the last of its incarnations, that is to say, to see it dissolve into seriality.

2 *The Circularity of Dialectical Investigation*

This enables us to reach the concrete at last, that is to say, to complete our dialectical investigation. We now confront not the real concrete, which can only be historical, but the set of formal contexts, curves, structures and conditionings which constitute the *formal milieu* in which the historical concrete must necessarily occur. Or rather – since nothing is *settled* except *past being* – we are at last encountering the set of structures of *transcended-being* which historical *praxis* transcends when it produces itself as a constituted dialectic in accordance with laws imposed by the constituent dialectic on the basis of *this* transcended-being, so as to constitute themselves as the conditions for a new *praxis*, with the same statute of *transcended-being*.

And if it is asked how our basic investigation, as such, can be completed (that is to say, since it is *also* a *praxis*, why it can be completed and entirely identified with its results), our reply is that the obvious criterion of its totalising value is its circularity. In fact we have seen how the first and most concrete characteristics of the individual as an abstract reality lie in alienation to the practico-inert; but the practico-inert, as a non-dialectical thickening of Being, enables sociality to be created as the common work of groups on series, and allows alienated freedom to reappear as a violence exerted upon necessity. And this common *praxis* gave its practical truth to the field of serialities: it unveiled it and constituted it as *what has to be dissolved*. But our study of the different structures, in an order of increasing complexity, has shown inertia reappearing inside groups, at first as the free violence of freedoms against freedoms and then becoming *a common being* in a reciprocally created inertia. This is what we have called freedom as necessity. On this basis, and through the force of inertia itself, this necessity, freely accepted under the pressure of increasingly urgent circumstances and in the milieu of scarcity, becomes pledged faith, and an agent of the re-exteriorisation of interiority (organised and institutionalised relations) until the most extreme mode of exteriority (the institution) produces in its own institutional statute the conditions and means of re-interiorisation.

In fact, the sequence of the dialectical investigation has shown sovereignty as an agent of petrification, and as a consequence an essential factor of increasing seriality. And this seriality is not simply the formal development of pledged inertia in material conditions which demand it (separation, etc.): in so far as the group constitutes itself in direct contact with inert gatherings, alterity rises into it from its material. However just as the group as *worked* reciprocity is a human product rather than a given of nature, so its action on series produces the form of worked seriality which we have called other-direction. Thus the difference between a group whose unity becomes more and more like a seal impressed on a human wax which is solidifying, and a gathering whose very inertia turns into a source of energy, in so far as it is exploited for serial actions by a false unity which is induced within seriality, tends to disappear. So it appears that we left collectives in the moment where the group was extricating itself from them and where the common initiative (through its half-failure: practical success, or at least possibility of practical success, but ontological failure) forced us back to them, to the extent that the necessity of freedom implied the progressive alienation of freedom to necessity. But when we reach the end of our investigation, we do not find collectives as we left them: the mere constitution of a group at the epidermic surface of a series constitutes for other layers of seriality a kind of abstract, negative unity (that of the non-grouped); at every moment of the investigation, a group's practices and manipulations differentiate certain sectors of series by employing recurrence as a mystifying synthesis in the form of other-direction; and in the end petrified groups collapse into the series, *their practical unity* having become an inert seal of pure exteriority. In this way series preserve and serialise significations (totalisations which are either dead or else have become false totalities) just as worked matter preserves determinations produced by work or, in other words, series, in certain sectors, become inorganic, worked materiality.

To go back to the deepest origin of the group, there can be no doubt that, whatever its manifest aim may be, it produces itself through the project of taking the inhuman power of mediation between men away from worked matter and giving it, in the community, to each and to all and constituting itself, as structured, as a resumption of control over the materiality of the practical field (things and collectives) by free *communised praxis* (the pledge, etc.). From its first appearance as the erosion of the collective, it is possible to see in it – to use Marxist terminology – the project of removing man from the statute of alterity which makes him a product of his product, in order to transform him, *hot (à chaud)*, by appropriate practices, into a *product of the group*, that is to say – as long as the group is freedom – *into his own product*. This double concrete undertaking is realised, of course, in concrete circumstances and in the basic context of need and scarcity. But this is a dialectical development; it asserts itself and gets lost in the anti-dialectical being of the practico-inert and produces itself anew as the very negation of this being; and consequently, although this conditioning by need is both indispensable and strict (directly or indirectly), it does not *explain*, in the sense of positivistic reason, the constitution of *the particular reality* which is the group. And, indeed, we have seen how threats and needs can give rise to a negative unity in those layers of the gathering which are inert in so far as they are already unified (by the enemy, by a natural but totalising threat, etc.): and it is on the basis of these abstract significations of synthetic unity that every Other acquires the ability to liquidate the Other in himself. Thus, in serial impotence, the negative possibility of the group produces itself everywhere as that which denies this impotence, or as that which is made temporarily impossible by this impotence. The group defines and produces itself not only as an instrument, but also as a *mode of existence*; it posits itself for itself – in the strict determination of its transcendent task – as the free milieu of free human relations; and on the basis of the pledge, it produces man as a free common individual, and confers new birth on the Other: thus the group is both the most effective *means* of controlling the surrounding materiality in the context of scarcity and *the absolute end* as pure freedom liberating men from alterity.

These observations are intended to demonstrate the basic reciprocity between groups and the collectives. Since, in effect, the group constitutes itself with the *Others* of the collective, all the imposed external characteristics of the collective are transferred to the group itself, are interiorised and, having been adopted through the pledge, determine it in interiority. A revolutionary party, intent on liquidating certain prejudices and ideological tendencies (imposed on the exploited class by the exploiting class by means of propaganda), will be formed through the union of the exploited who are determined by such an ideology and such prejudices. In the concrete domain of the group, this passivity presents itself as Other-Being which remains an inertia in everyone and which has to be liquidated as such, by everyone and by specialised organisations. A resumption in freedom is therefore characterised – in this negative example – by rearranging the group so as to destroy the inherited characteristic. In this sense, it can be said that the tangle of passive determinations which constitutes the collective, is entirely reproduced *within the group* as a perspective for acting on itself (positively and negatively) in the context of a transcendent objective. The entire temporalisation of a practical community is characterised *from within* by the evolution of restructured alterities in so far as this evolution is conditioned by practice (that is to say, by acting on the objective and by its reactions). Thus, the First French Republic was proclaimed by royalists. Or rather, at the time of the flight to Varennes, the assemblies, clubs, etc., discovered their royalism as an unnoticed inertia and, in the course of the following year, reclassifications, liquidations, schisms and purges, conditioned by the movement of History, led these power-groups and pressure-groups to *make themselves republican by proclaiming the Republic.*

Conversely, seriality, in so far as the group *emerged from it*, is profoundly determined by this separation. The unity of the grouping movement is perceived in alterity and negatively: it creates fear, and every *Other* imagines he will have to pay for the Others; and the action frightens the torpid. But, at the same time, it establishes its own legitimacy by reasserting its freedom and, at the same time, designates the *exis* of the Other as the inert ensemble which engulfs it in seriality (and which must either be liquidated or readopted in freedom). Now, the alienation of the Other is sustained and lived by everyone through an alienated freedom: alienated in its objectification, in its results, etc., but free and constituent, in so far as it is lost so that the Other can exist. Thus for every practical freedom which exhausts itself in order to produce necessity as alienation, the group is the free possibility of integration (one can join it or sign on). Thus it depends, in alterity, on everyone's choice. And this individual in the series will thereby initiate, by himself and for himself (through the mediation of the group), a liquidation of alterity, according to circumstances and to the particular History; and the Other who strenuously rejects the group will have to adopt alterity *as if* it were the result of a free common *praxis*: he will have to behave as if *Other-Being* were a system of values and a practical organisation; and he will thereby negatively reflect the action of the group and contribute to the dissolution of alterity.

Dialectical exchanges of an osmotic nature therefore concretely occur between groups and serialities: the series infects the group with its passivity, and either the group interiorises it and transforms it into instrumentality or it is ultimately destroyed by it; the group, in all its forms, forces the statute of alterity to emerge from immediacy, and produces a *reflexion* in the collective as such. But we should not forget that the opposite reciprocal relation is possible: the series may show by still isolated agitations that it is approaching the point at which it will dissolve into a group; thus it may exert real pressure on the active community which 'represents' it, and the group which is in the process of petrification may become an obstacle to the dissolution of seriality in the collective on account of its own inertia. In any case, a directing group, as an epidermic emergence from the collective, produces a double structure of unity in it: one of them is positive but illusory, and is the mirage of totality in the milieu of other-direction; the other is real but negative and ambivalent, and is the totalisation of the non-grouped by their non-membership of the group, which will ultimately be lived by everyone either as an impotence which has to be transcended (a negation of the negative totalisation) or as a practical refusal to join the group (a constitution of alterity into a practical and totalising bond of interiority: counter-groups).[91]

Through its decline and relapse into seriality, the group, at a distance, causes pseudo-synthetic or negatively synthetic variations in the collective. The induced, phantasmal unity of the collective from which a fused group has just extricated itself – as the immediate connection of impotence to action, of free *praxis* to suffered alterity, etc. – is completely different from the unities of other-direction. In so far as a small group knows how to produce them according to rule, it can use these unities to exploit the immense potentialities of an indefinite series (in the strictly physical sense of transformations of energy) so as to bring about specific changes in the social field by means of machines. Thus the group, *as praxis*, reproduces itself at every level with the

---

91. Counter-groups cannot be groups, except when the sovereign integrates them into apparatuses of constraint. In themselves, they constitute *by their unity* the mirage of a hostile group. They may occasionally present themselves as directed groups (with guides, organisers, etc.). But despite these attributes of practical totalisation their structure is still serial. If they come into contact with an enemy group (but a *genuinely* practical one) they are immediately dispersed. The difference between them and pure seriality is simply due to the fact that everyone who is marching in step with the Others, and, in the last resort, in *other-step*, is ultimately affected by a practical and adopted alterity. But these two characteristics, being 'practical' and being 'adopted', are induced: it is free *praxis* which, from outside, forces inertia to become negative action, while the interiorisation of this determination becomes adopted alterity. In fact, nothing is adopted; it is simply that they remain other and try, *as Other*, to prevent the dissolution of the series *in the Others*.

statute appropriate to each, in one case other-direction, at a lower level pure seriality, and lower still, the strict, directed equivalence of two physico-chemical states.

The preceding paragraphs can be summed up by saying that the constituted dialectic presents itself as a double circularity. The first circularity is of a static order: we can observe that the group's structures and lines of action are defined by the features of the collective from which it has extricated itself; and at the same time, in its practical relation with the collective, the group reproduces itself as directed alterity and as the exploitation of passive activity at every level until it becomes purely and simply *the movement of the machine* and the rhythm of production.[92] The second circularity is the perpetual movement which will sooner or later degrade actual groups and cause them to collapse back into collectives. I will recall here that this circularity is conditioned only by the movement of History and that, regardless of their statute, groups can either arise from the practico-inert field or be reabsorbed into it; and there is no formal law to compel them to pass through the succession of different statutes described above. A fused group may either dissolve instantaneously or be at the beginning of a long development which will lead to sovereignty; and in the complex world glimpsed here, the sovereign group itself may arise directly from the collective itself (or rather from its sector of other-direction). But it cannot really arise unless all the formal rules of its statute (separation, the institution, the exteriorisation of practices, and reinteriorisation by the untranscendable third party) are given simultaneously in their mutual conditioning. But in itself this should cause no surprise, and only the whole historical complex can determine whether the group will emerge *already half-petrified*, since in concrete reality, that is to say, in every moment of a temporalisation, *all statutes of all groups*, whether alive or dead, and *all types of seriality* (with all their induced unities, whether illusory or real, whether negative or positive) are given together as a tangle of strict relations and as the dispersed raw material of the developing totalisation.

Thus every pledged group, which forms freely at the expense of a series, necessarily relates *in itself* to some less differentiated structures

92. In the totalisation of the common field, every group does of course also find its objectivity in every hostile or friendly group. But this horizontal circularity is too obvious to be worth dwelling on. What is important for us is vertical circularity.

and ultimately to the fused group, which is its fundamental form and its surety. But *fusion*, as the totalising moment of the regulatory/regulated third party, takes place in the pledge itself, or rather in the moment of the decision to pledge. The first third party to raise his hand immediately gives the series everywhere the opportunity to dissolve, and it dissolves *through the pledge as ubiquity*. The stage is not missed out; but it is the immediate basis of the second stage (and, if necessary, this of the third, etc.). In the same way, fusion and the pledge, with their masked crude violence, sustain the feeble contractual link of a group in the process of *organisation*: in fact we shall encounter them again in the intransigence of colleagues and leaders, in a period of rearrangement. It should also be added that, although all forms of group are in themselves *created* products, produced by human labour, each of them *re-produces* itself in practico-inert fields and in common fields which are already determined by analogous forms (dead or alive) and under the direct or indirect influence of their presence. And in fact we have just seen that no group of any form can produce itself without influencing all social fields, and that seriality itself is determined, either negatively or positively, by unitary schemata which will be taken up again by the practical movement of regroupment. It is this double circularity, static and dynamic, in so far as it is manifested in shifting relations at every level of every social concretion, which constitutes the final moment of the dialectical investigation and, therefore, the concrete reality of sociality.

This concrete moment of the investigation reintegrates all the abstract moments which we have reached and transcended one after the other; it replaces them within the concrete in their concrete function. In the first place, the free *praxis* of the isolated individual loses its suspicious appearance as a Robinsonade; *there is no such thing* as an isolated individual (unless isolation is treated as a special structure of sociality). But within the historical totalisation, the real disappearance of the isolated individual and his replacement by the *Other* or by the common individual is based on organic *praxis* both as constituent dialectic and as a mediation (at another level) between function and the transcendent object. We will never *encounter* an isolated individual except implicitly and negatively, as a relativity of the constituted dialectic, that is to say, as a basic absence of a group ontological statute and as the shifting exile of common individuals (Fraternity-Terror) and in the paradox that the group tries to dissolve the multiplicity of persons in the cult of personality. Thus we can now see that the concrete dialectic is that which is revealed through the common *praxis* of a group; but we also know that the impossibility (for a union of individuals) of transcending organic action as a strictly individual model is the basic condition of historical rationality, that is to say, that constituted dialectical Reason (as the living intelligibility of all common *praxis*) must always be related to its ever present but always veiled foundation, constituent rationality. Without the strict, permanent limitation of relating the group to this foundation, the community *is no less abstract* than the isolated individual: there are revolutionary pastorals on the group which are the exact counterpart of Robinsonades.

But, in the same way, examining groups independently of series would be just as abstract as examining series independently of groups. In reality, the historical production of one or several groups determines a new kind of practical field, which we call the *common field*, whereas seriality defines the field which we have called *practico-inert*. But the circularity which we have just explained makes it possible to see why the dialectic – as a formal law of movement – remains silent on questions of priority. There is actually no *a priori* ground for supposing that seriality is an earlier statute than the group, although it is true that the group constitutes itself in and against it. Not only do we always find groups and gatherings together, but also, *only* dialectical investigation and experience will enable us to determine whether the seriality in question is an immediate gathering or whether it is constituted by old groups which have been serialised. Indeed, we have seen that sooner or later they return to the statute of inertia. But are we to regard the tuff of seriality as the inorganic as a foundation of object-sociality (*socialité-objet*), or should it be reduced to a dust of degenerate dead organisms? And – as we perceive it in everyday experience – is there not a perpetual double movement of regroupment and petrification? We can ignore such questions: our purpose was to explain the intelligibility of these possibilities; and this we have done.

3 The Working Class as Institution, Fused Group and Series

At this level, it should be observed that the complex forms assumed, in and through circularity, by what are conventionally called *social realities*, need not be confined to any one specific level of intelligibility, and that it may be impossible to confine them to any particular practico-ontological statute. This is not just because groups have a serial destiny even in the moment of their practical totalisation, or because a particular seriality may, in some circumstances, be transformed into a community. The most important reason is that the group is always marked by the series, that it becomes its reality in the milieu of freedom, and that a series is determined, even in its totally inorganic practico-inert layers, by the sovereign self-production of the group. It is therefore necessary to conceive of a specific statute for certain realities whose real unity is manifested as a bond of interiority between *common* and *serial multiplicities*. This applies, for example, to social classes (when defined within a system of exploitation).[93] We have shown how class-being (for example, in the working class) is defined by the seriality of impotence in so far as it is qualified and determined by practico-inert exigencies: the primary, negative relation of the worker to the machine (non-ownership), the mystification of the free contract, and labour becoming a hostile force *for the worker*, on the basis of the wage system and the capitalist process. All this takes place in a milieu of serial dispersal and antagonistic reciprocities on the labour market. Alienation as a real and strict process within the system arises in and through *alterity* as infinite recurrence: it concretises the abstract structure in an entirely concrete historical movement; but the dispersive skeleton, as a relation of fleeting impotence amongst the workers themselves, is a necessary part of this concretisation. Industrialisation produces its proletariat; it drains it from the countryside, and regulates its birthrate. But, here as elsewhere, a statute of impotence is produced, through the serialisation of the proletarians.

But this serial, practico-inert statute would not lead to class *struggle* if the permanent possibility of dissolving the series were not available to everyone; and we have seen how a first, abstract determination of this possible unity emerges through class interest, as a possible negation of destiny. However, the transformation of a class into an actualised group has never actually occurred, even in revolutionary periods. But we have seen that seriality is always being eroded by action groups constituted at various levels and pursuing variable objectives. Trade-union organisation, as we saw above, is typical of the organised group

93. But it does not apply to classes as defined by sociologists or ethnographers investigating 'primitive' societies.

which becomes institutional and sovereign (and is in constant danger of bureaucratisation). There can be no doubt, however, that in its free production of itself it takes on the inert characteristics which define, in untranscendability, the class-being of workers. I have tried to demonstrate this, in particular, for anarcho-syndicalism. The readoption of a constitution – generally in ignorance – helps to define inert limits to common action: this too we have seen. Thus, the entire class is clearly present in the organised group which constitutes itself within it; and its seriality as a collective, as a limitation, is the inorganic being of its practical community. It is genuinely a case of *the class* having two forms; the community is not to be regarded as a Spinozan mode of the proletariat-substance, because, on the contrary, it constitutes itself as *its practical apparatus*.

But the relation between such apparatuses and the series from which they spring is more complex than is often supposed. Clearly it depends on the means of production; and for capitalists there is a necessity to transform these means constantly. Thus the bond changes with the type of machine. In fact, before 1914, with the universal machine, we can observe that trade-union practice was defined by the workers themselves *as they practised their trades*. Thus the dissolution of series appeared to be an accomplished fact. But really their unity was created at the top: it was that of the working-class élite (skilled workers produced by the universal machine); and each of them, as a member of the sovereign group, gathered around him the unskilled labourers who helped him in his work. But he did not form a true practical community with them (in union struggle), because they did not constitute a group in themselves and because they did not produce it inside the group, as instituted sovereign. In fact, trade unions as a union of the élite constituted their sovereignty in the very act which produced them; and this sovereignty, for unskilled workers, was neither legitimate nor illegitimate; it belonged to another world (that of the group), and in this other world it produced its own legitimation, and could only be accepted in impotence in the serial world. Grouped *from outside* by their foreman (*l'ouvrier suzerain*), the labourers remained serial – first among themselves, then in relation to other foremen (who, as the leading group, refused to allow them into the union), and then in relation to other labourers (in other workshops and other factories) linked to them only through the mediation of a group of which none of them were members. Thus they were doubly serial: serial because exploitation was always based on their competitive antagonism and impotence, and serial because obedience and trust for other foremen by other labourers conditioned their trust *here* (participation in the strike, etc.). It would therefore be a mistake to claim that, in the first years of this century, the French working class itself had produced its apparatuses of protection and that a union militant (as a common individual of *practical class-unity*) was indistinguishable from the worker (as a member of a passive, exploited seriality). In fact, a particular category of workers – the foremen – had constituted themselves into a sovereign group, *the practical embodiment*[94] of the working class. Through the mediation of its local agents this group imposed a common will on an unintegrated 'sub-proletariat' whose class-being was seriality. And the difference between these two modes was so great that the unions never noticed the new workers emerging from and amongst the unskilled labour force – the products of the second industrial revolution, the specialised workers who emerged as a result of the deskilling produced by specialised machines.

In this sense, the development of the working class in the twentieth century, the new characteristics of labour (harassment, etc.), and the disappearance of a sector of skilled workers (in France) gave rise to a new formula for unity which has wrongly been supposed to be radically different from the preceding one. The work of the union militant and that of the specialised worker are practically incompatible. A specialisation is required: the working class produces its own permanent paid officials. The trade union therefore became, for the conservatives, a group which was *foreign* to the working class. It is true that the permanent official *is no longer* a worker: this is a truism, since he *no longer works* as a worker. Besides, he passes into the ranks of the *institutionalised third parties* (being an integrating part of the sovereign group). But we have just seen that the only way an anarcho-syndicalist skilled worker could turn the class into a group was by deciding that he alone was a *worker* and by practically excluding 80 per cent of workers from the proletariat. This difference is entirely in the interest of the permanent officials who made the proposals and addressed everyone; whereas the anarcho-syndicalist imposed the decision of the

94. I say 'embodiment' rather than 'representation', because these workers considered that they *were* eminently the working class in so far as they still based their condemnation of exploitation on the skill of their work. For them, the skilled worker was a complete worker (and, one might say, a complete man); labourers were unfortunate and their condition was unworthy: but then they were not really workers.

few on the majority. Thus permanent officials avoided the statute of workers precisely to the extent that skill in work was no longer the basis of their demands, to the extent that individuals who are inter-changeable in function recognise that they have the same needs. The sovereign's attempts to manifest a kind of authoritarianism reflect the very interchangeability which makes it necessary to tighten discipline and to carry out truly massive actions to prevent the immediate replacement of strikers. And this authoritarianism is simply *Fraternity-Terror* as it exists in the masses themselves when they dissolve their seriality (by means of a strike or demonstration). The permanent official is therefore precisely the product of the working class in so far as that class is characterised as a mass. Inside the sovereign group he realises a real exigency of the situation which mass movements con-stitute out of fused groups by liquidating seriality. In himself, apart from a few special characteristics due to the trade-union and pro-fessional ensembles which he represents, he is simply the sovereign, abstract invitation to unification. His very universality – he, too, is interchangeable, as a local permanent official – is the transposition of serialising interchangeability into the necessity for practical totalisation of the masses.

Thus one can distinguish two stages, depending whether, in a working-class city at work – when the class is a collective – he repre-sents possible unity in the abstraction of his institutional being (and is characterised by his relations with Paris rather than by his relations with the locality) or whether he becomes, in a tense situation, the practical schema and signification of the unity which is to be realised. However, when this unity is achieved, it excludes him. He will be listened to, provided his views accord with those of the constituted group; but he will be transcended and left behind if he tries to divert the group from its chosen course. It is therefore useful to consider the working class as defined by variable statutes (in space or time). The trade union *is* the working class *objectified, exteriorised, institutionalised,* and possibly *bureaucratised,* but unrecognisable to its own eyes and realising itself as a pure practical schema of unity.[95] It is the sovereignty

95. And the multiplicity of trade-union apparatuses – in France, for example – transposes the real divisions of the working class (divergences of interest, charac-terising certain partial ensembles 'within' the proletariat) into *praxis*. This means that these divisions, lived in the seriality of impotence by workers themselves, become practical antagonisms when embodied in organised groups.

of the class, but it is cut off from it, and produces itself elsewhere, in the pure milieu of common *praxis*. This *group* – defined by a statute of *separation* (local permanent officials who 'go to Paris' from time to time, controlled on the spot by *missi dominici*, etc.) – usually has no control over masses in serial flight. In favourable circumstances, every agent attempts to determine local disturbances (improvised meetings, posters, etc.): this is what is called agitation; but in fact, such disturbances are simply circuits of recurrence. In this moment, the working class exists under a double statute since, in its dispersive seriality, the union officials (*délégués*) are *external* guarantors of its possible interiorisation. When, in a period of social conflict, the workers of a given city unite in a common decision (taken in an atmosphere of violence-freedom: public voting, and the obligation on the minority to dissolve in unanimity), the working class *exists in fact* as a practical totalisation. It might be disastrous if the 'movement' were not taken up in other cities: but, from a formal point of view, local unification through the *praxis* of a strike or insurrection is enough on its own to posit *the group* as a possible permanent statute for the proletariat, even though, for the actual proletariat and in present circumstances, this group may manifest itself as a fused group (or at most as a pledged group), and maintain its systems of organised, institutional relations *outside itself*. In fact it will never re-absorb the union or *follow* the instructions of the unionists; apart from the fact of being institutional, permanent officials seem rather similar to the agitators whom the people required to reflect their practical thought, between 1789 and 1794.

This will lead us, as a synchronic determination, to treat the working class – at any given moment of the historical process – *not only* as an institutionalised organisational group (the 'cadres'), but also as either a fused or a pledged group (the constitution of the *soviets*, in 1905, appears as an intermediary between a pledged group and an organised group), and as a seriality which is still inert (in certain sectors), but which is profoundly affected by the negative unity of the pledged groupings. The institutional group, as an abstract skeleton of the united class, is a permanent invitation to unity; indeed it is the sovereignty of the class if it is entirely serial; and, secondly, it may reflect their absolute sovereignty to the fused groups (and to their concrete developments) and display their decisions to them in the framework of a more distant future, in relation to indirect objectives. But this reflection is not done by a regulatory third party to a group to which he belongs, but by a member of a group – in so far as he is the signifier/signified of the group – to another group which produces its own sovereignty. In other words, the appearance of the group as a developing totalisation of the working class – even though it may be the result of the work of the unions, and even though the group may set itself objectives which are laid down by 'central organs' – immediately makes union sovereignty redundant, but without re-absorbing the institutional group (and it will play a part in the material organisation of strikes and in establishing contacts with the employers). *It is this concrete group,* in fact, which becomes the concrete sovereignty of the working class, and which exercises it; the material conditions of conflict, and power relations with the other class and the apparatuses of constraint which it produces are all strictly determined through it, and they define the situation itself (as a relation of sovereign groups embodying hostile classes and as a relation between these groups and the serialities from which they arose).

In effect, the real efficacity of the common *praxis* here will depend on the abstract, totalising action of the fused group on the series which surrounds it. In fact, each member of the group is, through innumerable complex relations, also a member of the series at the same time as belonging to the group. One can easily see this when one remembers that the member will belong to a family, to a residential area, to various associations and, through all these more or less inert communities, to series of alterity which extend everywhere. Thus if he is a member of the combat group this will determine these series, practically, though abstractly. Similarly, the mere production of the group, in so far as the organs of diffusion (possibly of the institutional group) spread the news of it, becomes the practical sovereign reunification of the working class in a *here* for any *elsewhere* of the series. The process as a whole will then be manifested either through the serial passivity of large working-class concentrations or through a shifting agitation which begins to dissolve collective impotence into a truly revolutionary unification. But the important point here is that the practical constitution of the group (that is to say, the *Apocalypse*) is – in itself and in its being-outside-itself – the production at a distance, through the series and throughout it, of a schema of totalisation as an abstract ubiquity (and a rigid obligation for everyone to adopt either seriality or unity, even if, in the place and function he occupies, his impotence is insurmountable). And the new groupings which are to be constituted in opposition to seriality (and within it) differ from the first at least in that they are induced, and in that the totalising schema was already present in every Other as the possibility of rejecting all alterity. Of course, this does not prevent the groups from producing a new seriality (in separation, and in the variety of situations, of local interests, of circumstances of struggle, and of power relations – each group determining the other groups as others by its limited *praxis*),

As we saw in *The Problem of Method*, it was this seriality which aborted the peasant movement in Luther's Germany. In the case of the seriality of groups, the trade-union apparatus regained its importance, and its co-ordinating, organisational activities transformed isolated groups into organised *sub-groups*. But in itself it remained an *other-group* (*groupe-autre*) rather than an interior sovereignty. Similarly, the dissolution of series may often be the result of a serially propagated contagion (as with the strikes of 1936, when the working class came closest to a total synthetic unification). In this situation reflexivity does not occur till later, in the milieu of the resulting immense group; and the structure of a massive group (that is to say, a group which arises from the masses and is composed of them) has to be studied separately because it is characterised not only by a deep integration, but also, on occasion, by real separation. (Factory occupations in 1936 showed this double character: the occupation of a particular factory occurred within the practical awareness of totalisation and ubiquity; it was *the same*; *everywhere the same*, here. But they also made communications between sub-groups difficult; many intermediaries were necessary.) But the rebirth of seriality in its very dissolution may in turn occasion liquidating actions. I mention these abstract possibilities only in order to raise the question of the intelligibility of the concrete – in this case, of class. Of course, the terms of the problem are clear: class manifests itself not only[96] as an institutionalised apparatus, but also as an ensemble (serial or organised) of direct-action groups, and as a collective which receives its statute from the practico-inert field (through and by productive relations with other classes) and which receives its universal schema of practical unification from the groups which constantly form on its surface.[97] And these three simultaneous

96. On the terrain of the struggle for reforms, of course.

97. For greater simplicity, I am not taking account of workers' parties or of splits within the working class: these essential characteristics of historical proletariats are themselves material determinations. It does not make any difference

statutes arise in practical and dialectical connection with one another, through a process which is itself conditioned by the historical conjuncture as a whole. In fact, language *always* presents class too simply, either as always united and ranged against the exploiters, or as temporarily demobilised (having completely relapsed into seriality). May it not be that these imperfect and incomplete concepts are an accurate reflection of our inability to understand this unique triple reality of a developing historical class? May it not be that in this confrontation between groups as constituted dialectic and as series (as anti-dialectical), we run up against the very limits of intelligibility?

I do not think so; and the incompleteness of these concepts or determinations of language simply expresses political attitudes (that of the militant, that of the oppositionists, etc.) which as such do not concern us here. But this presents no difficulties on either the ontological or the practical plane.

On the ontological plane, there are not three beings, or three statutes of being: class-being is practico-inert, and defines itself as a determination of seriality, as we have seen. The two kinds of group (fused and pledged, organisational and institutional) have no inner-group-being; their statute is that their being-outside-themselves (the only group-being) lies in the series from which they have emerged and which sustains them (and which affects them even in their freedom). Of course, the fused group negates the series within itself since it dissolves it; but it also relates to it ontologically because it is *its actions as a series,* the activity *for the whole series in a particular situation* of this moving, changing, violent formation, whose future is still indeterminate, but which is the audacity of the series *here,* the success or failure of all who reject impotence, massification, and alterity *here.* In other words, the group's class-being lies outside it in the series, and inside the group the series is both the negation and the affirmation of its being through practical transcendence. We have seen how the practical individual always realises class-being in everyone; a working-class woman who has an abortion carries out the sentence which the exploiting classes have passed on her. But in a common action (whether reformist or revolutionary), there is both a realisation of class-being and freedom: the working-class woman now recognises her being as a

---

whether we are dealing with a trade union or a party; what is important is the relation of the *objectified class* (the trade union or any other institutionality) to the fused class.

worker – defined by her wages and her work – and she recognises it in the demands themselves; but she transcends it *through the demand* – however minimal – which is the common practice for bringing about a general change, and above all by grouping *with a view* to getting satisfaction.

The dissolution of the serial may in certain cases be the act of uniting with others, or a total liquidation (at least a temporary one) of the previous seriality (especially in the case of what contemporary sociologists call 'micro-organisms'), but then it is just a matter of transcending seriality. However, this transcendence may be intended to last longer than a demonstration or even than a strike. It may manifest itself in a rebellious practice, and become a revolutionary action: and on this basis, especially if the Revolution is not a failure, and develops according to its own laws, there will be a radical metamorphosis, and everything will shift into a different social world. But with the struggle of a dominated against a dominant class, seriality will always be the product of exploitation and the statute which maintains it, *even more than internal dissension. It is seriality* which must be overcome in order to achieve even the smallest common result (such as averting too rapid a fall of purchasing power). But *it is seriality* too which sustains the group making demands, in its very passivity, as a source of possible energy – the group, in fact, from the practical point of view of its action, can no longer conceive it except in the synthetic form of potentiality. *It is seriality* which appears to it *as producing it* – to the extent, as I have shown, that it is still engulfed in it *by the other serial relations of its members. It is seriality* which the group totalises *in exteriority*, that is to say, for the group and in its connection with seriality, in so far as it conceives the serial unity (of dispersal) in terms of the dialectical reasons which engender it materially and dialectically (historical conditions of the capitalist process). Lastly, it is seriality which, in the dialectical perspective of union struggles and of everyday labour, defines its future as its death and permanent resurrection (the group will dissolve into seriality when the workers – victorious or defeated – resume work; and it will be reborn from seriality when, having learnt from this experience, the workers become active again).[98]

98. Although the lie is spread for purely propaganda purposes, it is not true *today* that, in a factory constituted by a majority of skilled workers, it is possible *both* to do the work which, in the context of capitalist exploitation, enables the worker to live, *and* to exert constant *common pressure* on employers. It is true that social bonds remain (and a past too, as we shall see) and so does *a class attitude*

This means that *class-being*, as past, present, and future seriality, is *always* the ontological statute of the worker and that *group praxis*, as a surface dissolution of the relation of alterity inside the class (and therefore on the surface in the worker) and as a conservative transcendence of serial being, is either the present practical reality of the common individual or his future possibility as an induced signification and as an abstract unification coming to the series from the depths of the future. As for the institutional group (union, etc.), it *practically* represents this possibility in its permanence: and this means that the task of the institutionalised third parties who compose it is not only to maintain, through separation and by means of their centralised unity, this possible unity as a sovereignty, but also to realise, as far as possible, and in all circumstances, the local conditions which make this unity possible.[99]

From this point of view, the apparatus as a whole is the practical

---

on the part of each and all. But it is either a lie or a dream to claim that this amounts to working-class pressure: workers exert pressure from the moment in which the threshold of the dissolution of seriality is crossed. *Or at least* in the case of professional workers who are indispensable to the factory (which simply takes us back to the very special circumstances of pre-1914 syndicalism), such pressure may be exerted during work through the intermediary of skilled representatives who negotiate *on the basis* of constantly possible but avoidable strike-action. Or else, in the case of the masses, when circumstances, the pressure of need, etc., *have already produced* common *praxis*: negotiations with employers then turn on the concessions which they are prepared to make in order to *prevent the workers' action*. Victory (as in the case of the semi-official strike of the electric welders at Saint-Nazaire in 1954) obviously involves a new *exis*, that is to say, the threshold is lower, seriality is lived as temporary, and *class attitudes are already* the abstract connections of a community less [serial] than ever and always possible. This does not mean, however, that this attitude is as such revolutionary: and the proof of this is that the proud aggression of the anarcho-syndicalists (expanded production manifested and expressed itself in the fact that the proportion of successful strikes *never* fell below 50 per cent) had its final expression in the practice of reformism. And, above all, we must also accept the truth of the opposite case: which is that the failure of a strike (in particularly serious conditions) actually leads to a reinforcement of the serial statute (after an unsuccessful strike, a few years earlier, also at Saint-Nazaire, the unions lost nearly all their members and for a very long period the workers sank into almost total inertia). This all means that the militant action of the group is aware that even when they win, naked seriality is, like some 'seasonal condition', one of the terms of the choice which limits the possibilities for the proletariat.

99. This is not a question of politics: I do not need to determine whether they can do better or do something else. This is a pure problem of intelligibility.

unity of interiority (realising itself locally and in successive temporalisations) in so far as it is objectified, exteriorised and universalised. It is the sovereignty of the united proletariat, in so far as it produces itself in the milieu of integrating totalisation when it is in the milieu of seriality. But this objectifying exteriorisation, on the terrain of Being, does not raise any new questions: this institutional group has no *being-one*. If it were a fused group, its being would lie in inert seriality. Its apparent autonomy is due simply to its seriality. In effect, a trade union, as an institutional group, in itself presupposes structures of recurrence and alterity, grounded on separation and serial circularity; and these groups were investigated above. But the institutional-being of its members is simply inertia and can never act as group-being. This inertia – which has nothing to do with the way they apply themselves to their task or with their results – is precisely the basis of the permanence of working-class unity as a possibility which is always accessible to the series: the permanent official himself is this unity in so far as his mandate (whatever the mode of recruitment or appointment) is not connected in its institutional duration either with individual characteristics or with organic *praxis*. Elected or appointed for a two year period, for example, his activities, whatever their nature, are the transcendence and affirmation of a material and institutional inert unity which is both the *Other-Being* (being of seriality) of the sovereign in his local agent and the *being-one* of the series grasped in one of its members *in so far as he has become Other*. Thus the being of a permanent official is nothing like *the being of an institutional group*: this group-being has no reality: but *as such* the serial-being of the local official acts as an inert support (like wax to a seal) for the synthetic, sovereign unity of the class as a permanent possibility, that is to say, as the abstract, passive perseverance of being-one in his being. The unity of the exploited class is in fact *practical*: but if it is maintained in opposition to it, it is given an inert support which makes it resemble a being.

Ontologically, the situation is perfectly simple: between the trade unionists and the working people there exists an agreed inertia; class-being, which is serial, is an inert conditioning and tends to make unity appear as an other ontological statute: the being-unity of the class (the true goal). The tension which mutually determines the serialised sovereign and the series which inertly receives the inert sign of its unity, makes the liquidation of seriality, under specific circumstances, permanently possible. It is on this basis that a group which exercises its own sovereignty appears and destroys trade-union sovereignty (equally its own as other) while preserving the statute of an agitator for the permanent official. At the same time, it throws back its own inertia into the depths; but at least it retains its dependence on all in the form of transcended and preserved *class-being*.

Practically, there is no problem either: the *praxis* of action groups will define itself dialectically in terms of seriality as resistance which has been or is to be transcended and in terms of trade-union instructions, as external objective significations which have to be either rejected, interiorised or transcended. The important point for us is that in everyday action, the working class defines its practical unity *as a totalisation* of objective but inert practical significations, issuing from a sovereign who himself exists only in exteriority and as a patient dissolution of serial forces of inertia which are also no more than the class itself *in its being*, in the course of a regroupment which is aimed at a transcendent objective which has to be defined as *praxis-process*. The working class is neither pure combativity, nor pure passive dispersal nor a pure institutionalised apparatus. It is a complex, moving relation between different practical forms each of which completely recapitulates it, and whose true bond with one another is totalisation (as a movement which each induces in the others and which is reflected by each to the others).[100]

From the point of view of dialectical intelligibility, the differences of statute which separate and unite this single reality in its various forms imply, in the first place, that a single *praxis* – even *through the objective* – produces itself differently at different practical levels. This means that – even in the exceptionally simple case in which it remains unchanged – it will differ at every level through temporalisation (speed, rhythm, etc.), in organisation and internal structures, in its real bond with its objective (through all the means involved) and, consequently, in the very objective which ensures its unity. And this objective itself refers, according to its level, to other more or less distant objectives. It is as if activity had a statute of plurality (with large social ensembles) and developed in every dimension at once. It is *a single action*, in a period of social conflict, which *works* the series (in the same sense as one can say that wood works [*que le bois travaille*]), and which manifests itself in activities of co-ordination and organisation which have

___

100. In a chapter on diachronic totalisation in Volume Two we shall discuss what we shall call the *memory* of the group.

accrued to unionists (building up 'contacts', improvised, impromptu meetings, discussions of objectives with representatives of pledged groups, the determination of a practical plan, which will probably never be carried out, attempts to define the state of the forces involved, so as to give information to the masses, or, depending on the situation, to withold it from them, mediation between Paris and its general objectives concerning *the* French proletariat and local concentrations with their own interests, etc.) and which is encountered again at its own level of full efficacity, with no inertia other than pledged faith, in the common practice of workers. In these three forms, it is also indispensable to the practical struggle: in each of them, at various levels of practical importance, and with an appearance which refers to relational systems (alterity, concrete reciprocity, organisational systems), the same relations to the object, to the future, and to the transcendent world recur; it is just that the *production* of such relations in these practical milieux with their different indices is different, and their reality therefore becomes a heterogeneous and irreducible *production-refraction* in everyone.

The direct, concrete bond between action groups and the series from which they emerge is expressed for and in the group by internal production and by the reflexive grasp of its ontological connection with the proletariat; it *is* the proletariat, simultaneously active and inert, acting as a perpetual transcendence of its inertia as an exploited class. And this ontological structure of immanence-transcendence occurs in the really practical milieu of the determination of ends (to the extent that ontological and practical statutes condition one another in the closest unity, the latter being the practical actualisation and transcendence of the former). It is lived and transcended as a hierarchy of objectives (or fidelities, etc.): the group defines the struggle it will wage, and its exigencies, and it reveals itself at a certain inner 'temperature' in connection with its serial being-outside-itself. It is the suffering class, but above all it is the struggling class. In it, the suffering class transcends itself towards unity in struggle. It shows it to be a serial totality to the extent that the group totalises itself through the dissolution of seriality. In pure recurrence, in effect, class reality is, at most, lived in alienating dispersal. Thus the serial class is the group itself (as practice) and also more than the group (as a much larger gathering). The serial class, for the group, is its very action, its struggle as a negation of its seriality and an embodiment of the serial ensemble in its sovereignty; the serial class is also *its* fidelity (it is faithful to the class in so far as it is an *absence*, in so far as it does not manifest itself entirely at its level of unity in struggle) and *its* danger (it must itself group, unite and struggle everywhere against eroding seriality; it may lose its battle because of seriality, not here but over there and everywhere, for lack of support). Thus concrete, local action, *inside the group*, unites the particular objective – the demand – with the total objective (the mobilisation of the working class). But the connection arises directly in fused and pledged groups: it is an ontological connection transcended as a practical connection. In acting for the common interest of some local workers, the group acts for the whole class: it *is* the class in action. It cannot even conceive of a direct, violent action *betraying* the interests of the working class: if it can be done, then it *must* be done (class exigency). Conversely, it is also unable to recognise seriality – except in its immediate environment, in the *Others* it is in contact with – as a betrayal of its struggle by the class (in so far as the seriality of impotence prevents the concerted undertakings which, from one concentration to another, might have assured their victory).

There is in fact a deep relation of ontological identity, of practical ubiquity and of contradiction in movement; and, as a developing process, this is what, in Marxism, is called proletarian self-emancipation. But, in this case, although the most comprehensive and abstract objective is here, as with the institutionalised group, a foundation which will be determined by the immediate objective (the overthrow of the bourgeoisie and the accession of the working class as the meaning of the struggle are determined by the demand for a particular wage-increase, as the specific possibility which has to be realised in the existing context of the struggle), the relation within the combat group is immediate and always positive: the possibility that an action in support of some demand may go against the general interests of the proletariat (that it may compromise – for the present, though not for ever – the struggle for its accession to power), cannot be produced by the group and in the interiority of the group as a practical, reflected possibility, as a possible determination of the action undertaken, that is to say, as the object of a practice of control and study. On the other hand, a permanent official, in so far as he is sovereign in his institutionalised being, and in so far as he is in communication with Paris, that is to say, with the centre, produces himself in and through the organisation for which he is a local agent as the permanent working class. Inert and prodigiously active, his functions, abilities, and experience – all of which relate to the universal, that is to say, to the partially indeterminate possibility of demands – link him directly with the class as a totalised inertia: he produces himself as the possibility that the class will challenge and destroy the destiny of the workers. Thus the *local* official is everywhere, because he is the class itself or – in other words – because he is everywhere in the form of another permanent official (an institutionalised being whose unity is with all the Others in Paris), the class in movement pre-exists in him in its being-everywhere (at Oyonnax or Le Mans, at Nantes or Alès) in all the local agitations which are merely specifications which have to be considered and judged in themselves. The *opportuneness* of a local movement therefore appears as something which has to be questioned *in terms of* the overall situation (power relations *in France* between the working class as a whole and other classes, etc.). In short, the permanent official is identified with the class itself as a passivity of which he is the active sovereignty, and he affirms himself as qualified in his being to judge the immediate action of the class. Moreover, inertia as serial-class-being cannot challenge the sovereignty of the institutionalised group. Thus the union produces itself as the permanent sovereignty of the class. On the other hand, the fused group puts paid to trade-union sovereignty: the permanent official becomes no more than a temporary agent. Thus a contradiction is immediately established between the class as institutionalised, and partially serialised, sovereignty and the class as a living combat group, particularised by its very action and producing through agitation its free, fraternal sovereignty. This group, from the standpoint of the institutional group, will appear as a particular determination of the class (and therefore as limitation and finitude), and as having to be governed by the sovereignty of the trade-union institution in accordance with the general interests of the class itself.

This conflict of sovereignty therefore implies *not only* that *praxis* is different at every level, but also that these differences are produced fundamentally as contradictions whose effect is to constitute living oppositions, conflicts, transcendences, and struggles between the various forms of a single action – in short, to constitute action through a dialectic in depth in and through the same movement of dialectical transcendence which organises it in relation to its transcendent object. On this basis, comprehension becomes increasingly complex for each level of *praxis*; practical development, at the level in question, produces itself as a transcendence of certain structures (institutions, seriality, etc.), which themselves express certain material conditions *at this* level.

But as a temporalising tension, as an organised transcendence in a moving field of forces, in a directed transformation, it is determined from outside by each practical level, in so far as the whole process produces itself there in another form, at a different degree of compression, with other rhythms, etc. For example, the practical process of the pledged group, in the very milieu of its development, supports the abstract and sovereign activity of the institutional group. It supports this activity because it is itself produced as a transcendence of a material situation through the reorganisation of a common field which has been and still is organised by the sovereign activity as a class *praxis* which has become total objectivity.

Thus the group is defined from outside through and by institutional practice (trade-union practice, for example): it sustains it within itself as a determination of its actions; and from this angle, the group may either support it as inertia, as its own inert exteriority (which may end up by dissolving it entirely and liquidating the exterior sovereign), or interiorise it as one of the internal relations of reciprocity which condition the development of the process. In effect, this interiorisation can occur only as a determination in reciprocity, since the group is always defined by its mediated reciprocities. But there is nothing magical about the projection of the practical institution into the objective act: it simply occurs, in particular conditions, when certain third parties (whether a majority or a minority) adopt the practical maxim of the exterior sovereign and make him into *the reciprocal connection* which unites them within the pledged group as an organising sub-group. When this happens, it is possible to see how the sub-group may impose its common will (that is to say, the *other-will* (*volonté-autre*) of the objective other which has become a reflexive structure within the community). It is also possible – in the absence of any complete determination – that the interiorisation of transcendent sovereignty in *one* sub-group, far from giving an untranscendable authority to the sub-group thus constituted, occasions contradictions (violent or otherwise), and obstacles or splits within the pledged community and, with other factors, leads it to a revival of seriality.

These determinations appear only in the development of the historical event. For us, the important point is that these are all *intelligible possibilities* and that the composition of significations within the group is also intelligible – not by means of analytical reason, however, but dialectically. For, ultimately, the practical signification of the transcendent sovereign is sustained and produced by the fused group (or

the pledged group) as a part, by a living totality, whether this signification remains on the surface of the group as its exteriority or is
integrated into it as an interiorisation and a free re-creation. And in so
far as the group is structured on the basis of inert characteristics which
it has dissolved and readopted in common freedom, the sovereign
action – whether exterior or interiorised – is itself deformed by the
curvatures of the group, and can be determinant only by conforming
to the lines of action, the practical vistas and the webs which constitute
the community as the instrument of its own action. But *at the same
time*, as a determination which has been adopted by agents as common
individuals and in the free reciprocity of internal exchanges, it is
impossible that the sovereign action should not be a factor of constant
modification both for the common *praxis* and for the curvatures of
the internal space.

Now, it should be added that this institutional action is not a passive
determination deriving its only practical reality from the pledged community and living in the group only *with the life of the group*: it is in
fact *already praxis*; it is *the same praxis* in the abstract milieu of the
external institution. Thus its reproduction or reinteriorisation by the
pledged group produces it not as the product of the group but as an
intrusion into the group by an alien intention (by an alien free project). In so far as – for very simple, material reasons (that the 'permanent official' has supporters and 'contacts' them, and that they
establish a line of action within the pledged community, etc.) – the
action of the other group (that is to say, of the class as other) is
necessarily produced inside the pledged group as the emergence and
development of an other-freedom, it *transcends* every signification
which is directly produced by the common freedom (of every third
party as the same); and, conversely, every initiative *of the same* can
either transcend it, change it into a reified signification, or liquidate it.
But in so far as this sovereignty still has to be supported by third
parties who wish to remain *the same* and who claim to project themselves, as the same as all, through this interiorised project, the struggle
takes place between two free, practical projects, each of which has the
same abstract right as the Other. It is the concrete, material ensemble
which will determine the winner, the compromise or the balance of
impotence. This last remark is simply meant to indicate the ambivalence
of sovereign freedom when repeated inside the combat group: it is both
the actual freedom of an Other and the immanent project of the third
parties. The sub-group which proposes it as its own *is the same as all*;

but each third party knows it to be his own in so far as it is that of the Other. But there is nothing incomprehensible about this – on the contrary; and everyone has experienced it.

It may be asked whether, given the formal intelligibility of these dialectical determinations, it is now possible to grasp the reciprocal transformations to which the two practical modalities (in our example, the institution and the struggling community) subject one another. Or should we now admit that they elude the mind because they are so complicated?

The answer must be no. In fact, any re-production (whether external or interiorised) of the sovereign action must be *comprehensible*. This means that *comprehending* union instructions by reference to ends, to the future, to the relation to the working class both as an institution and as seriality, is no different from *producing* them as a possible regulation. But such *comprehension* is the temporalisation of common structures (of the pledged group); and so, though its principle may be invariant (being the dialectic itself), it particularises itself through practical schemata which ultimately express an inert or quasi-passive constitution. Thus the first necessity, for the situated investigator (assuming that he has the necessary information and that he is approaching his facts within a period whose main features are already known), is to comprehend the comprehension of the regulatory third party. He must grasp it as a free group *praxis*, that is to say, as a transcendence which preserves the conditions it transcends. Furthermore, he must comprehend the project of the Other (of the institution) in its real unity (within the institutional group) and on this basis he must be able to grasp the *transcended conditions*, in a new comprehension, as a determination within the pledged group of the comprehended project by the comprehension which re-produces it. But this operation (comprehending the comprehended signification to the degree that it is particularised by the particularities of a comprehension) is simply comprehension itself: there is only one single dialectical process in this grasp of free re-production and only the rigidity of language could make one suppose that there is some reduplication of comprehensions. The *sole* limitation on the power of comprehension here is due not to the complexity of the object, but to the *position of the observer*. This means that his comprehension determines a double objectivity: his own and that of the group which is his object. But this *de jure* and *de facto* limitation does nothing to diminish intelligibility – on the contrary; for the dialectic, if it is not to sink into the dogmatism of exteriority, must produce itself as a practical relation between free, situated organisms. Moreover, in the present case, it is clearly as a situated organism that, through my situation as conditioning my project, I comprehend the comprehension of the Other and his dependence on his being-situated.

On this basis, the conception of the pledged group as a *milieu of comprehension* makes it possible to treat the dialectic of projects (of the institutional project and the pledged practice) as an antagonistic relation of partial significations within a developing totalisation. The shifting oppositions between regulatory third parties within mediated reciprocity totalise themselves in these conflicts of significations, where every project tends to become identical with the signifying milieu as a whole so as to dissolve the Other in itself, and where everyone who is re-integrated into the Other becomes a negative force in him and destroys him. (The prudence and prevarication of the unions may, in a given case, be reinteriorised and become, within a more militant *praxis*, a system of obstacles and diversions. Conversely, an attempt to 'contain' mass enthusiasm may be interiorised and act as a negative schema of totalisation; but it is by virtue of this totalisation that an insurrectional movement may suddenly erupt.) In fact, counter-finalities have practically the same structure as teleological practices: so even if they are not produced by any human intention, they may have the structure of a project and of intentional transcendence. We discovered this when we were dealing with the practico-inert field. Thus there is no difference between the comprehension of a finality and that of a counter-finality, except for one crucial point: the second has to include the negation of every *author*. Thus it is possible to comprehend, as a determination of a level of action by an Other, the signification and objectives of the reinteriorised *praxis*, the movement of dissolution which is initiated (*contained* insurrection) and the counter-finality of this reinteriorisation (the exasperation of the demonstrators, etc.). This is to prepare oneself for comprehending the sequence of 'operations', the attempts despite everything to reinforce sovereignty as unity from above, their failures, the counter-attempts, etc.: and, on this basis, to comprehend (at least in so far as the groups in question are its agents) the signification either of the slowing up, the defections, and the total or partial failure of the undertaking or, on the other hand, that of the sudden eruption of an insurrection, of its propagation, and of its partial or total success, etc.

However, if every moment of this development is in itself intelligible, and if historical rationality is simply its comprehensibility, it must be acknowledged that the total development of the process is in danger of becoming *non-signifying*. But this is by no means necessary: the action group may submit completely to the authority of the union leaders; on the other hand, it may eliminate them and choose its own regulatory third parties. We will find either obedience (as the unity of institutional groups), or *praxis* in fusion (as a perpetual re-creation of *praxis* by the group through the third parties); and in either case, we shall be dealing with what we have called *praxis-processes*. But unity at *one* level of action means suppression of *the other level*; when the levels of action remain alive and practical during the entire undertaking, the plurality of signifying systems and their perpetual attempts to envelop each other produce results which belong to no system (not to those which are in conflict, nor to a new one), since each particular moment of such a *praxis* is constituted by non-totalisable complexes of *diminished* significations (each being half dissolved in the Others). The demonstration will not be as violent as the demonstrators wish, and neither will it be as calm and level-headed as union leaders recommend. It will not achieve its goal but it will give the employers an opportunity to drive the government to repressive policies. But the result may not be either sufficiently serious or sufficiently clear-cut to be comprehended in reverse as a counter-finality: it will then become clear that the entire process, in its futility, with lost hours of work, possible demoralisation, etc., is practically *devoid of meaning*. This means that the synthetic ensemble of directed temporalisations will ultimately appear *as a thing*, or rather, as a series of irreversible transformations in a physico-chemical system. We should then return to analytical Reason: in fact, it is on the basis of these de-signified processes that positivist history establishes its 'causal' sequences. It does not treat human *non-signifying* as a collection of truncated significations: on the contrary, it holds that signification is an epiphenomenon, an anthropomorphic illusion and that the processes without meaning are the positive truth of supposed human 'action'.

The positivist point of view has to be accepted as a negative limit of constituted dialectical Reason, at the moment where, in numerous, but strictly defined cases, the objective process, considered at one level of History and from beginning to end, effectively appears in itself as a non-dialectical result of an interior dialectic which has devoured itself. But this point of view corresponds only to an arrest of the total process of comprehension. It should be noted, in fact, that we have treated action only at one level – that of the pledged group – and that we have examined it at this level only in so far as it is conditioned by *one* other level, without reciprocity. Now, it is obvious that the conditioning of the institutionalised agent and the combat group is *reciprocal*, the fate of the sovereign as such (and in relation to the central apparatus itself) depending necessarily on his relations to the pledged group. Thus, the success or failure of a particular strike is not just an essential date in working-class history (in general); it is also crucial for the history of the trade-union movement in a particular country. But we would come back to the irrational here – the 'chance' of the positivists – if we assumed that the fate of a particular social movement depended simply on the relation between the leadership and the demonstrators and strikers. In fact, the events we have studied occurred at a particular moment of the historical process, in a particular practical field defined by class struggle; and the class struggle itself takes place between men who are produced by the contemporary mode of production, and is determined by a situation which itself relates to conflicts of interest and power relations. Conversely the working class defines itself by and through this struggle by its degree of emancipation, that is to say, both by its practices and by its consciousness of itself (which amounts to the same thing). But *in truth*, the workers' tactics, the militancy of the proletariat and its degree of class-consciousness are determined *not only* by the nature, differentiation and importance of the apparatuses (unions, etc.) but also by the more or less immediate opportunity for *serial individuals* to dissolve their seriality in combat groups, and by the aggressiveness, violence, tenacity and discipline of *these groups themselves* in the course of the action they undertake. All this, of course, relates to *class-being* not only as a passive constitution of the proletariat by the machines it uses but also, as a consequence of what I said above, as a material condition of everyone's *situation* within a class and as a *limit* of his practical comprehension.

We suggested earlier that, in relation to itself as a rapid regroupment for struggle, the working class as an institutionalised being (the permanent official, for example) adopted a particular attitude (which we arbitrarily assumed to be that of prudence tainted with mistrust). In fact, the attitude of a class-institution to the class-Apocalypse is always strictly conditioned by the entire process, but *primarily* by the relations of both to the class-collective. The relation between a union and workers who unite in order to strike must necessarily pass through its relations to the 'non-organised' masses. The percentage of workers unionised, their union practice and experience, discipline, and aggressiveness or passivity – all these are important; the present is deciphered in the light of recent struggles. Conversely, a trade-union militant will calculate with more or less precision the influence of the institution on the masses and, in particular, that of the tactics of agitation and struggle laid down by the central organs. To consider only the working class (and ignoring its power relations with employers in a particular case), the entire trade union will define its attitude to various groups in accordance with mass attitudes towards them and it. It may fear that in a period of decline, the most militant instructions will not really be followed; or equally, that some popular, 'wild' power – that of agitators, always the same but never 'elected' or in any way institutionalised – may substitute itself 'illegitimately' for the legitimate sovereignty of the union confederation. Or else, in contrast, it may notice – too late for its liking – that the wild elements have acquired an influence which it would be impolitic or disastrous to oppose, etc.

In this sense we must say that the practice of the trade union, as such, is produced *on the basis* of seriality, as class-being. In so far as, at certain moments, and in certain periods, the proletariat tends to blame its representatives for everything – because the situation makes it initially conscious of its impotence – this very impotence is communicated to the sovereign and the institutional group becomes bureaucratised. In a fused proletariat, the trade-union agents either disappear or obey. They always represent permanence, and they fill the gap: their policy towards the pledged group faithfully represents their comprehension of the situation. The contradictions will be sharper the more uncertainty there is in various quarters as to the general possibilities of mobilising the workers. If there is a temporary disappointment, the officials will use serial apathy to discourage group initiatives; but if there is agitation on a national scale, union resistance, if there is any, will be dissolved in the combat-groups. In fact, a 'wild' group itself comprehends its class as seriality in so far as it has just produced it as a group on the basis of series. This self-production immediately implies a comprehensive grasp either of the obstacles they have encountered or else of the encouragements and help they have received. They still feel in themselves the clay of which they are made. And this comprehension is a precise index of their militancy, that is to say, of their relations to the enemy class and to their own class as an institutionalised group. Thus the non-signifying process – which we just now located at the basis of analytical Reason, as a residue of contradictory interactions – is not devoid of meaning unless historical research stops at it. If we pursue it, however, the process is in itself the most valuable of indices: it defines the working class's deep relation to itself (that is to say, the relation of the institution to the 'wild' groups through the mediation of seriality and conversely, as well as the relations of 'wild' groups to seriality through the medium of unions, etc.). From this point of view, non-meaning itself has a profound meaning: the greater its contribution to the practical result, the more uncertain of itself the working class. What is supposed to be chance does not express a disorder of causes, but is, rather, produced by a common attitude: indecisiveness based on ignorance. Through this central index, we are referred back to the objective structures of labour, to the instruments, relations of production, etc., and, at the same time, to real wages, standards of living, and prices. At the same time, as I noted above, the indecisiveness of active groups is recapitulated in seriality as increased impotence; and this means that, in so far as he is other than the Others, everyone feels in the failures or semi-failures of the group the impossibility of dissolving the series. On the other hand, since it manifests the real timidity of the 'wild' committees in relation to the permanent officials, the failure strengthens the institution and bureaucratises or tends to bureaucratise it.

The practice is therefore still entirely comprehensible, at the level at which we have chosen, provided that, having studied it in itself to the point of finding this final residue, we perceive in this residue an indication of the task to be done, that is to say, of the interpretation in totalisation. At whatever level it is taken, class action is not intelligible unless it is interpreted in terms of all the other levels and unless it is itself regarded as a practical signification of the relations between other levels. And this totalisation – which completed an initial approach to the concrete – does not fall from the sky or from any pre-established dialectical law: class is *praxis* and inertia, dispersal of alterity and common field. Now, under pressure of need and in the urgency of the class struggle, groups (whether spontaneous or institutional) which form *on it* can emerge only by totalising it. It is not only their *praxis*, the infinite material of their practical field, and therefore the object of their totalisation, but also the *possible* totalisation – still inert, but eroded by the phantom unity which they induce in it – of their diversity and separations. For the situated observer, the totalising movement is *comprehension* because in any moment of the class struggle the practical local action is always the totalising *praxis of the* proletariat.

From this point of view, the various levels of action readily yield up their intelligibility, once it is understood that the *praxis* is both *the same and other* at every level: for in fact this vertical hierarchy dissimulates the reciprocal unity of circularity. The situated researcher must, in short, totalise the totalising action. At any given level, action has, so to speak, an abstract and superficial incomprehensibility ('What are they waiting for?', 'Why are they letting us disperse without giving instructions?', 'Why are they adhering to this demand given that another one makes it superfluous?', etc.) which relates to comprehension in depth (the determination of the action at each level by its production of itself at every other level). This comprehension would frequently lead to a new incomprehensibility if it were not that it reveals the circularity of the conditionings and if the action produced at every level did not *manifest* the real tensions which determine the class as a *totality to be totalised*. Thus the hierarchy of levels, a pure system of exteriority, curves in on itself and becomes their circularity. And the various 'embodiments' of the action (at each level) are superimposed *only in appearance* (for example, for employers who sack unionised workers but who believe that when there is a dispute the only people worth talking to are the union delegates). The situated observer may, in the abstract, grasp the hierarchised unity of the different levels of action in the practical bond with the transcendent objective: it must be because of the local increase in transport costs; the class in a particular locality is affected by it at every level and especially in its passivity as a collective. The *common project* of acting on the municipal authorities to make them withdraw their pernicious measures, or on the employers to make them adjust wages to this new rise in the 'cost of living', may be treated in exteriority as present at every level: *lived as an impotence 'to be overcome' in seriality*, as *mobilisation in support of demands* at the level of groups, and as a *particular local objective* which (in its urgency and in its relative importance) has to be settled in terms of more distant and more fundamental objectives (the working class *in this locality*, its chances of victory, the importance of this particular struggle for the future of local struggles, the struggle of the French proletariat as a whole, on all fronts) at the level of the apparatus.

At the same time, it is clear that the limits of this hierarchical intelligibility lie in the hierarchy: after all, *is it really the same object* which is seen in the immediate struggle as an absolute exigency for the pledged parties while it is seen by the permanent official (even if he is thoroughly informed) as an immediate, limited and relative objective?

In fact, intelligibility is re-established if this structure of the object (as determined by the sovereign) is regarded as defined in actions (depending whether the union supports or obstructs the action in support of the demand), and once it is recognised that in this way it in fact objectifies the relation of the local concentration of workers to the French proletariat as a whole and the determination of this same proletariat (as an abstract practical object and as its own institutionalised-being) by the union leaders of the locality (and thereby by the centralised sovereign). But then it must be understood that class action cannot acquire its complete signification unless comprehension becomes totalising and grasps action in its circular development: for it is not the pure production of a group by a *praxis* and of a *praxis* by a group (a combat group, a 'wild-cat' strike). In the union context or in opposition to it, class-action constitutes itself in its reflexivity through the mediation of the permanent officials: as a local reflexivity (tactics or realistic demands are determined within the actual power relations), 'spontaneous' action becomes 'experienced'. At the same time (depending whether it is helped or hindered by the actions of local or national union leaders), this absolute, immediate urgency reinserts itself into the tactical and strategic ensemble which is the practical determination of the class. This means that the action here receives its abstract knowledge of itself and of its objectivity in exteriority (either preserving it as a mark or interiorising it). But, at the same time, action *at this level* involves *in itself* a comprehension of the proletariat: not only as a seriality dissolving into a practical group (which is not distinguishable from the production of the group as itself), but also as a seriality without a future and which has been transcended (we shall come back to this), and whose acquired constitution – as the present condition of its being – determines and particularises the permanent possibility of its separating itself from its Other-Being (rate of transformation under a given pressure, in given circumstances, the possibility of horizontal and vertical expansion, etc.). In one way, this comprehension has the same object as the abstract knowledge of the sovereign, since, in effect, it *is* this object and *knows it* only in so far as it produces it in producing itself.

These two totalisations (each of which comprehends the other) may conflict even at the level of the pledged group: indeed, there is no reason why they should have the same content. But if it is true that even contradictions and confrontations threaten to make the process unintelligible in its residual abstraction, it is also true that the comprehension which is given in the group and which corresponds to its transcendence of serial-being (and to the preservation of this being as the bond of alterity and immanence), through practice (involving either agreement with or resistance to the sovereign), involves *a power of withdrawal* which is a transcendence of its immediate presence proximate to Being. This is obviously a simple abstract form, but (if, for example, it *contradicts* union plans) its interiorisation realises the real action of the combat-group as aware of itself and judging itself in relation to all the forms and practical levels of the class. This does not mean, of course, that the practical knowledge, as a system of real possibilities of distance from oneself, of withdrawal, etc., cannot manifest itself in a dangerous action based on mistaken calculations. But practical knowledge (in so far as it regulates action in pursuit of demands by itself on the basis of a future totalisation of union knowledge and of the *living comprehension* of the group) relates to the developing experience of the class as a serial-being, realising itself *not only* (and in mutual conditioning) as a *signification* of the collective as it produces itself in and through its relations with the sovereign ('Ten years of union practice have taught me . . .', etc.), *but also as a connection of interiority between the group and the series* (the being-outside-itself of the former lies in the latter and lives this transcendence in interiority), *and, thirdly, as an abstract possibility of the series negating itself* and negating its impotence in favour of common freedom, in short as the intensity of the forces of massification and reification in so far as they are lived by everyone at the level of alienation.

Obviously this third experience is also conditioned by the other experience which the series has of the groups which arise from it, and of their strength and multiplicity. At this level, the other becomes known in the collective through the undertakings of groups. And to become known obviously means *knowing oneself* – deciphering, through the groups themselves, through the multiplicity of actions, the violence which is still contained in impotence and the historical conditions which, for example, give a revolutionary aspect to the situation; but above all it means *making oneself* on the basis of the circumstances which condition the development. Thus *praxis* as totalisation has *both* the sense of a particular operation involving more or less important personnel and defining a historical moment by defining *itself*, *and* the practical signification of a *bet* which – as a result of the inadequacy of the withdrawals, of ambiguous experiences (even more so than contradictory ones: I indicated the meaning of such ambiguities in *The Problem of*

Method) and of distinct practical structures – each level must engage with the reactions of the other two, in which its own reaction figures – as it knows – as the object of a bet.

Is this one of those circuits of alterity which we noted in the practico-inert (anticipation of the conjuncture, etc.)? The answer is no; for there is constant communication and the *other* may always become *the same* (perhaps at a meeting of workers who *recognise* the union delegate because he is confined to the role of a regulatory third party, or in the reciprocal relations of two workers one of whom is committed to action while the other is still hesitating). In fact, this *bet* is made by the class on itself; it is *the decision* as a transcendence of an imperfectly known given and as a totalisation either in the negative unity of the conflicts, errors and failure, or in the mutual reinforcement of partial bets (at different levels) through the developing objectification and the final success. The action which forms the object of the bet in effect totalises itself in so far as it is determined *not only* as a short-term local undertaking, but *also* as the production of a concrete and temporalised relation between class-collective and class-conflict, *and* as the signifying mode of the class at a national level (an index of combativity, etc.). And the totalisation itself refers us, beyond the formations considered, to the comprehension (in reciprocity) which everyone has as a free, practical organism (who may be a permanent official, or aged and resigned) performing, in his whole *praxis* (even if it is a *praxis* of pure obedience), a totalising transcendence of every level by the other, and of all in the unity of common decisions. However, in so far as every practical organism remains inconceivable for the investigation (except abstractly and negatively), and concealed behind alienation, seriality, and the pledge or sovereignty as an institution, there is never a totality, but only a developing totalisation and we cannot discover any totalising apparatus and interrupt the circularity in it.

Let us be quite clear about this: this totalisation is always an attempt to dissolve the other in the same (even the resignation of a sick or old man is realised only through a totalising evaluation and *then negated*); and it is performed on synthetic schemata of unity which have penetrated right to the depths of seriality, on the basis of a common past (we shall come to this shortly), etc. So it is certainly a *real* and constant totalisation, though it necessarily contains complexities of its own, inertias which have to be dissolved, and contradictions. In this sense the working class can be said to be a developing totalisation *everywhere*. At the present level of our investigation, this does not mean either that it must or that it can attain a higher degree of integration or militancy; but it does not mean the opposite either. It is simply that we are not yet equipped to consider such a possibility. Before the perspectives of a History are given, a developing totalisation means that all levels of *praxis* are everywhere mediated and totalised by the inaccessible practical organism which they conceal and which, by means of its free individuality, sustains all the alienations which steal away its *praxis* and all the common functions which are imposed upon it (and therefore all groups in so far as they integrate it in Fraternity-Terror).

The totalisation of the working class is therefore *comprehensible*: the synthetic action by which the situated witness or historian totalises effectively does no more than reproduce a *praxis* of totalisation towards various objectives, on the basis of given conditions. This totalisation consists not in transforming an infinite series into a group, but in creating a circularity of control and perpetual readaptation for the common action through the determination of its possibilities at every level in accordance with the others. The action is controlled in that, for example, the series (as a national collective) is the arbiter and mediation in conflicts between local leaders and 'spontaneous' groups: this means that the final action (whether an ordered *praxis* or an apparently incomprehensible disorder) is a three-dimensional process where the meaning of each dimension lies in the other two. It is possible to repress a working-class movement (that is, possible for its own leaders to do so), but only in some cases and through the dispersive complicity of the whole class; and in other cases, it is impossible for the same reasons, that is to say, because of the signification assumed by the local movement within the national class. And this possibility, or impossibility, does not affect the leaders and strikers from outside, as a *fatum*: it realises itself practically as their comprehension of their situation within the class. In other words, they do whatever *they can and no more*, but it is necessary for them to *do it* in the dialectic of a reciprocal and antagonistic *praxis*, which, itself, is experienced by the freely totalising individual within serial alienation and totalised either as a rejection of seriality or as a resigned surrender to impotence. Let there be no mistake: in so far as the action of impossibility which is adopted by institutionalised and action groups is manifested by a disorder-index of *praxis*, it turns on alterity and is readopted within it in its serial dispersal as a new determination: but it is not possible to determine *a priori* whether this negativity of assumed impotence will or will not result in a reinforcement, in the series, of the negation and passivity of which it is the index. In fact it may bring about a positive regroupment: only the entire material circumstances – past and present – combined with the *praxis* of the enemy class, can, in each case, and in the context of a concrete historical development, provide the elements of an answer. What the formal investigation has to say is simply that class practice – even strictly localised actions – is comprehensible in a circular totalisation, as a new type of *praxis*: the *praxis* whose unitary and dialectical temporalisation (on the basis of its objective) develops in the unity of pluridimensional reciprocities between heterogeneous structures each of which contains the others. Or, metaphorically, the action of the free, practical organism – considered in itself and in the abstract – has no depth, and is temporalised in a two-dimensional space; but class-action – even ignoring the enemy class or diachronic determinations – develops in an n-dimensional space (we have observed three of them, but there are others,[101] though this is not relevant here). But the second is as comprehensible as the first, since, ultimately, it is produced by us, and, also, we are the pluridimensional space in which it temporalises itself. And this comprehension is based on the fact that everything is *practice*, that is to say, that the class practically recapitulates its class-being – and all the practico-inert characteristics it has been given – in the very movement of *praxis* as its orientation and its individual practical essence. The innovation of 'factory occupations' for example, as a tactic in the struggle, is a practice which recapitulates and transcends the passive constitution of the proletariat-collective following the second industrial revolution (that is to say, here, the interchangeability of specialised workers).

But this *praxis* is *constituted*: this is clear, and it is the very limit of its intelligibility. The plurality of its dimensions conflicts with the untranscendability of free, organic practice as constituent dialectic. This is precisely the free *praxis* which is produced as a totalisation of multiple dimensions in mediated reciprocity. Depending on the point of view, this means either that it stretches into the multiplicity of the dimensions and, in being stretched, preserves the organic unity of reciprocal, circular determinations, or that it folds itself back over a nascent dispersal as a reintegration of the signifying unity of interiority

---

101. We have, in fact, remained in abstraction, because we have assumed that the interior milieu of the class is homogeneous and that it lacks contradictions (divergences or conflicts of interest between various permanent officials, specialised workers, etc.).

through a retotalisation through the various dimensions. And there is nothing surprising in this, since free *praxis*, as a *dialectical temporalisation in a plane space*, is a rearrangement of the transcendent through a three-dimensional practical field.[102] This is why we have referred to class-action as '*praxis*-process': as a practical totalisation the comprehension of it can be the totalising *praxis* of an individual witness; but in so far as this totalisation, through its very objectivity (as it might appear to an observer situated in a space with $n + 1$ dimensions), eludes the agents as well as the observer, we can grasp it only as *process*, that is to say, as a limit of dialectical comprehension. In effect, the $n + 1$ dimensional observer does not and cannot exist; and, if he *did* exist, he would be completely alien to us. Yet it is to him alone that the practical reality of class would manifest itself as hyper-organic, if only this were not an absurdity; it is to him alone that an ontological statute of intelligibility might appear which would be inaccessible to the agents within this reality.

For us, situated inside or outside the class, the hyper-organic statute does not exist; it does not in fact manifest itself in any practical effect either on the agents or on the action. But in order to establish its total objectivity, it would also be necessary to be able to totalise from outside, that is to say, from a space of which this *n*-dimensional social space would be a particular case. The necessity and impossibility of grasping the class in struggle as a total objectivity produce within it *a negative external limit* or, so to speak, the possibility of having an *exterior*. And this exterior, as an abstract frontier which in principle

---

102. Or *n*-dimensional: I gave examples of this in *The Problem of Method*. Two-dimensional *praxis* is an abstraction: Robinson Crusoe building his hut. From the moment where we consider concrete man, his sociality, functions, powers, possibilities, etc., transform his project into a pluridimensional unity of the multiple conditions which he transcends – so that a return of the constituted to the constituent (in so far as the constituted is preserved in being transcended), by deploying complex spaces in the project itself, ends up by creating a fresh homogeneity between common action (and the internal multiplicity of its interactions) and *socialised* individual action. Nevertheless, the conditions which are transcended in the project are connected and totalised by the project itself, whereas multiplicities of individuals totalise *themselves* by totalising the common *praxis*. This is where comprehension comes to an end, both for the observer and within active groups, since this internal totalisation through interaction does not produce any new ontological statute in the group. In other words, the comprehension of class action by the observer who *reproduces* it is *both sufficient and inadequate*.

eludes us, is in fact the same as the frontier which separates dialectical Reason from analytical Reason when the conditions of knowledge prevent us from making the latter an integral part of the former. At this level, the process is the indeterminacy of the totalisation conceived in exteriority which cannot be either the pure, dialectical development of a free, individual *praxis*, or a totalised totality, or an irreversible and non-signifying series of determinations in exteriority. However, precisely because of this indeterminacy, it presents itself as the abstract possibility of the unity of all these characteristics: a strict and directed development, the complete determination of the present by the past and, equally, by the future, and therefore, over-determination; absolute necessity and free finality; a totality which is given (as inertia marked by a seal) and which produces its own temporality in exteriority as totalisation; practico-inertia conceived as *praxis*; the unity of the undertaking and of the outcome; and the unity of passive activity and active passivity.

Thus, as a result of the multiple passivity which reinvades the level of the group and intensifies in a class, penetrating *praxis* with various layers of inertia and restricting it to its statute of constituted practice, *process* (as a pure negative limit of investigation) becomes, for many anthropologists, the other side of the coin, the obverse which they will reach one day, or which they believe can be reached, the *hidden reality* of men and societies, in which all contradictions merge into each other although they have not been joined together by any synthetic transcendence: that inhuman objectivity of the human in which finality and 'causality', necessity and freedom, exteriority and interiority interpenetrate. This hidden reality, a fusion of meaning and non-meaning, is almost indistinguishable from Spinoza's substance. But it is absurd to substantify processes, giving a positive content to an abstract limit of comprehensibility and prematurely eliminating the contradictions in the investigation by looking at man from the point of view of God. The *process* is inseparable from the *situation* of the agent or observer: the process defines their situation negatively by reference to its limits and we cannot grasp it in itself without desituating ourselves in relation to everything. It also demonstrates the impossibility of integrating the project of a social multiplicity except by comprehending an individualising schema. Lastly, it relates to the exteriority which transfixes interiority from all sides, and to a set of facts which are purely physico-chemical (or at least capable of being abstractly treated as such), transmutations of energy and, at other levels, the destruction and expenditure of energy in the practico-inert field, appearing as the projection of ensembles which are not only inorganic, but also organic and social, into the inorganic. It represents, as it were, the impossibility of grasping common action in terms of its multiplicity and passivities by means of a constituent, dialectical comprehension; and, on a practical level, it indicates the risks of any common action (which it may itself produce): alienation, and the collapse into seriality. However, this *external* presence of the anti-dialectical (the practico-inert) and the non-dialectical (analytical Reason) as a permanent threat to the human cannot be grasped except *from the standpoint of the situated-being*, through *praxis* and as a living contradiction between constituent Reason and constituted Reason. This limitation of comprehensibility can be revealed only in and through the total practical success of comprehension itself. And I have made these remarks at this point because this is where they can have their simplest, most abstract form; but we shall have to return to them when discussing the historical process in order to avoid both relativism and dogmatism.

4 Economism, Materialism and Dialectics

But we have not yet left abstraction behind, since we have spoken of the class's internal relations to itself at the level of class struggle without introducing into the schema of intelligibility the hostile action of the enemy class (or classes; I assume a duality for the sake of simplicity). Now, it is quite clear that, in its social struggles, every class is both an interiorisation and a transcendence of the material conditions which produced it and of the characteristics occasioned in it by the other; and it is equally clear that particular objectives, as well as the means of struggle, tactics, etc., are always determined in the reciprocity of conflict and on the basis of an even more general conflict of interests. Thus every class is present in the other in so far as the *praxis* of the other tends, either directly or through the medium of a contested object, to modify it. But is there any intelligibility here? We have seen how a totalisation can occur in the working class because it bears on the same action at different levels and because the secondary conflicts are, *ex hypothesi*, subordinated to a basic agreement. But how can we *comprehend*, that is to say, unite within a single totalisation, the *results* of an action by the employers and the *significations* which the *praxis* of the bourgeois class produces as alien realities within the proletariat itself? Above all, how can we assume – as dialectical rationality requires – that there is a larger totalisation, unifying these hostile, irreconcilable classes in negative reciprocity itself? It is to this problem that we must now turn.

Now, the essential point is to establish *whether there is any struggle.* Engels makes fun of Dühring for speaking somewhat hastily of *oppression.* But, in trying to correct him, he goes to the opposite extreme: economism. If both classes are in themselves an inert, or even practico-inert, product of economic development, if both are created in similar ways by transformations of the mode of production, the exploiting class bearing its statute in passivity, as a constitutional law, the impotence of the haves reflecting that of the have-nots, then struggle will disappear: the two serialities will be completely inert, the contradictions of the system being realised through them, that is to say, through each as an other and in alterity. The resulting opposition between capitalists and wage-earners does not merit the name of *struggle* any more than that between the shutter and the wall it beats against. In *Anti-Dühring*, moreover, Engels takes these schematic ideas to extremes, and goes so far as to disband class struggle in the moment where the rising class, securing the development of the means of production, groups the whole of society around itself. Disagreements will appear gradually, and the gap will widen until it splits the whole of society, to the extent that the mode of production itself produces and develops its contradictions. It would then be possible to speak of *struggle* – in the narrow and purely metaphorical sense of molecular agitations tending in two opposite directions and producing *an average result* – once the contradictions become explicit. The rest of the time, History would be determined by the development of the mode of production in its fragile unity and in so far as the consequences of this development produce differentiations within classes and cause various transformations in different human groups. The unity between two activities which are equally passive (induced), but one of which determines a particular form of action among the workers while the other determines a particular type of reorganisation of means of production amongst employers, would be quite simply the *economic process.*

And, in a sense, this would provide History with complete intelligibility, in that the opposition between phenomena would be reduced to the action of a single set of external forces on various objects. But this economistic intelligibility is a mere illusion; *in the first place*, it takes Engels back to analytical Reason. The dialectician crowns his success with the splendid result that he kills the dialectic twice over to make sure it is dead – the first time by claiming to have discovered it in Nature, and the second time by suppressing it within society. The result of both attacks is the same: claiming to have discovered the dialectic in physico-chemical sequences amounts to the same thing as claiming to be a dialectician while reducing human relations to the functional relations of quantitative variables. But, *secondly*, we do not even get the real direct intelligibility of number and continuous quantity, for we are thrown straight back into the practico-inert field. In other words, the conventional transformations and definitions of economic thought are intelligible as long as they are *supported* by the concrete movement of a human, historical dialectic, provided they are not seen as any more than a temporary employment of analytical Reason, and that analytical Reason is itself presented as an abstract moment of dialectical Reason (the moment in which human relations are alienated and reified, and can be treated in exteriority, from the point of view of reinteriorisation). But when they are presented as principles or as basic definitions, and when strange quantitative inversions are treated as natural facts (rather than as a *superficially natural* aspect of social facts), then language itself ceases to signify: economic inversions and all the determinations of discourse to which they lead derive from nothingness, directly, on the basis of physico-chemical and biological laws but without it being possible to identify any movement (dialectic of Nature) capable of producing this mutilated analytical Reason on the basis of the other. In short, if analytical Reason is to become economic Reason without losing its rationality, it must be within dialectical Reason, and as produced and supported by it. Thus economism as a fundamental rationality collapses into empirical irrationality ('*This is how things are*').

Obviously this does not mean dissolving objective, material contradictions (productive forces $\longleftrightarrow$ means of production $\longleftrightarrow$ mode of production $\longleftrightarrow$ relations of production, etc.) in a kind of dialectical idealism. It is a matter of reinteriorising them and making them into the motors of the historical process in so far as they are the *internal foundation* of social modifications (as fundamental determinations of the relations of reciprocal interiority combining free, practical organisms in the 'episodic' ('*à tiroirs*') field of scarcity). But this reinteriorisation itself transforms their signification: the line of economism thus resembles the abstract relational skeleton which the informant, a member of an exogamous society, draws on the sand for the ethnographer. Their concrete, intelligible reality, at the level of *praxis*, is worked matter as a mediation between practical organisms and as the alienation of one to the other, or, in a word, of the collective. And the collective is neither dialectical nor analytical: it is anti-dialectical. It does not appear *initially* as a fundamental structure of human relations: but it constitutes itself through a complex dialectic, whose course we have traced as the dialectic running around and turning against itself, in short, as the *anti-dialectic*. And this anti-dialectic would not be intelligible if we did not produce it ourselves in the fleeting moment of false material unity, of alienated labour and serial flight. The practico-inert can be treated *as a process* (and this is already far removed from the pretensions of economism: for economic 'facts' were simply physico-chemical phenomena made unintelligible by negations of interiority parading as determinations of exteriority), but this process, in so far as it is *already* passive action, presupposes the entire *praxis* (as a relation with the material, practical field and with the Others), which it reabsorbs and transforms in the object, while still being based on its real, abstract pullulation.

In short, if the mode of production is the infrastructure of every society in human history, this is because labour – as a free, concrete operation which becomes alienated in the collective and which already produces itself as a transcendence of an earlier alienation to this collective – is the infrastructure of the practico-inert (and of the mode of production), not only in the sense of diachronic totalisation (and because a given machine with its special exigencies is itself the product of labour), but also synchronically since all the contradictions of the practico-inert and especially those of the economic process are necessarily constituted by the constant re-alienation of the worker in his labour, that is to say, by practice in general in this *other world* which it constructs, sacrificing itself so that it can exist (constituting its multiplicity into serial alterity through inorganic matter, and appropriating impotence with the full use of its sovereignty). From this viewpoint, if the foundation of the class struggle is to lie in the practico-inert, this is in so far as the objective conflict of interests is both received and produced by passive activity and reveals itself in labour (or in all kinds of behaviour) as a reciprocity of antagonism – possibly in a petrified form and, for example, as an exigency of the tool or machine.

Circularity – as a structure of the social as a human product – produces its intelligibility through a double determination. *On the one hand*, it is obvious that thoughts and activities are inscribed in worked matter (in so far as it produces a system of alterity through the *others*). This is why racism is not a mere 'psychological defence' of the colonialist, created for the needs of the cause, to justify colonisation to the metropolitan power and to himself; it is in fact *Other-Thought* (*Pensée-Autre*) produced objectively by the colonial system and by super-exploitation: man is defined by the wage and by the nature of labour, and therefore it is true that wages, as they tend towards zero, and labour, as an alternation between unemployment and 'forced labour', reduce a colonised person to the sub-human which he is for the colonialist.[103] Racist thinking is simply an activity which realises in alterity a practical truth inscribed in worked matter and in the system which results from it. But, *on the other hand*, and conversely, since the elementary structures of the simplest forms *are inscribed* in inorganic matter, they refer to various activities (both past and present) which either indefinitely reproduce or have helped to produce these human *seals* as inert thoughts: and these activities are necessarily antagonistic. The racism which occurs to an Algerian colonialist was imposed and produced by the conquest of Algeria, and is constantly recreated and reactualised by everyday practice through serial alterity. Of course, the conquest of Algeria in itself can only be taken as a complex process dependent on a certain political and social situation *in France* as well as on the real relations between capitalist France and agricultural, feudal Algeria. Nevertheless, the colonial wars of the nineteenth century *realised* an original situation of violence for the colonialists as their fundamental relation to the natives; and this situation of violence produces and reproduces itself as the outcome of a collection of violent practices, that is to say, of intentional operations with precise aims, carried out by the army – as a group-institution – and by economic groups supported by public authority (by the delegates of the metropolitan sovereign). Of course, this violence, the cruelty towards Algerian tribes and the systematic operations which aimed at taking over their land, was itself no more than an expression of a still abstract racism. This was due primarily to the state of war

103. There is just one difference: this sub-human is *all human*, and the colonialist, as a *superman*, is just a huge cripple. But this inversion will appear only in higher forms of the struggle.

('pacification' was long and bloody), which changed the statute because the fundamental relation was armed struggle; and this negative racism constituted *the enemy* as inferior rather than as a supposed 'French citizen'. They were either 'devils' or 'mindless savages', depending whether they had won a victory, showing them in their *activity* or whether, on the contrary, they had suffered a temporary defeat, which is in itself an affirmation of the conqueror's superiority. In either case, this Manichaean action, separating the hostile troops by the absolute negation of a line of fire, makes the Muslim *other than man*.

On the other hand, for reasons relating to its own history and to the development of capitalism within it, French society was at first quite undecided as to how to make use of its conquest. Colonial settlement? Penal colony? No practice had been defined up to 1880. Essentially, therefore, the Muslims still had to be respected, and subdued, and their slightest murmurs of revolt had to be suppressed. But they were more likely to be exterminated than employed – at least on a large scale. In any case, repressive practices, the policy of division and above all dispossession soon destroyed feudal structures and transformed this backward but structured society into an 'atomised crowd', and, before long, into an agricultural sub-proletariat. And this new (practico-inert) form of Muslim society is a real expression of violence; it objectively signifies the violence suffered by each of the serial *Others*, whom it produced. When our capital finally settled on capitalist colonisation as a partial solution to its problems and as a source of new profits, this new form of exploitation was explained, developed, diffused, and practised *by pressure groups*. There is an undeniable link between Leroy-Beaulieu's book,[104] the politics of Jules Ferry,[105] and the constitution of the first colonial banks and of sea transport. But, at the same time, other social milieux, with other interests, rose up in violent revolt against the policy of colonial conquest.

What this implies is that the colonial system, as an infernal machine which was to develop its own contradictions right up to a final explosion, corresponded to the objective needs of the French capitalists *in general*, but contradicted many particular interests. If it was to be imposed and set in motion, it had to be *promoted*; and the transition from objective interest, as an empty exigency, to the construction of the system was produced by a common practice, and corresponded

104. Paul Leroy-Beaulieu, French liberal economist, 1843–1916. [Ed.]
105. Jules Ferry, French statesman, 1832–93. [Ed.]

historically to a real, organised dialectic linking a number of financial groups, statesmen and theoreticians in one *organised task*. And it would be wrong to schematise everything by simply saying that these groups were the expression of the interests of their class. For, in one sense, this is indeed what they were, and even all that they were. But they were not mediums, puffed up by some kind of spiritual fulness, or dragons with the class spirit which filled them pouring from their throats: their class was necessarily determined *by their common creation* of the system. This does not mean – as a voluntarist idealism would assert – that the exposition of the system automatically transposed itself into a general practice of the class: on the contrary, it is well known that it took patient efforts to impose it (propaganda, victories to wipe out the memory of defeats, initial advantages, etc.). It means, quite simply, that by the practical unity of organisations and apparatuses which it had itself produced (the sovereign as the present temporalisation of the State, technicians or ideologists, and economic pressure groups), the class found itself in the process of elaborating new tasks, and, regardless of its divisions, also found that it was in a state of *minimal* resistance to the system it had created: in effect, it profited from the practical power of the most respected and active institutions and organisations (the subjection of the fiercest milieux was already the future fate of their resistance), from its precise, pluridimensional elaboration (ideology, action by public powers, initiatives of private groups) in the face of sporadic, uncertain, and often contradictory resistance, and lastly, from the light which these new practices threw on the economic and social problems of the metropolis (new outlets for production, special circuits of exchange from the colony to the metropolitan power, and conversely).

5   *Racism and Colonialism as Praxis and Process*

To make myself clear, I shall say that *all the relations* between the colonialists and the colonised throughout the colonial system are an actualisation of practico-inert characteristics which are introduced and defined by common actions – or in other words, that both sociology and economism must be dissolved *in History*. If some contemporary work of sociology says that 'pauperisation', as the destruction of the social structures of the Muslim community, was a necessary result of contact between two particular societies, one backward (or under-developed), agricultural and feudal, the other industrialised, then intelligibility and necessity are both absent from this type of deter-mination. The two can be connected only in so far as the real, conscious activity of each colonialist (especially on the economic plane) is seen as realising, by itself, in particular cases, for limited objectives, but in the light of a common objective, the 'pauperisation' which the contact between two societies (those beings of reason) could not produce apart from individual contacts between the individuals who compose them. But this means that the term 'pauperisation' and the pseudo-concept which underlies it become utterly useless: they are both designed to take us modestly back to the *process*. But the sole intelligible reality, the *praxis* of men, puts paid to both of them; and it relates to two quite distinct types of action: past, transcended action and present action. In fact, what should be said *first* is that the contact between the industrial society and the agricultural society was achieved by Bugeaud's soldiers, and by the atrocious massacres perpetrated by these soldiers; and that the destruction of the forms of inheritance proper to the Muslim tribes did not emerge from some idealistic interpenetration of two different juridical systems, but from the fact that merchants, encouraged by the State and supported by our armies, imposed the code on the Muslims *the better to rob them*. Only on this basis can one comprehend that the colonial goal *was* to produce and to sell food[106] to the metropolitan power at less than world rates and that the *means* of achieving this goal was the creation of a sub-proletariat of the desolate and the chronically unemployed (which itself explains the notion of pauperisation). And this operation was complemented by that of the commodity merchants – whom we have just mentioned – and by the policy of the military authorities (destroying all structures which might permit regroupment or resistance, maintaining a supposed feudality of collaborators and traitors, accomplices of the French, preserving the appearance of a locally-based sovereignty and exploiting, in their own interest and that of their masters, an impoverished, impotent mass which had been reduced to a molecular statute). Thus the system (as an infernal machine of the practico-inert field) became the undertaking of a nation through its institutional groups (war), through the 'hot' creation of a new form

106. Or minerals and other 'raw materials'.

of imperialism based on a new politics (involving a new relationship between individuals and public powers), through the systematic, concerted destruction of a community and, of course, the installation of a new mechanism of exploitation (new colonialists) by appropriate organisations (banking, credit systems, government favours, etc.).

Now, in all these practices, violence and destruction were an integral part of the desired objective. At the three different levels of this action, this involved (1) the physical liquidation of a number of Muslims and the dissolution of their institutions, while they were not allowed to 'enjoy' ours; (2) depriving indigenous communities of land ownership and transferring it to the newcomers through the brutal and deliberately over-rapid application of the civil code; and (3) establishing the true bond between the colony and the metropolis (sales of colonial products at minimum prices, and purchases of manufactured goods from the metropolitan power at high prices) on the basis of systematic super-exploitation of the native. In other words, for the child of the colonialist, violence was present in the situation itself, and was a social force which produced him. The son of the colonialist and the son of the Muslim are both the children of the objective violence which defines the system itself as a practico-inert hell. But *if* this violence-object produces them, if they suffer it partly as their own inertia, this is because it used to be violence-*praxis* when the system was in the process of being installed. It is man who inscribed his violence in things as the eternal unity of this passive mediation between men.

The proponents of 'pauperisation' may claim that the development of French society in the middle of the nineteenth century was precisely such as to prevent it from conceiving of any relationship to the Muslim peasants of Algeria other than one of violence. This is true, in that the bourgeois of the last century were very harmoniously ignoble in *all* their activities. And this ignominy was obviously partly due to the fact that the bourgeois were themselves alienated products of the capitalist system which characterised the metropolitan society: how could the objective characteristics of the system – the conditions of labour which he imposed on his workers, the senseless waste of human lives which was characteristic of the 'iron and coal' period – fail to produce bourgeois who had no feelings for the natives of North Africa? If the bourgeois was a man, while the worker, his compatriot, was merely sub-human, how could an Algerian, a distant enemy, be anything but a dog?

But the answer must be *first* that sociology has inverted itself in order to correspond to History: if bourgeois society pauperises feudal society, this is not a result of its superiority (acting on the Arab community, in fact, *in spite of itself* and by its mere existence) but of its inferiority, of the revolting brutality which so clearly characterised capitalism in its origins. And precisely because of this, the *negation* returns in the colonising class. Thus it necessarily refers to action: strictly speaking one might, from some idealist, Aristotelian point of view, countenance an attraction at a distance by the positive plenitude of an object which, in its distant connection with this plenitude, reinteriorises and reflects its inadequacies. But when *negativity* becomes the source in one object of modifications (either positive or negative) in the other, then this negativity will produce its effects only in an action or system of actions which determines itself on the basis of it and which preserves it in itself as the *negative* orientation of the expenditure of energy. It is true that the bourgeois are products (but when we shortly return to class we shall see that these products are also agents); it is also true that these children of violence were produced by the violent *praxis* of their fathers – which takes them back to the History from which they wished to escape.

But it is also true that this rapacious violence was not a cerebral circumvolution, or a proper power of social institutions (although it is realised in institutions *too*). Either it is the capitalist process itself (to the extent that, as we shall see, the exploiter readopts the practico-inert) or, if there are new developments in the system (for example, in colonialism), it *temporalises* itself in common (or even individual) real activities which realise it in objectivity. Violence, as bourgeois *exis*, exists in the exploitation of the proletariat as an inherited relation of the dominant class to the dominated class (but we shall see that it is also a *practice* at this level); and violence, as the *praxis* of this bourgeois generation, lay in colonisation. But the *exis*, in itself, was no more than a diachronic mediation between two cycles of *praxis*. And colonial undertakings, as the plural temporalisation of bourgeois violence (as the violence of one class against another within a community) is also its dialectical enrichment and expansion. In new conditions, where exploitation must start on the basis of oppression, this violence renews itself; it will *extend* to mass extermination and torture. It must therefore *create itself* in order to maintain itself, and change in order to remain the same. Conversely, it will return as practical violence to be used immediately in the metropolitan power against the exploited masses as soon as there is a lull in the colonial war. As is well known, Bugeaud appeared to the high bourgeoisie of 1848 as the dreamed-of destroyer of the Second Republic; and it is not an accident that Franco came from Morocco.

The evolution of violence is clearly expressed here: first a structure of alienation in the *practico-inert*, it is actualised as *praxis* in colonisation; and its (temporary) victory presents itself as the objectification of the practical ensemble (army, capitalists, commodity merchants, colonialists) in a *practico-inert* system where it represents the fundamental structure of reciprocity between the colonialists and the colonised. But *in alienation itself*, this new serial *exis* cannot exist unless everyone realises and adopts it as *other* in his everyday *praxis*. This means, in the first place, that it becomes its own idea in the form of *racism* – in other words, that the colonialists constantly actualise the practices of extermination, robbery and exploitation which have been established by previous generations, and transcend them towards *a system of other values*, entirely governed by alterity. But still it would be no more than an ineffectual transcendence of the *objective exis* if the situation did not involve a reciprocity of violence. In other words, the colonialist discovers in the native not only the Other-than-man but also his own sworn Enemy (in other words, the Enemy of Man). This discovery does not presuppose resistance (open or clandestine), or riots, or threats of revolt: the violence of the colonialists itself emerges as an indefinite necessity or, to put it another way, the colonialist reveals the violence of the native, even in his passivity, as the obvious consequence of his own violence and as its sole justification. This discovery is made through hatred and fear, as a negative determination of the practical field, as a co-efficient of adversity affecting certain multiplicities in this field, in short, as a permanent danger which has to be avoided or prevented. Racism has to become a practice: it is not contemplation awakening the significations engraved on things; it is *in itself* self-justifying violence: violence presenting itself as induced violence, counter-violence and legitimate defence. The colonialist lives on an 'Island of Doctor Moreau',[107] surrounded by terrifying beasts created in the image of man, but botched, and whose poor adaptation (neither animals nor human creatures) is expressed in hatred and cruelty: these beasts *wish* to destroy their beautiful image, the colonialists, perfect men. The immediate practical attitude of a colonialist is

107. Cf. H. G. Wells, *The Island of Doctor Moreau*, (1896), in which an island where gruesome experiments are conducted is described. [Ed.]

therefore that of a man confronted by a sly and vicious beast. First, one has to defend oneself against the blindness of the metropolitan power, which cannot distinguish false men from true. The colonialist phrase, 'We know the Arab', like the Southerner's, 'The Yankee doesn't know the nigger', *is an action*: a juridical (and *intimidated*) rejection of any possibility that the metropolitan power should find solutions to colonial problems in the metropolis. What this basically means is: the colonialist and the native are a couple, produced by an antagonistic situation and by one another. No one (except the army, if the colonialist calls on it as a weapon) can intervene in their duel. And this is precisely the theme of the racist propaganda that the colonialist spreads in the metropolitan power itself: his portrayal of the native (always *negative*) is designed to 'open people's eyes' and to disorientate metropolitan opinion. Furthermore, at a more complex level, the practical operation involves a rejection of any *political* solution to the colonial problem (the basis of the problem being, *of course*, social).[108] The colonialist wants the *status quo* because any change in the system (which, at the present time, is everywhere on the decline) can only hasten the end of colonisation: integration and assimilation (full recognition of *all our rights* for the colonised), as much as independence, *immediately* results in the end of super-exploitation, and therefore of low wages, and therefore of the low prices which are the *raison d'être* of the 'colony-metropolis' economic circuit. The activity of racism is a *praxis* illuminated by a 'theory' ('biological', 'social', or empirical racism, it does not matter which) aiming to keep the masses in a state of molecular aggregation, and to use every possible means to increase the 'sub-humanity' of the natives (a religious policy favouring the most superstitious elements; an educational policy designed not to educate the natives *in our culture* and at the same time to deprive them of the possibility of becoming educated in their own culture, etc.).

What is important to us here are the two following aspects of *colonial praxis*:

(a) First, the *praxis* of oppression which we have just described complements the process of exploitation and merges into it. By 'process of exploitation' I mean the practico-inert functioning of the system

---

108. Yet the colonialist prefers to evoke possibilities of social improvement because he knows that the demands of the natives are primarily political. And they are primarily political because the natives are aware that 'politics', in the colonies, is quite simply the installation and the regular functioning of an enormous repressive apparatus which *alone* permits super-exploitation.

once it has been installed: strictly speaking, the big (colonialist) land-owner does not – at least in Algeria – *force* the natives to work for him for starvation wages; the deceptive system of free contract on which the capitalist process is based has been acclimatised in Algeria, or so it seems. In fact, demographic pressure is producing an under-nourished population, in a state of chronic unemployment (or semi-unemploy-ment) and the natives come to offer themselves to the employers, poverty creating a competitive antagonism which forces them to accept, or even propose, the lowest wages. Owing to poor industrial development – which is also characteristic of the colonial system – this mainly agricultural sub-proletariat cannot overcome these antagon-isms in a unity of demands. Working-class emancipation goes hand in hand with industrial concentration: in a colonised country, the pauperisation of the masses destroyed the structures of the old society, and removed the means for reconstituting another, based on different structures and on different relations of sociality.

In this sense, therefore, it is possible to claim that exploitation by new generations of colonialists of new generations of natives realises itself as a process: in the framework of an economic and social system, wage levels will be settled on the basis of specific material conditions which elude the action of the colonialists as much as that of the natives (the economic conjuncture *and* the demographic thrust, for example, etc.). But the *process* is mainly conditioned by the atomisation of the native masses; and is based on the following duality: the disintegration of the old communities, and the constant dissolution of any new groups which attempt to form, and a rejection of integration into the colonising society. In short, it is necessary that the colonised people should be *nothing*, except a labour force which can be bought for less and less. Now this necessity, which conditions the entire process, may have manifested itself, in the great days of colonialism, as an inert exigency within the system. But, in fact, this exigency is *fulfilled*; and if it is fulfilled, this is *specifically* both because it is the object of an oppressive *praxis* and because it was the objective (now achieved and transcended) of *past* oppression. This oppressive *praxis*, past and present, with its objective future, did not initially set itself the long-term objective of producing a native statute which would favour the establishment and autonomous functioning of the colonial circuit. In fact, as we have seen, the violence of 'conquest' was accompanied by considerable uncertainty as to the aim of colonisation, and this uncertainty was partly due to the fact that the violence occurred at a moment before that in which the economic organisation of France enabled it to define a colonial policy. But the fact remains that the practices of extermination and plunder atomised Muslim society and politico-financial committees created the system on the basis of this atomisation. In other words, the radical impotence and the poverty of the masses were at least implicit among the fundamental factors which the banks and the State combined and transcended in the project of a rational exploitation of the colonies. Thus, when one reaches the key-condition of the colonial undertaking, low wages, it is notable that the *process* on the basis of which they were settled was a necessity of the practico-inert only in so far as an oppressive *praxis* had deliberately produced a situation which made the process necessary. Or rather, the victory of arms was not enough; it had to be renewed every day. It would be even more effective and economical to *maintain* it by institutionalising it, that is to say, by endowing it, for the natives, with the character of a practico-inert statute: and this could not be done without affecting the Algerian army itself with institutional inertia. Inorganic inertia, as a permanent feature of the *praxis*-institution, reproduces itself as an inert perpetuation of untranscendable impotence among the natives. The molecular constitution of the masses, as a material, inorganic, and necessary condition of the process of super-exploitation presents itself as the inert result of a strict determinism (and so one comes back to positivist reason): but in reality this inertia – however inorganic it may be – is constantly produced by the petrified violence which is constituted by the presence of the army. And the internal consequences of this induced impotence (poverty, disease, competitive antagonism, the birth-rate, etc.), though they present themselves as serial and as a determination of the practico-inert field, are, as a whole, a controlled process. The old violence is reabsorbed by the inertia-violence of the institution, and its uncertainties disappear in the objective certainty of colonialism, which is the thought of the army itself, that is to say, its *raison d'être* and the signification – both global and in detail – of its practices and organisation.

To the extent that the presence-institution of a metropolitan army is a *praxis* which occasions inorganic inertia amongst the colonised masses, the natives themselves will treat this inertia both as their destiny and as an oppressive practice of the enemy. Even if an individual interiorises it as a feeling of inferiority (adopting and accepting in immanence the sentence which the colonialists have passed), even if he sees his *colonised-being* as a negative determination and an original statute of sub-humanity, and even if he tries to get closer to his conquerors, and to resemble them (in short, if he seeks to be assimilated), he does not cease to experience this condition, this ontological statute, as the inexorable and unforgivable violence done to him by a hard-hearted enemy. This is because this violence is *specifically* directed so as to deprive him of any possibility of reacting, even by admiring his oppressors and seeking to become like them. Thus, in their practical, everyday life, the exploited experience oppression through all their activities, not as alienation, but as a straightforward deliberate constraint of men by men. And to the extent that the army-institution[109] is a force which is displayed so that it need not be used (or so that it is immediately ready for use), the practical display is the common *praxis* of all soldiers and is expressed both in their group operations and in their individual relations with Muslims (so we re-encounter a practical racism – though at a different level and with a different meaning).

A young soldier who 'did his military service' in Algeria (I am thinking of the heyday of colonialism, between 1910 and 1935) was himself *ambivalent* in his discovery of himself and of the Others: it was as an institutionalised being that he was there, in a given town, in a given barracks and even, in his 'free-time', in a particular street or brothel. But, at the same time, the living historical *praxis* of the African army (which presents itself as an apparatus of counter-violence) appeared to him through the repeated operations he was made to perform, the instructions he received: the a-temporal inertia of institutionalised Being is realised and produced through a historical, practical orientation. This orientation was determined by the relations between colonialists and the natives *everywhere*, which are reflected by news of military exercises, on a given morning, in a particular barracks at Blidah or Philippeville, both as an *index* of the universal tension and as a concrete factor of it. The soldiers see *this* particular riot as *the sign* which enables them to decipher the other signs which have appeared directly in their experience, and as the enemy action which will determine their immediate fate ('confined to barracks', 'despatched with two other regiments, to restore order') or their long-term fate (insurrection is brewing, it will break out). Through such news, they are *signified* as agents of a common *praxis* (a repressive expedition,

109. An army is both an institution and an institutional group. If I refer here to an army-institution, this is in so far as the general functions of an army are specialised by institutions peculiar to Algeria (administrative functions, etc.).

battles, etc.); in other words, they see themselves – in so far as they have *the power* to unleash counter-violence – as sovereign members of the sovereign. Since this sovereignty is, in effect, being rejected by the natives – by the revolt in some other town – it reverts to being the pure, common power of the individual and the group to rearrange the practical field unconditionally. And as this power is real and concrete only in so far as it is limited, in reciprocity, by that of the Other, it becomes here an abstract violence, through the decision to treat the colonised masses as objects. *They* have destroyed the relationship, according to the sovereign ideology, by suddenly rejecting military sovereignty: and by this action, they have put themselves outside the law. Thus the re-establishment of reciprocity presupposes a moment of pitiless violence, that is to say, of the bloody dissolution of native groups: for reciprocity takes place, for the sovereign, between two inertias, one of which is the pure, serial impotence of the native, while the other is the freely agreed passivity of the army which retains its force. The slightest regroupment, as a negation of serial inertia, is a breach of contract. But for the soldier, as institutionalised-being, the distant revolt gives a sort of negative unity to this molecular crowd, by defining (more or less exactly) the degree of tension between the troops and the colonised masses. It becomes wholly a group, or a possibility of producing armed groups, or an unfathomable sea concealing armed groups. Thus the point of application for counter-violence is really everywhere *here*, and the lived relationship between the soldier and the masses must everywhere be that of the sovereign to rebels. This means that the army, on the slightest suspicion, recognises itself in its entirety as a practical unit for repression, as an agent of the perpetual dissolution of communities in favour of serial alterity. Thus the impotence-revolt of the masses and the inertia-violence of the army both deserve the name of '*praxis*-process'.

The colonialists themselves, however, with or without military help (or rather with passive or active military help) had to defend the atomisation of the masses against any metropolitan initiatives. Here, the *process* was no longer the *product* of a *praxis*, but its autonomous development had to be *protected* by strenuous activities: political allies had to be found in the Assembly or in the government, support had to be found in economic groups uniting the big colonialists and certain metropolitan capitalists, and the acceptance of 'assimilating' or 'inte-grating' reforms had to be prevented. And if, in spite of everything, some law was passed which tended to 'liberalise' the régime and to

recognise Muslim political rights, its implementation would have to be
prevented – for example, by organising rigged elections whenever the
electors were consulted in Algeria. If social reforms were being proposed (redistribution of land, etc.), the colonialists might also be able
to turn them to their own advantage. Lastly, since all these violent
operations had to take place in a climate of violence – that is to say,
they could be undertaken only by violent men – propaganda had to
reflect this universal violence, and reflect his own violence to the
colonialist as the simple manly courage, resolute in all things, of an
embattled minority; and it had to present everyone with the *other-
violence* of the natives as constantly endangering the colonialists
everywhere. That is to say, it struck permanent fear into the colonialists
and presented this angry fear as pure courage. These indispensable
operations as a whole required organisms and vigilance apparatuses,
and these produced themselves, in specific circumstances, as a dissolution of seriality among the colonialists themselves. I have already said –
when speaking of the practico-inert – that the colonialists (as a super-
exploiting *class*) – like the natives, by the play of competitive antagonisms and recurrence – were engaged in a series of series and that racism
in this series was *other* thought (of and through the Other), in short,
process-thought. But *the common interest* was always present for all in
that they were engaged in a double relation to the metropolitan power
and to the natives, and that they had either to disappear or to remain
the sole necessary mediation between the two.

   Their basic contradiction lies at this level: the 'liberal' régime of the
metropolitan power corresponds to the historical development of
French capitalism, to the metropolitan bourgeoisie; and it is also useful
for the colonialists, out there, when they are represented and defended
in France, and when they try to create and finance pressure-groups in
Paris. But such a régime – which is possibly the most practical kind for
a society based on exploitation – is not at all suitable for a society based
on super-exploitation. So, in the name of bourgeois democracy, the
metropolitan power has to be prevented from democratising its
colonies; in the name of the heroic sovereignty of those who are
besieged, the rare liberal institutions in the colony must be besieged.
This conflict, this complex *praxis*, the manifestation of class interest,
of the interest of *all classes of colonialists*[110] is concretised in *groups of*

---

110. This interest common to all classes is manifested to all the colonialists in

violence at the slightest provocation. And by this I do not mean groups which *realise* real violence (though there are such groupings: provocateurs, counter-terrorists, etc.), so much as practical communities whose role is to perpetuate the climate of violence by making themselves *violence incarnate*. Such groupings can be regarded as having the function of systematically lowering the threshold of class seriality, so as to allow more effective groupings (economic groups and pressure-groups) to constitute themselves despite competitive antagonisms; they represent the extreme possibilities for the colonialist: the extermination of the natives and the extermination of the colonialists. In one respect, these possibilities are in fact equivalent: they both lead to the destruction of colonisation; it is precisely the colonialist's need for the super-exploited native which transformed the wasteful, uncontrolled violence of the colonial conquests into economic, controlled violence. But the *violent groups* embody the extreme possibilities and can be described as *extremist* in the sense that in the light of the conflict which they make permanent, any *praxis* of conciliation must appear as a terrible mistake: the only action which can bear fruit is one which is based on coercion and repression. Thus the organised groups formed a sort of one-way barrier: while constantly presenting violence to the colonialists as the very foundation of their situation and as the sole means of preserving it, they tended to create *in Africa* a milieu completely impenetrable to liberal institutions; but since they were based on French nationality, these organisations enabled every colonialist to defend his right to violence in Algeria, in terms of his rights as a free citizen of the metropolitan power.[111]

This operation of protection is indispensable if *the process* of super-exploitation is to develop according to its practico-inert laws. But if we connect the past *praxis* which is preserved by the serial inertia of the exploiters and exploited, and which has *become* passive activity (inanimate matter as a mediation between men), to institutional *praxis*, as violence held in an inertia which is forever temporary, and also to extremist activities (agitation, propaganda, and the defence of the Algerian colony *against* the metropolitan power), then we can see super-exploitation as a process which realises itself on the basis of a

---

the simple fact that in Algeria the average income of the colonialists is ten times higher than that of the natives.

111. He may also use these rights in order to claim economic aid from metropolitan France.

praxis which produced and directed it, under the protection of an institutional action and in non-reciprocal isolation which has been artificially produced by common practices. In short, it becomes the anti-dialectical moment determining itself in the milieu of the constituted dialectic or, so to speak, the practico-inert moment as the common objective of convergent practices and as *their artificial product*. And, of course, it is also their mediation or, in other words, the unity of their being-outside-it. But we also see that the groups in question are linked to one another by relations of interiority (there are diachronic and [synchronic] connections amongst the officers, and between them – as representatives of different generations and practices – and the soldiers; there are synchronic connections between extremist groups and the officers, etc.) and also to the colonialists in general (we shall come back to this in the next paragraph).

Thus it is *true* that the process involves both the super-exploiters and the native sub-proletariat in an anti-dialectical movement which constitutes the future as an inexorable destiny for everyone and for every collective. It is *true* that, from this point of view, it is the system and the conjuncture which bring about the ruin of *this* particular colonial undertaking and, thereby, blindly, the unemployment of *these* particular Muslims, and their poverty, and the death of their children through malnutrition, etc. Thus, in a way, the entire apparatus of violence will have served to constitute a sort of closed field in which practico-inert forces crush the individual enterprise of certain colonialists. But this is itself the goal, since the problem is to sustain and isolate, as in a laboratory experiment, an 'economic world' which obeys rigid laws and is based, in reality, on the continued annihilation of the super-exploited (on the practical refusal to treat them as subjects with rights, whatever the right). This 'economic world', in which super-exploitation is meticulously concealed, and which presents itself in the vague guise of classical liberalism, is simply the abstract set of competitive or semi-competitive relations between colonialists, either directly or through the mediation of the metropolitan power. To take things on this terrain (that is to say, deliberately ignoring colonialism *as a system* and History as the basis of every human process), the repressive apparatus and the groups of violence must in effect protect *the freedom* to produce, to sell and to buy, and *therefore* the possibility that any given colonialist may be ruined, in specific circumstances and in accordance with very strict rules. On the other hand, this abstract, false economics is nothing but the *common interest* of the colonialists, that is to say, it enables them to develop their individual antagonisms without these conflicts ever being able to benefit the over-exploited who have to pay the price.

It is now clear that we must distinguish between three levels within colonisation as developing History: the play of flat appearances which can be studied by economic Reason has no intelligibility except in relation to the anti-dialectical system of super-exploitation. And this in turn is not intelligible unless one begins by seeing it as a product of human labour which created it and continues to control it. And, unlike the forged tool, or worked matter, it does not by itself introduce alterity and recurrence between the groups which supervise its autonomous development: in fact it realises itself as a complex ensemble of connections between series (super-exploiters and super-exploited, the connections between the former on the basis of their relations with the latter and conversely, the connections with metropolitan importers and exporters, etc.); but the groups which ensure its functioning are connected by relations of interiority – springing from their practical tasks – and therefore cannot be *serialised* by its mediation.[112] Thus it is perfectly clear here that super-exploitation as a practico-inert process is nothing but oppression as a historical *praxis* realising itself, determining itself and controlling itself in the milieu of passive activity.

(b) This brings us to our second observation: the relations between the oppressing groups are always the conditioned conditions of serialities of series, that is to say, of the inert gathering of the 'occupants'. It should be noted, in fact, that they are aimed at a certain common objective through the various practices and in accordance with different assessments of the situation. Their racisms – though all of them are based equally on the sub-humanity of Muslims – are nevertheless divergent. The extremism of some – which arises from adopted function – can be contrasted with the apparent moderation of others (of the officers, or of some of them) which, apart from periods of disturbance and repression, appears as a *quiet strength* which is put on display so that it need not be used. On the other hand, the officers need not be 'colonials'; and if they are, they are not necessarily connected to any particular colony. Lastly, they are functionaries of the metropolitan

112. Which does not mean that they cannot, in other connections, be serialised by the process itself: the virulent member of a group of violence may suffer his destiny (receiving the economic sentence which he causes to be passed on him by the system) in so far as he is *also a producer of agricultural goods* and suffers *as a colonialist* from the competition of large-scale mechanised production.

power rather than landowners or shopkeepers who are established in Africa.[113]

But it should be stated quite specifically that the African army was the violence of the colonialists and that the colonialists were for the army the legitimacy of this violence. It should also be observed that the set of colonial exploiters includes all social categories and that all of them (from the French worker to the judge and the farmer) are bound by the same privilege, which the soldiers share with them: they are better paid than in France, and their relative comfort is based on the poverty of the Muslims. Thus the unity of all groups of colonialists (from accidental, ephemeral groups to institutional ones) was conditioned by the *climate* of the colony, that is to say, by the Other-Being of the series. To what extent could this *Other-Being* be dissolved in fused groups? And to what extent is it, on the contrary, unsurmountably rigid and passive? It is easy to imagine the array of intermediaries: to each moment there corresponds a different relation between the practical communities: opposition and tension – relaxation, quasi-serial co-existence – the more or less advanced unity of integration. But the being of the series, in the world of violence, is determined on the basis of its relation of antagonistic reciprocity with the masses whom it oppresses. This relation, in effect, as a *real antagonism*, is in no way reducible to the practico-inert ensemble of the process of exploitation: but it cannot be regarded as a genuine reciprocal *praxis* of struggle since it pits against one another series still paralysed by alterity. This is, in fact, a tension which is both immediately detectable and impossible to determine, and which appears as a common signification of reciprocal individual actions. This common signification, however, is not *directly* realisable, since it does not in itself relate to any community of which any of the agents might form part as a common individual. It consists, rather, of actions which, in themselves and in their strict individuality, involve a negation of seriality: they appear incapable of being carried out except on the basis of a previous agreement or an order; but the particular experience in which they occur does not allow them to be related to any organised group. In fact, these reactions do not, in general, transcend the level of atomisation or seriality, but they are evidence of a change in the serial bonds – for example, the strength of everyone's anger – which is expressed in his

113. And lastly, pressure groups, economic groups, etc., do not readily link themselves to extremists, although extremists help their work.

bearing – being derived from that which he attributes to the oppressed other and to all the others, as might happen, for example, the day after a mosque has been profaned by drunken soldiers, or after a brawl between soldiers and Muslims resulting in Muslim deaths. The employer[114] was worried that day; the behaviour of his employees (or employee) appeared to him as a sign; and his anxiety was soon to turn into violence: and this transition from anxiety to the will to repress is itself an act of alterity. But it is on the basis of these reactions, each of which bases its violence on that of the other, that insurrectional or punitive groups can constitute themselves within the series itself. In effect, everyone's serial reaction consists in confusing community and series, and interpreting the behaviour of the enemy as the *praxis* of a group, of which this particular antagonist is a common individual. This supposition induces the group into each series as a negative unity, that is to say, as the sole means of struggling against the groups which are hidden in the Other. Of course, historical conditions as a whole will determine the liquidation of seriality *here* or *there*; what is certain is that the liquidation, wherever it takes place, immediately occasions a liquidation of the same order in the adversary. Thus pressure-groups, violent groups, and institutional groups, in their relation of reciprocity and reciprocal mediation, provide an exact index of the reciprocal determination, beyond the process, of colonialists and colonised, that is to say, an index of violence.

But as tension increases, the unity of these heterogeneous groups tightens until it *becomes a real unity of action*. In this moment, this synchronic, pluri-dimensional *praxis* really becomes *the praxis* of the

---

114. The employer may curse or beat his workers, for example. He does this because that is *what one does*; he is the Other, the fleeting, unrealisable character called *the* colonialist. The employee allows himself to be beaten, also in so far as he is an Other. If he were insulted or struck by a Muslim, he would react as a particular individual (or as a member of a particular family). But he feels the blows of the colonialist in so far as other men of his religion are, also, at that very minute, being beaten, like him; in so far as these provocations are addressed through his person to *the native*, a character who is as little *realisable* as the colonialist himself. Thus, *through the two individuals*, the Other relates to the Other; and both are alienated to serial unities which cannot even be realised here and which, dislocating and generalising, remove the event from itself and constitute it as the formula of the recurrence and as an archetype which exists elsewhere. But conversely, if the serial action of the colonialists is beating their servants and if a particular colonialist does not strike his, the serial and inert truth of his relationship to him is *to strike him*, and to be the *Other who strikes*.

colonialist group. It adopts two serial determinations and takes them into itself in order to dissolve them: (1) Its deliberate violence cannot descend lower than that which the super-exploiters manifest every day in their relations to the exploited, and which constitutes what one might call a bond of inert interiority between the two serialities. Serial violence dissolves, like seriality, into *minimal violence* as a primary determination of *praxis*. (2) The group adopts, as its own project, the violence of the series in *this* precise moment of the history of the colony, turning it into its cohesion and the orientation of its *praxis* (in becoming the serial madness of a lynching, panic will be contained *in the Others* by army forces and will become, in the military group, in institutional forms (sanctions to be taken, etc.), the upper limit of its repressive activity).

Thus, the seriality of the colonialists is not dissolved *elsewhere*: everyone remains the Other, imprisoned in his impotent anger – whereas the groups as a whole (from the army and constituted bodies to the groups of violence) maintain the serial inertia of the *Others* (who are the passive individuals who *have to be defended* and whose defence requires them to be confined in their passivity). But the practical unity of the constitutive bodies and organisations, in its temporalisation, thereby becomes *the colony* itself, as oppression and repressive violence. The *apparatus* transforms the violence of flight and panic into a synthetic, sovereign project for re-establishing order by violence; in the repressive violence of the apparatus, the *Other* recognises his own *as Other*, he discovers the blind lynching to be the serial signification of the summary execution. He remains external to the armed force which defends him; but in the dimension of the Other, that force becomes the unity of everyone and of the Others, as an *other* synthesis (*other* mode of Being); it becomes the activity of all the Others as the other side of their passivity. Thus inert violence, as frequentative and as the dated connection between colonialists and colonised, *is recognised* as sovereignty inside repressive practice; and the latter, legitimated by the need to defend the Others, gives violence-process its first statute of operation. But, to conclude, if violence *becomes a praxis* of oppression, this is because it always was one. The first groupings of natives that occasioned repressive practices themselves appeared against the background of their daily deteriorating situation; and this deterioration could occur only as long as their molecular non-being was *forcibly* held in the framework of a political and economic *status quo* while demographic pressure constantly lowered their standard of living. *The impossible,* as the negative reality of their condition, was a *product*: it was molecular exile at the boundary of life and death. The only possible way out was to confront total negation with total negation, violence with equal violence; to negate dispersal and atomisation by an initially negative unity whose content would be defined in struggle: the Algerian nation. Thus the Algerian rebellion, through being desperate violence, was simply an adoption of the despair in which the colonialists maintained the natives; its violence was simply a negation of the impossible, and the impossibility of life was the immediate result of oppression. Algerians had to live, because colonialists needed a sub-proletariat, but they had to live at the frontier of the impossibility of life because wages had to be as close as possible to zero. The violence of the rebel *was* the violence of the colonialist; there was never any other. The struggle between the oppressed and oppressors ultimately became the reciprocal interiorisation of a single oppression: the prime object of oppression, interiorising it and finding it to be the negative source of its unity, appalled the oppressor, who recognised, in *violent rebellion,* his own oppressive violence as a hostile force taking him in turn as its object. And against his own violence *as Other,* he created a counter-violence which was simply *his* own oppression become *repressive,* that is to say, reactualised and trying to transcend the violence of the Other, in other words his own violence in the Other. We have thus shown, in the simple example of colonisation, that the relationship between oppressors and oppressed was, from beginning to end, *a struggle,* and that it was this struggle, as a double reciprocal *praxis,* which ensured – at least until the insurrectional phase – the rigid development of the *process* of exploitation.

It will no doubt be objected that I have chosen the most favourable example: where exploitation is super-exploitation and where it is necessarily accompanied by conquest and oppression. The very fact of *conquest* presupposes military struggle. No doubt it will be said that what I have found at the end of my search is what I carefully put there at the outset. But in reality, I discussed the practice and system of colonialism because I wanted to show, by reference to a simple example, the possible importance of substituting History for economic and sociological interpretations, or generally for all determinisms. For the first time in this investigation, I wanted to give an outline of an initial description of the formal structures of the concrete. Lastly, I wanted to show that we should no longer cheat with such precise and true words as *praxis* and *struggle.* Either we have endless equivocation, and *praxis* signifies almost the same as 'process' and *struggle* as 'contrary double alienation of two serialities in the practico-inert'; in which case everything is definitively obscured: action and History lose their sense and words no longer have any meaning. Or else we allow words their meanings, defining *praxis* as an organising project which transcends material conditions towards an end and inscribes itself, through labour, in inorganic matter as a rearrangement of the practical field and a reunification of means in the light of the end. Then the idea of *struggle* between classes must be given its fullest meaning; in other words, even in the case of economic development within one country, even though the gradual constitution of the proletariat is taking place among the poorest sections of the peasant class, and even though the worker 'freely' sells his labour power, exploitation must be inseparable from oppression, just as the seriality of the bourgeois class is inseparable from the practical apparatuses which it adopts for itself. Economism is false because it makes exploitation into no more than a particular *result*, whereas this result could not be maintained, and the process of capital could not develop, if they were not sustained by *the project of exploitation*. And I certainly mean that it is capital which is expressed through the mouths of capitalists and which produces them as projects of unconditional exploitation. But on the other hand it is capitalists who sustain and produce capital and who develop industry and the credit system through their project of exploiting in order to realise a profit. This is the circularity which we have encountered everywhere. We shall meet with it again. But we must recall its movement in order to understand the bond between process and *praxis*. We shall shortly be inquiring what type of intelligibility this bicephalous being called struggle can have, especially when it involves not individual combat, but practical contradiction splitting every nation and the world. But, above all, we must return to this notion of 'class struggle': if it is a practico-inert structure (a passive contradictory reciprocity of conditioning), or if it is *exis*, the human order is strictly comparable to the molecular order, and the only historical Reason is positivist Reason, which posits the unintelligibility of History as a definite fact. But, on the other hand, if it is *praxis* through and through, the entire human universe vanishes into a Hegelian idealism. In order to get out of the difficulty, let us attempt to employ all the discoveries which our investigation has given us, at every level of formal complexity.

8

Class Struggle and Dialectical Reason

1 Scarcity, Violence and Bourgeois Humanism

The 'discovery' we have made in the course of our dialectical investigation (but is it really even a discovery? is it not the immediate comprehension of every *praxis*, individual and common, by any agent whether internal to the *praxis* or transcendent?) has revealed, at different levels, the double character of human relations: apart from the determinations of sociality, as simple relations between real but abstract individuals, they are immediately reciprocal. And this reciprocity – mediated by the third party, and then by the group – must be the basic structure of the community. But, on the other hand, reciprocity is neither contemplative nor affective. Or rather, affectivity and contemplation are the practical characteristics of particular actions in particular circumstances. Reciprocity is a *praxis* with a double (or multiple) epicentre. It can be either positive or negative. It is clear that its algebraic sign is determined by previous circumstances and by the material conditions which determine the practical field. And it is clear that the conditionings of antagonistic reciprocity are, as a whole, and *in the abstract*, based on the relation of the multiplicity of men to the field of action, that is, on scarcity. We have also seen that scarcity, as a mortal danger, produces everyone in a multiplicity as a mortal danger for the Other. The contingency of scarcity (that is to say, the fact that relations of immediate abundance between other practical organisms and other milieux are not inconceivable *a priori*) is reinteriorised in the contingency of human reality. A man is a practical organism living with a multiplicity of similar organisms in a field of scarcity. But this scarcity, as a negative force, defines, in commutativity, every man and partial multiplicity as realities which are both human and inhuman: for instance, in so far as anyone may consume a product of primary necessity *for me* (and for all the Others), he is dispensable: he threatens my life to precisely the extent that he is my own kind; he becomes inhuman, therefore, as human, and my species appears to me as an alien species.

But, in reciprocity and commutativity, I discover the possibility, in the field of my own possibilities, of myself being objectively produced by the Others as a dispensable object or as the inhumanity of the human. We have already remarked that the primary determination of morality is Manichaeism: the intelligible and threatening *praxis* of the Other is what must be destroyed in him. But this *praxis*, as a dialectical organisation of means with a view to satisfying need, manifests itself as the free development of action in the Other. And it is clear that it is this freedom, as my freedom in the Other, which has to be destroyed if we are to escape the *danger of death*, which is the original relation between men through the mediation of matter. In other words, the interiorisation of scarcity as a *mortal* relation between men is itself performed by a free, dialectical transcendence of material conditions and, in this very transcendence, freedom manifests itself as a practical organisation of the field and as perceiving itself in the Other as other-freedom, or as an anti-*praxis* and anti-value which has to be destroyed. At the most elementary level of the 'struggle for life', there is not blind instincts conflicting through men, but complex structures, transcendences of material conditions by a *praxis* which founds a morality and which seeks the destruction of the Other not as a simple *object* which is dangerous, but as a freedom which is recognised and condemned to its very root.

It is precisely this that we have called *violence*, for the only conceivable violence is that of freedom against freedom through the mediation of inorganic matter. We have seen, in fact, that it can take on two aspects: free *praxis* may directly destroy the freedom of the Other, or place it in parentheses (mystification, stratagem) through the material instrument, or else it may act against necessity (the necessity of alienation), that is to say against freedom as the possibility of becoming Other (of relapsing into seriality), and this is Fraternity-Terror. Thus *violence* is *always* both a reciprocal recognition of freedom and a negation (either reciprocal or univocal) of this freedom through the intermediary of the inertia of exteriority. Man is violent — *throughout* History right up to the present day (until the elimination of scarcity, should this ever occur, and occur *in particular circumstances*) — to the anti-human (that is to say, to any other man) and to *his Brother* in so far as he has the permanent possibility of becoming anti-human himself. This violence, contrary to what is always claimed, envelops a practical self-knowledge because it is determined by its object, that is to say, as the freedom to annihilate freedom. It is called *terror* when it defines the bond of fraternity itself; it bears the name of oppression when it is used against one or more individuals, imposing an untranscendable statute on them as a function of scarcity. This statute is always[115] abstractly constituted by the same practical determinations; given a scarcity of food and of labour certain groups will decide to constitute, with other individuals or groups, a community defined both by the obligation to do surplus labour and by the need to reduce themselves to controlled under-consumption. Now, this oppression constitutes itself as a *praxis* which is conscious of itself and of its object: whether or not it passes over the fact in silence, it will define the multiplicity of dispensable workers not *despite* their reality as free practical organisms, but *because* of it. The slave, the craftsman, the skilled worker, and the specialised worker are of course produced by the mode of production. But they are produced precisely as that more or less considerable area of free control, free direction or free supervision which must fill the gap between instrumental-being and man. It is certainly possible for a man to replace an animal in work which an animal could do (the gold carriers in the sixteenth century on the routes which crossed the isthmus of Panama). But this new distribution of tasks is constrained, self-conscious, and a deliberate choice based on scarcity. It is decided by the organisers and by those in charge that he who used to work *as a man* should freely make himself inferior to man. For constraint does not eliminate freedom (except by liquidating the oppressed); it makes freedom its accomplice while allowing it no option but obedience.

These considerations are not intended to make oppression into the direct, historical origin of class division and exploitation. Far from it. On the contrary, we recognise – because it is obvious – that the practico-inert field of exploitation constitutes itself, through counter-finalities and through the mediation of worked matter, as a passive synthesis of serial relations. Whether we are dealing with slavery as an institution or with the consequences of the division of labour, it is impossible to treat the material, technical, demographic, etc., development

---

115. At least, as Engels would say, in historical societies. [Engels's note to the opening sentence of the *Communist Manifesto*. (Ed.)]

of a given society as the objectification of the free *praxis* of an individual or group. It is undoubtedly true that – as Engels says – slaves appear at the moment when the development of the techniques of agriculture makes them possible and necessary, that is to say, that an institution is a response to the practico-inert exigency of an already constituted field of passive activity. Nor can there be any doubt, though Engels is very simplistic on this point, that exploitation, in its many historical forms, is basically a process which corresponds to a differentiation of functions, that is to say, ultimately, to the development of the mode of production. When the 'iron and coal complex' began, the use of coal as a fuel determined the transformation of the system of mineral extraction from outside and as an other-exigency (that is to say, as an independent variable).[116] It was this demand for coal, as a serial process (propagated *by a lateral competitive antagonism*, and therefore by alterity rather than by common decision) which, within half a century, produced the mine-owners as *major capitalists*, owning a key-industry; this is what forced them – as we have seen – to introduce steam pumps to replace beasts of burden and men. Scientific discoveries, technical innovations immediately put to use, customers as seriality: no more was necessary for the mine to emerge as a fabulous inheritance, owned by one man; for the first machines to appear there, overthrowing techniques and imposing a set of exigencies and constraints on both capitalists and workers; for the need for labour to multiply the manual workers and for the contradiction which is at the root of capital to constitute itself *in seriality*. On the one hand there is the employer, the owner of the mine and the machines, whose interest is constantly to reduce costs, expand output and increase profits; on the other hand, there is the uprooted peasant, with no rights over the product of his labour and who receives in wages the minimum necessary for his subsistence. And to precisely the extent that the personnel at the mine are serialised by competitive antagonisms *induced* by material conditions as a whole, the employer is thrown into an equally serial competition, since his new power suddenly reveals *other competitors* to him, hundreds or thousands of miles away, whose power is as recent as his and who have suddenly been brought close to him by technical and economic changes.

116. In fact, circularity reconditions the variable and the system has a 'feedback' device. But at first, and for the mine-owners, it is demand which is the variable: it is demand which increases enormously and forces the mining industries to change.

So there can be no doubt as to the practico-inert character of the process of exploitation. But this is not what concerns us at the moment. What concerns us is that this process established itself *against a background of scarcity* (scarcity of coal for customers, over-rapid exhaustion of coal seams forcing suppliers to sink new shafts, scarcity of *time* necessitating use of steam pumps) and *by men* (that is to say, by practical organisms who have interiorised and readopted scarcity in the form of Manichaean violence). The transformation of the mine owner *comes to him from outside*, but he has to interiorise it and realise it practically by transforming his mine and the techniques of extraction, which implies a reorganisation of the labour-force. Now this *praxis* is precisely that of a being of violence, which means that his free response to the exigencies of the situation can be realised only in the form of oppression. When I speak of his *free-praxis*, I do not mean that he has a concrete possibility of refusing to make the necessary transformations: I simply mean that the necessary transformations will objectify themselves in the mine through a calculated adaptation of means to the end, and a set of dialectically organised actions, with the mine, the competitors, the exigencies of the market, etc., as their practical field.

When I emphasise *scarcity*, at the very moment where our man is transformed into a fabulously rich heir, I do not mean that he is still at the stage at which famine and death threaten every individual. Scarcity here is expressed in terms of temporalisation as *urgency*; dispersal, poverty of means, and the resistance of matter constitute impediments which threaten to slow down a production which the exigencies of demand require to be considerably accelerated. For the heir, scarcity is the possibility of not coming into his inheritance unless he reorganises his field of action as soon as possible. In this way any antagonistic activity by an Other (from 'force of inertia' to active resistance), in threatening to increase these impediments, appears as the *praxis* of an anti-human. Indeed, it would be true to say that the class-being of the worker (the pauper and future proletarian, who is as yet still wandering the roads or being fed by the village community) was already produced by the mine, just as that of the colonised native was produced by the colonial system. It is also true that, just as *racism* is a passive constitution in things before being an ideology, a certain idea of the working class is produced by technical changes. And this idea is simply class-being, in so far as it will be known and transcended by the owner, and known, adopted and negated by the working class. But, to be exact, this *class-being* could not be accepted and realised by the *praxis* of the industrialist unless the worker represented another species, an anti-human. It is absurd to attempt to settle the question by referring to egoism or by declaring that the employer 'pursues self-interest' blindly. For his interest – as being-outside-himself-in-the-factory – is constituted in and by the developing transformations; it is only for later generations that it will pre-exist whoever inherits the mine or factory as the very determination of his bourgeois-being. As for egoism, the word is devoid of meaning. First, it would have some semblance of significance only on the hypothesis of absolute social atomism (a creation of analytical Reason at the time of Condillac). And in any case, it cannot explain anything here, for it is not true that the employer was unconcerned about his workers and their situation; on the contrary, he concerned himself with them constantly, in that he incessantly took precautions against theft, sabotage, strikes and other 'social troubles'.

It should in fact be noted that the practice of the wage-contract 'freely agreed' by both parties and characteristic of the industrial era posits the freedom of the worker as an absolute principle. Contractual reciprocity goes further because – at least formally – each freedom is guaranteed by that of the Other, and this presupposes that the employer would find in the worker a freedom equal to his own, or in other words, recognise him as a member of the human race. At first sight, this seems very different from racism in that colonial super-exploitation is based upon the 'sub-humanity' of the natives. In the case of racism, the contradiction derives from the fact that the colonialist finds himself forced to use the 'sub-human' whom he oppresses as such for properly human activities. The contradiction of early capitalism, however, is that the employer, under cover of a proclaimed reciprocity, treats the worker as an enemy: the free contract, at this period, concealed what was really forced labour. Labour was recruited by constraint, iron discipline was imposed on it, and employers protected themselves by perpetual blackmail and, frequently, by repression.

The contradiction therefore is both to recognise that the worker is free and to introduce him by compulsion into a system in which it is *also* recognised that he will be reduced to a sub-human level. At the same time, the viciousness of preventive or repressive measures shows that the worker is condemned *in advance* for any *possible* tendency to revolt, while at the same time his protestations are apparently seen as legitimate. This takes us a long way from egoism and from the 'hard-ness' for which it is customary to reproach the capitalists of the 'palaeotechnical' period, as if their barbarity had been buried with them. It is not a question of a character trait, but of a class-hatred which, for English employers, preceded the true development of the working class. Either they had to see this freedom, which they wished to use (and mystify) in the moment of the wage contract, in order to bind it later and crush it under constraints, as the freedom-for-evil of the anti-human, or they had to discover the Evil and the Inhuman in their own *praxis*, on the basis of the hatred of the exploited for them. In other words, what they primarily hated in the men whom they constituted as sub-human was the freedom which would define *them* as anti-human; and this hatred was practical: it was aimed at suppressing the freedom of the Other by constituting it practically as bad freedom or as the freedom of impotence. But, on the other hand, they could not destroy it (by constant physical compulsion or extermination) and treat their men as beasts: the process of alienation requires that the worker should be regarded as free at the moment of the contract, in order to be reduced to a commodity later.

Thus man freely becomes a commodity: he sells himself. And this freedom is *absolutely* necessary: not on the superficial plane of law or civil society, but at a deeper level, because this freedom governs output. A slave, always fed, and always as badly fed, did not make a close connection between his need and his work for his master. Of course, he worked in order to be fed, in order to avoid blows, but still the quantitative relation between his output and the satisfaction of his needs was indeterminate: he did *just enough* to avoid punishment or inanition. Freedom of labour, in contrast, is to be found after the contract, as its consequence, even in the human-commodity, to precisely the extent that his own free effort (free in relation to physical constraints, though closely conditioned by his needs and by the situation) can increase his output. Within a strictly defined quantitative system, his wage will depend in effect on the increase of his production.[117] Thus the freedom of the manual worker, in other words his humanity, is a necessary exigency of industrial production. But in so far as everyone's activity, alienated and engulfed in the practico-inert field, becomes a process, it is also, necessarily, the neutralisation of this freedom: for it might, in effect, constitute itself through the group as a violent negation of alienation. This possibility is given *a priori* – even

117. And, in any case, the 'skill' of his work is what will enable him to triumph in the market of competitive antagonisms.

if the historical conditions for consciousness are not all fulfilled – by the formal dialectic itself, which, always and everywhere, produces the group as a constituted negation on the basis of constituent *praxis* and its alienation.

At this level, and from the earliest phase of the industrial revolution, the proletariat is the enemy in so far as its resistances are produced within the employer's enterprise as a restriction on the sovereign freedom of the proprietor through the other freedom of the wage-earner. The incredible ferocity of English proprietors, the poor laws and the *free forced* labour which resulted from them, express an anticipation of hatred. The wastage of human lives, so stupefying for us (even from a purely economic point of view), corresponded to the universal wastage of the 'iron and coal' period; it was a kind of limited extermination of a non-human species in so far as it did not create an immediate crisis of man-power. I am not referring only to the so-called 'iron laws' of classical economics, but also to really wasteful practices – some negative, like the systematic refusal to reburn toxic fumes, others positive, like the use of children (which had the *visible* result of destroying them in two or three years and, with them, future workers). To the extent that, as Sauvy rightly says, a society chooses its dead, the extraordinary indifference of nineteenth-century society for the mortality which it produced and maintained in its working populations cannot be attributed to anything but a will to exterminate. The aim was in fact to defeat resistance by fear of dismissal and unemployment; and for unemployment to be really threatening, it had, quite simply, to signify mortal danger (either for the worker or for his family).

On the other hand, repressive practices within factories (in particular the rule against speaking to one's neighbour, on pain of dismissal, which was common in English factories) make it perfectly clear that the employer *already* regarded the worker as a rebel; that is to say, he was *already* aware of creating an intolerable situation by employing him. A colonialist lawyer said to me recently: 'We have committed too many unpardonable errors, too many acts of cruelty, and too many crimes ever to hope that the Arabs can be reconciled to us, and love us; there is only one solution: terror.' This state of mind is just the same as that of the English employer at the end of the eighteenth century and the beginning of the nineteenth; except that the formation of the English proletariat was itself preventive terror. We have seen one sign of this attitude in the fact that mechanisation appeared to many as a means of intimidating the masses. Of course, this is not what it was initially or primarily; above all, it enabled costs to be reduced and production increased. But in the practico-inert result of mechanisation (the reduction of costs), employers immediately actualised the practical and human element: technological unemployment, in so far as it created a constantly available mass which made every worker aware of his replaceability, that is to say, of the impotence of his freedom.

So we can see that the first phase of the process of industrialisation, in so far as it was realised by individual employers, by pressure groups or by the State, manifested itself in England as a *praxis* of systematic oppression. It is completely wrong to interpret the cruelty of the English employers as indifference, blindness or contempt: it was in fact quite deliberate. And if we speak of indifference or blindness in circumstances such as these, we shall be reverting to the belief that exploitation is a pure process and that the exploiters, its products, are completely *separate* from its other products, the exploited, and separated by a mere *inert privation*. The mistake of some Marxist theorists is, in fact, that they describe the practico-inert process either as producing workers in relation to their condition as wage-earning producers and, thereby, in relation to the employers' class in its historical reality, *or* as producing capitalists through the evolution of capital itself and, thereby, in relation to the contemporary determinations of the working class, but that they never mention (except perhaps as an epiphenomenon) the real action of the first on the second or of the second on the first. But the determinations which come to the employers from the working class do not come to them through practico-inert reality alone; nor do the determinations which come to the workers from the employers. What is involved is not two parallel modes with opposite signs whose substance is unity and which can never communicate except through their unity: in fact, the practico-inert system realises itself as the system of the other through the employers' real actions on the workers and those of the workers on the employers. It is at precisely this level that we must understand how, from its origins and installation, the process of exploitation is a practice of alienated and serialised oppression.

Capitalist society is characterised by the systematic non-organisation of production (even if trusts, combines or partial planning enter its development). From the point of view of positivist rationality, one might say that social capital is simply the sum of innumerable individual capitals. But, at the practico-inert level, our investigation shows that, regardless of the individual action of various capitals, the general movement behaves as a unity. In particular, the *total product* is not, for the capitalists as a whole, the sum of the products of society: for the class taken as a whole, it is essential that this product should have a particular form of use – that it should include both means of production for the renewal of the labour process and means of consumption (for capitalists and workers). This necessarily implies that simple reproduction is incompatible with capitalist production. The total product of capitalist society implies 'expanded' reproduction, that is to say, the accumulation or allocation of an increasing portion of surplus value to functions of production.

All this is true: the lack of coherence between individual enterprises is only apparent; their coherence is fundamental in so far as they all contribute to the *total product*. But it must be noted here that this coherence is *serial*. From this point of view the capitalist process is a collective. How could it be otherwise, seeing that total production differs precisely *in its common organisation* from non-organised production? Surplus-value, accumulation, competitive markets, and the circulation of commodities are relations of alterity. The mediation in fact is money, which represents the *faux frais* of the private economy and which the latter produces as a regulator of its anarchy. But money is matter-mediation and is necessarily the Other. The circulation of money is a reinforcement of seriality. I have made these points before, but it is necessary to return to them in order to recall that the process of capital, taken as a social ensemble, *is not a whole, but a flight* and that a totalising language can only mislead us here. The unity of the process *always* lies precisely *in the other*; and accumulation, in so far as it is aimed at increasing fixed capital at the expense of variable capital, has no aim other than lowering costs and increasing production in a competitive field which is entirely polarised by the other. Thus accumulation, at the level of the social ensemble rather than of the individual capitalist, is a profound alterity in its being, in so far as it is an infinite unity of seriality: it is a false totalisation, by a passage to infinity, of a triple alterity (manufacturers, consumers, producers). But precisely for this reason, this recurrent unity brings us back to the individual capitalist in that it regulates his *praxis* (alienation, alteration) and in that this *praxis* alone sustains the rule and the product. The *other*-action of the manufacturer comes to him as other in so far as everything in it is defined *by the others*: importing a machine because the Other (the competitor) has done so, or has not yet done so, or because the Other is a buyer (the customer as seriality), in a moment where events are inscribed in the conjuncture *as other* (expansion, recession, etc.), is precisely, for the individual manufacturer, *to accumulate*.

But, to precisely the extent that this action eludes him with its significations of alterity, it remains *his free organised choice*: in fact it implies consultations with experts and technicians, the formulation of a production schedule, discussions with subordinates, decisions, etc. It is, therefore, *a direct action* with marginal alienation: its serial meaning will be revealed to him later, through the development of an economy which is united in alterity, whether in the form of increased exigencies (accumulation requires its own increase) or, in a crisis, in the form of destiny. But in itself the operation presupposes speculation on the other by practical thought as other; and this thought itself – as an objective relational system of alterity – is used (like a calculating machine) by a direct, synthetic *praxis* which *manipulates* it (as we have seen at various levels of our investigation). At this moment, Other-Thought (*la Pensée-Autre*) is merely a means which is transcended towards a direct result: profit, as a direct result, is still conditioned by the Other; and this very *praxis*, despite its reflexive knowledge of the rules of alterity, will become alienated to the serialised process. The process is the *lateral*, *material being* which is produced in passivity from each individual *praxis*. And this individual *praxis* is in fact directly exercised by the employer over his workers. In choosing to import a machine or to buy one in his own country, the industrialist contributes, as an Other, to increasing the portion of social capital invested in means of production compared to the portion invested by society in wages. But *directly*, and in so far as he is the individual proprietor of a particular factory or plant, his action causes redundancy and consequent unemployment for a number of workers, possible deskilling and a reduction in wages for those who remain. The term 'cause' is itself improper, since this is not an unexpected result of his action, in some way external to his objective: in fact, *it is the objective itself*. To reduce costs is to cut the number of one's workers. In other words, *it is directly with* future unemployment that he purchases his machines; not, as is sometimes said, 'without caring what happens to them', but, on the contrary, caring explicitly, in so far as every employer in this period wished to create a reserve proletariat by increasing the number of unemployed.

From a legal point of view, this action is irreproachable: in a society based on private property, the employer has the right not to renew the work contract (as, indeed, does the worker). At this time (the first half of the nineteenth century), the employers were so careful about legality that they even made daily contracts. But, at a deeper level, beneath liberal atomism, the manufacturer, by sovereignly withdrawing their real possibility and *social power* (power to purchase as a right which depended on fulfilling a function) from other free social organisms, perpetrated oppressive violence against them. Violence was constitutive of his act in so far as it was not only its means, but also its (partial) objective result and one of its immediate ends: the distress of those who were dismissed directly intimidating those who remained. Thus at the level of society (that is to say, of one or more nations, or of the whole world, depending on the moment under consideration), every action of the individual capitalist enters into the constitution of the social process, not as a free reciprocal contribution, but, on the contrary, in its *transitivity*, that is to say, in so far as, determined by others elsewhere, its sociality lies in the determinations which it brings to others elsewhere and in so far as this transitivity necessarily plunges it into anonymity – that is to say, into alterity – and prevents it from finding rest or consistency except in the process as the *transfinite reality of recurrence*, as this reality is revealed to *praxis* in a passage to a limit (the final operation of recurrent action). This transfinite reality is not accessible only to the historian, since, in a way, it is the foundation of all calculations of alterity (the point at infinity where all series meet): so in a way, and in so far as every *praxis* requires some rationalisation (the historical rationalisation which defines contemporary *praxis* and is defined in it), there is a univocal relation of polarisation between the individual capitalist and social capital, between individual practice and the overall process, and this relation is produced in and by action itself. Furthermore, accumulation as an aspect of an individual enterprise would be senseless and would in any case be a risk taken in ignorance (how could one tell whether social production of means of production and consumption would allow this accumulation to be maintained, and therefore to increase?), unless accumulation imposed itself on every manufacturer and on all as the essential characteristic of capital. Not only because *this* local increase of production requires overall expansion, but also because it necessarily contributes to it.

When Marx says that capital speaks through the mouth of the capitalist, he must be taken as meaning that the practical economics of capitalism constitutes itself as seriality and expresses itself as a particular serial system of polarised relations in a transfinite unity. But although producers come into the calculation in the form of commodities and therefore as pure quantities, capitalist thought – as the practical calculation of the manufacturer – like capitalist *praxis* (which involves practical calculation as its own knowledge), cannot exist except as the constant alienation, constantly lived and instrumentalised, of a constitutent *praxis*. Alienation is there at the beginning (in this capitalist world, it is always given for all *as already there*, with its exigencies and its characteristics – with the inherited mine whose value increases while its wealth begins to decline and the cost of extraction increases) and at the end; it is present as an individual operation in every moment and finally becomes the very calculation which makes it possible to estimate and predict results at the level of the Other. But, at the same time, direct free action unfolds in freedom. And free action is simply the practical organism who can and must be alienated in the collective *through his objectification*. Now, one man or a small group of men (family capitalism) can act on men in full self-consciousness through the mediation of worked matter; their action sovereignly selects this worked matter to deliver it from the freedom of the others (positively, because this freedom – which allows output to increase – is, also, what makes the human commodity more expensive than the machine; and negatively, because the possibility of replacing increasing numbers of workers by machines is equivalent to perpetual repression).

This is the dual practical character of the individual action of capitalists: the production of free workers in the form of human commodities in rigid, reciprocal conditioning, with a systematic preference for the machine over human labour, wherever the latter can be replaced by the former. Now, this dual character of the operation *as living praxis* is *precisely* what defines *oppression*: the power given to worked matter of (double) compulsion over free individuals in so far as they have been recognised (the free contract) in their freedom remains fundamentally unchanged, whether this worked matter is a machine (or the money to buy one) or a gun. And this oppression can be realised only in the form of permanent violence, that is to say, in so far as it is practised against an anti-human species whose freedom is essentially the freedom to do evil. In the milieu of class seriality and as the transitive relation of the Other to the Other, this free, direct oppression gives itself its practico-inert being as *exploitation*, that is to say, as a process. In fact, in the milieu of the Other, that is to say, in the pseudo-totality of competitive flight, oppression turns into an inability not to oppress or, as it were, experiences its necessity: it is no longer *I* who oppress, but the Other; it is always the Other, in fact, who makes use of machines or who is capable of using them. Finally, to grasp and produce this practical experience on the basis of the collective as transfinite, oppression is subordinated to exploitation as the infinite necessity of alterity, that is to say, as men being controlled by things (by laws of exteriority).

Serial flight, seen as necessity, becomes 'the ruthless play of economic laws'. This 'ruthlessness' is mentioned by all sorts of writers and in all sorts of statements in the nineteenth century: it is a fundamental structure of liberal ideology. But it is not things which are ruthless, it is men. Thus alienation transfers the principal feature of oppression – which *must* be ruthless in order to exist – into the process itself and thereby betrays its human origin: it is only through the practico-inert (multiple actions deriving inertia from material, inorganic, mediation) that a necessity can be affected by the practical quality of ruthlessness. This is what misled Engels in his hasty replies to Dühring: the bourgeois, in effect, acts on two levels: he is ferocious to those who frighten him and whom he wishes to subjugate and, at the same time as realising and living this ferocity in the translucidity of his action, he lives it as necessity. He becomes the ferocity of the Other, that is to say, the indifference of natural law to human suffering. But, at the same time, he preserves this ferocity as Other and *in seriality itself* because, in the name of liberalism, his theorists offer him a political and social doctrine based on optimism. Liberalism, in fact, posits two contradictory principles. The first, based on the exteriority of 'economic laws', says that it is they, in their ruthless rigidity, which are responsible for any particular disaster (some people even went so far as to treat working class mortality rates and their increase in periods of recession in this light). The second, aligning itself with the point of view of social capital and its social product, aimed to treat society as a totality in which the 'natural laws' of the economy performed a regulatory function by means of a sort of constant readjustment of exchange, through the ruin or poverty of particular individuals or groups. This second principle expresses the correspondence which each capitalist requires between his own product and the social product which integrates and conditions it. Now this correspondence (as an abstract statute concealing insurmountable contradictions[118]) cannot be realised except

118. The correspondence exists at the level of production: each capitalist expects to find on the market the raw materials and machines which he needs to increase his production. And in fact he finds them – normally, at least – not

through accumulation. Each capitalist requires accumulation as Other (that is to say, as a collective, at the same time as resisting it in his competitors). He considers it *good* because it is social enrichment, but at the same time he requires that the enrichment should be limited to the privileged classes. And, from the pseudo-totalitarian point of view of this enrichment, he dismisses, as negligible, the cost of crises and 'readjustments' in human lives.

Thus, in the bastard ideology (half analytic, and half falsely synthetic) which crowns the system (and which is simply the system thinking itself according to its own determinations and specific limitations), synthetic features are attributed to the analytic exteriority of legal relations: ruthless (exteriority *adopted* by individuals) and good (as structures of a false totality, their *functions* are to *regulate*, and they have the *powers* of an administration), these legal relations, which are really oppression turned into a process of exploitation by serial flight, bear the mark of the individual actions which they alienate and dissolve, as a pseudo-interiority of exteriority. And this duality is sufficient indication of the employers' profound acceptance of what would then be called the 'iron laws'. This acceptance was not in fact an act in itself, but it was the alienation of the reflexive and ethical commitment of each employer to his individual practices of oppression. In other words, oppression as a practical relation of the proprietor to his workers laterally preserved exploitation as a process and *based itself* on it; but it will never be able to dissolve the indelible marks of oppressive *praxis* and of the conscious consent of the employers to their own violence in its practico-inert necessity. As *praxis* absorbed into a process, the capitalism of accumulation can always be grasped *here* as oppression and its real foundation is always *elsewhere* as exploitation.

Of course, oppression itself, as pure violence (and apart from its economic objective), becomes serialised: the thought of the worker-as-the-Other becomes of itself an *other thought*. Commonplaces circulate about the worker as they do about the native. Or rather, they do not circulate. But, as we have shown, everyone becomes Other by re-affirming them: and on this basis the government, in so far as it carries out a class politics, exploits their value for re-initiation and perpetual

---

through some pre-established harmony, but through the practico-inert process of accumulation. But the first non-correspondence appears at the level of consumption. But we need not go into the details here.

re-cognition (of the Other by the Other as Other both in me and in the Other) as elements of other-direction. Now, it has to be recognised that, subject to the reservations outlined above, the State is the permanent apparatus of the bourgeois class – and that pressure-groups constantly form and dissolve in class seriality. And the constant reason for the existence of such groups is in effect the practico-inert evolution of capitalism with its counter-finalities: thus, in France at about the middle of the last century, a set of objective factors negatively adumbrated, in the object, the form of association known as a 'limited company' (*société anonyme*); and within seriality itself, the emergence of these companies, which threatened individual capitalism and 'family capitalism', gave rise to new groups, designed to maintain the power of the families. These might be called matrimonial associations: a whole exogamous system was formed, intended to create economic alliances (which in reality left everyone free) based on alliances between families. Sometimes these alliances served the general movement of horizontal concentration, while sometimes they were early adumbrations of what would later be called vertical concentration, of which the limited companies at the time did not have even an abstract idea. Thus these two types of groupings, both advanced and backward in relation to one another, developed in simultaneous struggle and interdependence. And this evolution, by clarifying divergences of interest within the dominant class, was to occasion a transcendence of the antagonisms between individual and homogeneous interests (competition), towards organised groupings whose interests (as the *common* interests of each organisation) are opposed in their heterogeneity (one sector of production requires protectionism, another Free Trade, etc.).

Thus the internal contradictions of the class are never lived in seriality: when they emerge, it is in and through the *praxis* of groups (unions of individuals or sub-groups under threat). And if this *praxis* is not purely economic and technical, it takes the form either of pressure on the State or of pressure on series (that is to say, on *one* class, or on several classes, or on all). Of course, this also means the opposite: pressure on the State tends to occasion State pressure on the series; and pressure on series may tend to occasion pressure on the State by series. Thus the bourgeois class (in alliance with other classes, and therefore only *partially*, if it is taken in isolation from them) is the milieu of the capitalist process as a practico-inert development; in other words, the bourgeois class realises the process, for its part, as seriality. But this seriality is itself a perpetual object of local dissolutions which produce organised groups defending the interests of a particular milieu. It goes without saying that these groups themselves are, from a formal point of view, in an indeterminate relation: it may be that, on the basis of particular circumstances, various agreements, defeats, etc., will constitute a hierarchy; but it is also possible that their relations will remain antagonistic and (through these negative reciprocities) *serial*. Groups emerge from the series and a seriality of groups may be constituted in its turn, etc. But this is not what interests us here. For us, the essential thing is that these economic groups cannot determine their reciprocal action except *other things being equal*, that is to say, here, without having one fundamental object at the heart of their antagonism: keeping the proletariat in its statute of impotence. It is as if everyone's *praxis* had two components: one horizontal and opposed to the *praxis* of the adverse group; and the other vertical, an oppressive and repressive force against the proletariat. But this oppression by a group is never direct: it depends on mediation by the State, by public force or by the series themselves. So the series, which produced oppression as an activity of its individual members and alienated it to the collective process as exploitation, ultimately encounters it again, beyond exploitation, *induced within it* as other-direction. In so far as the groups (or the State, if they have control of it) determine the practice of oppression in everyone through the Other and as a means of being absorbed by the Other with all the Others (the bourgeois as Other), the practice returns to haunt the individual other (that is to say, the exploiter) as a legal ghost with a social function.

In one way, in the milieu of individual *praxis*, exploitation becomes the mediation for everyone between oppression as a Manichaean sovereign practice, and *other-oppression* as an adumbration of a 'right-duty' system which defines the other, everywhere, that is to say elsewhere, as a *common individual*. In reality, no individual is common except within a group. But common-being here is an *objective illusion*. It corresponds to a real determination, that is to say, to the solidarity in alterity which is produced in everyone by other-direction, and whose rule is oppression as the legitimate exercise of a function. At this level, every bourgeois considers his class both as an infinite decompression (molecularity) and as an always potential totality which, as an ever possible common future, produces him and the powers which define him. This potential totality is *never actualised* and the individual has an ambivalent attitude to it: if his class practice requires him to, he negates it in the name of positivist or serial Reason; but, if the resistance of the workers seems more dangerous, he will regard *the whole* (the totalised class) as the only real possibility for the bourgeoisie, whose actualisation has always been negated, prevented by *individuals*, or by *particular groups*, antagonisms, mistakes, etc. Thus the power of oppression (that is to say, of repressing evil) and the common individuality which appears as a relation of interiority to all, remain merely potential determinations, indices of separation and impotence: 'Decent people are too stupid!' or 'The bosses are too selfish, none of them sees anything but his own interest' – so say all decent people, that is to say, every employer as a common individual whose practical non-reality depends solely on the Others. But, at the same time, they *signify* for the organic individual his own individual *praxis* of oppression as a certain way of doing his whole duty despite the failings of Others and, thereby, of realising, in his own person and in opposition to the oppressed, his own class as a sovereign totality. At this level, we can trace the roots of bourgeois humanism, which is abstract violence and a rule of oppression, because it identifies the bourgeois with man in opposition to the *other-species*, that is to say, to the anti-human, the worker. Humanism is the counterpart of racism: it is a practice of exclusion. But, at the same time – like racism – it is a product of other-direction, of seriality. Unable to extricate his oppressive power from a real totality which appears to define him as the typical social sovereign (like the noble or the priest in systems of aristocratic or theocratic oppression), the bourgeois serialises and replaces the absent totality by the fleeting, abstract unity of a concept. In effect this immediately leads to two contradictions:

(1) Individuals falling under the same concept stay, as such, side by side in an identity of indifference, whatever relations may subsequently be established between them. But we have seen that Other-Being and mere contiguity are two different statutes of co-existence. In fact, in a humanity which was a true totality, men *would be men through each Other*; which means that the concept of man would disappear. And, inside the class, the bourgeois is bourgeois in so far as he is Other and flees to the Others; and so humanity is simply this infinite flight (circular recurrence). A humanist bourgeois in the nineteenth century accepted his humanity as a practico-inert bond with the series and claimed to embrace it as his essence. But in fact, it lay outside him in the impotence of the Other; so ultimately it constituted his own inertia. But this inertia itself had violence inscribed in it, as the violence of a hurricane or a cataclysm. Bourgeois humanism as a concept crumbles

and disappears; as a practical inertia, it is a passive activity of exclusion and rejection.

(2) It would be inaccurate to say that bourgeois humanism excludes the worker *a priori*: capitalist society, precisely because it is based on free contract, retains a relative homogeneity through class struggle and by means of it. On the one hand, the structure of the system, the single market, the circulation of commodities, money as a universally accepted system of signs; and on the other hand, the necessary equality of employer and employee in the abstract moment of the wage contract, in short, the set of conditions necessary for production – from the point of view of accumulation – all require a moment of equivalence and solidarity between classes. And, in fact, the bourgeois will never cease to proclaim this solidarity. In this abstract, fleeting instant, the worker is integrated into humanism: the bourgeois defines him as his fellow by the very act of transforming him into commodity. But the contradiction is realised in the next instant because the human commodity can no longer express his freedom except to negate his state of being a commodity, and therefore as a negation of the human order in which the worker freely became a worker by selling his labour power to the bourgeois. The freedom of the worker-commodity therefore conflicts with the human freedom of the worker before and during the signing of the contract, that is to say, with his human reality (fidelity to freely contracted commitments, etc.). Thus bourgeois humanism lays its contradictions at the door of the proletariat: the worker is the being who lays claim to humanity only to destroy the human in himself; he is anti-human: no one but *himself* has excluded him from bourgeois humanism. All that is indeterminate (circumstances alone will decide it) is whether the aim of repression will be to *force him* to remain human or whether it will be *to treat him as anti-human*.

Bourgeois humanism, as a serial ideology, is solidified ideological violence. As such, it is a stereotyped determination of everyone by the other and this contagion spreads from industrialists to landowners, to liberal sections of the petty bourgeoisie, etc. It would be pointless to illustrate manifestations of this oppressive violence as a linguistic determination in the writers, judges, barristers, journalists, etc., and through the innumerable statements which have come down to us from the nineteenth century. I will just recall a curious article by the literary critic Saint-Marc Girardin, after the revolt of the silk-weavers: the author cynically acknowledges that the condition of the proletariat is intolerable; but it must be maintained: the proletarians *are our barbarians.* So, in the name of the great civilising task of *modern man* (the man of culture, the humanist who has studied the 'humanities'), and in order to defend the cultural wealth of this limited humanity, it is necessary vigilantly to oppress new barbarians. This article and hundreds of others, read as other (collectives), will have been interiorised in inert anger, in permanent fear, in abstract vanity by their readers: and should danger threaten, they will allow the threshold for the dissolution of seriality to be lowered. We come across them in frozen shouts, in the angry written cries of Flaubert (a small land-owner outside Rouen): like all others of his kind, he has 'eaten workers' *without even knowing it,*[119] without any relation of exploitation having been directly involved; simply because for the propertied classes as a whole, the action of groups caused seriality to be lived as complicity.

2   Malthusianism as the Praxis-Process of the Bourgeoisie

(i) June 1848

On this basis, we can comprehend how, through bourgeois dispersal and seriality, the practices of a group can become determinations of the collective, in such a way that a reciprocity of perspectives is created between the common *praxis* and the recurrent process. Elsewhere I have tried to show how the Malthusianism of the French employers – seen in a national context – was a genuinely repressive practice whose origin lay in the bloody repressions of the nineteenth century. On this subject, readers have often asked what could be meant by Malthusianism as the *praxis*-process of a class, given that I rejected both the idea of an agreement between individuals – which would have made the class into an actual group – and that of a hyper-organism whose individual actions would reflect hyper-individual decisions. In the light of the observations above, it is easy to answer these objections.

119. He 'ate' the bourgeoisie too. But I will show in another work that he did so with less appetite.

One characteristic which is common to exploitation and colonisation (as super-exploitation) is that the necessary limit of the rigorous repression of the dominated by the dominators lies in the latter's need for the former. Colonialism would be ended forever by the extermination of the Muslim population of Algeria. But this dependence still allows quite appalling acts of brutality. The peculiarity of the relation between the bourgeoisie and the proletariat in nineteenth-century France was that the economic dependence of the former on the latter had been complemented by a political dependence since 1789. Certainly, as we have seen, the working class was in the process of formation, but, at the time of the Revolution, it was not sharply distinct from the craftsmen and petty bourgeois who were then referred to as 'the people'. But, as historical development gave it a clearer political consciousness, economic development gradually gave it its statute as a proletariat. Its political victory of 1830 was immediately appropriated by the liberal bourgeoisie: but the apparent solidarity of liberal bourgeois and the people against the great landowners prevented the French capitalists from recruiting by violence, as the English had been doing for thirty years; the *praxis* and ideology of repression were not to be manifested until the revolt of the Lyon silk-weavers. Then a new class alliance occurred in the political field: the petty bourgeoisie, excluded from public affairs, became republican and secretly united with the first workers' organisations. The crucial role of the French proletariat in the first half of the century developed and nourished the militancy and class-consciousness of the workers: its triumph was the February Revolution.

But, to the extent that repression was suspended or restrained by political alliances, and in so far as one can follow Marx in contrasting the militancy of the French workers with the semi-passivity of the English workers, the basic character of oppression – always more or less concealed – suddenly had to explode in all its violence and find expression in real extermination. June 1848 represents the repressive-oppressive explosion: the struggle of the classes was stripped bare; having been hidden for so long, the fact that it was *a struggle to the death* was revealed in all its brutality. And, to all appearances, this is what it would remain until the last years of the century: Louis-Napoleon Bonaparte's coup d'état and the systematic massacres of 1871 were added to the June massacres. In the second half of the nineteenth century, the social policy of the bourgeoisie was aimed entirely at destroying the power (militancy, class consciousness) which it had allowed its erstwhile political ally, the working class, to win. Bloodshed provokes hatred, and hatred reinforces hatred: and French employers distinguished themselves from employers in other countries by the peculiar character of their oppression. They sought the death of the working class, though they had to exploit it, and they lived the oppression-exploitation tension to the limit – that is to say, to the point where the first, carried to its extreme, was entirely contradicted by the second, its alienation. And by their bloody practices (against a class which was in the process of emancipation, and conscious of the role it had played since the beginning of the century), they had, in twenty-five years, made the French proletariat quite different from other proletariats. The French working class was conscious of itself as exploited by bloodthirsty employers – in so far as the economic fact of exploitation was immediately supported not by impersonal laws of classical economics, but by a government supported by troops.

At the same time – as I have shown elsewhere – the treason of the petty bourgeoisie in 1848 discredited *politics* in the eyes of the exploited – all politics was bourgeois, even when practised by politicians who claimed to be socialists. This was the conviction of the skilled workers who would later become anarcho-syndicalists. The class-struggle must be waged in the field of work and by *direct action*, involving *sometimes mortal* danger. At the same time, the hatred aroused in the peasants by Catholic propaganda (the so-called *partageux*[120]) convinced the proletariat of its isolation, and so made it interiorise its real situation: – isolated in French society, and confronted by an exploiting class which, with the complicity of other classes, practised naked, colonial violence against the producers. This consciousness, leading to an *original* practice of the class-struggle (from anarchistic terrorism to anarcho-syndicalism) and supported by a particular structure of the contemporary proletariat (the skilled worker as an overlord to his labourers), appeared to the bourgeois in *the other*, in the class-object, in so far as he *too became its object* or might do so. This was not contemplative knowledge, but practice: the employer interiorised his bourgeois objective being when, on the occasion of social disturbances, and in particular circumstances, the proletariat showed its strength, that is, when a particular, isolated employer became its object. The strength of the proletariat includes the possibility of killing; the employer knows this, and he also knows that this possibility (which is implicit in all

120. Partisans of equal distribution of wealth and property. [Ed.]

class struggle, though nowhere so obviously as in France and Italy[121]) is simply an *active* temporalisation of a transcended past which the worker bears as a determination of his being (he is a son or brother of someone who was massacred in June 1848 or in the Commune). In 1871, and for a long time afterwards – at least until today – when tension increases, the employer realises himself concretely (if only in the project of seeing his situation clearly) as an object of hatred (and as a criminal object, stained with blood) for his workers – and not as a particular individual, but *as a common individual.*

Thus the past intervenes here (having been resuscitated and reproduced ever more violently by the present) to produce, despite seriality, the common-being of the bourgeoisie which, as we saw a little while ago, had hitherto been only an inert indetermination, an indication of an impossible task of regroupment. But it intervenes *in a double form*: as everyone's historical being (as the agent or beneficiary of repressive oppression), and as everyone's objective social being – in the eyes of the other class. Now, the members of *the other class* do not hesitate to attribute complete cohesion to the employers' class. They are as they were *produced*, in fact, by the action of the government in lending its military power to the bourgeoisie; this action made them, in their historical being, *survivors of the massacre* (or of the sons of the massacred, etc.). This systematically executed, deliberate action, which was approved by the majority in the Assembly, made them see the *agent* as an organised group. The workers knew very well that the process of exploitation involves antagonisms and possibly violent struggles within the possessing class: but they had also learnt what the class could do if it transcended its antagonisms and was suddenly unified by hatred and fear. In fact, we know that their seriality could not be dissolved and that the class supported its action by thinking and approving it in a serial dimension, through the thought and practice of recurrence (we shall come back to this, since it is *precisely this question* that has to be settled). The organised action was that of the *State apparatus*, thereby revealing itself as a class apparatus, whereas the bourgeoisie, terrified by universal suffrage and the rise of the petty bourgeoisie, was ready to disown it. But the worker was subjected to the action in so far as it was approved by the series, and thus he

121. The problem arose in a similar form in Italy, with the political struggles of the nineteenth century uniting liberals, nationalists, bourgeois, and workers in secret societies.

interiorised it in his being as a class-action, as an actual totality (*totalité en acte*), or as the only possible totalisation of the bourgeois class: divided in the process of exploitation, it was one and indivisible in oppression.

Thus every *other* bourgeois, through his object-being for the other class, saw himself as a co-responsible member of a concrete group which was none other than his class. Of course, the sign has to be reversed: the criminal member asserts himself as law-abiding and an upholder of social values. Nevertheless, hatred as the practice of the oppressed class constituted him as a common individual through a common past and future. But he cannot derive *this common-being* from the other class as such unless he himself regards it as an active totality, producing its actions and selecting its adversaries in the unity of a constituted practice. Now, on this point, his experience is confused: working-class concentrations frighten him, but he has tactics of massification to resist them; his workers offer him not only an image of dispersal and indefinite multiplicity of isolation, but also one of integrated members of more or less large and clandestine groups (union apparatuses did not yet exist). Inside the factory itself there are individual distinctions (he does not work with them himself, but he is aware of them): on the basis of competitive antagonisms in the labour market, he knows that some workers are *good* workers, while others are stubborn, or 'trouble-makers'; but it is the class as a whole (despite its heterogeneity – workers born peasants, workers born workers, etc. – of which he is perfectly aware), as a class, which strikes fear into him, for repression is used *against it*. He is bemused by this working-class reality which collapses, crumbles and turns to dust, and then reforms in some hidden union, or totalises itself in revolutionary action, etc. And to this bemusement there corresponds the vacillation of his own common being in so far as it is induced by the Other and interiorised. In other words, there is a perpetual indeterminacy in *this* structure of his common-being in so far as it reflects an indeterminacy in the total-being of the other-class and at the same time an empty signification coming from outside, through the *praxis* of the Other, to constitute this common-being as a permanent possibility.

But this permanent possibility is simply that of readopting his *common-individuality* as a common, transcended responsibility (a past, preserved inert determination) in a historical *praxis* of repression. It can never be produced and preserved as an *actual* possibility of re-constituting the group. In fact it relates to a past group which, in the *past present (le présent-passé)*, never existed. It refers to the historical-being of the employer after June 1848 as a sort of common *re-birth* of the employers' class today, a persistent and inert determination of everyone by seriality. In other words, the *sociality* of common-being for each employer depends on the historicity of this being as an ineradicable past common-being. But in the past – at the time of the massacres of June 1848 or of the military revenge of the Versaillais – this *common-being* was not a product of a total dissolution of the series or of a pledge: there was a change of class *statute* (an unveiling of oppression) occasioned by government action. And this action was itself brought about by pressure-groups. But at the same time it was supported by the series itself, in the classic form of passive activity: panic turning into violence without ceasing to be serial. If we examine, for example, the 1848 Revolution and its consequences in June, it is clear that it was the bourgeoisie of the notables which sparked it off; and it is also clear that it was this bourgeoisie rather than the insurgents who drove things to the point of revealing the concrete reality of class struggle, by forcing the workers either to be exterminated on the spot (or die of hunger in resignation) or to overthrow bourgeois power.

But it must also be recognised that their aim was to regain their lost power and the property franchise *(le régime censitaire)* on which it was based, by separating the republican petty bourgeoisie from the workers and making them betray their allies. In reality, neither the organisation of labour advocated by Louis Blanc, nor the number and concentration of workers, nor the spread of orders and tactics of revolt were such as to genuinely disturb the proprietors. The fright of the upper bourgeoisie, as described by Tocqueville, was a panic which emerged, in seriality, in all the possessing classes, in the countryside and among the petty bourgeoisie. Lefebvre is right to compare this panic to the 'great fears' of the French Revolution: it arose from 'the possible mob' composed of the poorest elements of the population, under the double influence of the economic crisis and of direct provocation (the closing of the national workshops). The bourgeoisie did not themselves experience this great fear so much as exploit it; or rather pressure-groups were immediately formed within it to control it by other-direction.[122] In the Assembly, Marrast, Trélat, Falloux, etc., became

122. 'I had always believed that it would be wrong to hope to regulate the movement of the February Revolution gradually and peacefully, and that it

their tools. But on this basis, and in a movement of directed (other-directed) panic, the provincial national guard marched on Paris. May 15 sowed terror. After this provocation, the national guards of Amiens, Pontoise, Senlis, Rambouillet, Versailles, Melun and Meaux encamped in the city. They were to fight and continue the occupation even after the defeat of the insurrection. Others, like the volunteers from Coutances, were to arrive at the close of the battle.

It seems that the bourgeoisie showed little militancy: their indignation was directed mainly at prisoners, whom they massacred without compunction. But, even in the field of repression, they were outstripped by the *Gardes Mobiles*, a *lumpen proletariat* engaged to oppose the Parisian population. Thus the attitude of the bourgeoisie (of the upper bourgeoisie manipulating the petty bourgeoisie) is historically ambivalent: it was really both an attitude of ferocity (clear recognition of the need to crush the popular forces and compromise the republicans, choosing the moment, deliberate provocation, the ruthlessness of the repression) and one of manipulated cowardice (exploited panic).

The children of this bourgeoisie never finally settled the significance of this civil war. But what interests us here is that the panic – propagated in seriality – led to a determination of the Other: the provincial action was a forward flight but, as Other, it involved all the Others, all the national guards who did not leave and who were, over there, *those other guards who were fighting*; it produced practices of violence in everyone, normally verbal ones, and these were, *here*, as Others, the reality of the oppression *by Others over there* as a clash followed by a massacre. The reaction of the individual proprietor was to reinteriorise this unity of alterity: he took every (repressive) precaution to prevent any disturbances in his own factory appearing as the reality *here* of the insurrection of the Others.

He had three links with this oppressive *praxis*. First, the action of the government and troops produced him here, at a distance, in the *impotence-value* of an *end which had to be defended*. And the *end* here being private property as the general interest of capitalism, this action determined the proprietor through a passive 'right-duty' system: the action of the sovereign reactualised the definition of the proprietor as

could only be ended abruptly with a great battle waged in Paris. I said so immediately after February 24; what I saw then proved not only that the battle was inevitable, but also that the moment was near and that it would be best to wage it at the first opportunity.' (Alexis de Tocqueville).

a *common individual*. But this common-being is conferred on him by a sovereign group which acts on him by a synthetic operation (totalising those it defends in the practical movement which totalises those it oppresses) rather than by a genuine dissolution of seriality.

The second link is the panic circulation of the Other. Strictly speaking this does not unite him with those who carried out the Paris massacres in a reciprocally devised and realised differentiation. Rather, it makes *him* one of the murderers – not that he approved of the massacres or even knew about them: the news from Paris may not yet have reached him – but because *he carried them out*. He did not go to Paris, but this omission was accidental (a matter of distance, difficulties of communication, personal reasons); but he was there as Other: here, he was afraid; *there*, in the person of some other, he was proud in his bourgeois courage. This identity in alterity, which was described above, nevertheless continues through events of which he is still unaware: tomorrow he will learn that he has killed a man. This passive mark which is imprinted in his Other-Being is exactly what people have vainly attempted to capture with the term 'collective responsibility'. Clearly this is impotence and an inert identification with the criminal. Its being depends on the absence of a negation: if he tried to regroup democratic bourgeois in order to protest against the massacres, and to oppose the repressive measures, he would escape this passive qualification. But we have seen that it is impossible to interpret or explain it by a negation in exteriority such as a pure absence (a signification revealed only to the historian). And this identity-alterity is really an opaque plenitude. And since his *Other-Being* merges with his *class-being* here, the class as a collective of oppression is produced in him as *oppressive-being*. This *production* takes place through a historical event: it affects him as an irreversible temporalisation: and it *makes him Other* in alterity. In alterity he reveals what he is as inert becoming through what he has done as passive activity.

This brings us to the third link. Through the series, he is connected to the pressure-groups, that is to say, *he implements their long-term policy* through his panic action over there as Other, and the organised oppression which he initiates here in his factory. From our formal point of view, it is irrelevant whether he senses, guesses, or actually knows this policy. Either way, it is *implemented*. What is much more important is that it rigidly defines the class statute – whereas panic massacres reveal oppression in chaos – and that he is subject to this statute in so far as he is its means or passive agent as Other. The definition of the class by the pressure groups (through their use of directed seriality) becomes the meaning of the repression in Paris. Now, the meaning of repression, lived as Other-Being (class-being), is the concerted transcendence and exploitation of seriality for the purpose of a class *praxis* by an organised grouping (or a multiplicity of groups connected by definite relations). Thus everyone lives his practico-inert statute as transcended-being (transcended by a common *praxis*); and conversely, this *praxis*, which is not really *his praxis* and which transcends him only in so far as he is a tool of the group, becomes *contaminated* because he produces it passively (in the same sense as the instrument produces the operation through the use made of it by the worker), or because, so to speak, he is a passive mediation between a dissimulated action (an other, common action) and its effects. It becomes contaminated with instrumental inertia, and in the unbalanced unity of a tension between contradictory elements, it is a *praxis* which is also a being and conversely.

Today this *praxis* is well known: there is a convergence of documents and evidence. The rebels were provoked by the closure of the national workshops, whose immediate objective had been to give work and bread to the workers. But on this basis, Louis Blanc had carefully defined more distant social objectives too: they were a first step towards the organisation of labour, towards a society which would take responsibility for its unemployed and provide them with systematic assistance; and he went even further, foreseeing that the state would co-operate in workers' production associations. These ideas were not socialist; on the contrary, they presupposed the capitalist process and would be meaningless outside bourgeois society. In a socialist society, state assistance to the unemployed would either be irrelevant (in the utopia where unemployment would necessarily be eliminated) or it would be such an obvious necessity that it could not be the object of a specific promise; in the same way, state aid to production associations is, from the purely schematic and abstract point of view of utopian socialism, either a truism or an absurd promise. But this depends on one's socialist *dream*: is it an enormous association of associations? But in this case (such is the anarchist dream) the State will have disappeared. And if it has not *quite* disappeared, if it is only in the process of regression, then its only function will be to destroy itself by strengthening the powers and freedoms of the free producing associations. On the other hand, if one regards it as necessary that the proletariat should exercise dictatorship through a State apparatus for a more or less extended period and if one hopes that the economy will be reorganised by centralised action, then co-operatives and autonomous associations of producers might appear incompatible with the process of reorganisation. In fact, these supposedly socialist objectives were merely *social*: the basic idea of Louis Blanc, as expressed in these declarations, was that of a bourgeois society 'integrating' its proletariat while acknowledging its duties towards it and which, to this extent, would transform the dangers of Revolution into a vista of indefinite evolution.

The systematic sabotage and destruction of the national workshops led directly to the expected insurrection. The immediate, concrete motive is well known: 'Work or bread!' At a real but more abstract level, the provocation drove the skilled workers (of whom there were many in the workshops) to revolt, because the work to which they would have been sent in the provinces would have had the same effect as systematic deskilling. And it is also true that as this rebellious crowd organised itself, it glimpsed a more general, more distant goal – and one which, in the moment of struggle, was much more abstract. From their headquarters in the *mairie* of the 8th *arrondissement*, the rebels demanded the withdrawal of troops from Paris and 'free association of labour assisted by the State'. It was what Louis Blanc had promised – no more, no less. Looked at more closely, this meant accepting, in exchange for the creation of a co-operative sector in the economic field of capitalism, their subjection as a working class to the authority and close supervision of a capital-dispensing State. Socialism was wiped out by the sociality of the Republic. A bourgeoisie which had wished to cut its costs, and to set the proletariat on an endless path of controlled evolution, *could now take the risk of negotiating.*

This is where pressure-groups came in. Their strange relations have been described countless times (the notables deprived of their franchise privileges over the petty bourgeoisie; the manufacturers against the bankers who reigned under Louis-Philippe and against the proletariat which they mobilised; a frantic petty bourgeoisie, doing the dirty work, through certain specific alliances of which we have evidence and whose exact circumstances might be revealed by a more detailed study.) The main thing is that they immediately stigmatised negotiation as a terrible crime; it was a betrayal which the proprietors at least could not accept without also renouncing their property rights. Everyone now knows that this is untrue, and that historical evolution has implemented most of Louis Blanc's projects without the structure of capitalist property being modified (even by nationalisation). The evolution of property since the second industrial revolution has had very different causes, as we know. And after 1848 the upper bourgeoisie which these groups represented in their sovereignty were themselves not unaware of this. On the contrary, they *knew* that, if they sought a confrontation, this would lead irrevocably to a new and radically violent world. But Tocqueville's text shows that their 'experts' preferred confrontation to negotiation. One has only to read Guillemin's book on *Le Coup du 2 décembre*[123] to discover an abundant harvest of similar texts: thus the groups determined the position of the bourgeoisie as a class (and, consequently, particular agreements based on different interests) and made it *radically negative*. What they rejected *a priori* was *sociality* in all its forms; the paternalist idea of that memorable mystification which would, a hundred years later, be called 'class collaboration', was not even conceivable for them, and neither was the idea of a community which, under an otherwise bourgeois régime, would take responsibility for its members. What they disliked most in the national workshops was the idea that a liberal State could take an interest in poverty and unemployment. The economic fact of poverty did not concern anyone apart from the pauper, and the priest who collected *generous* gifts for him. The only possible bond between employers and workers was the wage contract and this had to be respected in its entirety, though it was, in itself, a radical negation of human relations. Since, from the point of view of liberalism, economic crises represent a process of automatic readjustments of exchange; and since in any case it is normal that this beneficial process (for society as a whole) should mean poverty and death for many workers; and since, finally, this increased poverty and mortality were bound to drive the masses to desperation, and might in certain circumstances lead to armed revolt, the pressure-groups concluded that the government and the dominant classes could only take one course of action against poverty: ruthless repression which would allow the iron laws to do their work and benefit the survivors by increasing their market value and eliminating unemployment together with the unemployed. The role of the forces of order could be strictly defined: they were to act *with* poverty, which was the negative aspect of the process of readjustment, and *against* the wretches who would be selected by famine if they were resigned, and by controlled massacre if they revolted.

What the bourgeoisie was defending was not even capitalist pro-

123. Henri Guillemin, '*Le Coup du 2 Decembre*', Paris, 1951. [Ed.]

perty; it was liberalism. And it was in terms of liberalism that the groups defined, quite precisely, the role of the State: non-intervention in the economic activities of the dominant class, and permanent repressive intervention against the working class. This interventionism would be practically invisible in a period of stability, provided the standard of living remained constant (so at least they believed); but it would manifest itself in all its harshness when 'numerical readjustments' of the working population became necessary. In short, the groups determined the intransigence of the French bourgeoisie: they claimed that capitalist economics required that the proletariat should be left entirely at the mercy of economic laws and that no attempts to attenuate their harshness should even be considered. In fact, *they went beyond* them: even then the capitalist economy, taken as a pure practico-inert process, did not require quite this; it required it only in the sense that it occasioned extremist action-groups within bourgeois seriality and that these defined and *radicalised* the class position. Without them, the class would have remained conditioned by economic and social events, like any series, and its intransigence would be expressed only as a danger signal. In other words, *the class as a practico-inert process of exploitation*, even if it had its own government and institutions (since they would be capable of positing themselves for themselves and partially acting against it), was in danger of suffering the effects of its passive activity as a destiny (and ultimately, if the balance of forces were reversed, as a sentence passed on it by the exploited class) – unless *otherwise unreliable* pressure-groups, emerging both from internal tensions and from contradictions with other classes, defined *a common systematic practice of oppression* in constantly questioned agreements, and undertook, in the reciprocal differentiation of tasks, to realise it *not only* by economic, social and political control of the executive apparatus and of the Assembly, but also by provocations (through government action) which would cause violent and more or less concerted reactions in the exploited classes, and by the systematic exploitation of panic and other serial processes occasioned in their own class and in allied ones, with a view to tightening their control over the executive and supporting government action by direct action.

The Other, the provincial employer, may or may not know this, and may or may not adopt it into his 'political thinking'. Even his newspaper will not describe it. *In any case*, however, in so far as he becomes the instrument of the group's *praxis*, that is to say, in so far as he has *in fact* fought the workers demanding bread in Paris, or condemned them in what he has said, thus making himself one of the *murderers*; to the extent that he, as an Other, has spread the calumnies invented in Paris about the cruelty of the rebels, or in so far as he has already *accepted* and *repeated* everywhere the idea, often whispered about before 1848, but suddenly trumpeted by Falloux from the Assembly rostrum, at least a week before the insurrection ('The workers are *lazy*. The workshops have failed because they could not succeed, owing to the *sloth* of the workers'); in short, in so far as he spread this new attribute of the anti-human, free to perpetrate Evil, as widely as he could, he glimpsed (or clearly saw, depending on his intelligence and his economic and political position in his province) the *praxis* of the groups as his class *practical-being*, and he discovered – as the obverse of his activities and as their class meaning, as a seal of their inert alterity – the radical negation of the proletariat as a radical necessity if his free activity as a manufacturer was to continue and if he was to enrich bourgeois society with his products, in the framework of the capitalism of accumulation. Thus there is a signification which is reflected to him by the future and which will henceforth be the meaning of all his activities: whatever he does, he *must* repress; the proletariat is Evil and the bourgeois class cannot compromise with it without destroying itself. This bourgeois, in his free, organic *praxis* as a captain of industry, will indefinitely recreate the radicalism of the groups as an abstract inertia and an untranscendable, but suffered, limitation on his own activity. The activity which once manipulated him by other-direction now appears to him as an inert class duty: the passive, but ever present, limitation of the oppression which is his daily individual practice lies in the permanent possibility that if there are new disturbances it will take the form of a social necessity for bloodshed. In a way, the June days presented him with extermination as the social truth of his practices of oppression. To sack workers by closing a workshop was a sovereign action which implicitly actualised the basic right to kill. The worker is of course, as Marx says, the secret of bourgeois society; but in France in 1848, the bourgeois first constituted himself as the secret of the worker; he appeared to his wage-earners as the necessity that they should live the impossibility of living, or as the impossibility of their struggling against poverty without running the risk of being exterminated on his orders. Thus the employer had either to confine the proletariat completely to anti-humanity or to allow the proletariat to cast him into it. The employer became a murderer; so the worker became a criminal.

After 1848, therefore, employers were a curious historical product of the massacres for which they were collectively responsible without actually having committed them. They might have been employers, exploiters and oppressors before the February Revolution: but a sort of common upsurge – initiation, new birth – irrevocably produced them as active members of a group of murderers. However, though the murderers existed, the group did not (if it had done, it would have been the entire class). Thus they perceived their historicity as a sudden differentiation which produced and differentiated them on the basis of a synthetic unity which was completely illusory (that is to say, on the basis of the event as a *unity* of repressive oppression). Their class-being became historical through an initiation by murder. The initiation took place in three different directions: the employer was the absolute objective of the sovereign, and as such, his class-being was a legal entity, though his passive right was that of an object. Secondly he was the ambiguous Other, mad with fear and thirsty for blood – which he had never lived in all its homicidal madness, but which he found in all the Others just as the Others found it in him: in other words, he was *the* bourgeois in so far as this was defined as *the* victor of June (and *the* coward and *the* murderer). Lastly, as a manipulated instrument, he saw just beyond himself his use-truth (*vérité d'usage*) as the living truth of his relations with his workers; the foundation of these basically oppressive relations lay in bloodshed; it was a relationship of struggle and necessarily involved a reciprocity of hatred. And the hatred of the oppressor sentenced the oppressed: and the possibility of either killing or being killed became the extreme limit of the tension. We must therefore explain the relations between French capitalists and workers in the second half of the century not only in terms of the process of capital and exploitation, but also in terms of the historical impossibility that either should go back and undo the massacres, and therefore as a rigid determination of future struggles: if social disturbances reappeared, they would once again take the form of civil war and bloody conflict.

It was structures based on this situation that were inherited by the second generation of employers. The transcended past of their parents, and their developed, irreversible class-being became for them an *a priori starting-point* to which they were bound (we shall come back to this) by an ambivalent link (interiority-exteriority): it was not *his* starting point, but that of his class; and this negation permitted a reflexive withdrawal by everyone in relation to his class-being (since there was an incongruence between this being as a diachronic and a synchronic determination). But reflection presupposes an identity between the reflected and the reflector, in the case of a class as much as in that of a group or individual. It is the *opposite* of real division (as manifested, for example, in the reproduction of protozoa): in fact it should be considered as a *praxis* of interiority aimed at reproducing a *limited scissiparity* in order to increase its control of integration or totalisation. Reflection never gives the reflected to the reflector except as the quasi-object *which it is.* Thus the new employer, who, through an interiorisation of exteriority, has acquired an untranscendable class-being from memory, social training and everyday experience – on a basis of interests which he had even before his birth and in the light of a process which began before him and will continue after him and which assigns him his place *today* as a function of the overall movement – is forced by this contradiction of temporality to assume an abstract distance in relation to the quasi-object which he is for himself as himself. But the aim of the total operation is to destroy this contradiction: class-being as a non-temporal generality (that is to say, as an inertia with no temporal determination) *has* to be identified with class-being as an urgency which appears irreversibly through the behaviour-destiny of the parents. Reflection is *the means* of unifying; but, at the same time, it is itself the unifying *praxis*: through it, the free practical organism mediates between synchronic class-being and diachronic class-being from the point of view of a totalisation. This is enough to bring about a synthetic rearrangement of past being as a sacred objective, as repressive panic and as use-truth, controlled by inert, a-temporalised class-being, that is to say, as an abstract ontological scheme. Of course, this synthesis is mythical in so far as the event becomes archetypal and temporality and evil are introduced into the peaceful eternity of the bourgeois paradise by the workers.

But from our point of view this brings about an important internal change: the reflexive totalisation is not characterised by class *knowledge* – since class is a quasi-object – but rather, expresses the general schemata of a *situated comprehension*; and the relations we have analysed – *oppression* (historicity, *praxis*) and *exploitation* (process), the mortal struggle of killers and killed (in the light of the ever-possible reversal of relations), and negative radicalism as an affected inability to tolerate the slightest change in the régime – become orientations of comprehension. For the father, they were three distinct and irreducible levels of reality. For the son, they become operational indications which are always *complementary*: simply because any synthetic practical reinteriorisation of a practico-inert plurality always has the effect of dissolving the real multiplicity in favour of a negated, organised multiplicity. In other words, social *praxis* – whether it originates in an enterprise, a group, or a party – is always to be understood not in its pure, practical dialectic, but through the particular determinations which qualify and interpret it in its pluri-dimensional unity. Comprehension here means *evaluating public action in relation* both to the absolute necessity for the class never to surrender (either by abandoning *one particular individual* or by general withdrawal) and to the irrevocable past which constantly threatens to produce a future of death for the dominant class, in so far as these two practico-inert conditions necessitate a *praxis* of permanent oppression (the constitution of pressure-groups, control of the sovereign, and oppression as a social *praxis* supported by public forces of oppression). Thus when the massacres were reinteriorised, they took on a synthetic signification which they did not have for the generation which committed them; the pressure-groups which had been formed spontaneously in the time of the fathers became, in the reflection of the sons, a practice demanded by the situation. The absolute refusal to retreat, as a use-truth revealed by the action of the fathers, was adopted by the sons as a double inert limit, that is to say, as an impossibility and as a pledge.

Of course, such an individual act of reflection did not and could not constitute the oppressive class as a group, either totally or partially. They were isolated operations, temporalised through the relation of each heir to his factory. And when this has effects, when their practical thought is thrown back to them by the 'mass media', or by a newspaper article, etc., this is always as an *other-thought*, that is to say, as alienated to the infinite flight of recurrence. As for the pledge, as an adopted impossibility of opting out, it is not in fact *really made*, since the structure of pledged faith presupposes the group and mediated reciprocity. It would be better to say that the collective class impossibility which everyone adopts as a ferocious refusal to withdraw or surrender constitutes itself as a quasi-pledged inertia. The pledge is not given to anyone, but the quasi-pledged structure is apparent in the fact that individual freedom, interiorising its collective limitation, appears – as in the case of pledged faith – to be the source of its own negative inertia. But in one way this reinforces alterity: since any concession is liable to spark off a fatal development, everyone is threatened in the Other: he may learn, in fury, that an employer (in another industry and another area) has surrendered on one point to the demands of his workers. Conversely, he rejects them *also* as Other and because the fate of the Others is threatened in his person and by his *praxis*. The bourgeois (or the manufacturer) becomes the formula of the series, the Other acting elsewhere.

(ii) *Bourgeois 'Respectability' in the late Nineteenth Century*

But some kind of integration has occurred: the bourgeoisie has become aware of itself as a class. This means that the class is just Other-Being and that the *praxis* of every Other, through the limitations it assumes and claims to adopt, displays it and realises it for him as the signification-exigency of whatever he undertakes and as a norm by which to judge what every Other does. Moreover, class as the limitation and norm of every *praxis* itself becomes the solidified intelligibility of every economic and social action, in the form of *total praxis* (everyone's simultaneous reinteriorisation of the irrevocability of the past and of the use-truth which becomes the objective which has to be achieved through the mediation of every real and present practice). This means that every capitalist has his individual, practical comprehension of every operation (his own and those of the Other) on the basis of oppression as historicity (past-future [*passé-avenir*]) and of exploitation as a process (the present and a prediction of later presents). Thus, whatever the other manufacturer does, he knows it immediately, because *the Other also* acts on the basis of an untranscendable refusal to surrender: he *does him justice*, and if, in its individuality, the action of the Other realises the oppressive *praxis* which History requires, he will recognise it – *it will be his own over there*. At this level, of course, the oppressive *praxis* in its particularity is expressed in various forms and through different actions: it is still the signification of individual actions in so far as they are performed in a milieu of alterity (the choice of markets, of a place to live, of clothes, social 'connections', and life-style).

The bourgeoisie in the second half of the century had a lay-puritan attitude to life, and its signification was immediately oppressive: *respectability (distinction)*. The respectable man is an object of *choice* (by superiors): he is an individual who is recruited by class co-option (or kept in his class by constant acknowledgement). But he is not *born* (even if he is in fact a bourgeois, a son of a bourgeois). The aristocracy derived its privileges from nature and from birth. However, in the 'democratic' capitalist world, Nature represents universality, which means that, *at first sight*, the worker is a man just like the bourgeois. Respectability is anti-nature: the bourgeois becomes *respectable* (*distingué*) by suppressing his needs. In fact, he suppresses them partly by satisfying them and partly by concealing them (and sometimes by displaying a certain asceticism): he exercises a dictatorship over his body in the name of non-need; in other words, a dictatorship of culture over Nature. His clothing is *constraining* (corsets, stiff collars, top hats, etc.); he advertises his *sobriety* (young ladies eat beforehand when they go out to dinner, so that they can fast in public), and his wife does not conceal *her frigidity*. This constant violence against the body (which is real or fictitious depending on the individual: what is essential is that it should be public) is an attempt to crush and negate it in so far as it is universality, that is to say, in so far as, through the biological laws which govern its development and especially through the needs which are characteristic of it, it is the presence in the oppressor of the oppressed in person. The employer *distinguishes* himself from the workers by exercising his freedom in relation to his needs. But this freedom, as a real possibility of satisfying them at will, is not what he wishes to put on public display; and he conceals it by another power, which is in fact based on it: the supposed power of *negating* these needs.[124] Now this *praxis* was oppressive: in the first place, it enabled the bourgeoisie to affirm their Other-Being in relation to the exploited; they defined themselves by action and thought; they were culture without nature: respectability is bourgeois preciousness (*préciosité*). And preciousness is always a collection of practices in special milieux, intended to base the questionable prerogatives of the dominant class on a single, exquisite quality of its members. Secondly, the self-control which everyone is supposed to exercise serves as a justification of his control over his workers ('as hard on himself as on Others'); if he has vanquished flesh and need in his own body, he has the right to demand and

---

124. I am not claiming that *respectability* (the style of bourgeois life in the second half of the nineteenth century) was a complete sham: it may be that some employers really practised a humanist puritanism and that they allowed only a minimum satisfaction of their needs. But it must be remembered that the problem of asceticism and regularity could only exist in an economic situation which gave ample and permanent assurance of the satisfaction of these needs. The ascetic is a man who is rich enough to be poor only of his own free will.

require similar practices of the workers. Lastly, more directly and profoundly, the act of social oppression is itself repeated here together with all its significations: he is really oppressing the workers when he subjects the universality of his own body to countless constraints; it is the worker as the universal class that he destroys within himself or conceals under *artificially* produced particularities; and it is the repression of the workers' revolt against hunger, cold, fatigue, etc., which he exercises here against fatigue, cold and hunger, as revolts *of his body*.

But what concerns us here is not so much the description of this life-style and its history (the transition from utilitarian to puritanical humanism with the expansion of the capital of accumulation [*capital d'accumulation*]) as its universality in the upper bourgeoisie (and in the upper strata of the middle classes) in the period around 1880. How should we think of the being and the mode of appearance of this practice? How can we establish the relationship of respectability as a public attitude and its signification (oppression freely used by the oppressor against himself in so far as he thereby bases the oppression of the worker by the employer on the oppression of nature by culture)? Is it just *us* who see this meaning *today* through a diachronic totalisation of the last century? Or did the 'respectable' themselves see it as the common beyond of their peculiar practices? In the case of the *heir*, these two questions are easy to answer. In the first place, respectability is both individual *praxis* and seriality: individual *praxis* alienating itself to seriality and, conversely, the actualisation of seriality in everyone's individual creation. The respectability of a given individual, in fact, can exist only by and for the Other: what is at stake is public appearances (which at this time were often accompanied by very inadequate personal hygiene), and one became respectable through those who were respectable (this appearance was certainly not intended for the oppressed). But this reciprocity was a reciprocity of flight, since respectability never came from oneself alone to the Other alone (or *vice versa*); it always came to everyone through the Other, from Others – from me as Other and from my neighbour as respected by Others. Ultimately, one is respectable elsewhere in the respectability of the Other, and fashions are simply 'other-directions' enabling one to acquire a minimum respectability as serial conformity to certain ready-made schemata.

If one were attempting a historical study of respectability, the first thing to do would be to trace its origins to the individual activities of particular *heirs*, on the basis, in fact, not only of the material conditions constituted by the evolution of capital in a period of accumulation, but *also* of transformations in the class which were due to the fact that its class-being was an inherited-being. From this point of view, I would connect respectability with the increase of social (bourgeois) wealth, which enabled the dominant class to multiply the non-productive professions and which brought about the economic liberation of the manufacturer (enabling him to choose between more and more markets). But, above all, I would see it directly as a practice devised by heirs who wished to assert their right to their inheritance against the exploited classes and to deny the supposed birthright of the former dominant classes. The heirs could not in fact pride themselves on their birth (they were not *born*) or on their merit (since society would then prefer technical graduates). Their right had to be based on a merit which was birth and a birth which was merit, that is to say, on a non-acquired merit which would justify the class in maintaining them in their fathers' posts. But they had to find their immediate, distinctive merit in the historical situation where their class-being had become what it was: systematic oppression, justified by previous oppression and extermination, and positing itself as the only possible way of preserving exploitation as a practico-inert process. Apart from this, the heirs were not far from bourgeois utilitarianism, that supposed ethic which was simply based on the need to reinvest the largest possible share of profits in machines. The hardness of their fathers survived in their way of life, although they had the opportunity to live better. Thus the free individual *praxis* of respectability can easily be perceived in its movement: the new freedom (freedom for the proprietor to increase his unproductive consumption) will simply be the basis for the free resumption of paternal austerity. For their fathers and grandfathers, this austerity was a necessary *means*; readopted in the absence of economic necessity, it became a *virtue* but, at the same time, it was taken up and reactualised as a nature-against-nature, as a family *exis* transformed into *praxis*. And this self-control immediately became control over their workers: the employer's self-imposed living standards became an uncrossable threshold, and determined the various standards of living at the different wage levels. So this was *an individual creation*, a free practice. It was anticipated and required by the situation; if one transcended the given one would arrive at self-repressive austerity. Ultimately, everything was turned upside down: free austerity became the basis of their fathers' right to their property. Their fathers had denied themselves so that their sons could adopt puritan humanism in freedom. Respectability justified the heir's inheritance.

It is irrelevant for our purposes whether this simple, necessary practice was generalised from a few exemplary leaders of the bourgeoisie or from countless local innovations: only History and historical investigation could settle this question. What is important is that their *praxis* was immediately alienated. *Respectability* as serial reason became the dictatorship of the other. At first, *I* was oppressing *my* body; this became the oppression of my body by all the Others. Free innovation solidified into *cant* once it was propagated and serialised by imitation. Respectability became in everyone the right of inheritance of the entire class. The individual *praxis* was aimed at justifying the individual inheritance. But this justification involved the class as a whole, since it was to the class that the heir had to show his title-deeds. Thus the class as a whole, as the justification of each by all the Others, claimed, by a passage to infinity (already performed by every heir who wished to be accepted), to justify itself as the inheriting generation. In other words, the justification of each by all raises the question of the justification of all; but this justification is not totalising: by definition, it makes the transfinite Other (*the* bourgeois heir) the goal of serialised justification.

We can now raise our second question, which is one that concerns us very deeply: once respectability has become practico-inert, once it has become the inert limit in everyone of his daily *praxis*, and an index of his serial dependence, does the respectable individual still see his social signification as a determination of what was, for his father, a use-truth? Can he interpret what is really only an individual activity which has been alienated in recurrence as the unitary action of his class considered as a political grouping? There can be no doubt as to the answer: he can do so, and, moreover, he cannot prevent himself from doing so. The totalising practice of pressure-groups, readopted in reflection, becomes the *inert limitation and the guiding schema* of his comprehension; and this means that *he* comprehends all class practice – and therefore the entire passive activity of seriality – both in recurrent flight (as we have just seen) and as a tactic of organised oppression. He must also be able to comprehend his clothes and his manners, as the 'respectability' imposed by recurrent alterity, in terms of the untranscendable, solidified signification of the organised practice of class-totalisation. This practice is not directly translated into pressure against the enemy class: rather, it is a recurrent act of legal consecration. But in so far as the inert limitation which is the practical unity of the class-totalisation forces him to interpret everything in terms of radicalism (the intransigence which totalises a class-subject, and totalises the other class as its object), every respectable attitude (whether his own or that of an Other) is seen as a radical, oppressive negation of the working class by the bourgeois class. In any such attitude, he sees his class totalising itself in the form of culture and rejecting physical bodies from itself in the very movement by which it makes the workers keep their distance. And in any such attitude, he discovers and produces the following total determination: my body is simply one of my workers, and each of my workers is no more than a body.

It would be easy to give further quotations and documents, but it would be pointless: it is clear from reading any declaration (whether in the Assembly, in a newspaper, in an employers' meeting, or in con-temporary literature) that every bourgeois used his respectability as a legal foundation for class oppression and as an internal tactic of radicalisation. The difference between the diachronic and the syn-chronic totalisation here lies in the fact that the diachronic totalisation, being situated today in a developing evolution of capitalism and of classes, with very different methods of struggle, sees the signification of the respectable *exis* as a partial moment and as a privation whose truth lies in subsequent developments of the struggle. This significa-tion thereby regains a negative, inert autonomy, and becomes an objective mystification, before finding its true place within a moment where it will dissolve. The synchronic totalisation, however, which does not in fact exist here, and is performed by everyone on the basis of a false past unity (the rebirth), is expressed implicitly in action itself (in each respectable practice) without even positing itself for itself, as a positive plenitude and as the totalising beyond of every practical moment. The extreme seriousness of the ceremonies of respectability would not even be comprehensible if we did not regard each celebrant as performing each gesture in the light of the unformulated beyond of the class's self-totalisation as justified oppression. But in fact, such ceremonies (*salons*, dinner parties, etc.) are never *produced* by groups: their place is taken by temporary atomisation through recurrence – balls, receptions and '*soirées*' – mere collectives. But every other in these collectives sees the circular recurrence of which he is an integral part as a temporarily serial embodiment of the class *praxis* as totalisa-tion.

The example of *respectability* enables us to go further and to define what might be called *objective class spirit*, provided the word 'spirit' is shorn of its spiritualistic associations so that it simply means a medium for the circulation of significations. And in so far as a general practice like respectability – which is simultaneously *exis* and *praxis* – is *comprehended* by everyone in the movement which actually produces it, as a particular moment of a total action (whose signification as a simple beyond *goes before it*), this total action exists as everyone's inert beyond and its untranscendability appears in everyone as common. But this does not mean that it avoids this serial being: an inert determination, even if it takes on a total form, cannot produce a community; it is the common dissolution of the serial which produces meanings as real unities of *praxis*. But its serialisation does not modify its structure, since it is no more than the sign of totality as the inert beyond of all activity (whether free and individual or passive). And ultimately, in the transcendence of recurrence, it presents itself as the *other totality* of the practices of the transfinite Other who is the bourgeois. The effect of this opposition between the serial and the total is simply that it creates a contradictory tension in the unity of alterity as the double beyond of all references. And, since the signification-totality is still the untranscendable beyond of every practice, it is not only the general practice (or *exis*) of respectability which the man of respectability relates to it, but also every other individual *praxis*, every small innovation, and every addition (in clothing, for example).

These ephemeral creations and rapid events refer of themselves to generalised practice and through this to the totality-limitation which provides their full meaning. At this level, and from the serial point of view, it does not matter at all whether the innovation appears here or there, whether it is to be attributed to this individual or to that one, since it will always have been created *elsewhere* by *the Other*. Certain 'expressions' may appear, and be used by every *Other* for a season, in so far as he has received them from Others; or rather – as I have said – they do not move, but are indices of recurrence to which every Other refers; a certain walk is adopted – by nobody; everyone adopts it and then it is abandoned; a particular painter or actor is in vogue for a period, and is then forgotten. Each of these small serial events is of course rigidly conditioned beneath its apparent indeterminacy – like 'best-sellers', or personalities, characterised by some activity, immediately becoming alienated in the whole series, becoming objects of enthusiasm and then disappearing. The important point here is that everyone relates each of these manifestations to the untranscendable totality as the basic meaning of which it is a particular actualisation. And in one sense this is not false, since those who produced these objects or actions did so in a milieu which was already polarised by this totality, which, it is clear, is simply the class becoming the radical negation of the Other. Thus an ability for everyone to penetrate all products and manifestations comes to be constituted, in the milieu of the Other, as an adaptation of comprehension to practice.

Of course, the object is produced as other (through attempts to predict the taste of the Others by serial thinking or to determine it by other-direction) and it is comprehended and evaluated as other since everyone considers it from the point of view of whether it pleases the Others, and in order to make himself Other like them. This means that the structure of comprehension as practice remains unchanged, but that this practice becomes an *other comprehension*.[125] However, the *alterity* here is simply class-being: thus one comprehends a given picture or book *as a bourgeois*. In this way, class practice (the inert beyond) is reaffirmed, and the object comprehended is the concrete mediation between the one and the other. The result is not communication and *never* can be: there is nothing to communicate, since the same comprehension is present in everyone. Rather, every class event has a circular, shifting permeability for everyone, and every class 'mode' has a *solubility* in the class-substance. This class-substance, of course, is simply the inertia of a totalising rejection of any possibility of living for the other class; but the mere fact that each event (for example, the increasing influence of the Church between June 1848 and the end of the century) occurs within this limitation and is radicalised within it, means that there is a kind of tension peculiar to the bourgeois event:

125. This other-comprehension must not be confused with the comprehension of the Other. The latter, when direct, comprehends the Other as the same. I comprehend an action because I perform it or re-enact it. Complications may arise, especially when we try to base our comprehension on a situation or a history which is foreign to us. But in any case, if I make myself the Other by comprehension this is in order to transform him into myself. Other-comprehension, by contrast, is indirect: one is not trying to grasp either the object or the act as an immediate and real manifestation, nor is one trying to grasp the real actions of *the Other who comprehends them* (as a teacher might do if he was trying to find out why a pupil made a mistake). What one seeks to comprehend is the new manifestation; but one wants to do so through Others who have comprehended it and by re-enacting their process of comprehension. In fact, the practical movement is still a free operation but, in so far as I am alienated to the series, its limits come from the Other rather than from the object.

whether as *praxis* or as process, it is lived, produced, and comprehended as impelling itself towards a limitation which in fact represents its inner power of affirmation, its practical efficacity. And as this event is necessarily elsewhere and will transform the *here* into an *elsewhere* if it appears here (whereas a real, practical totalisation makes every local event a *here*), the inert totality – as a correlative of serial-being – becomes the determination of a homogeneous milieu of circularity (which is actually produced by the circulation of commodities, money and people) in which the event, as an index of radicalisation, is *produced* by everyone as Other in the equivalence between every elsewhere and every here (in the dissolution of every here in every elsewhere). *I* become the author of an action performed elsewhere in so far as I readopt it in a radicalising transcendence. This kind of *other-comprehension* is in fact peculiar: it arises as a transcendence of the comprehended fact towards a sort of 'third kind' of knowledge of this fact (in fact, this knowledge-mirage can be reduced to oppression as a rejection of the transcendent Other) and hence as a transcendence of the individual who comprehends towards membership of the class-totality (this totality being the inheritance of an ancient murder).

If I were to extend the study of this *milieu* (that of inert totalisation determining flight in alterity), I would refer to the various remarks I have made about serial thought at the practico-inert level of our investigation. All that needs to be observed here is that such thought contains a certain *truth*. In effect, the unity of radicalism, though it exists in the milieu of alterity, implies that the producers of the action or event (those directly responsible) completely transcend their own individual practice and passive activity to the degree that the other witnesses (those who are indirectly responsible) carry out this transcendence in comprehension. In the seriality of the heirs, comprehension and production are inseparable; especially as production very often involves reproduction. And, since we have already mentioned, in passing, the way people turned to the Church, especially after 1871 (though we should remember the Falloux law[126] after the June massacres), it is important to notice that there were always a few groups or individuals, from Thiers to Maurras, who cynically spelt out the meaning of the movement: a religion for the people. It should also be noticed that this signification-limitation (oppression through maintain-

126. A law of March 1850, permitting state funds to be given to Church schools, named after its author, Alfred Frédéric, Comte de Falloux (1811–86). [Ed.]

ing the people in superstition and ignorance) was communicated to the whole of the bourgeois class. In fact it had been present in all kinds of writings *ever since Waterloo*, beginning with Chateaubriand. Thus, as an inert and ancient shadow, it became a reference point, or in other words an Idea (in the Platonic sense), though an inert one, of the tasks which had to be performed *elsewhere by Others* (the priest, for example, who was responsible for supporting military oppression). But, at the same time, everyone became, *as Other*, a means of this Idea in the movement by which he comprehended it: he *helped* the Church. He made gifts to its local representatives and, like a government, tried to constitute their powers. Normally this was impossible unless the manufacturer himself became a Christian (so as not to be accused of Machiavellianism); in other words, his comprehension of the action of the sovereign and of quasi-official declarations was both that the proletariat had to be changed by the priests *so as to avoid* changing the bourgeoisie, and that the bourgeoisie could not avoid change unless it changed itself and grounded the new authority of the priest on the dissolution in it of the (serial) movement of de-Christianisation and on the emergence of a different recurrence (that of faith). For some of them, this comprehension was cynical; and it *could* be cynical for all, since its cynical signification was already present as a simple, *direct* connection between the measures taken or planned and the totalised signification as an inert negation which guided them. But equally, it *could* be lived, *by everyone*, in non-cynicism: this depends entirely on the particular circumstances. The need for a religion for the people might be connected with individual feelings of frustration, anxiety, etc. In this case, the need would become man's need for a religion. But within this universalisation, the Christian bourgeois would be re-asserting the class utility of faith in a way that was *scarcely* different: the worker who is also a believer is *integrated*, and his belief in heaven compensates for the vanity of his terrestrial existence; the wicked people who had infected the lower classes with atheism not only offended God, but also, necessarily, set the workers against the employers.

In order to see how easy it was in the nineteenth century to make the transition from the one signification to the other, one need only read one of the first texts to pose the question – Alfred de Musset's *Confession d'un enfant du siècle*. He attacks the bourgeois Revolution for having de-Christianised France: he sees this de-Christianisation as one of the main factors of the sickness of the age (that is, the bourgeois sickness, his own anxiety) and, at the same time, as an attack both on the rights of the poor and on the social order; the poor had the right to a faith which promised those who deserved it an eternity of happiness. If they were deprived of this faith, there would be terrible disorders which would have to be repressed in order to save society. But did Musset regard *this faith*, the only right of the exploited, as a genuine revelation of religious truth, or simply as an illusion which should not be dissipated – which would bring him very close to cynicism? Alfred de Musset did not choose: he resented the atheists for being right and he resented God for justifying them by his silence; he saw an equivalence between the dissipation of his own life and the revolts of the workers: both would disappear if the Church were to regain its strength. This *middle* position involved a complete comprehension of the *class signification* of a given conversion or individual action. From one moment to another, and in a single individual, it can disintegrate either into a mysticism of pure isolation (for one moment), or into a negativity against the individual himself (Musset's ethylism was partly due to his 'loss of God') or else it may dessicate into Machiavellian cynicism: all for the sake of mystifying the poor. But all these forms of objective class-spirit are equivalent in that they all contain the same determination to force the people to believe; and none of them – least of all the Machiavellian one – could claim to be the privileged form, expressing the relation of the practices to the signification-limitation in its purity: in effect, since this relation exists *everywhere*, all its practical realisations are equivalent. In other words, the relation: 'religion for the people ↔ practice of oppression' is immediately given, but as the simple orientation of an indeterminate transcendence; the determinations will be equivalent *a priori* until one or other of them shows itself to be more effective as the religious means of oppression.

It is not surprising that this *comprehension* on the part of the heirs made them open to every *group* practice aimed at maintaining oppression. In fact, its origin lies in the *use-truth* of the previous generation in so far as it is reinteriorised by the heirs as a free limitation on their freedom. And this use-truth was already grasped through the other-direction of the other by pressure-groups (and possibly by the sovereign). Taken up as a totality-limitation (class obligations, oppression as everyone's duty towards the other, etc.), its community determination lies in the class action of a practical community. And through the comprehension of the common action, the other is determined as a common individual in seriality. This inert determination, received from outside, does not change his statute, but it constitutes itself in alterity, as jointly responsible, in so far as he reinteriorises the *praxis* of the group (making it his own as Other). We have in fact seen the objective class-spirit defining itself in the form of a *current*; but, in that case, its origin was at infinity. In this new experience, however, seriality is manipulated by groups, that is to say, it is other-directed. The difference between the two generations is that the heirs are conscious of this other-direction and *comprehend* it in so far as they become its agent (by acting on themselves and on Others).

If we now return to French Malthusianism as the practice of the heirs, we can now comprehend all the conditions of the problem. We did not see how this practice could have a common meaning grasped by all the agents, while it is realised partly in different production-groups and partly by seriality.

(iii) *Class Struggle in the Twentieth Century*

At the end of the nineteenth century, class hatred in France was as virulent as ever and the third generation of employers saw themselves as constituted in their diachronic and *past* unity by two memorable massacres which themselves produced a future of bloodshed. But, on the other hand, material circumstances changed in the process of exploitation. Up to 1914, industry enjoyed a new period of expansion (owing to circumstances which have been thoroughly analysed by economists). The result was an intensification of the contradiction between oppression and exploitation. We have already seen how oppression supports and constitutes the process of exploitation in the milieu of the collectives. But of itself the movement of oppression leads to the extermination of the oppressed if they should revolt, while exploitation demands their (at least partial) co-operation as a work force. The contradiction was particularly acute since the entire social history of nineteenth-century France produced the exploited as objects of bloody violence and, consequently, as possible subjects of a ruthless insurrection at the moment when industrialisation and concentration were expanding the proletariat and increasing the value of the human-commodity (labour power). This contradiction was deepened after the 1914–18 war, because the advent of specialised machines led to further deskilling: the employers gained from this transformation in so far as it tended to destroy the old union structures and the practices of the anarcho-syndicalist struggle; and they lost partly because pre-war unionism had tended to demand State intervention, which entailed control of the unions by the sovereign apparatus, and partly because, if it continued unabated, deskilling would increase the homogeneity of the working class, so that the (relatively limited) activities of the skilled élites would be replaced by the more profoundly revolutionary activities of the masses, which would always be more dangerous for the régime. On the other hand, the capitalist process itself – if it was not interfered with – would develop itself to the full – as the development of the United States in that period proved. How could there be limitation of exploitation without limitation of profits? This question is revealing: this limitation is imposed on the process from outside and is not produced by the process itself in its practico-inert development. On the contrary, this development, in its passive activity, leads to mass-production, the transformation of the working class and agreements between employers (trusts, cartels, etc.), etc. Malthusianism was an oppressive and radical response based on a rejection: French capitalists rejected the free development of the process in order to save their class. This rejection was already present, as an inert-limitation of any change; it appeared, so to speak, as an *a priori* determination of the objective spirit and as an immediate schema for the comprehension of the Other by the Other and for his radicalisation. This limitation on industrialisation had the significance of an oppression: it attempted to limit the increase of the working population, and, if possible, to reverse the demographic movement so as to reduce the danger of concentrations; it was aimed at halting the transformations of the working class which were developing under the influence of the means of production in such a way as to maintain heterogeneous sectors within it and to oppose these milieux with conflicts of interest; it was a refusal to perform its historical function (specialised machine ↔ mass exploitation-production) and to contribute to raising the standard of living, in so far as it had the power to prevent it. This effectively meant:

(1) That the dominant class wished to have strict control of births in the working class. In fact, in spite of official hypocrisy, working-class households were forced to adopt Malthusian practices in the inter-war period. This explains the example given above. I said that the working woman who had an abortion was executing a sentence passed by the bourgeoisie. What we can now comprehend is why it is *a sentence*. The abortion is violence both to the woman and to a life, and

it is the violence of bourgeois society. The woman herself, and the friend who finds help for her, and the nurse (*faiseuse d'anges*) if one can be found, will discover this violence (as fury and despair) only by interiorising the *concerted* impossibility of a working-class household providing for the needs of an additional child. Since the economic process, by leading to mass-production, increases the demand for manpower, halting the process, so as to keep labour under a perpetual threat of unemployment and so as to keep it always slightly larger than the number of jobs available, *is an oppressive use of the right of life and death*. This oppression is complemented, of course, by the attitude of the dominant classes to working-class mortality: as we know, every society selects its dead. But the choice is made at the level of the upper classes (both through the sovereign – overall policy, budget, improvement of working conditions, hygiene – and through class-seriality – the improvement of premises, hygiene, workers' protection laws, attempts to eliminate fatal risks or occupational diseases). This means that the French employers – in the historical perspective of a bloody struggle, which was never forgotten, and which might be resurrected at any time – proceeded, after the troubles of 1919, to a controlled extermination of the working class by controlling births and by deciding not to prevent deaths.

(2) This practice was inseparable from the refusal to expand the market. Precisely because production *remained the same*, there was a convergence between industry's refusal to take on new workers and the deliberate and sustained impossibility of the working-class family having another child. If we approach this second aspect of the oppressive practice without referring to any of the recent, mistaken interpretations of the law of immiseration, and if, *like Marx himself*, we interpret it as relative, and recognise the undeniable fact that industrialisation raises everyone's standard of living, then it is important to recognise a truth which economism conceals from us: that the deliberately oppressive practice of the French bourgeoisie perpetuated an *abnormally low* standard of living (contradicting both the practico-inert consequences of the second industrial revolution and the standards of living of other 'advanced' capitalist countries). It oppressed the population as a whole in order to keep the working class in chains.

(3) In the context of this *managed scarcity* (the deliberate intensification of scarcity as a negative force), the contradictions between the workers as individual sellers of their labour power, already overcome by union practice, were transformed into contradictions between

different working-class *milieux* (skilled workers against specialised workers, state employees against workers in private industry, workers on fixed wages against workers on piece-rates, etc.) and the unions, confirming these splits with their own progressively petrifying sovereignty, themselves became agents of disunity for the working class. But they derived their destructive violence from the practice of the employers. Their conflicts installed the oppressive force which perpetuated the splits by impeding the economic process within the working class. The oppression, here, consisted in perpetuating temporary dissensions by perpetuating the French *situation*. It was a case of divide and rule. Aborting, starving and dividing, the bourgeois class continued the massacre. It arbitrarily expanded the already overfull tertiary strata at the expense of the secondary ones in order to aggravate the class tension between white-collar and blue-collar workers (*employés et prolétaires*). It reduced the enemy class to impotence, that is to say, to realising its class-being as a condemnation by the enemy.

This radical oppression is obviously *class-totality as praxis* and as the untranscendable signification of every proprietor's activities. In this sense, it might be said that oppression in its new form is automatically defined for everyone as Other (as alienating his own activity) in terms of new circumstances and as a rigid exigency. Since there has to be a permanent, controlled adaptation of the proletariat to production (and of production to the proletariat), repressive extermination could not be accomplished by means of massacres: discontinuous, brutal blood-lettings such as these do not have the value of a constant readjustment and progressive diminution of the working class. What was required was clearly a permanent, controlled blood-letting. And above all, since the historical past of the working class gave it a considerable experience of violence and consequently an equal though only potential violence, French *radicalism* continued to define itself as the impossibility of change, as the obligation to maintain the *status quo*. Around 1930 *all* employers interpreted *all* the practices of *the Other* employers in this teleological light.

But we have now demonstrated the contradictory exigencies without explaining the *praxis* which transcends these contradictions. How could the rate of profit be sustained or even increased while the rate of production growth fell to zero?

I have already explained elsewhere the Malthusian solution: large-scale industry increases productivity without increasing production; thus it reduces costs and manpower. But in retaining its poor French markets – without bothering to seek other outlets – it made more or less clandestine pacts with the small manufacturers whom its Malthusianism preserved and who produced the same commodities at higher cost: large-scale industry would fix its prices to match those of these small, out-dated enterprises whose very existence was gradually damaging the French economy. Oppression took the form of a double mystification: for the public, the small enterprises were covers for the big firms which were guaranteed considerable profits through selling what cost them least at the *highest* price (which *was the lowest* from the point of view of the small manufacturers). By increasing individual productivity (purchases of improved machinery, rationalisation, productivity bonuses, etc.), while maintaining production at a constant level, the industrialists forced workers to become agents of the controlled extermination in their own class. In fact it was *through the workers* – through their efforts to earn as much as possible, thereby raising the norms for their kind of work – that the probability of any given worker finding employment in the totality of French industry was rigidly determined in the domain of serial alienation. And of course in all phases of capitalism, the engagement of one worker represented negatively for an Other the possibility of not getting any work (except in a period of full employment, that is to say, in specific circumstances and at very special times). But this was a mere truism and it was the worker as an inert commodity (even before he began work) who eliminated an other human-commodity. In the case of Malthusianism, this mystification led the worker to destroy, unwittingly, the possibility of life and work for some *Other* member of the working class since the effect of this would not have been – as in unimpeded mass-production – to develop production itself and indirectly to increase the manpower needs of an industry in full development; on the contrary, his free organic adaptation to tasks, norms and new machines was necessarily expressed for the employers as a cut in their manpower requirements.

Such, then, was the *device*. By this I mean the real practice which resolved the modern contradictions between oppression and exploitation, between profit and the *status quo*, to the detriment of the working class and of the entire French population. There can be no doubt about its oppressiveness. Or rather oppression initially presented itself as a radical rejection of all change. Within this totalising obligation, various economic groups developed Malthusianism as the means *for them* (for a given large-scale industrial organisation) to surrender to the class exigency, and especially to secure their own control of their workers. Here again, everything is perfectly intelligible: it is simply a matter of translating a determination which is already inscribed in the practico-inert into *practice*. But if this practice by certain groups became a class practice, involving all other groups (or individuals) as others, this is because it presented itself as immediately interpretable in the serial milieu of the objective class-spirit, and because everyone comprehended it and transcended it towards radical negation both as untranscendability and as the common end of the totalised class (and of each group or person). But this comprehension must be the production *over there* of other action in so far as everyone, as Other, is the Other who produces it, and it must also be the re-production *here* (that is to say, in the elsewhere that contains my Other-Being for the Others), in so far as everyone is responsible to the class (for the radical rejection, as the limit which must never be crossed for fear of betraying the class), by and for all the Others. There was no conspiracy, no deliberation, no communication, and no common regroupment, except in the case of the powerful groups which created and inaugurated the practice. Everything took place serially, and *Malthusianism* as an economic process is seriality. But whenever possible, the activity of each local group or of each individual freely re-produced the movement of comprehension and was frequently indistinguishable from it.

Thus we come back to the case of collective responsibility which we considered above. It was in fact the comprehension of the Malthusianism of the Others and the deliberate (and not just imposed) adaptation of production *here* (for example, as the production of objects of immediate consumption) to production *over there* and *everywhere* (Malthusian production in mining industries, in machine-tool factories and, ultimately, everywhere) which, in the domain of the Other, became the Malthusianism of everyone. The contraction of production was a circular phenomenon: everyone anticipated the Malthusianism of the Others in determining his own production, and he conditioned this Malthusianism by basing his own production (and the needs which it engendered) on it in advance. Through this circularity, every manufacturer or group of manufacturers not only *created* Malthusianism but also perceived it *elsewhere* as a process to which he had to adapt. Everyone's Malthusianism was *induced*: I could not produce any more because I would run out of raw materials, means of production, etc. and, ultimately, of customers. But it also *induces*: I am the Other by reference to whom the Other will regulate his production. *At the same time*, everyone's mere adaptation to circular Malthusianism, as the practical comprehension of Malthusianism-*praxis*, is an act of oppression everywhere: everyone artificially limits production or its rate of increase by free practices of violence through which there appear two inert significations, one in laterality ('I must adapt myself to the other'), and the other as a totalised limit ('I comprehend the activity and I contribute to it through the class imperative') and as the intelligible beyond of every living activity. Determined by the deliberate (but still careful) *praxis* of inducing groups, Malthusianism as the circular reduction of production (in that each producer regulates *social production* both by his own production and by the wages he pays) is realised and continued, as a process, by the ready comprehension of the original action, that is to say, by its reproduction as a brutal limit of spending power, and therefore of the workers' possibility of living. Malthusianism is oppression in so far as the *a priori* limit imposed by the factory on its production is determined for the manufacturers by the limit beyond which their class would no longer be possible, that is to say, by the limit which their class imposes on the other *by oppression*. Malthusianism is a *praxis*-process in so far as this historical particularisation of the *praxis* of oppression necessarily implies various practico-inert modifications in the process of exploitation. There are of course other forms of oppression, specifically in those countries which have experienced class oppression without civil war (paternalism and neo-paternalism, 'human engineering', etc.). These have developed from existing circumstances, on the basis of existing conditions of production and power relations, and within perspectives which have been partially transformed by techniques and property relations. I will not describe them here (or even the attempts, in France itself in certain sectors of industry, to bring about, simultaneously, deconcentration, neo-paternalism and the destruction of Malthusianism). All we should notice here is that the individual practices of *struggle* (in a given society, organisation, etc.) necessarily support the marginal and circular process of exploitation, and that individual oppression itself is comprehended, quite innocently, as conditioned everywhere else (it is not me, it is the Others, I have *no choice* but to close this workshop) and also, in unitary good conscience, as the realisation *here* of untranscendable class-being, in so far as the individual *praxis* inscribes itself in an imperious and totalised practice.

I have used the example of Malthusianism in order to illustrate the *minimum* meaning which must be given to *class struggle* if it is to be described as the motive-force of History (rather than simply saying that this motive-force lies in the economic process and its objective contradictions). In fact, this is the whole point. Although our dialectical investigation, having made its first approaches to the concrete, is very far from being complete, we can now say (without having even encountered historical fact yet, except as a simple temporalisation, solidified in the past and transcended), that it is possible to discover something like meaning in the development of societies and men provided we recognise that the reciprocal relations of groups, of classes and generally of all social formations (collectives, communities) are *basically practical*, that is to say, that they realise themselves through reciprocal activities of mutual aid, alliance, war, oppression, etc., regardless of their type and mode of realisation apart from this (we have noticed the complexity of the practice of oppression, which constantly evolves with History and with the process). That *reification* will, in some circumstances, be one of the results (in alterity) of such a practical relation between multiplicities – whether structured or not – and that it should be interiorised everywhere as the absolute exteriority of human relations, in both the oppressed and the oppressing classes, and that the relation which unites the multiplicities (whether allied or hostile) may consequently contain an induced inertia, an interiorised exteriority which of itself tends to reification – all this is necessary; or rather, it is the necessity (as far as it is revealed) of universal alienation in practical multiplicities which are mediated by inorganic materiality. But if one were to reduce the relations of practical multiplicities to simple contradictory determinations, produced, whether simultaneously or not, by the development of a process – for example, if one were to suppose that the proletariat must be the coming destroyer of the bourgeoisie simply because the progressive diminution of variable and increase of fixed capital, by increasing the productivity of the worker and decreasing the overall spending power of the working class, will, from one crisis to another, produce the economic catastrophe in which the bourgeoisie will be engulfed – one would end up by reducing men to pure anti-dialectical moments of the practico-inert.

However, our dialectical investigation shows the double determination of constituted *praxis*. At every level, even inside a group as soon as it ceases to be fused, constituted *praxis* is characterised by lateral flight, that is to say, by various forms of inertia, alterity and recurrence. *At the same time*, and *even in a collective*, constituted *praxis* retains its basic character as a dialectical activity which transforms the practical field by an *intelligible* reorganisation of means for an end and which sees the end as an objective determination of the field of future possibilities on the basis of needs, dangers, 'interests', etc., conditioned by previous circumstances as a whole. *Praxis*, as the action of a multiplicity, is far from being an opacity in dialectical rationality. On the contrary, dialectical rationality implies the basic priority of constituted *praxis* over Being and even over *exis*, simply because in itself this rationality is nothing but the *praxis* of the multiplicity in so far as it is maintained and produced by free organic *praxis*. Without constituted *praxis*, everything would disappear, including alienation, since there would no longer be anything, even reification, to alienate, since man would be an inert thing by birth, and it is impossible to reify a thing. This does not mean that there is no point in making a careful distinction, in each case, between individual *praxis*, common, constituted *praxis* and *praxis*-process. But it does mean that these three modalities of human action are in themselves distinct from the practico-inert process and that they are its foundation. It is even possible – as we have just shown – to see one and the same development both as a *praxis* (oppression) and as a process (exploitation), and that the process constantly conditions the *praxis* (the economic crisis of the last years of the July monarchy as an infantile illness of capitalism producing, for the bourgeois class, the need for repression and its avowed character as civil war). Provided one takes care to determine what modes of rationality one is employing, all of this is still completely intelligible – *provided* that analytical Reason and economic Reason are finally dissolved in the constituted dialectic or (and this amounts to the same thing) that the transformations and avatars of *praxis* are always resumed in circularity and that its alienations, at every level, as a series of necessities of which it is both the mystified victim and the fundamental support, are demonstrated. Whatever kind of multiplicity men may belong to, their individual and common relations, whether reified or not, are *primarily practical*. Whether it is mediated or not, what exists between them is a reciprocity. And this reciprocity may be either an alliance or a conflict.

In a society in which one class owns the instruments of labour while others use them to produce commodities for a wage, it is precisely matter and the practico-inert object *which mediate between men*. And this is apparent in the investigation itself, since – insurrections and massacres apart – the pressure of each class on the Other is manifested in relation to machines: imports of English machines by French weavers in 1830, and of American semi-automatic machines about 1913, were determinations of the proletariat by the employers (wage cuts, deskilling); machine-breaking (as the uncontrolled reaction of a proletariat which was still unconscious of itself), the occupation of the factories in 1936 (as the devising of a tactic appropriate to a new situation) – these are all forms of working-class resistance. But the permanent presence of the forces of order is the real reason for these visible breakdowns: when they are outmanoeuvred, the employer and the worker stand face to face, without intermediary. Oppression, as a *praxis* based on the existence of armed forces, consists precisely in using this violence at rest (and not unleashing it unless it is unavoidable) so that the antagonistic relations remain at the level of the machine, that is to say, of the practico-inert, of necessity, etc.

If the working class is able to respond, its response is anti-repressive, organised violence: strikes are violent – as I have shown elsewhere – in that they present themselves as a breach of contract. Of course, strikes are violence against violence, but in the context of bourgeois democracy, even when they are legal, they appear as *the first violence.* This violence is an action: not against the machines, but against the employer himself (and, through him, against the enemy class), in so far as he is identified with his interests (alienation) and in so far as he is capable, from this point of view, of a practical reassessment of the forces involved, the risks incurred, and the possible concessions. Finally, it is an innovation in that its form varies with the historical development of the process and the consequent changes in the working class. From this point of view, and to complement the example of Malthusianism, it would be possible to show how the strikes of 1936 were *both* a serial transmission *and* an anti-repressive action of *the* working class. After years of recession and repression, the presence of popular parties in the government created everywhere an equivalent of class totality as the inert beyond of their activity. But on this basis the worker saw both the future of his class and his own future as an opening-up of the field of possibilities, that is to say, as a *future to be made.*

After the compression of the previous years, this was the determination of future practice as *common freedom.* It was in this climate that the first strikes occurred; they were not immediately imitated, on account of the embarrassed semi-silence of the left-wing press; but as soon as the socialist and communist organs had been forced to reveal them, the movement spread to the whole of France. Now this was obviously a serial movement. Of course, the occupation of a particular factory represented a dissolution of the series in favour of a pledged group. Nevertheless, there was a seriality of groups, in so far as the material circumstances of the new practice separated each occupying group from every Other, not only by distance but also by the walls of the occupied factory. But what corresponded to the totalised class as the radicalism of everyone's comprehension was that the comprehension of the new practice *was itself radical – first*, because it was inseparable from the production by everyone of the particular group; *secondly*, because it appeared in serial alterity as the new tactic, and, in its real movement, defined not only the material conditions which it transcended (the struggle against the abstract interchangeability of specialised workers) but also the meaning of this transcendence as a compensation for the structures of weakness by a reorganisation of methods of struggle (the transformation of the practical constitution of strikes, etc.); and *lastly*, because it saw this restructuring of action in terms of the indefinite opening-up of the field of possibilities.

In relation to the radicalisation of the exploiting class, this radicalising comprehension is the only true, living radicalisation, since it presents the totality of the exploited class in the light of an infinite task: up to that time, reality had merely been the necessity of living the impossibility of living, but it now became the *need to attempt* the practical realisation of a world where the impossibility of human life would be the only impossibility. And this realisation was not only *entirely present* as the complex meaning of the Popular Front and of the factory occupations (for the staff, occupying the factory is, ultimately, allowing oneself to be determined in the present by the future, as common freedom and no longer as destiny), but also the infinite beyond of every action for the individual and the constitution, by the future which was to be made, of the present activity *as a beginning* for the entire group. Everyone remembers that the occupation movement was accompanied, at least at the beginning, by disregard for union sovereignty. Consequently, an institutional, organised unification of the class, or attempt to transform the contagional tactics of the groups into a class strategy, was completely impossible. So there is no justification for comparing the working class to a practical community – though seriality was everywhere fused. Series of individuals were dissolved and series of groups were formed. And, from this point of view, that is to say from the point of view of the class ensemble, every organised *praxis* of occupation everywhere supported a process by which every group was affected as Other by the Others. Nevertheless:

(1) every member of every group discovered the objective class-spirit as the permeability of every common undertaking to comprehension; and (2) everyone saw his class totality as an infinite temporalisation, that is to say, both as a genuine task (whereas for the oppressors their inert totality is an illusion) and as common freedom; and (3) the practical unity of the occupations as *praxes-processes* (which were both contagious and realised by free pledged communities) lay in the receptivity of the other class, in so far as it *suffered* a complete cessation of production as a totalising negation (a counter-violence objectifying itself in the other class).

In this last sense, if we reduce the number of classes to two in order to simplify the schema, we might say that each class finds its unity in the Other, in a double form and in perpetual disequilibrium – both as a unifying threat of extermination, and as a totalisation which is sovereignly totalised by the action-process whose objective unity lies in the totalised object. Now, the contradiction between these two unities (negative and positive, suffered and produced), the temporal development of this contradiction, the internal tension which it causes and the reciprocity of this existence-outside-oneself-in-the-other are intelligible only in and through the lived, practical bond of antagonistic reciprocity. In fact, in so far as the objectification of a *praxis* occurs in a hostile milieu and through the organisation and reorganisation of enemy groups (whether or not there is also a seriality of these groups), it is very different from any objectification which may arise through the physico-chemical determinations of inorganic matter or through the modifications of a collective (by work on the impotent inertia of seriality): it is, in fact, *suffered* and *readopted*. For example, the working class was able to grasp its own unity, through the action of the employers, during the strikes of 1936, that is to say – roughly speaking – through the Matignon agreements. In other words, the action of the defeated, being both free and totally constrained (or required), produced the free unity of the victor by free surrender and through this freedom. The victorious working class *really was united* in the exigency-constraint which was maintained and produced as its limit by the action of the employers. The working class here was a totalising re-interiorisation of the serial propagation of strikes by the qualified delegates of the employers. It was united *for itself*, rather than for the employers – for it does not matter whether the employers believed in the real unity of the class or whether they believed that they were conceding to some passing disturbance; it does not matter much whether they were trying to prevent social revolution or whether they were making temporary concessions with the intention of winning them back one by one afterwards. What counts is what they did, and it was their real *praxis* of surrender which designated the proletariat to itself as a unity and a power. This was the unity which is produced by serial operations, and which returns to constitute them in and for themselves as a unified class *praxis* through the mediation of the Other. But the other unity (as a perpetual developing unification and as the danger of being exterminated or reduced to impotence and shaped as a collective which can be manipulated according to practico-inert laws) always manifested itself – even at the moment of temporary defeats – as the already reviving initiative of the other class, as a free *praxis* whose means and immediate objectives were still unknown or were only gradually revealing themselves: demobilised too soon by the unions and by associated parties, the working class after 1937 not only discovered its sovereign unity as a subject in the practices which it imposed on the employers, but also perceived the danger of being sovereignly totalised, in the disquieting and ever more numerous indications that the employers were gathering their forces for some underhand and uncontrollable action (price rises, etc.). At this level, in effect, the *praxis* of the employers was seen as a determination of the working class by and through its serial impotence, and the class found itself to be designated as though this impotence had been produced by the employers' *praxis* itself. The balance of forces constantly determined the tensions between the unity-power of the class-subject and the unity-impotence of the class-object. But in any case this double, contradictory unity *came to each class through the Other* and its tension indicated the objective dangers of the current undertaking, that is to say, the relations between the two extreme possibilities of total victory and total defeat. We have already seen how the objectifying totalisation (the project of extermination as a unity through the totalising *praxis* of annihilation) came to each series on the basis of the enemy group and, by itself, caused a dissolution of seriality in fused groups. This is because the series, through every Other, perceived its negative totalisation as entirely imposed (practico-inert), whereas in reality, defeat was partly imposed (the massacres of June 1848) and partly reinteriorised and reproduced by free actions which were both demanded and inevitable. Thus the class was haunted by its totalised being as a collective in so far as it could always be produced by the Other as long as it accepted it in seriality. But, in reality, its defeat would be temporalised in and by it through common actions (of submission, sham death, etc.) which would be performed in its name by a few groups, or by the sovereign group, where there was one.

In this way, one can see that the unity of two struggling classes is a fact of antagonistic reciprocity and that this contradictory unity of each in the Other is occasioned by *praxis* and by *praxis* alone. In other words, it is conceivable – as a pure, formal, logical hypothesis – that there should be a Universe in which practical multiplicities would not form themselves into classes (for example, a Universe where *scarcity* would not be the basic relation between the practical agent and his environment). But *if classes do exist,* then it is necessary to make a choice: *either* they should be defined in inertia as strata of society with no more unity than the compact inertia revealed by geological sections; *or* their moving, changing, fleeting, ungraspable yet *real* unity comes to them from other classes in so far as each is bound to all the others by a practical reciprocity of either a positive or a negative kind. If the unity of each is not directly occasioned by the *praxis* of the Other and if it is not produced through everyone's own *praxis* as his real action on the Other, then, on our abstract assumption (two classes, negative reciprocity), everything will scatter to infinity – and *first* of all the practico-inert itself. This means that the unity of each class depends on that of the Other and, above all, that this dependence is due not to some dialectical magic but to a real project of violence which incorporates the other unity as a practical factor of its own.

3 *Class Struggle as a Conflict of Rationalities*

We have been considering two classes. In each we have observed three concrete types of multiplicity: the group-institution or sovereign; combat-groups (or pressure-groups, propaganda-groups, etc.); and seriality. And we have observed, in the first place, that for both classes, each type of multiplicity is the mediation and the totalising signification of the other two. This has led us to see class unity not as a gathering together of inert molecules through the efforts of an institutionalised sovereign, but as the circularity of a movement of mediation, containing reversals such as seriality itself, despite its fleeting being, becoming the mediating unity between sovereign groups and pledged groups. As we have said, unity, at all levels, exists *in mediation*; and the circularity of the mediations is expressed both by a circular simultaneity *and* by a cyclical movement of the unities. The former tends to remultiply unity, while the latter gives it its dialectical truth, which is *temporalisation*. But this dialectical, practical temporalisation will lack both meaning and effective reality unless it is a *real action*, and this real action cannot exist unless the need for it arises from the situation as defined by the action of the Other. Thus it is a *reaction* to an action of the hostile class aimed at totalising it as an inert object. But this reaction also leads it to experience itself in the index of tension which represents its contradictory unity (subject-object) *in the enemy himself* through the significations he produces in it and through the reinteriorisation of his practices. If, for example, the class, in the course of a victorious battle, perceives its freedom as the inert limitation which penetrates the freedom of the Other, it is through the circularity of synthetic mediations that it will perceive itself as a free common unity; that is, the synthetic freedom of the victorious *praxis* will itself be the unity of unifying mediations. But this unity (the sovereign as group and the series as sovereign both refer, through their diverse structures, to the sovereignty of *their* class over the Other) is necessarily *in the Other* since it is, in fact, the falsification and alteration of his freedom. Thus the class is connected to its transcendent unity through the mediation of the other class. It is *united* outside itself in the suffered freedom of the Other.

But we have also seen the serial process of radical comprehension, in so far as it reproduces class actions on the basis of a radicalising totalisation, as the objective class spirit, or as the condition of the class's permeability to itself. This totalisation represents class-being as a limitation, that is to say, as a negation of the Other. And this negation is not only an inertia, but also a remanence, as a past particularisation of a particular class history, that is to say, of certain actions and their mortgages of the future. Now, it is precisely this transcended practice which creates the inert impossibility of surrender (the *threshold* which cannot be crossed (*dépassé*)) *in so far as*, in the past, it produced the other class and its history (as the inert unity of its temporalised temporalisation and of the mortgages of the future which it has engendered). The intransigence of French employers at the end of the nineteenth century was due to the massacres of 1848 and 1871. But this means that they *comprehended in the other class* what it is to have the past of a massacred class. And, conversely, this impossibility of surrender gradually developed, through the actions of the bourgeoisie, working-class radicalism. On the basis of a past of civil war, this radicalism, as a concrete unity of practical comprehension (as the permeability of all action to every comprehension *in the class*), was the impossibility of tolerating the impossibility of living, that is to say, the necessity of creating another reality by destroying *this present reality*. By absolutely rejecting change, the bourgeoisie constituted change – any adjustment that might be called for here or there on the basis of the pressure of needs – as the radical rejection of the bourgeoisie, if not in its detailed aspect (a rise of X per cent still being perfectly *possible* within the framework of capitalist exploitation, and scarcely affecting the profits of the enterprise) then at least in a vista of infinite change.

No doubt it will be objected that the radicalisation was mainly due to the discovery by the workers of their class situation, of the consequences of exploitation, and of the absolute necessity of transforming this situation. And there can be no doubt that the work of the militants (unionists and politicians) consisted throughout the nineteenth century in producing class reflexivity in the working class *on the basis* of the determinations which it suffered in impotence. And the first phase of this awareness was to be the systematic interpretation of practico-inert processes. But, in so far as the proletariat was a series, and thus affected, like all series, with impotence and with a tendency to limit action and to be satisfied with superficial, temporary advances; in so far as, in the field of appearance produced by bourgeois oppression, reality appeared to the proletariat as the impossibility of being other than it is; in so far as the concrete changes called for were always modest for everyone, the workers were affected by a spontaneous reformism. And this reformism simply expresses something which exists in everyone in his relations with every other (except for the oppressor in relation to the oppressed): the practice of conciliation (generally reinforced by the existence of mediating third parties). In a sense, the oppressed who were born into oppression, heirs of the oppressed, would be content with slight improvements: they would see these improvements as in themselves a total transformation of the situation. Obviously, in fact, they *believed* that they would be content with them. Nevertheless, an exploiting class which was immediately favourable to improvements (even after one or two generations) would have produced a completely different working class (with the same structures, but different internal relations, a different tension) and might perhaps have postponed revolutionary radicalisation for a time.

The reformism of the British proletariat seems to be due to several related factors: I will just mention the colonial super-profits which prevented Britain from suffering international crises with the violence which, in France, produced the February revolution, and British foreign policy, which meant that it got involved in only a few, distant actions in Europe, with limited objectives, and that these never did, or even could, place the country itself in danger in the way that our war against Prussia did.[127] In fact, the hypothesis of a progressive bourgeoisie is in itself absurd, at least as far as the nineteenth century is concerned. Today the possessing classes, through neo-paternalism and the practices of 'Human Engineering', attempt to reconcile the two roles in which they have cast the masses (as customers, and as wage-earners). They attempt to construct a mobile and complex system in which concessions are always possible (and may even anticipate demands), thus concealing from the exploited the radicalism of the exploiter. But this neo-paternalism presupposes a certain level of industrial development; it was not conceivable in the nineteenth century and, in the scarcity which was so brutally revealed during crises (poverty in 1845–8, poverty and war in 1870–1), the bourgeoisie produced itself as having either to kill or to disappear. By taking this line (which was undoubtedly an interiorisation of the situation by heirs whose reaction was already determined by their interiorised past), the bourgeoisie produced *at a stroke* a reciprocity of radicalisation. (This might even, from an otherwise abstract and purely formal point of view, taking no account of inertia, appear as an infinite to-and-fro.) In any case, the inducing class was *the bourgeois class*. And no doubt it will be said that accumulation (as a process) could not fail

127. Each proletariat derives its constituted violence (what might be called its violence-character) not only from the real conditions of production and from the structures proper to the worker, but also from its own history. The glorious, violent history of the French bourgeoisie and the glorious, violent history of the Italian bourgeoisie and people in the nineteenth century have been interiorised by the proletariats which have always been the real agents of social transformations. In both cases, internal violence has been an excuse for the bourgeoisie to shed blood and has thus been reinforced by this mediation. The impotence of the bourgeoisie in Germany, particularly in Prussia, when confronted by a military landed aristocracy, is also expressed in the rather mild reformism of social democracy, of trade unions and of a large section of the proletariat, etc.

to cost millions of human lives, that it required the poverty of the worker as a condition for social enrichment. No doubt this is broadly true, but we can see that it is never quite true in detail (the refusal to reburn toxic smoke, for example). In other words, capitalists in this period assumed that it was necessary for Others to be poor; and to assume the poverty of others is to acquiesce in producing it, and thus to *transcend* the assumed necessity by a free adoption of its laws and its themes; it is to justify this free transformation of necessity into oppression in terms of a class Manichaeism which designates the oppressed as anti-humans who *deserve their oppression*, and thus to condemn them to it. Lastly, it is to make this necessity-freedom even more intolerable for the oppressed, in that it presents itself as a *condemnation* of the exploited (a free human sentence) *by things* (the 'inexorable' laws of liberal economics).

Oppression based on radicalisation (as an assumption of scarcity by a still undeveloped capitalism) was to be the real force permitting a radicalisation of the practices of workers' struggle. One important fact of nineteenth-century history is that the workers experienced the absolute intransigence of the employers. They wished (initially) *to reach a mutual understanding as men*; and they gradually realised that this was impossible, *because, to their employers, they were not men*. This class racism is essential for the comprehension of the workers' movement in the nineteenth century: at first it was animated by a respect for property, faith in the employers (those members of the bourgeoisie who, thanks to the strength of the working-class, had improved the political system and still claimed to be the universal class). In about 1830, even the most advanced workers appear not even to have dreamed of introducing a socialist *sector* into the capitalist economy; they simply wished to insert a few production co-operatives amongst the employers' factories. Most of them were religious (many were straight from the country), and they used to criticise the bourgeoisie for their atheism. But, in France, the reversal of their position, or its radicalisation, has a very obvious origin: between 1830 and 1871 the bourgeoisie passed sentence on them. This means that their policy of brutal oppression was carried out through compulsion and in the workers' milieu as their condemnation of the workers by the supreme tribunal. So from this point of view too, oppressive activity was crucial: it burnt significations into the hearts of the oppressed class. These significations were ethical judgements (as the abstract general form of the considerations which would be the basis of real judgements meted out after repressive trials in the name of the constitution and of religious or moral principles) and these judgements were supposed to involve the oppressed themselves: had he not voted, for example? Was he not represented in the Assembly and therefore in the government? Had he not broken the social compact by striking, rioting, or rebelling? Had he not himself provided a justification for the precautions by men of order against his disruption?

This is how the judgement was formulated. The working class was thoroughly familiar with the system of values it related to and with the facts on which it was based. They learnt the first from propaganda, and the second was their own doing. The consequences of the assessment were widely diffused by newspapers: death sentences, imprisonments, deportation, etc. It was possible to mystify the proletariat: the worker appeared to have accepted the liberal system, Free Trade and the free wage contract; and since the employers apparently used no compulsion (*no one* is forced to work for him; and if someone makes trouble, the employer does not punish him, but simply regards the contract as broken, etc.), violence seems to arise in society, at times of crisis, from popular uprisings, strikes, etc. Did not, as Saint-Marc Girardin said, this *original* Barbarian violence justify apparatuses of permanent oppression (intended also, of course, to protect the workers against themselves)? In other words, we have seen how, for the oppressor, oppression is inseparable from the hatred he must feel for the oppressed. And this active hatred produces a number of significations and communicates them, *through reciprocal violence*, to the oppressed themselves. These unitary significations, at a certain level, represent a totalising conception of society, of classes and their respective roles. And, of course it is worth adding that the temporarily defeated class will always contain some individuals or even groups who will interiorise this conception.

Thus in the mid-nineteenth century the practice of struggle created in the working class the possibility of evaluating itself as the bourgeoisie did, that is to say of knowing itself, through the mediation of the Other and his Manichaeism, as the *absolutely other Object*; that is to say, as a servile-will, bound-to-do-evil, and ultimately as Other than man. When this characterisation was taken up and adopted, the mirage of the *Other-Unity* would disappear: this borrowed unity would dissolve into an *anti-humanism* whose universality would correspond point for point to bourgeois humanism and would justify it. But this synthetic ensemble of significations would still remain synthetic, since class practice would interiorise it and then reject it. In fact, as a material and totalised ensemble, and as a system, it is its own negation, produced in it as an imperative by the Other (through concrete exigencies: for example denouncing a given strike or insurrection) both because it refuses to give the statute of man to all workers and because it creates new divisions amongst them by distinguishing between the trouble-makers and the masses (who are stupid rather than vicious), between the bad worker (who is faithful to his class) and the good worker, who is a sort of tame animal who has achieved humanity by adopting the values and orders of the employers' humanism.

Now, it would be utterly inconceivable that this system should be interiorised, that it should – even for an instant, at a particular time and for specific people – present itself as a temptation, unless it is seen as more than an epiphenomenal ideology arising amongst the employers through the process of exploitation. In fact, in the struggle, the em-ployers really do see the workers as the absolute Other. Initially, this is the meaning and justification of their *praxis* in so far as every *praxis* produces its own justifications; but above all one of the objectives of the employers' *praxis* (and certainly not the least important) then becomes the introduction of splits and insecurities into the ranks of the workers by infecting the proletariat with a being-outside-itself in bourgeois class-consciousness taken as the absolute standard of what is human and what is not. Thus, for every grouped worker induced radicalisation is a radical negation of his being-for-the-bourgeoisie and this negation involves a set of difficult activities which are quite inseparable from one another: to refuse to define oneself as evil is to reject bourgeois Manichaeism; but this Manichaeism is simply another name for the humanism of the dominant class, and it has to be rejected as humanism. Now, an abstract rejection would still be an acceptance: in rejecting humanism as such, a worker *would be admitting* that he was non-human.

The new exigency, born of the transcendence of this contradiction, is that the rejection should be inscribed in the production of a true and positive humanism; and this presupposes that the worker takes away from the bourgeoisie the privilege of stating the truth of man for all, that is to say, truth itself. However, the bourgeois claims to be human by virtue of intelligence, culture, scientific knowledge, technical abilities, etc.: and while these powers must belong to everyone, the workers partly lack them. Furthermore, the idealist intellectualism of the bourgeoisie depends on analytical Reason: analytical Reason determines what is true. Thus the worker must either allow his class to be dissolved by a positivistic atomisation and allow himself to be defined as isolated in ignorance and malevolence *or* he must recreate Reason, dissolve analytical rationality in a larger complex and, without losing the hope of escaping ignorance some day, find non-intellectual criteria and foundations for truth. Of course, as Marx said, the problems are not formulated until the means of resolving them are present; but *everything is already present: praxis* as the measure of man and the foundation of truth, and dialectic as the permanent dissolution of analytical Reason. And then it must be recognised that the day-to-day expression of the radical reaction of the oppressed is in particular concrete skirmishes: and there is no need to be a Marxist in order to resist cuts in real wages. However, everyday practice itself would be affected by bourgeois propaganda unless the class which is totalised by the Other dissolved this alien unity by a real movement of totalisation.[128]

This is the only point of view from which the effect of the oppressed class on the intellectuals from the petty bourgeoisie – a class which is in tutelage to the capitalist class – can be comprehended. It is through their new production of the universal as exigency that the oppressed class preys upon them and detaches them in the name of the incomplete humanism produced by the bourgeois class. We will not labour the point here: let us simply indicate the action in reciprocity without which this nurturing and attraction of the theoreticians would lose all practical signification. In other words, the fascination which the proletariat has for petty bourgeois intellectuals – which is not well described by Marx and the Marxists – does not derive from particular material interests, but from the fact that the universal is the general material interest of any intellectual and that this universal is realised in potentiality (if not in actuality) by the working class. The intellectuals, in other words, are products of bourgeois universalism and they *alone* in the bourgeois class are *aware* of the contradictions of humanism, that is to say both of its unlimited extension (to all men) and of its limitations. But if, like Marx, the theorist *produces* a materialist and dialectical interpretation of History, it is because it is *required* by the materialist dialectic as a rule for working-class *praxis* and as sole foundation of true (that is to say future) universality. In other words,

---

128. We shall see later, in a section on the 'Critique of Dialectical Investigation', how the dialectic can be historical Reason at the same time as being historialised at a particular moment of History.

it is because a circulating comprehension, as the permeability of every worker's *praxis* to all, is already anti-analytical, and because the dialectic, and its realisation, *praxis*, emerge as a reaction to analytical Reason by each and all, and as its dissolution.

It must not be supposed that this provides an escape from the need for *situated realism*. This practical dialectic can be seen forming itself, for example, in the unity of the Lyon silk-weavers from 1830; and their very unity will manifest itself to them in the development of a *praxis* (to live working or to die struggling) which will leave them victorious and stunned. Dialectic and *praxis* are one and the same; in their indissolubility, they are the reaction of the oppressed class to oppression. Does this imply that oppression is really analytical? Obviously not. The bourgeois class conceals the operation of the dialectic under the atomising rationality of positivism, whereas a theorist of the proletariat will demand explanations in the name of the dialectic itself. Thus, at one level of abstraction, class conflict expresses itself as a *conflict of rationalities*. But let us be spared the classic imbecility which consists in contrasting science to bourgeois idealism. Science is not dialectic; and until the historical emergence of the USSR, it was exclusively bourgeois. Finally, in spite of the unfortunate theory of proletarian science, it remained the one area of agreement between Soviet and bourgeois scientists. This is not where the contradiction lies. The contradiction is between the bourgeois determination to stick at scientific positivism, and the progressive effort of the proletariat, of its theorists, and of socialist countries, to dissolve positivism in the dialectical movement of human *praxis*. In reality, this is simply a matter of the existence of a self-conscious dialectic in the movement of the working class, and of the tactical negation of this reason in the (actually dialectical) movement of the bourgeois class. In effect, it is dehumanisation by bourgeois oppression which leads the workers to unity and to organised *praxis* as constituted dialectic (that is to say, to a positive transcendence of abstract destructive Reason); conversely, this same dialectic as *praxis*-totalisation reinforces analytical Reason in the bourgeoisie. This is why abstract theoretical discussions between historians about particular events in the French Revolution (atomised crowds with 'ring-leaders', or totalising class-reactions?) are abstract expressions (and actually philosophically incomplete and false) of the deep conflicts between the totalisation (proletariat) and the dissolving faculty of analytical Reason (the action and propaganda of the bourgeoisie).

We can conclude by saying that the dialectic, as the practical consciousness of an oppressed class struggling against its oppressor, is a reaction which is produced in the oppressed by the divisive tendency of oppression – but not at any arbitrary time or place: later we shall discover the material conditions which make this consciousness possible. But at any rate it is a transcendence of contemplative truth by effective practical truth, and of atomisation (accompanied by serial agreement) towards the synthetic unity of the combat-group. This practical *comprehension* of workers' activities by workers (however cloudy it may be and however erroneous it may remain) is actually *the objective spirit* of the working class in so far as it is created as an extreme need and a necessary negation of its de-humanity. But, unlike that of the bourgeois class, this spirit is not, in itself, alterity: it is an attempt everywhere to dissolve alterity. In his every action, the worker naturally discovers dialectical development: being exploited, he discovers the constituent dialectic as a creation through his work (which is finally alienated from him). Alongside other exploited men, he sees his work as determining, as Other, the work of the Others (through norms), and he discovers this from the point of view of the rejection of alterity. If a worker says, 'I shall avoid doing more than the Others, in order not to require the Others to do more than they can, and in order that I shall not be required to do more than I can by an Other', he is already a master of dialectical humanism, not as theory but as practice and in spite of the negative twists which characterise this rationality in its empirical beginnings, as a dissolving practice directed against analytical rationality.[129]

Our aim is to define the formal conditions of History; we need not dwell on the relations of material reciprocity between classes in their real historical development. What has been established by our

129. This example illustrates how the dialectic is rejected, but then instrumentalised and exploited, by the employers, as well as the mystification of positivism. The employer sets out from the analytical point of view of atomisation and competition: everyone is free to work harder than his neighbour, if he can, and so to earn more; and the neighbour is free to compete with him. But dialectical Reason, as a carefully disguised mystery, actually ensures, on behalf of the employers, that if a work norm is increased for and by certain individuals, then it is increased (to a lesser degree) for all. This also applies to socialist societies: the bureaucracy pretends to be concerned with the improvement of output by individuals (Stakhanovism is positivist reason) but knows perfectly well that the activist will transform the production group as a whole (dialectical Reason proclaimed in theory, but negated in fact).

dialectical investigation is that for there to be any such thing as classes, they must be determined in reciprocity, whatever the mediating process may be. Besides, we know that the only intelligibility of their relationship is dialectical. From this point of view, analytical Reason can be seen to be an oppressive *praxis* for dissolving them, and its inevitable effect is to make the dialectic into the rationality of the oppressed class (on the basis of circumstances which have yet to be determined). The emergence of dialectical Reason in the working class as a dissolution of analytical Reason and as a determination of the bourgeois class in terms of its function and practice (exploitation-oppression) is induced; it is an aspect of the class struggle. But, conversely, if the bourgeois class clings theoretically to analytical Reason, dialectical Reason returns to it as its own fascination through its traitors (that is, its intellectuals) and it gradually becomes self-conscious in the very class which negates it. The permanent, but variable contradiction (increasing or diminishing tension) between these two types of rationality *inside the bourgeoisie* would merit a place of its own in a history of culture. Concrete examples would show not only positive Reason quietly being dissolved by the dialectic (in historians like Marc Bloch or even Georges Lefebvre), but also the dialectic being used *officially and theoretically* as a purely linguistic determination concealing an analytical calculation. (One of our best ethnographers uses the phrase, 'the dialectic of this dichotomy . . .', thus unintentionally *reducing* the dialectic to analysis.) But this is not relevant to our subject: what is important for us is to show that dialectic, as the controlled development of *praxis*, cannot experience itself (either as constituent or as constituted) except in and through the *praxis of struggle*, that is to say, antagonistic reciprocity. Of course, this does not mean that other practical organisms, in different worlds, differently constituted (without scarcity, for example), could not have a different consciousness of it (without the mediation of antagonistic reciprocity). But it does mean that in *our* world (governed by scarcity), it appears at the moment in which the group emerges from the oppressed series as a dictatorship of freedom. In other words, it *is* the *praxis* of the oppressed in so far as they are common individuals rooted in a seriality of impotence, and, in spite of their efforts, it *cannot fail to be* the practical reaction of the oppressors, in so far as they have to become dialectical Reason in order to foresee the behaviour of the oppressed. Exploitation as a practico-inert process is a reality which has to be dissolved both theoretically and practically in dialectical Reason, whereas it is struggle, as genuine human *praxis* and reciprocity of antagonism, which produces the unity of everyone through the Other. It is the movement of dissolution (or extermination), as the unification of the attacker, which produces the dialectical practice of the attacked. The conclusion of this investigation is that *the only possible intelligibility* of human relations is dialectical and that this intelligibility, in a concrete history whose true foundation is *scarcity*, can be manifested only as an antagonistic reciprocity. So class struggle as a practice necessarily leads to a dialectical interpretation; and, moreover, in the history of human multiplicities, class struggle is necessarily produced on the basis of historically determined conditions, as the developing realisation of dialectical rationality. Our History is intelligible to us because it is dialectical and it is dialectical because the class struggle produces us as transcending the inertia of the collective towards dialectical combat-groups.

4   The Intelligibility of History: Totalisation without a Totaliser

Now it may be suggested that the struggle in itself, that is to say, the temporalisation of reciprocity, although it creates both dialectical experience and the consciousness of it, may *transcend* the dialectical comprehension of the agent, observer, or historian. The investigation has shown us the translucid rationality of constituent organic *praxis*; and it has also revealed that of common *praxis* (in so far as it is assumed to be objectifying itself in an inert or practico-inert material which passively accepts its determinations). But there is no proof that a *praxis* of antagonism and reciprocity still has its rationality because each group (or class) signifies in its free *praxis* the practical freedom of the Other, and vice versa. In other words, it involves a twin-headed temporalisation each moment of which represents *not only* a *praxis*, but also its negation by the other *praxis*, and the beginnings of the transformation of the former in order to outwit the latter and of the latter in order not to be outwitted by the former. But even if this strange reality, the practice of no one, can be related, in a divergent double intuition, to the two agents when two individuals are involved (thus we can *comprehend* a boxing match provided we are familiar with the sport), can there be a *dialectical* comprehension of it? Is there not in fact a sort of private negation at the heart of this monster, each out-witting and mystifying the Other, seeking to disarm his freedom and make it his unwitting accomplice, and acknowledging the sovereignty of the Other only so as to get an opportunity of treating him *as a thing*? And then, even if this individual struggle (between individuals of the same profession, the same age, in a closed field) can *really* be decoded, will the same apply to the complex phenomenon which has to be described as a *praxis-process* and which sets classes in opposition to one another as circular totalisations of institutions, groups and serialities? Is it possible to have any clear comprehension of the complex modifications which each class derives from the Other (passively received and actively transformed) and which change the internal relations of different class structures to the degree that they are changed by them? Lastly, let us not forget that class, as such, is *also* a human product of a product and that, to this extent, its practical reactions temporalise the class-being of its members. Now, this class-being – as practico-inert – belongs to the domain of the anti-dialectic. How are we to grasp the intelligibility of a *praxis* which' has been mortgaged by a passive constitution?

We must reply to these theoretical questions like Diogenes, by walking. Or rather, by recalling that we are constantly struggling for or against *our* class and that the intelligibility of the struggle is essential to the action of the combatants. This does not mean that the intelli-gibility is given equally clearly in institutional groups, on combat- (or pressure-) groups, and in series. There is a weakening correspond-ing to internal transformations. But it must be *complete* in the case of class circularity (not only for the sovereign group, for example, but also for it *in so far as* the series mediates between it and combat- or pressure-groups), for a very simple reason which is itself dialectical: if *praxis ceases to be aware* of its end, its means, of the means and end of its adversary, and of the means of opposing the hostile *praxis*, it simply becomes blind and therefore ceases to be *praxis*; it is simply an un-conscious accomplice of the *other action* which overwhelms, manipu-lates and alienates it, and turns it against its own agent as a hostile force. (The simplest example is that of a lost regiment, cut off from the main army, fearing the enemy everywhere, imagining that everything is possible, but lacking any means of anticipating an unpredictable action. Such a regiment is no longer a group: it is a herd; but if it receives information and is able to locate the enemy troops, then – even if the enemy are numerically superior – it becomes a practical community again.) Thus the common *praxis* – wherever it is manifested – determines itself in the dimension of alterity because it adapts to the free *praxis* of the Other (in so far as it can predict it). The difficulty is that this is not a matter of predicting a physical effect – an inert repercussion of human work – but of predicting a freedom which is itself predicting this prediction. But this is neither other-direction nor alterity: it is reciprocal freedom which is computed and predicted. But the prediction will, if possible, be based on circumstances, knowledge which it will have both of the opposite *praxis and* of the inert structures from which it emerged (as either sovereign freedom or as fraternity-terror in a fused group). And though this prediction may be precise, it will still be dialectical in that it conceives material conditions, the situation, and knowledge as inert givens which are transcended by a freedom which retains them within it as its orientation and qualification. Thus the enemy is even more directly comprehended than the ally, although, of course, it depends entirely on material conditions whether such comprehension is *possible*, whether it is abstract and general or real and concrete (for example, information transmitted by intelligence agencies, indications of the relations of forces). And the enemy's comprehension of his enemy is also present in this fundamental comprehension (all traps and tricks presuppose such a comprehension in the Other). This means that *our* activity as a *praxis-subject* (I use this word to refer not to a subjectivity, but to activity itself as self-elucidating) must always include knowledge of itself as a *praxis-object* (that is to say, as objective movements of groups or troops, seen, for example, from an exclusively quantitative point of view[130]) and transcend this objectivity as a purely material condition. In a sense, the fundamental intelligibility of the struggle can be said to represent a development of dialectical comprehension: it necessarily implies that the *praxis* of each adversary is determined in accordance with his

---

130. This applies to ambushes in classical warfare: the action of the enemy is known; it is known that he is going to move to a particular place in order to attain a specific objective. But for us this objective is simply the spring of the trap which will make him go through a particular mountain pass, for example. And, from this point of view, in order to see whether the trap is to be set and *worked* (whether it is necessary to attack from both sides of the pass), one will – if one has sufficient information – come down to calculating *inert quantities*: the number of soldiers, weapons, etc. And of course the enemy has his own cards: he will foresee the trap and we will foresee his foresight.

objectivity for the Other. In other words, in the atomised, massified or serialised crowds which surround us, our reality as subjects remains abstract because we are paralysed by our practical impotence and our reality as objects resides in the evasion which is the Other. The subject-object relation, however, as a variable but ever intense tension, though it is not, or need not be, expressible in words, is immediately given in the *praxis* of antagonistic reciprocity. But conversely, I comprehend the enemy *through the object which I am for him*. Or rather, the dialectical moments of the investigation merge into one another: I predict my objectivity for him on the basis of the objective structures which I know to exist in him; and, through costly mistakes, gradual corrections, etc., I predict what he is on the basis of his former actions on me (that is to say, of the predictions which are their intelligible signification). My knowledge is the best *possible* if I can make a prediction not only of what he will do, on the basis of what he is, but also of what he is on the basis of what he has done, and, finally, of what he will do (predictions based on previous experience).

Thus reciprocal action is characterised, in its basic antagonistic structure, by the fact that it encloses the agent as an object and the Other as a subject in the prospect of a reversal which has to be produced (the Other becomes a pure passive object, the agent asserts himself as free *praxis*); in other words, the free practical dialectic of the one involves a grasp of the free dialectic of the other both *as freedom* and as a *double means* (a means of predicting the enemy action and thus outwitting it, and a means of making *the Other* an accomplice in an action aimed at subjecting him, by proposing a false goal for his freedom). In its basic principle, struggle is, for everyone, an opportunity to develop the multiplicity of human dimensions in a synthetic tension, since one has to be an object-subject for a subject-object who is the Other, and since one interiorises an other comprehended freedom within one's own freedom. But, this does not prevent one from being *materialist*. That is to say, it is *essential* to determine (*a*) the action of the Other on the basis of the inorganic reality of the conditions in which the Other exists, (*b*) one's own action against the Other on the basis of one's own initial material and inert conditions, and (*c*) the Other's prediction of the action undertaken on the basis of possibilities which have been calculated (or established as precisely as the situation allows) that the Other has precise information as to material conditions, etc.

Struggle is the only human practice which realises everyone's relation to his object-being in urgency (and sometimes in mortal danger). And, of course, the object that I am for the Other is altered by the fundamental structures and material conditions which have given the Other a constitution as an object. However, objectivity for this other tends to approximate indefinitely to objectivity pure and simple (such that synchronic and diachronic totalisation can establish it in the very tension of their contradictions) in so far as it is not the Other determining it in me but myself tending to produce it under the pressure of the Other. In particular, on the relatively simple plane of military conflict, an army, through its leaders, must always have a strictly objective awareness of its *being* (number, arms, means of communication, relation to bases, and everyone's combativity – in connection not only with the past and, for example, with good or bad supplies, but also with the future, that is to say, with the real meaning of the struggle it is engaged in for each soldier) and this consciousness must be as lucid, and *at least* as strict as that of the enemy (for the enemy may be ignorant of certain weaknesses, it may be poorly informed). In short, an army which did not see *its praxis* and its limited range of choice as strictly defined by its *object-being*, and which, consequently, did not interiorise its entire objectivity as its being-outside-itself in the practical field, and which did not produce its action as a transcendence of this objectivity (in so far as it is strictly determined and known) – in short an army which was ignorant about itself in the way that an individual – apart from individual conflicts – is ignorant of himself (slightly, though not completely, by mistaking his own capacities, etc.) – would be heading for defeat. In fact, the practical project must also define, in a synthetic bond (the determination of a tactic or strategy) the objectivity of every army, through the *praxis-subject* of the Other; and this involves not only – though this is the basic structure – calculating the *relation of forces*, but also calculating it in the prospect of a particular action. In the same way, and in the same perspective, one not only has to realise one's own objectivity on the basis of a particular action by the enemy (the enemy attack on a particular formation, in a particular place, reveals this formation in its objective fragility as a point which may be breached and, as such, as needing reinforcements), but one also has to reassess the *praxis*-subject of the Other *as object*, that is to say, as the means of a *praxis* directed against the enemy (one allows him to advance in order to cut him off from his bases; thus one benefits from the enemy plan itself in so far as it is a project).

However, in so far as the enemy *praxis* is capable of becoming a means of its own failure, that is to say, in so far as it can become a *praxis*-object, it must itself be conditioned in itself by inertias, shortages, and ignorance – which of course is true of every *praxis*. Relative ignorance of the future and incomplete knowledge of the past are the material conditions enabling freedom to be treated as freedom-object (by a freedom which is better situated in relation to the past and the future). This is alienation, as a moment of struggle; but this alienation – which transforms the *praxis* of a group into passive activity, that is to say into a practico-inert process – comes to the *praxis through the opposite praxis* and through its action on the material conditions. The narrow pass is a passivity of the enemy *praxis* through the ignorance of the army leaders; the ambush transforms this passivity into a destiny through work (transportation of troops, weapons, etc.). On this basis, the free *praxis* of the enemy is no more than *his* illusion; it disguises an instrumental process which presents itself to the soldiers doing the ambush (and, after a certain moment, to those who fall into the trap) as a passive activity produced by the manipulating group within the manipulated group.

However, this freedom which has become a thing, that is to say freedom seen from the point of view of its alienation and through the realisation of this alienation, retains the signs of freedom as its seal. In fact this appropriated freedom, in so far as it has walked into the trap, becomes *for both groups* the means of its own liquidation as *praxis*. So from this point of view one can see an agreement about *the object* gradually being realised in the course of struggle. When the *praxis* of the surrounded group reveals its alienation, it still does not destroy itself; when it is surrounded, the organised group seeks to defend itself, to avoid extermination if possible, to hold out as long as it can, etc.; in short, it treats its own previous action as a past alienation which *has to be transcended* (if only in a hopeless battle or in surrender), and which therefore *has to be preserved* in the transcendence, at the very moment when the group which laid the ambush is trying to draw the consequences of this practico-inert activity of the Other, as the objective result of its own practice. Thus the agreement – which manifests itself in combat – arises, here, from the fact that alienated freedom has become *for one of the groups and through the other* the objective mediation between the two groups, that is to say, the object of antagonistic actions. (In this moment, any action by the surrounded group presupposes an admission of its own 'mistake' as a betrayal by common freedom and a recognition of enemy *praxis* as constituting a dangerous passive activity which is identical with 'the mistake' and is simply a means of eradicating it).

Thus we arrive at a first level of intelligibility in struggle in that the dialectical intelligibility of a project comprehends the comprehension of the project of the Other. This particular form of dialectical rationality is obviously an irreducible moment of the investigation: the bond between the two actions is both dialectical and anti-dialectical in each action considered on its own. It constitutes itself, in effect, as a negation of the Other to the degree that the Other is already *in* it as its negation. At this level this is not a genuine organic *transcendence* of an objective, existing condition, such as, for example, the transcendence by *my project* (by *my praxis*) of the previous moment of this *praxis* itself as mere *transcended-being*. The struggle is in itself the attempt by one free *praxis* to transcend another free *praxis*, and conversely; and consequently there can be no formal determination of the relationship between these two transcendences of transcendences, which necessarily include in themselves the permanent possibility (actualised in the moments of the struggle) of being transcended. For *the transcendence itself* is called into question by the Other, both in himself and in the Other, in so far as it only requires some lucky action which fully exploits the real situation to transform it, alive, into a practico-inert object (matter worked for the Other). Here in fact one can see, against the background of scarcity, the profound threat which man presents to man: man is the Being by whom (by whose *praxis*) man is reduced to the state of a haunted object – to the state of a worked matter whose functioning is determined and which is penetrated by ineffectual dreams (that is to say *whose human transcendence (transcendance)* would always be there, though as a self-confessed illusion which was incapable of disappearing).

An individual undertaking may, of course, produce results which apparently resemble the action of a group on inanimate matter: a mountaineer may lose his way or make mistakes which lead him to fall into a crevasse. But in fact the resemblance is quite superficial: *praxis*, by definition, has ignorance and error as basic structures. In this case, the coefficient of adversity of matter is a special case of the adversity of the world as man's environment, and failure is still action proclaiming itself, if only in despair, as action.[131] Defeat in struggle, in contrast,

131. A woman jumped out of a train. She fell under a carriage, and was

is produced by freedom and is comprehended as such. At this level, there is only one man: the man who realises himself as a man (as free *praxis*) by transforming the Other into a non-human object. And this man is in fact seen by his victim as the free realisation of humanity, producing itself through the de-humanisation of the Other. Thus struggle involves a reciprocal possibility that one of the two combatants will become a man and create the rule of man through the other's becoming-inert: and in the *developing* struggle, man and the destruction of man are given as abstract reciprocities which will be determined by concrete circumstances. It is this affirmation of dialectical Reason based on the negation of dialectical Reason in the Other (and comprehended as the possibility of being negated by the Reason of the Other) which we call the level of the anti-dialectic, that is to say, the irreducibility in each of the *praxes* of both.

On the other hand, the *praxis* of the individual (or group) is *always* a comprehension of the Other (and tends to be a totalising comprehension: the limits are fixed only by the conditions of the struggle, and in any case they vary) and produces itself as a transcendence of the material results achieved by the Other in so far as it comprehends this *praxis* in the light of its own objectives. In other words, the signification of an antagonistic action necessarily includes the signification of the Other, in that each of them is both signifier and signified. In the simplest and most theoretical case, that of a game of chess, the arrangement of the white pieces, at each move, defines its intelligibility through the double depth of the future: *to comprehend* a move is to see it in terms of the responses it ought to elicit from black (in so far as it is a specific modification of a determinate field in which the power relations are strict and completely known), but these responses themselves have practical significations only in so far as they allow white to occupy new positions. So there are, in principle, two series (two successions of moves, white and black). But in practice move No. 1 (by white) is made in the prospect of a complex of subsequent operations; and since these operations can be carried out only if the complex of black positions is rearranged, this first move (the first in this particular operation, not the first in the game) is played in order to elicit a certain response from

---

terribly injured; she died saying over and over again: '*I shouldn't have jumped,*' which was, in the midst of frightful agony, a pure and simple affirmation of the practical power of man over things.

black (a displacement of pieces) to make way for move No. 2 by white. Now, this second move, which was planned from the very 'conception' of the project, is itself a means of provoking a certain defence by black whose function for white will be to make way for move No. 3,[132] that is to say, the development of the attack, etc.

Thus this is a miniature practical field which gains in rigour and precision what it loses in extension and complexity and which is always seen (by every adversary) both in its synchronic and in its diachronic totalisation. Every *move* is really a complete rearrangement, a transformation of the relations of all the pieces within the synthetic field. The future is relatively limited (in theory the game might go on for ever; but in practice the drama is quite short), but within the double, reciprocal temporalisation one can discern one series of successive objectives (each white move being directly aimed at a certain response by black, this response enabling white to achieve a second objective, etc.). Now, *from the point of view of white*, who is on the offensive, the temporal succession of white moves intertwines with that of black's responses until they become one: in effect, each position strictly implies the other. Thus, in so far as the options for black are gradually narrowed down to *one* (that is to say, to necessity), as in chess problems and 'end-games' and (this is partly the same thing) the more manifest the practical superiority of white, the whole operation will appear to reduce to the work of a single player on a material whose laws have been determined in advance. It suffices that the practical movement is defined by its end (check-mate), and this end by the rules of the game. Then it is possible to treat the black defence as a series of *negative and predictable reactions*, which can and must be governed, controlled, and elicited by white, that is to say, in short, as a negative, indirect instrumentality which white must be able to exploit in order to achieve his ends. At this level there is no longer any adversary: in chess problems, indeed, the player is usually alone, and *exploits* the black defence in order to reach the solution as quickly as possible: 'mate in three moves', etc. The way is open for a mathematics of games. But this mathematics is itself subordinate to action: it appears only when action is intentionally eliminated in favour of simple succession (that is to say, to

132. But the project is really more complex: the choice of the Other intervenes as an *intelligible* possibility; after a given move, he may chose three replies. But if he chooses the first, I will reply by a particular attack, and if he chooses the second, he will be enabling me to make a particular manoeuvre, etc.

allow analytical Reason to determine certain relational systems which have to be reactualised by *praxis*).

What concerns us in this example is not the abstract moment where *praxis* effaces itself before rigid relations; it is the moment where it becomes practically indifferent whether to attribute the complex of practical operations to a reciprocity of combat or to the isolated activity of an individual on an inert and strictly determined material. What is taking place? Simply this: if one of the adversaries is able to predict precisely the reactions of the other and elicit them by his action, and if his prediction corresponds for the enemy to the *necessity* of his reactions (that is to say, to their alienation), reciprocal and antagonistic action tends to become identical with individual action. But this can only mean that the dominated adversary has become no more than an object: and a basically similar transformation of the defeated takes place, only with less rigour, in the relations between a victorious army and a routed enemy. It is the relative unpredictability of the adversary – in so far as this unpredictability is comprehended and constitutes the ignorance of the Other – which allows struggle to retain its reciprocity. However, the mere fact that the limit-objective of everyone's action involves the integration of that of the Other as a simple indirect means shows that the comprehension of the other is the dialectical intelligibility of everyone's own action as its obverse, its organ of control, and its means of transcendence. And at the same time this comprehension posits itself as temporary because it takes place in the prospect of integrating the enemy into its victorious *praxis* and turning him into an inert, docile means of carrying victory to the limit.

In short, between the two limit-possibilities (becoming an isolated agent, and being transformed into worked matter by enemy *praxis*), each of which reduces the struggle to a mere practical rearrangement of the field by the sovereign and which are also the goals pursued by each of the adversaries (and sometimes realised by one of them), the *praxis* of struggle arises in everyone as the comprehension of his object-being (in so far as it exists for the Other and threatens to enclose him one day in the Other) through his practical existence as a subject. In its attempted transcendence of this concrete objectivity (which only succeeds in so far as it is not prevented by the Other), the *praxis* of struggle awakens, actualises, comprehends and transcends (*transcende*) the constitutive *praxis* of the Other in so far as he is himself a practical subject; and in its action against the Other, on the completion of this very transcendence and through the mediation of the field of materiality, it reveals and produces the Other as an object. From this point of view, the anti-dialectical negation appears as a moment in a more complex dialectic. At first, in fact, this negation is precisely what is transcended: the *praxis* is constituted for both as the negation of a negation: not only through everyone's transcendence of his object-being, but practically through everyone's attempts to *liquidate* the practical subject in the Other outside and from the outside and to recover his objectivity through this transcendent (*transcendante*) destruction. Thus the antagonistic negation is grasped by everyone as a scandal which has to be transcended. But at the level of scarcity its origin does not lie in this revelation of scandal: it is a *struggle for life*; thus the scandal is not only grasped in its appearance as scandal, but also profoundly comprehended as the impossibility that the two should co-exist. Consequently the scandal is not, as Hegel supposed, the mere existence of the Other, which would take us back to a statute of unintelligibility. It lies in suffered (or threatened) violence, that is, in interiorised scarcity. In this respect, although the original fact is logically and formally contingent (scarcity is only a *material given*), its contingency is far from impairing the intelligibility of violence. What is important for the dialectical comprehension of the Other, is the rationality of his *praxis*. Now this rationality appears in violence itself, in so far as this is not the contingent ferocity of man, but *everyone's* intelligible reinteriorisation of the contingent fact of scarcity: human violence is *meaningful* (*signifiante*). And as this violence is a negation of the Other in everyone, negation, in its reciprocity, becomes meaningful in and through everyone, as scarcity turned practical agent, or in other words as human-scarcity. Thus practical negation is constituted as a negation of scandal-negation both in so far as the latter is the Other in everyone and in so far as this Other is interiorised scarcity.

From this point of view, what is indissolubly negated by *praxis* is negation as the condition of man (that is to say, as a conditioning readopted in violence by the conditioned) and as the freedom of an Other. And in fact the scandal of the presence in me (as a mark of my object-being) of the Other's freedom as the freedom-negation of my freedom, is itself a determination in rationality in so far as this negative freedom actualises in practice the impossibility of our co-existing in the field of scarcity. In short, on the basis of scarcity, and in the prospect of the annihilation of the Other, struggle is, for everyone, a deepening of the comprehension of others. To comprehend, in an immediate sense, is to grasp the *praxis* of the Other, through its ends and means, as a simple, objective, transcendent (*transcendante*) temporalisation. To comprehend in struggle is to grasp the *praxis* of the Other in immanence, through its own objectivity and in a practical transcendence. I now comprehend the enemy *through myself* and myself *through the enemy*. His *praxis* does not appear as a pure transcendent (*transcendante*) temporalisation which I reproduce without participating in it; urgency forces me to discover my objectivity and adopt it in every detail; it forces me to penetrate, as far as concrete circumstances permit, the activity of the enemy. Comprehension is an immediate fact of reciprocity. But as long as this reciprocity remains positive, comprehension remains abstract and external. Struggle, in the field of scarcity, as negative reciprocity, engenders the Other as Other than man, or as anti-human; but at the same time I comprehend him, in the very springs of my *praxis*, as a negation of which I am a concrete practical negation, and as mortal danger.

For each of the adversaries, this struggle is intelligible; or rather, at this level, it is intelligibility itself. Otherwise, reciprocal *praxis* would in itself have no meaning or goal.[133] But what concerns us is the general problem of intelligibility, particularly at the concrete level. Now, *if a situated dialectic* is possible, then social conflicts, battles, and regular conflicts, as complex events produced by the practices of reciprocal antagonism between two individuals or multiplicities, must *in principle* be comprehensible to the third parties who depend on them without participating, or to observers who see them from outside without being in any way involved. From this point of view, nothing is fixed *a priori*: the investigation has to be continued. In fact every adversary *realises* the intelligibility of the conflict because he totalises it *for himself* in and through his own *praxis*; but the reciprocal negation is, for the third party, the very reality of struggle. We have seen how

---

133. Of course, this formal feature does not prevent there being varying degrees of reciprocal comprehension among enemies. This depends on circumstances; and people may be 'treated like children', 'tricked', etc.; or they may take part in absurd wars (as in the Late Middle Ages) in which the peculiar contradictions of the period resulted in the mutual incomprehension of the armies (who avoided confrontations). And as a result of failing to comprehend a technical improvement the French nobility were decimated by English archers. This much is obvious; or rather the enemy could always depend on a new weapon, an unexpected, uncomprehended manoeuvre, to give it victory. But *for this very reason* we should recognise that struggle as reciprocity is a function of reciprocity of comprehension. If one of the adversaries should cease to comprehend he would become *the object of the Other*.

the mediation of the third party realises the transcendent (*transcendante*) objective unity of positive reciprocities. But is this unity still possible when each action is aimed at destroying that of the Other and when the observable results of this double negation are nil or – as usually happens – when the teleological significations which each adversary has inscribed in it have been partly erased or transformed by the Other, so that no trace of concerted activity is any longer to be seen? Similarly, to take the example of individual combat, each blow dealt by the one is dodged or parried or blocked by the Other – but not completely, unless they differ greatly in strength or skill. And the same observation – as we saw in *The Problem of Method* – applies to most of the historic 'days': they often ended indecisively. Thus the effects cannot be attributed entirely either to the rebels or to the government forces, and they have to be comprehended not as the realisation of a project, but in terms of how the action of each group (and also of chance, accident, etc.) prevented them from realising that of the Other, that is to say, to the extent that they *are not* practical significations, and that their mutilated, truncated meaning does not correspond to any one's practical plan so that, in this sense, they fall short of being human. But if this is what the historian recreating the 'days' of 20 June or of 10 August 1792 has to do, is it really appropriate to call this recreation *intellection*?

These questions bring us at last to the real problem of History. If History really is to be the totalisation of all practical multiplicities and of all their struggles, the complex products of the conflicts and collaborations of these very diverse multiplicities must themselves be intelligible in their synthetic reality, that is to say, they must be comprehensible as the synthetic products of a totalitarian *praxis*. This means that History is intelligible if the different practices which can be found and located at a given moment of the historical temporalisation finally appear as partially totalising and as connected and merged in their very oppositions and diversities by an intelligible totalisation from which there is no appeal. It is by seeking the conditions for the intelligibility of historical vestiges and results that we shall, for the first time, reach the problem of totalisation without a totaliser and of the very foundations of this totalisation, that is to say, of its motive-forces and of its non-circular direction. Thus, the regressive movement of the critical investigation has demonstrated the intelligibility of practical structures and the dialectical relation which interconnects the various forms of active multiplicities. But, on the one hand, we are still at the level of synchronic totalisation and we have not yet considered the diachronic depth of practical temporalisation; and on the other hand, the regressive movement has ended with a question: that is to say, it has to be completed by a synthetic progression whose aim will be to rise up to the double synchronic and diachronic movement by which History constantly totalises itself. So far, we have been trying to get back to the elementary formal structures, and, at the same time, we have located the dialectical foundations of a structural anthropology. These structures must now be left to live freely, to oppose and to co-operate with one another: and the reflexive investigation of this still formal project will be the object of the next volume. If the truth is *one* in its increasing internal diversification, then, by answering the last question posed by the regressive investigation, we shall discover the basic signification of History and of dialectical rationality.

Annexe

Sartre's Preface to *The Problem of Method* and *Critique of Dialectical Reason*

I fear that the two works included in this volume[1] may appear to be unequal in importance and scope. Logically, the second should have come before the first, since it is intended to supply its critical foundations. But I was afraid that this mountain of notes might seem to have brought forth a mouse: why waste so much breath, use so much ink, or fill so much paper, simply to produce a few remarks about methodology? Moreover, since the second work did in fact grow from the first, it seemed best to preserve the chronological order – which, from a dialectical point of view, is always the most significant.

The Problem of Method was an occasional piece – hence its somewhat hybrid character, and the fact that it seems to approach problems somewhat indirectly. A Polish journal decided to devote its Winter 1957 issue to French culture, intending to give its readers a panorama of what we still refer to as '*nos familles d'esprit*'. Many different writers were invited to participate, and I was asked to write on 'The situation of Existentialism in 1957'.

I do not like speaking about existentialism. Inquiry ought to be indefinite: to give it a name and a definition is to button it up; and what remains of it then? A past, peripheral cultural fashion, not unlike a special brand of soap; in other words, an *idea*. I would not have accepted the Polish invitation if I had not seen it as an opportunity to explain, to a country with a Marxist culture, the present contradictions

---

1. Sartre refers here to the French edition of *The Problem of Method* and *Critique of Dialectical Reason*. [Ed.]

of philosophy. From this point of view, I thought it might be possible to group the inner conflicts which divide philosophy around a single major opposition, between existence and knowledge. But my approach would have been more direct if arrangements for the special 'French' issue had not required me to concentrate on the existential ideology, a Marxist philosopher, Henri Lefebvre, having been invited to 'situate' the contradictions and development of Marxism in France in these years.

My article was subsequently republished in the review *Les Temps Modernes*, but I altered it considerably to suit French readers. It is this version which is published here. The title has been changed from *Existentialisme et Marxisme* to *Questions de Méthode* (*The Problem of Method*).

Finally, my intention is to raise one question, and only one: do we now possess the materials for constituting a structural, historical anthropology? This question is located within Marxist philosophy, for – as will become clear – I regard Marxism as the untranscendable philosophy for our time, and I believe that the ideology of existence, along with its 'comprehensive' method, is an enclave within Marxism itself, both produced and rejected by Marxism.

The ideology of existence inherited two exigencies from the Marxism which revived it, and these in turn are derived from Hegelianism: if there is to be any such thing as a Truth in anthropology, it must have *developed* (*devenue*) and it must be a *totalisation*. Obviously this double exigency defines the movement of being and knowledge (or comprehension) which, since Hegel, has been known as 'dialectic'. Thus, in *The Problem of Method*, I have taken it for granted that such a totalisation is constantly developing both as History and as historical Truth. On this basic assumption, I have tried to explain the inner conflicts of philosophical anthropology, and at some points – in my chosen field of methodology – I have outlined provisional solutions to the problems. But obviously these contradictions, and the synthetic transcendence of them, will have no meaning or reality if History and Truth are not in fact totalising, and if – as positivists would claim – there are *several* Histories and several Truths. For this reason, while I was drafting *The Problem of Method*, I came to feel that I ought to tackle the fundamental problem – whether there is any such thing as a Truth of humanity (*une Vérité de l'Homme*)?

Not even empiricists have restricted the word 'Reason' to some kind of order amongst our thoughts. And any 'rationalism' would require that this 'order' should correspond to, or constitute, the order of being. From this point of view, if the correspondence (*rapport*) between the historical totalisation and the totalising Truth is possible, and if this correspondence is a double movement in both knowledge and being, we shall be justified in calling this changing relation Reason. Consequently the aim of my inquiry will be to establish whether the positivist Reason of the natural Sciences is the same as the Reason which is to be found in the development of anthropology, or whether the knowledge and comprehension of man by man involves not only special methods but also a new form of Reason, that is, a new relation between thought and its object. In other words, is there such a thing as dialectical Reason?

But it is not a matter of *discovering* a dialectic: Dialectical thought became conscious of itself, historically, at the beginning of the last century; and besides, historical and ethnological investigations have themselves brought to light various dialectical domains in human activity. However, on the one hand, investigation cannot, in general, establish more than partial, contingent truths; and on the other, dialectical thought has, since Marx, directed its attention to its object rather than to itself. We are facing the same difficulty which confronted analytical Reason at the end of the eighteenth century, when it became necessary to prove its legitimacy. But our problem is made harder by the fact that we have the solution of critical idealism already behind us. Knowledge is a mode of being; but for a materialist it is out of the question to reduce being to knowledge.

However: anthropology will continue to be a mere confusion of empirical data, positivistic inductions and totalising interpretations, until the legitimacy of dialectical Reason has been established, that is to say, until we have earned the right to study a person, a human group or a human object in the synthetic reality of their significations and of their relations to the developing totalisation; in other words, until we have proved that any isolated knowledge of men or their products must either transcend itself towards the totality or reduce to an error of incompleteness. Our approach will therefore be *critical* in that it will be an attempt to determine the validity and the limits of dialectical Reason, and this will mean identifying both the oppositions and the connections between this Reason and positivist, analytical Reason. But it must also be dialectical, since dialectic is necessary for dealing with dialectical problems. This is not a tautology, as I shall show later. In the first volume of this work, I shall simply outline a theory of practical ensembles, that is to say, of series and groups as moments of the totalisation. In Volume Two, which will appear later, I shall approach the problem of totalisation itself, that is to say, of History in its development and of Truth in its becoming.

Glossary

alienation	the condition in which free *praxis* is taken over and controlled by the other or by the practico-inert.
alterity	a relation of separation, opposed to reciprocity
analytical reason	the form of reason appropriate to the external relations which are the object of the natural sciences
anti-dialectic	the result of a *praxis* being turned against itself by the practico-inert
class	the developing totalisation of three kinds of ensemble: institutionalised groups, pledged groups and series
comprehension	the understanding of a *praxis* in terms of the purposes of its agent or agents (cf. 'intellection')
collective	a passive structure of the practico-inert corresponding to a series
common individual	a member of a group (cf. 'group')
constituent dialectic	the dialectic of individual *praxis*
constituted dialectic	the dialectic of group *praxis*

destiny	a future inscribed in the practico-inert (cf. 'interest')
dialectic	the intelligibility of *praxis* at every level
ensemble	a collection of individuals, however related
exigency	a necessity imposed by the practico-inert
exis	an inert, stable condition opposed to *praxis*
fraternity-terror	the relation of an individual to a pledged group to which he belongs
fused group (*groupe en fusion*)	a newly formed group, directly opposed to seriality, and unstructured
gathering (*rassemblement*)	a series which is capable of constituting a group
group	an ensemble each of whose members is determined by the others in reciprocity (in contrast to a series)
immanence-transcendence	the ability at once to command a group and to merge with it, characteristic of members of a fused group
institution	a group which develops from a pledged group through the ossification of its structures and the emergence of sovereignty and seriality within it
intellection	the explanation of a *praxis*, not necessarily in terms of the purposes of its agent or agents (cf. 'comprehension')

interest	being-outside-oneself in the practico-inert (cf. 'destiny')
investigation (*expérience*)	the process of understanding History, as corresponding to the historical process itself
multiplicity	a collection of individuals, however related
organised group	a group based on a pledge
other-direction (*extéro-conditionnement*)	the manipulation of a series by a sovereign
pledged group	a group which develops from a fused group through an organised distribution of rights and duties enforced by a pledge
practico-inert	matter in which past *praxis* is embodied
praxis	the activity of an individual or group in organising conditions in the light of some end
project	a chosen way of being, expressed in *praxis*
scarcity (*rareté*)	the contingent impossibility of satisfying all the needs of an ensemble
series	an ensemble each of whose members is determined in alterity by the others (in contrast to a group)
sovereign	an individual (or group) who (or which) manipulates series within an institutional group
statute	the condition of an individual (or ensemble) in so far as it is prescribed by the

	kind of ensemble to which he (or it) belongs
structure	an adopted inertia, characteristic of organised groups and open to investigation by analytical reason
third party (*tiers*)	an individual who unifies a group by observing or commanding it
totalisation	the constantly developing (*en cours*) process of understanding and making history, (obscured, according to Sartre, by the 'scholastic' notion of totality employed by Lukács and others)
transcendence (*dépassement*)	the process of going beyond present conditions towards a future which at once negates and incorporates them
transcendent (*transcendant*)	escaping from given conditions
univocal	one sided, non-reciprocal

Index

Comparative Pagination Chart

English	French	English	French
15	135	420	519
20	140	430	529
30	149	440	539
40	158	450	547
50	166	460	557
60	175	470	566
70	184	480	576
80	194	490	585
90	203	500	595
100	213	510	603
110	222	520	613
120	232	530	622
130	242	540	632
140	251	550	641
150	261	560	651
160	271	570	659
170	280	580	668
180	290	590	677
190	300	600	686
200	310	610	696
210	320	620	705
220	329	630	714
230	339	640	724
240	348	650	733
250	358	660	743
260	368	670	752
270	377	680	762
280	387	690	771
290	396	700	781
300	406	710	791
310	416	720	800
320	426	730	810
330	436	740	819
340	445	750	829
350	454	760	838
360	463	770	848
370	472	780	858
380	482	790	867
390	491	800	876
400	501	810	886
410	510